THE CAMBRIDGE RAWLS LEXICON

John Rawls is widely regarded as one of the most influential philosophers of the twentieth century, and his work has permanently shaped the nature and terms of moral and political philosophy, deploying a robust and specialized vocabulary that reaches beyond philosophy to political science, economics, sociology, and law. This volume is a complete and accessible guide to Rawls's vocabulary, with over 200 alphabetical encyclopaedic entries written by the world's leading Rawls scholars. From *basic structure* to *burdened society*, from *Sidgwick* to *strains of commitment*, and from *Nash point* to *natural duties*, the volume covers the entirety of Rawls's central ideas and terminology, with illuminating detail and careful cross-referencing. It will be an essential resource for students and scholars of Rawls, as well as for other readers in political philosophy, ethics, political science, sociology, international relations, and law.

JON MANDLE is Professor of Philosophy at the University at Albany (SUNY). He is the author of *Rawls's A Theory of Justice: An Introduction* (2009) and co-editor of *A Companion to Rawls* (2014).

DAVID A. REIDY is Professor of Philosophy at The University of Tennessee. He is the co-editor of *Rawls's Law of Peoples: A Realistic Utopia* (2006) and *A Companion to Rawls* (2014).

THE CAMBRIDGE
RAWLS LEXICON

EDITED BY

Jon Mandle
SUNY Albany

AND

David A. Reidy
University of Tennessee, Knoxville

CAMBRIDGE
UNIVERSITY PRESS

University Printing House, Cambridge CB2 8BS, United Kingdom

One Liberty Plaza, 20th Floor, New York, NY 10006, USA

477 Williamstown Road, Port Melbourne, VIC 3207, Australia

314-321, 3rd Floor, Plot 3, Splendor Forum, Jasola District Centre, New Delhi - 110025, India

79 Anson Road, #06-04/06, Singapore 079906

Cambridge University Press is part of the University of Cambridge.

It furthers the University's mission by disseminating knowledge in the pursuit of
education, learning and research at the highest international levels of excellence.

www.cambridge.org
Information on this title: www.cambridge.org/9780521192941

© Cambridge University Press 2015

This publication is in copyright. Subject to statutory exception
and to the provisions of relevant collective licensing agreements,
no reproduction of any part may take place without the written
permission of Cambridge University Press.

First published 2015

A catalogue record for this publication is available from the British Library

Library of Congress Cataloging in Publication data
The Cambridge Rawls lexicon / edited by Jon Mandle, SUNY Albany and
David A. Reidy, University of Tennessee, Knoxville.
pages cm
Includes bibliographical references and index.
ISBN 978-0-521-19294-1 (hardback)
1. Rawls, John, 1921–2002 – Dictionaries.   1. Mandle, Jon, 1966– editor.
II. Reidy, David A., 1962– editor.
B945.R283Z863   2014
320.01 – dc23   2014020026

ISBN 978-0-521-19294-1 Hardback

Cambridge University Press has no responsibility for the persistence or
accuracy of URLs for external or third-party internet websites referred to in
this publication, and does not guarantee that any content on such websites is,
or will remain, accurate or appropriate.

Contents

List of abbreviations for Rawls's texts	xiv
Introduction	xv

A

1.	**Abortion** *James Boettcher*	3
2.	**Advantage, mutual vs. reciprocal** *Colin Macleod*	5
3.	**Allocative justice** *Pete Murray*	7
4.	**Altruism** *Jon Mandle*	9
5.	**Animals** *Daniel Dombrowski*	11
6.	**Aquinas, Thomas** *Daniel Dombrowski*	14
7.	**Aristotelian principle** *Steven Wall*	17
8.	**Aristotle** *Daniel Dombrowski*	20
9.	**Arneson, Richard** *Dale Dorsey*	23
10.	**Arrow, Kenneth J.** *Iwao Hirose*	25
11.	**Autonomy, moral** *Catherine Audard*	27
12.	**Autonomy, political** *Catherine Audard*	32
13.	**Avoidance, method of** *Henry S. Richardson*	40

B

14.	**Barry, Brian** *Rex Martin*	45
15.	**Basic liberties** *Peter de Marneffe*	47
16.	**Basic needs, principle of** *Rodney G. Peffer*	50
17.	**Basic structure of society** *David A. Reidy*	55

VI / Contents

18. **Beitz, Charles** *Matt Lister* — 59
19. **Benevolent absolutism** *Walter J. Riker* — 61
20. **Berlin, Isaiah** *Daniel Weinstock* — 63
21. **Branches of government** *Martin O'Neill and Thad Williamson* — 65
22. **Buchanan, Allen** *Helena de Bres* — 69
23. **Burdened societies** *Michael Blake* — 71
24. **Burdens of judgment** *Michael Blake* — 74

C

25. **Capabilities** *Henry S. Richardson* — 81
26. **Care** *Victoria Costa* — 84
27. **Catholicism** *James Boettcher* — 87
28. **Chain connection** *Jon Mandle* — 90
29. **Circumstances of justice** *Faviola Rivera-Castro* — 92
30. **Citizen** *Matt Lister* — 97
31. **Civic humanism** *Victoria Costa* — 100
32. **Civic republicanism** *Victoria Costa* — 102
33. **Civil disobedience** *David Lyons* — 104
34. **Close-knitness** *Rex Martin* — 108
35. **Cohen, G. A.** *Jon Mandle* — 111
36. **Cohen, Joshua** *Helena de Bres* — 115
37. **Common good idea of justice** *Walter J. Riker* — 117
38. **Communitarianism** *Daniel Weinstock* — 119
39. **Comprehensive doctrine** *Paul Voice* — 126
40. **Conception of the good** *Pete Murray* — 130
41. **Congruence** *Andrew Lister* — 133
42. **Conscientious refusal** *David Lyons* — 139
43. **Constitution and constitutional essentials** *David A. Reidy* — 141
44. **Constitutional consensus** *George Klosko* — 147
45. **Constructivism: Kantian/political** *Larry Krasnoff* — 149
46. **Cooperation and coordination** *J. Donald Moon* — 157
47. **Cosmopolitanism** *Darrel Moellendorf* — 162
48. **Counting principles** *Jon Mandle* — 169
49. **Culture, political vs. background** *Micah Lewin* — 171

Contents / VII

D

50. **Daniels, Norman** *Martin O'Neill and Juliana Bidadanure*   179
51. **Decent societies** *Gillian Brock*   182
52. **Deliberative rationality** *Henry S. Richardson*   186
53. **Democracy** *Jeffrey Bercuson*   190
54. **Democratic peace** *Walter J. Riker*   195
55. **Deontological vs. teleological theories** *David A. Reidy*   198
56. **Desert** *Jon Mandle*   202
57. **Desires** *Alan W. Grose*   206
58. **Dewey, John** *Robert B. Talisse*   209
59. **Difference principle** *Anthony Simon Laden*   211
60. **Distributive justice** *Pete Murray*   217
61. **Dominant end theories** *David A. Reidy*   222
62. **Duty of assistance** *Darrel Moellendorf*   226
63. **Duty of civility** *James Boettcher*   229
64. **Dworkin, Ronald** *Peter de Marneffe*   234

E

65. **The economy** *Gerald Doppelt*   239
66. **Egoism** *James P. Sterba*   248
67. **The environment** *Jon Mandle*   252
68. **Envy** *Steve Wall*   256
69. **Equal opportunity, democratic interpretation** *Rex Martin*   259

F

70. **Facts, general (in OP argument and as part of justification)** *Jeppe von Platz*   267
71. **Fair equality of opportunity** *Shlomi Segall*   269
72. **Fairness, principle of** *David Lyons*   273
73. **Faith** *Daniel Dombrowski*   277

VIII / *Contents*

74. **Family** *S. A. Lloyd* — 279
75. **Feminism** *S. A. Lloyd* — 284
76. **Formal justice** *Jon Mandle* — 288
77. **The four-stage sequence** *Miriam Ronzoni* — 290
78. **Freedom** *Jon Mandle* — 293
79. **Freedom of speech** *Colin Macleod* — 300
80. **Freeman, Samuel** *Jeppe von Platz* — 304
81. **Fundamental ideas (in justice as fairness)** *Pablo Gilabert* — 306

G

82. **Games** *Anthony Simon Laden* — 311
83. **Goodness as rationality** *Pete Murray* — 314
84. **Guilt and shame** *David A. Reidy* — 318

H

85. **Happiness** *David A. Reidy* — 325
86. **Harsanyi, John C.** *Iwao Hirose* — 327
87. **Hart, H. L. A.** *Matt Lister* — 329
88. **Health and health care** *Norman Daniels* — 332
89. **Hedonism** *Helena de Bres* — 336
90. **Hegel, G. W. F.** *Sibyl A. Schwarzenbach* — 339
91. **Higher-order interests** *Adam Hosein* — 342
92. **Hobbes, Thomas** *S. A. Lloyd* — 346
93. **Human rights** *Gillian Brock* — 349
94. **Hume, David** *Jon Mandle* — 354

I

95. **Ideal and nonideal theory** *James W. Nickel* — 361
96. **Individualism** *Peter de Marneffe* — 365
97. **Institutions** *Miriam Ronzoni* — 368
98. **Intuitionism** *Chris Naticchia* — 371

Contents / IX

J

99.	**Just war theory** *David Lefkowitz*	377
100.	**Justice and interpersonal comparison** *Iwao Hirose*	382
101.	**Justice, concept of** *João Cardoso Rosas*	385
102.	**Justification: freestanding/political** *Jonathan Quong*	388
103.	**Justification vs. proof** *Jonathan Quong*	390

K

104.	**Kant, Immanuel** *Larry Krasnoff*	395
105.	**Kantian interpretation** *Larry Krasnoff*	399
106.	**King, Martin Luther, Jr.** *Kevin Vallier*	403
107.	**Kohlberg, Lawrence** *Walter J. Riker*	405
108.	**Kymlicka, Will** *João Cardoso Rosas*	407

L

109.	**Law of Peoples** *Gillian Brock*	411
110.	**Law, system of** *David A. Reidy*	417
111.	**Least-advantaged position** *Paul Voice*	420
112.	**Legitimacy** *J. Donald Moon*	422
113.	**Legitimate expectations** *Martin O'Neill*	428
114.	**Leibniz, G. W.** *Jon Mandle*	431
115.	**Leisure** *Kristi A. Olson*	433
116.	**Lexical priority: liberty, opportunity, wealth** *Andrew Lister*	435
117.	**Liberal conception of justice** *Micah Lewin*	440
118.	**Liberal people** *Walter J. Riker*	442
119.	**Liberalism as comprehensive doctrine** *Todd Hedrick*	445
120.	**Liberalism, comprehensive vs. political** *Micah Lewin*	447
121.	**Libertarianism** *Peter Vallentyne*	452
122.	**Liberty, equal worth of** *Adam Hosein*	457

x / *Contents*

123. **Liberty of conscience** *Kevin Vallier* — 460
124. **Locke, John** *Bas van der Vossen* — 464
125. **Love** *Paul Voice* — 468
126. **Luck egalitarianism** *Véronique Munoz-Dardé* — 471

M

127. **The market** *Andrew Lister* — 481
128. **Marx, Karl** *Rodney G. Peffer* — 486
129. **Maximin rule of choice** *Jon Mandle* — 493
130. **Migration** *Michael Blake* — 496
131. **Mill, John Stuart** *Catherine Audard* — 499
132. **Mixed conceptions of justice** *Véronique Munoz-Dardé* — 504
133. **Moral education** *Victoria Costa* — 507
134. **Moral person** *David A. Reidy* — 512
135. **Moral psychology** *David A. Reidy* — 520
136. **Moral sentiments** *David A. Reidy* — 528
137. **Moral theory** *Paul Voice* — 533
138. **Moral worth of persons** *Faviola Rivera-Castro* — 539

N

139. **Nagel, Thomas** *Alan Thomas and Martin O'Neill* — 543
140. **Nash point** *Anthony Simon Laden* — 546
141. **Natural duties** *Faviola Rivera-Castro* — 548
142. **Natural duty of justice** *David Lyons* — 551
143. **Natural talents** *Adam Hosein* — 553
144. **Neutrality** *Peter de Marneffe* — 557
145. **Nozick, Robert** *Helga Varden* — 561
146. **Nussbaum, Martha** *Alan W. Grose* — 565

O

147. **Objectivity** *Daniel Weinstock* — 571
148. **Obligations** *Miriam Ronzoni* — 574

Contents / XI

149. **Okin, Susan Moller** *Michael Blake* — 577

150. **The original position** *Anthony Simon Laden* — 579

151. **Outlaw states** *Darrel Moellendorf* — 586

152. **Overlapping consensus** *Rex Martin* — 588

P

153. **Paternalism** *Peter de Marneffe* — 597

154. **Peoples** *Helena de Bres* — 599

155. **Perfectionism** *Steven Wall* — 602

156. **Plan of life** *Faviola Rivera-Castro* — 606

157. **Pogge, Thomas** *Jon Mandle* — 608

158. **Political conception of justice** *Micah Lewin* — 612

159. **Political liberalism, justice as fairness as** *J. Donald Moon* — 616

160. **Political liberalisms, family of** *Micah Lewin* — 623

161. **Political obligation** *George Klosko* — 628

162. **Political virtues** *James Boettcher* — 631

163. **Practical reason** *Larry Krasnoff* — 635

164. **Precepts of justice** *Jon Mandle* — 640

165. **Primary goods, social** *Andreas Follesdal* — 643

166. **The priority of the right over the good** *Jaime Ahlberg* — 648

167. **Procedural justice** *Jon Garthoff* — 651

168. **Promising** *Adam Hosein* — 654

169. **Property-owning democracy** *Rodney G. Peffer* — 656

170. **Public choice theory** *Kevin Vallier* — 662

171. **Public political culture** *Ryan Prevnick* — 664

172. **Public reason** *Blain Neufeld* — 666

173. **Publicity** *Jon Garthoff* — 673

R

174. **Race** *Kevin M. Graham* — 681

175. **Rational choice theory** *Iwao Hirose* — 683

176. **Rational intuitionism** *Jon Mandle* — 685

177. **Realistic utopia** *Catherine Audard* — 688

XII / *Contents*

178. **The reasonable and the rational** *Larry Krasnoff* — 692
179. **Reasonable hope** *Paul Voice* — 698
180. **Reasonable pluralism** *Andrew Lister* — 700
181. **Reciprocity** *J. Donald Moon* — 703
182. **Reconciliation** *Todd Hedrick* — 707
183. **Redress, principle of** *Steven Wall* — 709
184. **Reflective equilibrium** *Norman Daniels* — 711
185. **Religion** *Daniel Dombrowski* — 717
186. **Respect for persons** *Nir Eyal* — 723
187. **Right: concept of, and formal constraints of** *Jeppe von Platz* — 725
188. **Rights, constitutional** *Frank I. Michelman* — 728
189. **Rights, moral and legal** *Alistair Macleod* — 731
190. **Rorty, Richard** *Robert B. Talisse* — 737
191. **Ross, W. D.** *Adam Cureton* — 739
192. **Rousseau, Jean-Jacques** *Jeffrey Bercuson* — 741
193. **Rule of law** *David A. Reidy* — 745
194. **Rules (two concepts of)** *Daniel Weinstock* — 750

S

195. **Sandel, Michael** *Robert B. Talisse* — 755
196. **Scanlon, T. M.** *Peter de Marneffe* — 757
197. **Self-interest** *Adam Cureton* — 760
198. **Self-respect** *Faviola Rivera-Castro* — 762
199. **Sen, Amartya** *Pablo Gilabert* — 765
200. **Sense of justice** *Jon Mandle* — 768
201. **Sidgwick, Henry** *Catherine Audard* — 773
202. **Sin** *Daniel Dombrowski* — 777
203. **Social choice theory** *Iwao Hirose* — 779
204. **Social contract** *Andrew Lister* — 781
205. **Social minimum** *Walter E. Schaller* — 785
206. **Social union** *Sibyl A. Schwarzenbach* — 788
207. **Socialism** *Rodney G. Peffer* — 791
208. **Society of peoples** *Chris Naticchia* — 795
209. **Soper, Philip** *Walter J. Riker* — 798
210. **Sovereignty** *Matt Lister* — 800

Contents / XIII

211.	**Stability** *Larry Krasnoff*	804
212.	**Statesman and duty of statesmanship** *Jon Mandle*	811
213.	**Strains of commitment** *David Lefkowitz*	813
214.	**Supreme Court and judicial review** *Todd Hedrick*	817

T

215.	**Taxation** *Martin O'Neill and Thad Williamson*	825
216.	**Thin and full theories of good** *Paul Weithman*	828
217.	**Toleration** *Daniel Weinstock*	838
218.	**Truth** *Henry S. Richardson*	842
219.	**The two principles of justice (in justice as fairness)** *Pablo Gilabert*	845

U

220.	**Unity of self** *David A. Reidy*	853
221.	**Utilitarianism** *Rahul Kumar*	858
222.	**Utility** *Jon Mandle*	866

W

223.	**Walzer, Michael** *Daniel Dombrowski*	871
224.	**Well-ordered society** *J. Donald Moon*	874
225.	**Wittgenstein, Ludwig** *Martin O'Neill*	878

Bibliography	882
Index	893

Abbreviations for Rawls's texts

When referring to Rawls's works, we have used the following abbreviations in this volume:

BIMSF   *A Brief Inquiry into the Meaning of Sin and Faith*, ed. Thomas Nagel (Harvard University Press, 2009)

CP   *Collected Papers*, ed. Samuel Freeman (Harvard University Press, 1999)

JF   *Justice as Fairness: A Restatement*, ed. Erin Kelly (Harvard University Press, 2001)

LHMP   *Lectures on the History of Moral Philosophy*, ed. Barbara Herman (Harvard University Press, 2000)

LHPP   *Lectures on the History of Political Philosophy*, ed. Samuel Freeman (Harvard University Press, 2007)

LP   *The Law of Peoples* (Harvard University Press, 1999)

PL   *Political Liberalism*, expanded edition (Columbia University Press 2005; original edition, 1993)

TJ   *A Theory of Justice*, revised edition (Harvard University Press, 1999; original edition, 1971)

Introduction

John (Jack) Bordley Rawls was born on February 21, 1921, in Baltimore, MD. His father, William Lee Rawls, was a self-taught lawyer who had managed a successful career and achieved some political influence. His mother, Anna Abell Stump Rawls, though primarily a homemaker, was politically active on her own as well. She was also an artist. Of the two parents, Rawls was closer to his mother.

Rawls had four brothers, one older and three younger. Two of his younger brothers died in childhood, both from infectious diseases that then claimed many more lives than today. In 1928, Rawls was ill with diphtheria. His closest younger brother and "great companion" Bobby contracted the disease from him and died. Only a year later, Rawls was ill with pneumonia after having his tonsils removed. His next youngest brother Tommy then came down with pneumonia and did not survive. Very shortly after, Rawls developed a stutter that would be with him to one degree or another for the rest of his life. The stutter forced him as a university professor meticulously to handwrite out and then read his lectures, a discipline that, especially when conjoined with constant and wide reading and an inability to resist the temptation to revise lectures in the light thereof, contributed to his immense and deep learning. All too cognizant of the risks of error when it comes to self-understanding, Rawls neither affirmed nor denied claims linking his stutter to a sense of guilt over his brothers' deaths, though he allowed that their deaths no doubt affected him profoundly.

Rawls did well in elementary and secondary school. He attended mostly private schools, attending public school only for a two-year period, middle school or junior high, while his father was President of the Baltimore School Board. He boarded at the Kent School in Connecticut for high school, where he found himself insufficiently challenged academically and without enough personal freedom. It was a High Episcopalian school. Rawls found uncongenial the severity of the school's headmaster, but the religious orientation suited him and he began to contemplate a future in the Episcopalian priesthood. In 1939, he followed his older brother from Kent to Princeton. He tried and did reasonably well in a number of subjects, including chemistry, math, art, and music (leading to a run as the music critic for the *Daily Princetonian* student publication). But he did not excel and he eventually settled into philosophy. Among the philosophy teachers who made an impact on the young Rawls were Walter Stace and Norman Malcolm. Stace was a British empiricist with utilitarian leanings who, perhaps oddly, had written an early book on Hegel and who retained a lifelong interest in mysticism arising out of an early religious experience. Malcolm had studied under Wittgenstein and was instrumental in bringing Wittgenstein's thought to the US. Increasingly drawn toward philosophical-theological inquiry, and writing under Stace's direction, Rawls wrote his undergraduate senior thesis, titled "A Brief Inquiry into Sin and the Meaning of Faith: An Interpretation Based on the Concept of Community," on the idea of sin as the refusal of, and faith as an openness to, genuine community and so personality, the spiritual core of the universe. He graduated in philosophy *summa cum laude*.

He graduated early in January of 1943 so that he could enlist in the US Army and join the fight in World War II against what he judged great evils. He served from 1943 to 1946, experiencing fierce hand-to-hand combat as an infantryman and then infantry radioman in the Pacific theater – New Guinea, Leyte, and Luzon – and earning a Purple Heart and a Bronze Star. As part of the occupation force of Japan, he passed through Hiroshima not long after the bomb, just one of several war experiences that challenged Rawls's belief in a personal theistic God to whom one might pray. He left the Army freed of his previous ambition for the seminary.

He entered the graduate program in philosophy at Princeton in 1946. Troubled by the rise of emotivist and other noncognitivist accounts of our moral capacities and nature, and by their implications for the rationality and so reasoned criticism of political deliberation, judgment, and authority, Rawls began to work toward a refutation of such views by counterexample. He would demonstrate the possibility of representing our moral judgments as the outcome of a rational procedure, a reasoning machine, with which we might freely identify and which we might even internalize as a regulative part of our self-understanding. By so doing, he would establish a rationalist, cognitivist alternative to emotivist and other noncognitivist accounts of our moral capacities and nature and would thereby undermine a tempting post-war invitation to cynicism about the ideal of democracy as reasoned self-rule. Such were his ambitions as a graduate student.

Notwithstanding his other interests, and a year (1947–1948) spent as a visiting graduate student at Cornell, where Malcolm and Max Black were then spreading Wittgenstein's teachings and influence, Rawls worked steadily, albeit in fits and starts, on his project. In 1949 he defended his dissertation, "A Study in the Grounds of Ethical Knowledge: Considered with Reference to Judgments on the Moral Worth of Character." He imagined the dissertation, written under Stace's direction, as the first installment of a three-part project, the other two taking up the grounds of ethical knowledge with respect to judgments regarding right actions and final ends. During this time, Rawls's substantive normative views were largely Millian in spirit and he thought of himself as a kind of, even if an unorthodox, utilitarian.

While a graduate student at Princeton Rawls met Margaret ("Mardy") Warfield Fox, a student at Pembroke College, Brown University. Like Rawls's mother, she was intelligent, interested in history and politics, and an artist. Jack had taken to painting and their shared passion for it was a source of both union and the occasional vigorous debate. They married in the summer of 1949. Their first child was born late autumn of 1950. By the summer of 1957, they would add three more, giving them two boys and two girls. Mardy and Jack remained married until his death. Always a full partner, Mardy played a significant role not only as a homemaker and financial manager during his active career years, but as a fulltime caregiver and editor and intellectual assistant in his later years of declining health.

Rawls spent 1949–1950 as a post-doctoral fellow and then 1950–1951 and 1951–1952 as an instructor at Princeton. He published a revised section of his dissertation under the title "Outline of a Decision Procedure for Ethics." And he began to read widely and to sit in on lectures as he was able. Economics, political and legal history, and the then emerging fields of decision and game theory drew special attention. In 1951 Rawls met the Oxford philosopher J. O. Urmson, who was visiting at Princeton. Urmson urged Rawls to apply for a Fulbright in order to spend a year at Oxford. Rawls applied, secured the Fulbright, and spent 1952–1953 as a member of the High Table at Christ Church College, Oxford. It was a pivotal year for Rawls, setting him on the path to what would become *A Theory of Justice*. The rich intellectual environment of Oxford and important relationships forged with Isaiah Berlin, H. L. A. Hart, Stuart Hampshire, Gilbert Ryle, and others served Rawls well. In brief, it was while at Oxford that Rawls became convinced of the need for a theory of institutional justice and began to worry that his own preferred version of a Millian utilitarianism was inadequate to the need.

The need for a theory of institutional or social or distributive justice arose from several sources. One was the insight, which Rawls credits to his reading of Rousseau and Marx, that culpable individual behavior cannot by itself explain, and so its elimination cannot ensure our overcoming, the great evils of the world. Another was the growing worry that his dissertation project, which aimed at a rationalist, cognitivist explanation of our moral capacities and nature, presupposed as data to be explained moral judgments that themselves stood in need of explanation. To serve the role he assigned them in his theory, certain moral judgments needed genuinely to express our moral capacities and nature rather than forces of indoctrination or manipulation. But this could only be asserted if the background conditions against which they arose were favorable to the free development and expression of our moral capacities and nature. To be sure, he held, a just constitutional liberal democracy would constitute favorable background conditions. But how might one publicly verify that any given polity was in fact a just constitutional liberal democracy? Without a theory of institutional justice, one suited to a democratic society and capable of underwriting an objective public judgment as to whether any given democratic society is in fact a just constitutional liberal democracy, one could never be sure that the moral judgments given a rationalist, cognitivist explanation were a free expression of our moral capacities and nature.

Rawls came to think his somewhat unorthodox Millian utilitarianism inadequate as a theory of institutional justice in several respects. These included an insufficiently secure public justification for the priority of liberty and, relatedly, the absence of any principled public constraint on what might count as a legitimate exercise of democratic citizenship, since with the right informational inputs the principle of utility might justify virtually any proposal or action as conducive to the common good and thus legitimate as an exercise of democratic citizenship.

Upon return to the US, Rawls took a position as an assistant professor of philosophy at Cornell. He began to work toward an adequate theory of institutional or social or distributive justice. After the publication of his influential paper "Two Concepts of Rules," a paper Rawls judged an essential first step toward shifting his focus to issues of institutional justice, Rawls was tenured and promoted at Cornell. Though "Two Concepts" was for Rawls an essential first step in his then just unfolding project, few readers recognized it as a promissory note on the project. But by 1958, Rawls's project was, in its first basic outline, available to all, in the form of his widely read paper "Justice as Fairness." Rawls would over the next twelve years complete the project, which would receive its full expression in his masterpiece *A Theory of Justice*. He would study carefully Aristotle, Aquinas, Hobbes, Locke, Hume, Rousseau, Kant, Hegel, Marx, Mill, Sidgwick, the British Idealists, nineteenth- and early twentieth-century political economy, Wittgenstein, Dewey, Quine, and much else. It would all find its way, synthesized, imaginatively reworked, sometimes repurposed, into his masterpiece.

In the late 1950s, Jack met Burton Dreben, then at Harvard, and Dreben helped to arrange an invitation to Rawls to spend 1959–60 as a visiting faculty member at Harvard. Dreben and Rawls would become close life-long friends. Rather than return to Cornell in 1960 after his Harvard visit, Rawls accepted a position as professor of philosophy with the then fledgling philosophy department at MIT, where he hired, among others, Hilary Putnam, who would later join him at Harvard. After just two years at MIT, Rawls left for a permanent position at Harvard, beginning there in the fall of 1962 as professor of philosophy. For the next eight years he worked steadily on drafts of what was to be *A Theory of Justice*. He also devoted considerable time to opposing the 2-S student deferment of draft military service in Vietnam on the grounds that it worked to distribute unjustly liability to military service. And with colleagues Tom Nagel, Marshall Cohen, Ronald Dworkin, Frank Michaelman, Owen Fiss, Charles Fried, Michael Walzer, Robert Nozick, Tim Scanlon, and a few others, he met regularly for what would become a most influential and long-lasting reading group, from which in the early 1970s would be born also the influential journal *Philosophy and Public Affairs*. Rawls spent a sabbatical year at Stanford in 1969–70 where he completed the final draft of *A Theory of Justice*. Remarkably, the manuscript (typescript in those days) was almost lost to a fire and, waterlogged, had to be set out page by page to dry. Rawls then returned to Harvard with *TJ* just published and facing a four-year term as Chairperson of the Philosophy Department, during politically turbulent times at Harvard (like most college campuses) and for the nation, an administrative task that he did not much enjoy.

Rawls spent much of the 1970s explaining and defending *TJ*, which he often felt was not well understood, and receiving recognitions and awards. He had hoped to move on to work in moral psychology. But by the late 1970s, he came to think incorrect a key piece of *TJ*, the so-called "congruence argument" given in part III's account of how a society faithful to the principles of justice as fairness could reasonably be expected to be stable in the right way. The defect proved challenging to correct. The process of correcting it unfolded over a little more than a decade's worth of papers and led eventually to Rawls's second book, *Political Liberalism*, first published in 1993, two years after he retired to Emeritus status at Harvard. Before readers had been able to fully absorb the lessons of *TJ*, Rawls had put in their laps another dense, rich, careful work of political philosophy. Inevitably, debates opened over its meaning, methods, motivation, and relationship to *TJ*.

Just as *Political Liberalism* was hitting the shelves, Rawls delivered in 1993 an Oxford Amnesty Lecture he titled "The Law of Peoples." In the lecture, he endeavored to extend his view, now to be understood as a political liberalism, to issues of international relations, or more specifically, to issues of foreign policy as confronted by a just, stable, and pluralist constitutional liberal democracy. The lecture, which was published, drew attention, mostly critical. The lecture surprised and disappointed even some of Rawls's closest students and most careful expositors and defenders, since he rejected a direct application of his principles of domestic justice, including the difference principle, to the question of global justice. And so the debates over *Political Liberalism* were forced to compete with, and were often folded into, the debates over Rawls's foray into foreign policy and international justice.

Rawls taught part-time in Emeritus status at Harvard until 1994. In 1995, just two days after a large conference celebrating the twenty-fifth anniversary of *A Theory of Justice* and attended by colleagues, students, admirers, critics, and the like, he suffered a stroke. He would suffer two more, amidst difficult and slowly declining health, before passing seven years later. However, Rawls had planned to publish not only a new introduction to *Political Liberalism*, but another treatment of the idea and ideal of public reason, so central to it and his project more generally. Both were underway at the time of his first stroke. And he had intended to work up his Oxford Amnesty Lecture into a short monograph treatment of international justice and foreign policy from the point of view of a democratic people committed to political liberalism. The stroke put all this in doubt. With the assistance of his wife Mardy, his close friend Burton, and others, he was able to get all this work done. His new introduction to *Political Liberalism* appeared in 1996. His essay "The Idea of Public Reason Revisited" appeared in 1997. And his short monograph *The Law of Peoples* appeared in 1999.

Students and colleagues had long urged Rawls to draw together and republish in one volume his many papers and to publish his course lectures, so carefully written out and developed over many years. Initially reluctant, he finally agreed. His *Collected Papers* appeared in 1999, edited by his past student Samuel Freeman. Under the editorial supervision of his past student Barbara Herman, his *Lectures*

Introduction / XXI

on the History of Moral Philosophy were published in 2000. His, by then widely circulated in mimeograph form and well-known, lectures on justice as fairness from the survey course on political philosophy he regularly taught at Harvard, and updated on each iteration of the course, were published in 2001 under the editorial supervision of his past student Erin Kelly under the title *Justice as Fairness: A Restatement*. Samuel Freeman had already begun work on Rawls's lectures in the history of political philosophy, but they would not appear in print before Rawls's passing. He passed away, his wife Mardy at his side, on November 24, 2002. Under Freeman's editorial supervision, his lectures on Hobbes, Locke, Hume, Rousseau, Mill, and Marx appeared as *Lectures on the History of Political Philosophy* in 2007. After Rawls's passing, his undergraduate thesis on sin, community, and the meaning of faith was discovered in both the Princeton and Harvard archives. After discussion, Mardy and his literary executor, Tim Scanlon, agreed to the publication of the thesis, not because Rawls would have wanted it published but because it was publicly available in university archives and likely to attract scholarly attention in any event. Better to supervise the publication and get the material properly introduced and contextualized. In 2009 the thesis was published as *A Brief Inquiry into the Meaning of Sin and Faith* and introduced by Joshua Cohen and Thomas Nagel, with Robert Adams providing a contextualizing essay in the intellectual history of philosophical theology. The volume included also Rawls's own brief late life statement of his religious orientation, a short essay titled "On My Religion."

Since Rawls's passing, nearly every major publisher has ventured one or more volumes offering a systematic reconstruction, a rethinking, or a new contextualization or fresh assessment of his work. With scholars now also actively working through his archived papers, more can be expected. All this is to the good, for it can hardly be doubted that much of this recent work has been insightful and productive and there remains much of value still to be drawn out of engaging his work.

We have prepared this *Lexicon* with the intention of contributing to the value of future engagements with Rawls's work, whether done by students or scholars. Rawls was an exceedingly careful philosopher and writer. He was very deliberate in his choice and very disciplined in his use of words. He took immense care with his own and others' ideas. In the course of so doing, he produced a terminologically and often technically rich and distinctive body of work. The terminology and technical aspects of Rawls's work can sometimes prove challenging, for both students and scholars. We have attempted in this volume to provide a reliable resource for dealing with such challenges. We have not attempted to resolve genuine interpretive or substantive debates. We have attempted only to set out clearly how Rawls used various terms, including terms of art, and presented key ideas. Inevitably, of course, this may seem to some as weighing in on a substantive or interpretive debate. We can say only that with respect to debatable matters, we have tried to avoid taking positions and instead have indicated that the matter is debatable. But not everything is debatable. And it is part of the aim of this volume to enable students and scholars to better distinguish what is debatable from what is not and to bring the latter more fully to bear on the former.

Rawls saw his work as a single painting, one he worked on over the course of his life. All the elements, as diverse as they often were – methodological, substantively normative, metaphilosophical, historical, sociopsychological, institutional, and so on – were meant to fit together systematically into a unified view. The painting was the result of Rawls's efforts, both for himself and with the communities of which he was a part, toward self-understanding and self-constitution, activities inseparable from one another. The vision, both of what we are and what we might be, answers our needs for both reconciliation to and reasoned reform of our shared social world. To the extent that it finds a regulative place within the self-understandings and conception-dependent desires of successive generations, there need be no talk of late modernity as a period of disenchantment with the world.

Rawls rightly recognized that his principles of justice were not particularly novel or controversial. Indeed, only the so-called difference principle represented a substantial departure from what one might have characterized as the enlightened center of mid-twentieth-century democratic thought. What was novel in Rawls's work was his ability to draw everything together and to overcome all manner of false dichotomies and divisions within philosophy. He could find a way to draw together both Humean and Kantian insights, to honor fully the priority and autonomy of practical reason without making a metaphysical commitment out of so doing, to articulate a meaningful conception of the common good and civic friendship for late modern democracies awash in self-centered individualism and base materialism, and to make clear why Lincoln was right about our last best hope.

Rawls received many honors and awards over his life. He received two honorary professorships from Harvard. He received honorary degrees from Harvard, Princeton, and Oxford and was a member of the Norwegian Academy of Science and Letters. He received the Ralph Waldo Emerson award from Phi Beta Kappa, the Ames Prize from Harvard Law, and the Lippincott Award from the American

Introduction / XXIII

Political Science Association. In 1999 he was awarded the National Humanities Medal by President Clinton and the Rolf Schock Prize by the Royal Swedish Academy. But apart from the awards, it was the painting – not the thing but the activity, one pursued both alone and with others – that animated the life.

JON MANDLE and DAVID A. REIDY

A

1.

ABORTION

A MUCH DISCUSSED footnote to the first edition of *Political Liberalism* takes up the "troubled question of abortion" in order to illustrate how norms of reasonableness and public reasoning apply to comprehensive religious and philosophical doctrines (*PL* 243 n.32). Rawls suggests that because the equality of women is an "overriding" value in this case, "any reasonable balance" of the relevant political values – not only equality, but also respect for human life and the ordered reproduction of society and the family – is sufficient to establish at least "a duly qualified right" to first-trimester abortion. According to Rawls, comprehensive doctrines that would deny such a right are "to that extent unreasonable" and citizens who vote on doctrinal grounds to effect this denial thereby violate requirements of public reason (*PL* 243–244 n.32).

Even shortly after the publication of *Political Liberalism*, this analysis had become something of a focal point for a variety of critical challenges to Rawls's idea of public reason. Critics argue that public reason unfairly excludes religious believers and convictions from politics and that it remains far too incomplete to resolve especially difficult moral-political controversies like abortion.

In both the "Introduction to the Paperback Edition" of *Political Liberalism* and "The Idea of Public Reason Revisited" Rawls clarifies and in some ways corrects the analysis of the earlier footnote, which is said to have aimed mainly at "illustration" and to have expressed an "opinion" rather than an "argument" (*PL* liii–liv n.31; *PL* 479 n.80). He repeats an earlier claim that comprehensive doctrines may be reasonable on the whole even though they yield an unreasonable conclusion with respect to a particular issue. Moreover, citizens should be able to respect abortion rights as part of legitimately enacted law even as they continue to argue against them. Forceful resistance to a legitimate right to abortion would be unreasonable (*PL* lv).

More important, in this later analysis Rawls observes that political opposition to abortion rights does not necessarily violate requirements of public reason. Citizens who oppose abortion on religious or moral grounds may indeed advocate against abortion rights politically, but only if they satisfy the proviso and identify sufficient public reasons for their judgments. Citing an essay by Cardinal Joseph Bernardin, Rawls acknowledges that there are in fact arguments within the domain of public reason against legalizing abortion (*PL* liv n.32). Rawls does not attempt to evaluate the soundness or reasonableness of these arguments or of the constitutional arguments against *Roe* v. *Wade* (*CP* 618). Nor does he provide any indication that these arguments would ultimately be sufficiently compelling to justify the denial of abortion rights. Thus even this later discussion of the abortion issue suggests that in Rawls's considered view the stronger arguments are those that would support abortion rights on the basis of the political values listed in the original abortion footnote (*PL* liv n.31).

An earlier discussion of moral personality from *Theory* would also seem to be relevant to the question of abortion. Moral persons are defined in terms of their capacity for realizing the two moral powers, at least to a minimum degree, and this capacity for moral personality is sufficient for entitling one to equal justice (*TJ*, 442–443). This is why infants and children are owed duties of justice while animals are not. However, with his main goal of identifying principles of justice for the basic structure of a society into which persons are born, Rawls does not apply this account of moral personality to the ethics of abortion.

James Boettcher

SEE ALSO:

Catholicism
Duty of civility
Feminism
Public reason
Religion
Supreme Court and judicial review

2.

ADVANTAGE, MUTUAL VS. RECIPROCAL

RAWLS TREATS SOCIAL cooperation as voluntary activity between citizens of a common polity that generates benefits for cooperators. Fair social cooperation is regulated by public rules and procedures that all can freely accept as appropriate. Rawls's principles of justice apply to the basic institutional structures of society that define the fair terms of social cooperation. An accurate representation of the fundamental idea of society as a fair system of cooperation is thus essential to understanding the overall character of Rawls's theory. Rawls maintains that justice as fairness adopts an understanding of social cooperation that is animated by an idea of reciprocity or reciprocal advantage. He locates reciprocity between an idea of impartiality and an idea of mutual advantage. The contrast between these ideas lies in the different relation citizens engaged in cooperation can stand both to one another and to the benefits that cooperation generates.

Reciprocity assumes that citizens in a well-ordered society view each other as free and equal persons who are jointly committed to establishing fair terms of cooperation. Each citizen is concerned to advance her own good through cooperation but this concern is tempered by an acknowledgement of the reasonable claims of others. So each citizen need not extract the maximum benefit from a scheme of social cooperation that they can secure via rational bargaining in order for a scheme to be fair. Reciprocity requires both that all contribute to social cooperation and that social cooperation be beneficial to all. However, the benchmark for assessing whether cooperation benefits all is an equal division of social benefits.

Impartiality acknowledges the equal standing of persons engaged in social cooperation but treats the persons engaged in cooperation as altruistic and moved by promotion of the general good. As such, impartiality does not require that all persons benefit from participation in cooperation: an acceptable cooperative scheme may leave some persons worse off than they would be under an equal division. Similarly, whereas impartiality may allow some to free ride on the cooperative efforts of others, reciprocity does not.

Mutual advantage, unlike both reciprocity and impartiality, assumes that persons approach cooperation as rational maximizers who are solely concerned with promotion of their own good. Mutual advantage does not demand that cooperators view one another as free and equal persons and it does not accept an equal division as the benchmark for gauging how cooperation yields benefits to persons. Instead, mutual advantage treats the prior distribution of benefits, even if it is highly unequal or the result of injustice, as the relevant benchmark. Whereas reciprocity allows that the transition from an unjust society to a just one can leave some less well off than they were under an unjust society, mutual advantage holds that persons must benefit relative to the prior division of benefits. Rawls claims that no reasonable conception of justice could satisfy such an idea of mutual advantage and he insists that the idea is alien to justice as fairness.

Colin Macleod

SEE ALSO:

Cooperation and coordination
Reciprocity

3.

ALLOCATIVE JUSTICE

JOHN RAWLS INTRODUCES the concept of allocative justice in order to note the contrast with how justice as fairness treats distributive justice. Rawls says, "[A]llocative justice applies when a given collection of goods is to be divided among definite individuals with known desires and needs" (*TJ* 77). A wealthy person deciding which charities to include among her beneficiaries when drawing up her will, for example, faces a problem of allocative justice. No charity has a prior claim to any portion of the inheritance, so the person might consider the relative importance of the needs that each charity addresses, and how far her legacy would go to address these on the basis of different allocations.

Justice as fairness understands distributive justice differently. It applies its principles of justice to the institutions of the basic structure of society. Distributive justice concerns the distribution of various primary social goods already built into the basic structure of society, which is conceived of as a cooperative system for their production and distribution. If the distribution of these goods already built into the basic structure is just, then whatever particular allocation of them that results from the free activity of citizens within that structure, consistent with its rules, is a just allocation, or "distribution." He says, "A distribution cannot be judged in isolation from the system of which it is the outcome or from what individuals have done in good faith in the light of established expectations" (*TJ* 76). Note that while Rawls distinguishes distributive from allocative justice, he often uses the terms "distribution" and "allocation" interchangeably, such as the use of "distribution" in the previous quote, where "allocation" would be the better term. A just allocation is, then, for Rawls, a matter of pure procedural justice. An allocation of primary social goods to particular individuals is just so long as it follows from the just procedure of free, rule-governed activity within a basic social structure that is distributively just.

When the question is of the justice of the basic rules of society – those rules that are constitutive of the institutions of the basic structure – neither the stock of goods nor the desires of citizens are fixed. The design of the basic structure will impact the kind and amount of goods produced. Likewise, while it is possible to identify desires that are stable across different institutional designs – for example, some concern for the primary goods – citizens' more particular sets of desires will be impacted by their institutional environment. These differences make the problem of distributive justice distinct from that of allocative justice, and Rawls goes on to interpret the problem of distributive justice as one of pure procedural justice.

Rawls notes two values that might be held central to a conception of allocative justice: efficiency and equality. If efficiency is the end of allocative justice, then we are led to endorse some form of utilitarianism. The idea is that utilitarianism will lead to an allocation that maximizes the aggregate level of utility (which can be understood in various ways). If we take allocative justice to be aimed at equality, then on one class of interpretations of equality we are led to some form of luck egalitarianism. Rawls rejects both utilitarianism and luck egalitarianism in favor of justice as fairness as the most reasonable conception of distributive justice. Apart from arguments from the original position, one way to understand Rawls's rejection of these two is that for Rawls distributive justice is a matter of pure procedural justice, and so no account of allocative justice can serve also as an account of distributive justice.

Pete Murray

SEE ALSO:

> *Distributive justice*
> *Primary goods, social*
> *Procedural justice*

4.

ALTRUISM

ALTRUISM IS THE sacrifice of one's own interests or good for the benefit of others. Egoism, concern for one's own good alone, is its opposite. In general, altruism does not require that one promote the interests of others equally, so an altruist may, for example, sacrifice her own interests for those of the members of an exclusive group such as family or community members. Rawls says that classical utilitarianism "is the ethic of perfect altruists" (*TJ* 165). The suggestion is that a "perfect" altruist would be a perfectly impartial altruist, although as a technical matter, utilitarianism allows one's own interests to count on equal terms with the interests of others.

Any moral doctrine that requires individuals to sacrifice their own interests for those of others will incorporate altruistic elements, although not necessarily raised to a first principle. Justice as fairness certainly may require individuals to make sacrifices, but it does so in accordance with an ideal of reciprocity. Reciprocity, Rawls holds, "lies between the ideal of impartiality, which is altruistic (being moved by the general good), and the idea of mutual advantage understood as everyone's being advantaged with respect to each person's present or expected future situation as things are" (*PL* 16–17). He also associates reciprocity with the idea of the reasonable: "Reasonable persons, we say, are not moved by the general good as such but desire for its own sake a social world in which they, as free and equal, can cooperate with others on terms all can accept" (*PL* 50).

Understood in terms of the satisfaction of desires (as opposed to interests or goods), altruism is a second-order desire, in that it aims at the satisfaction of the first-order desires of others. Thus Rawls notes the following "peculiar feature of perfect altruism": "A perfect altruist can fulfill his desire only if someone else has independent, or first-order desires" (*TJ* 165). This parallels a feature of Rawls's understanding of justice. The virtue of justice (or fairness) is needed in conditions of moderate scarcity when the (reasonable or permissible) conceptions of the good of different individuals conflict. Justice (or fairness) is then a second-order good that aims at resolving the conflicting ground-level interests or goods fairly. This is why the parties in the original position are assumed to be mutually disinterested. It is not because actual persons are not or should not be concerned with one another. It is because the virtue of justice only arises when there are actual or potential conflicts among conceptions of the good.

Jon Mandle

SEE ALSO:

> *The reasonable and the rational*
> *Reciprocity*
> *Self-interest*
> *Utilitarianism*

5.

ANIMALS

RAWLS IS CLEAR in *A Theory of Justice* that the basis of equality does not extend to nonhuman animals (hereafter: animals). This is because they are not moral persons with the two basic moral powers: the ability to develop a conception of the good and a sense of justice or the right. Strictly speaking, equal justice applies only to those with these two powers. Hence animals are left out of Rawls's famous social contract experiment. Another way to put the point is to say that it is those who can give justice who are owed justice (*TJ* 15, 441–449; also *LP* 92, 171).

In an earlier piece, "The Sense of Justice" (1963), Rawls asked the question, "who is owed justice?" His response was that the capacity to be just was a necessary and sufficient condition for receiving justice. He admits that establishing that the capacity to be just is a necessary condition for receiving justice is much more difficult than it is to establish that the capacity to be just is a sufficient condition for receiving justice. (In *TJ* Rawls is not explicit that the two moral powers are necessary for being owed justice, only that they are sufficient for being owed justice, although the necessary condition may be implied in *TJ*.) Nonetheless he concludes that we have no duty of justice to animals, as there might be in utilitarianism where possession of sentiency seems to be a sufficient condition for being a full subject of rights (*CP* 112–116).

Rawls is aware of the fact that high-level criteria for being owed justice, like the aforementioned two moral powers, have implications not only for animals but for some human beings as well. Once a certain minimum level of the two moral powers is met, citizens are entitled to equal justice, Rawls thinks. In *TJ* he does not examine those who do not meet this minimum level, but he does say that the vast majority of human beings have the capacity for, if not the actual ability to enact, the two moral powers. Thus, for practical purposes, he thinks, "all" humans "originally" possess moral personality. And the capacity for love and affection are universal among human beings. Once again, he chooses not to examine those who have lost these capacities through congenital defect or illness or accident (*TJ* 441–449; *CP* 112–116).

Although animals are not owed justice, and this because they do not have a moral status equal to human beings with the two moral powers, they should be afforded some protection. Because they are capable of feeling pleasure and pain, Rawls holds that we have duties of compassion and humanity toward them and thus we ought not to be cruel to them. And destruction of a whole animal species is a great evil. But Rawls thinks that the protections that we ought to give to animals are not the result of a duty of justice on our part. Rather, a conception of justice is only one part of an overall moral theory and there are moral virtues besides justice. That is, the principle of humanity is more inclusive than justice (*TJ* 441–449; *CP* 112–116).

In *PL* Rawls expands on the relatively narrow concerns of *TJ* by treating four problems of extension, three of which are amenable to resolution, he thinks (by extending the principles of justice to future generations, by expanding them so as to include the law of peoples, and by covering the health care needs of citizens). But concerning the fourth problem of extension, he doubts if animals can be brought within justice as fairness as a political conception. He admits that this may be due to a lack of ingenuity. If we start with full persons in adult society with the two moral powers, he cannot see how animals can be included in the social contract (*PL* 21, 244–246). The ambiguity in *TJ* is removed in *PL*: the two moral powers are necessary (not only sufficient) to be owed justice (*PL* 302). He does not consider the efforts by Donald Vandeveer and others to develop a revised original position where "marginal" human beings and animals, although not moral agents, are nonetheless seen as moral patients who are the beneficiaries of decisions made in the original position.

Also in *PL* he treats two contrasting views that have implications for animals. The traditional Christian view, on his interpretation, sees animals as subject to our use, as in the biological and medical knowledge that they make possible. By way of contrast, the view of natural religion (which is either a separate comprehensive doctrine from the traditional Christian view or a countercultural tendency within that view) is one wherein animals are seen as the loci of rights and are hence brought within the scope of justice. But this view, Rawls claims, cannot direct us toward a constitutional essential in that it is like opposition to abortion on strictly religious grounds. That is, the values cherished by the natural religionist are nonpolitical. Rawls does not state explicitly that the traditional view of animals is also nonpolitical, leading some to wonder whether this was the view he endorsed at a political level (*PL* 244–266). This is reminiscent of the open question in *TJ* regarding how to fit justice as fairness within a metaphysical system that explains humanity's place within the natural world (*TJ* 448–449).

Rawls admits, relying on evidence provided by ethologists, that animals resemble human beings in their desire for self-realization. In a way the Aristotelian principle also applies to them, as is borne out by the facts of everyday life and which can be given an evolutionary explanation. In effect, natural selection, he thinks, would have favored animals concerning whom the Aristotelian principle would have applied (*TJ* 378–379).

The undergraduate Rawls saw a wide gap between human beings and other animals in that he opposed what he saw as the superficial modern view that human beings were merely biological animals. Human beings, he thought, were not so much biological animals as they were persons (*BIMSF* 217–218). This view is continuous with his later Kantian view that we are not dignified as animals, but as personal beings with the two moral powers.

Daniel Dombrowski

SEE ALSO:

Aristotelian principle
The environment
Moral person

6.

AQUINAS, THOMAS

THE MATURE RAWLS viewed St. Thomas Aquinas' *Summa Theologiae* as a "magnificent" achievement. Just as Leibniz rendered the scientific discoveries of the seventeenth century compatible with Christian orthodoxy, Aquinas (1225–1274) confronted the new Aristotelianism of the thirteenth century so as to restate Christian theology in Aristotelian terms (*LHMP* 12, 106).

This praise of Aquinas contrasts with the very early Rawls, who opposed the naturalism of Plato, Aristotle, Augustine, and Aquinas to Christian personalism. Rawls defended the latter and denigrated the former. By "naturalism" Rawls did not mean "materialism." Rather, naturalists like Aquinas were those who saw human beings as essentially oriented toward an abstract good instead of toward a personal God (and toward human persons). The danger, he thought, was that naturalists like Aquinas turned God into an object and, because of this depersonalized character of naturalism, encourage egoism and hence the destruction of community (*BIMSF* 119–120, 161–162, 178, 182, 189, 209, 217, 220–221).

Both the very early Rawls and the 1997 Rawls of "On My Religion" opposed the predeterminism of Aquinas (alleged to be every bit as severe as that of Calvin) as well as Aquinas' effort to offer rational proofs for God's existence. Throughout his life Rawls seemed to remain a fideist (*BIMSF* 224, 247, 263–264).

Rawls thinks that his own view that justice is a complex of three ideas – liberty, equality, and reward for services contributing to the common good (once primary goods are fulfilled regardless of contribution) – is compatible with Aquinas' political philosophy. But Aquinas failed to draw out the implicit egalitarianism of these three ideas. What is needed is not merely the announcement of these ideas, but also their interpretation and application (*CP* 193).

Rawls's view is compatible with Aquinas' stance regarding the common good and solidarity *when it is expressed in terms of a political value*, rather than in terms of a value associated with a particular comprehensive doctrine. It can thus be said that Rawls's view is that of a (political) common good of (various comprehensive and sometimes conflicting) common goods. In this regard Rawls's view is also compatible with the stances of Thomists like Jacques Maritain and John Finnis (*CP* 582–583; *LP* 142).

In a similar vein, Rawls's view is compatible with Aquinas' stance regarding the dignity of the human person *when it is expressed as a political conception* of the person, rather than in terms of a conception of the person peculiar to a particular comprehensive doctrine. Regarding the latter, Thomists tend to say that all human beings desire, even if unknown to themselves, the vision of God, just as Platonists tend to say that all human beings desire a vision of the good. Political liberalism sets aside comprehensive accounts of human nature such as these, although it should also be noted that it permits them as long as they are reasonable (*LP* 172).

Rawls's view is especially at odds with Aquinas' (along with Plato's, Aristotle's, St. Augustine's, and the Protestant reformers') stance that there is only one reasonable and rational good such that political institutions are justifiable to the extent that they promote this good. On this basis, intolerance of those who impede this good is justifiable. This sort of intolerance, which is based on (very often dogmatic) confidence in one's own comprehensive doctrine, is different from (very often reluctant) intolerance based on a concern for justice in a liberal society. Decision-making in the original position favors equal liberty of conscience that can be limited only when it interferes with public order and the liberty of others. Or again, liberty can be constrained only by liberty itself (*TJ* 189–190; *PL* 34).

A dramatic example of the difference between Aquinas and Rawls on the basis of intolerance is provided by Aquinas' defense of the death penalty for heretics on the ground that corrupting the soul is worse than counterfeiting money – the latter of which was a capital crime in the thirteenth century (see *Summa Theologiae* IIaIIae, q. 11, a. 3). The view that intolerance of heretics is necessary for the safety of souls is only apparently reasonable, according to Rawls, in that it relies on one comprehensive doctrine that is forced on everyone else (*TJ* 189–190; *CP* 91).

Likewise, in Rawls's later works comprehensive liberalism, in contrast to political liberalism, is utopian in the pejorative sense and is no better than the comprehensive religious views of Aquinas or Luther when these are imposed on others (*CP* 490; *JF* 188). But Rawls anticipated this point even in *TJ* in his rejection of the "omnicompetent laicist state" (*TJ* 186).

Rawls agrees with Aquinas on the good when simpler cases are involved, concerning which reasonable people do not disagree (e.g. that cruelty is wrong). Here he is also in agreement with philosophers who have been positively influenced by Aquinas like Philippa Foot (*TJ* 350–351). And he also agrees with Aquinas that play and amusement are crucial in the effort to moderate one's pursuit of a dominant end in life, otherwise such a pursuit, according to Rawls, tends to lead to fanaticism or irrationality (*TJ* 484–485).

The importance of natural duty in Rawls (*TJ* 293–301) also indicates overlap with Aquinas' view of natural duty. But because the compatibility between Rawls and Aquinas lies at the level of *political values*, rather than at the level of comprehensive doctrine, there is no overlap between Rawls and Aquinas regarding the latter's belief that eternal law is the basis of ethics and politics, regardless of whether eternal law is defended in terms of divine command theory or natural law theory. That is, natural duty in Rawls is affirmed without a metaphysical account of its underlying basis. Such a basis, if there is such, is left for those who adhere to any one of a number of comprehensive doctrines (*LHMP* 7; *TJ* 293–301). Nonetheless Rawls appreciates the monumental contributions to a politically liberal society made by Martin Luther King, who held the Thomistic view that unjust laws were those that violated eternal law, including natural law, as in Jim Crow laws that denigrated blacks (*PL* 250).

Daniel Dombrowski

SEE ALSO:

> *Aristotle*
> *Catholicism*
> *Justice (common good idea of)*
> *Faith*
> *Religion*

7.

ARISTOTELIAN PRINCIPLE

THE ARISTOTELIAN PRINCIPLE purports to be a basic principle of human motivation, one that describes a strong, and not easily counterbalanced, tendency or desire. The principle states that "other things equal, human beings enjoy the exercise of their realized capacities (their innate or trained abilities), and this enjoyment increases the more the capacity is realized, or the greater its complexity" (*TJ* 374). To illustrate with Rawls's own example: if people can play both chess and checkers, they will tend to prefer the former over the latter, since chess is a more complex game, one that draws on a wider range of abilities. The Aristotelian principle also has a companion effect. "As we witness the exercise of well-trained abilities by others, these displays are enjoyed by us and arouse a desire that we should be able to do the same things ourselves" (*TJ* 375–376). Rawls introduces the Aristotelian principle and its companion effect in part III of *TJ*. The principle and its companion effect, he claims, add content to the formal definition of a person's good, help to account for our considered judgments of value, and contribute to the stability of a well-ordered society.

Since the Aristotelian principle purports to be a basic principle of human motivation, the question of its justification, Rawls claims, does not arise. We should not ask whether the principle is a good principle. Rather, we should ask whether it accurately describes human psychology; and Rawls not only suggests that it does, but also that an evolutionary explanation can be given for its truth. Natural selection "must have favored creatures of whom this principle is true" (*TJ* 378). But, interestingly, Rawls also makes a number of claims about the principle that strongly indicate that it has normative force. For instance, he claims that the principle conveys Aristotle's idea that the exercise of our natural powers is a leading intrinsic human good. He observes further that Mill's doctrine of higher pleasures comes very close to stating the principle, and he allows that the principle bears a certain resemblance to the idealist notion of self-realization. These claims all suggest that the Aristotelian principle is a perfectionist principle. It not only describes human nature, but also tells something important about the content of a good human life.

Yet Rawls himself resists characterizing the principle as perfectionist. He does so for two principal reasons. First, the principle does not identify any particular activities as valuable. Different people will be drawn to develop different capacities and talents, and the Aristotelian principle does not rank them as better or worse. It states only that people's rational plans will include activities that allow them to develop their talents, and that they will tend to prefer more to less complex achievements. Second, and more fundamentally, Rawls claims that his account of the good for persons does not depend on the truth of the Aristotelian principle. If the Aristotelian principle did not apply to a person – if the person did not have the psychological tendencies it postulates – then the good for that person would not include activities that allow him to develop his powers and talents. This is illustrated by Rawls's example of the man who only finds pleasure in counting blades of grass. A rational plan of life for this person would not be one in which he developed his natural talents and capacities to any significant extent. The Aristotelian principle must find its place within Rawls's subjectivism about the human good.

The grass counter, to be sure, is a fanciful example. For human beings as we know them, we can safely assume, or so Rawls claims, that the Aristotelian principle is a deep feature of their motivational makeup. For this reason, rational plans of life generally must take it into account; and, in the design of political and social institutions, "a large place has to be made for it" (*TJ* 377).

The companion effect of the Aristotelian principle further illustrates its significance for rational plans of life. Since human beings take pleasure in one another's development of their natural talents and capacities, they will tend to value the plans of life of others only if these plans achieve a certain measure of self-development. And if one's plan of life is not valued by others, then it will be impossible, or at least very difficult, for one to maintain the judgment that it is worth carrying out. That is why the Aristotelian principle "ties in with the primary good of self-respect" (*TJ* 380). Although Rawls does not say so, these claims suggest that the grass counter would not have a good life, for his activities would not be valued by others and so he would not be able to have a secure sense of his own worth, which is itself a condition for a good human life.

The companion effect of the Aristotelian principle also explains how living in a well-ordered society contributes to the good of its members. A well-ordered society is, to use von Humboldt's phrase, a social union of social unions. No one person can develop all sides of his nature, but the wide range of associations that exist in a free society make possible a broad and deep development of human potentialities and talents. By participating in a society of this kind, each member "can participate in the total sum of the realized natural assets of the others" (*TJ* 459). Following von Humboldt, Rawls claims that this a great good for each member, but it is a good that can be realized fully only if each member acknowledges and affirms the regulative role of the principles that make a social union of social unions possible. These are the principles of justice. In this way, the Aristotelian principle and its companion effect contribute to the stability of a well-ordered society. They help to establish the congruence between a commitment to justice, on the one hand, and a desire to lead a good human life, on the other.

Steven Wall

SEE ALSO:

Conception of the good
Congruence
Natural talents
Perfectionism
Self-respect
Stability

8.

ARISTOTLE

IN AT LEAST five different ways Rawls's thought is indebted to Aristotle's (384–322 BCE). First, Rawls's overall method of reflective equilibrium goes back to Aristotle's dialectic in *Nicomachean Ethics*, as interpreted by W. F. R. Hardie (*TJ* 45). Second, his theory of primary goods relies heavily on Aristotle (*TJ* 79, 351). Third, Aristotle's belief that the fact that human beings possess a sense of justice is what makes possible a *polis* is analogous to Rawls's belief that humanity's common understanding of fairness is what makes possible a constitutional democracy (*TJ* 214). Fourth, Rawls relies on Aristotle in thinking that justice consists in refraining from *pleonexia* – i.e. unfairly gaining at the expense of others (*TJ* 9–10). And fifth, Rawls relies on Aristotle's idea that no one should tailor the canons of legitimate complaint to fit his or her own special conditions (*CP* 200–201).

The chief point of conflict between Rawls's views and Aristotle's lies in the latter's perfectionism, as Rawls interprets Aristotle (*TJ* 22, 286). He notes that Aristotle was interpreted as a teleological and metaphysical perfectionist at least until the time of Kant (*CP* 343). Because perfectionism is a type of teleological doctrine, it comes under the sway of Rawls's critique of teleological doctrines, in general, which is one of the main aims of *TJ*.

Aristotle's eudaemonistic perfectionism (along with Aquinas') is connected to his commitment to the common good. This commitment is compatible with political liberalism as long as it is expressed in terms of *political* values, rather than in terms of a particular comprehensive doctrine. In the latter case it is subject to the restrictions on comprehensive doctrines, in general, that are required in a condition of reasonable pluralism (*CP* 583; *LP* 142).

Nevertheless, Rawls acknowledges that Aristotle's treatment of happiness as an inclusive end for a human life (rather than as a dominant end) is the most influential in the history of philosophy (*TJ* 481), and even influences Rawls's own treatment of a rational plan of life.

Aristotle's perfectionism led him to affirm only one reasonable and rational good, on Rawls's interpretation. Institutions were justifiable to the extent that they promoted this good (*PL* 134); and intolerance of those who did not promote this good was permissible. Aristotle thus set the tone in at least two ways for classical moral philosophy: human beings by nature desired to know and knowledge in ethics centered on the idea of the highest good in the pursuit of true happiness (*LHMP* 4, 47). Rawls uses these features of classical moral philosophy to better understand Kant and Hegel. For Kant, contra Aristotle, the religious or the holy in some fashion transcends happiness. And for Hegel, along with Aristotle, the highest good is desired for its own sake and is self-sufficient (*LHMP* 160, 371).

The rational intuitionism of Aristotle, wherein moral concepts are not analyzable in terms of nonmoral concepts and first principles of morality are self-evident propositions, is not Rawls's view. This "self-evidence," if there is such, is subject to the constraints of reflective equilibrium, in general. Rawls would hold this view even if W. D. Ross is correct in claiming that moral decisions almost always rely on intuitions regarding a balance of reasons (*CP* 343, 350). In fact, such a balance is very close to what Rawls means by reflective equilibrium.

There are at least two different types of contemporary political philosophy that are heavily influenced by Aristotle and concerning which Rawls's view can be contrasted. *Classical republicanism* (or civic republicanism) in the tradition of Aristotle affirms the priority of ancient liberties to modern ones, such that we should encourage active participation in public life in order to preserve basic rights and liberties. Rawls's thought is consistent with this view, at least when classical republicanism is balanced by a commitment to modern liberties. However, political liberalism is much more likely to be at odds with *civic humanism*. This latter view is a type of essentialist Aristotelianism wherein a human being's nature is most fully achieved in participation in political life. Because civic humanists like Hannah Arendt see politics as a privileged locus for our complete good, such that without vigorous participation in politics one's *telos* cannot be achieved, it is itself a comprehensive doctrine that must be held in check along with other comprehensive doctrines in a condition of reasonable pluralism (*PL* 205–206, 410; *JF* 142–143).

Rawls is also affected by Aristotle's treatment of particular vices, like envy, which implies badness of character from the start in that it does not admit of a mean (*TJ* 466). In a way, spite is the flip side of envy in that if envy consists in negative feelings toward the good fortune of others, spite consists in the pleasure brought about by the bad fortune of others (*TJ* 468). Rawls, along with Aristotle, thinks it is virtuous, however, to prefer a short yet noble life to a long life of vice or to many years of "humdrum existence." In this regard he uses Aristotle in his critique of hedonism as a dominant end (*TJ* 488).

It should also be noted that in Rawls's undergraduate thesis he exhibited a very negative attitude toward Aristotle in many different passages. We should stop "kow-towing" to him, Rawls thought, in that "an ounce of the Bible is worth a pound (possibly a ton) of Aristotle." He was mainly critical of Aristotle's "naturalism," by which he did not mean "materialism." Rather, naturalism in ethics refers to turning desire to its proper object, the good. According to the very early Rawls, this misses the spiritual or personal element in ethics. In effect, Aristotle turned God into the good, he thought. Rawls feared that this depersonalizing tendency in Aristotle would eventually lead to egoism and to the destruction of community (see *BIMSF*, especially 107, 114, 227).

Daniel Dombrowski

SEE ALSO:

Aquinas, Thomas
Aristotelian principle
Civic humanism
Political virtues
Rational intuitionism
Reflective equilibrium

9.

ARNESON, RICHARD

RICHARD ARNESON (b. 1945) is an important figure in contemporary political philosophy, and a critic of Rawls's and Rawlsian theories of justice. Arneson's views diverge in three important ways from Rawlsian approaches.

First, Arneson rejects Rawls's two principles in favor of a weighted-maximizing welfarist conception of political justice. In particular, Arneson is critical of the two lexical priorities found in Rawls's principles: the lexical priority of the first principle to the second, and the lexical priority of benefits to the worse-off in comparison to the better-off. With regard to the first, Arneson holds that the freedoms guaranteed by the first principle of justice (such as the freedom of speech, say) are only important to justice insofar as they allow citizens to live better lives than they otherwise would. Hence to say that such freedoms lexically dominate other concerns of justice is to grant these freedoms a level of priority that is insensitive to concerns about life quality, and is hence unjustified. This applies, according to Arneson, also in the case of democratic freedoms, or the right of political participation (Arneson 1993). Furthermore, Arneson rejects Rawls's difference principle. According to Arneson, the difference principle would require massive transfers from the better off to the worse off, even in cases in which the benefits to the worse-off will be comparatively small. According to Arneson, Rawls's maximin approach is "implausibly extreme." Instead, Arneson accepts what he deems a "broadly egalitarian" understanding of distributive justice, in which benefits to the worse-off are given some, but not lexical, priority to benefits for the better off (Arneson 2000b).

Second, Arneson rejects Rawls's reliance on primary goods as the index of political distribution. Arneson argues that the capabilities approach, championed by Sen (1980) is superior to the primary goods approach. Arneson also believes, however, that a welfarist approach is superior to the capabilities approach (Arneson 2000a). According to Arneson, we should measure the justice of a given society not by the extent to which individuals have the capability to achieve particular goods, but rather by their actual achievement of objectively valuable welfare states. Related to this, Arneson rejects Rawls's insistence that political morality should be neutral with respect to considerations of the good, or considerations of substantive ethical conceptions (Arneson 2003).

Arneson's welfarist consequentialism is enriched by his embrace of the importance of individual responsibility in determining just patterns of welfare distribution. Arneson has developed this view in many stages; currently he proposes a version of "responsibility-catering prioritarianism" (Arneson 2000b), which holds that benefits to the worse-off matter more than benefits to the better-off, but that benefits to those who have displayed forms of irresponsibility or who fail to deserve such benefits matter less than benefits to those who are so deserving.

Dale Dorsey

SEE ALSO:

Capabilities
Lexical priority: liberty, opportunity, wealth
Luck egalitarianism
Primary goods, social

10.

ARROW, KENNETH J.

KENNETH J. ARROW is an American Nobel-laureate welfare economist (b. 1921). He is the founder of modern social choice theory, and his General Possibility Theorem influenced Rawls's *TJ*. Arrow claims that there exists no collective decision-making rule that satisfies four seemingly uncontroversial conditions that any democratic society should satisfy (Pareto, unrestricted domain, independence of irrelevant alternatives, and non-dictatorship). In Arrow (1973), he raises a set of the earliest, and still most fundamental, criticisms to Rawls's *TJ*.

First, Arrow argues that Rawls's argument against John Harsanyi's justification of average utilitarianism is false. According to Rawls, in order for average utilitarianism to be chosen in the original position, Harsanyi and other defenders of average utilitarianism must assume that the attitude of the parties is risk-neutral, whereas Rawls contends that the parties would have a risk-averse attitude and thus choose the two principles of justice. Arrow, however, argues that the von Neumann–Morgenstern function for assigning utilities under uncertainty can incorporate a risk-averse attitude into its determination of utility. Rawls's principles of justice, including the priority of liberty, are perfectly consistent with a general form of utilitarianism and cannot be seen as a rival theory to utilitarianism. Second, Arrow criticizes Rawls's notion of primary goods. Rawls believes that primary goods can avoid the problem of interpersonal comparison that utilitarianism would encounter. However, Arrow argues that if primary goods are used as the basis for interpersonal comparisons, then a healthy person and a chronically ill person, who requires many resources to maintain a normal level of functioning, will be deemed equally well off insofar as their possession of primary goods is at the same level. Primary goods cannot accurately capture the diversity of what each person derives from a given bundle of primary goods. Therefore, primary goods cannot avoid the problem of interpersonal comparison. Third, Arrow raises an epistemological problem. In the original position, the parties are supposed to know the basic laws of sociology, economics, and psychology, but not their actual position or psychological disposition. However, individuals may well disagree about the facts and laws of the physical and social world. For example, if I endorse Marxism (or laissez-faire capitalism) as the true economic principle, I would support suppressing other positions in the original position. Rawls would not want to allow for such varying opinions about basic laws.

Arrow (1977) proposes the notion of extended sympathy (to define an extended preference ordering over pairs of individual identities and states of affairs) as the basis of interpersonal comparison of utilities, but does not endorse it because it does not take autonomy seriously. Rawls (1982) discusses Arrow's observation in order to illustrate the contrast between the utilitarian and Kantian concepts of autonomy.

Iwao Hirose

SEE ALSO:

Harsanyi, John C.
Justice and interpersonal comparisons
Primary goods, social
Social choice theory
Utilitarianism

11.

AUTONOMY, MORAL

SUBSTITUTING THE KANTIAN ideal of autonomy for the Millian ideal of individuality is one of the most innovative moves accomplished by Rawls, deeply modifying the self-understanding of classical liberalism and overcoming the opposition within it of "ancient" and "modern" liberties (*PL* 5). This definition of liberty is borrowed from Rousseau and Kant: "Kant's main aim is to deepen and to justify Rousseau's idea that liberty is acting in accordance with a law that we give ourselves" (*TJ* 225).

Rawls's thinking about autonomy can be roughly divided into two phases. In his earlier papers and in *TJ*, he argues that, in contrast to utilitarianism, the social contract doctrine he advocates is based on a Kantian conception of the autonomous moral person (*TJ* 221). However, his thinking takes a new turn when, in the 1980 Dewey Lectures and in *PL*, he begins to question this Kantian interpretation of autonomy and introduces a distinction between moral and political autonomy as well as between various subcategories of the concept.

A deeply ingrained ideal of democratic regimes is that a just and well-ordered society is one that treats its members as autonomous agents, "respecting their wish to give priority to their liberty to revise and change their ends, their responsibility for their fundamental interests and ends, their autonomy, even if, as members of particular associations, some may decide to yield much of this responsibility to others" (*CP* 260 and *TJ* 456).

Now, how does autonomy lead to justice as impartiality and objectivity in the treatment of others? For Rousseau and Kant, it is the autonomy of the will that constitutes the morality of the act, not its conformity to an external given order of values. Similarly, Rawls writes that: "properly understood the desire to act justly derives in part from the desire to express fully what we are or can be, namely, free and equal rational beings with a liberty to choose" (*TJ* 225). This is a major argument against utilitarianism and in favor of the priority of basic rights and liberties over welfare. To assume that people are capable of autonomy, of being moved not simply by their immediate natural interests, by the desire for welfare and happiness, but by a higher-order interest to express their nature as free and equal, as rational and reasonable beings, is to see them as moral agents, capable of justice as impartiality and objectivity without appealing to a given order of moral values (*TJ* §78). "Thus in a Kantian doctrine, a relatively complex conception of the person plays a central role" (*CP* 346). "In a Kantian view, autonomy has a further sense as part of the conception of persons as free and equal moral persons...which has no part in the utilitarian principle of justice" (*CP* 383). "A person is acting autonomously when the principles of his actions are chosen by him as the most adequate possible expression of his nature as a free and equal rational being...not because of his social position or natural endowments" (*TJ* 222).

Rawls's task is to refine Kant's view on justice and autonomy thanks to the device of the Original Position (OP). "This defect is made good, I believe, by the conception of the original position" (*TJ* 224). He shows that the question of justice can be solved if it is assimilated to a rational choice problem along Kant's views. "The real force of Kant's views lies elsewhere...in the idea that moral principles are the object of rational choice" (*TJ* 221). The ideal of autonomy should be applied in the procedure for choosing principles "defining the moral law, or more exactly, the principles of justice for institutions and individuals" (*TJ* 225). If acting morally, for Kant, is acting autonomously and expressing our nature as free and equal rational beings, then, this is "displayed when we act from the principles we would choose when this nature is reflected in the conditions determining the choice. Thus men exhibit their freedom, their independence from the contingencies of nature and society, by acting in ways they would acknowledge in the original position" (*TJ* 225). If the conditions of choice are suitably chosen, then, the choice procedure itself as an autonomous procedure will determine what justice is. "The original position may be viewed, then, as a procedural interpretation of Kant's conception of autonomy and the categorical imperative within an empirical theory" (*TJ* 226) and as "the point of view from which noumenal selves see the world" (*TJ* 225).

The main features of the choice situation in the OP, the veil of ignorance, the assumption of mutual disinterest, the conditions of publicity and so on, are all interpretations of what it means to be an autonomous person in Kant's sense "as the veil of ignorance deprives the persons in the original position of the knowledge that would enable them to choose heteronomous principles" (*TJ* 222). For instance:

> the assumption of mutual disinterest is to allow for freedom in the choice of a system of final ends. Liberty, in adopting a conception of the good, is limited only by principles that are deduced from a doctrine, which imposes no prior constraints on these conceptions. Presuming mutual disinterest in the original position carries out this idea ... This premise also connects up with the Kantian idea of autonomy. (*TJ* 223–224, 511)

As a consequence, "the principles of justice are also analogous to categorical imperatives" (*TJ* 222). "To act from the principles of justice is to act from categorical imperatives in the sense that they apply to us whatever in particular our aims are" (*TJ* 223). There are only two departures from Kant, however: "the person's choice as noumenal self is a collective one" (*TJ* 226) and "it is subject to the conditions of human life" (*TJ* 226).

The link between autonomy and justice as impartiality and the congruence between reason and freedom are the major philosophical features of the Kantian concept of autonomy and adopting it distances Rawls's theory from utilitarian or intuitionist doctrines. Not only is there "no antinomy between freedom and reason" (*TJ* 452–453), but Kant's famous Copernican revolution firmly connects the two in describing the autonomous and rational agent as producing truth and objectivity (*Critique of Pure Reason* Preface to the second edition and *PL* 102). "Kant is the historical source of the idea that reason, both theoretical and practical, is self-originating and self-authenticating" (*PL* 100). More specifically, "practical reason is concerned with the *production* of objects according to a conception of those objects – for example, the conception of a just constitutional regime taken as the aim of political endeavor – while theoretical reason is concerned with the knowledge of given objects" (emphasis added, *PL* 93; Kant, *Critique of Practical Reason* Ak: V: 15).

In *PL*, Rawls describes this position as constructivist, a term not used but implied in *TJ*: "in constructivism, the objective point of view is always understood as that of reasonable and rational persons suitably specified" (*PL* 115). This is explained in contrast to rational intuitionism, which, for Kant is heteronomous.

> Kant's idea of autonomy requires that there exists no such order of given objects determining the first principles of right and justice among free and

equal moral persons. Heteronomy obtains not only when first principles are fixed by the special psychological constitution of human nature, as in Hume, but also when they are fixed by an order of universals or concepts grasped by rational intuition, as in Plato's realm of forms. (*CP* 345)

As central as the ideal of autonomy may be, it would be a mistake to see it as a moral foundation for the whole doctrine of justice as fairness. Such a theoretical foundation would be contradictory with the very ideal of autonomy and the autonomous choice of principles of justice in the OP. This is the reason why Rawls says as early as in *TJ* that no moral doctrine of respect for autonomy is the source of the principles of social justice. "The principles of justice are not derived from the notion of respect for persons, from a recognition of their inherent worth and dignity... the notion of respect is not a suitable basis for arriving at these principles. It is precisely these ideas that call for interpretation" (*TJ* 513). It is only in *PL* that Rawls will dissipate this ambiguity with his idea of "doctrinal autonomy" (*PL* 98), namely that the doctrine itself has to be autonomous.

Autonomy plays a central role in *TJ*'s conception of stability and in the sense of justice that it relies upon. It underpins Rawls's view of moral education as progress toward autonomy. "Moral education is education for autonomy" (*TJ* 452). The morality of principles is the source of a developed and stable sense of justice, not subject to biases and arbitrary preferences. It is "a process whereby a person becomes attached to these higher-order principles themselves... and wishes to be a just person" (*TJ* 414 and §72). The sense of justice is autonomously acquired (*TJ* §78).

> No one's moral convictions are the result of coercive indoctrination...A person's sense of justice is not a compulsive psychological mechanism...Following the Kantian interpretation of justice as fairness (§ 40), we can say that by acting from these principles, persons are acting autonomously: they are acting under conditions that best express their nature as free and equal rational beings. (*TJ* 452)

> A well-ordered society affirms the autonomy of persons and encourages the objectivity of their considered judgments of justice. Any doubts that its members may entertain about the soundness of their moral sentiments... may be dispelled by seeing that their convictions match the principles which would be chosen in the original position or, if they do not, by revising their judgments so as they do. (*TJ* 456)

However, Rawls will come to realize that the central role played by autonomy in his conception of justice needs to be reformulated as it risks imposing one dominant view of the good at odds both with his own deontological view and with the plurality of religious, moral and philosophical doctrines that flourish in an open and free society. In the papers dating from 1980 to 1989 and in *PL*, he will offer a distinction between moral autonomy as part of a moral doctrine and political autonomy as a right for all citizens, even if they may reject autonomy in their private nonpolitical lives (as they may reject equality) (*CP* 409; *PL* xliv; *LP* 146; *CP* 586).

Catherine Audard

SEE ALSO:

Autonomy, political
Constructivism: Kantian/political
Freedom
Kant, Immanuel
Kantian interpretation
Moral education
Moral person
Practical reason

12.

AUTONOMY, POLITICAL

POST-TJ, RAWLS DEVELOPS his new views on autonomy on numerous occasions where he feels the necessity to introduce new subcategories. First, in *PL* and in his 1980s papers, he introduces the central distinction between moral and political autonomy (*PL* xliv and 29–35). Second, he develops the idea of "doctrinal autonomy (*PL* 98 and 110–116). Third, he describes the Kantian interpretation of autonomy as "constitutive" and as different from his own political constructivism (*PL* 99 and 125). Fourth, he introduces a distinction between the rational autonomy of the parties in the OP and the full autonomy of citizens as a way to lift misunderstandings on his view of rationality (*PL* 72–81). Then, he answers the crucial question of the conflicts between personal identity and political autonomy with an appeal to autonomy (*PL* 140). In his "Reply to Habermas" (*PL* 396–421), he proposes further elucidations that insist on the convergences between political liberalism and civic republicanism as both guaranteeing citizens' full autonomy. In *LP*, finally, he builds his argument against both cosmopolitanism and political realism on a conception of peoples as entitled to political autonomy and self-determination as well as the respect that goes with it in view of their moral identity (*LP* 79, 118, 146, and 106–112).

In *PL* and in the 1980s papers, Rawls introduces a new and central distinction between moral autonomy as part of a comprehensive doctrine, and political autonomy, as a freestanding conception of citizens, in response to the fact of reasonable pluralism. Addressing at this stage the issue of stability, Rawls recognizes the existence of a liberal paradox (*PL* 190 and *JF* 153). "Historically one common theme of liberal thought is that the state must not favor any comprehensive doctrines and their associated conception of the good. But it is equally a common theme of critics of liberalism that it fails to do this and is, in fact, arbitrarily biased in favor of one or another form of individualism" (*PL* 190 and 221 n.8). One such form is the individualistic ideal of autonomy. In *TJ*, Rawls deals mostly with political conflicts between particular individuals and the authority of the State such as civil disobedience (*TJ* §55) and conscientious refusal (*TJ* §56), conflicts expressing the moral autonomy of persons. However, he now recognizes that conflicts between communities and the State run even deeper, in particular religious and civic education may clash (*PL* 199–200) and that "many citizens of faith reject moral autonomy as part of their way of life" (*PL* xlv). He claims that "political liberalism is unjustly biased against certain comprehensive doctrines only if, say, individualistic ones can only endure in a liberal society or they so predominate that associations affirming values of communities or religion cannot flourish" (*PL* 199).

The answer to this major problem consists in separating "the special domain of the political from the personal, the familial and the associative realms and their values" (*CP* 482; *JF* §54; *PL* 137). This is a distinction that utilitarianism does not make (*TJ* §26) and that was missing in *TJ* (*PL* xliii n.8). "Whatever we may think of autonomy as a purely moral value, it fails to satisfy, given reasonable pluralism, the constraint of reciprocity, as many citizens, for example those holding certain religious doctrines, may reject it. Thus moral autonomy is not a political value, whereas political autonomy is" (*CP* 586). Moral autonomy as "a comprehensive moral ideal, is unsuited for a political conception of justice" (*CP* 409). "Moral autonomy is purely moral and characterizes a certain way of life and reflection, critically examining our deepest ends and ideals . . . it is not a political value" (*CP* 586).

In contrast, autonomy as a political value means only "the legal independence and assured integrity of citizens and their sharing equally with others in the exercise of political power," something a majority of citizens should be able to connect to their reasonable conceptions of the good (*CP* 586). Rawls distinguishes three aspects of citizens' political autonomy (*PL* 29–34, *JF* §7.4). (1) "They conceive of themselves as having the moral power to have a conception of the good" (*JF* 21). (2) They are "capable of revising and changing this conception . . . if they so desire. As free persons, citizens claim the right to view their persons as independent from and not identified with any particular conception of the good" (*JF* 21). "They regard themselves as self-authenticating sources of valid claims" (*JF* 23). (3) "They are viewed as capable of taking responsibility for their ends and . . . of adjusting their aims and aspirations . . . of restricting their claims in matters of justice to the kinds of things the principles of justice allow (*PL* 33–34).

A major consequence of this distinction is to reveal what was lacking in *TJ* and led to its revision: justice as fairness was not presented as a political and autonomous doctrine (*PL* xlii and xliii). In an autonomous doctrine, "the political values are not simply presented as moral requirements externally imposed... but as based on citizens' practical reason" (*PL* 98). In contrast to utilitarianism and teleological doctrines, "there exists no standpoint external to the parties' own perspective from which they are constrained by prior and independent principles in questions of justice that arise among them as members of one society" (*CP* 311).

In a "neutral" or "autonomous" and "freestanding" (*PL* 374) or purely "political" conception of justice, citizens only rely on (1) principles and ideas constructed by their own practical reason and reflected in the original position (OP) set up, and (2) on "the fundamental ideas that are present in the public political culture of justice as fairness or at least implicit in the history of its main institutions and the traditions of their interpretation" (*PL* 78). *TJ* failed to conform to this requirement that complements the view of citizens as politically autonomous.

This leads Rawls to review the relations between Kant's moral constructivism and his own version as he saw them previously (compare *CP* 340–358 and *PL* 99–102). He discusses Kantian constructivism and the Kantian interpretation of autonomy as "constitutive" in the 1980 Dewey Lectures, in his 1980s papers, and in *PL*, where he gives the most sophisticated and extensive presentation of his political constructivism.

Kant's constructivism is not "doctrinally autonomous" (*PL* 98) in that it does not solely represent "the order of political values as based on principles of practical reason in union with the appropriate conception of society and person" (*PL* 99). It requires a further metaphysical thesis on the capacity of human reason as "constitutive" (*PL* 99). "Constitutive autonomy says that the so-called independent order of values does not constitute itself but is constituted by the activity, actual or ideal, of practical (human) reason itself" (*PL* 99). Whereas Rawls recognizes that "not everything then is constructed; we must have some material, as it were, from which to begin" (*PL* 104), for Kant's transcendental idealism, reason itself constitutes the order of values. "Reason is self-originating and self-authenticating" and "alone competent to settle questions about its own authority" (*PL* 100, 101, 120 n.26). This cannot be widely acceptable as a basis for a normative political conception or for an overlapping consensus.

Rawls offers a better understanding of the conception of the person used in the OP, where the parties are said to be autonomous. Does this mean that they

Autonomy, political / 35

share a particular comprehensive Kantian moral doctrine or that a Kantian conception of persons is involved, which could be inferred from the Kantian interpretation in *TJ* (*TJ* §40)? Rawls now insists that this was a misunderstanding (*PL* 28) and that we have to suppose that "the parties are rationally, not fully autonomous" (*PL* 72–77), that is, "citizens' rational autonomy is modeled in the original position by the way the parties deliberate as their representatives" (*PL* 77). There are two ways in which the parties "model citizens' rational autonomy" (*PL* 75). (1) "Citizens themselves (via their representatives) are to specify the fair terms of their cooperation" (*PL* 72). "Parties are free within the constraints of the original position to agree to whatever principles of justice they think most to the advantage of those they represent" (*PL* 75). (2) "In estimating this advantage they consider those persons' higher-order interests" (*PL* 75). This answers Schopenhauer's criticism of Kant that external values such as prudential interests are implied in rational choices, making them heteronomous (*PL* 72–77 and 104–107). Rational or artificial autonomy as a device of representation should, then, be clearly distinct from citizens' full autonomy, as a subcategory of political autonomy (*PL* 77–81).

However, political autonomy is a source of major conflicts that threaten the stability of a democratic society. With the acquisition of the new rights of political autonomy, citizens now have divided allegiances. "Citizens' overall views have two parts": as private individuals, a comprehensive doctrine, as members of the collective body, a political conception of justice, which is "regularly imposed on citizens as individuals" (*PL* 38 and *CP* 482). As private persons, citizens may have deep attachments to their communities and their comprehensive doctrines that may contradict their rights as autonomous citizens. "They may regard it as simply unthinkable to view themselves apart from certain religious, philosophical, and moral convictions, or from certain enduring attachments and loyalties" (*JF* 22). This conflict is at the heart of Rawls's questioning: "how is it possible for those affirming a religious doctrine that is based on religious authority also to hold a reasonable conception that supports a just democratic regime?" (*PL* xxxix) Some religions or groups may make it impossible to revise one's conception of the good without losing one's moral and personal identity, whereas when considered as citizens, "their public or legal identity as free persons is not affected by changes over time in their determinate conception of the good" (*JF* 21 and *PL* 30–31).

Whereas *TJ* gave the false impression that a theory of justice could answer these conflicts, Rawls now states that: "these two aspects of their moral identity citizens must adjust and reconcile" (*JF* 22 and *CP* 485). In the name of autonomy, "it is left to citizens individually, as part of their liberty of conscience, to settle how they think the great values of the political relate to other values within their comprehensive doctrines" (*PL* 140 and *CP* 485). "It is left entirely open to citizens and associations to formulate their own way of going beyond or of going deeper, so as to make that political conception congruent with their comprehensive doctrine" (*PL* 378). They must give an autonomous solution to the conflicts between their political autonomy and their moral attachments. In that, they may be helped by the procedure of public justification in the OP and by the use of deliberative reason (*PL* 315) and of public reason, in cases that are questioning constitutional essentials (*PL* 214), even if public reason has only a limited result (*PL* lx and 215). They may, then, reach an overlapping consensus between their comprehensive views and the public conception of justice that overrides it.

In his "Reply to Habermas" (*PL* 396–421), Rawls gives further elucidations of this answer that exhibit a degree of convergence between political liberalism and civic republicanism as both guaranteeing citizens' full autonomy (*PL* 420 and *JF* 146 n.16, 150).

Habermas starts his critique of Rawls with a definition of full political autonomy as including "the rights of political participation and communication" (*PL* 403). He objects to Rawls's conception because, having selected their first principles in the OP, citizens "cannot reignite the radical democratic embers of the original position in the civic life of their society" (*PL* 399–400) as "they find themselves subject to principles and norms that have ... already become institutionalized beyond their control" (*PL* 397). As a consequence, "the use of public reason does not actually have the significance of a present exercise of political autonomy but merely promotes the nonviolent preservation of political stability" (*PL* 400). A second criticism concerns "the rigid boundary between the political and non-political identities of the citizens" (*PL* 403) and "the dialectical relation between private and political autonomy" (*PL* 409). Habermas explains this rigidity and the problems it creates for citizens trying to adjust their two sets of political and nonpublic values, by the so-called priority of private autonomy over political autonomy, that Rawls as a liberal is assumed to advocate. For Habermas, private autonomy, as specified by the liberties of the Moderns, is founded on human rights. On the other hand, the public (political) autonomy of citizens is derived from the principle of popular sovereignty which liberalism opposes, invoking "the great danger of the tyranny of majorities rule and has simply postulated the priority of human rights as a constraint on popular sovereignty" (*PL* 410). Habermas's solution, instead, is to treat public and private autonomy as "co-original" and of "equal weight" (*PL* 410).

Rawls's answer is "first, that citizens gain full political autonomy when they live under a reasonably just constitution securing their liberty and equality" (*PL* 402). They have, obviously to work on these principles and they should not remain passive. "Whenever the constitutions and laws are, in various ways, unjust and imperfect, citizens with reason strive to become more autonomous" (*PL* 402). He mentions the well-known contrast between constitutional politics and ordinary politics and the role of people's participation as constitutive of political autonomy, drawing a parallel between Jefferson and Habermas (*PL* 408). Crucially, the ordering of the principles of justice shows that there is no priority of one set of liberties over the other and that "the liberties of both public and private autonomy are given side by side and unranked in the first principle of justice...as rooted in the two moral powers" (*PL* 413). Rawls concludes his Reply by saying: "we both have a normative ideal of democracy that grounds an internal connection between the two forms of autonomy" (*PL* 419).

It is interesting to note that, in his thinking about international justice, Rawls remains committed to the ideal of autonomy, but applied now to peoples rather than to individuals. His first point is that the addressee of international justice is not the individual, as is the case for cosmopolitanism, or states, as is the case for political realists, but peoples. The reason is that peoples have a moral status, a lasting autonomy over time, which is not the case for states. "Peoples (as opposed to states) have a definite moral nature. This nature includes a certain proper pride and sense of honor; peoples may take pride in their histories and achievements as what I call a 'proper patriotism' allows" (*LP* 62).

In order to present an "ideal theory" of international relations (*LP* 4–5), he asks what a "well-ordered" people could be. Is it limited to a people with liberal institutions? Are its present institutions the only criterion? In that case, only democratic peoples are "well-ordered." Or are autonomy and self-determination in their past history also important? Ex-colonial countries suffer from a huge deficit of self-determination and self-respect inasmuch as their independence was "given" to them, whereas nations that have fought and struggled for it are obviously in a different position. Thus the moral status of "well-ordered" peoples should not depend upon their present institutions being liberal and democratic. Rawls views "well-ordered" peoples as having a moral status because their institutions, good or not so good, are the result, up to a point, of their autonomous development, of their own history. The point is that self-determination and autonomy are crucial to the status of a people. A people is a people when it possesses a sense of being the author of its own history. "Self-determination, duly constrained, is an important good for a people" (*LP* 85 and §16) in the same way that "it is a good for individuals and associations to be attached to their particular culture" (*LP* 61).

This is why Rawls stresses the importance of the notions of respect and self-respect in international relations. Respect for peoples' autonomy is what separates Rawls from cosmopolitans. Thus, showing equal respect and consideration for peoples' institutions and traditions, within the framework of the Law of Peoples, even if they are not liberal and democratic and do not recognize all their members as free and equal persons, is not contradictory. It is important to recognize peoples' relative autonomy and self-sufficiency in bringing about these nonliberal, but decent, institutions and traditions: this is what makes them peoples and not just a collection of individuals and, in that sense, they can see themselves as equal to any other.

> If all societies were required to be liberal, then the idea of political liberalism would fail to express due toleration for other acceptable ways (if such there are, as I assume) of ordering society...Provided a non-liberal society's basic institutions meet certain specified conditions of political right and justice and lead its people to honor a reasonable and just law for the Society of Peoples, a liberal people is to tolerate and accept that society. (*LP* 59–60)

> The danger of error, miscalculation and also arrogance on the part of those who propose sanctions must, of course, be taken into account...decent societies...deserve respect, even if their institutions as a whole are not sufficiently reasonable. (*LP* 84)

Respect for the political autonomy of peoples is central in Rawls's three guidelines for the duty of assistance to burdened societies, which is the last principle in the Law of Peoples (*LP* 106–112). (1) A well-ordered society need not be wealthy. Just institutions are more important for justice than wealth (*LP* 106–107). (2) Assistance should respect the people's political culture (*LP* 108–110). (3) Help should be directed at aiding burdened societies to manage their own affairs. The principles of international justice should serve as principles of transition to a people's political autonomy (*LP* 118). Where cosmopolitans would like to see an open-ended process of assistance to less well-off peoples, he proposes a "target and cut-off point" conception of assistance in the name of respect for their autonomy (*LP* 119).

Catherine Audard

SEE ALSO:

Autonomy, moral
Citizen
Civic republicanism
Comprehensive doctrine
Freedom
Kant, Immanuel
Peoples
Political conception of justice

13.

AVOIDANCE, METHOD OF

LTHOUGH RAWLS MENTIONED the method of avoidance only in a few places, the idea is important to understanding his hopes for political liberalism and to avoiding confusions about his stances on metaphysical issues. An outgrowth of his presidential address to the American Philosophical Association, "The Independence of Moral Theory" (1975), this "method" counsels avoiding philosophically controversial topics insofar as this is possible.

In "Justice as Fairness: Political Not Metaphysical" (1986; *CP* 395), Rawls wrote that he was seeking to generalize the kind of stance he had earlier taken (in his 1980 Dewey Lectures) about the idea of objectivity, aiming to finesse issues about moral truth by characterizing objectivity "by reference to a suitably constructed social point of view" (*CP* 356). In a similar effort to side-step metaphysical controversies about "the nature of the self," he was putting forward a political conception of "citizens as free and equal persons" (*CP* 395). In both of these cases, as Rawls commented, "the hope is that, by this method of avoidance, as we might call it," we may find a basis for reasonable public agreement on fundamental matters of justice (*CP* 395).

Does not avoiding deep issues about moral truth and the nature of persons entail embracing an objectionable skepticism? In his 1987 essay, "The Idea of an Overlapping Consensus," Rawls invoked the method of avoidance to explain why it does not: "In following the method of avoidance, as we may call it, we try, so far as we can, neither to assert nor to deny any religious, philosophical, or moral views, or their associated philosophical accounts of truth and the status of values" (*CP* 434).

The hallmark of the method of avoidance, then, is neither asserting nor denying anything about the controversial matter in question – at least insofar

Avoidance, method of / 41

as that is possible. In addressing the limits of neutrality, Rawls interestingly invoked the method of avoidance at a higher order. A footnote in *Political Liberalism* (29 n.31) noted that although political liberalism attempts to proceed "without presupposing...a particular metaphysical doctrine," some might assert, for instance, that its political conception of persons as free and equal citizens embeds certain metaphysical commitments. The "precept of avoidance," Rawls there suggests, counsels neither affirming nor denying this. To respond otherwise would be to get drawn into controversial metaphysical territory. Although Rawls's second book mentioned the method or "precept of avoidance" only in that footnote, it employs it pervasively. Rawls regularly highlights that his political liberalism "neither asserts nor denies" this or that controversial, metaphysical point (*PL* 126; cf. 113, 375). This stance of avoidance is crucial to any hope for overlapping consensus (*PL* 150).

It is curious, therefore, that the just-cited passage in *Political Liberalism*, which otherwise corresponds to the one introducing the method of avoidance in "The Idea of Overlapping Consensus," describes the method but removes the label, "the method of avoidance." Although Rawls does not explain this excision, the method of avoidance itself suggests a possible explanation. That the method of avoidance is an apt method for a political theory of justice is itself a controversial assertion. Accordingly, the method of avoidance counsels avoiding any assertion that the method of avoidance should be followed. Of course, it also counsels avoiding denying that it should be followed. Instead, one should simply follow it, as *Political Liberalism* did, without trumpeting the fact.

Henry S. Richardson

SEE ALSO:

> *Citizen*
> *Objectivity*
> *Overlapping consensus*
> *Political conception of justice*
> *Truth*

B

14.

BARRY, BRIAN

B RIAN BARRY (1936–2009) was born in London and educated at Oxford. Barry first met John Rawls when Barry was a Rockefeller fellow at Harvard in 1961–1962 (see Kelly 2009).

Later, Barry was invited to write a review article on Rawls's *A Theory of Justice*, but he decided that a serious overall judgment of it required book-length treatment. Barry focused on the "central doctrines" (1973, 128) of *A Theory of Justice*, emphasizing the formulation and derivation of Rawls's two principles of justice. Barry offers a number of helpful expository points (especially in 1973, ch. 7) and some trenchant critiques in the course of the book. Perhaps the best known of his critiques concerns "the derivation of the maximin criterion" in the Rawlsian original position (Barry 1973, 87). I think Barry gets the derivation wrong (he didn't have the advantage of Rawls's second thoughts as spelled out in *TJ* (xiv) and in *JF* (part III). But he did make a plausible argument for saying that the parties in the original position would prefer a modified version of the principle of maximizing average utility over Rawls's own difference principle (Barry 1973, 93–95, 103).

Fair equality of opportunity was rejected (in Barry 1973, ch. 8) as adding nothing of value. But it became, in Barry's next book (1989, ch. 6), the *basic* idea. Barry argues that the point of fair equality of opportunity is to achieve impartiality by removing all morally arbitrary differentiations between persons (especially those based on genetic endowment, initial social circumstance, or brute luck). We must start then from the benchmark idea of a strict equality in the distribution of social primary goods. Developments away from strict equality are allowed when they're beneficial for everyone, up to the point of reaching the maximum benefit of the least well-off group. Achieving this maximum benefit is the *only* thing that makes a scheme of unequal incomes permissible.

Barry's review essay (1995) of Rawls's second book, *Political Liberalism*, is a bracing root-and-branch critique. Barry finds no place for Rawls's idea of a "family" of liberal conceptions (and instead focuses *exclusively* on one conception in particular, justice as fairness). Barry alleges (1995, 913, also 910–911) that Rawls, in order to secure an overlapping consensus, simply abandons his second principle of justice. However, Barry thinks that, since overlapping consensus is not required to secure stability (see 1995, 891, 896, 901), there is no role for overlapping consensus at all in *Political Liberalism*. Barry is unwilling to allow that Rawls's account of critical moral justification in *A Theory of Justice* might be problematic – in assuming convergence on a single comprehensive moral doctrine (see *PL* xv–xvii) – or that Rawls in *Political Liberalism* might have hit upon an interesting solution to this problem.

Barry's discussion of international justice follows lines laid down in his discussion of Rawls (Barry 1973, ch. 12; 1989, ch. 5). Here Barry develops such ideas as a global difference principle (see Rawls *LP* 82 n.28 for comment) and joint human ownership of natural resources. See Dowding *et al.* (2004) for citations to Barry's relevant articles.

It might be useful, finally, to look at some additional points where Rawls refers to Barry. In *Theory of Justice*, Rawls cites Barry (1965) as an example of intuitionism – that is, of a pluralism which lacks any objective basis for weighing plural principles against one another (*TJ* 30 n.18, 33 n.19, 291 n.53); as stressing how the social system not only satisfies existing desires but shapes them as well (*TJ* 229 n.2); as defining "ideal-regarding principles" (*TJ* 287 n.52), and as contributing to the notion of pure procedural justice (*TJ* 74 n.14). Other references, of interest, by Rawls to Barry can be found in *PL* (17 n.18; *JF* 43 n.5, 69 n.37).

Rex Martin

SEE ALSO:

> *Congruence*
> *Difference principle*
> *Fair equality of opportunity*
> *The original position*
> *Political conception of justice*

15.

BASIC LIBERTIES

THE IDEA OF a basic liberty is central to Rawls's theory of justice. Rawls distinguishes basic liberties from other liberties and from liberty in general, and holds that basic liberties – and only basic liberties – are entitled to special protection. They are given special protection in his theory by the principle of equal basic liberty and its "lexical priority" over fair equality of opportunity and the difference principle. This means that a basic liberty may be limited only for the sake of a basic liberty, and not to equalize opportunity or wealth. Rawls also speaks more generally of the "priority of liberty," which means that a basic liberty may be limited only for the sake of a basic liberty, or to make the system of basic liberty as a whole more secure, and not to promote equality, or the general welfare, or human excellence or perfection.

Rawls formulates the principle of equal basic liberty differently in different places, but the final formulation is this: each person has the same indefeasible claim to a fully adequate scheme of equal basic liberties, which scheme is compatible with a similar scheme for all (*JF* 42). Rawls specifies basic liberties by a list, but presents different lists in different places. The following liberties appear on at least one list: freedom of thought; liberty of conscience; freedom of association; freedom of the person (also called "the freedoms specified by the liberty and integrity of the person" (*PL* 291)); the freedom to own personal property; political liberty, including the right to vote and to be eligible for public office, freedom of political speech, and freedom of assembly; and the rights and liberties covered by the rule of law, including freedom from arbitrary arrest and seizure. What justifies including a liberty in the list of basic liberties, according to Rawls, is that its recognition and protection by the government is necessary to secure the social conditions necessary for the full development and exercise of our two moral powers, a capacity for a sense of justice and a capacity for a conception of the good. To illustrate, we will not fully exercise our capacity for a sense of justice unless we are free to discuss and reflect on what government policies justice requires, which requires freedom of thought and discussion; and we will not fully exercise our capacity for a conception of the good unless we are free to act on our convictions about what is required of us by our religious beliefs, which requires freedom of conscience.

According to Rawls, the strongest argument for the superiority of his conception of justice over any form of utilitarianism is that it provides a more secure foundation for the basic liberties than utilitarianism does. This is because any utilitarian theory must permit the government to limit a basic liberty whenever it is sufficiently clear that doing so (or that allowing limitations of this kind) will maximize utility. Why, though, do parties in the original position care so much about their basic liberties, given that, behind the veil of ignorance, they don't know their conceptions of a good life? Rawls answers in *TJ* that basic liberties, as primary goods, are rational to want whatever else one wants. But it seems that someone might have a consistent set of informed preferences that could be satisfied without having some basic liberty – the right to vote, for example – which suggests that not all basic liberties are rational to want *whatever* else one wants. Why, in any case, do parties in the original position rank basic liberties higher than other social goods, as the priority of liberty presupposes? Suppose that everyone will have more money if only those who are educated about economics have the right to vote. Wouldn't some rational person be willing to give up his vote in exchange for more money?

Rawls answers these questions in *Political Liberalism* as follows. Parties in the original position are assumed to have "higher-order interests" in developing and exercising their two moral powers fully, and so in securing the social conditions necessary to do so. Because the basic liberties are necessary social conditions, parties in the original position choose principles that guarantee the basic liberties; and because basic liberties are more essential than other social conditions (once a certain level of material prosperity has been reached), parties in the original position agree to the priority of liberty. This explanation also enables Rawls to answer H. L. A. Hart's puzzle about how to resolve conflicts between basic liberties (Hart 1975, 239). Imagine there are two systems of basic liberty, A and B. In system A, basic liberty 1 is more extensive, but only because basic liberty 2 is curtailed, whereas in system B, basic liberty 2 is more extensive, but only because basic liberty 1 is curtailed. Which system should be established, according to Rawls's theory? *TJ* answers that it is the one that the "representative equal citizen" would prefer (*TJ* 204). But, Hart asked, which system is this, given that citizens have different goals and find themselves in different situations? *PL* provides an answer: that system should be established that better secures the social conditions necessary for the full development and exercise of the two moral powers.

Peter de Marneffe

SEE ALSO:

Constitution and constitutional essentials
Freedom
Freedom of speech
Hart, H. L. A.
Higher-order interests
Lexical priority: liberty, opportunity, wealth
Liberty of conscience
Moral person
Rights, constitutional
Two principles of justice (in justice as fairness)
Utilitarianism

16.

BASIC NEEDS, PRINCIPLE OF

N TJ RAWLS does not mention a "principle of basic needs," although he does speak of "needs" and the "precept of needs" (as one of the competing traditional canons of distributive justice) (*TJ* 244, 271–273).

> The social minimum is the responsibility of the transfer branch [of government]...The workings of this branch take needs into account and assign them an appropriate weight...a competitive price system gives no consideration to needs and therefore it cannot be the sole device of distribution...the transfer branch guarantees a certain level of well-being and honors the claims of need." (*TJ* 244)

However, even though Rawls clearly believes that the application of the difference principle will ensure that people's basic needs are met (in all but the poorest societies), this is not stated or required in his two principles themselves.

Neither does *TJ* speak of "subsistence rights" (or a right to have the opportunity to meet one's basic needs) or even of a right to life (in general) in his two principles. Nevertheless, it is arguable that Rawls's theory of natural duties implicitly promulgates a right to life in both its negative and positive aspects (*TJ* 98–101, 293–301). His duty not to harm (i.e. not to cause unjustified avoidable substantial harm to people) seems clearly to correlate to the "negative" right to life (i.e. to security rights), while his proposed duty to aid the severely deprived (if one can do so without great risk or cost to oneself) seems clearly to correlate to the "positive" aspects of the right to life (i.e. to subsistence rights). (See Peffer 1990, 20.) Another property of these natural duties that makes it suitable to interpret them as entailing security and subsistence rights, respectively, is that "they

Basic needs, principle of / 51

hold between persons irrespective of their institutional relationships; they obtain between all as equal moral persons. In this sense the natural duties are owed not only to definite individuals, say to those cooperating together in a particular social arrangement, but to persons generally" (*TJ* 99). This property correlates to the universal nature of human rights.

However, in *Political Liberalism* Rawls does recognize and elaborate a Basic Needs Principle as part of a more general Basic Rights Principle when he states that his "first principle covering the equal basic rights and liberties may easily be preceded by a lexically prior principle requiring that citizens' needs be met" (*PL* 7). Arguably, Rawls is here endorsing a Basic Rights Principle covering both security and subsistence rights since in this context he writes "For the statement of such a principle, as well as instructive fuller statement in four parts of the two principles, with important revisions, see Rodney Peffer's *Marxism, Morality, and Social Justice*, Princeton University Press, p. 14" (*PL* 7 n.6; cf. *JF* 44 n.7), and Peffer's first principle of his version of Rawls's theory stipulates that *both* the security and subsistence rights of people must be respected and protected.

Later in *PL* Rawls claims that the constitutional consensus – a precursor to the overlapping consensus – must include "principles covering certain essential needs" of citizens (*PL* 164) and that "a social minimum providing for the basic needs of all citizens is also a [constitutional] essential, [whereas] what I have called the 'difference principle' is more demanding and is not" (*PL* 228–229; cf. *JF* 47–48). In this context he several times approvingly cites Frank Michelman's articles which argue for constitutionally protected "basic welfare rights" (*PL* 166, 237, 339, and *JF* 162). It is important to note here that the social minimum is determined *not* by the difference principle (as some have suggested) but by a determination of people's needs that must be fulfilled for them to be normally functioning persons (adequate nutrition, potable water, basic health care, etc.) and citizens (these conditions plus opportunities for a sufficient level of education, for participating in politics, etc.). In a relatively poor society these could turn out to be the same, but normally the level set by the difference principle will be higher than that established as the social minimum by the basic needs principle. In this context, the "needs of citizens" refers to the primary goods necessary to ensure for "all citizens the adequate development and full exercise of their two moral powers and a fair share of the all-purpose means essential for advancing their determinate (permissible) conceptions of the good" (*PL* 187). Moreover, while some authors – including Michelman, Scanlon, Shue, Jordon, Waldren, and Peffer – argue for the acceptance of basic welfare rights (or subsistence rights) on the bases of both their intrinsic value and their instrumental value, Rawls consistently only argues the latter: "[The justification of] the constitutional essential here [i.e. the social minimum or Basic Needs Principle] is . . . that below a certain level of material social well-being, and of training and education, people simply cannot take part in society as citizens, much less equal citizens" (*PL* 166).

Unfortunately, in *Justice as Fairness* Rawls also states that "the difference principle specifies a social minimum . . . This specifies at least the basic needs essential to a decent life, and presumably more" (*JF* 130). This makes for a bit of confusion; but here Rawls is using the term "social minimum" differently than he usually does. For example, at another point in *JF* he writes: "a social minimum providing for the basic needs of all citizens is also a constitutional essential . . . the difference principle is more demanding and is not so regarded" (*JF* 47–48). Unfortunately, Rawls does not suggest a convenient terminology to differentiate these two uses of "social minimum" and, thus, prevent confusion. Although awkward, one can always refer to them as "the social minimum as determined by the difference principle" versus "the social minimum as covering [only] the needs essential for a decent human life" (*JF* 129). In this context Rawls also speaks of the latter as "What is owed persons in virtue of their humanity" (*JF* 129) and the former as "what is owed them as free and equal citizens" (*JF* 129). Here he again adverts to his theory of natural duties in the first case (which apply universally) and, presumably, to his obligation from fair play in the second (which applies only to people within a cooperative institutional framework). He also claims that "it is possible that the social minimum specified by these two concepts will not be very far apart in practice . . . [they] may be very much the same" (*JF* 129). While this may be true in relatively poor societies, it is difficult to imagine how this could be true in wealthier societies. To be true in a wealthy society one would have to construe people's "essential needs" to include a great many things that we normally don't place in that category, or else one would have to estimate the minimum level set by the difference principle to include only enough income, access to health care, etc. to meet one's essential (basic) needs. Neither of these seems very plausible as interpretations of Rawls's intentions. Thus, contra what Rawls claims here, it seems extremely likely that the minimum set by the difference principle in a wealthy society will be substantially above that set by a basic needs principle.

Rawls also connects this discussion with his concept of a property-owning democracy as opposed to welfare capitalism. "While a social minimum covering only those essential needs may suit the requirements of a capitalist welfare state, it is not sufficient for what . . . I call a property-owning democracy" (*JF* 130).

Finally, we need to determine if in his final published work, *The Law of Peoples*, Rawls advocates a universal, globally applied basic needs principle (or, equivalently, the subsistence rights component of a basic rights principle). In this

Basic needs, principle of / 53

work Rawls distinguishes five types of contemporary, large-scale societies: (1) liberal peoples (i.e. democratic constitutional societies protecting an extensive list of rights and accepting political liberalism); (2) decent (but hierarchical) peoples, that may operate on a comprehensive view of the good (and of justice), but which protect a limited list of essential human rights and have a "decent consultation hierarchy," which gives it legitimacy from the perspective of its members; (3) benevolent absolutisms that protect a more limited list of human rights and are not externally aggressive but which have no "decent consultation hierarchy"; (4) burdened societies (that don't presently have the social, economic, political, and/or cultural conditions to be well-ordered societies, i.e. either liberal or decent societies); and (5) outlaw states that, by definition, are unjustifiably externally (militarily) aggressive and/or extremely internally repressive toward their own members.

By definition, a well-ordered (i.e. liberal or decent) society "secures for all members of the people...human rights...Among the human rights are the right to life (to the means of subsistence and security)...including minimum economic security" (*LP* 65). Moreover, "subsistence rights are basic" (*LP* 65). In nonburdened societies this mandates, among other measures, that "Basic health care [is] assured for all citizens" (*LP* 50).

Within a society (association) of liberal and decent peoples, "Certain provisions will be included for mutual assistance among peoples in times of famine and drought and, insofar as possible, provisions for ensuring that...people's basic needs are met. These provisions will specify duties of assistance [between these societies]" (*LP* 38). So both *within* and *between* liberal and decent societies provisions exist to try to make sure that everyone's basic needs are met by, first and foremost, arranging background institutions such that people are able to meet their basic needs (and those of their dependants) by their own efforts and, second, by receiving appropriate assistance from society or the state to meet them, if required.

Moreover, "[liberal and decent] peoples have a duty to assist other peoples living under unfavorable conditions that prevent their having a just or decent political and social regime" (*LP* 37). Here Rawls is speaking of people living in "burdened societies." The aim of "the duty of assistance...is to help burdened societies to be able to become members of the Society of well-ordered Peoples. This defines the 'target of assistance.' After it is achieved further assistance is not required even though the now well-ordered society may still be relatively poor" (*LP* 111). It is debatable whether this duty – together with the duty of liberal and decent peoples to meet their members' basic needs and to aid each other in time of need to make sure this can be done – is equivalent to a universal, globally applied basic needs principle (or, equivalently, to the subsistence rights component of a basic rights principle).

The main problem is that so far in his analysis Rawls doesn't claim that this duty applies to either benevolent absolutisms or outlaw states. In fact, Rawls further confuses this issue by writing that "the 'duty of assistance' applies only to the duty that liberal and decent peoples have to assist *burdened* societies" (*LP* 43 n.53). This would seem to indicate (A) that the duties of liberal and decent peoples to aid each other is not to be called a "duty of assistance" (a constraint that Rawls clearly does not abide by) and (B) that no such duty exists with respect to benevolent absolutisms or outlaw regimes, a claim that Rawls clearly violates later in *LP* when he writes "I do accept...goals of attaining liberal or decent institutions, securing human rights, and meeting basic needs [for all people everywhere]. These I believe are covered by the duty of assistance" (*LP* 118) and

> The list of human rights honored by both liberal and decent hierarchical regimes should be understood as universal rights in the following sense: they are intrinsic to the Law of Peoples and have a political (moral) effect whether or not they are supported locally. That is, their political (moral) force extends to all societies, and they are binding on all peoples and societies, including the outlaw states. An outlaw state that violates these rights is to be condemned and in grave cases may be subjected to forceful sanctions and even to [military] intervention [in extreme cases]. (*LP* 81)

Thus, it is most reasonable to interpret Rawls in *LP* to be advocating a universal, globally applied basic needs principle (and basic rights principle); i.e. that he is still accepting, as he holds in *PL* and *JF*, that respecting and protecting peoples' security and subsistence rights is the first and foremost principle of social justice.

Rodney G. Peffer

SEE ALSO:

Branches of government
Law of Peoples
Lexical priority: liberty, opportunity, wealth
Primary goods, social
Property-owning democracy
Social minimum

17.

BASIC STRUCTURE OF SOCIETY

RAWLS MAINTAINS THAT the basic structure of society is the first subject of justice. A society is a more or less independent, closed and self-sufficient, ongoing system of cooperation between persons within which it is ordinarily possible for a person to live out a complete life. A society's basic structure is the network or system of institutions, taken as a whole and in dynamic relation to one another, that forms the institutional background within which individuals and associations interact with one another. It includes political and legal structures, economic systems, civil society, the family, and so on. It is the total institutional structure of a society as an ongoing cooperative venture carried out by a particular people.

A conception of justice for the basic structure of society is a conception of social justice. Social justice concerns justice in the production and distribution of the goods for the sake of which a people cooperates within and through the basic structure of its society. Rawls distinguishes social justice from local or transactional justice (a conception of justice for a particular kind of institution or transaction within a society), on the one hand, and international justice (a conception of justice for the relations between societies), on the other. He begins, but does not end, his inquiry into justice with an inquiry into social justice. Rawls's two principles specify a conception of social justice, "justice as fairness."

Rawls distinguishes between the basic structure of society (basic social structure) and the basic structure of the international society of peoples (global basic structure). The latter refers to the network or system of institutions, taken as a whole and in dynamic relation to one another, that forms the institutional background within which peoples or legitimate states and other international actors (corporations, nongovernmental organizations, particular persons) interact with one another globally and across borders. The global basic structure is the total institutional structure of the international order as an ongoing cooperative venture carried out by particular peoples or societies. It includes the United Nations system of institutions, the World Trade Organization, the International Monetary Fund and World Bank, various global governance institutions, various regional trade regimes, the system of international law, the so-called global civil society, and so on. The principles of social justice do not apply to the global basic structure. They apply only to the basic structure of society. Principles of international or global justice, Rawls refers to them as "the Law of Peoples," apply to the global basic structure.

The principles specifying a conception of social justice also do not apply directly to interpersonal, noninstitutional relations (friendships) or to individual actions (whether one cultivates one's talents or not). What justice requires, if anything, in these areas is not a question that Rawls addresses.

Rawls has been criticized for treating social justice as a subject distinct from local and transactional justice, international justice, and justice in interpersonal relations and individual conduct (Pogge 1989; Cohen 1997; Murphy 1998).

The principles specifying a conception of social justice do not apply directly to particular components or elements of a society's basic structure taken one at a time; they apply directly only to the whole structure. And they apply to the whole structure taken as a dynamic system over time. While the family in whatever form it is legally and socially recognized is part of the basic social structure, the principles of social justice do not apply directly to the internal structure of the family isolated from the rest of the basic structure. Rather, they apply indirectly insofar as they apply to the total set of institutional relations constituting the basic social structure of which the family is a part. The same holds for churches, the market, business corporations, and so on. They must all satisfy the principles of social justice, but only as parts of the unified, dynamic system, the institutionalized social world that is the basic social structure. Of course, the application of the principles of social justice to the basic social structure as a whole may still have immediate consequences for the internal structure of particular institutions. So, for example, it may be that the basic structure as a whole cannot adequately secure basic liberties as required by justice unless particular institutions within the basic structure, perhaps the family or churches, honor those liberties within their own internal affairs. There is, however, no a priori reason to think that the internal structure of every particular institution ingredient in the basic structure must itself directly conform to the principles of social justice in order for the basic structure as a whole to conform to them. Of course, particular institutions must also always satisfy whatever principles of local or transactional justice apply specifically to them.

Within the basic structure of society, the legal–political structure occupies a special place. It is through its legal–political structure that a society makes explicit and binding decisions regarding the principles and design of its basic structure, and thus the particular institutions belonging to it. So, for example, a society properly determines the design of its economic markets through its legal–political institutions. It does not properly determine the design of its legal–political institutions through its economic markets. Within the legal–political institutions of a society, Rawls distinguishes between constitutional institutions that are more or less fixed and placed beyond the reach of ordinary legal–political processes and other institutions subject to ordinary legal–political processes. While the principles of social justice apply always to the basic structure of society taken as a whole, these distinctions play an important role in understanding how they are applied to that structure.

Because they apply directly in the first instance only to the basic social structure, the principles of social justice do not determine directly the allocation of particular entitlements or obligations to specific individual persons. Provided the basic structure of their society is not too unjust (no basic social structure to date has been fully just), individuals acquire obligations and determinate entitlements by what they do subject to the rules of the particular institutions within which they act. They so acquire obligations and determinate entitlements as a matter of fairness or fair play. In a more or less just basic social structure, the rules of particular institutions conjoined with the voluntary actions of individuals give rise to legitimate expectations. And fairness or fair play requires that these legitimate expectations be met, whether as obligations performed or entitlements delivered. So, for example, when conjoined with the rules of contract in the market, the voluntary actions of Smith and Jones may give rise, as a matter of fairness or fair play, to an obligation on the part of Smith and an entitlement on the part of Jones regarding the salary Smith owes Jones for work performed. Rawls refers to justice in the allocation of particular entitlements and obligations to specific individual persons as "allocative justice." He distinguishes "allocative justice" from "distributive justice." The latter refers to justice in the design of the basic social structure, or social justice. Rawls believes that it is not possible to solve the problem of allocative justice in general solely by reference to substantive reasons relating particular persons to particular goods. The problem is too complex to admit of any such general solution. Accordingly, he holds that the solution to the problem of allocative justice is given as a matter of pure procedural justice once just institutions have been established. As a matter of allocative justice, each person is to have just those entitlements and obligations that flow directly from her and others' voluntary conduct within just institutions.

Perhaps the primary reason that Rawls takes the basic social structure to be the first subject of justice is that societies inevitably allocate the particular goods they produce to specific individual persons by reference to some combination of various factors including the content and strength of their desires, their desert or merit, and the social value of their natural abilities. But in every society each of these will be shaped to a very great degree by the basic social structure. Suppose you were raised in a society with a basic social structure very different from the basic structure of your present society. You would likely have different desires. You would likely come to deserve things and merit praise through different forms of conduct and character traits. And your natural abilities would likely be valued by others in different ways. But if societies allocate social goods to particular individuals by reference to socially produced factors that vary from society to society, then the justice of a society as a whole cannot be determined by whether or not it realizes allocative justice. It can be determined only by an inquiry into the justice of the basic social structure from which those factors emerge, that is, by an inquiry into social or distributive justice.

David A. Reidy

SEE ALSO:

Cohen, G. A.
Distributive justice
Fairness, principle of
Family
Feminism
Fundamental ideas (in justice as fairness)
Law of Peoples
Political conception of justice
Procedural justice

18.

BEITZ, CHARLES

CHARLES BEITZ (b. 1949) is Professor of Politics and affiliated professor of philosophy and director of the University Center for Human Values at Princeton University. Before moving to Princeton Beitz taught in the political science departments at Swarthmore and Bowdoin Colleges. He earned his Ph.D. in Politics from Princeton University in 1978, where he studied under Dennis Thompson and Thomas Scanlon, and attended Scanlon's early important seminar on *TJ*.

Beitz is best known in relation to Rawls for his innovative extension and adaptation of ideas from Rawls to the global realm. In his early work *Political Theory and International Relations* (1979, second edition 1999) Beitz provides the first detailed attempt to work out a "globalized" version of the view presented in *TJ*, and in his recent work on human rights, culminating in the book *The Idea of Human Rights* (2009), Beitz develops what he calls a "practical conception" of human rights, significantly developing and extending ideas drawn from the comparatively sketchy account of human rights presented by Rawls in *LP*.

Although the idea of "globalizing" Rawls's account from *TJ* had already been discussed by Thomas Scanlon and Brian Barry, Beitz, in *Political Theory and International Relations*, provided the first sustained and detailed attempt to work out the view. Beitz there argues that ideas developed by Rawls in *TJ* could and should be applied at the global level, and should not be applied merely within "closed societies." Beitz suggests two ways in which Rawlsian principles could be globalized: first, within an international "original position" with states as members; second, in a cosmopolitan original position, where all individuals in the world would be represented as individuals.

In the first case, Beitz argues that even if we assume that societies are largely self-sufficient, as he takes Rawls to assume, parties to the second, "global," original position would insist on a global resource distribution principle which would function in a way somewhat analogously to how the difference principle works in domestic society. This argument is motivated by the idea that the distribution of resources is both "arbitrary from the moral point of view" and that access to sufficient natural resources is necessary for a society to be successful. In the other case, Beitz argues that there are strong reasons to reject the "self-sufficiency" claim he finds in Rawls, and holds that we should take individuals as the subjects of a truly global original position. (Beitz has consistently rejected the idea that toleration of states, nations, or "peoples" should have any priority over the pressing claims of individuals.) A global original position leads, Beitz claims, to a global difference principle, one ultimately addressed to individuals, though states might still play an important intermediary role. In *LP*, Rawls rejected both of these challenges to his view, arguing that global resource distribution was not of primary moral or practical importance, and further developing his arguments as to why the difference principle is inappropriate on the global level. Despite Rawls's reservations, however, Beitz's work has been and remains deeply influential in the developing global justice literature.

Beitz has recently taken on certain aspects of Rawls's account of human rights, as set out in *LP*, and used them to develop a distinct "practical conception" of human rights, grounded in the idea of "public reason" and based on the role that human rights play in the discursive interactions among relevant participants. This approach, contrasted by Beitz with "naturalistic" and "agreement" approaches, offers another potentially fruitful extension of Rawls's ideas in the global realm.

Matt Lister

SEE ALSO:

Human rights
Law of Peoples
The original position

19.

BENEVOLENT ABSOLUTISM

I N THE LAW OF PEOPLES, Rawls develops an account of the fundamental principles of the foreign policy platform of a well-ordered liberal democratic society. In organizing this effort, Rawls identifies five types of societies, each of which presents its own type of foreign policy challenge for a liberal society. One type of society he identifies is the benevolent absolutism (*LP* 4, 63, 92). However, Rawls spends little time on benevolent absolutisms, as they are not his primary concern.

Benevolent absolutisms are societies that honor and respect most human rights, domestically and internationally. Thus, benevolent absolutisms are nonaggressive. Their evident peacefulness, coupled with their honoring of most human rights, gives them a right to wage war in self-defense. Nevertheless, they do not deserve full and good standing in the international community because they are not well-ordered.

Benevolent absolutisms are not well-ordered because their members are not given any role in political decision-making. Even if some benevolent absolutism were structured in accordance with some principles of justice, these principles could not be voluntarily affirmed by the members of that benevolent society, just because the members would have no say in political decisions. What we have, then, even where the content of human rights is reliably supplied, is not a genuine scheme of social cooperation, but an (admittedly benevolent) exercise of power. Social cooperation requires at least some small measure of reciprocity, not just of advantage or benefit, but also of reason-giving. But reciprocal reason-giving is missing in the case of benevolent absolutisms, because political decision-making is an entirely one-sided affair. This prevents benevolent absolutisms from being well-ordered, and further keeps them from attaining the status of "people" (artificial, corporate moral person).

Commentators have said little about benevolent absolutisms. One issue that has arisen is whether it is appropriate for Rawls to describe benevolent absolutisms as genuinely respecting or honoring human rights. Since members of benevolent absolutisms have no political participation rights, it seems that the content of other rights must be supplied to them only contingently and not as a matter of right. The delivery of the content of these rights does not seem to be secured at all, but seems instead to depend completely on the continued benevolence of the ruler. This leaves members of benevolent absolutisms open to domination as Pettit describes it, i.e., susceptible to arbitrary exercises of control or force by others. Such control is arbitrary because it tracks the interests or worldview of the controller and not of the controlled. Securing rights through the institutionalization of political processes (such as Rawls's decent consultation hierarchy) promotes freedom by preventing domination. Since domination is not consistent with Rawls's goal of a world of constitutional republics, his position on the human rights situation in benevolent absolutisms is somewhat puzzling.

In any event, since benevolent absolutisms deliver at least the content of human rights to their members, unlike many burdened societies and outlaw states, and are peaceful, unlike outlaw states, they represent in many ways the least urgent of the foreign policy problems confronting liberal societies.

Walter J. Riker

SEE ALSO:

Law of Peoples
Cooperation and coordination

20.

BERLIN, ISAIAH

SAIAH BERLIN (1909–1997) was a Latvian-born political theorist and historian of political ideas. He was the Chichele Professor of Social and Political Theory at Oxford University between 1957 and 1967. Though the bulk of his writing had to do with the political ideas of thinkers of the Enlightenment and of the Counter-Enlightenment, he is perhaps best known among political philosophers for a relatively small number of essays that were published in the volume *Four Essays on Liberty* (Berlin 1969).

In these essays, Berlin defended a view of political life that emphasized the irreducible plurality of ends legitimately pursued by human agents. In Berlin's view, pluralism puts paid to certain forms of political rationalism, according to which reason militates in favor of one of these values, or a small subset thereof. He viewed this kind of rationalism as insufficiently attentive to the plurality of ends, and as potentially politically noxious since the belief in a single rational end can fuel tyrannical political forms aimed at "freeing" human subjects from the hold that illusory desires and ends have upon them.

Pluralism is one of the grounds of Berlin's preference for a negative as opposed to a positive conception of liberty. Negative liberty obtains when no one stands in the way of my doing what I want to do, whereas positive liberty has to do with the quality of my will, and with whether I truly want what I rationally ought to want. Some critics have urged that Berlin's espousal of both pluralism and negative liberty is inconsistent, since a real pluralist would be indifferent as between the two conceptions (Gray 1996; Weinstock 1997).

Rawls did not engage systematically with Berlin's thought. In his earlier work, Rawls often cites Berlin's influential essay on liberty, but ends up endorsing MacCallum's attempt to reconcile positive and negative conceptions by defining liberty as being fully specified only when agent, restriction, and object are specified (MacCallum 1967; *TJ* 177 n.4).

In his later work, Rawls sometimes invoked Berlin's pluralism, and in particular the idea that there can be "no social world without loss" (*PL* 57, 197; *CP* 462, 477). The idea that humans legitimately pursue a diversity of ends was seen by Rawls as underwriting two claims that are central to the later formulation of his views. First, the recognition by Rawls that societies in which basic civil freedoms obtain would inevitably be marked by a diversity of reasonable "comprehensive conceptions" of the good life. For Rawls, the recognition of plurality, arguably underemphasized in *A Theory of Justice*, changes the way in which principles of justice must be justified. Rather than showing that these principles flow from some shared conception of rationality or of the good, they must be shown to be at the center of an "overlapping consensus" between the plurality of comprehensive conceptions.

Second, Berlinian pluralism was invoked by Rawls in his claim that just social and political institutions could not possibly have entirely neutral effects on reasonable conceptions of the good. There is on this view limited social and institutional space with which to accommodate the full diversity of such conceptions, and it is unavoidable that even in an ideally just society some will fare better than others.

It is unclear, however, that Rawls took Berlin's pluralism fully to heart. Rawls saw the overlapping consensus as needing to encompass not just the principles of justice themselves, but also the justificatory apparatus he preferred, including the original position. A thinner consensus would have in Rawls's view been unstable, on the order of a *modus vivendi*. It may be, however, that *modus vivendi* liberalism is more in keeping with the spirit of Berlin's pluralism.

Daniel Weinstock

SEE ALSO:

> *Burdens of judgment*
> *Freedom*
> *Neutrality*
> *Overlapping consensus*
> *Reasonable pluralism*

21.

BRANCHES OF GOVERNMENT

RAWLS DOES NOT provide a detailed account of the structure of political and economic institutions that would be needed in order to secure stable conditions of justice as fairness. However, his account of the "Background Institutions for Distributive Justice" (*TJ* §43, 242–251) does provide at least a sketch of the central institutions for governing the economy in a property-owning democracy. In delineating a number of distinct "branches of government" Rawls is explicitly following Musgrave's approach to public finance (Musgrave 1959). It should be stressed that these various "branches" may each involve the activities of a number of distinct government agencies (*TJ* 243). Each branch is defined functionally (*TJ* 243–244) and should not be thought of as being equivalent to a traditional government department. While Rawls's specification of the branches of government is for a property-owning democracy with private ownership of land and capital, he thinks that a slightly amended scheme could also secure social justice under a liberal socialist regime (*TJ* 243, 247–249).

The four main branches of government are the (1) allocation, (2) stabilization, (3) transfer, and (4) distribution branches. These four branches, taken together as constituting one integrated scheme, constitute the "supporting institutions" required for achieving pure procedural justice (*TJ* 243), when operating under a just constitution that secures the equal basic liberties, and together with other institutions needed to secure the fair value of the political liberties and fair equality of opportunity.

The allocation and stabilization branches are designed to work together "to maintain the efficiency of the market economy generally" (*TJ* 244). The allocation branch does this by regulating the economy so as to keep prices competitive, avoiding monopolies or other concentrations of "unreasonable market power," by means of "suitable taxes and subsidies and by changes in the definition of property rights," so that prices may be made more fully reflective of social costs and benefits (*TJ* 244). The stabilization branch is associated with the traditional Keynesian goal of securing "reasonably full employment" through the management of "strong effective demand" (*TJ* 244).

The transfer branch is there to provide the "social minimum," and can be seen as embodying some of the traditional functions of the welfare state. The transfer branch is necessary because the efficient market outcome that could be secured by the allocation and stabilization branches working together "gives no consideration to needs" and therefore requires supplementation by a system of social transfers. Here, Rawls envisages a "division of labor between the parts of the social system in answering to the common sense precepts of justice" whereby "different institutions meet different claims" (*TJ* 244). There is thus an interesting sense in which Rawls sees the task of specifying a just basic structure as being in part about setting the appropriate balance, or proper division of labor, between these different functional branches of government activity. Rawls's commitment to this division of labor leads him to favor certain policies over rival ways of addressing the same problems, as where he endorses a combination of the market determination of wage rates with a system of social transfers to those with low market incomes, rather than addressing claims of need through regulating income by minimum wage standards (*TJ* 245).

The distribution branch is there "to preserve an approximate justice in distributive shares by means of taxation and the necessary adjustments in the rights of property" (*TJ* 245). It does this in two main ways. First, in order to act to secure fair equality of opportunity and fair value of the political liberties, it imposes substantial gift and inheritance taxes, and restricts the right of bequest. Second, in order to raise the revenue required for the provision of public goods and for the transfers undertaken through the transfer branch, both of which are required by the difference principle, it institutes a general system of taxation. With regard to this second function, Rawls expresses a (tentative) preference for a proportional expenditure tax over more familiar approaches, such as progressive income taxation (*TJ* 246). This further division of labor between the two parts of the distribution branch corresponds to the division between the two parts of the second principle of justice; here again, what we may describe as Rawls's architectonic commitments direct him towards certain policies and away from others (for example, inheritance taxation is on Rawls's view to be used only with the aim of redistributing wealth and not for the purpose of raising general government revenues for the provision of public goods (*TJ* 245)).

Branches of government / 67

A fifth and final branch of government, the exchange branch, stands alone from the others, and is brought into operation only once the foregoing branches have together secured conditions of social justice. It is comprised of "a special representative body taking note of the various social interests and their preferences for public goods" (*TJ* 249) and hence has a distinct institutional basis, separate to the parts of the basic structure of society governed by the two principles of justice (*TJ* 249–251). This representative body undertakes a process of bargaining to decide upon discretionary expenditures on optional public goods, according to Wicksell's unanimity criterion, whereby, for each proposed expenditure, a scheme must be found for which (at least approximately) unanimous approval can be found over the conjunction of the public activity in question and a specific proposal for spreading the costs of that activity through extra taxation (Wicksell 1958). This extremely demanding Wicksellian standard of approximate unanimity is very far from the vision of "ordinary legislation" that one sees later in Rawls's thought, as with the specification in *Political Liberalism* that the strictures of public reason need not apply (or not apply "so strictly" (*PL* 215)) when polities decide on questions that do not implicate the constitutional essentials of a just society, as with "establishing national parks and preserving wilderness areas and animal and plant species; and laying aside funds for museums and the arts" (*PL* 214). Rather than an exchange branch operating against tight criteria of permissibility, we are instead confronted with a more familiar kind of democratic legislature, exercising (majoritarian?) discretion across a wide ambit of political questions, where constitutional essentials are not at stake.

It is interesting to note that, although there is a discussion of property-owning democracy and the institutions of a just basic structure in *Justice as Fairness* that is in important respects more detailed and developed than that in *A Theory of Justice*, Rawls does not mention these branches of government in that later discussion (see *JF*, part IV, 135–179, esp. 135–140). One might therefore justifiably speculate as to whether Rawls's conception of the institutions of a just basic structure in fact retained these particular functional divisions between distinct branches in his later thought. (See O'Neill and Williamson 2012.)

While discussion of the specific functions of the different branches of government is largely absent in Rawls's later work, the Introduction to the paperback edition *Political Liberalism* includes, in the specification of the institutional requirements for a stable just society, an amplification of the function of the stabilization branch. Going beyond ensuring "reasonably full employment" by means of Keynesian demand management, justice requires that, if citizens' self-respect is to be preserved, we must ensure "society as employer of last resort through general or local government, or other social and economic policies" (*PL* lvii). It therefore seems reasonable to conclude that Rawls's understanding of the institutional requirements of a just society continued to develop beyond the rather schematic sketch of the branches of government offered in *A Theory of Justice*.

Martin O'Neill and Thad Williamson

SEE ALSO:

Basic needs, principle of
Basic structure of society
Distributive justice
The economy
Fair equality of opportunity
Four-stage sequence
Property-owning democracy
Social minimum

22.

BUCHANAN, ALLEN

ALLEN BUCHANAN (b. 1948) is James B. Duke Professor of Philosophy and Public Policy at Duke University. He works in three chief areas: the philosophy of international law and justice, biomedical ethics, and a new field he has christened "social moral epistemology." Buchanan attributes his turn toward political philosophy in his first year of graduate school to the publication of Rawls's *A Theory of Justice*. In his extensive work since, he acknowledges a large debt to Rawls, even as he extends or challenges key elements of the Rawlsian program.

Buchanan's work in the philosophy of international law, where Rawls's influence is strongest, centers on the nature and justification of human rights, the legitimacy of international law-making institutions and the use of force in international relations. Buchanan criticizes Rawls's account of human rights in *The Law of Peoples* for its minimalist content and its refusal to ground human rights in characteristics that all humans share. Both features, Buchanan argues, derive from a misuse of the political liberal notion of "reasonableness." We can construct a more robust and intuitive account of human rights without violating a commitment to respecting reasonable moral and metaphysical disagreement. On the topic of international governance, Buchanan draws on Rawls's distinction between justice and legitimacy in *Political Liberalism* to develop an account of what, if anything, might render the rule of international legislative bodies acceptable. In his work on the morality of war, Buchanan has done much to extend the narrow focus of traditional just war theory to novel questions concerning humanitarian intervention, preventive war, and forcible democratization.

In international political philosophy more generally, Buchanan is critical of what he terms Rawls's "Westphalian" conception of global politics in *LP*, according to which societies are economically self-sufficient and distributively autonomous units, between which no principles of international distributive justice apply. Buchanan argues that the existence of a "global basic structure" undermines these assumptions and supports an egalitarian account of global justice that is much closer in content to the theory of domestic justice that Rawls had advocated in *TJ*. Rawls is also criticized for glossing over the existence of intrastate conflict, a theme that connects to Buchanan's early groundbreaking work on the ethics of secession.

In medical ethics, Buchanan has written on decision-making on behalf of impaired patients, biomedical enhancement, and the just domestic and international distribution of health care.

Buchanan's writing is informed by a distinctive methodological commitment, the development of which is an independent focus of his research. He argues that philosophers – including Rawls – have underestimated the role of institutions not simply in implementing political norms but also in justifying them. For instance, the moral attractiveness of a norm permitting preventive war or an expansive list of human rights crucially depends on the nature of the institutions available for specifying and enforcing such norms. Good political theorizing requires *social moral epistemology*: an empirically grounded comparative evaluation of alternative "norm-institution packages" in terms of their effectiveness at achieving our goals. Buchanan is himself accustomed to marrying philosophy with institutional knowledge, having served as a consultant to several national bioethics commissions in the US, and to Canada, Ethiopia, and the EU on issues relating to secession and political self-determination.

Helena de Bres

SEE ALSO:

Distributive justice
Human rights
Law of Peoples
Legitimacy

23.

BURDENED SOCIETIES

URDENED SOCIETIES – OR, societies burdened by unfavorable conditions – are societies lacking the necessary means to fulfill the human rights of their citizens. As such, these societies are not well-ordered. The well-ordered members of the Society of Peoples have a duty to assist these burdened societies, providing them the means by which they might become well-ordered themselves. The concept of a burdened society, and the duty of assistance that extends toward them, is at the heart of Rawls's analysis of international distributive justice.

Two aspects of the concept of a burdened society are worth noting. The first is that the burdens these societies face are not primarily a matter of simple material deprivation. Rawls argues that there are no societies – except, perhaps, the Arctic Eskimos – who do not have enough material resources to form a well-ordered society. The circumstances that prevent a society from being well-ordered, Rawls argues instead, are generally aspects of its social and political culture. In particular, Rawls argues that the causes of a people's wealth are to be found in its political culture, in the "religious, philosophical and moral traditions that support the basic structure of their political and social institutions," and in the "industriousness and cooperative talents of its members, all supported by their political virtues" (*LP* 108). This analysis also entails that even severe crises of material goods, including famines, are best understood as resulting from political failures and a lack of respect for human rights – a conclusion which echoes Amartya Sen's work on famine (*LP* 109). Given that the duty of assistance demands that well-ordered people work to help burdened societies become well-ordered, it is clear that the content of the duty of assistance will be considerably more complicated than a mere command to share material goods. The members of the Society of Peoples have the obligation to do what is necessary to help burdened societies become well-ordered; this duty might entail many things – technological transfer, direct provision of expertise, even the conditioning of aid on the protection of certain human rights norms, including gender equality (*LP* 110–111). The direct provision of material goods, though, will rarely be a part of this assistance; the burdens faced by burdened societies cannot be fixed by such transfers.

The second aspect of the burdened societies worth noting is that the existence of such societies is placed within the category of nonideal theory. Rawls's vision of the Law of Peoples as realistic utopia imagines a world of self-determining peoples, each of which respects the principles governing the Society of Peoples. This vision is compatible with significant differences in well-being or happiness between the inhabitants of different societies. The duty of assistance applies only towards societies that are not well-ordered, and then only to the extent required to make such societies well-ordered. The duty of assistance demands that burdened societies be made well-ordered; it does not require that these societies be made wealthy.

Rawls's concept of the burdened society is thus at the heart of his theory of international distributive justice. Much of the response to the idea of the burdened society has been a response to Rawls's overall analysis of international distributive justice (see generally Martin and Reidy 2006). Some critics have focused more directly upon the idea of a burdened society, however, and have argued that this concept conceals injustice to which Rawls should be attentive. Thomas Pogge, in particular, has criticized Rawls's concept of a burdened society for embodying what he calls the Purely Domestic Poverty Thesis – namely, the thesis that the causes of poverty are to be found within the traditions and norms of a political society. In contrast to this, Pogge argues that the poverty of those peoples Rawls would call burdened is best explained with reference to international rules and practices. These norms were set in place by the wealthy states of the world for their own benefit, and have a causal role in the replication and maintenance of global poverty. As such, Pogge argues, it is morally shortsighted of Rawls to assert that the poverty of a burdened society is due to its own culture and virtues; this account ignores the causal role of wealthy societies in ensuring that other societies continue to be underdeveloped (see generally Pogge 2008). Rawls's response might be to note that he understands himself as writing ideal theory; if the causal story he uses in this story fails to describe our actual world, then his theory cannot directly be applied to it. Rawls is, on this view, not committed to the Purely Domestic Poverty thesis as a descriptive fact in our own,

Burdened societies / 73

nonideal, world. This defense may save Rawls's Law of Peoples from Pogge's criticism, but the strategy is risky: Rawls is no longer writing about a world similar to the one we inhabit, and as such we cannot easily use Rawls's work to derive moral conclusions about that world.

Michael Blake

SEE ALSO:

Duty of assistance
Human rights
Ideal and nonideal theory
Law of Peoples
Pogge, Thomas

24.

BURDENS OF JUDGMENT

THE BURDENS OF judgment are considerations intended to explain the persistence of reasonable disagreement, and to motivate parties to obey the constraints of public reason in the face of this disagreement.

Public reason constrains political agents, when those agents seek to engage the coercive machinery of politics. In particular, political agents are enjoined to restrict the reasons they invoke (in certain political contexts) to those that do not rely crucially upon comprehensive doctrines about which the parties can be expected to disagree. The ideal of public reason involves a principled refusal, on the part of political agents, to invoke their own controversial moral and political views when arguing about constitutional essentials and matters of basic justice.

The burdens of judgment are intended to support the commitments of these political agents, by giving a series of explanations for the existence of a reasonable pluralism of comprehensive doctrines. The burdens of judgment help these agents avoid the temptation to regard their own comprehensive doctrines as a sufficient justification for political coercion exercised over those who reject that doctrine. To accept the burdens of judgment, he argues, is to commit oneself to the shared task of seeking standards of justification that can be accepted by a plurality of reasonable comprehensive doctrines. Reasonable people commit themselves to the search for these standards, even in circumstances in which they might be able to rely upon their own comprehensive doctrines as justifications for public policy. The burdens of judgment are intended as a set of considerations to provide support for reasonable agents in this search. The notion that this is a "burden" is meant by Rawls quite literally: we must be aware, in our political judgment, of the temptation to regard our own worldview as natural and correct,

Burdens of judgment / 75

and competitors as simply mistaken. To accept the burdens of judgment is to forestall this easy sort of injustice.

Rawls provides six considerations as representative examples of the considerations that should lead us to accept the burdens of judgment; this list provides what Rawls takes to be the most obvious sources of reasonable disagreement – Rawls makes no claims that the list is exhaustive. Rawls argues that the following facts are true about disagreements over fundamental matters, as found in the disagreement between comprehensive doctrines:

a. The evidence – empirical and scientific – bearing on the case is conflicting and complex, and thus hard to assess and evaluate.

b. Even where we agree fully about the kinds of considerations that are relevant, we may disagree about their weight, and so arrive at different judgments.

c. To some extent all our concepts, and not only moral and political concepts, are vague and subject to hard cases; and this indeterminacy means that we must rely on judgment and interpretation.

d. To some extent (how great we cannot tell) the way we assess evidence and weight moral and political values is shaped by our total experience, our whole course of life up to now; and our total experiences must always differ.

e. Often there are different kinds of normative considerations of different force on both sides of an issue and it is difficult to make an overall assessment.

f. [Any] system of social institutions is limited in the values it can admit so that some selection must be made from the full range of moral and political values that might be realized...[W]e face great difficulty in setting priorities and making adjustment. Many hard decisions seem to have no answer. (*PL* 56–57)

Several things are worth noting about these ideas. The first is that, while the considerations given here are intended to explain why disagreement over matters of comprehensive doctrine is inevitable, they emphatically do not also say that all comprehensive doctrines are equally valid. Rawls wants to avoid relativism and skepticism; his commitment is to a society that treats disagreeing parties fairly – not to the more radical notion that each side in the disagreement is equally correct.

The second is that the idea of the burdens of judgment is simultaneously epistemological and moral. It is epistemological, in that it relates to how we can expect human beings to decide upon questions of ultimate value, and why we can expect free persons to arrive at differing comprehensive doctrines. It is moral, though, in that the proper response to these considerations is intended to be a political commitment to treating those with whom we disagree with fairness. In recognizing the inevitability of disagreement, we are supposed to ensure our commitment to avoid the sorts of injustice that come about when we insist that our own doctrines are sufficiently obvious that they might be used to ground political coercion.

The relation between the moral and the epistemological elements of the burdens of judgment, though, is not always easy to make out. Why, exactly, does recognizing the epistemological fact that people are likely to disagree with us about morality give us reason to give principled respect to our opponents? That such disagreement is predictable, by itself, gives us no ethical information about how such disagreement should be treated. (We can imagine a theist who accepted Rawls's epistemological story, and saw in it only an account of how many people are predictably led astray by a wicked and fallen world.) Rawls is not entirely clear about how the link between the epistemological considerations and the normative considerations is to be made.

One possible strand here involves the idea that one's comprehensive doctrine is so basic that the "errors" made here cannot be fixed by reason; Rawls does suggest that the burdens of judgment make it "not in general unreasonable" to affirm one of a number of comprehensive doctrines (*PL* 60). We must keep the burdens of judgment in view, on this strand, to remind ourselves that those with whom we disagree are not making errors that we could hope to fix. This is true, of course, but provides no independent moral reason for us to respect the mistaken view; the theist above could agree that the error was not fixable, while rejecting public reason as the appropriate response. The burdens of judgment are – on this account – only useful to us once we are already committed to public reason. Another strand invokes the idea that our most basic moral commitment is to use our political apparatus in ways that could be justified to all, based upon reasons they could in principle find motivating. On this account, the burdens of judgment are important because they remind us that the free use of human reason will inevitably issue in disagreement at the level of comprehensive doctrine; we should, therefore, look for a methodology of political justice that does not begin in any such doctrine. This is likely true, but it is not clear that the acceptance of the burdens of judgment is morally required for us to act as reasonable political agents. On the contrary: it might be true that the burdens of judgment, as described by Rawls, are rejected by some reasonable comprehensive doctrines. The Roman Catholic Church, for example, is doctrinally committed to freedom of conscience – but emphatically rejects the burdens of judgment, on the doctrinal

Burdeneds of judgment / 77

rationale that God's law is available to all clear reasoning agents (see, on this, Wenar 1995). A final strand emphasizes the difficulty of the task of developing a comprehensive doctrine, and the importance of this task for a person's life. The burdens of judgment emphasize how much any particular comprehensive doctrine reflects value choices and weightings that are the result of that person's life and experience; to respect that person, on this account, is to respect what she has created for herself – namely, her comprehensive doctrine, however wrong it may appear to us. The burdens of judgment, on this account, give us reason to think that a commitment to respecting persons is a commitment to respecting even their mistaken answers to foundational questions. This strand is not especially developed within Rawls's writings, but is a potentially fruitful area of analysis.

Michael Blake

SEE ALSO:

Political conception of justice
Public reason
Reasonable pluralism
Religion

C

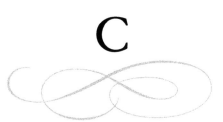

25.

CAPABILITIES

I N THE LATE twentieth century, theorists' attention was drawn to a new way of thinking about individuals' relative level of advantage or well-being. Instead of assessing either of these on the basis of the resources (such as income and wealth) available to people or on the basis of what they have achieved (by way of satisfying their interests, preferences, or plans, as utilitarians would, or by way of functioning in one way or another, as Aristotle did), the new thought was to do so on the basis of what people are able to do or to be: on the basis, that is, of their capabilities. Amartya Sen (1982) introduced this idea of capabilities partly via a critique of Rawls's reliance on the idea of primary goods, and specifically of his suggestion that income and wealth can serve to index inequalities for purposes of the difference principle. Consequently, it is sometimes thought that the "capabilities approach" that has grown up around Sen's constructive suggestions and those of Martha Nussbaum is inimical to Rawls's approach. Nussbaum, however, has recently written that since "for Rawls the primary goods are just one element in a highly complex overall theory, it is perhaps best not to invoke his theory" as a foil for the capability approach (2011, 56–57).

As a practical matter, the capabilities approach has gained its influence largely by addressing the weaknesses of a much simpler foil, development economists who assessed nations' economic progress on the basis of their gross domestic product. Sen helped develop the United Nations' Human Development Index (HDI), which takes account of individuals' health and education in addition to their income and wealth. (Although inspired by Sen's work on capabilities, the HDI has been forced to work with information about individual achievements which – unlike information about what people would have been able to do or to be, if they had only chosen to – is available in national statistics.)

Theoretically, Sen and Nussbaum have taken the capabilities approach in two quite different directions. Nussbaum has elaborated a list of ten basic capabilities and developed an account of minimal justice according to which governments have a responsibility to see to it that their citizens reach minimum thresholds in each of the ten categories (Nussbaum 2006). This proposal arguably complements Rawls's theory of justice, which is not focused on minimal justice and which added a highest-priority basic needs principle only as an afterthought (*PL* 7). Nussbaum stresses that she embraces Rawls's effort to develop a liberalism that is political, not metaphysical (e.g. 2011, 89). In contrast to Nussbaum, Sen has resolutely refused to specify which capabilities are most central to human advantage or well-being. Instead, he emphasizes that capabilities embody an important aspect of freedom, for they indicate the range of what a person could choose to do (Sen 1985, 200–203). This form of freedom is more abstract, and more closely related to consumer choice, than any of Rawls's basic liberties.

Sen's central criticism of Rawls's use of lifetime expectations of income and wealth in indexing advantage for the purposes of the difference principle, and of reliance on the primary goods more generally, was that this approach to indexing advantage is informationally impoverished, and hence insensitive to variations that it should be sensitive to. These variations, most prominently, involve people who "convert" resources such as income and wealth into advantage or well-being at different rates. It seems that someone suffering from disabilities or from severe health problems will get less advantage or well-being out of a given set of resources than someone not facing such difficulties and that, likewise, a disabled person with a "jolly disposition" will get more out of the resources than will a disabled person with a sour disposition (1982, 365, 367). Intuitively compelling as these cases are, one must remember that Rawls put forward the primary goods as part of his "thin" theory of the good. Taking it that people disagree quite deeply about the nature of the good, he avoided developing principles that rely upon a prior, detailed conception of human advantage or well-being. Instead, he defined each individual's good in terms of the rational plan that that person would choose with deliberative rationality. If, however, we take *this* as the basis for our working understanding of advantage or well-being, how can we possibly know whether a disabled person is less likely to live a good life than someone without a disability? We would need to know how people's plans vary with their disability or lack thereof and whether those variations tend to be irrational (in the way, say, that adaptive preferences are).

Of course, pinning the complaint of informational poverty upon Rawls's use of income and wealth to index advantage for the purposes of the difference principle is potentially unfair, as it ignores how his other principles address the other primary goods. Sen noted that Rawls's first principle is addressed to the basic liberties, but ignored the principle of fair equality of opportunity (1982, 365) – which is ironic, since the idea of people's opportunities is at least very closely related to that of their capabilities. In a careful response to Sen's critique, which seems so far to have been ignored in the secondary literature (apart from a possible allusion in Sen 2009, 216), Rawls argues that accessible medical care is "necessary to underwrite fair equality of opportunity" (*JF* 174). More fundamentally, he argues that his account of primary goods, as recast in his later writings, rests on an idea of basic capabilities, namely "the capabilities of citizens as free and equal persons in virtue of their two moral powers" (*JF* 169). It is presumably for these sorts of reasons that Nussbaum has concluded that Rawls's theory is not an apt foil for the capabilities approach.

Henry S. Richardson

SEE ALSO:

Higher-order interests
Moral person
Nussbaum, Martha
Primary goods, social
Sen, Amartya
Thin and full theories of good

26.

CARE

PHILOSOPHICAL THEORIES CENTERED on the notion of care were initially inspired by the research of psychologist Carol Gilligan, who challenged Lawrence Kohlberg's theory of moral development. Kohlberg's theory presupposed that when people reach full moral maturity their moral reasoning will appeal to notions such as duty, rights, justice, universality, and impartiality. Kohlberg's theory also assumed that the core of morality is deontological and that the most important aspects of morality are to be understood in terms of these same notions. Gilligan argued that this way of understanding morality – which she termed "the ethics of justice" – led Kohlberg to overlook or misinterpret important moral concerns that some research subjects were expressing. In particular, Gilligan claimed that her research with women revealed a different moral voice – an "ethics of care"– which reflected distinctive moral sensibilities:

> In this conception, the moral problem arises from conflicting responsibilities rather than from competing rights and requires for its resolution a mode of thinking that is contextual and narrative rather than formal and abstract. This conception of morality as concerned with the activity of care centers moral development around the understanding of responsibility and relationships, just as the conception of morality as fairness ties moral development to the understanding of rights and rules. (Gilligan 1982, 19)

Gilligan suggested that the ethics of justice and the ethics of care involve two competing ways of seeing the moral world. Gilligan appeals to empirical studies in which most people tend to make notably greater use of one framework than the other, and in which there are gender-related differences in the framework that predominates (Gilligan 1987, 25–26; 2011, 23–24). Although Gilligan's research methodology has been criticized, along with her account of normative phenomena, her work has had an enormous impact on feminist moral and political philosophy. An important line in feminism advocates the development of moral and political theories centered on the notion of care. It holds that theories that incorporate the value of care are more representative of the concerns and perspectives of women than traditional theories produced by male philosophers. Care theorists criticize the emphasis that contemporary moral and political philosophy places on universal and impartial principles of justice and rights. Instead, they argue for the theoretical centrality of interpersonal relationships, as well as the importance of a set of dispositions and capacities to attend to the particular needs of concrete others. They also react against the conceptualization of moral subjects as rational and independent individuals, offering an alternative account of moral subjects as interdependent and in need of emotional and material support.

Care theorists have raised a number of criticisms to Rawls's theory of justice, objecting to the description of the parties in the original position as disembodied and disembedded, and their reasoning as limited and male-biased (Benhabib 1987). They argue that the thought experiment presents itself as universal and accessible to everyone, while in fact it excludes the experiences and moral concerns of women. It is possible that these criticisms have some force against Rawls's early work, in which he hints at the possibility of developing a general moral theory that makes use of the original position to generate moral principles (*TJ* 93–101). However, after the political turn, Rawls makes it clear that his theory is meant to apply only to the functioning of the basic structure of society, and is not intended to offer a complete account of the moral domain. Still, certain aspects of Rawls's later political work have also been the target of criticism by care theorists. For example, they object to his idealized account of citizens as free and equal, because it abstracts from the basic fact that human beings are highly dependent on the care of others (Kittay 1999).

A related set of challenges to contemporary political theories focuses on the topic of care understood as a kind of activity. Some feminists argue that the activity of care should be acknowledged both as work and as socially indispensable. Although some of the work of tending to children and those who are sick, disabled or elderly is paid, an enormous amount of such work is not. Unpaid care work is disproportionately performed by women. The social distribution of unpaid care work may be explained by the fact that predominant social norms and social arrangements function in ways that reinforce a gendered division of labor. It may also reflect the actual considered choices and priorities of many women. Either way, those who do a significant amount of unpaid care work tend to be disadvantaged; they tend to have fewer opportunities to obtain desirable or well-paid jobs, less control of economic resources, and less leisure time. Moreover, these disadvantages tend to increase in cases of divorce (Okin 1989, 134–169).

Feminists have pointed out that Rawls's theory fails to acknowledge unpaid care work and the burdens and vulnerabilities associated with it. Although Rawls notes the essential contribution of parents' love and care for children in their acquisition of the sense of justice, he fails to examine issues of justice generated by the division of paid and unpaid work within families and the social and economic consequences of this division. Iris Young has argued that the source of this failure is Rawls's focus on the end-state distribution of social primary goods, and a correlated blindness to the social processes that produce such distributions. For instance, the principle of fair equality of opportunity does not consider how the occupations themselves should be defined, what kinds of labor will be valued, how long and under what conditions workers are expected to work, and so on. The theory also ignores the question of whether care work is the private responsibility of families or a matter of public policy. The problem to which Young is pointing is not precisely that gender roles and expectations might end up disadvantaging women even in a context of just political institutions. Rather, it is that Rawls's account of a well-ordered society seems to take for granted that its institutions will be, in essentials, the same as those we are familiar with today.

Victoria Costa

SEE ALSO:

Family
Feminism
Kohlberg, Lawrence
Okin, Susan Moller
The original position

27.

CATHOLICISM

RAWLS'S MATURE WORKS treat the topic of Catholicism only in a few brief passages and several extended footnotes. Yet his view of the Catholic Church – its history, institutional structure, doctrine, and social teaching – seems to have influenced his thinking at several points, particularly his understanding of political liberalism and public reason. It is noteworthy that one of the very few interviews given by Rawls, and the only one published in his *Collected Papers*, appears in the Catholic magazine *Commonweal*, where Rawls discusses (with Bernard Prusak) the relationship between religion and liberalism (*CP* 616–622).

In the terminology of political liberalism Catholicism is a comprehensive religious doctrine – it is connected to a recognizable tradition of thought and involves the exercise of both theoretical and practical reason to address the major aspects of human life (*PL* 59, 175; *JF* 14). Depending on how it is interpreted, Catholicism may be affirmed reasonably or unreasonably (*PL* 60 n.14). Among their other features, reasonable comprehensive doctrines should acknowledge the burdens of judgment and key liberal-democratic political values and commitments (*JF* 191; *BIMSF* 267). Especially in its refusal to join forms of comprehensive liberalism in celebrating moral autonomy as a central value (*PL* xliii), Catholicism is precisely the kind of worldview addressed by the fundamental question of political liberalism, namely, how those who affirm a religious doctrine based on religious authority might also accept democratic rule guided by a reasonable political conception of justice (*PL* xxxvii).

Familiar chapters in the history of both Christianity and the Catholic Church reveal the urgency of this question as well as the possible answers to it. Citing the Crusades, the Inquisition, early campaigns against heresy, and the religious violence of the St. Bartholomew's Day massacre, Rawls concludes that a "persecuting zeal has been the great curse of the Christian religion," as evidenced historically in religious coercion and persecution by both Catholics and Protestants (*LP* 21; *PL* 476–477 n.75). Neither political society nor religious communities will ultimately flourish if the Church becomes "part of the repressive state apparatus" (*CP* 621).

In fact Rawls locates one of liberalism's main origins in the Reformation and the sixteenth- and seventeenth-century Wars of Religion that played a key role in the formulation of modern ideas of religious toleration and liberty of conscience (*PL* xxiv; *LHPP* 11; *LHMP* 7). This interpretation is markedly different from views that would reduce liberalism's beginning or essence to a kind of possessive individualism. Nevertheless a *modus vivendi*, the model of toleration initially forged in the conflict between Catholics and Protestants, is plainly inadequate for contemporary liberal-democratic societies that aspire to remain stable for the right reasons (*PL* 148, 459).

At the same time, the historical experience of the Catholic Church illustrates the possibility of an alternative model, namely, a genuine normative commitment to freedom of religion, understood as fully consistent with – and implied by – religious doctrine. Rawls refers to the fundamental changes brought about by Vatican II and expressed in conciliar documents such as the 1965 "Declaration on Religious Freedom" (*Dignitatis Humanae*). With respect to religious pluralism, the longstanding teaching of the Church had been that "error has no rights." John Courtney Murray, a Jesuit theologian widely regarded as the most influential contributor to the "Declaration," describes the political implication of the Church's pre-Vatican II position as "intolerance whenever possible" and "tolerance whenever necessary" (1965, 12).

Rawls cites Murray in a note discussing the significance of Vatican II, which resulted in the acceptance of religious freedom on moral, theological, and political grounds (*PL* 477 n.75; *LP* 22 n.15). Indeed several of the ideas embraced by Murray in the 1950s and 1960s anticipate key features of political liberalism – not only religious liberty but also Murray's endorsement of constitutionally limited government, his distinction between private and public morality, his conception of civil society as a realm of freedom distinct from the state, and his attempt to articulate a consensus providing the shareable premises essential to the public discourse of a pluralistic democracy. Discussing public reasoning in the context of Catholic opposition to abortion, Rawls cites Murray's intervention into debates about the decriminalization of artificial contraception (*PL* 480 n.83). In appealing to a distinction in judgment not unlike what would be expected in Rawlsian public reason, Murray had argued that Catholics should not oppose decriminalization, even as they hold firm to the belief that artificial contraception is morally wrong.

Rawls even mentions "Catholic views of the common good and solidarity" as a potential form of public reason, provided that "they are expressed in terms of political values" (*PL* 451–452). Presumably the idea of the common good, already developed by Aquinas and expounded further by Catholic philosophers and theologians, might serve as the foundation for – or perhaps be interpreted directly in terms of – a reasonable political conception of justice, thereby providing the content of a citizen's public reasoning. Rawls's suggestion is a reminder of the similarities between justice as fairness and certain elements of Catholic social teaching, with its strong emphasis on the needs of the marginalized and its call for a preferential option for the poor. What is not clear is whether other elements of Catholic social teaching or doctrine, particularly with respect to sexuality and the family, could be easily translated into the values of a reasonable political conception.

These political questions are not addressed in Rawls's undergraduate thesis, which remains his most extensive investigation into theological topics. The young Rawls criticizes Augustine and Aquinas for relying on the impersonal ethics of Plato and Aristotle and for conceiving of God as an object of natural desire (*BIMSF* 161–162). While the undergraduate thesis examines the views of philosophers who have most influenced Catholicism, and even includes occasional references to the Catholic Church (*BIMSF* 197), it is by no means a study of specifically Catholic theology or doctrine. As Robert Adams observes in his commentary introducing Rawls's undergraduate thesis (*BIMSF* 24–101), the work is best understood as situated within the "intellectual climate" of neo-orthodox Protestant theology and as expressing a "classically Protestant" focus on the ethical evaluation of human attitudes and motives (*BIMSF* 30–32).

James Boettcher

SEE ALSO:

Abortion
Aquinas, Thomas
Common good idea of justice
Comprehensive doctrine
Culture, political vs. background
Public reason
Religion
Sin

28.

CHAIN CONNECTION

JUSTICE AS FAIRNESS takes the problem of distributive justice to concern the prospective shares of primary social goods that various representative persons (or social positions) are expected to receive over a complete life. "Chain connection" and "close-knitness" are simplifying assumptions that Rawls makes concerning the dynamic relationships among these different social positions. A society is "close-knit" if whenever there are changes to one position, all other positions change as well. There is no requirement that they all gain or lose together. Close-knitness holds whether a change to one position results in gains or losses to the other positions, as long as there is some change. In contrast, chain connection holds only if every change that results in gains to both the least-advantaged position and to the most-advantaged position also results in gains to all of the intermediate positions. It says nothing about what happens to the intermediate positions if there is a gain to the least-advantaged position but a loss to the most-advantaged position. Rawls's defense of the two principles of justice does not depend on assuming that the society is close-knit or that chain connection holds. Nonetheless, he makes these simplifying assumptions to help clarify the content of the difference principle.

If close-knitness fails, it is possible to have a situation in which a policy results in gains to one (or more) of the more-advantaged positions without any effect on the least-advantaged position. It might be somewhat unclear whether the difference principle would allow such a policy. Rawls introduces the "lexical difference principle" to clarify that such an inequality should properly be permissible. However, he believes that such a situation will be rare, since "when the greater potential benefits to the more advantaged are significant, there will surely be some way to improve the situation of the less advantaged as well" (*TJ* 72).

Chain connection / 91

If we assume that there are only two relevant social positions, we can say that the difference principle selects the most egalitarian from among the efficient distributions. ("Reply to Alexander and Musgrave" in *CP* 247) With more than two relevant social positions, when chain connection and close-knitness hold, this result generalizes: the difference principle selects the most egalitarian from among the efficient distributions. (See Martin 1985, appendix.) However, this is not always true when chain connection fails. When chain connection fails, it may be possible to increase the shares for the least- and most-advantaged positions, but only by lowering the shares of intermediate positions. Although the difference principle would allow such a change, it may appear to be in some tension with the requirement of reciprocity. Furthermore, depending on how equality is measured, it may or may not result in an increase in inequality. For example, there may be many members of the intermediate groups who fall from a position just below that of the most-advantaged to a position just above that of the least-advantaged. When chain connection fails, slight variations in the precise formulation of the difference principle can result in very different requirements, and there is some controversy in the secondary literature concerning which is the best interpretation of justice as fairness. (See Martin 1985, ch. 5; Williams 1995.)

Jon Mandle

SEE ALSO:

Close-knitness
Difference principle
Distributive justice
The original position

29.

CIRCUMSTANCES OF JUSTICE

THE CIRCUMSTANCES OF justice are the background conditions in which the question of justice arises. This is the question about how to distribute the benefits and burdens of social cooperation as well as about the rights and duties that persons should have in the basic institutions of society. These conditions make mutually advantageous cooperation both possible and necessary and, for this reason, give point to the role of justice. If they did not hold, "there would be no occasion for the virtue of justice" (*TJ* 110). The circumstances of justice capture the relations in which persons find themselves without assuming any particular theory of human motivation. In particular, there is no assumption that the need for principles of distributive justice arises because persons are egoistic. On the contrary, these conditions describe the relations in which individuals stand to each other regardless of their particular motivations.

Rawls divides these circumstances into two kinds: objective and subjective. The objective circumstances are the following: individuals share a defined geographical territory; they are roughly equal in physical and mental powers or, at least, their capacities are such that none can dominate the rest; they are vulnerable to attack and are subject to having their plans blocked by the united force of others; and they coexist in a condition of moderate scarcity, which means that resources are neither extremely abundant nor extremely scarce (*TJ* 109–110). The subjective circumstances include the fact that persons have needs and interests that are either roughly similar or, at least, complementary; they have plans of life or conceptions of the good that lead them to make conflicting claims on the natural and social resources in order to pursue their own and mutually diverging ends and purposes; they suffer from various kinds of shortcomings in knowledge, thought, and judgment in ways that are natural or usual; there exists a diversity of philosophical and religious beliefs as well as of political and social doctrines (*TJ* 110). These conditions, both objective and subjective, make human cooperation possible and necessary. On the one hand, individuals share ends and interests, the pursuit of which would be greatly improved if they were to cooperate with one another. On the other hand, there is moderate scarcity and conflicting claims on resources, which together make principles of distribution necessary.

In the pursuit of their conceptions of the good or long-term rational plans of life, individuals need natural and social resources. The conflict among them is inevitable because they are entitled to press on each other what they take to be their rights regarding the benefits and burdens of social cooperation in a condition in which resources are scarce. It is crucial to Rawls's account that this conflict is unavoidable regardless of whether individuals are egoistic or not. The conflict arises because the ends that individuals pursue oppose one another. In attributing to individuals an interest in pursuing their own rational plans of life, Rawls does not commit himself to any particular theory of motivation but only to the uncontroversial claim that people are interested in the pursuit of the ends that they set for themselves. In particular, he is not committed to the assumption that people are rational egoists. Whether their motivation is egoistic or not will depend, he maintains, on the content of their final ends. His own examples of egoistic final ends are one's own wealth, position, influence, and social prestige (*TJ* 111). The need for principles of distributive justice arises because of the relation in which individuals stand to one another when the circumstances of justice hold regardless of the content of their particular motivations.

This is a familiar theme from social contract theory: the need for cooperation and agreement among individuals is motivated by a combination of shared interests and conflicting claims. However, Rawls maintains that in offering his account of the circumstances of justice he follows Hume, a critic of contractarian approaches, and "adds nothing essential to his much fuller discussion" (*TJ* 110). As Hume before him, Rawls is explicit that in an extreme condition of either abundance or scarcity, mutually advantageous cooperation and, therefore, justice, become either unnecessary or impossible. If, on the one hand, natural resources were extremely abundant such that there was plenty to meet everyone's needs, there would be no need for principles of distributive justice because there would be no occasion for conflicting claims. If, on the other hand, natural resources were so scarce that there could not possibly be enough for everyone, justice would be impossible. In this case, "fruitful ventures must inevitably break down" because the benefits of cooperation would not be enough to meet the needs of everyone

(*TJ* 110). For a scheme of social cooperation to work and be stable over time, it must be mutually advantageous such that "one person's or group's gain need not be another's loss" (*CP* 256). If people perceive no advantages either because they have plenty or cannot get enough, the scheme turns out unnecessary or impossible.

Though Rawls does not make it explicit in *TJ*, he seems to agree with Hume's further claim that justice would also be unnecessary or impossible if people were extremely benevolent or rapacious. If people were extremely benevolent, justice would not be necessary because they would not press their rights against each other. In agreement with this, Rawls stipulates that people are not altruistic. In "Justice as Reciprocity" he remarks that "among an association of saints, if such a community could really exist, disputes about justice could hardly occur" (*CP* 205). Though he does not make it explicit, in later writings he seems to abandon the claim that there could be situations in which justice would not be necessary: when he includes the fact of reasonable pluralism among the circumstances of justice, which fact he claims to be "permanent."

As regards Hume's claim that if people were rapacious, justice would be impossible because they could not be moved to observe the rules, Rawls does not make his own position explicit, though it is safe to assume that he does not disagree. For social cooperation to work it is not enough that it be mutually advantageous: it is also necessary that people perceive such advantages, as Hume would put it. People who are extremely rapacious presumably do not perceive them. His agreement on this point is not inconsistent with the claim that he is not assuming any particular theory of human motivation. He does assume, however, that people are motivated in ways that we would find familiar and uncontroversial: when social cooperation is mutually advantageous and resources are scarce, individuals press their rights against each other when they come into conflict.

The solution to the conflict in the circumstances of justice is a set of principles of justice that assign rights and duties to individuals and determine a scheme of distribution. In Rawls's theory, such principles are chosen in the original position, which is a point of view that models, among other elements, the relations in which individuals stand to each other when the question of justice arises. For the principles to serve as a solution, they must be addressed to the features that characterize the problem. The original position models the conflict among individuals by presenting the parties as mutually disinterested. The parties know that the circumstances of justice hold and are interested in pursuing the conceptions of the good of the persons they represent. They know that their altruism is limited. The condition of mutual disinterest is not a motivational assumption of reciprocal egoism, but models the condition of conflict of interests. This means that the parties are not willing to have sacrificed to others the interests of those they represent and see themselves as defending the basic rights and liberties of the latter.

In *TJ* and in previous writings Rawls presents the circumstances of justice as conditions that could arise in any society. Accordingly, the principles of justice as fairness appear to address the universal problem of justice that any human group faces when cooperation is possible but there is moderate scarcity as well as a conflict of interests. However, beginning in "Kantian Constructivism in Moral Theory" he restricts his account to the historical conditions of modern democracies. Among the subjective circumstances, he now stresses that individuals affirm "not only diverse moral and political doctrines, but also conflicting ways of evaluating arguments and evidence when they try to reconcile these oppositions" (*CP* 323). This is the fact of reasonable pluralism that characterizes a modern democratic society. While the conflict over scarce resources can be said to be common to all human societies, the conflict that arises in light of a plurality of comprehensive moral doctrines, which are incommensurable, irreconcilable, and reasonable, is the historical outcome of democratic institutions, according to Rawls. In the *Restatement* he says that "we are to think of the circumstances of justice as reflecting the historical conditions under which a modern democracy exists" (*JF* 84).

By including the fact of reasonable pluralism, Rawls significantly narrows the scope of the problem posed by the circumstances of justice and, consequently, the scope of the principles of justice that are meant to solve it. The principles of justice as fairness are now explicitly addressed to the problem of justice that arises in a modern democratic society. This does not imply, however, that roughly similar circumstances of justice would not hold in nondemocratic societies or that the principles of justice as fairness could not be relevant for them, but he does not pursue these points. As mentioned above, by including the fact of reasonable pluralism among the circumstances of justice, Rawls closes the possibility that a modern democracy could conceivably attain a condition beyond justice. He stresses that this fact is a permanent feature that cannot be changed without the oppressive use of state power (*CP* 329). In this way, he offers a response to some communitarian and Marxist critiques, which are arguably motivated by the idea of reaching a condition beyond the circumstances of justice. Against communitarians, he can be taken to hold that the fact of reasonable pluralism is the inevitable result of democratic institutions. Against Marxists, he can be taken to imply that this fact is a definitive component of the circumstances of justice for a modern democracy in a way in which the conflict over scarce resources is not.

He appears to grant that the objective circumstance of moderate scarcity may be overcome when he claims in "A Kantian Conception of Equality" that the state of technology is a factor that determines whether the fruits of cooperation may be abundant or scarce (*CP* 256). However, the fact of reasonable pluralism makes it impossible that a modern democracy could conceivably attain a condition beyond justice.

Faviola Rivera-Castro

SEE ALSO:

Advantage, mutual vs. reciprocal
Altruism
Cooperation and coordination
Egoism
Facts, general (in OP argument and as part of justification)
Hume, David
Reasonable pluralism
Social contract

30.

CITIZEN

I N TJ, THE idea or role of a citizen, as opposed to that of a "moral person," does not play a major role. The term does not appear in the index, and though it appears in the book several times, it is not a fundamental idea. This is not to say it is of no importance at all to the early Rawls. In particular, the idea of a citizen as setting an important role that people have appears on several occasions, including the idea of the "representative citizen," who is used as a standard for evaluating the basic liberties (*TJ* 179, 211), and in the idea of "equal citizenship," which is used as one of the relevant social positions in evaluating the two principles of justice (*TJ* 82). Important as these uses of the idea of a citizen are, however, they are not central to the argument and do not come in for sustained analysis in *TJ*.

All of this changes when we turn from *TJ* to *PL*. With the development of a political, as opposed to comprehensive, liberalism, Rawls moves the idea of a citizen to the center of his analysis. In fact, one of the best ways to understand the development from *TJ* to *PL* is to focus on Rawls's shift from the idea of "free and equal persons" in *TJ* to the idea of "free and equal citizens" in *PL*. The increasing importance and centrality of the idea of a citizen in *PL* is both central to and indicative of the move to political liberalism. In *TJ* Rawls had envisioned a "well-ordered society" as one made up of people who see themselves as "free and equal moral persons" who not only take themselves to be sources of moral claims on others, but also "conceive of themselves as free persons who can revise and alter their final ends and who give priority to preserving their liberty in this respect" (*TJ* 475). As Rawls came to realize, this conception of the person was not one that everyone in a democratic society could accept. The move from the comprehensive liberalism of *TJ* to the political liberalism of *PL* is mirrored and expressed in the shift from the focus on a particular understanding of persons as "free and equal" and with particular higher-order values in the former, to the focus on "equal citizens" in the latter, where this is understood to be a thorough-going political conception of a person, not dependent on any underlying comprehensive understanding.

Many of the attributes that Rawls attributes, in *TJ*, to "persons" are attributed to "citizens" in *PL*, making the distinction somewhat subtle. It is, nonetheless, fundamental. To say that a "person" is one who conceives of herself as "free and equal" and able to "revise and alter her final ends" is to attribute a particular and controversial view about the nature of persons and what is most important to them to the subjects of political philosophy. This is, arguably, a Kantian conception of the person, one that is rejected by some religious views and some more conservative conceptions of the good. In *PL* Rawls describes citizens as conceiving of themselves as "free" and as "independent from and not identified with any particular . . . conception with its scheme of final ends" (*PL* 30). This seems similar to the conception of a person in *TJ*, but, as this is now cast in terms of a "political" conception, one limited to the "domain of the political," there is an important difference. The shift in focus from "persons" to "citizens" frees Rawls from an unreasonable commitment to a particular conception of the person. Free and equal citizens may have many diverse conceptions of the good and of the person, and yet maintain a shared political conception of justice.

If the conception of citizens in *Political Liberalism* is not a metaphysical or controversial philosophical one, as the conception of the person was in *TJ*, where does it come from, and why would it be acceptable to people with diverse and incompatible comprehensive conceptions of the good? It is found in the nature of a democratic society, one where members accept a "duty of civility" and apply a "criterion of reciprocity" to each other, and only insist on terms to govern their relationships that each could accept (*LP* 135–136). This democratic and political conception of a citizen does not require accepting any particular comprehensive conception of the good, but only a willingness to cooperate with others in a democratic society on fair terms, a recognition of reasonable pluralism, and the "burdens of judgment" that come with this recognition (*PL* 54–58).

Finally, in *LP* Rawls explains how the idea of free and equal citizenship is only made complete and secure in the context of an effective Law of Peoples. (*LP* 10) We see here an implication of Rawls's account in *LP* that is often missed by critics – the nature of peoples, at least for the liberal states that first formulate the Law of Peoples. The Law of Peoples is made by representatives of liberal peoples (*LP* 23). "Peoples" are not states, as traditionally understood, because they lack certain of the traditional powers of sovereignty. But they are also not, as some have thought, nations, but rather the collective body of citizens, where this is understood in the political sense discussed above (*LP* 23). A nation would be, essentially, the equivalent of a particular conception of the person at the level of the Law of Peoples. But peoples, as understood by Rawls, are essentially political bodies, and liberal peoples are the collective manifestation of liberal, free and equal democratic citizens (*LP* 23). This shows how the idea of a citizen becomes central to Rawls in *PL* and plays a deeply important, though often missed, role in *LP* as well.

Matt Lister

SEE ALSO:

Freedom
Law of Peoples
Moral person
Political conception of justice

31.

CIVIC HUMANISM

THIS EXPRESSION REFERS to a particular interpretation of the core normative commitments of the republican tradition of political thought, which is a topic of significant debate among historians of ideas. Based on what they take to be the experience of civic life in Ancient Athens, and inspired by Aristotle's work, civic humanists claim that human beings are essentially social and political beings, and that they can only lead flourishing lives if they engage in virtuous political activity aimed at the common good. One might interpret this thesis weakly to mean that citizens' political participation is necessary to sustain well-functioning political institutions and the social conditions favorable to the enjoyment of good lives. After all, it would be difficult for people to flourish if they lived in societies plagued by injustice and corruption. But the civic humanists' thesis is stronger. It is that any good or flourishing life must include political participation as a key element. Political participation is considered not only intrinsically valuable, but also something whose absence would seriously diminish the value of citizens' lives. This view of the intrinsic value of political activity has been attributed to Jean Jacques Rousseau and Hannah Arendt, among others.

In Rawlsian terms, civic humanism is a partially comprehensive doctrine that recommends political activity and its associated virtues as fundamental personal goods. Against this doctrine, Rawls argues that some reasonable citizens may freely choose to take an active part in public life, but that others who are equally reasonable may prefer to give less value to political activity. Rawls rejects the civic humanist thesis as part of a political conception of justice, claiming that it should be up to individual citizens to determine, using their own capacities for practical reasoning, whether engaging in political activity is part of their complete good or not. Rawls's theory remains agnostic as to whether political participation is

Civic humanism / 101

a necessary and significant part of the good life. It intentionally avoids giving any definite answer to the question of how people should live their lives, insofar as their behavior is consistent with maintaining just institutions over time. Rawls acknowledges that the political activity of citizens contributes to the good of society, and indeed that the adequate functioning of democratic institutions requires that a certain number of citizens take part in public life. But he is confident that just and democratic institutions can be sustained over time by leaving citizens free to decide which talents to cultivate and which goals to pursue. Moreover, if widespread political participation and the cultivation of civic virtues were in fact necessary to preserve democratic institutions and the public good, then Rawls would advocate them as part of our natural duty to support just institutions. But this is not an endorsement of the civic humanist thesis, since the reasons it offers for valuing political participation and its associated civic virtues are public reasons, and not reasons that stem from a comprehensive doctrine of the human good (*PL* 205–206, 420–421; *JF* 142–145).

Victoria Costa

SEE ALSO:

Aristotle
Basic liberties
Civic republicanism
Comprehensive doctrine
Political virtues

32.

CIVIC REPUBLICANISM

THIS EXPRESSION REFERS to an interpretation of the republican tradition of political thought that is often contrasted with the civic humanist interpretation of the same tradition. Civic republicans argue that in order to sustain a political regime that secures the central rights and liberties of citizens, it is necessary for citizens to participate actively in politics and to cultivate certain civic virtues. The kind of virtues they have in mind include the dispositions to be informed about public affairs, to be vigilant about the behavior of public officials, and to support the rule of law. They warn that society's effective pursuit of the common good is undermined when citizens are corrupted by luxury, ambition, excessive self-interest, and factionalism. Civic republicans defend the value of political participation and of civic virtues by appealing to their fundamental contribution to the establishment and maintenance of a free society. In other words, they defend them primarily in instrumental terms, rather than presenting them as essential components of a comprehensive view of the human good. Among the historical figures who offered this kind of argument for civic engagement are Cicero and Machiavelli.

There are many significant affinities between civic republicanism and justice as fairness. Rawls agrees with civic republicans that in order to sustain a just democratic regime over time, it is necessary that citizens be politically active. Rawls and civic republicans endorse similar ideals of deliberative democracy, and share a concern to design political institutions in ways that encourage deliberation in pursuit of the common good. Another important similarity is that Rawls accepts the view that citizens having equal political liberties is central to the preservation of their other basic liberties and rights, pointing out that when vulnerable groups in society are disenfranchised they are likely to have other basic rights and liberties denied as well. The first principle of justice guarantees citizens fair opportunities to participate in politics, on the assumption that without such a guarantee those with more wealth and power will tend to control political life and dominate others by shaping laws and policies to benefit their factional interests. The institutions of a property-owning democracy recommended by Rawls are very similar to the economic arrangements supported by civic republicans, who argue that personal freedom and independence are not possible without controlling a certain amount of property.

The primary disagreements between justice as fairness and civic republicanism have to do with the relative weight of certain political values and some related empirical questions: what type of political engagement by citizens is necessary to secure their liberties; how extensive must this engagement be; how should democratic institutions be designed to encourage such engagement? To give a concrete example, some civic republicans claim that voting should be mandatory, while Rawls thinks of voting as a moral obligation of citizens, but an obligation that should not be enforced by law (*PL* 205–206; *JF* 142–146, 150).

Victoria Costa

SEE ALSO:

Basic liberties
Civic humanism
Political conception of justice
Political virtues
Property-owning democracy

33.

CIVIL DISOBEDIENCE

IVIL DISOBEDIENCE RECEIVES Rawls's most careful and extended consideration in *A Theory of Justice*. It is there defined as "a public, nonviolent, conscientious yet political act contrary to law usually done with the aim of bringing about a change in the law or policies of the government" (*TJ* 320). It "is engaged in openly with fair notice" (*TJ* 321) and involves a "willingness to accept the legal consequences of one's conduct" (*TJ* 322).

This is as narrow a conception of civil disobedience as one might find, and Rawls acknowledges that it excludes some acts that have usually been regarded as civil disobedience. An example is Thoreau's tax refusal, protesting his state's complicity in unconscionable federal policies. Rawls classifies Thoreau's act and many other kinds of principled disobedience as "conscientious refusal," which he treats separately (*TJ* 323–326, 331–335).

Rawls's theory of civil disobedience relates directly to the principal project of *TJ*, which is to identify "the principles of justice that would regulate a well-ordered society" (*TJ* 8). The basic institutions of such a society satisfy the principles of justice, its members knowingly share that conception of justice, and they are morally committed to maintain institutions that respect its principles. That is the setting for what Rawls terms "ideal theory" (*TJ* 397). One of Rawls's central concerns is the stability of a well-ordered society.

Rawls's treatment of civil disobedience carries this concern over into "nonideal" theory. He regards civil disobedience as a stabilizing rather than a disruptive force, at least in a society that is "nearly just" – "well-ordered for the most part but in which some serious violations of justice nevertheless do occur" (*TJ* 336f., 319). Rawls emphasizes that his theory of civil disobedience "is designed only for" this "special case" (*TJ* 319). A nearly just society is indeed special, for it is the best that one might hope for. As Rawls observes, it is impossible to design a constitution that excludes the possibility of governments enacting unjust laws, which, Rawls seems to say, are inevitable in the real world.

As Rawls conceives of a nearly just society, its members knowingly agree about the basic criteria of social justice. This enables him to assume that one who engages in civil disobedience "invokes the commonly shared conception of justice that underlies the political order," "addresses the sense of justice of the majority of the community and declares that in one's considered opinion the principles of social cooperation among free and equal men are not being respected" (*TJ* 320f.). "The persistent and deliberate violation of the basic principles...over any extended period of time...invites either submission or resistance. By engaging in civil disobedience a minority forces the majority to consider whether it wishes to have its actions construed in this way, or whether, in view of the common sense of justice, it wishes to acknowledge the legitimate claims of the minority" (*TJ* 321). One who engages in civil disobedience (so circumscribed) identifies respects in which the majority has deviated significantly from the shared conception of justice, tries to persuade the majority of the need for reform, and stresses the importance of the issue by her willingness to accept the legal penalties that are expected to follow. Given the shared moral commitments, the nonthreatening character of civil disobedience, and the willingness of the protesters to accept the burden of legal sanctions for their acts (which demonstrates their sincerity as well as the gravity of the situation), Rawls believes that in "the special case of a near just society" civil disobedience would perform a "stabilizing" function by preserving social unity and promoting justice in the basic institutions (*TJ* 336f.).

Civil disobedience requires moral justification because, Rawls holds, in nearly just societies there is (or would be) a moral presumption favoring obedience to law, including unjust laws. Because civil disobedience is supposed to persuade, Rawls believes that it can be justified only when the injustice complained of is difficult to deny. He accordingly suggests that the grievance must concern "a clear violation of the liberties of equal citizenship, or of equality of opportunity, this violation having been more or less deliberate over an extended period of time" (*TJ* 329). "By contrast infractions of the difference principle are more difficult to ascertain" (*TJ* 327). Other conditions must also be satisfied. One must seek legal recourse first – at least where feasible. Some of Rawls's cautionary comments concern contingencies that he acknowledges are unlikely (*TJ* 329). He worries, for example, that civil disobedience engaged in simultaneously by several aggrieved groups might destabilize the society. It is difficult, however, to imagine that clear, grave injustices imposed by a persistently unresponsive majority could become so massive in a society that is, in Rawls's terms, *nearly* just. In societies that are not nearly just, of course, there is no moral presumption favoring obedience to law and civil disobedience is easier to justify (if justification is required at all).

Rawls first presented his theory of civil disobedience in 1966 (Bedau 1969, 240 n.), during the height of the civil rights movement, when protests against US intervention in Vietnam were intensifying, dissidence was often loud and was sometimes unlawful. Most philosophers who then discussed the nature and justification of civil disobedience seemed to believe that their theories had immediate application. Given Rawls's active social conscience (Pogge 2007 [1994], 19), the timing of his work on civil disobedience, and the fact that he followed the definition of one of the theorists just referred to (*TJ* 320 n.19), one might reasonably assume that he too meant his theory to have immediate application. But the evidence is ambiguous.

For Rawls to have intended his theory to have direct political relevance, he would have had to regard the United States as a nearly just society (in his sense of that term). He would have had to suppose that all Americans were consciously united on the basic principles of social justice, and would have had to believe that they were all subject to a moral requirement of obedience to law. Rawls gives some reason to conclude that he viewed the United States differently.

Rawls says, for example:

> one of the main defects of constitutional government has been the failure to insure the fair value of political liberty. The necessary corrective steps have not been taken, indeed, they never seem to have been seriously entertained. Disparities in the distribution of property and wealth that far exceeded what is compatible with political equality have generally been tolerated by the political system...Political power rapidly accumulates and becomes unequal; and making use of the coercive apparatus of the state and its law, those who gain the advantage can often assure themselves of a favored position. (*TJ* 198f.)

This seems to imply that the first principle of justice has long been violated systematically, because the less advantaged are unable to effectively exercise their political rights, with no reform likely.

Another significant passage occurs in Rawls's discussion of "the duty to comply with an unjust law" (*TJ* 308–312). Rawls observes that some entrenched injustices are incompatible with such a duty. He says that "in the long run the burden of injustice should be more or less evenly distributed over different groups in society, and the hardship of unjust policies should not weigh too heavily in any particular case." What this seems to mean is that systematic discrimination does not obtain in a nearly just society. He continues:

> Therefore the duty to comply is problematic for permanent minorities that have suffered from injustice for many years. And certainly we are not required to acquiesce in the denial of our own and others' basic liberties, since this requirement could not have been within the meaning of the duty of justice in the original position, nor consistent with the understanding of the rights of the majority in the constitutional convention. (*TJ* 312)

Rawls seems to allude here to the system of racial subordination known as Jim Crow, which was enforced by terror, coercion, harassment, and brutality, and which had been tolerated at *all* levels of government for generations. When Rawls was completing *A Theory of Justice*, the federal government had only recently and for the first time renounced the doctrine of white supremacy and had only just committed itself to ending Jim Crow. (The first major civil rights acts since Reconstruction were enacted in 1964 and 1965.) Much hard, dangerous work was needed to test that commitment and, it was hoped, to realize the promise of equal rights. But the attempt to dismantle Jim Crow was facing massive resistance. That fact plus the fact that the United States had abandoned its brief, Reconstruction-era commitment to civil rights would have prevented a knowledgeable observer from being confident of the outcome. It would have been implausible to regard a society with such deeply entrenched, violently supported racial discrimination as nearly just. This evidence suggests that Rawls did not assume that American society was ready for his theory of civil disobedience.

David Lyons

SEE ALSO:

Conscientious refusal
Ideal and nonideal theory
King, Martin Luther, Jr.
Political obligation
Stability
Well-ordered society

34.

CLOSE-KNITNESS

IN RAWLS'S INITIAL formulation, the difference principle specified that the distribution of income and wealth, via the basic structure, was to be to "everyone's advantage" ("Justice as Fairness" [1958] in *CP* 48, 50; *TJ* 53). In subsequent discussion in *A Theory of Justice* Rawls amended this formulation. He notes that the phrase "everyone's advantage" suggests that the expectations of the various income groups are "close-knit"; they go up and down together, and "there's no loose-jointedness, so to speak, in the way expectations hang together" (*TJ* 70).

"Close-knitness," had been assumed, Rawls says, "to simplify the statement of the difference principle." He, of course, had in mind here his own initial formulation of the difference principle, as aimed at achieving a benefit literally for everybody as regards income and wealth. But Rawls immediately adds, it is "clearly conceivable" that some groups – (for instance) those least well off – "are not affected one way or the other by changes in the expectations of the best off although these changes [may] benefit others" while having no effect on the least well off (*TJ* 72).

This failure of close-knitness, in fact or in hypothesis, forces a revision on Rawls's initial formulation of the difference principle. A very general revision would say that every group is to benefit, or at least none becomes worse off. Accordingly, Rawls's principle of "everyone's advantage" needs to be revised to accord with this more nuanced understanding of mutual benefit. Thus, as some people improve their situations, others should continue to improve, to become better–off, or at least none becomes worse off. "Everyone's advantage" or mutual benefit so understood is an ongoing process.

However, at this particular point in the argument, Rawls's main move is to state what he calls the "lexical difference principle" (*TJ* 72). This principle specifies a fixed sequence: one of the income groups (initially, it's the least well-off one in Rawls's analysis) goes up to a certain level (its maximum level, as it were) and plateaus there; in turn and in serial order, each of the other income groups experiences the same state of affairs, ending with the best-off group (whose prospects in that situation are allowed to be improved, up to their maximum level). Derek Parfit (in his 1991 Lindley Lecture) glosses this lexical version of the difference principle as saying "if we cannot make other groups better off, we should, if we can, make the best-off group even better off" (Parfit 2002, 120).

In the original edition of *A Theory of Justice*, Rawls's discussion of the lexical difference principle, intended as a response to the failure of close-knitness as a simplifying assumption, simply stops with the statement of that principle. But in the revised edition (of 1999), Rawls goes on to say that in actual cases the lexical principle is "unlikely to be relevant, for when the greater potential benefits to the more advantaged are significant, there will surely be some way to improve the situation of the least advantaged as well" (*TJ* 72).

Rawls regards the situation described in the lexical difference principle as unlikely because it goes against the background ideas with which the difference principle is bound up. The difference principle works in tandem with prior principles – equal basic liberties, fair equality of opportunity – and with basic structure practices, like "workable competition" (*TJ* 72; also *JF* 61, 66–68) already in place; thus, when these prior principles and practices are satisfactorily installed, "cases requiring the lexical principle will not arise" (*TJ* 72).

In short, Rawls, immediately after introducing it, drops the lexical difference principle and says (in both the original edition of *TJ* (83) and the revised edition (72)) that he will "always use the difference principle in simpler form." Just after making this point about a "simpler form," Rawls goes on to describe the difference principle, anew and for the first time, as specifying that "social and economic inequalities are to be arranged so that they are ... to the greatest benefit of the least advantaged" (*TJ* 72, 266–267). Probably this is the best-known and the most-cited version of the difference principle.

Given Rawls's discussion here, I cannot accept Gerald Cohen's claim (2008, 17, 156–161) that the lexical difference principle is the "canonical" form of the difference principle so far is Rawls is concerned. Nor can I accept Andrew Williams's contention (1995, 259) that the lexical version represents Rawls's "considered view" and that the simpler version of the difference principle, just referred to, is employed merely for "convenience in presentation."

Rex Martin

SEE ALSO:

Chain connection
Difference principle
Least-advantaged position

35.

COHEN, G. A.

G. A. ("JERRY") COHEN (1941–2009) was a Canadian philosopher and the Chichele Professor of Social and Political Theory at Oxford from 1985–2008. Cohen was born into a Communist Jewish family in Montreal, where his "upbringing was as intensely political as it was antireligious" (Cohen 2000, 22). He received his BA from McGill University in Politics and Philosophy in 1961, and then his BPhil in philosophy at Oxford, where he studied with Gilbert Ryle. Cohen's first book, published in 1978, was *Karl Marx's Theory of History: A Defence*. This became a central work among the so-called "Analytical Marxists" who, in the 1980s, sought to apply the tools of analytic philosophy to critically reconstruct the insights and approaches of Karl Marx. While there was – and is – a debate concerning whether Marx's theory implicitly relies on normative principles of justice or rejects such moralizing, in the introduction to a collection of his essays published in 1995, Cohen writes that he never had any doubt: "I did not think that Marxists could be indifferent to justice. On the contrary: I was certain that every committed Marxist was exercised by the injustice of capitalist exploitation, and that Marxists who affected unconcern about justice, from Karl Marx down, were kidding themselves" (Cohen 1995, 2–3).

Cohen reports that it was an encounter with Nozick's "Wilt Chamberlain" argument that "began a process that, in time, roused me from what had been my dogmatic socialist slumber" (Cohen 1995, 4). Cohen did not renounce his socialism, and indeed, he concluded his short 2009 book *Why not Socialism?* with these words: "Every market, even a socialist market, is a system of predation. Our attempt to get beyond predation has thus far failed. I do not think the right conclusion is to give up" (Cohen 2009, 82). But upon learning of Nozick's argument, he resolved that when he completed his first book, "I would devote myself in the main to political philosophy proper" (Cohen 1995, 4–5). In 1977, he published what he would describe as "my first exercise in normative political philosophy" (Cohen 1995, 12), entitled "Robert Nozick and Wilt Chamberlain: How Patterns Preserve Liberty" (reprinted in Cohen 1995). Cohen argues against Nozick that not all distributive outcomes brought about by individually just transactions from an initially just distribution are necessarily just. Voluntary self-enslavement, to take an extreme example, would not be just (Cohen 1995, 21). More generally: "Among the reasons for limiting how much an individual may hold, regardless of how he came to hold it, is to prevent him from acquiring, through his holdings, an unacceptable amount of power over others" (Cohen 1995, 25).

In 1989, Cohen published what is arguably his best-known article, "On the Currency of Egalitarian Justice" (reprinted in Cohen 2011). There, he argues not only that equality is necessary to limit the power that some have over others – to eliminate exploitation – but also that equality is itself a direct requirement of justice: "I take for granted that there is something which justice requires people to have equal amounts of, not no matter what, but to whatever extent is allowed by values which compete with distributive equality" (Cohen 2011, 3). Following Dworkin in distinguishing brute luck (which is "not the result of a gamble or risk which...could have been avoided") and "option luck" (for which an individual is responsible), Cohen writes: "I believe that the primary egalitarian impulse is to extinguish the influence on distribution of both exploitation and brute luck" (2011, 5).

In defending his version of luck egalitarianism, Cohen offers a revealing criticism of Rawls's reliance on primary goods. Rawls acknowledges that "citizens' income and wealth [and primary goods more generally] is only a rough indicator of their level of satisfaction" (*CP* 369). Other things equal, an equal share of resources will result in a lower level of satisfaction for those with expensive tastes compared to those who can more easily satisfy their preferences. But this is as it should be, Rawls holds, for: "as moral persons citizens have some part in forming and cultivating their final ends and preferences. It is not by itself an objection to the use of primary goods that it does not accommodate those with expensive tastes" (*CP* 369). Cohen acknowledges the influence individuals can have in forming their own preferences, but points out that they only have *some* influence. He concludes that we should differentiate the (expensive) preferences for which we are responsible from those for which we are not. "We should therefore compensate only for those welfare deficits which are not in some way traceable to the individual's choices. We should replace equality of welfare by equality of opportunity for welfare" (Cohen 2011, 11). He acknowledges that by taking this approach, "we may indeed be up to our necks in the free will problem" (Cohen 2011, 32).

There was another criticism of Rawls implicit in Cohen's luck egalitarianism that he developed in a series of articles incorporated into *If You're an Egalitarian, How Come You're So Rich?* (Cohen 2000). For if there is "something which justice requires people to have equal amounts of," then anything that affects the distribution of that good (whatever it is – for example, opportunity for welfare) should be of concern to justice. Certainly, the basic structure of society is likely greatly to affect the distribution of this good, but individual conduct and the ethos of a society will do so as well. Rawls has no grounds, Cohen argues, for singling out the basic structure as the primary focus of the principles of justice: "justice cannot be a matter only of the state-legislated structure in which people act but is also a matter of the acts they choose within that structure, the personal choices of their daily lives" (Cohen 2000, 122; cf. 142). Furthermore, "there is no good reason why the very principles that govern the basic structure should not extend to individual choice within that structure" (Cohen 2008, 359). This extension of the application of the difference principle (in particular) to individual choices significantly limits permissible inequalities. In fact, he argues, that the extension of the difference principle to individual choices "implies that justice requires (virtually) unqualified equality itself" (Cohen 2000, 124). The difference principle will allow a structural inequality only when it is necessary for generating an increase in the share of primary goods for the least advantaged (relative to a baseline of equality). An inequality can only generate such an increase in primary goods for the least advantaged if it somehow influences the behavior of various individuals, for example, by offering an incentive for people to act in certain beneficial ways. If individuals governed their behavior directly by the difference principle, however, they would act in those beneficial ways without the need to introduce an inequality. So the inequality is necessary only if the difference principle is applied to the basic structure alone and not directly to the behavior of individuals within the basic structure.

In *Rescuing Justice and Equality* (2009), Cohen extends his radical egalitarian critique of the difference principle, but he also explores an even deeper contrast with Rawls. Justice as fairness aims to identify the principles of justice that citizens of a well-ordered society should use when deliberating over possible reforms to the institutions of the basic structure of their society. Constructivism holds that "a conception of justice is framed to meet the practical requirements of social life and to yield a public basis in the light of which citizens can justify to one another their common institutions" (*CP* 347). Since the principles have "a wide social role as part of the public culture" of a well-ordered society, they should satisfy the publicity requirement and "cannot be so complex that they cannot be generally understood and followed in the more important cases" (*CP* 347). Cohen insists, in reply: "it is a fundamental error of *TJ* that it identifies the first principles of justice with the principles that we should adopt to regulate society" (Cohen 2008, 265; cf. 301). Publicity, for example, "is *at most* a desideratum of the rules regulating society, and not a proper constraint on the content of *justice*" (Cohen 2008, 22). The fundamental principle of justice, Cohen insists, is independent of any factual assumptions or conditions. "Until we unearth the fact-free principle that governs our fact-loaded particular judgments about justice, we don't know why we think what we think just is just" (Cohen 2008, 291). Where Rawls holds that the justification of the principles of justice is "based essentially on practical reason and not on theoretical reason" (*PL* 93), Cohen asserts that "the question for political philosophy is not what we should do but what we should think, even when what we should think makes no practical difference" (Cohen 2008, 268).

Jon Mandle

SEE ALSO:

>*Basic structure of society*
>*Difference principle*
>*Luck egalitarianism*
>*Primary goods, social*
>*Practical reason*
>*Socialism*
>*Utility*

36.

COHEN, JOSHUA

JOSHUA COHEN (b. 1951) studied under John Rawls, taught at MIT for twenty-nine years, and is currently Marta Sutton Weeks Professor of Ethics in Society and Professor of Political Science, Philosophy, and Law at Stanford. Much of Cohen's work is inspired by Rawls and his own writing significantly influenced the development of Rawls's mature thought.

Three contributions are central. The first is Cohen's distinctive "deliberative" conception of democracy. Against those who present democracy as simply a method of producing collective decisions through preference aggregation, Cohen argues that democracy is an activity of reasoning amongst equals on matters of common concern. As such, it is not merely an institutional procedure, but also – and more fundamentally – a type of society and a compelling normative ideal.

A second, related contribution is an original account of political legitimacy. For Cohen, the moral authority of democratic decisions derives from their source in a process of mutual justification in which citizens argue for policies on the basis of reasons they can expect other citizens, understood as equals, to accept. Rawls had argued that the fact that citizens endorse conflicting moral and metaphysical doctrines constrains the role that appeals to justice may play in politics. Cohen strengthened this idea by emphasizing that only "reasonable" disagreement places limits on the types of justification that can legitimately be offered in political argument. The idea that citizens of a diverse range of persuasions can converge on a shared understanding of the content of democracy's "public reason" is key to Cohen's project of showing how democracy can organize and justify other political values. For instance, many liberals understand basic rights, such as freedom of speech and religious liberty, as independent constraints on democratic decisions. For Cohen, however, such rights are intimately connected to the democratic ideal. The standard sorts of reasons used to restrict a person's peaceful exercise of her religion, for instance, come out as fundamentally undemocratic, once we understand the limits that reasonable pluralism places on political justification.

A third, more recent, contribution involves the extension of the Rawlsian "political liberal" framework sketched above to global politics. Here, Cohen stakes out a moderate position that avoids two popular extremes. Against some, Cohen argues that contemporary globalization involves relationships to which norms of justice apply. Against others, he claims that the content of these norms cannot be read off the standards of domestic justice that hold within liberal societies, but must be respectfully negotiated within the bounds of global public reason.

Cohen's work involves a degree of engagement with social science, constitutional law, history, and contemporary politics rare among political philosophers. In connection with the fundamental philosophical issues mentioned above, he has written on many current controversies, including campaign finance, workplace democracy, and the regulation of pornography. He is also co-editor of the political-literary journal *Boston Review*. Throughout, Cohen's writing expresses a conviction, shared with Rawls, that political philosophy is a practical endeavor, in which the aim is to guide public conduct, the constraints are the demands of mutual respect and practical possibility, and the hope is that we can achieve the aim, in accordance with the constraints, without doing violence to our central values.

Helena de Bres

SEE ALSO:

Democracy
Political liberalism
Public reason
Reasonable pluralism

37.

COMMON GOOD IDEA OF JUSTICE

N THE LAW OF PEOPLES, Rawls holds that every society has a common end it tries to achieve for its members, or a set of special priorities that guide its development as a society (*LP* 71). Decent peoples seek to realize some comprehensive conception of the good at the societal level. For example, Rawls's "Kazanistan" has priorities it observes, which include establishing itself as a decent people – specifically as a decent Islamic republic – that respects its religious minorities (*LP* 75–78). The common good idea of justice puts restrictions on a society's pursuit of its end or priorities (*LP* 71).

A society's end determines whether many opportunities are open to members. Decent societies may have state religions that control much domestic policy (*LP* 74). Thus, members of the established religion may have privileges denied to others, though no religion is persecuted. In Kazanistan, Islam is the favored religion, so only Muslims can hold important political or judicial positions (*LP* 75). Nevertheless, Kazanistan may not do just anything in pursuit of its priorities. The common good idea of justice encourages peoples to pursue their ends, but it also assigns basic rights to all of their members (*LP* 65, 78–81, 38 n.47). Further, it requires that peoples pursue their ends according to institutionalized procedures which protect basic rights (*LP* 71). For decent hierarchical societies, this means that ends must be pursued through Rawls's "consultation hierarchy" (*LP* 71–72). The assignment of rights and institutionalization of political processes ensures that the end is maximized only to the extent consistent with social and political cooperation (*LP* 65). This cooperation implies both reciprocity in advantage, i.e. some commitment to the basic physical and psychological welfare of all members, and reciprocal reason-giving, expressed partly through the political participation rights secured for all by the consultation hierarchy.

Even non-Muslim members of Kazanistan regard its priorities as important, though they are less committed than Muslim members (*LP* 77). But their commitment to these priorities, and to their common good conception of justice, gives Kazanistan a public (decent) conception of justice. A slave society is not like this (*LP* 65). Where there is no reciprocity in advantage or reason giving, rules are mere commands imposed by force. In decent societies, the legal system has genuine normative force, imposing bona fide duties and obligations on all, because the legal system is administered according to the consultation hierarchy and is seen by all (including political and judicial officials) as not unreasonably consistent with the society's priorities and common good conception of justice.

In order to ensure that public officials take seriously the common good conception of justice, all members of decent societies have a right to express political dissent, e.g. to challenge policies as not consistent with their society's end or as generated in violation of appropriate political procedures, and to expect conscientious replies from officials (*LP* 72). These conditions preserve reciprocity of advantage and reciprocal reason-giving and give even minority members of a decent society some good reason to see their legal system as providing genuine normative direction.

Walter J. Riker

SEE ALSO:

> *Cooperation and coordination*
> *Decent societies*
> *Liberal conception of Justice*
> *Political conception of justice*

38.

COMMUNITARIANISM

THE TERM "COMMUNITARIANISM" refers to the writings of a number of political theorists who, in the 1980s and early 1990s, sought to critique what they saw as the excessively individualistic aspects of liberal theory in general, and of Rawls's arguments in particular.

Beyond this very general characterization, it is hard to identify a core set of substantive claims to which all of the theorists who have been described as communitarians subscribe. The claims of communitarians are addressed at diverse dimensions of the liberal project, from the putative metaphysical assumptions that lie at the basis of the liberal project, to the substantive policy prescriptions to which liberalism allegedly gives rise.

While it is clearly not exhaustive, the following list of claims is at the heart of what came in the 1980s to be known as the "liberal/communitarian" debate.

(1) *The metaphysics of the self.* According to some communitarians, most notably Michael Sandel (Sandel 1982), liberals go wrong by placing a deficient conception of the moral and political agent at the core of their theories. Liberals, the argument goes, see the self as "unencumbered," that is as related to its cultural and historical entanglements in a contingent rather than a constitutive manner. According to the view attributed to liberals by communitarians, the self is metaphysically "prior" to its ends, and to the conceptions of the good that are prevalent in its community. In Sandel's view, nowhere is this conception of the self more obvious than in Rawls's notion of the "original position," in which individuals who are defined as reasonable and rational and as capable of separating themselves from their contingent conceptions of the good and other aspects of their social selves, deliberate in order to

determine what principles of justice will govern their community. This deficient conception of the self, according to Sandel, has a range of deleterious implications for Rawls's theory of justice as a whole, chief among them being the inability of this conception of the self to underwrite the principles of distributive justice that Rawls seeks to defend.

(2) *The conception of community.* According to a second objection, which was formulated most forcefully in Alasdair MacIntyre's *After Virtue* (1984), what is problematic is not so much the liberal conception of the self, but rather the liberal conception of *community*. According to Rawls, social institutions are to be governed by a conception of the right, rather than by a conception of the good. Individuals have a diversity of conceptions of the good, which are defined by their subjective preferences, and these conceptions can lie at the basis of legitimate claims upon others only to the extent that they satisfy criteria of rightness. On MacIntyre's view, however, it is impossible to disentangle conceptions of the right and of the good as cleanly as Rawls does. As a consequence of this, a community whose members do not share a conception of the good, of what gives life meaning and point, will be unable to sustain a conception of justice. MacIntyre famously concludes his book by presenting citizens of modern societies with a stark alternative: St. Benedict or Nietzsche? Either we will be able, despite modern pressures toward fragmentation, to reconstitute cohesive communities ordered around a shared conception of the good, or we will have to resign ourselves to societies marked by a kind of nihilism, in which normative claims are taken to have no backing more substantive than that found in people's preferences.

(3) *Sham universalism.* According to a criticism of Rawls's views that were articulated most forcefully by Michael Walzer (1983), the principal flaw with Rawls's theory has to do with the manner in which he argues for principles of distributive justice. According to Walzer's criticism, Rawls holds that such principles can be derived in a universal manner, simply by reflecting upon what reasonable and rational individuals would agree to. Walzer's objection has to do not so much with the conception of the self that was decried by Sandel, but with the conception of the goods that are at issue in theories of distributive justice. For Rawls, the goods that lie at the center of a theory of distributive justice are ones that can be characterized in universalist terms as "basic primary goods." These are goods that it is rational for an agent to want, regardless of whatever else she wants. According to Walzer, the task of figuring out what principles should be employed to govern the distribution is impossible unless we attend to the meanings that

attach to specific goods, and which are defined by shared social understandings and interpretations. For example, health is an important *distribuandum* for a theory of social justice, but the good of health is neither understood nor ranked the same way in different societies, nor do different societies agree as to whether a good such as health can be "traded off" against other goods. Thus, in order to carry out the work that Rawls claims to be able to carry out on the basis of an abstract and culturally decontextualized conception of "basic primary goods," we must instead attend to the ways in which specific goods are understood in specific communities.

(4) *Self-defeatingness.* A final criticism of the liberal project that I want to briefly describe is due in large part to the work of Charles Taylor (1985). According to Taylor, liberals err in seeing their favored theory as standing above particular conceptions of the good, as a kind of neutral arbiter of these conceptions. Thus for example, liberals see themselves as privileging autonomy not because they consider an autonomous lifestyle to be preferable to other lifestyles, but because autonomy is a (purportedly neutral) condition of agents being able to choose among available goods. According to Taylor, liberalism is, however, itself a conception of the good. A society that protects individual rights so that people can lead lives according to their own lights embodies a partial, historically and culturally situated, conception of the good, rather than standing somehow "above" such conceptions. What's more, according to Taylor, the failure to recognize that liberalism is a conception of the good, one that has historical and institutional conditions of possibility, ends up being self-defeating, as citizens of liberal societies who cleave to the view that liberalism is a neutral framework might be less inclined to stand up for the institutions that make liberalism possible (Taylor 1989).

Some communitarian criticisms were directed at liberal theory and practice as a whole, whereas others were aimed at the writings of particular liberal theorists, Rawls chief among them. Indeed, Michael Sandel's *Liberalism and the Limits of Justice* develops its argument on the basis of an extended analysis of *A Theory of Justice*, and Michael Walzer's *Spheres of Justice* emerged from a seminar that Michael Walzer taught on Rawls's work.

Though Rawls claimed that communitarian criticisms largely missed the mark as far as his work was concerned, it seems clear that much of the writing that Rawls published between 1985 (when the essay "Justice as Fairness: Political not Metaphysical" was published) and 1993 (which saw the publication of

Rawls's second major book, *Political Liberalism*) was concerned with reacting to these criticisms.

Rawls's responses can be divided into three types of philosophical moves. Some communitarian criticisms were deflected by Rawls as grounded in mistaken readings of his work. Others brought forth clarifications, wherein Rawls spelled out responses to communitarians which were latent in his work, but never fully articulated. Finally, it seems clear that Rawls was led to making some substantive changes to his theory, and in particular to its justificatory structure, in order to accommodate and integrate communitarian criticisms which exposed flaws in his theory.

Rawls's response to Sandel's criticisms to do with the "metaphysics of the self" is an instance of the first strategy. The original position, which lay at the core of the critique, was never intended by Rawls to represent anything like a theory of human nature or of human agency. It is already clear in *A Theory of Justice* that it is a "device of representation" whereby certain intuitions that flesh-and-blood citizens have about how to think about justice are operationalized. The original position should thus be read politically, not metaphysically, to advert to the distinction made by Rawls in his 1985 essay. That is, the original position, along with the veil of ignorance, performs very specific tasks in helping citizens reason and deliberate about what principles of justice should govern society's main institutions, those institutions that make up what Rawls called the "basic structure" of society.

To the criticism that a society well-ordered by principles of liberal justice lacks the kind of shared conception of the good needed (for example, in MacIntyre's view) to contribute to social cohesion, Rawls responds, most notably in the 1988 article "The Priority of Right and Ideas of the Good," that there are numerous teleological elements latent in his theory as it was formulated in *A Theory of Justice*. First of all, Rawls points out, the theory as a whole is articulated around the ideal of rational agents possessed of "a rational plan of life in the light of which they schedule their more important endeavors and allocate their various resources...so as to pursue their conceptions of the good over a complete life" (*CP* 451). The theory also articulates an ideal of citizens as free and equal, and a partially shared conception of rational advantage, expressed through the idea of basic primary goods.

Third, the theory, especially in its later formulation, takes for granted that citizens in a pluralist society all have different views about what gives life meaning. They have different "comprehensive conceptions of the good." Thus, the neutrality of the state, a key element in liberal theory, should not be interpreted as implying that liberals are indifferent to questions of the good. Rather, neutrality reflects the liberal state's commitment to providing its citizens with equal opportunities to pursue diverse permissible conceptions of the good.

Finally, Rawls makes plain that a society well-ordered by liberal principles of justice is in and of itself an important good. It is good for individuals in that they are able to exercise their moral powers within it, and because it represents a social good that can only be achieved through cooperation. It is also good in that it is the site through which citizens can display a distinctive set of political virtues that are instrumentally necessary in order to uphold just institutions.

This insight also provides Rawls with a response to the Taylorean concern according to which a republic bereft of a sense of a shared good might find it difficult to sustain the motivation on the part of citizens to uphold just institutions. As long as the display of civic virtues and participation in political life are viewed as instrumentally good, as in Rawls's construal of classical republicanism, rather than as having intrinsic worth, as in civic humanism, Rawls is perfectly willing to accept the idea that liberal institutions are not self-sustaining, and that citizens must be possessed of the dispositions and traits of character required to sustain them.

Rawls was, however, led to making a number of significant changes to his theory in response to the complaint that his way of arguing for his principles of justice embodied an untenable form of universalism. To begin with, though Rawls could easily deflect the Sandelean concern according to which his theory embodies a metaphysically suspect conception of the subject as only contingently related to her ends, the complaint according to which Rawls did not emphasize to a sufficient degree the motivational hold that comprehensive conceptions of the good have upon human agents, and that the development of such conceptions is a natural concomitant of the exercise of human rational and moral powers, may very well have led him to making that notion central to his later work, and most significantly to *Political Liberalism*. However, unlike Sandel, Rawls recognizes that the exercise of these powers in conditions of freedom of thought, conscience, and association will not lead citizens to form one conception of the good shared throughout society. Rather, given these conditions (and given also the "burdens of judgment," that is, the imperfect epistemic conditions within which human subjects reason and deliberate), a plurality of reasonable conceptions will emerge.

The recognition of the importance of the plurality of such conceptions leads to a change in the way that the principles of justice are to be justified. Rawls's theory of justification has always had two distinct dimensions (Weinstock

1994). First, Rawls believes that principles of justice are justified by their being in "reflective equilibrium" with considered convictions of agents, that is with moral judgments that are marked by a high degree of certainty. Second, he believes that such principles must be stable, which means that they must be shown to generate the motivational basis for their continued support over time.

With respect to the first of these aspects of the justification of principles of justice, the criticism of the universalism that many commentators saw as latent to *A Theory of Justice* led Rawls to making an important amendment to a key ingredient of his theory of justification, that of "considered moral convictions." As seen above, Rawls's theory of justification requires that principles of justice be in reflective equilibrium with considered convictions. Now, in his earlier work, Rawls held that considered convictions were moral judgments reached in ideal epistemic circumstances. Such conditions included, among other things, disinterestedness and the exclusion of emotional engagement. The hypothesis behind Rawls's view of justification was that moral agents' considered convictions would converge, that is, that differences in moral judgment were the result of moral agents forming these judgments in less-than-optimal conditions. The recognition of the pluralism of modern societies leads to Rawls eschewing the view that the citizens of such societies would spontaneously converge on shared considered moral convictions. The considered convictions are now seen as implicit in citizens' shared institutions. "We start ... by looking to the public culture itself as the shared fund of implicitly recognized basic ideas and principles" (*PL* 8).

The plurality of comprehensive conceptions makes it the case that Rawls must show not only that his principles are in reflective equilibrium with considered moral convictions, but also that they can attract the support of diverse reasonable comprehensive conceptions. To this end, Rawls develops the notion of an "overlapping consensus." In Rawls's view, the plurality of reasonable comprehensive conception does not necessarily mean that the stability of a society ordered by a liberal conception of justice is impossible. What must be shown is that there can be a diversity of paths to the espousal of liberal principles of justice. For some, these principles will flow quite naturally from their comprehensive conceptions, whereas for others, support will come from a looser connection between fundamental tenets of their comprehensive conceptions and principles of justice.

In sum, Rawls's principles of justice emerged unaltered from his confrontation with communitarian thought. But this confrontation did lead him to emphasize teleological elements of the theory that were implicit in the earlier

Communitarianism / 125

formulation of the theory, and to making rather substantive modifications to his view of how his principles of justice were to be justified.

Daniel Weinstock

SEE ALSO:

Comprehensive doctrine
Moral person
Neutrality
Political conception of justice
Political liberalism
Primary goods, social
Priority of right
Sandel, Michael
Social union
Unity of self
Walzer, Michael

39.

COMPREHENSIVE DOCTRINE

A COMPREHENSIVE DOCTRINE is a set of beliefs affirmed by citizens concerning a range of values, including moral, metaphysical, and religious commitments, as well as beliefs about personal virtues, and political beliefs about the way society ought to be arranged. They form a conception of the good and inform judgments concerning "what is of value in life, the ideals of personal character, as well as ideals of friendship and of familial and associational relationships, and much else that is to inform our conduct, and in the limit to our life as a whole" (*PL* 13). Rawls argues that in a society with a history of democratic institutions citizens will come to affirm different and incompatible comprehensive doctrines. This fact presents a problem for a theory of justice because it suggests that citizens will fail to agree on principles of justice to govern their institutions if they rely exclusively on their separate and incompatible comprehensive doctrines. Rawls addresses this problem by distinguishing between two points of view citizens can adopt – a comprehensive point of view and a political point of view. The comprehensive view is grounded in a comprehensive doctrine, while a political view is "freestanding," meaning that while it draws from reasonable comprehensive doctrines it does not affirm or deny any particular one. Thus, political liberalism articulates and defends a set of freestanding political values, rather than arguing for the truth of comprehensive values grounded in a particular comprehensive doctrine. The separation of comprehensive doctrines from freestanding political values allows Rawls to locate the source of stability in society in a consensus on political values, while allowing for a plurality of comprehensive doctrines.

Comprehensive doctrine / 127

Rawls makes a number of distinctions in kinds of comprehensive doctrines and their scope. First, he distinguishes between fully and partially comprehensive doctrines. Fully comprehensive doctrines constitute a "precisely articulated system" of beliefs. He offers the following as examples of a fully comprehensive doctrine: perfectionism, utilitarianism, Idealism, and Marxism. Liberalism, as formulated by Kant and Mill, is also fully comprehensive. These doctrines offer a complete, interconnected, coherent, and reasoned account of values. In addition, these fully comprehensive doctrines are general. By this Rawls means that they cover all (or most of) the major issues of human value, including moral, religious, metaphysical, and political values. They are grounded in an intellectual tradition and present an "intelligible view of the world."

In contrast, a partially comprehensive doctrine is "loosely articulated" and need not be general in the sense outlined above. Rawls assumes that most citizens affirm a partial comprehensive doctrine rather than implausibly thinking that citizens are expressly and knowingly committed to full and general comprehensive doctrines. Indeed, the looseness in citizens' comprehensive doctrines is important in explaining how they marry their comprehensive and their political views. Looseness is also important in understanding how citizens' comprehensive doctrines change over time.

Second, Rawls distinguishes between reasonable and unreasonable comprehensive doctrines. Reasonable people affirm reasonable comprehensive doctrines, meaning they propose terms in public political discourse that others might be willing to accept. In other words, they offer political rather than comprehensive reasons. To this end, they accept what Rawls calls the "burdens of judgment," which require citizens to acknowledge the fundamentally controversial nature of their comprehensive moral, metaphysical, and religious views. Reasonable people, therefore, do not assert the truth of their comprehensive views as decisive in public political discourse and consequently do not use state power to impose their comprehensive doctrine on others. A reasonable comprehensive doctrine, then, is one that accepts the distinction between the comprehensive point of view and the political point of view. In contrast, unreasonable citizens hold comprehensive doctrines that cannot be used as a foundation for offering political reasons. Consequently, they make political judgments, take political action, and argue for principles of justice solely from within the perspective of their comprehensive doctrines, and cannot or are unwilling to engage with others from the political point of view.

It has been argued that Rawls's sharp distinction between comprehensive and political doctrines is untenable. One of the most pressing complaints is that while citizens can affirm the truth of their comprehensive beliefs, they are not permitted to assert these sincerely held beliefs in political debate if they cannot be rendered into an acceptable political form. In response, Rawls revises the idea that the comprehensive and political spheres should be strictly separated by distinguishing between a narrow and a wide ideal of public reason. Rawls allows that citizens can draw on reasons that are exclusively framed by their comprehensive doctrines and offer these in public debate. However, he insists that the final justification advanced must be expressed by reasons that are political rather than comprehensive and offered as reasons that fellow citizens could reasonably accept. This answers the objection that construing public debate on the narrow, strict separation of the public and comprehensive reasons unnecessarily constrains political discussion and also perhaps silences points of view.

Thus, ideally, democratic citizens have two registers of values – their comprehensive values issuing in comprehensive reasons and political values issuing in public reasons. It is important to see how Rawls understands the relation and connection between these different sets of values and reasons. He says that political reasons are embedded in a comprehensive view in the sense that the justification for a political view can be grounded in comprehensive beliefs. So, for example, the political assertion that citizens are equal can be grounded in a metaphysical view about human nature or a religious belief about God's wishes, and so on. Citizens may therefore justify their political views in different ways. What matters for Rawls is that citizens converge on a platform of political values and thus are able to come to an "overlapping consensus" on principles and "constitutional essentials." There are two further features of comprehensive doctrines that should be mentioned. First, ideally, political reasons trump comprehensive values when these conflict. Citizens affirm the political values that ground democratic principles of justice and they treat these as "very great values" that form the "very groundwork of our existence" (*PL* 139). In nonideal circumstances Rawls allows that the order of priority may not be clear and that extreme circumstances may force difficult choices.

Second, Rawls says that while it is often appropriate to assert the truth of beliefs within a comprehensive doctrine, political beliefs are reasonable rather than true. This claim reaffirms Rawls's insistence that the problem of justice is principally a practical and pragmatic problem rather than a theoretical or epistemic problem.

Paul Voice

SEE ALSO:

Burdens of judgment
Liberalism as a comprehensive doctrine
Overlapping consensus
Political conception of justice
The reasonable and the rational
Reasonable pluralism
Stability

40.

CONCEPTION OF THE GOOD

A CONCEPTION OF the good is "an ordered family of final ends and aims which specifies a person's conception of what is of value in human life or, alternatively, of what is regarded as a fully worthwhile life" (*JF* 19). In justice as fairness, every citizen is assumed to have some conception of the good, some system of ends, aims, convictions, commitments and projects that provides the structure of values within which they make their decisions and plans. The idea of a conception of the good is tied to the Rawlsian idea of a rational plan of life. One's rational plan of life determines – or reveals – one's conception of good. That plan which one would select under ideal deliberative conditions, including full information about the consequences of one's choices and about one's own preferences, determines one's overall system of final ends and one's conception of the good.

The idea of a conception of the good is also related to the idea of a comprehensive doctrine. A comprehensive doctrine includes conceptions of what is of value in human life, ideals of personal character, of friendship and family, and much else; a doctrine is fully comprehensive if it ranges over and systematizes all recognized values and virtues. After *TJ*, Rawls describes one's conception of the good as embedded within one's comprehensive (or partially comprehensive) religious, philosophical, or moral doctrine, which provides the resources to develop such a conception and "in the light of which the various ends and aims are ordered and understood" (*JF* 19). In deliberation, one's comprehensive doctrine together with facts about the world and one's own preferences and desires are taken into account, resulting in a commitment to some particular ordered system of ends.

Both one's conception of the good and one's rational plan of life are a consequence of deliberative rationality.

The idea of a conception of the good plays three fundamental roles in justice as fairness. The first is that it figures in Rawls's account of the circumstances of justice in *TJ*. Rawls describes subjective and objective parts of the circumstances of justice. In *TJ*, the subjective part is described as a pluralism of reasonable conceptions of the good. The account of pluralism is recast in *PL* and beyond, where Rawls deepens the idea of a pluralism of conceptions of the good with that of a reasonable pluralism of comprehensive doctrines as a natural outcome of the free exercise of reason over time. The objective part of the circumstances of justice is the condition of moderate scarcity. Without these conditions, according to Rawls, "there would be no occasion for the virtue of justice" (*TJ* 110). However, while the objective conditions of moderate scarcity "might be overcome," the subjective circumstances will hold wherever people are allowed the free use of their own reason (*CP* 329).

The second role of the idea of a conception of the good is that it gives content to the motivation of the parties in the original position. The parties in the original position, or their constituents, are assumed to have some determinate and reasonable conception of the good that they seek to advance in society. But in the original position the parties are behind a veil of ignorance and do not know the content of their or their constituents' conceptions. This means that they cannot try to aim the principles of justice at advancing their particular systems of ends over those of other parties or constituents. Still, that they have some determinate conception of the good, and know that they have one, is important, because it provides their motivation for engaging in the task of arriving at principles of justice. They desire principles that will allow them rationally to form and pursue their reasonable system of ends whatever it turns out to be.

The final role is that the idea of a conception of the good is part of the specification of the two moral powers of citizens that are part of the foundation of a political liberalism. Citizens have the capacity for a sense of justice and the capacity for a conception of the good. These are the two powers required to be participants in a fair system of social cooperation. The latter power, which Rawls labels "the rational," is one's capacity to form, to revise, and to pursue a conception of the good. This is necessary in order to be able to specify one's rational advantage in a system of cooperation.

Within justice as fairness, each person is responsible for his or her own conception of the good and for revising his or her system of ends in light of reasonable expectations regarding anticipated shares of natural and social goods and pursuing his or her ends reasonably and rationally. But citizens are collectively responsible, as a body politic, for providing one another with a just basic social structure and a fair share of primary social goods.

Pete Murray

SEE ALSO:

Deliberative rationality
Goodness as rationality
Moral person
Plan of life
Primary goods, social
Priority of the right over the good
Thin and full theories of good

41.

CONGRUENCE

THE ARGUMENT FOR the congruence of justice and the good plays a central role in Rawls's argument for the stability of justice as fairness, and is crucial to understanding the evolution of his thinking. This entry will explain what congruence is, why it matters, and why we should think that justice as fairness is (more) congruent (than utilitarianism). It will also explain the controversy about whether the argument from congruence is necessary, and how Rawls's dissatisfaction with his case for congruence eventually led him to the ideas of political liberalism and overlapping consensus.

The general question of congruence is whether being a good person is a good thing for that person (*TJ* 349). In many situations, the answer is of course "no," since when faced with serious wrongdoing a commitment to moral principle may require personal sacrifice, even to the point of laying down one's life. Over a range of more favorable conditions, however, it is possible that the personal costs of being a good person are outweighed (in expectation) by the benefits. Rawls posed the question of congruence with respect to justice. Whether or not it is good *for me* for me to be just depends on what the conception of justice in question demands of me, in the range of conditions under consideration, and on which conception of the good we are using to evaluate the desirability of having a sense of justice, so specified. Rawls argued that justice as fairness was congruent with what he called the thin theory of the good, or in any case more congruent than was utilitarianism, justice as fairness's main rival. In a society well-ordered by justice as fairness, it would be good to have a sense of justice, whereas the greater demandingness of utilitarianism might make it fail the congruence test (*TJ* 501–502).

The need for a thin theory of the good results from the priority of right. Rawls's principles of justice are not derived by determining what will maximize the satisfaction of whatever preferences people happen to have. Rather, the satisfaction of a preference has value only if it is consistent with principles of justice. However, some notion of goodness is needed to describe the parties' motives in the original position. Rawls's thin theory of the good performs this role, and thus provides the basis for the identification of the primary goods. My good, in this thin, pre-justice sense, is determined by what is for me in the circumstances the most rational plan of life (*TJ* 79, 347), which is the plan I would adopt if I had full information about the consequences of the various possible courses of conduct open to me (*TJ* 366). Primary goods are thus those goods that are generally necessary for forming and carrying out a plan of life, those things it is rational to want whatever else one wants (*TJ* 380). A conception of justice is congruent when, in a society organized according to that conception, having the appropriate sense of justice is in one's interest according to this thin sense of goodness, which does not presuppose any commitment to justice. Thus, the congruence of justice as fairness would indicate that the attitudes associated with justice "are desirable from the standpoint of rational persons who have them when they assess their situation independent from the constraints of justice" (*TJ* 350). Evaluating the demands of justice from a standpoint independent of justice is not equivalent to evaluating justice from the point of view of the egoist who has purely selfish interests (*TJ* 497–498). The thin theory does not assume any commitment to justice, but is also highly generic, whereas the egoist is typically assumed to have concerns for things such as wealth, power, and status. Rawls later made it clear that his account of the primary goods depended on a moral conception of persons who as citizens have higher-order interests in developing and exercising the two moral powers, not just on claims about what typical persons tend to desire or would desire given full information (*TJ* xiii). The more moral content we build into our thin theory of the good, the more plausible it will be that justice is congruent with the good, but the less that congruence will have to say about the likelihood of compliance and stability in actual societies, in which people may not be committed to this conception of the person.

As this last comment suggests, the reason for caring about the congruence of justice as fairness is stability (*TJ* 350, 504–505). Other things equal, a conception of justice is preferable if it is more stable (*TJ* 6). A conception of justice is stable when public recognition of its realization by the social system tends to bring about the corresponding sense of justice in citizens, with the result that if any deviations from justice occur, there is a tendency for justice to reassert itself

(TJ 397–401). It is clear enough how the congruence of a conception of justice would support its stability, since congruence provides personal reasons for being glad that one has a sense of justice. It is somewhat puzzling that it should be necessary to consider the question of congruence, however, since Rawls had already made the case for stability on other grounds (Barry 1995, 883).

In Chapter 8 of *Theory*, Rawls relied on a broad empirical generalization about human psychology to argue that those growing up in a society well-ordered according to justice as fairness would tend to develop an effective and appropriate sense of justice. It is "a deep psychological fact" (*TJ* 433), presumably rooted in natural selection (*TJ* 440), that we have a tendency to "answer in kind," loving those that love us, and showing friendship to those who have shown us friendship (*TJ* 433). Our sense of justice extends this backward-looking, non-strategic form of reciprocity; we want to comply with the rules of institutions when we have benefitted from others likewise complying with these rules (*TJ* 414–419, 429, 433). Rawls claimed that this deeply ingrained disposition could be harnessed as a stabilizing force more easily by justice as fairness than by utilitarianism. If social inequalities benefit all, then people will tend to see others' compliance with society's rules as benefits that ought to be reciprocated, whereas under utilitarianism, some people will not see any benefit to themselves in other people following the rules. If, growing up in a society well-ordered by justice as fairness, I would most likely develop an effective sense of justice, why should I need to be shown that it is good *for me* for me to be just? The answer is presumably that even if there are psychological mechanisms in place to generate a sense of justice, it might not survive reflection at age of maturity. The question is why this should matter, to the question of what is just. On the one hand, I might conclude that only my own well-being matters, and that I will endorse my sense of justice only if it is good for me, in the circumstances. Yet doing so would mean that I had already renounced my sense of justice. Why should we potentially have to adjust our conception of justice, just because some people who don't really care about justice can't find self-interested reasons to be just? Brian Barry accused Rawls of accepting "the ancient doctrine that no act can be rational unless it is good for the agent to perform it" (Barry 1995, 884–885). On the other hand, after reading part 1 of *A Theory of Justice* and other works of philosophy I might conclude that I do have reasons that justify my sense of justice. Why would it then have to be shown that I have a personal motive for affirming my sense of justice? Either there is no independently justified sense of justice for my (thin) good to converge with, and congruence is illusory, or justice is a sufficient motive by itself, and congruence is unnecessary.

This objection can be answered if we bring in reciprocity and bounded reasonableness. The flip side of our commitment to returning benefits is an unwillingness to make unilateral sacrifices (*TJ* 236, 298). People may be willing to comply with just rules even when they think they could get away with breaking them, but they will not be willing to comply with such rules unilaterally, if others are not also complying. For a conception of justice to be feasible, then, people will need assurance about the conduct of others. The congruence argument gives us assurance that others can be counted upon to observe the requirements of justice that they recognize and endorse, but which they might be tempted to flout (Freeman 2003, 283). Suppose that I take myself to have most reason to do as justice requires, and (in order to avoid Barry's objection) that I do so for reasons independent of the congruence argument. Still, when justice conflicts in deep ways with other important values, I may be tempted not to do what I recognize I ought to do. If many people often face such conflicts, levels of compliance with justice may fall below the threshold at which I will not consider myself obligated to do as justice requires. The point of the congruence argument is thus to show that in a well-ordered society there are reasons for wanting to have a sense of justice, reasons independent of but not antithetical to justice, and thus to assure each other that our predictable weaknesses of the will are not so extensive as to push levels of compliance below the threshold of reciprocity.

Why think justice as fairness is congruent, or at least more so than utilitarianism? First, being liable to moral feelings such as guilt and indignation is essential to participating in relationships of trust and friendship (*TJ* 428, 499–500). Second, having a sense of justice is essential to participating fully in the life of a well-ordered society, which is a great good (*TJ* 500). Rawls reaches this conclusion by applying his "Aristotelian principle" to social institutions, in the context of "the social nature of humankind." People enjoy exercising their capacities, and this enjoyment increases with the skill involved and the complexity of the activity in question (*TJ* 374). No person can develop all of his or her potentialities, but we can appreciate each other's perfections, and by cooperating realize and enjoy more of our common nature than would be possible separately (*TJ* 457–458). Thus through social union "each person can participate in the total sum of realized natural assets of the others" (*TJ* 459). Given the rejection of perfectionism (i.e. "the acceptance of democracy in the assessment of one another's excellences" (*TJ* 462, 388)), the well-ordered society is not a social union based directly on shared ideals of human flourishing. It is nonetheless a social union of social unions, because participation in such a society is a shared end valued for its own sake. Participation in a well-ordered society is a shared end because a well-ordered society consists of a set of public rules that are as a matter of common knowledge conditions for the realization of everyone's nature in a manner consistent with justice. And such participation is valued for its own sake because the Aristotelian principle also holds for institutional forms. Complying with the rules of just institutions engages the cognitive ability to recognize rules as just and conducive to the common good, and to comply with them for that reason (*TJ* 4, 48–49). Finally, the Kantian interpretation of justice as fairness maintains that acting from principles that would be chosen in the original position expresses our nature as free and equal rational beings. Acting in accordance with justice thus allows us to affirm our dignity, as creatures who are not simply moved by causal forces, but can instead act as rational agents (*TJ* 503).

The remaining problem with Rawls's argument for congruence is that the conception of the good that it rests upon is not as thin as advertised, since it rests in part on a Kantian conception of autonomy. As a result, it does not provide assurance about the conduct of those who accept other reasonable comprehensive doctrines. The idea of the overlapping consensus was meant to solve this problem, but a number of critics have questioned whether overlapping consensus plays any independent justificatory role, assuming that the first-stage argument for political liberalism and justice as fairness is correct (Barry 1995; Habermas 1995; Quong 2011, 161–191). The first stage of Rawls's argument in *Political Liberalism* sets out the basic ideas of political liberalism, then aims to show that justice as fairness is the best political conception of justice. At the second stage, we are to check whether justice as fairness can become the object of an overlapping consensus of reasonable comprehensive doctrines (*PL* 390) Yet if the first-stage argument is correct, reasonable doctrines should accept justice as fairness or at least one of a family of liberal political conceptions, while acceptance on the part of the unreasonable is not necessary for stability. Either overlapping consensus is superfluous, or it holds political liberalism hostage to the unreasonable (Quong 2011, 162). One solution is to dispense with the two-stage model of justification, leaving overlapping consensus as simply the starting point for political liberalism. The other is to understand overlapping consensus as pluralistic congruence in the context of bounded reasonableness.

To simplify things, consider the ideal case of a well-ordered society, where all reasonable citizens find reasons within their own comprehensive doctrines to accept political liberalism and justice as fairness. Some people will nonetheless face difficult conflicts of values. Although every reasonable comprehensive doctrine supports justice as fairness given the fact of reasonable pluralism, doctrines that are not philosophically liberal would support quite different principles *were reasonable pluralism not a fact.* For each reasonable comprehensive doctrine, we could in principle measure the distance between the principles of justice as fairness, which the doctrine does support given reasonable pluralism, and the principles the doctrine would support absent reasonable pluralism. The extent of this gap in the case of a particular doctrine would measure the extent of the psychological tension experienced by those adhering to this doctrine, in acting according to the tenets of justice as fairness. If, for many doctrines, the extent of the gap were too great, predictable failures of reasonableness on the part of otherwise reasonable citizens might drive levels of compliance below the reciprocity threshold. It is thus possible to imagine a second congruence argument, this time not focused on the extent of the difference between the individual's thin good and justice, but rather on the extent of the difference between what would be just were there no fact of reasonable pluralism, and what *is* just given the fact of reasonable pluralism. On this account, achieving overlapping consensus means achieving a sufficiently high level of congruence between political and comprehensive justice, on the part of reasonable doctrines, such that predictable failures of reasonableness on the part of otherwise reasonable citizens do not undermine citizens' assurance that others can generally be trusted to act on principles of justice.

Andrew Lister

SEE ALSO:

Goodness as rationality
Overlapping consensus
Political liberalism, justice as fairness as
Reciprocity
Sense of justice
Stability
Thin and full theories of good

42.

CONSCIENTIOUS REFUSAL

R AWLS DEFINES CONSCIENTIOUS refusal as "noncompliance with a more or less direct legal injunction or administrative order" (*TJ* 323). This contrasts with civil disobedience, which he defines as "a public, nonviolent, conscientious yet political act contrary to law usually done with the aim of bringing about a change in the law or policies of the government" (*TJ* 320). Conscientious refusal thus differs – or, strictly speaking, *may* differ – from civil disobedience in several ways (*TJ* 324–325).

Unlike civil disobedience, conscientious refusal is not defined as a public act, though the government may know of it. But unlawful omissions may be publicized and their rationales explained, as Thoreau did of his tax resistance (Thoreau 1973 [1849], 63–90, 313). Some conscientious refusers may avoid publicity, as Thoreau wisely did in aiding escaped slaves (Harding 1982, 314–317). Rawls calls the latter cases "conscientious evasion" (*TJ* 324).

A second difference is that the motivating principles of conscientious refusal need not be political; they might, for example, be religious. But they can be political, as Thoreau's indeed were. A third difference is that the motivating principles may not be shared with other members of the community – though they might be. A fourth difference is that a principled omission need not be part of an effort to achieve reform. The point of aiding escaped slaves, for example, is to ensure their freedom, not the abolition of chattel slavery. Thoreau's tax resistance indicates, however, that conscientious refusal can be part of a line of conduct that seeks reform, e.g. by encouraging others to do the same.

In considering justifications for conscientious refusal, Rawls focuses on conscientious objection to military service and "general pacifism" (*TJ* 325, 331–335). Although Rawls allows for the possibility of just war, he acknowledges that pacifism "accords reasonably well with the principles of justice" in view of "the tendency of nations, particularly great powers, to engage in war unjustifiably" (*TJ* 325). "Given the often predatory aims of state power, and the tendency of men to defer to their government's decision to wage war," he says, "a general willingness to resist the state's claims [its rationales for war] is all the more necessary." Rawls thus endorses "a discriminating conscientious refusal to engage in war in certain circumstances" (*TJ* 335).

As defined by Rawls, civil disobedience and conscientious refusal do not encompass all familiar forms of principled resistance. For example, dissidents sometimes "bear witness" by publicly protesting immoral laws or public policies, even when the protesters do not expect to persuade others or to bring about the desired reform. Some actions, such as boycotts, seek reform by exerting economic pressure in order to persuade public officials or private parties to negotiate an end to protested practices, as in the Montgomery bus boycott of 1955–1956 and the Birmingham campaign of 1963. In such cases, officials may manipulate the law, seeking to make lawful actions illegal, as happened in both Montgomery and Birmingham (King 1987 [1958], 142–148; 2000 [1964], 56–63). Finally, Rawls mentions that, when nonviolent methods fail to achieve urgent reform, "militant" and "forceful" resistance may be appropriate (*TJ* 309, 321–322).

David Lyons

SEE ALSO:

Civil disobedience
Comprehensive doctrine
King, Martin Luther, Jr.
Political obligation

43.

CONSTITUTION AND CONSTITUTIONAL ESSENTIALS

FROM HIS DAYS as a graduate student at Princeton, Rawls's work was animated by a concern to understand and vindicate the possibility and promise of constitutional democracy. In a constitutional democracy, the constitution, whether written or unwritten, fixes, among other things, certain familiar basic individual rights and liberties and the general structure of government and the political process (*PL* 227). These are its "essentials," and there is a high level of moral urgency that these essentials be just and workable.

To be just, a constitution must in its essentials satisfy the two principles of justice. It will satisfy the first (so-called liberty) principle directly by (i) specifying a system of equal basic rights and liberties, (ii) imposing these (with fair value for the political liberties) as a constitutive constraint on the (presumably workable) general structure of government and the political process it sets out, and (iii) providing an institutional mechanism (e.g. judicial review by a Supreme Court) to secure the basic rights and liberties within, and to ensure their priority relative to the other legitimate ends pursued through, government and the political process. These other legitimate ends will include not only other matters of basic justice as set out by the second principle of justice, e.g. matters of fair equality of opportunity and of permissible economic and social inequalities, but also important matters of the common good, e.g. environmental protection or the preservation of culture.

A just constitution satisfies the second principle of justice, then, to the extent that the workable general structure of government and the political process it sets out, already made consistent with the first principle and ensuring and expressing its priority, reliably yields legislation and promotes the common good consistent with the second principle. The workable general structure of government and the political process may be regarded, then, as a kind of procedure designed to produce just results. Of course, there is no such procedure that will always produce just results. But, a just constitution will set out a form of government and a political process that, like a fair trial, not only honors basic liberties but reliably, if not perfectly, yields just results (*TJ* 194, 318).

This workable general structure of government and the political process is itself a constitutional essential, and while a constitution is just with respect to this essential only to the extent that the government structure and political process it specifies tends to yield legislation and policies consistent with both principles of justice, the second principle of justice is not itself embedded or entrenched as constitutional essential. Though it sets out requirements of basic justice, it need not, and on Rawls's view should not, be built into the constitution itself in the way the first principle is. Of course, citizens and other officials will properly refer to the second principle when proposing and voting for, and assessing whether their governmental structure and political process is reliable over time as a mechanism for generating, just laws and policies (*PL* 337–339).

In one respect Rawls's distinction between the two essentials of a democratic constitution – citizens' basic rights and liberties and a workable general structure for government and the political process reliably oriented toward just results – and other matters of basic justice is noncontroversial. The two principles, or basic justice, govern the entire basic social structure, and this includes a good deal more than the constitution as a political-legal institution and blueprint for government. It includes also the economy, the family, the general framework of civil society, and so on. And it includes the relations between these. So there will be many matters of ordinary legislation, regulation, adjudication, and policy that concern basic justice but do not involve constitutional essentials.

But in another respect the distinction is somewhat controversial. For one might think that the second principle of justice should be, like the first, effectively incorporated into and directly expressed by the constitution as a condition, even if not the first condition, on permissible law or policy. One might think, for example, that in a constitutional democracy with judicial review, the Supreme Court ought to be directed and empowered by the constitution to invalidate as unconstitutional not only laws that encroach on the basic rights and liberties or their priority but also laws that encroach upon fair equality of opportunity or that facilitate social or economic inequalities eliminable without loss to the least-advantaged social or economic position. Rawls rejects this view.

He offers several reasons for doing so. One is the different roles played by the constitution and the other institutions and activities constituting the basic social structure: ordinary legislation, regulation, adjudication, economic transactions, civil associations, family life, and so on. The constitution sets the more or less fixed framework for, and for the political and legal assessment and reform of, these other institutions. And so it is imperative that it be settled. Of course, one might suppose then that it ought to be settled in a manner that makes an explicit constitutional commitment to basic justice, enforceable if necessary by the Court or some other comparable institutional mechanism. Rawls rejects this on the grounds that it is much more important, much easier, and much better as a matter of institutional design to treat only the basic rights and liberties and the general structure of government and the political process as constitutional essentials (*TJ* 174). The rest of basic justice is best left to citizens and officials to pursue within that structure and through that process.

Structural social and economic inequalities are, of course, matters of basic justice and thus high-priority agenda items for citizens and other officials. And a constitution is not just unless it sets out a governmental structure and political process conducive to the production of laws and policies consistent with basic justice in these areas. But when it comes to social and economic policy, it is often very difficult, even for those who share a common public conception of justice, to determine and agree on what justice requires. The facts are complicated. Causal relations are difficult to determine. Predictions are uncertain. And so on. And what justice requires can change rather quickly in light of ordinary economic activity and the everyday evolution of social patterns. It is for reasons such as these that matters of fair equality of opportunity and economic justice are so regularly divisive, contested, and pushed center stage within ordinary politics.

By contrast, it is typically much easier to determine what justice requires in terms of basic rights and liberties and the general structure of government and the political process. To be sure, there will always be hard cases and thus a need for constitutional adjudication. And there will sometimes be a need for change to governmental structures and the political process. But what makes these cases hard is not typically complicated facts, indeterminate causal relations, or uncertain predictions, matters better resolved through extended legislative hearings and easily revised legislation than judicial decision upon written briefs and perhaps a morning of limited oral argument and fixed in place until another case presenting the same issue arises before the Court (*PL* 230–231). And typically it is not ordinary economic activity or the everyday evolution of social patterns that generates the need for change to governmental structures or the political process.

On balance, then, while there is much to be gained and little to be lost by treating the basic rights and liberties, and so the first principle of justice, as a constitutional essential to be enforced through judicial review by a Supreme Court or via some similarly effective institutional mechanism, there is, by contrast, much to be lost and little to be gained by treating fair equality of opportunity and permissible social and economic inequalities as constitutional essentials. Such matters of basic justice are better left to citizens and officials within the constitutionally defined domains of ordinary day-to-day legislative, regulative, and adjudicatory processes. Of course, citizens and officials may and should still assess constitutionally mandated structures and processes within these domains by reference to their tendencies to produce just results. And where constitutional reforms seem likely to improve dramatically these tendencies at little cost to political trust and stability, they ought to pursue them.

Here Rawls is keen to emphasize that with respect to the general structure of government and the political process as a constitutional essential, political philosophy is by itself inadequate as a guide. The reason is straightforward. While political philosophy can specify the aim at which the general structure of government and the political process ought reliably to be oriented, judgments about the efficacy of institutions with respect to that aim will necessarily be informed by historical experience, political psychology, institutional facts, and so on (*PL* 408–409.) Indeed, even where there is broad agreement over these matters, there may still be a number of ways in which to structure government offices and political processes in a just constitutional democracy – e.g. bicameral or unicameral legislatures, parliamentary or presidential systems, and so on. Of course, once these essentials are fixed, they should remain so absent compelling reasons of justice or the common good. Frequent controversy over or revision to such matters is likely to generate political suspicion and mistrust. Nevertheless, it is not difficult to imagine that, given certain demographic or other large-scale changes, justice or the common good might indeed justify revision or a call for change with respect to one or another aspect of the general structure of government and the political process.

By contrast, with respect to the basic rights and liberties, matters are more straightforward and less variable with respect to history, political psychology, institutional dynamics, and so on. Justice and the common good typically require the basic rights and liberties, for example, of thought and conscience – in the same form and with the same priority regardless of particular demographic or other large background facts. Accordingly, once constitutionally secure, these essentials may be understood as resolved and removed from the political agenda. This is not to say that they are somehow beyond the reach of the political power of citizens. It is rather to say that citizens and other officials publicly recognize that in the absence of a "supreme emergency" calling for, at most, a temporary revision to these essentials for the sake of preserving them for the future, they are always necessary, and necessary in basically the same form, to any constitution justified by and conducive to justice and the common good. They are thus properly enforced by the Supreme Court as a condition of ordinary politics. Indeed, Rawls speculates that they may even be enforced by the Court against attempted constitutional amendment, for the amendment procedure is arguably in place only to permit the addition of basic rights and liberties and revision to the structure of government and the political process, not to permit revocation of basic rights and liberties (*PL* 239).

As noted, in a constitutional democracy with judicial review as known and practiced in the United States, the Supreme Court will have the final word with respect to legal disputes over the meaning and force of both sorts of constitutional essentials. But while the Court may have the last legal word, in a constitutional democracy it ultimately answers, albeit not directly, as do the legislature and the executive, to the political power of the electorate, the people acting as free and equal citizens. The Constitution is not what the Supreme Court says it is but what the people over time allow the Supreme Court to say that it is (*PL* 237). The justice and stability of a constitutional democracy crucially depends, then, on the people and its political officials, including in the United States those serving on the Supreme Court, sharing a conception of political justice in terms of which at least the essentials of the constitution (and ideally other matters of basic justice) may be understood, justified, evaluated, debated, and reformed through constitutional and legal means (which in extreme cases may require of the people some measure of civil disobedience). For example, justice and stability in the United States depend crucially on a shared understanding between the people and political officials to the effect that the Article V amendment provisions of the Constitution do not permit amendments to revoke basic rights and liberties.

While acknowledging that political philosophy alone cannot settle all questions of the constitutional design of government and the political process, Rawls argues that it can settle some and set parameters on acceptable solutions for others. As noted, government and the political process must honor and express a commitment to the basic liberties and their priority. As applied to government and the political process, the priority of the basic liberties may be understood in terms of a principle of equal participation. This principle requires a constitutional commitment to elected representative bodies with law-making authority; limited terms for elected representatives; political parties oriented toward competing views of justice and the common good rather than factional interests; universal suffrage on a one-person, one-vote basis and so limits on gerrymandering; regularly scheduled elections rather than ad hoc plebiscites called at the discretion of those in power; a presumption of majority rule; and adequate provisions for public deliberation. It requires also a cultural if not constitutional commitment to the ideals of a loyal opposition and civic friendship across political divisions and disagreements. Rawls emphasizes that historically democratic constitutions fail most often with respect to the principle of equal participation by ensuring only formal or legal opportunities but not meaningful realizable opportunities for equal participation. To be just a democratic constitution must secure for all citizens fair value for the political liberties or rights to equal participation constitutionally established.

David A. Reidy

SEE ALSO:

Basic liberties
Basic structure of society
Democracy
Supreme Court and judicial review
Two principles of justice (in justice as fairness)

44.

CONSTITUTIONAL CONSENSUS

THE IDEA OF a constitutional consensus was developed in a 1989 article by Kurt Baier, "Justice and the Aims of Political Philosophy" (Baier 1989). The focus of Rawls's "political liberalism" is an "overlapping consensus," a conception of justice that is able to contribute to the stability of liberal society, in spite of inhabitants' fundamental disagreements over moral, religious, and political views. In Rawls's terms, the necessary "political" conception should be worked up from "fundamental intuitive ideas" in the public culture, and so independent of society's comprehensive views. It should also be rooted in moral principles, as opposed to a *modus vivendi*, which is conceived on the model of a truce, the outcome of political bargaining. While Rawls believes these conditions can be satisfied by justice as fairness, Baier presents an alternative. Contending that there is no consensus on Rawls's principles of justice in the US's deeply pluralistic culture, Baier argues that "there is a consensus on something else, namely, on the procedures for making law" and on the outlines of a judicial process for settling disagreements. Unlike a *modus vivendi*, this "constitutional consensus," as Baier calls it, "is valued for its own sake and for much the same reasons as a consensus on a principle of justice" (Baier 1989, 775). Although Baier recognizes that a constitutional consensus is mainly procedural, an agreement on means to adjudicate differences between adherents of different conceptions of the good, he also argues that political philosophy's practical aim, "stable political unity," can be achieved on the basis of something narrower and easier to obtain than the agreement on principles of justice that constitutes an overlapping consensus (Baier 1989, 775). Empirical evidence indicates that something like Baier's constitutional consensus exists among the vast majority of Americans (Klosko 2000).

Baier's argument raises important questions concerning the kind of consensus necessary for a stable society. As a rule, it is likely that a larger group of people can be brought to agree on a narrower – as opposed to a wider – set of principles, but are also likely to be less committed to their principles than would be members of a narrower but deeper consensus. A question, then, is how deep a consensus must be in order to accomplish Rawls's practical ends. Doubting the possibility of Rawls's hoped for overlapping consensus that is both broad and deep, Baier opts for a broad but relatively shallow agreement.

Because *Political Liberalism* had not been published when Baier presented his critique, Rawls was able to respond in that work. He argues that an overlapping consensus is not utopian. While a constitutional consensus is clearly superior to a *modus vivendi*, it lacks the depth of an overlapping consensus. As an agreement directly about procedures and principles, it is not rooted in specific conceptions of the person and of society. Although it provides for essential rights, the constitutional consensus leaves their parameters open to negotiation by the political process and so lacks the security of an overlapping consensus (*PL* 161). Although admittedly somewhat speculative, Rawls works out a process through which, over time, the convictions of adherents of a constitutional consensus could deepen sufficiently to give rise to an overlapping consensus (*PL* 164–168).

George Klosko

SEE ALSO:

Overlapping consensus
Political liberalism, justice as fairness as
Stability

45.

CONSTRUCTIVISM: KANTIAN/POLITICAL

N THE TITLE of his 1980 Dewey Lectures, Rawls famously characterizes his theory of justice as fairness as an example of "Kantian Constructivism in Moral Theory." This description clearly identifies constructivism as a particular option in moral philosophy, to be contrasted with other "familiar traditional moral conceptions, such as utilitarianism, perfectionism, and intuitionism" (*CP* 303). The description also implies that there can be different versions of constructivism, of which the Kantian form is only one. Since the Dewey Lectures, there has been great interest in constructivism as a potentially distinct option in moral theorizing, but little agreement about what constructivism actually is, or about whether it can ever be fairly described as Kantian.

The difficulties can be traced back to Rawls's own definition. "What distinguishes the Kantian form of constructivism is essentially this: it specifies a particular conception of the person as an element in a reasonable procedure of construction, the outcome of which determines the content of the first principles of justice" (*CP* 304). It is not so hard to see how this definition applies to Rawls's own theory of justice. He specifies a particular conception of persons as characterized by the two moral powers, possessing both a conception of the good and a sense of justice, and thus to be treated as free and equal. He then uses this conception of the person as an element in a procedure of construction, the original position, in which the free and equal persons themselves choose the two fundamental principles of justice, the principle of equal liberty and the difference principle. So a natural interpretation of Rawls's definition would seem be: a constructivist moral theory is one in which some suitably characterized set of persons selects moral principles for themselves, and the Kantian form of constructivism is one in which the set of persons is characterized in a specifically Kantian way.

149

This interpretation would seem to be confirmed by the fact that Rawls spends much of the first Dewey Lecture explaining how and why the parties in the original position should be described as autonomous, and by the fact that Rawls had, in *A Theory of Justice*, cited the autonomy of the parties in the original position as the reason that his theory of justice could be given a Kantian interpretation (*TJ* §40).

The problem with this interpretation, however, is that it seems to leave us with too weak an understanding of constructivism to identify it as a distinctive option in moral theorizing. Since constructivism here means a specified set of persons selecting principles under a specified set of conditions, the term would seem to apply to any moral theory in which persons could be described as rationally choosing moral principles. On this view, Hobbes would seem to count as a constructivist, because his favored moral principles, the laws of nature, are specified as the principles that would be rationally chosen by self-interested individuals under the conditions of uncertainty that characterize his state of nature. But utilitarianism, or at least rule-utilitarianism, might also be described as constructivist, because it justifies moral principles as what would be chosen by utilitarian calculators, by persons rationally determined to count each person's desires as having equal weight, and to find principles that would best satisfy those desires in the aggregate. Since Rawls introduces constructivism by way of a contrast with a set of more familiar moral theories that includes utilitarianism, this way of characterizing constructivism would then seem too weak for Rawls's purposes.

One response to this line of objection, of course, is simply to grant that constructivism in general already *is* a familiar option in moral theorizing, and to interpret Rawls as saying that it is just the Kantian form of constructivism that is the new and interesting option. There is some prior support for this interpretation in the way that Rawls uses the term "constructive" in *TJ* §7. There Rawls describes intuitionism as the view that moral theory is powerless to settle at least some practical conflicts in a principled way, since those conflicts will stem from competing intuitions that have the same primitive moral force. A constructive view is one that rejects this view of practical conflict and proposes criteria to settle disputes in a principled way. In *TJ* §7, utilitarianism is specifically identified, along with justice as fairness, as a constructive moral theory that rejects intuitionism in just this way. The difference, Rawls explains, is that utilitarianism proposes a single principle to settle practical conflicts, while justice as fairness proposes two distinct principles, arranged in lexical order. But it seems odd to use this difference between a pluralistic and a monistic account of practical principles to mark the difference between Kantian and non-Kantian constructivism. (Hobbes shouldn't

Constructivism: Kantian/political / 151

count as a Kantian constructivist merely because he identifies nineteen different laws of nature, or as rejecting constructivism in favor of intuitionism merely because he didn't arrange the nineteen laws in lexical order.) More importantly, constructivism as Rawls describes it in "Kantian Constructivism" seems to imply having a procedure of construction through which morally justifying principles are selected, and not simply the fact of having morally justifying principles at all. Suppose one held a kind of crude moral theory that idealized just one sort of person as virtuous in some way, and that defined good actions as ones that best promoted the development and flourishing of such persons. Such a crude theory would seem to be constructive in *TJ*'s sense, because it at least claims to have a principle of justification that should be deployed in every moral deliberation. But the theory would not seem to be constructivist in "Kantian Constructivism"'s sense, because there is no procedure through which the virtuous or any other persons select and thus construct the favored principle of justification.

Another response to the possible weakness of Rawls's definition, then, would be to deny that utilitarianism should count as constructivist, because it too lacks a properly constructive procedure. After all, the principle of utility is not constructed; it is not justified because it has been selected by a certain set of persons. What might seem to be constructed in the utilitarian calculus are the justifications for individual actions, or in the case of rule-utilitarianism, for the principles that are found to best maximize utility in general practice. But while those utility-maximizing principles might be said to have been chosen by the utilitarian calculators, it is also possible to understand their calculations as tracking an independent fact, the objective desirability of the principles. A similar story can be told about Hobbes's moral theory: the laws of nature that individuals agree to in the state of nature are really those that assure mutual security. These supposed procedures of construction, then, the means through which persons select moral principles, might well be understood as simply heuristic devices, means by which the theorist dramatizes the justification of moral principles by depicting them as chosen by persons committed to certain values. But the devices are merely heuristic, because the moral principles are ultimately justified by their independent rational connection to those values.

Is Rawls's theory any different? It is possible to read *TJ* and answer no. The original position is certainly a heuristic device, and it is possible to understand that device as merely heuristic, as simply dramatizing the selection of fair political principles. On this reading, the real justificatory work of the theory is done not by the original position, but by the independent value of fairness. In "Kantian Cconstructivism," however, Rawls explicitly rejects this reading. He argues that justice as fairness, with its device of the original position, should be understood as a practical response to divergent opinions about independent moral values, and in particular to divergent opinions about the meaning of freedom and equality.

> [W]e take our examination of the Kantian conception of justice as addressed to an impasse in our recent political history; the course of democratic thought over the past two centuries, say, shows that there is no agreement on the way basic social institutions should be arranged if they are to conform to the freedom and equality of citizens as moral persons. (*CP* 305)

Given this disagreement, there is no independent route by which Rawls's favored principles of justice could be derived from freestanding moral values like fairness, or freedom and equality. The original position, then, is not merely heuristic: it is introduced in a way that could settle disputes about the political meaning of freedom and equality, by depicting free and equal persons as choosing principles of justice for themselves. We do not say that these principles of justice express the true meaning of freedom and equality, in the sense of deriving directly from these moral values. Instead we say that the principles represent the outcome of a public agreement on what those values mean for us. This public agreement is justified in its own terms, in the way it allows us to collectively regulate our political life by means of shared reasons, and not because the agreement tracks some further value.

> Thus, whenever a sufficient basis for agreement among citizens is not presently known, or recognized, the task of justifying a conception of justice becomes: how can people settle on a conception of justice, to serve this social role, that is (most) reasonable for them in virtue of how they conceive of their persons and construe the general features of social cooperation among persons so regarded? (*CP* 305)

Constructivism, then, is not simply hypothetical proceduralism, the view that justified moral principles are those that would be chosen by a specified set of persons under a specified set of conditions. That sort of view, which includes any form of social contract theory and various forms of utilitarianism, is consistent with a realist account of moral value, with the constructive procedure a merely heuristic device in which the specified constraints model a person's properly rational relation to the moral truth. By making agreement on a public conception of justice the ultimate goal of his theory, Rawls is rejecting this sort of moral realism.

This is the reason why constructivism in recent years has come to be understood primarily as a form of anti-realism in moral theory, a version of the claim that moral truths are made and not found. Rather than holding that practical reason operates by accurately tracking an independent order of value, constructivism proposes that value is created through the operation of practical reason itself.

But it is just as misleading to describe constructivism as simply a form of anti-realism, to reduce its content to the practical aim of constructing public agreement on a shared conception of political justification. For it is not hard to imagine public agreements around conceptions of political justification that make no reference to hypothetically described persons, choosing according to a specified set of constraints. Constructivism as Rawls describes it in "Kantian Constructivism" is neither hypothetical proceduralism nor anti-realism *simpliciter*, but the special combination of those views: the view both that the aim of moral theorizing is a certain sort of public agreement, and that this aim is best satisfied through a theory that describes persons collectively choosing moral principles for themselves. This special combination is present in Rawls's original definition at *CP* 304, because the pure hypothetical proceduralism of the rest of that sentence is qualified by one crucial word. Rawls speaks not simply of a procedure of construction, but of "a reasonable procedure of construction," with a reasonable procedure crucially understood as a procedure that could be endorsed by a set of reasonable persons, a set of persons motivated to reach an agreement that they all could freely accept. For Rawls, constructivism is reasonable both because it seeks agreement on moral questions, and because it seeks that agreement through a shared choice of moral principles.

What makes Rawls's form of constructivism Kantian? On that point, our first reading of Rawls's definition was correct: it is the Kantian conception of the person, as free and equal, and therefore able to understand the moral principles we choose as free and equal persons as autonomously willed. It is certainly possible to imagine, as Mark LeBar has done, an Aristotelian form of constructivism, in which virtuous agents choose practical principles for themselves by deciding what would best contribute to *eudaemonia* (LeBar 2008). Such a constructivism is appropriately nonrealist, because its practical judgments refer not to what is true or good in an independent sense, but to their contribution to a flourishing life. It is appropriately proceduralist, because what contributes to a flourishing life is something which virtuous agents must choose for themselves. And it combines those elements in the appropriately special way: for LeBar, the good is constituted by the choices of the virtuous agent, reasoning about what would best contribute to a flourishing life. This kind of view substitutes an Aristotelian conception of the person, the virtuous agent reasoning about *eudaemonia*, for Rawls's Kantian conception of persons as free and equally legislating political principles for themselves.

What may be less clear, however, is the extent to which Rawls's own form of constructivism is Kantian in the sense of being faithful to Kant's own views. In his own work on Kant, like the essay "Themes in Kant's Moral Philosophy," Rawls describes the categorical imperative as a kind of constructive principle, but this kind of interpretation faces some important obstacles. For one thing, the categorical imperative is designed not to produce or select justified principles of action, but to place certain constraints on individual maxims without which they cannot count as justified. And the fundamental role of the categorical imperative in practical justification is itself to be justified, on many readings, in a fundamentally realist manner, as a commitment to the independent value of freedom or rationality. The identification of Kant as a constructivist thus depends on a particular reading of Kant, favored by students of Rawls like Onora O'Neill and Christine Korsgaard, which emphasizes the claim that for Kant, the good exists only as a property of the maxims of rational agents, choosing according to rational standards. For O'Neill, those standards are the ones that could serve as the basis for shared reasoning among a plurality of agents; for Korsgaard, they are the ones that are constitutive of a person's having a practical identity, or being an agent at all (O'Neill 1989; Korsgaard 1996, 2009). Much has been written about the plausibility or implausibility of these claims. Here what matters is just that both O'Neill and Korsgaard understand the categorical imperative as a procedure which (together with the hypothetical imperative, the principle of instrumental rationality) allows agents to understand their ends as good, and justify the categorical imperative as a means to satisfy a practical end, either providing a basis for shared reasoning (O'Neill) or the self-constitution of agency (Korsgaard). In each case, Kant is understood as affirming the special combination of views that characterizes Rawls's constructivism: invoking a procedural device to select practical principles, justified merely by reference to a shared practical aim.

To endorse one of these constructivist interpretations of Kant is to commit oneself to a deep claim about moral and indeed any form of value: that it has no existence outside the choices of rational agents, choosing according to certain shared practical aims. In his work after "Kantian Constructivism," Rawls recoils from this sweeping claim about value. He does characterize Kant as a moral constructivist – which presumably implies an interpretation of Kant along the lines favored by O'Neill or Korsgaard – but he denies that justice as fairness

Constructivism: Kantian/political / 155

requires any form of moral constructivism. Effectively dropping "Kantian Constructivism"'s reference to "moral theory," the later Rawls insists that justice as fairness implies only political constructivism: we need understand only political claims as justified by their ability to contribute to public agreement about justice. It is for this reason that justice as fairness is now characterized as political liberalism.

In an important sense, the domain of the political is defined negatively, in contrast with the larger domain of value which is the concern of practical reason, taken generally. Modern democratic societies, explains Rawls, are characterized by deep ethical disagreements, deriving from a diversity of religious and philosophical doctrines, none of which is able to command anything close to universal assent. Moreover, this pluralism of claims to value is reasonable pluralism: it is the natural and foreseeable outcome of the sincere exercise of practical reason in diverse modern societies. We should expect that even reasonable people, sincerely motivated to come to a rational agreement, will not be able to reach consensus on the ultimate sources of value and the ways in which they are to be justified. Given the fact of this reasonable pluralism, we are naturally led to the idea of a merely political conception of justice, a way of regulating the coercive effects of ourselves and our social institutions on one another, without resorting to comprehensive claims about the nature of value. But the depth of this pluralism is even more reason to understand a merely political conception of justice as constructed, as designed specifically to secure public agreement from a diversity of citizens, and justified on that basis alone. But political liberalism's rejection of moral constructivism implies that there will be no further argument for the sufficiency of public agreement as a practical value, as a claim in moral theory or practical philosophy more generally. In this sense, political constructivism is not an alternative to utilitarianism or intuitionism. Instead, the specifically political character of justice as fairness implies that the sufficiency of Rawls's merely political conception of justice is ultimately justified by an agreement of the diversity of individual citizens, reasoning in the diverse terms of their individual comprehensive doctrines. Such an overlapping consensus should finally be understood as more deeply supportive of the freedom and equality of each person than a comprehensive Rawlsian account of the political good, no matter how metaphysically thin.

Is this merely political constructivism still Kantian? The answer depends on which aspect of Rawls's political constructivism we choose to emphasize. If we look to the sort of nonrealist interpretation that O'Neill or Korsgaard give to Kant's moral philosophy, the answer is obviously no, because Rawls's political liberalism does not require an account of moral or practical value of the sort these contemporary constructivist readers find in Kant. But if one emphasizes the conception of the person that Rawls throughout his entire body of work emphasizes as Kantian, the answer looks very different. Autonomy, Rawls has suggested before, during, and after "Kantian Constructivism," consists in free and equal agents legislating practical principles for themselves. If Kantian constructivism is the view that free and equal persons can best agree on practical principles by choosing those principles for themselves, then Rawls's political constructivism is clearly Kantian. For in Rawls's political liberalism, justified political principles are those that free and equal agents would select as constituting the basis for a public agreement among themselves. That this agreement is merely political does not alter the fact that it is justified because it is self-legislated, which is just the claim of the Kantian form of constructivism.

Larry Krasnoff

SEE ALSO:

> *Kant, Immanuel*
> *Kantian interpretation*
> *Moral person*
> *Political conception of justice*
> *Practical reason*
> *The reasonable and the rational*

46.

COOPERATION AND COORDINATION

SOCIAL COOPERATION HAS always been an important concept in Rawls's political philosophy. In *A Theory of Justice* he conceives of society as "a cooperative venture for mutual advantage," whose members acknowledge "certain rules of conduct as binding," rules that "specify a system of cooperation designed to advance the good of those taking part in it" (*TJ* 4). In his later writings, however, social cooperation becomes even more central. The "idea of a society as a fair system of social cooperation over time from one generation to the next," he tells us, is the "most fundamental idea" in his conception of justice as fairness (*JF* 5). Indeed, it is even built into his conception of political philosophy, whose first task is to narrow "the divergence of philosophical and moral opinion at the root of divisive political differences" so that "social cooperation on a footing of mutual respect among citizens can still be maintained" (*JF* 2).

Social cooperation is best seen by contrast to "socially coordinated activity – for example, activity coordinated by orders issued by an absolute central authority" (*JF* 6). The key point is that all social life involves a division of social labor, not merely in the narrowly economic sense epitomized by Adam Smith's pin factory, but in a broader sense of differentiated social roles, each with its own responsibilities and powers. As Socrates tells Adeimantus in the *Republic*, society is necessary because no one is self-sufficient, and each of us must turn to others to meet one's needs (369b–c). Once social activity is divided, the separate types of activity must be coordinated through a system of rules so that members' activities are (more or less) complementary, enabling the society to produce the goods – broadly understood as the advantages of social life – necessary for the orderly reproduction of the society and its members.

A social system based on slavery is a system of social coordination, assigning individuals to certain roles and coordinating their behavior in such a way that society can sustain itself over time and meet the natural and, more specifically, the socially defined needs of its members. All systems of social cooperation, then, must be systems of social coordination, but a system of social cooperation is distinct in that the coordination it achieves "is guided by publicly recognized rules and procedures which those cooperating accept as appropriate to guide their conduct," in part because the rules enable them to realize their own good in ways they regard as fair. As Rawls puts it,

> Fair terms of cooperation specify an idea of reciprocity, or mutuality: all who do their part as the recognized rules require are to benefit as specified by a public and agreed-upon standard. (*JF* 6)

In a slave system, by contrast, there is no reason to suppose that the slaves "accept" its "publicly recognized rules and procedures," since the system obviously does not function to realize the "rational advantage, or good" of the slaves (*JF* 6). Reciprocity or mutuality does not necessarily mean that in a system of social cooperation people benefit equally; whether equality is required depends upon the publicly accepted standards, that is, the standards or principles of justice accepted in that society. The "role of the principles of justice" is "to specify" the "fair terms of cooperation" (*JF* 7). A society that is a system of social cooperation is "well-ordered."

In a system of social cooperation the principles of justice regulate the "basic structure of society," that is, a society's "main political and social institutions and the way they hang together as one system of cooperation" (*JF* 8). It is through the basic structure that the advantages and burdens of social life are produced and distributed. Thus, the basic structure largely determines individuals' life prospects by allocating advantages and burdens across different social positions. Perhaps even more important, its "effects are so profound and present from the start" (*TJ* 7) that they also shape "the sort of persons they want to be as well as the sort of persons they are" (*TJ* 229). Every society has a basic structure, but a society will be a system of social cooperation rather than coordination only if its participants "accept and regard" the principles governing the system, specifically the basic structure, as "properly regulating their conduct" (*PL* 108).

Any society that can be characterized as cooperative will respect certain basic or human rights (*PL* 109 n.15). Rawls does not specify these basic rights with any real precision; he lists the right to life (including "the means of subsistence and security"), the right to liberty (including "freedom from slavery, serfdom, and forced occupation, and to a sufficient measure of liberty of conscience to ensure freedom of religion and thought"), the right to "personal property," the right to "formal equality" (in the sense that "similar cases be treated similarly") (*LP* 65), and in other places he proposes additional rights, such as a right to emigrate (*LP* 74) and a right to participate in some way in a political process in which those who exercise power must justify their use of power in terms of the society's public conception of justice. Although protecting such vital interests as subsistence may not take the form or employ the language of "rights," without the protection of these basic interests, the social practices of the society would not be mutually beneficial, and the social order would involve "command by force, a slave system, and no cooperation of any kind" (*LP* 68).

What appears to unify this list is a common sense idea of agency: these rights in some form are necessary to protect the capacities that are presupposed by the idea of social cooperation, or willing participation in the social order. More specifically, without protecting such basic rights we would not "have a society with a legal system imposing what are correctly believed to be genuine obligations, rather than a society that merely coerces its subjects who are unable to resist" (*PL* 109). I say "common sense idea of agency" because in setting out an account of human rights Rawls is not attempting to ground a set of invariant moral principles in a theory of human nature, but to spell out in broad terms what is necessarily involved in the idea of a cooperative or well-ordered society.

Rawls suggests that there are two types of societies that could be systems of social cooperation. One type is based on what Rawls calls a "common good conception of justice." He does not develop an elaborate account of such a society, but what is essential is that (virtually) all of its members share a "comprehensive doctrine" that defines its "common good." Rawls refers to these systems as "decent" societies to distinguish them from well-ordered liberal societies. In the absence of a widespread acceptance of a particular comprehensive doctrine, participants could not accept the rules or procedures rooted in that doctrine as "appropriate to regulate their conduct," and so a society organized by a common good conception of justice would not be a system of social cooperation, but merely one of social coordination. In that case, a large number of its members would experience its norms as imposed upon them, and so they would experience it as a system of domination or mere coordination rather than cooperation.

The fundamental question addressed by Rawls's later work is to explain how a system of social cooperation would be possible in a society whose citizens do not share a comprehensive doctrine but "remain profoundly divided by reasonable religious, philosophical and moral doctrines" (*PL* 4). Because a pluralist society cannot be well-ordered in terms of principles of justice derived from a unified comprehensive doctrine, Rawls proposes the idea of a liberal but "political conception of justice," one that is "freestanding" and not rooted in any particular comprehensive doctrine, as the answer to that fundamental question. In justice as fairness, and political liberalism generally, citizens – "those engaged in cooperation" – are seen as "free and equal persons" (*JF* 5), which is another fundamental "companion idea" of justice as fairness. As free and equal persons, the "publicly recognized rules and procedures" must "be seen by all as fair terms of cooperation" that each person must "honor," even when it is not to one's immediate advantage to do so (*JF* 7).

The idea of a *system* of cooperation, which presupposes a group of individuals who share a basic structure, must be distinguished from the idea of social cooperation more generally. There are, however, spaces in which individuals may engage one another apart from the basic structure of a society. Individuals whose interactions are not part of a structured system of social roles, such as strangers encountering one another in public spaces, are subject to natural duties and obligations, such as the duty of mutual respect and the duty not to harm the innocent (*TJ* 93–101). In addition to these universal obligations, individuals may form or participate in voluntary associations and "less comprehensive social groups" (*TJ* 7) that may impose additional obligations on them, as well are conferring new powers and opportunities. To the extent that participants observe these norms they engage in social cooperation even if the relationships in question are not embedded in a basic structure.

Social cooperation is also possible at the global level, among societies and individuals from different societies. Although there is no global basic structure that has the pervasive impact of a domestic basic structure, social cooperation at the international or global level requires "publicly recognized rules and procedures which those cooperating accept as appropriate to guide their conduct." In his *Law of Peoples* Rawls sets out the basic principles of global justice to which these "publicly recognized rules and procedures" must conform, but in this area, like spaces of individual interaction not governed by the norms of institutions that are part of a basic structure, the requirements of "basic fairness" (*LP* 115) play the central role, rather than principles of distributive justice

Cooperation and coordination / 161

that govern the distribution of the advantages and burdens of a system of social cooperation.

J. Donald Moon

SEE ALSO:

Basic structure of society
Common good idea of justice
Political conception of justice
Publicity
Reciprocity
Well-ordered society

47.

COSMOPOLITANISM

Rawls's explicit discussion of cosmopolitanism occurs entirely within two brief sections of *The Law of Peoples* although he makes remarks related to the theme elsewhere in that book and in the preceding article, "The Law of Peoples." There is no commonly agreed upon definition of cosmopolitanism in political philosophy; but it is fair to say that it involves at least the views that duties of justice extend beyond compatriots to include noncompatriots and that individuals are the proper object of concern in accounts of global and international justice. When Rawls contrasts his Law of Peoples to cosmopolitanism he usually has in mind versions of cosmopolitanism that extend aspects of his justice as fairness to relations between noncompatriots. Rawls draws three contrasts between his views and cosmopolitanism. One is methodological; another concerns the substance of principles of international justice; and the third, merely implicit, regards the extent to which nonliberal states should be tolerated as full members of international society.

Regarding methodology, Rawls takes cosmopolitanism to be based upon a different constructivist justificatory account. Rawls develops the Law of Peoples by means of an account that employs an original position in which representatives of liberal and decent peoples decide in two separate steps on principles of justice. In contrast to this he imagines a cosmopolitan constructivism in which

> all persons are considered to be reasonable and rational and to possess what I have called 'the two moral powers' – a capacity for a sense of justice and a capacity for a conception of the good...[and] a global original position with its veil of ignorance behind which all parties are situated

symmetrically...[T]he parties would then adopt a first principle that all persons have equal basic rights and liberties. Proceeding this way would straightaway ground human rights in a political (moral) conception of liberal cosmopolitan justice. (*LP* 82)

The cosmopolitan method is individualistic; whereas Rawls's method of representing peoples is collectivist or corporatist. In distancing himself from the cosmopolitan method, Rawls is explicitly rejecting the claims of several of his commentators who argue that employment of the original position from his domestic account can be used to extend an account of justice globally (Beitz 1999; Pogge 1989).

The substantive contrast that Rawls draws between his view and cosmopolitanism focuses on whether distributive justice applies across states as well as within them. "The ultimate concern of a cosmopolitan view is the well-being of individuals and not the justice of societies. According to that view there is still a question concerning the need for further global distribution, even after each domestic society has achieved internally just institutions" (*LP* 119–120). This cosmopolitan view takes individuals and their well-being as the proper concern of global justice. "It is concerned with the well-being of individuals, and hence with whether the well-being of the globally worst-off person can be improved" (*LP* 120). Rawls is particularly interested in the claim that the difference principle should be applied internationally, a claim typically endorsed by the methodological cosmopolitans cited above. Rawls rejects this egalitarianism. In contrast, he takes international justice to require aiding burdened societies to become well-ordered (*LP* 111).

The third contrast with cosmopolitanism is merely implicit in Rawls's account of toleration of decent hierarchical societies. The methodological distinction highlighted above suggests that a cosmopolitan constructivism results in liberal principles with global scope. Hence, cosmopolitanism provides grounds for moral criticism of all non-liberal societies. Rawls characterizes such hostility to nonliberal regimes as the view that, "nonliberal societies are always properly subject to some form of sanction – political, economic, or even military – depending on the case. On this view, the guiding principle of liberal foreign policy is gradually to shape all not yet liberal societies in a liberal direction, until eventually (in the ideal case) all societies are liberal" (*LP* 60). In contrast, Rawls believes that certain nonliberal societies, decent hierarchical societies, should be tolerated as full members of international society.

[N]ot all regimes can reasonably be required to be liberal. If so, the Law of Peoples would not express liberalism's own principle of toleration for other reasonable ways of ordering society. A liberal society must respect other societies organized by comprehensive doctrines, provided their political and social institutions meet certain conditions that lead the society to adhere to a reasonable Law of Peoples. (*CP* 563)

In sum, Rawls's concerns about cosmopolitanism are focused on what he takes to be its methodological or justificatory individualism, its egalitarianism, and its refusal to tolerate non-liberal societies.

In his discussion of methodology Rawls is more interested in drawing the contrast between his own view and the cosmopolitan view than in mounting a refutation of the latter. After posing the question in "Peoples" of how a construction of principles of international or global justice proceeds, Rawls makes a tentative reply: "I think that there is not a clear initial answer to this question. We should try various alternatives and weigh their pluses and minuses. Since in working out justice as fairness I begin with domestic society, I shall continue from there as if what has been done so far is more or less sound" (*CP* 536). Rawls shows no great interest in moral arguments about the starting points – individualist or corporatist – of the two methods of justification. Rather, a refutation of cosmopolitanism, if there is to be one at all, would seem to exist in the favorable comparison that the fully worked out version of the Law of Peoples makes to a developed version of cosmopolitanism.

The idea that the best response to cosmopolitanism is to consider the developed accounts is further reflected in "Peoples" in the suggestion that the cosmopolitan method will issue in principles that will be judged infeasible by the public. "[P]eoples as corporate bodies organized by their governments now exist in some form all over the world. Historically speaking, all principles and standards proposed for the Law of Peoples must, to be feasible, prove acceptable to the considered and reflective public opinion of peoples and their governments" (*CP* 536). But this is a puzzling comment since the cosmopolitans that Rawls is responding to do not typically call into question the international state system.

Rawls's second explicit discussion of cosmopolitanism draws on arguments he makes in defending his view of distributive justice between peoples. Rather than endorsing the global application of the difference principle, Rawls defends the view that well-ordered peoples have a duty of assistance to burdened societies. The duty is stated as the eighth principle in *LP* (*LP* 37). Burdened societies "lack the political and cultural traditions, the human capital and know-how, and, often, the material and technological resources needed to be well-ordered" (*LP* 106). While the difference principle requires that an institutional structure be to the maximum benefit of the least advantaged, the aim of the duty of assistance is "to help burdened societies to be able to manage their own affairs reasonably and rationally and eventually to become members of the Society of well-ordered Peoples" (*LP* 111).

Rawls asserts that an advantage of the duty of assistance is that it has a cut-off point for assistance. In contrast, he doubts the appeal of an egalitarian principle that would require redistribution "without end" (*LP* 117) because such a principle is insensitive to the role that domestic policies play in creating inequalities between peoples (*LP* 117–118). The egalitarian principle would justify taxing a society that has become comparatively wealthy through free and responsible policy choices in order to improve the well-being of people in a society that is less wealthy also as a result of free policy choices (*LP* 118). Rawls's response to egalitarian cosmopolitans is based upon the claim that the wealth of societies is largely a matter of self-determined policy choice, or as he puts it "the political culture" of a society (*LP* 108, 117).

The emphasis on the political culture of societies is contentious for several reasons. One influential challenge comes from Thomas Pogge (2008), who argues that international practice and international laws contribute to corruption in many states by providing incentives to people to assume leadership positions by nondemocratic means. Regardless of how a leader arrives in office, he or she is recognized as legitimate for purposes of taking out international loans and selling natural resources on terms that might be quite favorable to the office-holder. Such incentives to power implicate the international community in what appears to be merely a matter of domestic corruption. Another empirical matter is whether a vision of autarkic societal development is plausible given global economic interdependence in which a mortgage crisis in the USA can lead to a global recession.

Because Rawls stresses the importance of the political autonomy of decent and liberal peoples (*LP* 118), the emphasis on the political culture of societies might not merely be an empirical claim. The idea might be that inequalities between societies are a possible outcome of an appropriate arrangement in which political societies are held responsible for their policies. A worry that cosmopolitans might have about this is that holding societies responsible could result in attributing responsibility to citizens when this is not appropriate. For example, it is unclear on what grounds adult citizens in decent societies are responsible for their societies' choices, when they have input merely through institutions of group consultation, but have no effective democratic control (*LP* 72–73). But even if there are good reasons for holding adults responsible, it may be problematic to hold the children in the society responsible. An alternative cosmopolitan view holds that, as a matter of global justice, the policy choices should no more affect the opportunities of children than, as a matter of domestic justice, the wealth of parents should affect them. Although perfect equality of opportunity seems impossible in both cases, this is not a reason not to approximate it (Moellendorf 2009, 85).

The plausibility of Rawls's rejection of cosmopolitan egalitarianism depends in part on his defense of his alternative principle of distributive justice, the duty of assistance, which is supposed to be chosen in the original position. The reasons why parties would choose the duty of assistance in this original position are unclear. If the parties assume ideal conditions, then it is unclear why they would select a duty of assistance. If nonideal conditions are entertained, it is unclear why burdened societies would not also be represented in the original position, perhaps as a third step. Moreover, in the first step of the original position, if the parties were assumed to represent egalitarian liberal peoples, it is unclear why a more robustly egalitarian international distributive principle would not be chosen (Moellendorf 2002, 13).

Despite the difference of moral principle between Rawls and egalitarian cosmopolitans, there is some room for agreement about the justice of international redistribution to eradicate absolute global poverty. For Rawls this is just if it is necessary in order to make societies well-ordered.

The third – implicit – contrast that Rawls makes between his view and cosmopolitanism involves his rejection of accounts of justice that render all illiberal societies – especially decent hierarchical societies – as in principle open to sanction of some sort, whether it be political criticism, economic measures, or military intervention. Such views are inconsistent with the liberal notion of tolerance extended to global affairs (*LP* 19). The conception of toleration in *Peoples* is not identical to the conception in justice as fairness, which conception rests heavily on the burdens of judgment – the inability to achieve rational agreement regarding comprehensive conceptions of the good – and on citizens conforming their conduct in accordance with the equal rights of others. According to Rawls, in domestic society toleration requires that principles of justice not be justified to others on sectarian grounds (*PL* 10, 154). In international society decent peoples are organized around comprehensive conceptions of the good and thus do not satisfy the liberal conception of tolerance. Rawls's view is that the toleration shown to decent peoples is an extension of the liberal notion of toleration, not an application of the same notion.

Rawls contends that decent peoples should be tolerated as full members of international society because they are (i) nonaggressive, (ii) respectful of a small set of human rights, (iii) sufficiently legitimate to impose real legal obligations on their citizens, (iv) adherents to a common good idea of justice that takes into consideration what it counts as the interests of everyone, and (v) in possession of a judiciary that has a sincere and not unreasonable belief that the law is guided by the common good idea of justice (*LP* 67). Additionally, Rawls holds that the condition that the judiciary possesses a sincere and not unreasonable belief that the law is guided by the common good idea of justice requires that decent societies include institutions of group consultation (*LP* 72–73).

To be tolerant requires, among other things, that one conform one's criticisms and policy justifications to a public conception of justice. The content of the Law of Peoples establishes the constraints on reasonable public criticism for international affairs. "The Law of Peoples with its political concepts and principles, ideals and criteria, is the content of the public reason in a society of liberal and decent peoples by means of which members debate 'their mutual relations'" (*LP* 55). Rawls takes the constraints on debate to apply "whenever chief executives and legislators, and other government officials, as well as candidates for public office, act from and follow the principles of the Law of Peoples and explain to other peoples their reasons for pursuing or revising a people's foreign policy and affairs of state that involves other societies" (*LP* 56). The constraints on public reason also apply to citizens considering such matters. "As for private citizens, we say, as before, that ideally citizens are to think of themselves *as if* they were legislators and ask themselves what foreign policy supported by what consideration they would think more reasonable to advance" (*LP* 56–57).

A cosmopolitan view that takes all non-liberal societies as open in principle to political, economic, or military sanction rejects the principled constraint on public reason that prohibits criticizing decent societies. Because cosmopolitans are often concerned with justice between individuals rather than peoples, its proponents sometimes claim that to reject in principle all criticism of societies that fail to respect a principle of liberal toleration is not standing on a principle of toleration, but, on the contrary, on a principle permissive of intolerance (Kuper 2000, 648–653; Tan 2000, 30–32).

Darrel Moellendorf

SEE ALSO:

> *Decent societies*
> *Difference principle*
> *Duty of assistance*
> *Human rights*
> *Law of Peoples*
> *Liberal people*
> *The original position*
> *Pogge, Thomas*
> *Toleration*

48.

COUNTING PRINCIPLES

RAWLS HOLDS THAT a person's plan of life is rational if it is consistent with the principles of rational choice and would be chosen with full deliberative rationality. Satisfying the principles of rational choice, which Rawls calls "counting principles," therefore, is necessary but not sufficient for a plan to be rational. The principles rule out some plans, but do not select one uniquely or rank them completely. The principles are formal in the sense that they do not dictate any particular content, but only the general shape or structure that plans must have if they are to be rational. Deliberative rationality is necessary to select a single plan from among the formally rational candidates. Deliberative rationality, as an ideal, requires one to determine "in light of all the relevant facts ... what it would be like to carry out these plans" and thereby allows an individual to select the plan that would "best realize his more fundamental desires" (*TJ* 366). The parties in the original position know that their plan of life will satisfy the counting principles. However, the veil of ignorance obviously deprives them of the information that they would need in order to engage in deliberative rationality.

A plan of life is not "a detailed blueprint for action" governing one's entire life. Rather, "It consists of a hierarchy of plans, the more specific subplans being filled in at the appropriate time" (*TJ* 360). So, we can see how the principles of rational choice operate by considering how we fill in short-term plans in light of broader, more abstract, and longer-range goals. We can think of the principles as guides to rational deliberation. Rawls considers three such principles.

The first principle is that of "effective means." It holds that when we have an objective, it is rational (other things equal) to take the most efficient means to that end. The second principle is "inclusiveness." The idea is that if one plan is likely to achieve all and more general ends when compared to another plan, then it is rational (other things equal) to adopt the former plan. And the third principle, "greater likelihood," holds that if two plans may achieve the same ends, but one is more likely to achieve one of them without any others being less likely, then it is rational (other things equal) to adopt the one that has the greater chance of success. In all three of these cases, we can think of the principles as guiding deliberation from more general ends to more specific means. At least in cases where our long-term goals are relatively fixed and we reason toward identifying effective, inclusive, and more likely means, Rawls takes these principles to be uncontroversial.

Rawls also holds that these principles properly apply to decisions about long-term decisions. He takes "effective means" and "greater likelihood" to be uncontroversial in these cases as well. But the principle of "inclusiveness" may seem more questionable because the plan that we select will itself affect the desires that we come to have. If an individual chooses a plan that does not develop certain further desires, she might turn out to be indifferent to their satisfaction, and from her point of view, it might seem that the more inclusive plan would not be the more rational choice. But Rawls argues that given the Aristotelian principle, it is rational for individuals to choose the plan that involves "the larger pattern of ends which brings into play the more finely developed talents" (*TJ* 364).

Thus, while the counting principles serve a formal function, preliminary to the discussion of deliberative rationality, they also reveal some important commitments. Rawls insists that "we can choose between rational plans of life. And this means that we can choose now which desires we shall have at a later time" (*TJ* 364). Rationality does not simply consist in identifying the most effective means to satisfy our existing desires any more than justice is a matter of maximally satisfying the aggregate of existing desires in a population.

Jon Mandle

SEE ALSO:

Conception of the goodness
Deliberative rationality
Goodness as rationality
Plan of life

49.

CULTURE, POLITICAL VS. BACKGROUND

RAWLS'S DISTINCTION BETWEEN political culture and background culture is important for understanding his conception of public reason; for being "attentive to where we are and whence we speak"; for the articulation and justification of politically liberal conceptions of justice; and for understanding the ways such conceptions can influence democratic societies (*PL* 382).

The public political culture of a constitutional democracy encompasses the society's political institutions along with its commonly recognized interpretive traditions (especially those of a supreme court) and commonly known political texts of enduring or historical significance (*PL* 13–14; *JF* 6). These components of the public political culture are understood as a "fund of implicitly shared ideas and principles" that "may play a fundamental role in society's political thought and in how its institutions are interpreted" (*PL* 14; *JF* 6). The public political culture thus incorporates a general tradition of democratic, political thought whose content and fundamental, intuitive ideas are relatively familiar and comprehensible to "the educated common sense of citizens generally" (*PL* 14; *JF* 5–6). These fundamental ideas and democratic principles can be used as the basic building-blocks of a political conception of justice (*JF* 27, 34–35; *PL* 8). A political conception of justice attempts to combine and organize these ideas in an innovative and insightful way so as to harmonize with our most firmly held, considered convictions at all levels of reflective scrutiny and thus seeks to provide us a basis for resolving deep disagreements (such as those regarding the proper understanding of freedom and equality) within the very political culture from which its basic ideas were sourced (*P*, 8–9; *CP* 393–394; *JF* 25–26). Accordingly, political principles and conceptions of justice, though formulated from ideas in the political culture, can play an edifying, self-clarifying role for the political culture and its citizens. This is especially so in public political debates and judicial decisions that grapple with basic, constitutional rights – matters where the political culture's otherwise implicit conceptions of citizen and society are most articulately bound up (*LHPP* 5; *JF* 122, 146–147; *CP* 571; *LP* 102–103).

The public political culture contains "the public political forum," which is the sole, discursive forum to which Rawls's idea of public reason applies, and then again, only to discussions of constitutional essentials and matters of basic justice therein (*PL* 442–443). This forum includes "the discourse of judges in their decisions, . . . the discourse of government officials, . . . and finally, the discourse of candidates for public office and their campaign managers" (*PL* 443). In order to follow public reason's ideal, politically moral (not legal) standards in the public political forum, a participant must, when debating matters of constitutional essentials and basic justice, decide upon and justify her official actions and decisions to her fellow citizens by gathering for them sufficient reasons that stem from what she sincerely believes to be the most reasonable conception of political justice and that she thinks her fellow citizens, as free, equal, and noncoerced, could at least accept as reasonable (*PL* 444–447, 450). The discourse of the political culture's public political forum is thus ideally limited to the content of public reason, which Rawls takes to be given by the principles and standards of a family of reasonable, liberal, political conceptions of justice (*PL* 450–451). Still, Rawls, takes a "wide view of public political culture" that permits beyond this, the contents of reasonable comprehensive doctrines to be introduced into discussions within the forums of the public political culture, recognizing that there may at times be positive reasons for their introduction, provided that "in due course [sufficient] proper political reasons," stemming from a reasonable political conception of justice, "are presented" (*PL* 462–466). All citizens can engage in the public political forum by politically advocating for particular candidates or parties (*PL* 215), but it is candidates and their campaign managers who are responsible to the standards of public reason for this advocacy done on their behalf (*PL* 443 n.9). Yet the ideal of public reason does hold "for how citizens are to vote in elections when constitutional essentials and matters of basic justice are at stake" (*PL* 215, 444–445), even though the *privacy* of the voting booth and its *secret* ballots are not public discussions and do not seem appropriately situated in the *public political forum* as opposed to, say, the wider, political culture (although Rawls never comments on this).

Distinct from the political culture is "the background culture," or the culture of civil society, that includes all citizens and their myriad associations, worldviews, discursive forums, and "full and open" discussions (*PL* 14, 382–4, 443–444). The background culture "is the culture of the social . . . the culture of daily life with its many associations," occupying the "point of view of citizens in the culture of civil society," where citizens can discuss anything and everything as protected by constitutionally enshrined fundamental liberties of speech, thought, conscience, and association, among others (*PL* 14, 382–383, 443–444). Rawls does not view such a wider, background culture as somehow pre-political or voluntary. Rather, civil society's background structure of basic institutions, including the fundamental liberties they embed, have a "prior and fundamental role . . . in establishing a social world within which alone we can develop . . . into free and equal citizens," realize our moral capacities, and first acquire our comprehensive worldviews and individual self-conceptions (*PL* 41, 43).

The background culture encompasses all of society's comprehensive doctrines: it is here that believers in a comprehensive worldview instruct new generations, explain their doctrines, and debate with others open-endedly about their respective views (*PL* 382). In the background culture, citizens affirming particular comprehensive doctrines may "urge far tighter standards of reasonableness and truth" based in their own worldviews than that of the political notion of reasonableness with which political-constructivist, liberal conceptions of justice operate, and "may regard many [other comprehensive] doctrines as plainly . . . untrue" based on their own worldview's standards (*PL* 60 n.13). Still, to be politically reasonable themselves, such citizens must countenance these rival comprehensive views as nevertheless *politically* reasonable (if they are so) in the public reason of the public, political culture. But the idea of public reason does not apply to the background culture and its reasoning (*PL* xlviii, 220, 382 n.13, 443–444). Instead, to the background culture belongs civil society's numerous associations and their many, respective "nonpublic reasons," i.e. reasoning that is nonpublic with respect to society's citizens *generally*, even though still social and public (not private) with respect to the relevant group's members (*PL* 220). The associations in civil society, which include universities, churches, professional societies, and groups of all sorts, each have their own nonpublic reason, with standards and procedures that vary based on the organization's nature and goals (*PL* 220–221).

In the background culture, "endless political discussions of ideas and doctrines are commonplace everywhere" (*PL* 383). Rawls thinks that political conceptions of justice can play an educational role for citizens within civil society (more extensive than its analogous role in the public, political culture), exposing them in schooling and elsewhere to certain ideal conceptions of constitutionally democratic citizenship, political society, liberty, and equality, which they can "bring to democratic politics" and the political culture when they begin to actively participate (*LHPP* 5–7; *PL* 382–384; *CP* 571; *LP* 102–103). It is in the background culture of civil society that, according to Rawls, we citizens freely discuss reasonable, liberal political conceptions of justice, such as "how justice as fairness is to be formulated, and whether this or that aspect of it seems acceptable" (*PL* 382). Rawls understands *justice as fairness* to address its arguments about political justice to the "audience of citizens in civil society" as "any democratic doctrine" must, and *justice as fairness* has the "primary aim" of being "presented to and understood by" this audience for their consideration (*PL* 384). Even though "citizens' debates may, but need not, be reasonable and deliberative" in the background culture, still the "overall criterion" of reasonableness for a political conception of justice is deeply considered, well-reasoned scrutiny and affirmation of the conception compared to its rivals (i.e. "full reflective equilibrium") by all citizens in civil society (*PL* 383–385, 443–444). Additionally, political conceptions of justice are discussed "often from within peoples' comprehensive doctrines" in the background culture (*PL* xlviii). Such discussions in civil society are requisite for the "full justification" of a political conception of justice, in which citizens embed the conception within their comprehensive views (*PL* 386–387). Discussions of the ways in which various political principles and settled convictions might be seen to have "their roots in comprehensive doctrines" are likewise part of the background culture (*PL* 151–152 n.16).

Mediating between the public political culture and the background culture, is the "*nonpublic* political culture" which includes "media – properly so named – of all kinds: newspapers, reviews and magazines, television and radio," etc. (*PL*, 443–444 n.13, emphasis added). In the nonpublic political culture, Rawls's idea of public reason does not apply. The idea of a nonpublic political culture is a late-coming and sparsely mentioned addition for Rawls, and it is likely (at least in part) a product of his exchange with Jürgen Habermas (see *PL* lecture ix). Indeed, Rawls asks us to compare his account of these three cultures to "Habermas's account of the public sphere" (*PL* 443–444 n.13). Habermas sees a *mediating* role, similar to Rawls's nonpublic political culture, for "informal public spheres," which are sensitive to problems and concerns raised by civil society's many associations (themselves attuned to difficulties of their members), and which distill these into publicly accessible considerations, communicating them to the formal, politically institutionalized public spheres that have more demanding institutional and procedural strictures on discourse and decisions (Habermas 1996, 307–314, 356–387).

Micah Lewin

SEE ALSO:

Basic structure of society
Comprehensive doctrine
Fundamental ideas (in justice as fairness)
Public political culture
Public reason

D

50.

DANIELS, NORMAN

NORMAN DANIELS (b. 1942), currently Professor of Ethics and Population Health at Harvard School of Public Health, is one of the philosophers who has done most to explore and enrich Rawls's approach to social justice. Daniels was a graduate student in the Department of Philosophy at Harvard, although his own dissertation was not in moral or political philosophy, but concerned with Thomas Reid's treatment of geometry, and was supervised not by Rawls but by Hilary Putnam. Over the course of his career, Daniels has stood in a number of relations to Rawls's theory – from early critic, to extender and systematizer, through to acting as a defender of Rawls against a range of later critics.

Daniels edited the first collection of critical articles on *TJ*, *Reading Rawls* (Daniels 1975), which brought together many of the most significant early discussions of Rawls's theory, including pieces by Nagel, Dworkin, Hart, and Scanlon. Daniels's own piece in this collection, "Equal Liberty and Unequal Worth of Liberty," stands as one of the most interesting and powerful challenges to Rawls's view from the left, and later earned a clarifying response from Rawls (*PL* 324–331; *JF* 148–152). Daniels has also been one of the leading defenders and developers of Rawls's philosophical methodology of reflective equilibrium (Daniels 1996).

Perhaps Daniels's largest contribution has been his extension of Rawls's theory to cover issues of health and the distribution of health-care resources. Rawls himself made the simplifying assumption that citizens are fully cooperating members of society, idealizing away from circumstances under which citizens fall below that threshold due to accident or illness (*JF* 175). Daniels extends Rawls's approach by relaxing that idealization, and considering citizens' entitlements of justice to access health-care resources that allow them to return to the

179

range of normal functioning. His suggestion, which Rawls seems to have found sympathetic (see *PL* 184–185; *JF* 175), is that one should approach these questions through the principle of fair equality of opportunity, with "species normal functioning" being seen as a precondition for an individual enjoying fair opportunities (see Daniels 1985).

Pursuing the agenda set by this research on the distribution of health care has led Daniels to develop important further work on rationing across age groups, and related problems of justice between overlapping generations. He has developed the "prudential lifespan account" of justice between age groups (see Daniels 1988), an idealized procedure in which prudent planners, operating behind a partial veil of ignorance, deliberate on how resources should be distributed to make their lives go as well as possible. Through this procedure, Daniels argues both that we must aim to preserve a "normal opportunity range" throughout our lives, and that age rationing can be a requirement of justice. As one of the most significant landmarks in the field of intergenerational justice, Daniels's work on justice between age groups has attracted a significant degree of critical attention, in response to which he has gone on to modify his account in recent years (see Daniels 2008b, 2009).

Daniels's recent work on health has broadened out from its earlier focus on medical interventions and health-care resources, toward a more holistic and sociologically informed concern with both public health and the social determinants of health, and with fair procedures for public deliberation and justification with regard to health-related priorities (see Daniels 2008a).

In his role as defender of Rawls's approach to justice against some of its more influential critics, Daniels's "Democratic Equality: Rawls's Complex Egalitarianism" (Daniels 2003) stands out for its force and sophistication. In it, Daniels shows how Rawls's theory can overcome some of the lines of critique advanced against it: from luck egalitarians concerned with the full eradication of morally arbitrary distributive contingencies; from advocates of Amartya Sen's capabilities approach; and from the specific criticisms of the operation of the difference principle associated with G. A. Cohen. In developing this defence of Rawls's "complex" egalitarianism, Daniels provides a rich account of the relationship between distributive questions and the question of how citizens relate to each other as democratic equals, and of the nature of a social ethos of justice.

Daniels stands out as a leading theorist of social justice in the Rawlsian tradition who extensively engages both with ideal theory and with the complex practicalities of social reality. In 1985, he wrote: "[a]n essay in applied philosophy has its risks – it risks frustrating both the professional philosopher and specialists in the area of application ... For some of them, the discussion starts a bit too close to the ground to really fly," while for others "this discussion is never down to earth enough." (Daniels 1985, xi) Daniels's work stands as an outstanding example for those who see value in an intermediate space, in which we both examine practical issues through a philosophical lens, and engage in philosophy with a sense of prevailing social realities.

Martin O'Neill and Juliana Bidadanure

SEE ALSO:

Difference principle
Fair equality of opportunity
Health and health care
Reflective equilibrium

51.

DECENT SOCIETIES

THE NOTION OF a decent people plays a key role in Rawls's views about international affairs. One central part of Rawls's project in *The Law of Peoples* is to determine the appropriate boundaries, extent, and nature of liberal toleration in shaping liberal foreign policy. A decent people or society is a theoretical construct that assists in understanding what liberal tolerance requires in the international sphere.

If we are aiming at peaceful coexistence and cooperation in the international realm, what kinds of societies must liberals tolerate? Are there any kinds of nonliberal societies which can be admitted as societies of good standing in the international community? Under what conditions, if any, may liberals defensibly decide not to tolerate certain regimes? In a world filled with much diversity, what kinds of peoples should we consider as legitimate, indeed perhaps as allies, in securing a peaceful world order? And are there some actions that are so repugnant that they might warrant coercive intervention? In order to answer such questions, Rawls introduces the theoretical construct of a people who are nonliberal and yet sufficiently committed to certain ideals that they can be accorded recognitional legitimacy and equal standing in international affairs. These are decent peoples.

Rawls distinguishes between several different kinds of societies such as liberal democratic societies, decent societies, outlaw states, and burdened societies. He argues that liberal societies should tolerate not only each other but also decent societies. Outlaw states, in contrast, are not to be tolerated and, indeed, "in grave cases may be subjected to forceful sanctions and even to intervention" (*LP* 81). Although decent societies do not accept liberal principles of justice, unlike outlaw states they have features that are sufficient to command the respect of liberal societies and admission into a Society of Peoples. Like the other models of societies, the idea of a decent society is a theoretical construction designed to highlight essential features that are relevant for determining the appropriateness of toleration. Rawls does not address the question of whether some – or any – actual society meets the criteria. Instead, he presents the hypothetical country of Kazanistan to illustrate the features that such a country might have.

Decent societies must meet several important criteria (*LP* 64–66). The first criterion is that they are peaceful societies. They neither embrace aggressive aims nor pursue their aims in aggressive ways. The second criterion has three parts. Decent societies: (a) have a common good conception of justice which includes securing human rights for all of their members; (b) impose bona fide moral duties on all persons within the territory beyond human rights; (c) administer the legal system in accordance with a common good conception of justice. All three parts of the second criterion require further elaboration, which follows.

Rawls claims, in the first part of the second condition, that the system of law and its idea of justice must secure basic human rights for all members of the people. Protecting such rights is a minimum condition for a decent scheme of political and social cooperation to be in place. At this stage in the argument the list of particular rights that Rawls *appears* to offer is very short (*LP* 65), however, it is commonly overlooked that Rawls in fact gives an indicative rather than an exhaustive list here. In describing these, Rawls includes the following: (i) the right to life, by which he means the rights to the means of subsistence and security; (ii) the right to liberty, which equates to freedom from slavery or forced occupation but also includes some liberty of conscience, enough to ensure freedom of religion and thought; (iii) the right to personal property; and (iv) the right to formal equality, by which he means only that similar cases be treated similarly. (See also *LP* 80 n.23.) Rawls believes all peoples (whether liberal or nonliberal) have reason to endorse this list of human rights and that the list is not parochial or infected by Western bias. The second part of the second condition that a decent people must satisfy is that a decent people's system of law must impose proper moral duties and obligations on all who reside within the territory. They recognize these duties as in accordance with their common good idea of justice rather than imposed by force. So their system of law embodies a decent scheme of political and social cooperation, rather in contrast with a slave society. The third part of the second condition is that judges and others who administer the legal system must believe that the law is guided by a common good idea of justice and should be prepared to defend the laws in public, should they be challenged.

Though not a formal part of the definition of decent peoples, Rawls does also devote a substantial section of the exposition (*LP* §9) to the idea of the importance of a decent consultation mechanism or what he frequently calls a "decent consultation hierarchy" (*LP* 71). A decent people should have a consultation mechanism whereby constituent groups are consulted in an attempt to reflect all groups' significant interests. The nature of the "should" is a bit obscure, but he does make additional remarks that suggest the consultation mechanism is indeed part of the requirements for the constitution of a decent people. He says for instance: "the legal system of a decent hierarchical people must contain a decent consultation hierarchy" (*LP* 71) and also "the basic structure of the society must include a family of representative bodies whose role in the hierarchy is to take part in an established procedure of consultation and to look after what the people's common good idea of justice regards as the important interests of all members of the people" (*LP* 71). The decent consultation mechanism allows opportunities for different, especially dissenting voices, to be heard. While this opportunity for input might well differ from mechanisms we view as central to democracy (such as equal opportunities to participate in elections), the mechanism must allow people to express their views, and this is important (inter alia) to ensure that the people's common good idea of justice is represented in the legal system.

Rawls describes a case of a hypothetical decent people, Kazanistan, that he believes fulfills his requirements. Kazanistan is an idealized Islamic people in which human rights are protected, but only Muslims are eligible for positions of political authority and have influence in important political matters, though other religions are otherwise tolerated and encouraged to pursue a flourishing cultural life (*LP* 76). Rawls believes Kazanistan can be admitted to the society of well-ordered peoples. Liberal societies should tolerate states such as Kazanistan. Anticipating that some might have trouble with the idea that such a society should be considered as a member of the Society of Peoples, Rawls remarks that "something like Kazanistan is the best we can realistically – and coherently – hope for" (*LP* 78). Moreover, Rawls believes that liberal peoples should "try to encourage decent peoples and not frustrate their vitality by coercively insisting that all societies be liberal" (*LP* 62). He argues that it is crucial that we maintain mutual respect among peoples.

The defining criteria that Rawls outlines for societies to count as decent well-ordered people seem appropriate. We cannot expect all societies to conform to *all* the norms of a constitutional democracy as a requirement of peacefully coexisting and cooperating with them. So, what are the essential criteria which must be satisfied for societies to be decent? The key ingredients are that they recognize essential elements of what it is to have a decent life and to enjoy a decent scheme of social and political cooperation. Clearly, the criteria picked out are salient: we can exclude aggressive societies pretty quickly as they are not committed to the peace necessary for decent lives. The core human rights Rawls picks out are central entitlements needed to secure a decent life, as are the other elements of the second criterion, centrally animated by a common good conception of justice, which also informs decent terms of cooperation.

Indeed, the criteria imposed on decent societies might be thought of as necessary ingredients for political legitimacy. Based on the idea of what is needed for social cooperation, a society which meets Rawls's criteria for decent peoples will enjoy widespread support, since it has public processes for collective decision-making that not only allow input and dissent, but also generate genuine duties and obligations and are animated by a conception of justice that includes consideration of the good of all members. These features mean that resulting laws are legitimate, in stark contrast with outlaw states where none of the legitimating features are present. (See Mandle 2005.) Decent peoples, being well-ordered, are equal members of the global Society of Peoples and deserve equal recognition status to liberal peoples. (Compare Freeman 2006a and Reidy 2004 with Pogge 1994 and Tan 2000.) By contrast, no such tolerance or recognition is owed to outlaw states. Importantly, decent peoples – in virtue of being decent – would have reason to accept Rawls's Law of Peoples as embodied in the eight principles that Rawls articulates. This further separates them sharply from outlaw states.

Gillian Brock

SEE ALSO:

Common good idea of justice
Duty of assistance
Human rights
Law of Peoples
Liberal people
Society of Peoples

52.

DELIBERATIVE RATIONALITY

N A THEORY OF JUSTICE (§64 and elsewhere), "deliberative rationality" is Rawls's name for our capacity of reflective choice – a capacity that transcends the various principles of rational choice of which it makes use. It operates on that range of choices still left over once the explicit principles of rational choice have been exhausted. Rawls gives a simple example of planning a holiday, one on which we want to study a certain kind of art. This aim rules out various possible destinations, but leaves us with Paris and Rome as equally good prospects. We also care about seeing Christendom's most famous church and its most famous museum; but since Paris and Rome each score one for two on these, this will not advance our decision. "[S]ooner or later," Rawls comments, "we will reach incomparable aims between which we must choose with deliberative rationality" (*TJ* 483).

In addition to being of interest in its own right, this conception of deliberative rationality plays two important roles in Rawls's theory, each motivated by the thought that the idea of goodness cannot be adequately captured by the principles of rationality that people have so far succeeded in articulating. First, it is an important working part of Rawls's definition of the good for persons, thus indirectly contributing to Rawls's account of the good of justice, and hence to his argument for the potential congruence between justice and the good in the well-ordered society of justice as fairness. Second, it does important work in Rawls's criticism of the kind of unity of self available to teleological (good-based) views, paving the way for his account of the superior unity of self offered by deontological theories.

Although Rawls does not purport to give an exhaustive list of principles of rational choice, his list is both interesting and surprisingly inclusive. Contrary to

Deliberative rationality / 187

the impression that part I of *A Theory of Justice* seems to leave with some readers, Rawls makes clear in part III that even rationality (as distinct from reasonableness) involves much more than simply narrowly selecting effective means to given ends. To this, he adds the "principle of inclusiveness" (if plan A achieves all of the ends achieved by plan B, plus more, then plan A is to be preferred) and a parallel "principle of the greater likelihood" (*TJ* 362). Rawls comments that these simple "counting principles," as he calls them, "do not require a further analysis or alteration of our desires" (*TJ* 364). He goes on, however, to suggest some additional rational principles and "devices" at our disposal for analyzing and criticizing our ends. Ends that are impossible to achieve are criticizable, as are ends that stem from "excessive generalization" from our past experience (*TJ* 368). A "principle of postponement" holds that plans that defer certain decisions until later are often to be preferred, as they allow us more flexibility in "fruitfully combin[ing our aims and interests] into one scheme of conduct," a process in which some of our ends "are weeded out" (*TJ* 360–361, 369). Finally, Rawls adds three temporal principles (*TJ* 369): a principle of prudence, which demands that one not operate with any pure time preference among the different stages of one's own life (*TJ* §45); a principle of continuity, which demands appropriate connections among different periods of one's life; and a principle of nondeclining expectations.

In introducing these many principles of rational choice, Rawls writes that they "are to be given by enumeration so that eventually they replace the concept of rationality" (*TJ* 361). Given his description of our deliberative rationality as a capacity that enables us to make choices even when the principles of rational choice have been exhausted, however, it is clear that he does not think that we have yet reached this eventuality. Our practical rationality clearly includes our deliberative rationality, which enables us to conduct "rational deliberation" (*TJ* 367) that extends beyond reliance upon enumerated principles and thereby gives rise to rationality in a fuller sense (*TJ* 370).

Deliberative rationality, as Rawls describes it, involves two core capacities that enable us to go beyond the principles of rational choice enumerated so far. One is the kind of "direct self-knowledge" that allows agents to assess the relative intensity of their own desires (*TJ* 365). This capacity is one to which we might well have recourse in settling an issue like whether to take our art-focused vacation in Rome or in Paris. The other is our capacity to analyze our aims, potentially enabling us "to find a more detailed or more illuminating description" of our aims and to "trim, reshape, and transform [them] in a variety of ways as we try to fit them together" (*TJ* 483). Although Rawls does not trumpet or elaborate the point, these passages provide the basis for a noninstrumentalist understanding of practical rationality, according to which our deliberative rationality enables us rationally to revise our ends. Crucially, in addition to transcending the enumerated principles of rational choice, deliberative rationality enables one to transcend one's initial set of aims, at least to an extent (cf. *PL* 85 n.33).

These observations about the potential reach of deliberative rationality help us see what is controversial and interesting in Rawls's definition of the good for persons, which importantly rests on the idea of deliberative rationality. In building up to the idea of the good for persons in chapter 7 of *TJ*, Rawls proceeds in a methodical and stepwise way that gives the account a dull and pedantic aura. First, he offers a fully general account of goodness as rationality, according to which, roughly, a good x has the features it is rational to want in an x. Then, after elaborating the notion of a life plan, he describes what it is rational to want in a plan of life, enumerating the basic principles of rational choice at that point and noting that these "principles are not in general sufficient to rank the plans open to us" (*TJ* 364). Finally, he characterizes a person's good in terms of the life plan that the person, having full knowledge and imaginative appreciation of the relevant facts, would choose with deliberative rationality (*TJ* 370; cf. 358–359). Since deliberative rationality importantly involves the capacity to revise our aims, this definition implies that one cannot adequately characterize a person's good simply by reference to a fixed set of ends or desires.

As Rawls himself emphasized (*TJ* 44), a mere definition cannot establish such an important substantive point. He defends this conclusion in chapter 9 of *TJ*, drawing on the idea of deliberative rationality as he does so. The relevant sections begin with the general idea of a so-called "dominant end" and build to a critique of the unity of the self afforded by good-based views. A dominant end would provide us with a way to make all of our choices by means of the counting principles. We could, in effect, simply select those options that would maximize the expected achievement of the dominant end. In criticizing this idea, Rawls reminds us that we seem to care about many different things and rely upon deliberative rationality to choose when this multiplicity of attachments prevents the counting principles from settling upon an answer for us. After substantively criticizing some of the prominent candidates for dominant ends (see also *TJ* 365–366), he concludes that pleasure is the only attractive one. Yet pleasure cannot serve as a dominant end, he argues, for buried under the label "pleasure" are the very same sorts of qualitative difference and evaluative incommensurability that make deliberative rationality inescapable in the general case (*TJ* 488).

Deliberative rationality / 189

The close of the section on pleasure contains one of the most notorious and difficult of Rawls's passages, one that a focus on the idea of deliberative rationality helps us understand. A person is not to be understood in terms of a fixed set of ends. "For the self is prior to the ends which are affirmed by it; even a dominant end must be chosen from among numerous possibilities. There is no way to get beyond deliberative rationality" (*TJ* 491). As Rawls had said when introducing the idea of deliberative rationality, "while rational principles can focus our judgments and set up guidelines for reflection, we must finally choose for ourselves" (*TJ* 365).

Henry S. Richardson

SEE ALSO:

Conception of the good
Congruence
Counting principles
Goodness as rationality
Plan of life
Thin and full theory of good
Unity of self

53.

DEMOCRACY

RAWLS'S TEXTS SAY very little about the day-to-day practice of democracy: there are only occasional, passing references to competitive multiparty elections, processes of political mobilization and public opinion formation, law making, the administration of justice, and so on. As Amy Gutmann points out, the index of *Political Liberalism* contains zero references to democracy, while *Theory*'s index contains only one – a reference to "democratic equality," to Rawls's own demanding interpretation of the second principle of justice (Gutmann 2002, 170; see also *TJ* §13). But the idea of democracy *is* clearly important to Rawls. In the Preface to the revised edition of *Theory*, he says that justice as fairness is meant to provide "a philosophical conception for a constitutional democracy" (*TJ* xi). And in the original Preface, Rawls says that justice as fairness "constitutes the most appropriate moral basis for a democratic society" (*TJ* viii).

Joshua Cohen helps us to fill in Rawls's meaning in these prefatory remarks (Cohen 2002, 91–103). Justice as fairness, says Cohen, is a theory for a democratic political community in three important ways. First, Rawls's theory outlines a democratic *regime*: justice as fairness requires institutional arrangements that secure and protect the standard bundle of democratic rights, including citizens' equal rights to participation and association, conscience and expression (*TJ* 174–175 and 194–196). Second, Rawls's theory outlines a democratic *society*, one that is animated by an egalitarian ethos, by the public recognition of all its members as free and equal co-authors of the basic structure of society (*TJ* 336 and 479–480). And third, Rawls's theory outlines a *deliberative* democracy: a society of conscientious reason givers, each of whom is committed to strategies of justification that respect the freedom and equality of all (*TJ* 17–18, 195–200, 229, and 313–318). Thus, in Rawls's view, a fully just society is one in which (1) every

Democracy / 191

citizen is in secure possession of the same bundle of political rights (the institutional argument); (2) the basic structure ensures the fair value of the political liberties for each citizen, there is fair equality of opportunity for jobs and positions of authority, and any structural inequalities in expected wealth and income are limited by the difference principle (the ethos argument); and (3) each citizen must be treated by others in ways that respect their status as free and equal (the interpersonal–deliberative argument).

(1) Rawls's first principle of justice is a principle for the guidance of democratic institutions: it states that "political liberty (the right to vote and to hold public office)" must be equally distributed to every citizen (*TJ* 53). Stated more fully: "all citizens are to have an equal right to take part in, and to determine the outcome of, the constitutional process that establishes the laws with which they are to comply" (*TJ* 194; see also *PL* §viii.2). But, for Rawls, the provision of formal political equality is not sufficient: what is essential is that all citizens can make *effective use* of their political liberties, that the political liberties of every citizen are fairly valued (*TJ* §36). *Having* a voice – the formal right to participate – is not enough; what matters is having one's voice *heard* (*PL* 361).

This important distinction is motivated by Rawls's deep sensitivity to the tendency of democracy to degenerate into plutocracy: "The liberties protected by the principle of participation lose much of their value whenever those who have greater private means are permitted to use their advantage to control the course of public debate...these inequalities will enable those better situated to exercise a larger influence over the development of legislation" (*TJ* 198; see also *PL* §§ viii.7 and viii.12). So far, the "fair value" argument is fundamentally an instrumental one: when political power and influence are unequally distributed according to wealth, "just background institutions are unlikely to be either established or maintained" (*PL* 328). For when individuals or economic factions regard political power as nothing more than the efficient means to accumulation, "citizens tend to become resentful, cynical, and apathetic," and the possibility of mutually beneficial social cooperation is negated (*PL* 363). In order for democratic processes "to yield just and effective legislation," political power must therefore be made independent of economic power (*PL* 328). Politics must be "set free from the curse of money" (*PL* 449).

According to Rawls, the "fair value" argument is also a better "fit with our considered convictions" about justice (*PL* 327). Here, Rawls takes his normative cue from the public culture and evolving political practice of the American republic: the "fair value" thesis, he says, is implicit, in the Constitution (Article 1, §2), in various amendments to the Constitution (especially the 14th

Amendment), and in many of the Supreme Court's interpretations of the Constitution and the amendments (*Wesberry* and *Reynolds*) (*PL* §VIII.12; see also *JF* §7.2, *LHPP* 1 and *PL* 453); hence Rawls's disappointment and dismay with the Court's failure (in *Buckley* and *First National Bank*) to act as the guarantor of the fair value of the political liberties (*PL* 359–360).

How, then, can we maintain the fair value of the political liberties? Rawls provides some suggestions, including institutionalized forms of economic redistribution to prevent the excessive concentration of money and power, as well as public funding to encourage free public discussion (*TJ* 198). Most crucially, the financial health and independence of political parties must be guaranteed through the legal provision of tax revenues: "If society does not bear the costs of organization, and party funds need to be solicited from the more advantaged social and economic interests, the pleadings of these groups are bound to receive excessive attention" (*TJ* 198–199; see also *PL* 328). Rawls sees clearly that this will likely require legal (and judicially upheld) constraints on certain (economically advantaged) citizens' (or groups') political activities (i.e. their ability to influence the political process through campaign donations). This may entail certain restrictions on their free speech, but this, he says, may very well be a worthwhile trade-off: "For how else is the full and effective voice of all citizens to be maintained? Since it is a matter of one basic liberty over another, the liberties protected by the First Amendment may have to be adjusted in the light of other requirements, in this case the requirement of the fair value of the political liberties" (*PL* 362; cf. Rawls's statement on the lexical priority of the first principle at *TJ* §11).

(2) For Rawls, democracy is not *merely* a set of institutional arrangements aimed at the common good (*TJ* 205–206). Democracy *also* describes a political society animated by a particular *ethos* and understanding of the common good. Its public culture recognizes the freedom and equality of all its members: "The grounds for self-government are not solely instrumental. Equal political liberty when assured its fair value is bound to have a profound effect on the moral quality of civic life...these [political] freedoms strengthen men's sense of their own worth" (*TJ* 205–206). Stated more fully:

> The basis for self-esteem in a just society is not...one's income share but the publicly affirmed distribution of fundamental rights and liberties. And this distribution being equal, everyone has a similar and secure status when they meet to conduct the common affairs of the wider society. No one is inclined to look beyond the constitutional affirmation of equality for further political ways of securing his status...a subordinate ranking in

Democracy / 193

public life would indeed be humiliating and destructive of self-esteem. (*TJ* 477)

Equal political liberties – when their "fair value" is secure – are the essential guarantor of citizens' self-respect (*TJ* 478; *PL* 318f.). And, of course, self-respect is the most important primary good. It includes:

> a person's sense of his own value, his secure conviction that his conception of his good, his plan of life is worth carrying out. And second, self-respect implies a confidence in one's abilities ... When we feel that our plans are of little value, we cannot pursue them with pleasure or take delight in their execution ... Without [self-respect] nothing may seem like worth doing, or if some things have value for us, we lack the will to strive for them. All desire and activity becomes empty and vain, and we sink into apathy and cynicism. (*TJ* 386; see also *PL* §vɪɪɪ.6)

Democracy is the regime of secure and widespread self-esteem: the institutional arrangements and egalitarian public ethos of democratic regimes thus maximize the possibility of human flourishing. Rawls's point is that we need to have respect for ourselves as ends-setters, and it is our status as an equal citizen that provides this essential primary good: the status of citizen is what gives us both the institutional space and psychological desire to explore, pursue, and revise our system of ends, individually and in conjunction with like-minded fellows (*TJ* §79 and *PL* §§vɪɪɪ.5–6).

According to Rawls, widespread self-respect is the foundation of political fraternity and fellow feeling. Why? Because "one who is confident in himself is not grudging in the appreciation of others" (*TJ* 387). When individual self-esteem is secure, the pleasures of community are apparent: "With the constant assurance expressed by [the principles of justice and the political institutions designed in light of them], persons will develop a secure sense of their own worth that forms the basis of the love of humankind" (*TJ* 438; see also *TJ* 403). The Rawlsian argument for democracy thus begins from individualistic premises – the individual's need for certain primary goods – and it is from the good of individuals that Rawls derives the social values and the good of community (*TJ* §§17, 41, and 81).

(3) How do citizens give expression to the social values? How is the good of community made manifest in the day-to-day practices of political life? The answer to these and related questions can be found in the idea of public reason,

which "belongs to a conception of a well-ordered constitutional democratic society" (*PL* 440). "How," Rawls asks, "is the ideal of public reason realized" in the public culture of civil society? (*PL* 444)? It is realized by citizens' willing fulfillment of the duty of civility – the (moral not legal/punitive) duty to "offer one another fair terms of cooperation," to publicly justify the coercive use of state power with reference to "reasons … shared by all citizens as free and equal," "reasons consistent with seeing other citizens as equals" (*PL* 446, 447, 448 n.21). And this is no easy feat: Rawls recognizes that human beings possess a natural "zeal to embody the whole truth in politics" (*PL* 442). And yet, given the fact of pluralism, civility requires that citizens combat – *self*-combat – their inclination to justify the exercise of power with reference to comprehensive moral and religious views.

In the end, being reasonable requires that we fulfill the duty of civility in order to give expression to an essential moral power, the sense of justice (*PL* §§II.1, VI.2, and VIII.6). And the widespread willingness to be reasonable – to abide by the constraints of public reason – is the essential precondition of the stability, and the source of the vitality, of democratic polities:

> Taking part in political life does not … answer to the ambition to dictate to others, since each is now required to moderate his claims by what everyone is able to recognize as just. The public will to consult and to take everyone's beliefs and interests into account lays the foundation for civic friendship and shapes the ethos of the public culture. (*TJ* 205)

Jeffrey Bercuson

SEE ALSO:

Basic liberties
Comprehensive doctrine
Political liberalism, justice as fairness
Public reason
Self-respect

54.

DEMOCRATIC PEACE

N THE LAW OF PEOPLES, Rawls argues that a world of liberal and decent peoples would be peaceful and stable for the "right" reasons (*LP* 44–54). He draws on the democratic peace thesis. This thesis holds that war is less likely to occur between two democracies than between either a democracy and a nondemocratic society or two nondemocratic societies. Another version of the thesis holds that democracies are simply more peaceful than nondemocratic societies. Rawls invokes this latter interpretation in his argument, though other interpretations may support his position too. (See Hayes 2011 and Ray 1998 for reviews of the democratic peace literature.)

The democratic peace thesis consists of a factual and a causal claim. The factual claim refers to the historical absence of war between democracies. Some trace this peace back to the early 1800s, while others hold that the post-World War II era is most significant, since few democracies existed before 1939.

The causal claim holds that some feature of democratic society causes the peace. There are several competing, and perhaps complementary, versions of the causal claim. One holds that shared values lead to trust between democracies. Another holds that constitutional restraints inhibit war. The economic interdependence view holds that war is unattractive because it interferes with trade and other economic relations. Reelection constraint accounts depend on democratic voting and the political consequences of unpopular wars.

Political realists reject the causal claim. They admit that the post-World War II era has seen a democratic peace, but hold that the cause is US world dominance during this period. On their view, the peace is at best a *modus vivendi*.

Rawls rejects this skepticism, and argues that liberal peoples are peaceful because they are "satisfied." A liberal people is satisfied when (a) there is fair equality of opportunity, especially in education and training, (b) citizens have the means to make effective use of their basic freedoms, (c) social security is available, (d) basic health care is assured, and (e) elections are publicly financed and information on policy issues is available. Under these conditions, the members of a liberal people have their basic needs met and have proper pride in their society. Further, their interests, now as a people, are compatible with the interests of other liberal peoples. They will not be moved by power or glory, nor will they seek to impose an ideology, such as a state religion, upon others. Further, they will not be driven by a need for ever greater wealth (*LP* 107–108), and, to the extent that they do seek to increase their wealth, will prefer peaceful commerce to conquest.

Liberal peoples have only two fundamental interests: first, to secure their independence as peoples and to guarantee the liberty, security, and well-being of their members, and, second, to have self-respect, which rests on their shared understanding of their achievements as a people (*LP* 34). To the extent that liberal peoples are satisfied, their fundamental interests are met and they will not be aggressive. As long as no society attempts to harm a liberal people, it will remain peaceful.

Wenar and Milanovic (2009) object to Rawls's claims about the actual economic interests of liberal peoples, holding that Rawls underestimates this. Further, they think Rawls is mistaken to deny that inequality between peoples will lead to wounded pride and undermine self-respect. They also question whether Rawls's understanding of liberal foreign policy-making is sufficiently realistic.

Rawls concedes that, historically, liberal peoples have gone to war, but holds this does not conflict with his argument. He draws a distinction between wars of self-defense (*LP* 48) and wars caused by shortcomings in actual constitutional democratic regimes, such as when the United States overturned democracies in Chile, Guatemala, Iran, and Nicaragua (*LP* 53). Wars of self-defense are started by satisfied societies, but for the sake of security and safety against some threat from an unsatisfied society. Other wars are caused by imperfectly democratic societies, societies that are unsatisfied in some way. Rawls attributes US interference in Latin America and Iran to monopolistic and oligarchic interests acting in secret. A world of satisfied societies, he maintains, would be peaceful.

Rawls includes decent peoples in his peaceful world order. This is a problem, because decent peoples are nonliberal and nondemocratic, and cannot be satisfied in the same way that liberal peoples can. Thus, it is not clear how their existence in a peaceful world order is related to the democratic peace.

Doyle (2006) and Wenar and Milanovic (2009) interpret Rawls as claiming that "peace-prone" liberal peoples will not start wars with decent peoples, just because decent peoples are nonaggressive. But Doyle objects that while liberal peoples may be peaceful toward one another, they may not be peaceful toward nondemocratic societies. Doyle sees democracies forming an exclusive club, rooted in common commitments and norms, which decent peoples and other nonliberal societies are excluded from. Wenar and Milanovic point out that Rawls does not argue that decent peoples will be peaceful toward others, but instead simply stipulates their peacefulness.

Riker (2009) offers a different interpretation, arguing that the democratic peace thesis should be extended to include decent peoples. Riker points out the democratic peace is secured not primarily through democratic institutions such as voting, but through several norms and practices common to democratic societies. He argues that analogs of some important norms and practices can be found in decent peoples, and that this renders them reliably peaceful too. Riker argues that decent peoples would be satisfied, though in nonliberal terms, and that they would have constitutional restraints on war.

Walter J. Riker

SEE ALSO:

Decent societies
Democracy
Human rights
Law of Peoples
Society of Peoples

55.

DEONTOLOGICAL VS. TELEOLOGICAL THEORIES

J USTICE AS FAIRNESS is a deontological view. Rawls defines deontological moral theories as nonteleological theories rather than nonconsequentialist theories because "all ethical doctrines worth our attention take consequences into account in judging rightness" (*TJ* 26). The difference between deontological and teleological theories lies, then, not in the latter's attention and the former's lack of attention to consequences, but rather in the distinctive ways in which each relates the two fundamental concepts of any moral theory, the ideas of the right and the good (*TJ* 21).

Rawls follows Frankena and defines teleological theories as those that specify the good independently of the right and then define the right as that which maximizes the good (*TJ* 22). A theory is deontological, then, on Rawls's view, if it either does not define the right as that which maximizes the good or does not specify the good independently of the right. Rawls characterizes his own view, justice as fairness, as deontological in the first way, since it does not define the right as that which maximizes the good, but rather in terms of mutually intelligible and acceptable relations between free and equal persons (*TJ* 26).

Of course, justice as fairness is also deontological in the second way; that is, it does not specify the good independently of the right. To be sure, it characterizes the good most generally or abstractly as the satisfaction of rational desire and so independently of the right. And it invokes only this "thin theory" of the good in accounting for the rationality of the parties in the original position and the primary goods with respect to which they assess candidate principles of right or justice (*TJ* 348f.). So it may seem as if justice as fairness defines the right in terms of an independently specified idea of the good. But this is but one idea or conception of the good at work in justice as fairness, and it is by itself incomplete as an account of the good. A theory is not teleological simply because it makes use of some idea or conception of the good in order to explicate its conception of the right or justice. If it were then it would be hard to see how any theory could be other than teleological. What renders Rawls's view deontological, or anti-teleological, in the second way is that in setting out its complete theory or account of the good it invokes an account of right or justice worked out prior to and independently of that complete theory.

Within justice as fairness, then, the right and the good are complementary notions standing in complex relations. To work out the idea of the right, one must invoke some notion of the good. But to complete an account of the good, one must have already in hand a complete account of the right. The complexity of the complementary relations between the right and the good in justice as fairness reflects similar relations between the right and the good that Rawls finds in Kant's moral theory. Rawls identifies several conceptions of the good at work in Kant's moral theory, the majority but not all of which presuppose an independent conception of the right or the reasonable (*CP* 506–510). Similarly, with justice as fairness, he identifies several analogous conceptions of the good at work in the theory, the majority but not all of which presuppose an independent conception of the right or the reasonable (*PL* 176f; *JF* 140–142). In both theories, the conception of the right is fixed prior to and as a condition on the complete or full specification of the good.

Teleological theories treat our judgments of value or the good as fully separable from and fully explainable without any reference to our judgments regarding right. Of course, different teleological theories will offer different accounts of our judgments of value or the good. Hedonist theories will characterize them as best explained in terms of pleasure. Eudaimonist theories will characterize them as best explained in terms of happiness. Perfectionist theories will characterize them as best explained in terms of various human perfections. Rawls understands the classical utilitarian tradition as characterizing them as best explained in terms of the satisfaction of desire, or perhaps rational desire. The classical utilitarian tradition then defines the right as maximizing the aggregate, or on some accounts the per capita average, satisfaction of desire or rational desire.

Of course, for Rawls and justice as fairness, the right is specified not in terms of maximizing the good but rather in terms of mutually intelligible and acceptable relations and interactions between persons as free equals, relations paradigmatically cooperative and aimed at the or a common good. Further, while at the most general or abstract level Rawls is prepared to accept the utilitarian identification of the good with the satisfaction of rational desire, he is, unlike the utilitarian, unwilling to stop there. Finally, unlike the utilitarian who presupposes of persons no constraints on their desires other than that they are rational, Rawls is concerned with and addressing himself to human beings with a desire reciprocally to interact only reasonably within a social world mutually intelligible and acceptable to one another as free and equal persons. If this desire is creditable as rational, then it is not possible to specify a complete or full theory of the good apart from or prior to specifying the demands and priority of right or justice. Given this rational desire, the good is conditioned on right or justice. The good is realized only through the satisfaction of desires consistent with the prior and independent demands of right or justice.

One might suppose that since Rawls's justice as fairness is a deontological theory (not only in the sense that it does not define the right in terms of maximizing the good but also) in the sense that it affirms the independence and priority of the right to the good that it must embody some essential tension between the right and the good. But Rawls argues that properly understood the right and the good are fully or at least sufficiently congruent within justice as fairness. Indeed, their congruence is what underwrites the stability and unity of a society governed by justice as fairness.

In *A Theory of Justice* Rawls argued that within a society governed by justice as fairness human beings will naturally acquire a (principle- and conception-dependent) desire to act reasonably and share with others a social world mutually intelligible and acceptable to all as free and equal persons. This desire they will be able fully and publicly to vindicate as rational. Everyone will know that wanting and doing justice is part of each person's good. Rawls came over time to see that this so-called congruence argument unreasonably presupposed of citizens within a society governed by justice as fairness more uniformity or homogeneity in their moral views than it was reasonable to presuppose. It presupposed of all citizens a moral view more or less deontological and Kantian in its structure and content. But surely some citizens would continue to affirm teleological views, utilitarian, perfectionist or otherwise. If so, how then, Rawls asked, can we account for the stability and unity of a society governed by justice as fairness?

In *Political Liberalism* Rawls recast the so-called congruence argument of *TJ* by focusing more narrowly on the desire of the citizen qua citizen to act reasonably in the political domain and share with others a political-institutional order mutually intelligible and acceptable to all as free and equal citizens. This more narrowly defined desire is also fully and publicly creditable as rational, or at least as not irrational, even for those who affirm perfectionist or utilitarian moral doctrines. Thus, citizens affirming a wide range of moral views, from Kantian or

liberal Thomist deontological views to various forms of utilitarian or perfectionist teleological views, might all be able publicly to see that the good of each and
all inclines toward honoring the demands of right and justice, at least in the political domain and in their relations one to another as citizens. Of course, this more
narrowly defined desire to be politically reasonable is potentially in conflict with
desires for transcendent or otherworldly goods, desires that are not obviously
irrational and so the satisfaction of which cannot be dismissed as other than good.
Here the right and the good threaten to come apart. Rather than insisting on their
congruence, Rawls simply emphasizes the great weight of the political and civic
goods associated with the satisfaction of the desire to be politically reasonable and
expresses the hope that the weight of these goods will be sufficient, at least over
time, to transform or tame conflicting desires for transcendent or otherworldly
goods.

David A. Reidy

SEE ALSO:

Congruence
Kant, Immanuel
Perfectionism
Priority of the right over the good
Right, concept of and formal constraints of
Thin and full theories of the good
Utilitarianism

56.

DESERT

IN A THEORY OF JUSTICE, Rawls observes that "There is a tendency for common sense to suppose that income and wealth, and the good things in life generally, should be distributed according to moral desert. Justice is happiness according to virtue." However, he continues, "justice as fairness rejects this conception" (*TJ* 273). While Rawls's so-called "rejection of desert" is well known, what exactly he is rejecting and why is often misunderstood.

The first thing to note is that Rawls uses the term "desert" more narrowly than is common. Ordinarily, the grounds on which we might say that someone deserves something are very wide: a worker deserves a raise for her hard work and loyalty, a student deserves an A because he answered all of the questions correctly, a team deserves to win for playing well, a criminal deserves to be punished for breaking the law, etc. But Rawls is interested in a single, narrow use: the idea that as a matter of justice, individuals' entitlements should be determined by their degree of moral virtue. He signals this narrow use by typically using the term "moral desert" (as above) and associating it with the idea of "virtue" (as above), and by contrasting it with the broader idea of "deserving in the ordinary sense" (*TJ* 64; cf. 276).

Many (but not all) of the ordinary senses of "desert" fall under Rawls's definition of "legitimate expectations." When a just (or fair) institution is in place, its rules will specify certain benefits and burdens to be placed on participants based on various criteria. The principle of fairness says that those who voluntarily accept the benefits of participating in just institutions must comply with their requirements and accept their burdens (*TJ* 96). Legitimate expectations "are the other side, so to speak, of the principle of fairness and the natural duty of justice" (*TJ* 275). That is, when an institution is just (or fair) and individuals comply with its requirements, when they fulfill their duties and obligations, they have a legitimate expectation that they will receive the benefits specified by the rules of the institution. Rawls rejects the idea of rewarding moral virtue as the standard of distributive justice, but he certainly thinks that just institutions will satisfy people's legitimate expectations. Thus, he says that while "it is incorrect to say that just distributive shares reward individuals according to their moral worth...what we can say is that, in the traditional phrase, a just scheme gives each person his due; that is, it allots to each what he is entitled to as defined by the scheme itself" (*TJ* 275–276). Note, once again, that this account assumes that the institutional scheme is just.

The most common interpretation of Rawls's rejection of desert points to the following passage:

> We do not deserve our place in the distribution of native endowments, any more than we deserve our initial starting place in society. That we deserve the superior character that enables us to make the effort to cultivate our abilities is also problematic; for such character depends in good part upon fortunate family and social circumstances in earlier life for which we can claim no credit. The notion of desert does not apply here. (*TJ* 89. This passage was revised from the original edition of *TJ* 104.)

Rawls thinks it is *obvious* that we don't deserve our natural abilities or our initial starting place in society. And it *is* obvious when we remember that this simply amounts to the claim that our natural endowments and our initial starting place in society are not based on our moral virtue. However, in this passage, Rawls goes further and apparently argues that our developed abilities are undeserved as well, since they depend "in good part" upon factors "for which we can claim no credit." Many critics interpret Rawls as holding that a claim to deserve something can only be based on factors that themselves are deserved. Since there are no grounds that are entirely free from contingency, strictly speaking there is *nothing* that we deserve, and desert cannot ground claims of justice.

But Rawls's point is not that the grounds of a desert claim must themselves be deserved or that there is nothing that we deserve. He never makes these claims. In fact, in this passage he is taking issue with those who hold that the more fortunate deserve greater advantages than what the difference principle allows. In reply, he points out that the sense of entitlement at issue is not moral desert (based on virtue) but rather legitimate expectations. Moral virtue is not the same as, nor indeed is it correlated with natural talents and abilities. So the objection to the difference principle cannot be that those with greater talent deserve (in the sense of moral virtue) greater rewards than what the difference principle allows, since there is no reason to think that those with greater talents are any more virtuous than anyone else. Instead, the objection must be based on the claim that the difference principle fails to give talented individuals what should properly follow from their superior talents. The problem with this argument, Rawls points out, is that we can only determine what follows from a given set of abilities if we know the institutional context in which they are to be exercised. A single set of natural talents and abilities would produce very different results when developed and exercised in different institutional contexts, and our question is precisely how to evaluate these different background institutional schemes. As Rawls explains in the revised edition immediately after the passage quoted above:

> To be sure, the more advantaged have a right to their natural assets, as does everyone else...And so the more advantaged are entitled to whatever they can acquire in accordance with the rules of a fair system of social cooperation. Our problem is how this scheme, the basic structure of society, is to be designed. (*TJ* 89)

Justice requires giving people what is their due. But what is their due depends not only on the exercise of their talents and abilities but also on the institutional scheme within which this takes place. Therefore, on pain of circularity, our standard for institutional design cannot be simply that individuals get what is their due.

Rawls also makes a related point. Part of our assessment of moral virtue concerns a person's compliance with the requirements of social justice. Rawls treats this under the headings of the natural duty of justice and obligations. The natural duty of justice, for example, "requires us to support and comply with just institutions that exist and apply to us" (*TJ* 99). But once again, this depends on a prior determination of which institutions are just. "Thus," Rawls writes, "the concept of moral worth [and therefore moral desert] is secondary to those of right and justice, and it plays no role in the substantive definition of distributive shares" (*TJ* 275).

The temptation to define justice in terms of desert may come from thinking that "distributive justice [is] somehow the opposite of retributive justice" (*TJ* 276). They are, however, "entirely different" (*TJ* 277). Principles of retributive justice are necessary in order to respond to violations of various ethical or legal standards. Violations deserve punishment or rectification according to standards of retributive justice. In contrast, principles of distributive justice are necessary even in the ideal, even under the assumption of full compliance. This is because the ends of reasonable citizens often conflict, and the principles of distributive justice are designed to adjudicate those conflicts fairly. The fact that different individuals exhibit different levels of moral virtue is irrelevant to the resolution of this problem. Although distributive justice requires giving people their due, it is not a matter of rewarding people according to their moral virtue.

Jon Mandle

SEE ALSO:

Distributive justice
Ideal and nonideal theory
Legitimate expectations
Redress, principle of

57.

DESIRES

N CHARACTERIZING the moral psychology of citizens as represented in political liberalism, Rawls articulates three kinds of desires that illuminate aspects of their moral sensibility as reasonable: object-dependent desires, principle-dependent desires, and conception-dependent desires (*PL* 81–86).

Object-dependent desires, on the one hand, are desires that "can be described without the use of any moral conceptions, or reasonable or rational principles" (*PL* 82). Such desires are potentially unlimited in number, ranging from desires for such mundane objects as food, drink, and pleasures of various kinds to more complex desires for objects or states of affairs arising out of social life, among which Rawls includes "desires for status, power and glory and for property and wealth" (*PL* 82). As Rawls's list suggests, these desires might be complex, some of them perhaps even being instrumentally related to other such desires. But the motivational force of these desires does not arise from a principle and no principle intrinsic to the object of the desire guides how the agent will pursue its satisfaction.

Principle-dependent desires and conception-dependent desires, on the other hand, are those in which the force of the desire involves a principle that is possible and intelligible only by virtue of an agent's nature as rational and reasonable. That principle is both intrinsic to the goal or aim of the desire and guides or regulates how the agent should act to satisfy the desire. Among principle-dependent desires, Rawls subdivides the group according to whether the principle upon which the desire is dependent is one of rationality or one of reasonability. As examples of desires dependent upon principles of rationality, he includes the desire to take the most efficient course of action or the desire to realize the greatest good. As examples of desires dependent upon principles of

206

reasonability, by contrast, he suggests the desires to act fairly or to act justly (*PL* 82f). Conception-dependent desires, in turn, are desires to act upon specific principles, but with the caveat that the choice of principle upon which one acts must be essential to realizing some more complex conception. One might desire to act upon the principles that articulate what it means to be a person of a certain kind, such as an exemplar of a specific vocation or comprehensive doctrine. The most pertinent example of a conception-dependent desire, of course, is the way in which acting from the principles of justice that define Rawls's conception of justice as fairness contributes to realizing the ideal of citizenship embraced by that conception (*PL* 84).

Acknowledging the possibility of principle-dependent desires and conception-dependent desires is important to understanding how a political liberalism is genuinely possible. Rawls notes that acknowledging these differing forms of desires means that "the class of possible motives is wide open" (*PL* 85). Emphasizing that the normative force of these desires arises from the moral powers of rationality and reasonability distinguishes them as authentic desires within the reasonable psychology of citizens in political liberalism. In the terms of an important distinction drawn by Bernard Williams, which Rawls cites, these desires count as reasons that are "internal," to "'a person's motivational set'" (*PL* 85 n.33 citing Williams 1981, 101–113). This is in sharp contrast, Rawls emphasizes, to conceptions, such as Hume's, that might deny that our reasoning nature can give rise to motivationally effective desires at all (*PL* 85 n.33).

Acknowledging such desires suggests also that citizens' desires may be acquired by a process of education. This could follow from the study or contemplation of a complex comprehensive doctrine, but also just as well from exposure to the background public culture of a particular society. Importantly, if it is reasonable to think that these desires may come to be genuine desires, this contributes also to an understanding of how citizens may develop trust and confidence in the motivation and intentions of one another. As a set of political institutions or cooperative social arrangements endures over time, citizens may reasonably gain greater confidence in their fellow citizens' commitment to those arrangements (*PL* 86). We should also perhaps note that this account of the development of motivation through education does not seem to contravene Rawls's earlier sense "that human actions spring from existing desires and that these can be changed only gradually. We cannot just decide at a given moment to alter our system of ends" (*TJ* 498).

This reasonable moral psychology also helps to understand the structure of the political motivation of citizens in a society marked by profound, but reasonable pluralism. For such a society to be stable for the right reasons, rather than as a mere *modus vivendi*, it must be characterized by the "fact of majority support," which indicates that "an enduring and secure democratic regime ... must be *willingly and freely* supported by at least a substantial majority of its politically active citizens" (*PL* 38, emphasis added). To the extent that it is reasonable to see how citizens might genuinely acquire conception-dependent desires of a politically liberal nature, we can also see how the essentials of a politically liberal society might be willingly and freely endorsed by citizens who disagree profoundly on other matters.

Moreover, this distinction among types of desires helps to clarify the extent and manner in which citizens may be satisfied with the outcomes of public reason. While it is not reasonable on the view of political liberalism to expect that all of the demands of one's comprehensive doctrine might be met, to the extent that one's principle-dependent and conception-dependent desires are genuine, their satisfaction will be genuine as well. Thus, this partial, but principled satisfaction illustrates how when the outcomes of public reason fall short of satisfying all of one's desires, one can nevertheless achieve the satisfaction of a sense of reconciliation Rawls distinguishes from simple resignation (cf. *JF* 3–4; *LHMP* 331).

Rawls emphasizes that this psychology is philosophical and not empirical. He notes that this conception does not arise from "the science of human nature but rather a scheme of concepts and principles for expressing a certain conception of the person and an ideal of citizenship" (*PL* 86–87). While this psychology cannot contradict empirically based science, its correctness does not depend on empirical claims regarding actual human behavior. It depends rather "on whether we can learn and understand it, on whether we can apply its principles and ideals in political life, and on whether we find the political conception of justice to which it belongs acceptable on due reflection" (*PL* 87).

Alan W. Grose

SEE ALSO:

> *Moral psychology*
> *The reasonable and the rational*
> *Reconciliation*
> *Stability*
> *Utility*

58.

DEWEY, JOHN

JOHN DEWEY (1859–1952) was an American philosopher, political activist, and public intellectual. After earning a Ph.D. in Philosophy from Johns Hopkins University, Dewey secured teaching positions at the University of Michigan (1884–1894) and the University of Chicago (1894–1904) before moving to Columbia University in 1905, where he remained for the remainder of his career.

Widely recognized as one of the three founders of pragmatism, John Dewey formulated a more systematic version of pragmatism than can be found in his pragmatist predecessors, Charles Peirce and William James. At its heart is Dewey's Darwinian conception of experience. Unlike sensationalistic forms of empiricism, Dewey's pragmatism begins with an organic conception of experience according to which experience is the continual doing and undergoing performed by each living creature within its physical and social environment. This conception allows Dewey to bring empiricism into line with what he regarded as the most important scientific advance of our time – Darwinian biology – while also eschewing many of the philosophical problems occasioned by traditional empiricism, including skepticism and mind–body dualism.

The centerpiece of Dewey's philosophy is the conception of inquiry that emerges out of his empiricism. According to Dewey, inquiry is fundamentally aimed at problem-solving rather than accurately representing facts or states of affairs. Dewey thought that inquiry is the directed attempt to address experimentally the *problematic* factors within an environment. Dewey held that scientific method was simply a more explicit and precisely designed version of inquiry in general.

Hence Dewey shares with the Logical Empiricists of his day the aspiration to make philosophy more scientific; however, his conception of science is rooted in his view of experience. Accordingly, the aim of making philosophy more scientific is, for Dewey, that of making philosophy more self-consciously aware of its own methodologies, categories, presuppositions, and biases. In this way, Dewey's pragmatism is in part a *metaphilosophical* view, focused on questions concerning the nature and limits of philosophy.

Dewey wrote extensively in political philosophy, producing several treatises as well as hundreds of journalistic pieces deriving from his public engagements. His work is focused particularly on democracy. His emphasis on inquiry gives his democratic theory a decidedly progressive, participatory, deliberative, and epistemic bent. According to Dewey, democracy is not merely a kind of state or a procedure for collective decision; it is rather a network of social and political habits, practices, norms, and attitudes appropriate for competent collective inquiry.

Dewey's influence on Rawls seems indirect. Rawls shares with Dewey a commitment to naturalism, roughly the view that philosophical theorizing must be continuous with natural science; consequently, like Dewey, Rawls is suspicious of the metaphysical commitments of Kantian moral philosophy. However, there is a case to be made for thinking that Rawls's methodology of reflective equilibrium has its source in Dewey's pragmatism; for Dewey held that the moral life was an ongoing and experimental dialectic between theory and practice. A similar argument can be made for Rawls's later aspiration to devise a "political not metaphysical" version of liberalism.

Robert B. Talisse

SEE ALSO:

Democracy
Kant, Immanuel
Political liberalism, justice as fairness as
Reflective equilibrium

59.

DIFFERENCE PRINCIPLE

THE DIFFERENCE PRINCIPLE is perhaps the best-known and most controversial element of Rawls's two principles of justice. It states that "social and economic inequalities are to be arranged so that they are...to the greatest benefit of the least advantaged" (*TJ* 266). As part of the two principles of justice, it has the lowest priority, which means that it cannot be satisfied at the expense of the equal provision of basic liberties, fair equality of opportunity or the just savings principle. It holds that if a society provides for the satisfaction of these other aspects of the two principles equally, and its institutions and the various regulatory procedures they establish yield, when followed, a class of people who have fewer primary goods than anyone else in their society (the worst off) but who have more primary goods than the worst off in all other comparable societies with different basic structures, then that society is, for this reason, just.

As with other well-known parts of Rawls's theory, such as the original position and the veil of ignorance, the difference principle is the subject of a voluminous secondary literature. Unfortunately, as with these other aspects of Rawls's theory, much of that literature takes the difference principle out of the context of the full theory or treats it as if it is the whole of Rawls's theory of justice (thus described as maximin justice). It is, for instance, important to an understanding of the difference principle that it applies only to the basic structure of a society as a whole, and that it serves to distinguish between the justice of institutional structures understood not as allocative schemes but as instances of what Rawls calls pure procedural justice. This entry places the difference principle within the context of the wider theory, explaining the role it plays there and the grounds for it within the larger theory. It then explains how the principle is to be applied.

In an early essay laying out the basic features of justice as fairness, Rawls characterizes a just society as one in which citizens can "face each other openly." We can face each other openly when we can offer reasonable justifications for the various institutions of the basic structure of our society, justifications that we can expect that our fellow citizens, insofar as they are reasonable, can accept. This means that in working out principles of justice, Rawls is always concerned that a basic structure that satisfies those principles is one that could be justified by those living within it to one another, no matter how they fare under its auspices. The difference principle can then be seen as part of Rawls's answer to the question: what levels of social and economic inequality could we justify to our fellow citizens? Note that phrasing the underlying point of the difference principle in this manner brings out an often overlooked fact about it: it is a principle of permissible inequality, not directly a principle of equality. It tells us when inequalities are justified, which means, among other things, that Rawls's theory accepts that some level of social and economic inequality might be justified.

Rawls offers two related kinds of considerations in favor of the difference principle and its place within the two principles of justice, both of which can be seen as giving us a way to justify the inequalities it permits to one another. First, he argues that the difference principle, in combination with the other principles of justice, rules out various bases for inequality that would be "arbitrary from a moral point of view." Second, he argues that it satisfies an ideal of reciprocity. I take each in turn.

The difference principle addresses a shortcoming of the principle of fair equality of opportunity in the possible arbitrary distribution of social and economic advantages. Fair equality of opportunity offsets advantages in one's social origins, so that being born into a wealthy family (something no one deserves) cannot be a source of social or economic advantage. It does not, however, correct for differences in people's natural talents or levels of motivation. Rawls claims that we no more deserve our natural talents than we deserve to be born into a certain family or class, and so distributing economic and social advantage on the basis of these features would also be "arbitrary from a moral point of view." This does not imply, and Rawls does not hold, that we are not entitled to the rewards a just system of rules offers us for the concerted use of those talents. It merely means the justice of a society is not a matter of respecting a supposedly natural relation between rewards and talents. A society's institutions determine what that relationship is, and principles of justice give us means for assessing the relationship it establishes in terms of justice. Once just social institutions are in place, we are entitled to what our talents and effort bring us (*TJ* 74, 76; *JF* 72).

Difference principle / 213

Rawls argues that our talents, our willingness to work hard, and perhaps most importantly, our ability to transform those talents and work into economic and social advantages depend on factors that are not up to us individually, and so are arbitrary from a moral point of view. To see the point, we might separate out four ingredients that go into an individual's so-called natural talents and willingness to expend effort: (1) genetic endowment, (2) family and other formative environment, (3) social resources, and (4) the social valuation of talents. Whatever portion of talent and character rests entirely on one's biological makeup is due to factors over which one has no control and are as arbitrary from a moral point of view as the class into which one is born. But this is also true of the formative environment in which we grow up. Some people are born into environments that nurture certain skills and habits, and others are not. Moreover, the further ability to translate my individual skills into anything productive depends on the larger infrastructure of the society in which I live. No one turns talents and hard work into economic and social success alone. Finally, there is no one proper or natural way of putting a social value on talents. The social value of particular talents is itself a feature of our social organization, which predates and shapes our particular development of our talents. I no more deserve to live in a society that values academic philosophical ability or the computational skills needed for computer programming than I deserve to be born into a particular class. So even the social value placed on the talents I develop is undeserved. (Again, this does not mean that I am not entitled to the rewards my society offers for the use of the talents I develop, but that I have no inherent right to a society that offers to reward these talents.)

The difference principle addresses the problem of inequalities due to talents by requiring that whatever benefits accrue to the more talented do so in a manner that maximally benefits the less advantaged. Rawls describes the resultant form of social equality as "democratic equality" and contrasts it with "liberal equality," the title he gives to a conception of justice that includes fair equality of opportunity but no difference principle (*TJ* 65f.).

Rawls calls the moral idea behind the difference principle (and, indeed, the two principles as whole) "reciprocity" (*TJ* 88). Reciprocity demands that we only exact from a scheme of social cooperation that which we can reasonably expect that others could agree to. It is thus tied to the basic idea of finding social institutions in which we can face each other openly. We can also see it as lying between a principle of total altruism, whereby everyone sacrifices for the good of others, and total egoism, where everyone uses whatever means she has at her disposal to get the best deal possible for herself. This idea of reciprocity captures the features of the traditional idea of fraternity that are appropriate for a democracy, where citizens recognize one another as free and equal, but are not necessarily bound by stronger ties of affection (*TJ* 90–91). This can be seen by the kinds of arguments that Rawls suggests the parties in the original position could make in favor of the difference principle over rival principles such as one that equated justice with maximal average levels of utility combined with a social minimum, or one that mandated complete social and economic equality. Rawls argues that pointing out that the institutions of the basic structure are organized so that they satisfy the difference principle gives citizens a reasonable way of justifying those institutions both to those who are least advantaged and to those who are more advantaged. To those who are least advantaged in a society that satisfies the difference principle, we can say that under any alternative arrangement, there would be people who do even worse than they are currently faring. To the most talented, who might object that under a more laissez-faire system of institutions, they could exploit their talents for greater economic and social gain, we can argue that under the difference principle, the talented do better than others, and better than they would themselves do under a purely egalitarian system. By hypothesis, any alternative system that allowed the talented to do even better would involve some people doing even worse than the worse off would do under the difference principle. The talented, then, in rejecting the difference principle, are demanding that others, who are worse off than they are, be made even worse off, so that they can derive extra benefits. In either case, those rejecting social institutions that satisfy the difference principle are demanding that others who fare worse than they do sacrifice so that they can do better. This is an unreasonable demand, and so we can reasonably expect the least advantaged to reject any such argument against the difference principle insofar as they are reasonable.

What, exactly, does the difference principle tell us to do? There are six points to keep in mind. First, the general aim is to assess the justice of basic structures in terms of how those who are worst off in them do. Given two societies that equally satisfy the other parts of the two principles of justice, the more just of the two societies is the one that provides the higher standard of living to those at the bottom. Second, we are not to look to the individual who is at the bottom, but to a representative member of the group at the bottom. In defining that group, we may want to use different criteria depending on what aspect of a social system we are evaluating. Thus, if the question involves the structure of the economy and the distribution of income and wealth, we might ask how unskilled workers fare. If we are asking about social institutions that create and perpetuate unequal systems of gender or race, then we should look to members of the gender or

Difference principle / 215

race who are disadvantaged (women, nonwhites). In *A Theory of Justice*, Rawls focuses on questions of economic inequality, and so he focuses on economic criteria to pick out the least favored group. Nevertheless, the least favored group is not definable by anything but its position in the distribution. Thus, if, in one society, unskilled workers are the worst-off group, and in another society, unskilled workers have a much higher standard of living, and people with advanced degrees find themselves the worst off, then the difference principle tells us to compare the plight of the unskilled workers in the first society with the plight of the people with advanced degrees in the second society. If the unskilled workers in the first society do better, then the first society is more just according to the difference principle, even if the unskilled workers in the second society would do better than the unskilled workers in the first society.

Third, we are to look at people's expectations over a complete life, and not at a particular time when they are badly off. Fourth, the difference principle is not the only principle governing the distribution of social and economic advantages. The first principle, which requires the equal protection of a set of basic liberties and a guarantee of the fair value of the political liberties, and the fair equality of opportunity principle, which requires that one's family background not have an effect on one's chances of attaining various positions of prestige and power in society, have enormous distributive implications, and the difference principle only comes into play once these have been attended to. (Think, for instance, of what would be required for everyone in a society to have the same ability to influence political decisions, and give the same opportunities in life to their children as a Bill Gates or a George Soros.) Fifth, social and economic advantages are to be measured in terms of what Rawls calls "primary goods." In *A Theory of Justice*, Rawls describes primary goods as "things every rational man is presumed to want whatever else he wants" (*TJ* 79). (In later work, he ties the primary goods to the development and exercise of the two moral powers, e.g. *PL* 178–190; *JF* 57–61.) Primary goods are meant to be things that are likely to be useful to any reasonable and rational plan of life. In addition, they provide an objective measure of well-being which allows for public comparisons of advantage. Since the principles of justice need to be the basis of a public conception of justice, they must refer to features of persons that are objective and publicly knowable. Finally, the difference principle, along with the rest of the two principles of justice are principles of what Rawls calls pure procedural justice. That is, they are not to be applied to particular states of affairs produced by institutions directly, but to the structure of the institutions themselves. To criticize the institutions of the basic structure for failing to meet the difference principle, we need to look, then, not only at the distribution of income and wealth throughout the society at a given time, but how the institutions of the society, including its laws, work together to shape that distribution.

Anthony Simon Laden

SEE ALSO:

Basic structure of society
Close-knitness
Least-advantaged position
Maximin rule of choice
Procedural justice
Reciprocity
Two principles of justice (in justice as fairness)

60.

DISTRIBUTIVE JUSTICE

JOHN RAWLS'S justice as fairness includes a theory of distributive justice for the basic structure of society – the collection of background social, economic, and political institutions within which citizens pursue their everyday activities. Rawls understands the concept of distributive justice to specify a property of these institutions. A basic social structure is distributively just when it properly balances the competing claims of citizens on it, understood as a cooperative system for the production and distribution of certain primary social goods (*TJ* 4–5). Importantly, for Rawls distributive justice does not specify a property of any particular allocation of primary social goods to nameable individuals. With respect to primary social goods, he understands the solution to this problem to be a matter of pure procedural justice: that is, a just allocation of primary social goods to nameable individuals is just whatever allocation follows from the fair procedure of their freely acting within, and in accord with the rules of, a distributively just basic social structure.

Rawls aims to identify the conception of distributive justice most appropriate for a democratic society, that is, a society within which each and every citizen has as a free equal the same claim on its basic social structure understood as a system of cooperation for the mutually advantageous production and distribution of primary social goods. As principles of distributive justice, Rawls's two principles of justice purport to specify key constraints on the institutional structure of a society within which the claims of all citizens, taken simply as free equals, are properly balanced at the most basic level.

Rawls claims that "Justice is the first virtue of social institutions" (*TJ* 3). That is, justice is the primary end at which the design of institutions must aim.

Here Rawls means to refer to distributive justice. Of course, distributive justice is not the only justice-based virtue of social institutions. Corrective and allocative justice matter too. But distributive justice is logically prior to these. Of course, it does not follow from the fact that justice is the first virtue of social institutions that it is the only virtue. Even if we include other dimensions of justice – e.g. corrective and allocative justice – justice is not the only thing that matters. Rawls claims that, "other things equal, one conception of justice is preferable to another when its broader consequences are more desirable" (*TJ* 6). So, while justice is the primary virtue for evaluating social institutions, and distributive justice is prior to other aspects of justice, other virtues such as efficiency are also relevant, at least to decide among otherwise equally reasonable or correct conceptions of justice.

The concept of distributive justice contrasts, first, with the concept of retributive justice. Retributive justice is concerned with the proper response to wrongdoing. Some hold that both of these ideas of justice are guided by a single principle: giving people what they deserve. Retributive justice concerns correcting wrongs or meting out punishment to wrongdoers while distributive justice concerns allocating rewards in proportion to virtue. Rawls does not interpret the contrast in this way. One reason is that retributive justice presupposes distributive justice, for we cannot know that a person deserves punishment for violating a rule without knowing something about the justice of the social structure of which the rule is a part. Another contrast between distributive and retributive justice is that principles of retributive justice are only invoked in response to particular instances of various kinds of wrongdoing. Rawls holds that in a well-ordered society of justice as fairness, distributive justice arises from self-authenticating valid claims that citizens make against one another. It is not based on what they have done, but simply on who they are, namely, moral persons who, for political purposes, understand themselves and each other to be free and equal. A third reason for resisting any interpretation of retributive and distributive justice as responsive to one and the same notion of desert is that while the rules of a distributively just basic social structure provide a common public measure for assessing retributive justice, there is in any free and democratic and so pluralist society no deeper or more basic common public measure of desert.

A second contrast with distributive justice is with allocative justice. Some might think the question of distributive justice concerns how to allocate a given set of social resources among the particular citizens of a society. Rawls refers to this as the question of allocative justice. For him, distributive justice instead concerns the design of the basic structure of society. The basic structure of society consists of the set of background political, social, and economic institutions that specify the procedures by which citizens gain entitlement to their share of social resources. Just allocations are then determined as a matter of pure procedural justice. Rawls holds that whatever allocation of the burdens and benefits of social cooperation that results from citizens acting justly within a background of just social institutions is itself a just allocation, again because the procedure under which that allocation came about was a fair procedure.

> A distribution cannot be judged in isolation from the system of which it is the outcome or from what individuals have done in good faith in the light of established expectations. If it is asked in the abstract whether one distribution of a given stock of things to definite individuals with known desires and preferences is better than another, then there is simply no answer to this question. (*TJ* 76)

Retributive and allocative justice each assign particular things to particular people, whether penalties or benefits. Both require an account of fair background conditions within which benefits and penalties assigned to particular persons can be just. For Rawls, distributive justice, then, has priority over allocative justice as well as retributive justice, in the sense that these other accounts cannot be completed without first taking up the question of distributive justice.

One might think that distributive justice applies primarily to economic benefits, but for Rawls, the focus of distributive justice is on primary goods, including rights, duties, political power, as well as wealth and economic power. Note that the institutions of the basic structure both create and distribute the various social roles and positions of authority of society. So, to arrive at a conception of the proper balance of competing claims on these institutions one must decide on rules that determine both what those roles, positions, burdens, and benefits should be as well as by what procedure they are to be allocated to particular individuals.

Rawls is careful to distinguish the justice of the basic structure from the justice of other kinds of relationships and associations. The conception of justice that describes the proper balance of competing claims for a democratic society is not assumed to be the right account of the proper balance of competing claims for a group of friends or a family, for a professional association or a church, for example. But he takes the justice of the basic structure – the social or political account of distributive justice – to be primary because it sets limits on permissible accounts of justice for citizens' other sorts of roles and associations.

Rawls claims that the basic structure of society is a primary subject of justice also because its effects are "so profound and present from the start" (*TJ* 7).

Commentators have noted that this is not reason enough to establish Rawls's claim that the justice of the basic structure is special and the primary subject of distributive justice. G. A. Cohen notes that the ethos of a society – which might be understood as a set of cultural norms and traditions that informs an individual's choices – also has profound effects and is present from the start of every individual's life. For Cohen, then, the same principles of justice that apply to the basic structure ought to apply also to the ethos of a society as well as to individual actions. Rawls, by contrast, thinks that his principles, though appropriate for evaluating the basic structure, may not be appropriate for evaluating a society's ethos or individual actions. A defense against such arguments might be found in Rawls's emphasis on the coercive nature of the rules of the basic structure, though these attempts too have been challenged.

Rawls's substantive conception of justice contains two principles that focus on different primary goods, although there is some overlap between them. The first principle holds that "each person has an equal claim to a fully adequate scheme of basic rights and liberties" (*PL* 5). The second principle requires equality of opportunity, understood not simply as the formal constraint of "careers open to talents," but as a substantive requirement that citizens who possess similar sets of talents and motivation should have an equal chance to attain the various offices and privileges in society. Equal opportunity does not require that two persons of similar talent have opportunities equal to each other if one is, for example, a harder worker. Nor does it require equality of opportunity between two persons who differ in their sets of natural talents. But note that the background structure of society has a tremendous impact on the benefits one may become entitled to on the basis of any particular instance of individual action.

The second principle also requires that structural inequalities satisfy the difference principle. This requires that any structural inequalities be to the greatest advantage of the worst-off representative person. By itself, the difference principle does not place any limits on the size of those inequalities as long as they maximally benefit the least advantaged. But when combined with the first principle and equality of opportunity, together with reasonable social assumptions, Rawls argues that inequality will be limited.

In any individual case, one's actual share of social resources will be a consequence of institutional design, individual talent and effort, and luck. The difference principle asks us to think at the level of social positions instead of individuals. These social positions are defined by the structural inequalities in shares of social resources associated with the various social positions defined by the basic structure. The difference principle allows a smaller share of resources for one social

Distributive justice / 221

position only when the worse-off group does better than the worse-off group would under any other distribution, including an equal distribution. When these conditions are met by a society's basic structure, then whatever particular share of resources any individual obtains in that society by following the rules of the institutions is a fair share, as a matter of pure procedural justice.

Pete Murray

SEE ALSO:

Allocative justice
Basic structure of society
Desert
Liberal conception of justice
Political conception of justice
Procedural justice
Two principles of justice
Well-ordered society

61.

DOMINANT END THEORIES

PREPARATORY TO HIS argument that justice, as understood within justice as fairness, is congruent with the good and happiness of those it governs, Rawls examines a family of closely related ideas: happiness, a rational life plan, a dominant end, hedonism, and the unity of the self. More specifically he considers and rejects a number of claims involving these ideas so as to set the stage for the place and content of these ideas within the so-called congruence argument he presents in favor of justice as fairness. One of the claims he considers and rejects is that without appeal to a dominant end to which rational persons subordinate all their other ends we cannot give meaningful content to the idea of a person's happiness in order to consider how justice may be related to it. Another is that we cannot account for the unity of the persons whose happiness we must show to be congruent with justice without appeal to a dominant end.

A person is happy, Rawls argues, when she is successfully carrying through her rational plan for her life and is confident that she will continue to be successful in her future efforts. Since her rational plan specifies her good, a person is happy when her good is realized and she is reasonably optimistic that it will continue to be so. Her plan for her life, which may be more or less developed, is given by her various ends. It is a rational plan insofar as it is both (i) a coherently ordered system of ends, or *a* plan, that is consistent with the counting principles of rational choice and (ii) *the* plan, assuming there are many plans that satisfy the foregoing condition, that she has chosen or at least would choose with full deliberative rationality. To choose with full deliberative rationality is to choose with complete awareness of all the relevant facts and after careful consideration of the total consequences of making each of the alternative choices available. Rawls notes several features of the exercise of full deliberative rationality and the ways in which these determine rational choice. But he argues that it may often be the case that no amount of deliberating rationally over all candidate plans, each of which satisfies the counting principles of rational choice, will free a person from having simply to choose among candidate plans, presumably guided by her own direct self-knowledge of what she most wants or values (*TJ* 483).

One consequence of the foregoing is that Rawls allows that a person's rational plan for her life, and so her good and her happiness, may often be at least partly a function of what she most wants or values. Rawls recognizes that this is a somewhat unsettling idea: that in the end a person may find herself forced to rely on her own direct self-knowledge of what she most wants or values as a criterion of rational choice among life plans, and so of her good and happiness. What is unsettling here is that the absence of a criterion or decision procedure for validating as rational what a person most wants or values may appear to sever the relationship between reason or rationality and a person's life plan and so her good and happiness. It is the unsettling nature of this idea that accounts, he suggests, for the attractiveness of the idea that irrespective of what any particular person happens to want or value there is a single dominant end, lexically prior to all other ends, capable of serving as a common evaluative standard and so grounding rational choice among life plans without any appeal to direct self-knowledge of what one most wants or values.

What the proponent of a dominant end, or a dominant end theorist, wants is a generally applicable first-person decision procedure sufficient to enable a person to identify, simply by following the procedure, the plan of life most rational for her (*TJ* 484). The counting principles of rational choice coupled with a commitment to the inclusion of one and the same objective dominant end in every person's life plan would yield such a procedure. But what might the dominant end presupposed by such a decision procedure be? It cannot be happiness, for happiness is simply the state a person is in when she is successfully executing her rational plan and confident that she will be able to continue doing so. Perhaps happiness is an inclusive end, but it cannot be our dominant end. Christian theology has urged service to God or the beatific vision or community with God as our dominant end. But on the assumption that God is a moral being, positing this as our dominant end simply restates the problem. Either we must appeal to divine revelation of God's moral ordering of ends, with no criterion for validating the order as rational other than our supposed direct knowledge of God's revelation of what God most wants or values, or we must rely on our natural reason, and so ultimately our own direct knowledge of what we most want or value, to confirm as rational the order revealed by God. In either case, we've provided no first-person decision procedure sufficient to enable a person to identify, simply by following the procedure, the plan of life most rational for her. The foregoing considerations, once coupled with the implausibility of power or wealth as a dominant end, tend to lead naturally to the hedonist thesis that pleasure, understood as agreeable feeling or consciousness, is the objective dominant end grounding rational deliberation and choice among candidate life plans. The rational life plan is the plan that maximizes pleasure.

So understood, pleasure appears to provide a serviceable measure of first-person rational deliberation. And because persons find pleasure in so many varied activities it appears to respect the fact that the human good is heterogeneous. But, Rawls argues, pleasure so conceived is also implausible as a dominant end. To want more than anything else the feature of agreeable consciousness picked out by pleasure so understood is unbalanced and inhuman. But even apart from this problem, pleasure so understood can serve as a dominant end only if we have a standard for measuring trade-offs between, say, the intensity and duration of a pleasure. The need simply to choose among incommensurable final ends based on what one most wants or values arises all over again, but now within the space of subjective feelings of pleasure (*TJ* 488). Hedonism thus fails as a dominant end theory. This, Rawls argues, should not come as a surprise. Citing Wittgenstein, Rawls notes that we should have anticipated that private inner experiences would prove ill-suited to serve as shared criteria for distinguishing rational from irrational life plans (*TJ* 489).

To be sure, Rawls allows that a person may choose with full deliberative rationality a life plan organized around an end that functions for her as a dominant end. But that choice will reflect what she most wants and values. It is neither required by the idea nor necessary to the possibility of a rational choice. As Rawls says, "even a dominant end must be chosen from among numerous possibilities" (*TJ* 491). There is no escaping the burden of deliberative rationality. And it is this that Rawls means to call attention to when he says that "the self is prior to the ends affirmed by it" (*TJ* 491).

Finally, it bears mentioning that within Rawls's conception of justice, justice as fairness, justice is not a dominant end. It is true that Rawls argues that rational persons will find the development and exercise of their capacity for justice, as governed by justice as fairness, fully congruent with their own good. And it is true that he argues that justice is the first virtue of social institutions and that persons have a natural duty to support and perfect just institutions. But none of this adds up to the claim that justice is a dominant end within justice as fairness. Justice as fairness leaves it to each person, in the exercise of her deliberative rationality, to determine the order and relations of her final ends, including her commitment to supporting and perfecting justice as the first virtue of social institutions.

David A. Reidy

SEE ALSO:

Deliberative rationality
Happiness
Moral psychology
Utilitarianism

62.

DUTY OF ASSISTANCE

RAWLS DISCUSSES the duty of assistance in the article "The Law of Peoples" and the book *The Law of Peoples*. The duty is merely mentioned subsequent to the list of seven principles in "Peoples" (*CP* 541). It is stated as the eighth principle in *LP* (*LP* 37).

Rawls distinguishes between ideal and nonideal theory. The former concerns relations between liberal and decent peoples – collectively referred to as "well-ordered peoples" – and the latter concerns relations between such societies and those which are neither liberal nor decent. Nonideal theory is directed towards the long-term goal of an international society comprising liberal and decent peoples (*LP* 89). The duty of assistance, like principles five (the right of self-defense) and seven (the duty to observe restrictions in war), applies only in nonideal conditions. This contrasts with Rawls's account of domestic justice in which strict compliance is assumed in the original position (*TJ* 125) and the principles selected are applicable only in ideal conditions. Rawls claims that, "Well-ordered peoples have a *duty* to assist burdened societies" (*LP* 106), which are lacking in the "political and cultural traditions, the human capital and know-how, and, often, the material and technological resources needed to be well-ordered" (*LP* 106).

The original position for the Law of Peoples has two steps (*LP* 63). In the first the parties represent only liberal democratic peoples, and are "guided by the fundamental interests of democratic societies...expressed by the liberal principles of justice for a democratic society" (*LP* 32). The second step includes representatives of decent hierarchical peoples. Their interests are related to their acceptance of a set of urgent human rights (*LP* 65) and their legitimate legal system incorporating a comprehensive conception of the good (*LP* 65–66). In the first step the parties "strive to protect their political independence and their free

Duty of assistance / 227

culture with its civil liberties, to guarantee their security, territory, and the well-being of their citizens." In the second step parties are guided by the interests of decent peoples (*LP* 34) and are motivated to protect their people's interest in their "proper self-respect of themselves as a people" (*LP* 34). In both steps parties are behind a veil of ignorance regarding the size of the territory, the size of their population, and their strength (*LP* 32).

The selection of the duty of assistance in this original position is beset with interpretive difficulties. If the parties assume strict compliance, it is unclear why they would select a duty of assistance. If nonideal conditions are entertained, it is unclear why burdened societies would not also be represented in the original position, perhaps as a third step. Moreover, in the first step, if the parties were assumed to represent egalitarian liberal peoples, it is unclear why a more robustly egalitarian international distributive principle would not be chosen (Moellendorf 2002, 13) since parties have a fundamental interest in a liberal conception of justice (*LP* 33). A requirement that liberal societies be egalitarian is rejected on grounds of the desirability of greater generality, but without a discussion of the importance of generality (*CP* 537).

Rawls states three guidelines for applying the duty of assistance. First, well-ordered societies need not be wealthy (*LP* 106). The aim of transfers of goods and knowledge is to establish the institutions of well-ordered peoples. So, the duty of assistance is directed neither by egalitarian considerations nor ultimately by poverty eradication, although Rawls expresses concern for both inequality and poverty (*LP* 117). But he takes lack of material resources to be a possible contributor to being burdened. So, the duty of assistance is instrumentally directed toward eradicating poverty insofar as that is required to create well-ordered institutions.

Second, "the political culture of a burdened society is all-important." (*LP* 108) Rawls maintains that the causes of wealth of a people are "in the religious, philosophical, and moral traditions that support the basic structure of their political and social institutions, as well as in the industriousness and cooperative talents of its members, all supported by their political virtues" (*LP* 108). This empirical claim is related to a moral claim about responsibility. If the causes of wealth and poverty are largely indigenous to the political culture of a society, then perhaps other societies have no responsibilities regarding such poverty.

The empirical claim is challenged by Thomas Pogge (2008, 118–122), who argues that international practice and law harm the poor by establishing incentives to corruption. Regardless of how a leader arrives in office, he or she is recognized as legitimate for purposes of taking out international loans and selling natural resources on terms that might be quite favorable to the office holder. Such incentives implicate the international community in the corruption in many states. Some argue that Pogge employs a dubious baseline for assessing harm (Risse 2005; Patten 2005).

The third guideline holds that the aim of assistance is "to help burdened societies to be able to manage their own affairs reasonably and rationally and eventually to become members of the Society of well-ordered Peoples" (*LP* 111). Rawls emphasizes the importance of self-determination and of individuals being attached to their particular cultures (*LP* 111). Moreover, he suggests that societies are responsible for the level of well-being of their citizens (*LP* 117–118). That the end of assistance is the production of well-ordered societies he takes to be an attraction of his account. In contrast, he doubts the appeal of cosmopolitan egalitarian principles requiring redistribution "without end" (*LP* 117). Such principles are insensitive to the role of domestic political cultures in creating inequalities between peoples (*LP* 117–118).

Darrel Moellendorf

SEE ALSO:

Burdened societies
Ideal and nonideal theory
Law of Peoples
Liberal people
Pogge, Thomas
Society of Peoples
Well-ordered society

63.

DUTY OF CIVILITY

THE DUTY OF civility refers to the set of moral requirements that are associated with Rawls's idea of public reason and its corresponding view of liberal-democratic political legitimacy. Indeed this duty is said to be one of the central "innovations" of Rawls's theory of public reason (*PL* 253). It applies to both government officials and ordinary citizens in the public political forum when they are resolving constitutional essentials and matters of basic justice. The duty of civility instructs them to "be able to explain to one another on those fundamental questions how the principles and policies they advocate and vote for can be supported by the political values of public reason" (*PL* 217).

A principal obligation of the duty of civility, then, involves the practice of public justification. Citizens and officials should identify and sometimes publicly communicate suitable justifying reasons for their exercise of coercive political power, at least with respect to constitutional essentials and matters of basic justice. Public justification is "not simply valid reasoning, but argument addressed to others" (*PL* 465). It proceeds on the basis of public reasoning, that is, by way of ascertainable evidence and reasons and arguments drawn from a reasonable political conception of justice, consistent with the liberal principle of legitimacy based on the criterion of reciprocity. According to this criterion, the exercise of political power is legitimate only when "we sincerely believe that the reasons we would offer for our political activities – were we to state them as government officials – are sufficient, and we also reasonably think that other citizens might reasonably accept those reasons" (*PL* 447).

Citizens and officials need not agree to the very same conception of justice in order to satisfy the duty of civility. Justice as fairness is part of a family of reasonable political conceptions of justice that constitute the content of public reason. Public justifications should be based on a reasonable political conception with a balance of political values that one believes other reasonable citizens might endorse or at least appreciate as not unreasonable (*PL* 226, 241, 253). Political conceptions of justice should also be complete in the sense of providing an answer to "all or nearly all" fundamental questions (*PL* 244, 454). In short, when fundamental political questions are at stake, citizens and officials discharge their duty of civility by honoring the idea of public reason and pursuing public justifications within the framework it establishes (*CP* 617).

A related requirement of the duty of civility is to maintain an appropriately deliberative attitude toward democratic politics. In the search for publicly justifiable political arrangements citizens and officials should remain sincere, fairminded, and willing to listen to others. They should also be disposed to making sound judgments and to modifying their own views in an effort to accommodate others (*PL* 217). Referencing Rousseau, Rawls suggests that the duty of civility is incompatible with the notion that voting is a purely private matter or that politics serves merely as an occasion for each strategically to advance his or her interests. It is also incompatible with the assumption that an individual's political activity should be determined simply by convictions derived directly from a religious or philosophical point of view (*PL* 219).

This last remark points to what has been the most controversial feature of Rawls's proposed duty of civility, namely, the requirement that citizens and officials sometimes exercise restraint in relying on comprehensive doctrine in political decision-making. The fact of reasonable pluralism suggests that free and equal citizens are likely to affirm different and incompatible moral, religious, and philosophical doctrines concerning questions of first philosophy, the divine, and the meaning of a well-lived life. No such form of nonpublic reason can legitimately serve as a shared basis for arranging the terms of political cooperation. Thus, with respect to constitutional essentials and matters of basic justice, citizens and officials in the public political forum should refrain from appealing solely to religious and other comprehensive doctrine in their deliberation, voting, and political advocacy. This requirement of restraint – a call to recognize the limits of public reason – is an implication of the duty of civility (*PL* 219).

Yet the restraint requirement, the target of much criticism in the secondary literature on political liberalism, should not be misinterpreted as a kind of gag rule intended to silence religious and moral contributions to important public debates. First and most obvious is the fact that the obligations imposed by the duty of civility are morally binding but not legally enforceable (*PL* 217). Legal constraints on the kind of reasons that citizens would affirm or offer to one another would be inconsistent with the content of public reason, that is, with reasonable political conceptions of justice that protect freedom of speech, liberty of conscience, and rights of political participation. Second, the idea of public reason is meant to regulate the public political forum of courts, public offices, legislatures, campaigns, and voting booths. Thus even as part of a moral ideal of citizenship it does not require restraint in the background culture of civil society where discussion is assumed to be "full and open" (*PL* 444).

A final point is that even where the restraint requirement does apply citizens are not thereby altogether morally prohibited from appealing to comprehensive doctrine. Rather, they should avoid relying *solely* on such doctrine in their political discourse and decision-making. According to Rawls's wide view of public political culture, which modifies and extends *Political Liberalism's* original "inclusive view" of public reason, religious and nonreligious comprehensive doctrines "may be introduced into public political discussion at any time" provided that "in due course" sufficient public reasons are also given in support of any laws and policies that are said to be doctrinally justified (*PL* xlix, 462). In addition to affirming this "proviso" concerning the political use of comprehensive doctrine, Rawls suggests that there are positive reasons for introducing nonpublic reason into political discussion, such as the mutual recognition of how reasonable comprehensive doctrines can nourish allegiance to liberal-democratic values. These contributions to public discourse are consistent with the duty of civility, which ultimately, at least for many citizens, will be morally grounded in their religious and philosophical views.

The duty of civility applies to both citizens and government officials but in somewhat different ways. It is part of the very structure of public reason that its various requirements apply directly to government officials and candidates for office. A supreme court charged with resolving constitutional controversies should reach its decisions only by means of public reasoning; the court is in this sense the "exemplar of public reason" (*PL* 233–234). Other government officials may sometimes turn to forms of nonpublic reasoning, depending on the circumstances and the issues under consideration. Yet these officials must still satisfy their duty of civility by explaining to others how their choices on fundamental questions are justified in terms of a reasonable political conception of justice. Rawls observes that whether officials succeed or fail in their duty is evident in their everyday speech and conduct (*PL* 444).

Citizens who are not government officials sometimes enter the public political forum as advocates, protesters or even as voters on referenda questions. But in a representative democracy the main way that ordinary citizens would fulfill the duty of civility is as voters who hold government officials accountable through periodic elections. As an ideal of citizenship, public reason instructs citizens to "think of themselves *as if they were legislators*" in order to determine which laws and policies are publicly justifiable and "most reasonable." From this standpoint they should "repudiate government officials and candidates for public office who violate public reason" (*PL* 444–445). Even in the case of a stand-off, in which there are compelling arguments on both sides of an issue, citizens should not allow religious or other comprehensive doctrines to tip the balance of relevant considerations in one direction or another. Rather, like judges deciding hard cases, they should "vote for the ordering of political values they sincerely think most reasonable" (*PL* 479).

The duty of civility is relevant to both voting and forms of public discourse and expression. Yet one ambiguity in Rawls's discussion of the duty is the extent to which ordinary citizens should regularly offer explanations for their political choices as would be expected of government officials. Insofar as citizens are to satisfy the criterion of reciprocity and hold officials accountable, they should support only those laws and policies that they take to be publicly justifiable. Citizens should thus aim to identify sufficient public reasons for favored laws and policies (and, presumably, for favored candidates for office). The duty of civility also implies that they should "have, and be ready to explain," the general framework of principles and guidelines associated with a reasonable political conception of justice (*PL* 226). What is not clear is, first, the extent to which ordinary citizens should communicate their explanations to one another and, second, whether they might legitimately defer to others whose political judgment and explanatory authority they trust. Similar questions may be raised about Rawls's proposed proviso concerning the political appeal to religious and other comprehensive doctrine. What does it mean for citizens to offer sufficient public reasons "in due course" and could those supporting public reasons be expressed instead by their compatriots?

Another question about the duty of civility is how its demands should be balanced alongside other goals and moral obligations, especially in cases that would appear to present citizens with conflicting duties. This question is particularly relevant to debates about whether requirements of public reason are unfair or overly burdensome to religious believers who take themselves to be obligated to abide by their religious convictions even in political deliberation and decision-making. Critics argue that for these religious citizens the duty of civility will sometimes conflict with the goal of maintaining a life of religious integrity. While Rawls never responds directly to this integralist objection to political liberalism, he does examine what he calls the "paradox" of public reason, that is, the difficulty of sometimes setting aside what one takes to be the "whole truth" when fundamental political questions are at stake (*PL* 216). One response to this dilemma is

Duty of civility / 233

to argue by analogy that there are other areas of social and political life, such as criminal trials, in which an appeal to the whole truth may be limited for good reason. A second is to stress the importance of satisfying the duty of civility in order to reach legitimate political decisions. Finally, Rawls observes that the political values of public reason are "very great values and not easily overridden" (_PL_ 218).

As a feature of political liberalism the duty of civility is not discussed in any detail in _A Theory of Justice_. There the duty of civility is only briefly mentioned in connection with the duty sometimes to comply with unjust laws. Insofar as constitutional and democratic arrangements do not exceed a certain threshold of injustice, there is a duty of civility not to take advantage of loopholes in the political system or to use its shortcomings as "a too ready excuse" for noncompliance (_TJ_ 312). More relevant to Rawls's later account of the duty of civility, however, is _Theory_'s presentation of the duty of mutual respect. The duty of mutual respect is a natural duty to respect others as moral beings capable of a sense of justice and a conception of the good. Respecting others calls for giving due consideration to their points of view and providing them with reasons for one's actions whenever their interests are "materially affected" (_TJ_ 297). In later writings, Rawls does not rely directly on a theory of natural duties – or, more generally, on any comprehensive moral doctrine – in setting forth the duty of civility. But he does observe that political cooperation "on the basis of mutual respect" implies justifying the coercive use of political power "in the light of public reason" (_JF_ 91).

James Boettcher

SEE ALSO:

> _Culture, political vs. background_
> _Justification: freestanding/political_
> _Legitimacy_
> _Natural duties_
> _Political liberalism, justice as fairness as_
> _Public reason_
> _Respect for persons_

64.

DWORKIN, RONALD

OTHER THAN RAWLS, Ronald Dworkin (1931–2013) is the most influential theorist of liberalism of the late twentieth century. In his remarks at the Harvard memorial service for Rawls, Dworkin credited Rawls with showing that it is possible to a give systematic, individualistic theory of justice, one that is not aggregative in the way that utilitarianism is. In virtue of their shared commitment to individualism, Dworkin agrees with Rawls that a just government must take individual rights to liberty seriously and must ensure a fair distribution of resources, but their views also differ in important ways.

First, whereas Rawls's individualism is represented theoretically by the view that justice consists of principles that equally situated, rationally self-interested individuals would rationally choose behind the veil of ignorance in the original position, Dworkin's individualism is represented by the principle that the government must treat each citizen with equal concern and respect.

Second, and as a consequence, whereas Rawls justifies specific rights, such as to freedom of thought and conscience, by the rational choice argument from the original position, Dworkin justifies specific rights, such as to religious and sexual freedom, as implied by the general right to be treated by the government with equal concern and respect. In his review of *TJ* (Dworkin 1975), Dworkin argued that, because hypothetical contracts do not bind, and because Rawls's argument from the original position presupposes that persons are entitled to be treated as equals, Rawls's argument from the original position is really best understood as a method for articulating what distribution of goods is required by the principle of equal concern and respect.

Third, whereas Rawls's difference principle allows only those kinds of inequality in wealth that function to benefit the least advantaged, Dworkin's "equality of resources" permits other inequalities in wealth. If, starting with an equal share of resources – which will require some compensation for bad luck in the natural distribution of talents – one person ends up with more money than another person as a result of their authentic choices – choices that accurately reflect their values – then that inequality is permitted by Dworkin's view, even if permitting inequalities of this kind does not function to benefit the least advantaged.

Fourth, whereas Rawls grounds individual rights on a political conception of justice that does not presuppose the truth of any "comprehensive moral, philosophical, or religious doctrine," Dworkin grounds rights on a particular view of what makes a human life go well – that a person succeeds in meeting worthwhile challenges (including the challenge of making do with no more than a fair share of resources) – which he calls "the model of challenge" (Dworkin 2000, 253). Rawls believed that liberalism is more likely to gain the principled support of most citizens in a modern democracy if it is understood not to presuppose the truth of any particular comprehensive doctrine (none of which is widely shared), but Dworkin believes that liberalism is more likely to gain principled support if it is understood to be grounded on an appealing conception of what it is for a person to have a good life.

Fifth, and as a consequence, the liberal idea of neutrality toward conceptions of a good life figures into their views in different ways. Whereas Rawls's argument from the original position is neutral toward different conceptions of a good life in that it does not presuppose the truth of any particular conception, Dworkin grounds a substantive right to government neutrality, which prohibits certain forms of official intolerance, such as laws criminalizing homosexual sodomy, on the model of challenge, which is itself an abstract conception of the good life.

Peter de Marneffe

SEE ALSO:

Difference principle
Individualism
Liberalism as a comprehensive doctrine
Luck egalitarianism
Neutrality
Supreme Court and judicial review

E

65.

THE ECONOMY

Rawls's conception of the economy plays an important role in *A Theory of Justice*. First, economic institutions constitute a part of the basic structure of society and as such must be regulated by principles of justice. Secondly, his conception sets the stage for his own institutional model of just economic relations and this model indicates the ways existing society would need to be transformed to conform to the demands of justice. Thirdly, the institutional model plays a key role in establishing that his theory of justice meets his test of stability and well-orderedness: the theory can be embodied in institutions that are stable because they generate voluntary support by its members based on their shared sense that they are just and are widely regarded as such (*TJ* 4–5, 192–933, 397–399; *JF* 8–10, 124–126, 184–188; Freeman 2007b, 245–253). Finally, Rawls's account of a just economy is the most provocative feature of his theory of justice, providing a litmus test of its rational acceptability. His account implies a sharp critique of existing capitalist societies and defends a radical transformation of the ways they distribute income, wealth, and economic and political power. Rawls's defense of political equality – equal civil and political rights – is an important but familiar liberal ideal. On the other hand, his defense of economic egalitarianism challenges the common idea that socioeconomic inequality is either an inevitable, desirable, or fair feature of modern society, based on unequal talent, productivity, merit, and desert – with "winners and losers." Rawls also rejects the idea that there are natural property rights and natural market relations that justify economic inequalities.

The basic structure of society – the primary subject of a theory of justice – encompasses the state and the legal system (constitutional fundamentals), the economy, and the family. These institutions constitute the basic structure because

(1) they have a profound effect on persons' life chances, what each can hope for and achieve over an entire lifespan; and (2) unlike voluntary organizations, they are regulated by rules that involve legal coercion, which provide some assurance that they will be followed even when it goes against the inclination or advantage of individuals (*TJ* 6–10; *JF* 10–12; Freeman 2007b, 101–102, 464). The profound effect of the basic structure on persons' life chances is largely a result of the fact that it distributes primary social goods among persons, such as basic rights and liberties, opportunity, income and wealth, economic power/professional authority, and the social bases of self-respect. Rawls characterizes primary social goods as all-purpose means to human ends in general, whose distribution can be controlled by society, rather than being the effect of nature, luck, and other contingencies. Rawls subsequently characterizes such primary goods as the preconditions and resources necessary for persons to freely form their own conceptions of the good and act effectively to realize their conceptions (*TJ* 78–81; *JF* 57–60, 88; Freeman 2007b, 152–154, 478).

Rawls's conception of the economy turns on his account of the primary goods distributed by economic institutions, which sets the stage for his own normative view of how a just economy will distribute these goods. On this account, the key economy-related goods are opportunity (for economic position), income and wealth, the powers and prerogatives of economic authority, and the social bases of self-respect (*TJ* 52–73; Freeman 2007b, 104–105, 467–468). The economy also indirectly affects the distribution of basic political and civil liberties; in particular the "fair worth" of these liberties to democratic citizens whose opportunity for an effective voice in political life may be undermined by excessive inequalities of wealth and economic power (*TJ* 197–199; *JF* 148–153; *PL* 336–337). Thus, the distribution of the primary economy-related goods includes their effect on the "fair worth" of political rights, otherwise governed by his first principle of justice requiring equal civil and political liberties. Rawls's first principle is lexically prior to the second, blocking the justification of any system that limits basic liberties or their equality for the sake of a higher level of income.

Rawls's conception provides a rich account of the various primary goods whose distribution defines the normatively salient features of modern economies. What then is a just economy? On his well-known second principle of justice, inequalities in economic position are just if and only if (1) they work out to make the worst-off positions better off than they would be under any alternative economic arrangement, and (2) all positions are open to everyone under the requirement of fair equality of opportunity (*TJ* 52–56, 266; *JF* 42–44, 61–64; Freeman 2007b, 99–140). This principle must be combined with a just savings principle to reconcile it with justice for future generations (*TJ* 251–267; *JF* 159–161). Within the second principle, equality of opportunity is lexically prior to maximizing the social minimum of income, blocking the justification of unequal opportunities which might raise the social minimum. What results is a bold distributive paradigm of economic institutions. We evaluate economic institutions from the point of view of their outcome on the distribution of the primary goods at stake. Whose positions are made better off or worse off by this or that system of economic rules and institutions, and is there an alternative that would improve the worst-off position?

Rawls's conception of economic justice requires that the background institutions and procedures governing the economy are structured to satisfy the difference principle and the arrangement of positions it implies. On this conception, when such background institutions are just, then, whatever distribution of goods to individuals results is by definition just. There is no independent criterion of just outcome, apart from the justice of the background institutions that generate these outcomes. Rawls aptly characterizes his conception as one of pure procedural justice, in the sense that a just procedure is taken to define the justice of its outcome, whatever it turns out to be (*TJ* 74–77; *JF* 50–51; Freeman 2007b, 126–127, 400).

Rawls's rich account of the primary goods at stake in the structure of the economy introduces some ambiguities and complexities into the meaning of the difference principle and its institutional implications. On the face of it, the goods of income and wealth, the powers and prerogatives of economic authority, the social bases of self-respect, and the fair value of political liberties seem to be distinct, independent, and incommensurable values, and dimensions of an economy. Which of these goods do we employ to define "the worst off," and what makes them "better off"? An inequality in the powers and prerogatives of authority – e.g. between owners of capital, managers, and workers – may make the worst off (e.g. workers making minimum wage) better off in terms of income, but worse off in terms of these very powers (e.g. the exercise of control over one's work), or in terms of work-related self-respect; and vice versa, less income but more power. If trade-offs among these goods are required, on what basis are they to be determined? Income and work-based authority play quite different, and irreducible, roles in persons' self-respect and well-being (Doppelt 1981, 267–272; 2009, 138–142).

Rawlsians may assume that there is a reasonable solution which might provide a balancing of these goods to yield a clear characterization of worst off, better off, and the difference principle. Yet without one in hand, how can we characterize a viable institutional model of a just economy – quite central to test the stability and well-orderedness of Rawls's theory? Altering the distribution of income is much less difficult than altering the relations of economic power, ownership, and control – which involves transforming the organization of production, property rights, economic liberties, etc.

Rawls addresses these issues in *A Theory of Justice* by making simplifying assumptions concerning the interpretation and institutional embodiment of the difference principle. He accepts the working assumption that economic positions which are worst off in terms of income are also worst off in terms of workplace authority (*TJ* 82–85; *JF* 59; Doppelt 1981, 270–271). If income and power are interdependent variables, then we might also assume that economic inequalities and arrangements that make the worst-off positions better off in terms of income also make them better off in terms of authority. The result is that Rawls reads the difference principle to say that inequalities of income and power are just if and only if they raise the income of those in positions with the lowest income to a greater degree than any feasible alternative economic arrangement. Worst off and better off are reduced to the homogeneous measure of income (Doppelt 1981, 271–273). In effect, the primary good of workplace authority drops out of Rawls's account of economic justice and a just economic order, except in so far as a social division of labor and authority (with inequalities of power) is instrumental in raising the income of the worst-off positions higher than would be possible in any alternative division of labor and power.

How about the ways economic inequalities may affect the distribution of equality of opportunity, the fair worth of equal civil and political liberties, and equality in the social bases of self-respect? Any of these primary goods may impose constraints on economic inequalities of income and power that are independent of those sanctioned by the difference principle. In *A Theory of Justice*, Rawls makes certain simplifying assumptions that free the formulation of the difference principle from these problems. Whatever inequalities of income and power work out to maximize the social minimum (income), they must be attached to positions open to all, under fair equality of opportunity (*TJ* 63, 73–78, 264–266; *JF* 43–44). Fair equality of opportunity is taken to require equal educational opportunities and the use of law to eradicate all forms of bias and discrimination in employment and the workplace (*TJ* 243). Aside from such measures, if certain inequalities of income and power that maximize the income of the worst-off positions nonetheless generate inequality of opportunity, there is no characterization of them and they do not explicitly enter into the difference principle of economic justice.

The economy / 243

Similarly, while Rawls clearly rejects economic inequalities that undermine the fair value of political liberties, there is no characterization of them that is worked into the statement of the difference principle. In the main, a just society will block *the uses* of wealth and economic power to monopolize political influence and subvert the fair and democratic worth of citizens' equal liberties. This can be achieved by laws and policies that create public funding of campaigns, limit the role of lobbyists, constrain privately funded political advertisements, and similar measures (*TJ* 198; *JF* 149).

Does Rawls's demand that justice require equality in the social bases of self-respect place independent constraints on acceptable kinds and degrees of economic inequality? He acknowledges that unequal income and authority may well affect the self-respect of those in lesser positions (*TJ* 468, 478–479). Rawls makes the simplifying assumption that the equal liberties of democratic citizenship, together with equal opportunity, will suffice as the social bases of self-respect in a just society (*TJ* 205–206, 477–478; Doppelt 1981, 261–264). This paradigm of self-respect as democratic citizenship underlies one of Rawls's main arguments for the lexical priority of the first principle over the difference principle, blocking any system of unequal or lesser liberties for the sake of a higher social minimum (*TJ* 477–480). So, the simplifying assumption of a citizenship paradigm of self-respect generates a distinctive feature of Rawls's whole model of a just society: the priority of political over economic institutions in guaranteeing the equal respect required in a just society. As a result, Rawls takes the principle of equal liberties to be a matter of the constitutional fundamentals of a just society, while the difference principle can be accommodated by economic legislation.

The substantial pay-off of these simplifying assumptions is that they allow a clear unencumbered statement of a difference principle with evident practical implications. They allow Rawls to provide a viable institutional model of a just economy and polity – namely a democratic welfare state capitalism with a far higher social minimum and much lower degree of economic inequality than what prevails in societies today. This is a great advantage for a political theory that claims to generate a more well-ordered and stable society than its rivals, and existing societies. Rawls holds that different forms of society may best realize his principles of justice, depending on social conditions: so, in principle the theory is consistent with some form of democratic capitalism, with private property in the means of production, and some form of democratic socialism, with ownership and control of the means of production dispersed among workers' councils and/or shared with democratic government bodies (*TJ* 242).

Nonetheless, Rawls provides a model of a reformed, democratic welfare-state capitalism to establish the practical import of his theory and its stability. Many readers have assumed that this institutional model lies at the heart of *A Theory of Justice* although Rawls characterized it as "a property-owning democracy" (*TJ* 242–251; Doppelt 1981; Sandel 1982; Freeman 2007b, 224–226). Rawls arrives at this model by adopting a familiar account of modern economic institutions that distinguishes their two key functions: the allocation and production of wealth, and its distribution. The central virtue of the economy directed at the allocation/production of wealth is maximum productivity, efficiency, and economic growth. For Rawls, competitive economic markets governing the allocation of land, capital, and labor – with whatever inequalities of income and authority they involve – are unrivaled in the production of wealth and economic growth (*TJ* 239–242). Indeed such competitive markets may be embraced equally by regimes with private ownership of the means of production and those with some form of public ownership (*TJ* 234–242; Freeman 2007b, 219–223). However, when market mechanisms also determine the distribution of wealth, the result is injustice – the malaise of modern societies – poverty, unemployment, homelessness, malnutrition, morbidity, etc. In modern political economy, we count on the state to correct the maldistribution of goods that results from unfettered market forces: hence, social security, unemployment insurance, a minimum wage and hours, public provisions for the sick, disabled, poor, etc. funded by taxation and other mechanisms of redistribution.

This understanding of political economy provides Rawls with a template for his own model of a just economy. Armed with the distinction between the allocative/productive and distributive functions of the economy, the difference principle allows whatever market-driven inequalities of income, wealth, and economic authority are necessary to maximize the aggregate wealth of society, provided that the state redistribute this aggregate such that those left in the worst-off positions end up better off in terms of income than they would be under any other organization of production, with lesser or greater inequalities of income and power. The relentless play of market forces, private ownership of capital, unequal incentives, the pursuit of profit, downsizing, liquidations, bankruptcies, hostile takeovers, etc. are not by themselves just or unjust – even if the result is an initial maldistribution of earnings and employment. For, Rawlsian justice relies on a redistributive political policy of "transfer payments," a negative income tax, or wage subsidies undertaken by the state to assure that the difference principle is fulfilled (*TJ* 243–247; Freeman 2007b, 231). Market-driven relations with the inequalities they entail are just provided that they maximize the aggregate wealth of society in a manner the state can feasibly use to guarantee that everyone, especially the worst-off positions, will end up better off after the transfers, and better off than they would be under any other organization of production. In this context, it is important to distinguish between Rawls's principle of distributive justice and the state's redistributive policy that is justified by this principle. Clearly the concept of redistribution applies to Rawls's institutional model, not his unitary principle of just distribution.

Rawls's institutional model does not validate the existing concentrations of economic wealth and power in capitalist societies such as the USA, even if they try to "buy off" the working and middle classes with some measure of material benefits. This is a mistake because Rawls's difference principle condemns the existing economic relations in so far as they (1) harm the worst-off positions, (2) do not function to make them better off, and (3) do not make them as well off as they could be with a lesser concentration of wealth and power at the top. Take the example of public outrage in the USA over the taxpayer bailout of the "too big to fail" Wall Street banks and their underwriters. Outrage was focused on the outsized bonuses the bankers are giving themselves with taxpayer money, the very bankers that wrecked the economy. Obviously their bonuses aren't making anyone better off except themselves. More to the point it was changes in our nation's laws, policies, and regulatory agencies that gave the banks the "powers and prerogatives of authority" to make grossly irresponsible and imprudent decisions (bad loans, toxic mortgage-backed securities, unsustainable debt, derivatives trading, extreme undercapitalization, etc.) that produced a disaster for the rest of us – and may continue to make many worse off. The point is that Rawls's institutional model of a more just form of democratic welfare-state capitalism does not only require a radical redistribution of income. It also implies a radical change in both the kinds and inequalities of economic power that now attach to the positions of those at the top of the economy, and sacrifice the income of the worst-off positions.

Some readers of *A Theory of Justice* may have worried that Rawls's institutional model of a just society might be too close to welfare-state capitalist societies with their claims to maximal productivity and large concentrations of economic power, wealth, and political power at the top. These considerations motivated Rawls in later work to emphasize that his model of a just society in *TJ* is a "property-owning democracy" and to reject its description as a democratic welfare-state capitalism, although he acknowledges that the distinction between the two models is not clear in *TJ* (*JF* 135–140). In any case, Rawls's property-owning democracy is clearly a model with private ownership and control of the means of production. A property-owning democracy is supposed to be society in which capital, economic power, wealth, and political power are more widely dispersed among persons and groups than what prevails in existing capitalist welfare states (Freeman 2007b, 224–233). Rawls was well aware of Marx's critique of capitalist society and intends that the notion of a property-owning democracy blunts the force of this critique (*JF* 176–179; Freeman 2007b, 27–28). Nonetheless, the institutions Rawls describes in *TJ* approximate the model of a democratic welfare state, albeit one with lesser socioeconomic and political inequality and a much larger social minimum than what prevails in these societies. Rawls emphasizes that his model of a society with private ownership of the means of production is an "ideal system" that does not imply that historical forms are just, or even tolerable (*TJ* 242). The notion of a property-owning democracy is never fleshed out in Rawls's work, nor is it characterized in any way that differentiates it from the restructured, ideal democratic welfare state described in *TJ*. This is no criticism of Rawls's model of a just economy – which gives his entire theory a concrete practical and social meaning that many political theories lack.

Rawls's provocative conception of economic justice raises fruitful issues for scholars today. By making certain simplifying assumptions, in particular that the key parameters of the difference principle – its notions of "worst off" and "better-off" – can be cashed out in terms of income, Rawls is able to sketch a plausible model of just economic institutions. If we set his simplifying assumptions aside, we arrive at some intriguing questions. Suppose we bring "the power and prerogatives of authority" back into our notions of the worst-off positions, and what makes them better off, treating this dimension of economic justice as independent of and incommensurable with income. This complicates our model of a just economy – not simply because we will need a reasonable view of trade-offs between income and power to determine which structure of economic institutions (e.g. division of labor and power) makes persons better off than in viable alternatives (Doppelt 2009).

Workplace power and authority are far more complex than income. Power covers several dimensions of the workplace: power/authority over the conditions of work; the pace of work and how it is performed; hiring and promotions; the goals of a firm and the nature of its products; opportunities within one's work for judgment, skill, and autonomy. Which aspects of a workplace are most salient in our model of a just economy that creates a high or tolerable "social minimum" of the powers and prerogatives of authority? Unlike income, power is typically a zero-sum good: an inequality of power gives some people power over others, and this results in the latter's loss of power over their own work and other aspects of the workplace. If it is easy to see how inequalities of power (and income) function to raise the income of the worst off, it is far from clear how such inequalities of power can function to raise the power of the worst off.

Rawls makes the simplifying assumption that equality in the social bases of self-respect can be provided by the equal rights of democratic citizenship, fair equality of opportunity, and the fair worth of equal political liberties. While these are plausible social bases of self-respect, it is far less plausible to detach self-respect from the powers and prerogatives of authority, employment, the source of one's income, and one's relative position in the distribution of income (Doppelt 1981, 2009). In the USA serious injuries to self-respect result from unemployment, welfare-dependence, powerlessness and subordination in work, demeaning mindless self-stultifying work, and the inability to provide an adequate standard of living for oneself and dependent family members through one's earnings on the market. Thus the challenging issue is how to build the social dynamics of self-respect into a feasible institutional model of a just economy and the principles of justice themselves.

Gerald Doppelt

SEE ALSO:

Basic structure of society
The market
Marx, Karl
Primary goods, social
Property-owning democracy
Socialism
Two principles of justice

66.

EGOISM

ONE OF THE goals of the Kantian tradition in moral and political philosophy has been to defeat the egoist by showing that morality is rationally required. Early in *A Theory of Justice*, John Rawls seemingly renounces this particular Kantian goal. Egoism, Rawls tells us, is logically consistent, and not irrational, and as such it is no part of his project in moral and political philosophy to defeat it.

Accordingly, although in *TJ*, Rawls initially includes three forms of egoism: first-person dictatorship egoism (Everyone is to serve my interests), free-rider egoism (Everyone is to act justly except myself if I choose not to), and general egoism (Everyone is permitted to advance his interest as he pleases) on his list of conceptions from which persons in the original position are to choose, he immediately tells us that these forms of egoism do not, strictly speaking, belong on his list. First-person dictatorship egoism and free-rider egoism obviously violate a generality condition, and general egoism violates an ordering requirement because if everyone is authorized to advance his or her aims, there is no overall ranking or ordering of competing claims. Given that Rawls assumes that any conception of justice must satisfy both a generality condition and an ordering requirement, these assumptions provide the basis for the quick elimination of these forms of egoism from Rawls's list (*TJ* 107). All the other conceptions on Rawls's list are clearly moral conceptions, and egoism, Rawls tells us, is "a challenge to any such conception." This might lead us to conclude that Rawls was simply not interested in considering any kind of challenge that egoism might present to his work. That conclusion would certainly accord with Rawls's previous work from "Outline of a Decision Procedure in Ethics" (1951) to *TJ* (1971).

Egoism / 249

It is bit surprising, therefore, to find that later in *TJ*, when Rawls is concerned with the stability of his conception of justice to find him asking whether people who have a sense of justice would also have adequate reason to act justly even if they were to evaluate their situation from a self-interested perspective (*TJ* 295–296). Egoism, of course, would maintain that such people would not have adequate reason to act justly, but Rawls hoped to show just the opposite in order to establish the stability of his conception of justice. However, Rawls did not want to test the stability of his theory by relying on premises that simply presupposed egoism, any more than he wanted to test his theory's stability by relying on premises that simply presupposed his theory (*TJ* 497–499). That is why Rawls ultimately sought to determine whether people who have a sense of justice would also have adequate reason to act justly even if they were to evaluate their situation from a self-interested perspective, or from what he, in a further refinement, began calling the point of view of a thin theory of the good as reflected in principles of rational choice (*TJ* 505). Thus, it is particularly significant that Rawls came to realize that he could not achieve that result; he was unable to show that people who had a sense of justice would also have adequate reason to act justly when judged from the point of view of a thin theory of the good as reflected in principles of rational choice, Rawls came to see that the arguments that he used at the end of *TJ* to ground acting justly depend on ideals of personal conduct, friendship, and association that themselves presuppose his conception of justice. This failure led Rawls to reinterpret his work in a political direction, culminating in his second book, *Political Liberalism*.

When Rawls came to realize that justice as fairness, as he had developed it in *TJ*, itself presupposed a partially comprehensive Kantian conception of the good, he further realized that the stability of justice as fairness was threatened, not just from a self-interested point of view, or the point of view of a thin theory of the good, but also from alternative comprehensive moral views that were opposed to a partially comprehensive Kantian conception of the good as well. This, of course, led Rawls to transform justice as fairness from a comprehensive conception to a political conception that he then could argue was supported by an overlapping consensus of reasonable comprehensive views. In this way, Rawls thought he had shown how his conception of justice as fairness, now understood as a political not a comprehensive conception, and supported by an overlapping consensus, would have the stability that his earlier conception of justice as fairness, now recognized to be a comprehensive conception, could never have.

Yet what about that initial question of whether Rawls's conception of justice as fairness could be shown to be stable from a self-interested point of view or from the point of view of a thin theory of the good? Rawls never explicitly returned to that question, even reformulated so that it was directed at justice as fairness as a political conception. Rawls might be interpreted as indirectly responding to this question when he claimed that he was now seeking to establish that justice as fairness is supported by "reasonable" comprehensive conceptions. Given that "reasonable" here means roughly "morally reasonable," evaluation simply from a self-interested perspective, or simply from the perspective of a thin theory of the good, would now just be excluded by definition. That would imply that Rawls was just no longer interested in seeking to answer his original question about the stability of justice as fairness now interpreted as a political conception.

Yet why the subsequent lack of interest in this question? Maybe Rawls came to think that there really was no way of showing that justice as fairness, even reinterpreted as a political conception, is stable from a self-interested point of view or from the point of view of a thin theory of the good. Maybe so. Still, there is at least one other way of thinking about Rawls's theory of justice, or at least a way of thinking about a more general variant of his theory, such that it would provide an adequate response to egoism or to a self-interested perspective.

In Rawls's theory, the normative standard of the original position is employed to decide whose interests should be served and to what extent they should be served. Self and others are thus purportedly treated fairly in Rawls's original position. However, this standard provides no response to the egoist.

Now consider another analogous normative standard that also arguably treats self and others appropriately. That standard is the principle of non-question-beggingness, a requirement for a good argument. Self and others are appropriately taken into account by this normative standard through a non-question-begging weighing of an individual's self-interested and altruistic reasons when they come into conflict. This it does by favoring high-ranking altruistic reasons over lower-ranking self-interested reasons and favoring high-ranking self-interested reasons over low-ranking altruistic reasons in cases of conflict. This standard tends to approve of similar normative requirements to those approved of by Rawls's normative standard of the original position. Yet by non-question-beggingly (hence, fairly) taking self-interested and altruistic reasons into account, this standard provides an adequate response to both egoism and altruism, thus securing for itself the same sort of stability that Rawls had first sought for his own normative standard in *TJ*.

James P. Sterba

SEE ALSO:

Altruism
Conception of the good
Congruence
The original position
The reasonable and the rational
Reciprocity
Self-interest
Sense of justice

67.

THE ENVIRONMENT

RAWLS'S CONCEPTION OF justice does not directly address our treatment of the environment. As a theory of social justice, and not a comprehensive account of morality, it focuses primarily on the basic structure of society. His main goal is to develop principles to regulate the shared institutions of a democratic society in which individuals are understood to be free and equal, reasonable and rational moral persons. Rawls apparently assumed that nonhuman animals lack the two moral powers necessary for full participation in a scheme of social cooperation. (This is not controversial for the vast majority of species.) Therefore, he assumed that reciprocity of social justice was not owed to them. This is emphatically not to say, however, that they are beyond moral consideration. As he observes in *A Theory of Justice*, while animals are not owed the rights of persons under his principles of social justice,

> it does not follow that there are no requirements at all in regard to them, nor in our relations with the natural order. Certainly it is wrong to be cruel to animals and the destruction of a whole species can be a great evil. The capacity for feelings of pleasure and pain and for the forms of life of which animals are capable clearly imposes duties of compassion and humanity in their case. I shall not attempt to explain these considered beliefs. They are outside the scope of the theory of justice, and it does not seem possible to extend the contract doctrine so as to include them in a natural way. A correct conception of our relations to animals and to nature would seem to depend upon a theory of the natural order and our place in it. (*TJ* 448)

The environment / 253

Although our proper relation to nature and the environment is a question that goes beyond the scope of justice as fairness, it is possible to develop important, although limited, conclusions concerning the treatment of the environment from within the theory.

A theory of "the natural order and our place in it" is (at least part of) what Rawls would later call a comprehensive doctrine. A well-ordered society is characterized by a diversity of conflicting comprehensive doctrines, so we should expect reasonable disagreement about the intrinsic value of natural objects and individuals, species, and nature itself. The ideas of public reason and the duty of civility put limits on the direct appeals in public political justifications to specific comprehensive doctrines. Therefore, it would appear that Rawls is ruling out arguments that appeal to the intrinsic value of nature. To be sure, there would still be room for arguments supporting the conservation of natural resources, but these would apparently have to be tied to some widely shared human interests that can be defended within the scope of a political conception of justice.

However, Rawls himself limits the scope of public reason to constitutional essentials and matters of basic justice. Whether and how public reason applies beyond these areas are questions that Rawls does not explore. At one point, he suggests that it may be desirable to apply the ideal of public reason more broadly, but he holds that this "may not always be so" (*PL* 215). More frequently, he holds that on matters of ordinary legislation, as opposed to constitutional essentials or basic question of justice, "citizens can vote their nonpolitical values and try to convince other citizens accordingly. The limits of public reason do not apply" (*PL* 246). Therefore, Rawls holds, a well-ordered society may choose to devote its resources to the preservation of the environment based on the comprehensive doctrines that are held by the majority of citizens. As an example of how legislators may appeal to perfectionist values to answer "suitably circumscribed questions... or certain matters of policy," Rawls writes:

> a bill may come before the legislature that allots public funds to preserve the beauty of nature in certain places (national parks and wilderness areas). While some arguments in favor may rest on political values, say the benefits of these areas as places of general recreation, political liberalism with its idea of public reason does not rule out as a reason the beauty of nature as such or the good of wildlife achieved by protecting its habitat. With the constitutional essentials firmly in place, these matters may appropriately be put to a vote. (*JF* 152 n.26)

When the requirements of social justice are secure, a democratic society may choose to devote resources to goals that are valued not simply as political goods, but as intrinsic goods as judged from the point of view of some particular comprehensive doctrine(s).

To find an argument that conservation of the environment is not merely permissible, as seen above, but is in some way a requirement of justice, we will have to remain within the limits of a political conception. And this does, indeed, mean ruling out appeals to the intrinsic value of nature. Still, there are two obvious ways in which this can be done. First, Rawls holds that a well-ordered society is "a fair system of cooperation over time, from one generation to the next" (*PL* 15). In order for a society to remain just over time, citizens have a duty of justice to ensure that future generations are in a position to maintain the justice and stability of their basic institutions. This means that they cannot deplete resources to the point that it would impose severe hardships on future generations that might imperil their institutions and the exercise of their liberties. Because the parties in the original position "have no information as to which generation they belong," they will choose a principle of just savings to address "the question of the appropriate rate of capital saving and of the conservation of natural resources and the environment of nature" (*TJ* 118–119). Rawls does not give a precise statement of a principle to govern this issue and only indicates some broad constraints. "Presumably different rates are assigned to different stages. When people are poor and saving is difficult, a lower rate of savings should be required; whereas in a wealthier society greater savings may reasonably be expected since the real burden of saving is less" (*TJ* 255).

Some environmental issues have an international dimension, as well. Climate change raises serious concerns of justice along both dimensions, as our present conduct will impose severe costs, both financial and human, in the future and these will be unevenly born among different societies. Rawls does not address this explicitly in *The Law of Peoples*, and some have doubted that his framework allows us to do so, but there are at least two ways in which it can be done. First, Rawls holds that well-ordered societies have "duty of assistance" toward "societies burdened by unfavorable conditions" (*LP* 106). The aim of this duty is "to realize and preserve just (or decent) institutions, and not simply to increase, much less to maximize indefinitely, the average level of wealth, or the wealth of any society or any particular class in society" (*LP* 107). It is an obvious corollary of this duty that well-ordered societies have a duty not to undermine the conditions necessary for the stability of just (or decent) institutions and the securing of basic human rights, which include, notably, "the right to life (to the means of subsistence and security)" (*LP* 65). There is now no doubt that the effects of climate change will result in the severe deprivation of many people in poor societies. To the extent that wealthy societies contribute to this, they are violating this corollary to the duty of assistance.

Climate change threatens to be catastrophic for some, but lesser environmental effects across borders can also be addressed in the Society of Peoples. Rawls envisions the creation of various "cooperative organizations" to establish "standards of fairness for trade as well as certain provisions for mutual assistance" (*LP* 42). Although not mentioned explicitly, it is not hard to imagine a similar organization to regulate international environmental disputes. One might object that such organizations would be dominated by the narrow self-interest of the most powerful societies. But in Rawls's Society of Peoples, the principles of these organizations are established from behind a veil of ignorance in which "no people knows whether its economy is large or small" (*LP* 43). Well-ordered societies, Rawls argues, will be moved to comply with the requirements of such fair organizations because they have "a moral character" (*LP* 25). They will "offer to other people fair terms of political and social cooperation. These fair terms are those that a people sincerely believes other equal peoples might accept also; and should they do so, a people will honor the terms it has proposed even in those cases where that people might profit by violating them" (*LP* 35). Moved by their moral character, well-ordered societies will not unilaterally impose costs – environmental and others – on others in violation of a standard of reciprocity.

Jon Mandle

SEE ALSO:

Animals
Duty of assistance
Law of Peoples
Political conception of justice
Public reason

68.

ENVY

ENVY IS A nonmoral feeling or emotion, one that is aroused by the recognition that others are faring better than oneself. Critics of egalitarian justice often charge that it springs from envy. The envious person would prefer to have less of some good than to have more of it if that meant having less than others. If egalitarian justice required worsening the position of the better off without raising the position of the worse off, then it might be motivated by feelings of envy. Rawls took this possibility seriously. He sought to show that the egalitarian conception of justice that he proposes and defends, "justice as fairness," is not one that is based on envy. As he allows, "strict egalitarianism, the doctrine which insists upon an equal distribution of all primary goods, conceivably derives from this propensity" (*TJ* 472). But justice as fairness does not, since there is an independent justification for it, one that does not appeal to envious feelings. This is shown by three basic features of the original position argument that Rawls advances in favor of his conception of justice. The first feature concerns the motivation of the parties in the original position. It is stipulated that the parties are mutually disinterested. They do not concern themselves with how others fare. It follows that the parties are not motivated by considerations of envy or spite. The second feature concerns the general design of the original position. Its design and the constraints it imposes have justifications that make no mention of envy. The third feature is the maximin decision rule that the parties rely on in justifying justice as fairness over alternative conceptions. Reliance on this rule is inconsistent with giving considerations of envy weight in one's deliberations, for the maximin rule, at least on its lexical formulation, directs one never to oppose or object to others having more than oneself if their having more does not leave one with less.

It is worth asking whether Rawls, with this response, really answers the critic. The critic might be making either one of two claims. He might be claiming (1) that a conception of justice springs from envy if it cannot be justified without appealing to envious feelings, or he might be claiming (2) that a conception of justice springs from envy if its proponents are led to accept it out of feelings of envy, irrespective of whether it can be justified in a way that makes no mention of envy. Rawls's response looks effective when directed against (1), but less so when directed against (2). Since Rawls allows that "the appeal to justice is often a mask for envy" (*TJ* 473), it might be the case that the envy-free justifications for his conception of justice are themselves rationalizations of this feeling.

The issue here is delicate, for a conception of justice both could be correct and one that attracts support because it springs from envy. The fact that a commitment to a particular conception of justice is best explained by feelings of envy toward others would not establish that that conception was misguided. Still, this fact might undermine one's confidence that the conception really was correct. Rawls, however, can point out that his conception of justice does not justify egalitarian proposals that would benefit no one and harm some. It therefore looks to be a poor expression of the vice of envy.

Two final complications can be mentioned. First, Rawls allows that the difference principle in theory could justify economic inequalities between the better off and the worse off that damaged the self-respect of the latter. In this circumstance, Rawls claims, the worse off can object to the inequalities. This would be an example of what he terms "excusable envy" (*TJ* 468). This concession, however, does not show that the argument for justice as fairness must, at some point, appeal to envious feelings; for the economic inequalities in question do come at the expense of the worse off. The inequalities damage the self-respect of those on the bottom, thereby harming them and making it untrue that the inequalities benefit some without adversely affecting any. Second, and intriguingly, Rawls sometimes formulates the difference principle in terms that are inconsistent with the maximin idea on its lexical formulation. Thus, at one point, he claims that the difference principle "does seem to correspond to a natural meaning of fraternity: namely, to the idea of not wanting to have greater advantages unless this is to the benefit of others who are less well off" (*TJ* 90). A commitment to fraternity, so construed, implies that the worse off can object to gains to the better off, even if these gains do not adversely affect them. The critic of justice as fairness, who surmises that it is a conception of justice that is based in part on envy, could be forgiven for suspecting that Rawlsian fraternity is a rationalization for the rancor of envy.

Steve Wall

SEE ALSO:

> *Difference principle*
> *Maximin rule of choice*
> *Moral psychology*
> *Moral sentiments*

69.

EQUAL OPPORTUNITY, DEMOCRATIC INTERPRETATION

I N RAWLS'S VERY first statement of his two principles of justice, the second principle says that social and economic inequalities are to be arranged so that "it is reasonable to expect that they will work out for everyone's advantage, and provided the positions and offices to which they attach...are open to all" ("Justice as Fairness" [1958] in *CP* 48). In subsequent writings in the 1960s and in his initial statement of the two principles in *A Theory of Justice* (*TJ* 53) the core formulation of the second principle, requiring "everyone's advantage" and positions "open to all," is retained.

Rawls recognizes the key terms, "everyone's advantage" and "open to all" (or "equally open"), require explication. He provides this by developing (*TJ* §§12 and 13) three different ways to interpret the second principle of justice, and in each of these interpretations the two key terms are linked together. Here he closely follows the pattern set in his important 1968 paper "Distributive Justice: Some Addenda" (*CP* 158–164).

The first interpretation is called by Rawls the system of natural liberty (a term he takes from Adam Smith). Two distinct themes are involved here. One is that positions are "equally open" where there are no legal or institutional or customary barriers that restrict entry into an occupation to one class or kind of individual and no formal restrictions on the taking of opportunities. The result of ending such restrictions would be "careers open to talents"; individuals would be free to exercise their talents or seize opportunities up to the limit of their own abilities. This leads directly to the second theme. In a system of natural liberty (assuming a self-stabilizing open and competitive supply–demand free market system), the ideal result would be a recurring tendency toward pareto-optimal efficiency in the exchange of goods and services. In an efficient and productive economy the economic well-being of all those involved would be advanced. The "correct" final arrangement is one that results from the actual use of aptitudes and talents by individual persons in a free market system under conditions of formal equality of opportunity, and nothing should be done which disturbs this resulting pattern (*TJ* 57–63).

Rawls makes two basic criticisms of the system of natural liberty. First, it gives too much weight to one's social connections and to one's established position. These are things one is born into; the fact of birth into a particular family or class, something no one is responsible for in their own case, should not be determinative of one's success in life or of one's development and use of talents to the degree that is allowed in the system of natural liberty.

The liberal interpretation, the second of Rawls's two interpretations, takes its rise from this claim. The leading idea is that "positions are to be not only open in a formal sense, but that all should have a fair chance to attain them." Something can be done to reduce the difference in advantage that accrues to individual persons in virtue of initial social circumstances. For example, the provision of public education for all at no special cost to the individual or to their family or taxation on inherited wealth would be effective toward such an end. The implicit ideal here is that initial social advantages (or disadvantages) should be mitigated up to the point that "in all sectors of society there should be equal prospects of culture and achievement for everyone similarly motivated and endowed" (*TJ* 63).

But after developing this idea of fair equality of opportunity, the liberal interpretation goes no further; it sticks with the emphasis on efficiency (at the level of practices and institutions in the basic structure) and with the laissez-faire approach characteristic of the natural liberty system (*TJ* 57, 63–64). This brings us to Rawls's second criticism of the system of natural liberty. Not only does it permit "distributive shares to be improperly influenced by…factors [social circumstances and such chance contingencies as accident and good fortune] so arbitrary from a moral point of view," but it also relies on a resultant scheme, efficiency, which is radically indeterminate and can, in some cases, be unfair. (For a brief account of efficiency, see *TJ* 59–62; also Dyke 1981, 91–98.) In any society there will be numerous points (indeterminately many) on an efficiency frontier. Each of them is equally efficient; on grounds of efficiency alone, then, there is no choice between them (*TJ* 58–63). The problem of indeterminacy is one that the liberal interpretation, given its commitment to efficiency and a laissez-faire approach thereto, shares with the system of natural liberty.

The liberal interpretation is problematic for another reason. Even if we actually did a good bit to provide fair chances by significantly reducing the differences

Equal opportunity, democratic interpretation / 261

between persons that accrue to them from their initial social circumstances, it "still permits the distribution of wealth and income to be determined by the natural distribution of abilities and talents" (*TJ* 64). The liberal interpretation still gives too much sway to the natural endowment of individuals. Why is it a matter of fair chances to attempt to reduce the gap between people as regards their initial social circumstances (and the undue advantage/disadvantage this brings) but to ignore such a gap in the case of their natural endowments? For the two sets of factors – one's starting social position and one's natural endowment – seem to be equally matters that individuals are wholly unresponsible for in their own cases (*TJ* 274); they are equally "arbitrary from a moral perspective" (*TJ* 63–65). Rawls concludes, "we may want to adopt a principle which recognizes this fact and also mitigates the arbitrary effects of the natural lottery itself. That the liberal conception fails to do this encourages one to look for another interpretation" of the second principle of justice (*TJ* 64).

This brings us to what Rawls calls "Democratic Equality" (*TJ* §13), the interpretation he prefers (*TJ* 64–65). The main feature of this interpretation is that it rejects efficiency per se as the end goal (and the entire laissez-faire approach, as regards outcomes). In place of efficiency Rawls puts the difference principle. This principle says that developments away from a hypothetical situation of strict equality in income and wealth should be taken when they're beneficial for everyone (or at least leave no one worse off), up to the point of reaching the maximum benefit of the least well-off group. This maximum benefit point is on the efficiency frontier for a given society; indeed, on that frontier, it is the optimally efficient point that is "closest to equality" – the point on that frontier that most reduces the inequality between the top-most and the bottom-most income groups (*JF* 68, 62, 123).

The difference principle accomplishes two things here. It is Rawls's solution to the indeterminacy of efficiency, the end goal shared by the two previous interpretations. And the difference principle is his main device for mitigating the inegalitarian effect of the two main contingencies (natural endowments and initial social circumstances). These contingencies powerfully affect a person's life prospects, advantageously for some and disadvantageously for others. Indeed, they are among the main sources of inequality between people.

What about fair equality of opportunity; does its basic formulation change at all in the move from the liberal interpretation to the democratic one? From what has been said, one would expect some change. But in *A Theory of Justice* Rawls says nothing explicitly (and offers no examples) suggesting a change.

This is not surprising when one considers the difficulties involved in dealing with differences in natural endowment. Clearly, it would be very difficult to work directly on the natural endowment of persons. Few examples of direct rearrangement come to mind (and these are highly controversial), such as benign procedures of genetic engineering designed to eliminate subsequent birth or health defects (Gutmann 1980, 255 n.27). The more promising strategy is to work indirectly on natural endowment, by rearranging through social measures those circumstances that are known to influence that endowment.

Rawls regards health as a primary *natural* good (*TJ* 54), and here some feasible and desirable ways to deal indirectly with people's natural endowment are available. For example, public health and other measures (sanitation, clean air and water, vaccinations, reduction of lead in the environment, adequate prenatal and childhood nutrition) would significantly cut the incidence of childhood diseases and other forms of impairment or even disablement. Such steps would be designed to mitigate disadvantages due to natural endowment or to one's prebirth or early life health history. In sum, there is certainly a biological or natural component of health. But there are obviously social bases of health, too, so health itself is a product of both natural and social influences. And Rawls does say, in his later writings, that provisions for health and medical care fall under fair equality of opportunity (*JF* 174).

The standard interpretation (insofar as it is based on *A Theory of Justice*) is that fair equality of opportunity aims at eliminating "inequalities that can be traced to class backgrounds and the wealth of one's parents"; it aims at preventing such social contingencies from "being transformed into unequal shares" of such social resources as positions and income and wealth (Mandle 2009, 27–29). But the democratic interpretation has a wider scope than that; it recognizes a broader set of opportunities over which fair equality is to be ranged than does the liberal interpretation and requires consideration of important differences in *both* social starting points and natural endowments.

One reason this point has not been widely seen is that Rawls lumps both the democratic and the liberal version together under the same heading: fair equality of opportunity (*TJ* 57). This has led readers to tend to think of fair equality of opportunity as the selfsame thing in each case.

More important, when Rawls glosses "fair equality of opportunity" he often describes it as involving a fair chance such that "those who have the same level of talent and ability and the same willingness to use these gifts should have the same prospects of success regardless of their social class of origin, the class into which they are born and develop until the age of reason" (*JF* 43–44). But, unlike his other iterations of this gloss (*TJ* 63; *LP* 115), Rawls says that "fair equality of opportunity here means *liberal* equality" (*JF* 44, italics added). There is a distinction in Rawls's mind between liberal fair equality of opportunity and *democratic* fair equality.

Democratic fair equality of opportunity focuses on both of the main contingencies, thereby differing from liberal fair equality (which focuses only on social contingencies, entirely ignoring natural endowment). Just as liberal fair equality of opportunity builds on and adds to the formal equality of opportunity characteristic of the natural liberty system, so democratic fair equality of opportunity builds on and adds to liberal equality of opportunity.

The point of democratic fair equality of opportunity is to try (through the institutions of the basic structure) to make people less unequal at the point where they actually enter into adult life, as citizens and as workers, and to make sure that everyone there, so far as possible, has the basic capabilities required to be contributing members of society. It is precisely where a fundamental equality in starting points cannot be fully and strictly achieved that concern for reducing the inequality of *resultant outcomes* is in order. The difference principle, operating on an agenda of reciprocity (*PL* 16–18), complements democratic fair equality of opportunity by reducing – and, ideally, minimizing – the gap between persons as regards outcomes.

In this discussion I have set out Rawls's exposition of fair equality of opportunity (from *TJ* chapter 2). I regard this "informal" exposition as basic, but it does not take account of other possible considerations for choosing fair equality that might have weight in the original position (*TJ* chapter 3). Democratic fair equality and the difference principle belong to Rawls's notion of justice as fairness, the interpretation of political liberalism that he prefers. But Rawls makes clear, in his later writings, that justice as fairness is only one of several variant interpretations of political liberalism; and democratic fair equality of opportunity and the difference principle will not figure in all of these (*PL* 6–7, 228–230).

Rex Martin

SEE ALSO:

Difference principle
Fair equality of opportunity
Health and health care
Least-advantaged position
The original position

F

70.

FACTS, GENERAL (IN OP ARGUMENT AND AS PART OF JUSTIFICATION)

THE CHOICE OF the parties in the original position is determined by their interests, their knowledge, and the available options. The knowledge of the parties is restricted to general facts (*TJ* §24; *PL* 22–28, 70; *JF* §§6, 11, 25–26, 35).

The original position models the reasonable constraints on the choice of principles of justice. Placed behind a veil of ignorance, the parties in the original position do not know particular facts about their gender, race, skills, what wealth they own, or similar facts about themselves or those they represent. The parties are also ignorant about particular facts about their society, such as the distribution of religious beliefs, what sorts of natural resources the society has access to, or the distribution of wealth and opportunities amongst different classes of citizens. The idea is to shield the parties from knowledge that could lead them to propose unfair terms of social cooperation, but let them know enough to choose principles of justice that can define the basic structure of a well-ordered society. So, the parties know that they have a conception of the good, but not what it is, and they know certain general facts: that they are in circumstances of justice, facts about human nature, psychology, and needs, the general laws of social theory and economics, and that the members of their society affirm a diversity of philosophical, religious, political, and social doctrines (*TJ* §24).

After *A Theory of Justice*, Rawls realized that the general fact of reasonable pluralism undermines the argument for stability presented in part III of that work. The burdens of judgment imply a cluster of general facts that together undermine the hope for stability based on shared affirmation of liberalism as a comprehensive doctrine (see *CP* 425, 445, 474–492; *PL* 36–38, 58; *JF* §11 and part v). The most important of these facts are, first, the fact of reasonable pluralism, that a pluralism of reasonable comprehensive doctrines is a permanent feature of democratic societies, and second, the fact of oppression, that societal consensus on a comprehensive doctrine only can be established through coercive state power. The facts of reasonable pluralism and oppression imply a third fact, namely, that the social unity and stability of a democratic regime must be based on support from within a diversity of comprehensive and political doctrines. In short, the hope for democratic community is unrealistically utopian; only a society well-ordered around a political conception of justice can be both just and stable (*JF* 187–188). To articulate justice as fairness as such a political conception, and to show how it can be the subject of a stabilizing overlapping consensus, are two of the main aims of Rawls's writings after *A Theory of Justice*.

Justice as fairness has been criticized for both being too fact-insensitive and too fact-sensitive. Utilitarians might favor a thinner veil of ignorance that allows the parties (or an impartial spectator) to know all particular facts, but secures impartiality by leaving them ignorant of (or disinterested in) what position they inhabit or represent. Discourse ethicists and realists might argue that the veil should be lifted altogether. Conversely, G. A. Cohen has argued that first principles of justice must be entirely fact-insensitive.

Jeppe von Platz

SEE ALSO:

> *Burdens of judgment*
> *Circumstances of justice*
> *Justification: freestanding/political*
> *The original position*
> *Political conception of justice*
> *Reasonable pluralism*

71.

FAIR EQUALITY OF OPPORTUNITY

THE IDEAL OF equal opportunity features in a number of places in John Rawls's theory of justice, but the most prominent one is, by far, the role it plays in his second principle of justice. The first part of that principle says that social and economic inequalities are just if and when they are attached to offices and positions that are open to all under conditions of, what Rawls calls, fair equality of opportunity (FEOP). Whereas the difference principle, the second part of Rawls's second principle, has received enormous attention, the FEOP has received nowhere near as much. This neglect is not entirely justified (some commentators have even referred to the FEOP as Rawls's Trojan horse).

The FEOP has at least two noteworthy features. The first and obvious one is Rawls's designation of his equality of opportunity as "fair." The designator distinguishes Rawls's ideal from "formal equality of opportunity" (which is sometimes referred to as the ideal of "careers open to talent") (*JF* 43). The latter holds when institutions place no formal barriers to individuals' attainment of scarce and competitive positions (e.g. jobs, admittance to university). This, in effect, nondiscrimination principle holds that no one should be barred from a position due to features such as skin color or sex. For Rawls this nondiscrimination understanding of equal opportunities was insufficient. This ideal of formal equality of opportunity, taken on its own, "means an equal chance to leave the less fortunate behind in the personal quest for influence and social position" (*TJ* 106–107). His FEOP, in contrast, is a much more substantive ideal. It requires not only the removal of formal barriers of discrimination in the competition for jobs and positions, but also something by way of leveling the playing field in the run up to these jobs. Imagine, to use a famous example (Williams 1962), a society in which enlistment to the army carries a lot of prestige and benefits. And suppose that trials for these military positions involve some physical test. Even if no formal discrimination is in place, it may well turn out that those who win these positions come predominantly from the higher rungs of the socioeconomic ladder, simply because they are better fed and thus in better physical shape. This de facto socioeconomic barrier to the attainment of positions of power is precisely what Rawls's FEOP sought to correct. So whereas formal equality of opportunity entails only the minimal requirement of "careers open to talent," Rawls's FEOP adds the requirement of "fair background." In practice, the FEOP would imply, for example, subsidizing private schools and the funding of a public school system (*CP* 141), as well as justifying certain means of taxation, such as on inheritance, and a negative income tax (*CP* 141, 143). The latter follows, says Rawls, because FEOP is jeopardized when inequalities of income exceed a certain range.

For some commentators, the FEOP represents a great progressive stride, whereas for others it still falls short of an adequate ideal. We may mention two points to that effect. First, Rawls recognized (following Plato), that the family is a major obstacle to equality of opportunity (*CP* 596). Should the family be abolished, then, he famously asked (*TJ* 511). Regardless of the (obvious) negative answer he settled for (*JF* 163), the very recognition of this question signals an important insight for our understanding of equality of opportunity, something which did not go unnoticed by feminists. On the other hand, some claimed that Rawls's ideal of equality of opportunity does not go far enough. FEOP, recall, does not rest content with removing formal obstacles to opportunities, and depicts socioeconomic obstacles as also unjust. But this conception of equality of opportunity sees no injustice with natural (or innate) impediments to opportunities. Having a lesser marketable talent compared to another is no infringement of equality of opportunity on Rawls's reading. This can be gleaned from Rawls's following characterization of FEOP: "those who are at the same level of talent and ability, and have the same willingness to use them, should have the same prospects of success regardless of their initial place in the social system, that is, irrespective of the income class to which they are born" (*TJ* 73). This is justified, on Rawls's view, because these inequalities of natural talent would be corrected for (or compensated) by the difference principle. But of course such a claim does little to convince Rawls's egalitarian critics. Consequently, these egalitarians to the left of Rawls have put forward a rival understanding of equality of opportunity, sometimes termed "radical" or "socialist" equality of opportunity (Cohen 2009, 17). Whereas Rawls's FEOP removes socioeconomic (as well as formal) obstacles to one's opportunities, the radical ideal of equality of opportunity supplements that requirement also with natural or innate barriers to one's opportunity set.

Fair equality of opportunity / 271

One noteworthy feature of Rawls's ideal of fair equality of opportunity, then, concerns its contrast to the more conventional "formal equality of opportunity" on the one hand, and the more radical "luck egalitarian" understanding of equality of opportunity. The second noteworthy feature concerns the relation between FEOP and the difference principle. Rawls's theory of justice famously speaks of two principles of justice, but commentators (Arneson 1999; Nagel 1997, 307) have noted that it contains, in fact, three: the principle of basic liberties, FEOP, and the difference principle. These three principles are held by a relation of lexical priority, namely, each principle must be exhausted before the next one is applied. This special relationship has important implications for the role played by the ideal of equal opportunities in the Rawlsian scheme. Now, there are different interpretations as to what Rawls precisely meant by lexical priority. On one, strict, interpretation the lexical priority between the FEOP and the difference principle implies that no deviation is allowed from strict equality of opportunity between the equally talented and motivated, even when the trade-off represents an enormous gain to the worse off in terms of primary goods. This would imply spending all available resources on improving FEOP before we are allowed to invest resources along the lines of the difference principle. To illustrate, the FEOP would require tutoring middle-class talented students in order to make sure they have the same chances of success as equally talented super-rich kids. As long as those resources would continue to improve FEOP, even when concerning inequalities between the rich and super-rich, these resources must not be spent on boosting the bundle of primary goods held by the worse-off members of society. That seems wildly counterintuitive (Arneson 1999, 82).

The Rawlsian account of equality of opportunity has not received as much attention as the implications of the difference principle, I said. But one important exception is the application of Rawls's theory of justice to the sphere of health care, undertaken by Norman Daniels (Daniels 1985). The obvious way of filling this particular lacuna left by Rawls (nobody in the original position, recall, is ever sick), would have been to identify health care as a primary good and thus place it under the auspices of the difference principle. Part of Daniels's innovative approach was to resist this move and to rather justify the distribution of health-care resources through the lexically prior FEOP. He justified doing so by identifying the important link between health and individuals' opportunities to carry out their life plans. (This strategy was later endorsed by Rawls himself (*PL* 184; *JF* 174).) Perhaps the most important implication of this strategy is that it justifies a strictly equal distribution (as the FEOP mandates) of health care, rather than merely a maximin one (as the difference principle would have required).

Rawls's ideal of equality of opportunity thus helps justify a strictly equal distribution of health care, something which does tally with egalitarian intuition (see for example Walzer 1983, 86–91).

Shlomi Segall

SEE ALSO:

Equal opportunity, democratic interpretation
Family
Two principles of justice

72.

FAIRNESS, PRINCIPLE OF

RAWLS'S THEORY OF justice primarily concerns the morality of institutions and secondarily the morality of conduct under them. A central theme of the latter is that "We are not to gain from the cooperative efforts of others without doing our fair share" (*TJ* 96.) This idea, its implications and Rawls's terminology evolve as his theory of justice develops. In 1964 Rawls presented what he then called "the duty of fair play" as the ground of a widely applicable "moral obligation to obey the law" (*CP* 117–128), whereas in 1971 "the principle of fairness" is said to ground an obligation of obedience to law that applies to only a limited subset of citizens (*TJ* 308–312). These changes are related to Rawls's distinguishing "obligations," based on fairness and incurred by voluntary actions, from "natural duties," which obtain independently of anyone's voluntary acts (*TJ* 96).

In "Legal Obligation and the Duty of Fair Play," Rawls says that fair play calls for compliance with the rules of an institution when (1) the institution is a "mutually beneficial and just scheme of social cooperation"; (2) compliance with its rules involves some sacrifice (if only some restriction on one's liberty); (3) the relevant benefits are created by general compliance with its rules; (4) free-riding is possible because it is possible for some to enjoy the benefits without complying; and (5) one has "accepted" such benefits (*CP* 122f.). In *A Theory of Justice*, Rawls says that the principle of fairness calls for compliance with institutional rules under similar conditions, except that Rawls modifies the last condition so that (5′) one is under an obligation to do what the rules require if one has not merely accepted (perhaps only passively received) such benefits but welcomes them and intends to continue accepting them or has actually sought them (*TJ* 301f.). The obligation is owed to those who have complied with the rules and contributed to

273

the production of the benefits (*CP* 123), who thus have a right to compliance by those who have accepted the benefits (1964 version) or (1971 version) by those who have welcomed the benefits and intend to continue accepting the benefits or have taken advantage of the opportunities offered (*TJ* 302).

Rawls's later account of fairness has narrower implications than his earlier account of fair play. In 1964 Rawls claimed that, when conditions (1)–(5) are satisfied, the duty of fair play grounds an obligation of obedience to law which applies to all citizens. In 1971, Rawls claims that, when conditions (1)–(5′) are satisfied, the principle of fairness grounds an obligation to obey the law for only a limited subset of citizens, such as entrepreneurs and those who successfully seek political office within the system, and that not fair play but the natural duty of justice grounds a moral requirement of obedience to law for citizens generally (*TJ* 98). In both cases, of course, the moral requirement of obedience to law is contingent upon the system as a whole being just or, in *TJ*, being "nearly just" (*TJ* 308).

In support of the general idea that appears to be represented by both conceptions (and by conditions (1)–(4), which they share), Rawls says that, as the relevant benefits have been created by the cooperation of many individuals, they belong to no one (*CP* 122, 127). In some cases it may be possible to distribute unassigned benefits in an equitable manner. But no one has the right to claim any of those benefits for herself by free-riding.

When Rawls held (in 1964) that the duty of fair play requires all citizens to obey the law, he did not indicate his reasoning, but some reconstruction of it seems possible. Rawls assumed "that there is, at least in a society such as ours, a moral obligation to obey the law" (*CP* 117). If we combine that with his claim that the duty of fair play grounds the obligation, he must have regarded societies like ours as mutually beneficial and just cooperative schemes.

But are they? It is unclear, for example, that many of those who obey the law do so in a cooperative *spirit*, which presumably means consciously striving together in order to achieve some common goal, as opposed to complying in order to avoid the legal consequences of noncompliance.

Viewed within the context of Rawls's developed theory of justice, his later reasoning seems easier to understand. In *Theory*, Rawls is preoccupied with "ideal theory," which endorses principles that would be chosen in the original position as ground rules for the "basic structure" of a "well-ordered" society. The members of such a society share the same (or nearly the same) sense of justice, they are aware that they do, and they are morally committed to complying with its principles, which they know that their society's principal institutions satisfy (*TJ* 397). Under such idealized conditions, those subject to law might plausibly be seen as participants in a cooperative scheme.

Fairness, principle of / 275

Both the earlier and the later lines of reasoning assume that the law promotes coordination that generates benefits. These might include security of one's person and privacy from illicit intervention. It is unclear, however, whether all of the benefits that are produced by governments arise from coordination. Some benefits may simply be purchased as revenue accumulates from taxation. Compliance with laws related to the latter benefits might be required by the natural duty of justice but not by a duty of fair play.

We do not need a special duty or obligation to comply with laws when they are just; the need arises when they are unjust. And, Rawls observes, it is impossible to design a constitutional system that excludes the possibility of unjust laws, which are inevitable. The moral requirement thus binds us to comply with *un*just laws – but only within limits. "By the principle of fairness," Rawls says, "it is not possible to be bound . . . to institutions which exceed the limits of tolerable injustice" (*TJ* 96). Thus Rawls's discussion of fairness ventures into a limited corner of what he calls "nonideal" theory, which concerns societies whose basic structures do not satisfy the principles of justice; specifically the part that concerns societies that are "*nearly* [not perfectly] just."

In his 1964 essay, Rawls did not distinguish between duties and obligations. In *TJ*, Rawls distinguishes the moral requirements that he calls "obligations" from "natural duties" (*TJ* 93–101). Obligations stem from voluntary actions, such as promises, whereas we have natural duties, such as the duty of justice, independently of anyone's voluntary acts. Rawls's use of this distinction helps to explain the displacement in his theory of a duty of fair play by the principle of fairness, which he regards as the ground of all obligations (so understood). Given that understanding, Rawls finds that most members of political communities do not perform a voluntary action that would bind them in fairness to comply with the law. We generally have no choice whether or not to receive many of the benefits afforded by just systems. Only a proper subset of citizens have committed themselves to accepting such benefits or have taken advantage of the opportunities afforded by the system. Rawls concludes that the fairness argument applies to that subset alone, not to all of those who are subject to the laws and who might benefit from their operation (*TJ* 301–303).

By contrast, the natural duty of justice unconditionally requires one to support and promote just institutions, and Rawls accordingly maintains that it can ground a widely applicable moral requirement of obedience to law (*TJ* 293–296). He observes that "the better-placed members of society are more likely than others" to be bound to comply by the principle of fairness *as well as* by the natural duty of justice. "For by and large it is these persons who are best able to gain political office and to take advantage of the opportunities offered by the constitutional system. They are, therefore, bound even more tightly to the scheme of just institutions" (*TJ* 302–303).

Although the principle of fairness plays a secondary role in *Theory*, Rawls there assigns it a central role in ethical theory, when he claims that all obligations are based on fairness (*TJ* 96). Rawls regards the principle of fidelity, for example, as "but a special case of the principle of fairness applied to the social practice of promising" (*TJ* 303). (This of course construes the "social practice of promising" as a mutually beneficial and just cooperative scheme.) That view of obligations is not developed further in his subsequent work.

In *A Theory of Justice*, Rawls appears to give up a second assumption of his earlier paper. In 1964 Rawls said that "there is, at least in a society such as ours, a moral obligation to obey the law" (*CP* 117). In *Theory*, Rawls neither says nor implies that, but on the contrary suggests the opposite by observing that our system tolerates injustices which imply that it is not "nearly just." He says, for example, that our system has failed "to insure the fair value of political liberty" and that "corrective steps … never seem to have been seriously entertained." He refers here to our system's toleration of gross "disparities in the distribution of property and wealth," which undermine political equality (*TJ* 198f.). Rawls thus sketches a grave, entrenched violation of the first principle. He also observes that "the duty to comply is problematic for permanent minorities that have suffered from injustice for many years," which seems to refer especially to African Americans under Jim Crow, a system of racial subordination that the federal government had only recently become committed to dismantling. As that new federal policy was facing massive and often violent resistance in a number of Southern states, it would have been premature to suppose that such serious, long-standing injustices would soon be rectified.

David Lyons

SEE ALSO:

> *Basic structure of society*
> *Natural duty of justice*
> *Obligations*
> *The original position*
> *Political obligation*
> *Promising*

73.

FAITH

ONE LEARNS ABOUT Rawls's own approach to religious faith in published writings at the very beginning and the very end of his career. In
his undergraduate thesis at Princeton (1942) he indicated a religious faith
under the influence of neo-orthodox Protestant thinkers like Emil Brunner. At
this stage he thought that faith in God was not sheer fancy and that one could give
reasons for religious belief, even if he did not have a great deal of confidence in
rational or natural theology. By "faith" he meant a spiritual disposition to be fully
integrated into community and to be rooted in the divine source which sustains
it. That is, faith is inherently personal, in contrast to "belief," which is a cognitive
attitude that holds certain propositions to be true or false. Strictly speaking, he
thought, one might believe *that* God exists, but one has faith *in* God as personal.
At this very early stage of his career, the opposite of faith was "sin," which he
defined as the destruction of personal community (*BIMSF* 113, 123–125, 214).

Late in life (1997) Rawls drafted an essay titled "On My Religion" in which
he described the history of his own religious beliefs and attitudes toward religion, including his abandonment of orthodoxy during World War II, largely due
to orthodoxy's inability to deal convincingly with the theodicy problem. Apparently his views changed several times over the years. Although it is clear that he
abandoned orthodoxy, it is not clear that he abandoned theism, in general. In
fact, he speaks of his "fideism" (*BIMSF* 261, 263). In addition to this late essay, it
also makes sense to suspect that Rawls's own religion is illuminated by his comments on "reasonable faith" in Kant in that Rawls's own comprehensive doctrine
seems to have been Kantian until the end of his life (*LHMP* 16, 147, 288–289,
306, 309–310, 319–322, 363).

Quite apart from Rawls's own religious faith or lack thereof, what is more important in his thought is his treatment of faith as a *political* problem. Indeed, he is quite explicit that the origin of political liberalism lies in the aftermath of the Reformation, when it became clear that the lack of toleration among both Catholic and Protestant leaders alike created a huge problem: how can people of faith live together in justice when they are divided, sometimes uncompromisingly so, in the comprehensive doctrines that they affirm? Rawls's solution to this problem is to take questions of the highest good off the table as *political* questions (*PL* xxv–xxxi, 159; *CP* 412; *JF* 192; *LHMP* 347–348). In this regard he was heavily influenced by both Locke's famous "Letter Concerning Toleration" and the not so well-known "Colloquium of the Seven" by the sixteenth-century Catholic thinker Jean Bodin (*PL* 145; *BIMSF* 266–269).

In that many or most of the people that Rawls wanted to bring within the scope of political liberalism were persons of faith of some sort, his hope was that, at the very least, a *modus vivendi* among all reasonable citizens could be established. Or better, he hoped that stability for the right reasons could eventually be reached among all reasonable citizens, both those who professed religious faith and those who did not (*CP* 616–622). That is, religious faith need not be fanatical or irrational or mad, although admittedly there is the possibility that it could exhibit these qualities (*TJ* 485; *LP* 126–127, 173).

Daniel Dombrowski

SEE ALSO:

> *Catholicism*
> *Comprehensive doctrine*
> *Overlapping consensus*
> *Political liberalism, justice as fairness as*
> *Religion*
> *Sin*

74.

FAMILY

Rawls included the family, understood as the primary venue for the rearing and educating of future citizens, as an essential part of society's basic structure. Ideally, the family serves as what John Stuart Mill called the first school of social justice by raising children through affection, example, and guidance to develop the cooperative virtues and sentiments upon which the just society depends (*TJ* §70). These include the desires to interact with their fellow citizens on fair terms, and also to participate as fully cooperating members of society. Children's education should further include practical measures to prepare them to become self-supporting, and knowledge of their equal constitutional and civic rights (*PL* 199), although these sorts of education may be provided outside the home by schools. It is the family's role in the formation of future citizens that justifies its inclusion among the institutions of the basic structure. In Rawls's words in "Public Reason Revisited," "the family is part of the basic structure, since one of its main roles is to be the basis of orderly production and reproduction of society and its culture from one generation to the next" (*CP* 595).

Rawls specifies a society's basic structure as the *system of interaction* among the main political, economic, and social institutions – how they operate together to form the background conditions against which associational and personal ends are pursued. Rawls's principles of justice apply *directly* to this system, but only indirectly to the basic structure's component institutions. So although the basic structure must satisfy the difference principle, requiring that inequalities work to the greatest advantage of the least well off, it is neither required nor appropriate for judges to apply the difference principle in deciding cases between litigants. Similarly, parents are not required to distribute family resources according to the difference principle. Principles of justice constrain individual institutions and associations, but usually do not internally order them. Rawls offers the example of churches; churches need not provide fair equality of opportunity for men and women or believers and nonbelievers to enter their priesthoods, and they may expel heretics or apostates. But they may not burn them, because apostates and heretics are also, and from society's point of view, principally, citizens. Citizens enjoy freedom of conscience and association, and thus the principles of justice constrain what churches may do.

Considering the point and purpose of the "family in some form," what forms of family are to be publicly authorized? Rawls is committed to answering this question functionally: whatever forms are capable of adequately rearing children to be citizens. Heterosexual couples, homosexual couples, single parents, adoptive parents, and grandparents rearing children clearly count as families by Rawls's functional criterion. The family's tasks being to nurture and educate the next generation of citizens, Rawls insists that "no particular form of the family (monogamous, heterosexual, or otherwise) is required by a political conception of justice so long as the family is arranged to fulfill these tasks effectively and doesn't run afoul of other political values" (*CP* 596 n.60). It should be noted that for Rawls, the public authorization of family forms does not depend on the notion of legal marriage.

Seeing that Rawls's principles of justice do not internally order families, the critical question is how permitting future citizens to be raised within families can be compatible with securing fair equality of opportunity. After all, there are good parents and bad parents. Some facilitate children's development while others stunt it. As Rawls himself notes, upbringing affects our sense of self-worth, our confidence, and even our willingness to make an effort to become fully cooperative members of society (*TJ* §12). Even if the society can correct for inequalities in the economic and social advantages of birth, these psychological differences seem intractable. Rawls recognizes that the requirements of fair equality of opportunity suggest that it might be best to abolish the family altogether (*TJ* §77) in favor of some more collective childrearing institution. He elects though not to take that course, and it is interesting to consider why not.

How does Rawls escape the radical conclusion to which his theory appears to commit him? The fact that most parents want to raise their children and would be made miserable if prohibited from doing so would count as a consideration against collective childrearing for a utilitarian theory, but has no purchase in Rawls's theory of justice, except perhaps by way of posing a problem of the "strains of commitment" of justice as fairness. In *A Theory of Justice* Rawls suggests that in the well-ordered society of justice as fairness, with the difference principle operative along with the principles of fraternity and redress, those disadvantaged by bad parents will feel much less aggrieved than they do under present circumstances, in which those disadvantages are exacerbated and magnified rather than ameliorated. He writes: "We are more ready to dwell upon our good fortune now that these differences [in family upbringing] are made to work to our advantage, rather than to be downcast by how much better off we might have been had we had an equal chance along with others if only all social barriers had been removed" (*TJ* 448). But this argument, that we can better cope with the bad fortune of having been reared in a disadvantageous family environment under justice as fairness than under societies ordered by alternate principles, even if true, goes only so far. It does not explain why justice does not require our adoption of a system of childrearing that better secures fair equality of opportunity. To say that a bad thing is not as bad as it might be is not an argument against adopting a better thing. It is not until he writes *Political Liberalism* that Rawls's principled reluctance to abolish the family begins to become clear.

Political Liberalism recasts justice as fairness as an answer to the question how a pluralistic society, deeply divided in moral, religious, and philosophical doctrines of how life is to be lived, may settle terms of social cooperation justifiable to all on the basis of equality that can remain stable in a principled way over time. It is a part of many moral and religious views that it is *the* primary duty of parents to effect the moral education of their progeny, to do their utmost to ensure that their children become good people with good values who live good lives at least in the present world, and possibly in the hereafter. What rights of liberty of conscience and free exercise of religion could permit a restriction on parents in the name of justice of such magnitude as to remove their influence from the education of their children? How is institutional socialized rearing of all children so as to privilege or disadvantage none compatible with the liberties of conscience and free exercise of religion?

It is here that Rawls provides some positive reason against abolition of the family that might supplement his earlier argument that the disadvantages of family rearing are mitigated under justice as fairness. The missing piece of Rawls's defense of the family "in some form" over socially collective childrearing is his earlier account of moral development. The development of the sense of justice and of the desire to participate in a fair system of social cooperation depends in the first instance, Rawls argued, on the child's perception of her caregivers' evident love for her and wish for her good. That, Rawls argued, was the basis of all trust, of willingness to accept authority, of readiness to emulate, and of acceptance of the values of the caregivers. These are the mechanisms by which future citizens' senses of justice and sociability are developed.

Now, what institution might we expect to be better suited, or more likely, to provide the personal dedicated love that is required for moral development on Rawls's account? Parents, or public institutions? Rawls never asked this question, but we can ask it. Do we believe that the provision of personal love is, overall or as a general rule (to which of course there are always exceptions), more reliable in the case of parents rearing their own children, or in the case of public institutions rearing all children? In our present society, social workers, live-in schoolmasters, overseers of juvenile facilities are supposed to do their best to rear children with the sort of attention needed for the development of their charges' moral faculties. So we need not think of this question as a matter purely of good will or intention. But as a structural question – and Rawls always sought to create background conditions against which personal choices would naturally not contravene the requirements of justice – which form of institution is better suited to fulfill the function of the moral education of future citizens? It is plausible to think that families, with their more personalized connection and attention, are generally better suited than large state institutions. Furthermore, it may be easier to remove children from harmful families than it would be to oversee and effectively reform large juvenile institutions.

Nevertheless, permitting children to be raised within families has the potential not only to compromise fair equality of opportunity, but more seriously, to subject impressionable children to sexist, racist, or other ideas that would compromise their development of the necessary sense of justice and make it difficult for them as adults to treat their fellow citizens as equals. Or children may be brought up under religious or cultural practices that undermine their equal sense of self-worth, and thus compromise their capacity to form, revise, and pursue a conception of the good. Or their families may deprive some members of opportunities to develop the marketable skills to be a self-supporting productive member of society.

One might treat egregious cases of these sorts as forms of child abuse, and grounds for removal of the child from the family. But in most cases, Rawls's requirement that a module of civic education be mandatory for every child as part of every public and private and home-school curriculum should suffice. This module of education will include education about their status as equal citizens with equal basic rights and liberties, including the rights to change their religion or reject religion altogether, their rights to work, to divorce or to refuse to marry, to freedom of movement and free choice of occupation, and so on. If needed, it may also include education to insure that children develop marketable skills, or the capacities upon which many such skills depend. In general, the module of civic education is designed to make clear to children that the society regards them as equal citizens whose rights do not depend on their conforming to the religious, cultural, or other traditions in which their family may have raised them. Rawls acknowledges that this sort of education may do harm to the perpetuation of some illiberal comprehensive doctrines, but justice requires it. One might add that it is a small price to pay for the benefits to adults of a system in which they are permitted to rear their own children.

Finally, it is important to appreciate that the role Rawls assigns to the family as an institution of the basic structure elevates the status of childbearing, childcare, and childrearing from a matter of private charity to one of public justice. Rawls explicitly acknowledges that "reproductive labor is socially necessary labor" (*CP* 595–596). The support of children is not to be left to the haphazard earning abilities of the inseminator and inseminatee alone, but is a collective social responsibility, just as care for wounded veterans is not the sole responsibility of them and their spouses, but, because military service is necessary for defense of the just society, a collective social responsibility. Aid to families with dependent children is thus not some sort of optional charitable handout, but rather a matter of social justice.

S. A. Lloyd

SEE ALSO:

Basic structure of society
Fair equality of opportunity
Feminism
Moral education
Okin, Susan Moller
Political liberalism, justice as fairness as
Sense of justice
Stability

75.

FEMINISM

RAWLS WAS PERSONALLY a feminist, and his theory of justice, justice as fairness, belongs to the category of liberal feminisms. (See Nussbaum 2003; Baehr 2004.) Understanding feminism as both the conviction that women are equal to men in value and entitled to all the rights and privileges of men, and also as the active effort to transform social reality to match that conviction, Rawls unequivocally embraced feminism. He educated and supported the professional careers of women philosophers on a scale that is both unprecedented and so far unsurpassed. Just by his teaching and mentoring alone, he did more to equalize the playing field for women in philosophy than anyone else. But more important is the way he transformed social contract theory from its sexually tone-deaf and conservative history. (See Pateman 1988.) His introduction of a "veil of ignorance" that deprived parties to the social contract of knowledge of their gender quite self-consciously forced the theory to treat women as equal citizens.

Rawls was surprised by the backlash from some feminists contending that justice as fairness perpetuated women's subequal status, writing:

> I have thought that J. S. Mill's landmark *The Subjection of Women* (1869)...made clear that a decent liberal conception of justice (including what I called justice as fairness) implied equal justice for women as well as men. Admittedly, *A Theory of Justice* should have been more explicit about this, but that was a fault of mine and not of political liberalism itself. (*CP* 595 n.58)

That is a fair assessment. He should have been more explicit about how justice as fairness does in fact secure women's substantive equality.

Although many feminists in the liberal tradition appreciated Rawls's advance in the basic social contract, some argued that it did not go far enough, because although it settled equal formal rights status for women, it did not mandate reform of the "private sphere" of family life, in which much of the oppression of women is perpetrated and perpetuated. The liberalism of Rawls's theory of justice disallowed internally ordering families so as to mandate equal regard for girls, or to prohibit religious or cultural indoctrination into sexist roles. Rawls refused to have the state mandate that men and women within families must equally work inside and outside the home, as a model to their children of equality. That, he thought, would be incompatible with the freedom of conscience, and free exercise of religion, required by a just society.

Some contemporary feminists then object to justice as fairness because of its liberality, or liberalness, for not imposing a comprehensive feminism on families to order their internal life. (See Lloyd 1994.) Sexist families can seriously damage the self-conceptions and aspiration of girls growing up within them, and by not requiring the imposition of his principle of fair equality of opportunity on the operations of parents within families, Rawls has contravened the force of his own theory of justice by giving *carte blanche* to illiberal parents to oppress and to stunt the development of their girls, and to undermine their boys' respect for females as equal citizens.

Another contemporary feminist objection to Rawls's theory of justice is that care, an historically and predominantly female concern, receives no attention, or at least inadequate attention, in justice as fairness. The entire approach to justification by means of a social contract amongst self-interested people who are equally free with equally potent bargaining power over the terms of social cooperation appears doomed when we see the real status in the world of women both historically and currently. Children, elders, and the sickly need care, and it is mostly women who provide this care. Much of this care goes uncompensated. Providing such care is socially necessary labor, yet much of this labor is provided by women outside of the market. The demands of providing this care not only compromise many women's market earning potential, but can make them entirely dependent on men for their own economic support, thus reducing their bargaining power over the terms of family life. Employers, suspecting that female employees will have caregiving duties that will make them less reliable or less productive workers, may offer them lesser pay than men in the same job. A theory of social justice should not turn a blind eye toward such a pervasive source of gender inequality as is women's role as caregivers.

Justice as fairness has the resources to address both of these concerns. The family does not belong to a "private sphere," but is rather an institution belonging to society's basic structure, meaning that it is part of a system regulated by Rawls's principles of justice. As such, families are constrained by the requirements of justice: "The equal rights of women and the basic rights of their children as future citizens are inalienable and protect them wherever they are. Gender distinctions limiting those rights and liberties are excluded" (*CP* 599). "Wherever they are" includes inside the family. Marriages are regarded as voluntary associations, so women's freedom of entrance and exit are protected. Justice may require that the pay of spouses working outside the home be split equally between them and their homeworking spouses, and divorce laws should be reformed so as not to disadvantage women, for "it seems intolerably unjust that a husband may depart the family taking his earning power with him and leaving his wife and children far less advantaged than before" (*CP* 600–601).

Of course, families are not voluntary associations from the perspective of the children raised in them, and children, as future citizens, receive special attention in Rawls's theory. All children must receive a module of education sufficient to make them aware of their status as equal citizens, with equal basic rights, liberties, and opportunities regardless of gender. They are to learn that they have freedom of conscience to reject the religious or cultural doctrines of their families. They must receive an education that ensures they have the skills to be self-supporting. These educational requirements constrain the degree to which parents can insulate their children from the larger society that affords them equal status with every other citizen.

The question remains whether these measures suffice to counteract the negative effects of sexist upbringings. Some feminists have recommended stronger intervention inside the family, through the regulation of parental division of labor, and the restriction of practicing religious or cultural views that subordinate females. (See Okin 1989.) Rawls rejected such measures as incompatible with political liberalism. As matters of liberty of conscience, association, and practice of religion, people must be permitted to pursue their comprehensive moral or religious doctrines, including the demands of those doctrines for the organization of family life and gender roles, so long as those doctrines are compatible with the recognition of political equality. In the well-ordered society of Justice as Fairness, where equal basic rights and liberties, fair equality of opportunity, and the difference principle are realized, any remaining gendered divisions of labor

Feminism / 287

or social roles must be respected as voluntary choices flowing from citizens' comprehensive doctrines and conceptions of the good.

S. A. Lloyd

SEE ALSO:

Care
Family
Liberalism as a comprehensive doctrine
Nussbaum, Martha
Okin, Susan Moller

76.

FORMAL JUSTICE

Rawls's principles of justice are designed to be applied to the institutions of the basic structure of society. An institution, for Rawls, is "a public system of rules which define offices and positions with their rights and duties, powers and immunities, and the like" (*TJ* 47). So the principles of justice aim to identify principles to be used in determining when these public rules are just. But even if the institutional rules are not fully just, the institutions may still realize formal justice. This is achieved when there is "impartial and consistent administration of laws and institutions, whatever their substantive principles" (*TJ* 51). Rawls follows Sidgwick in holding that "this sort of equality is implied in the very notion of a law or institution, once it is thought of as a scheme of general rules" (*TJ* 51). In the case of legal institutions, it is an aspect of the rule of law, which also includes elements such as generality, publicity, and due process. Rawls does not explicitly address whether these elements are also part of formal justice, but he does suggest the use of the phrase "justice as regularity" for the "regular and impartial, and in this sense fair, administration of law" (*TJ* 207).

Obviously, formal justice is necessary but not sufficient for full justice. The more difficult question is whether formal justice is a virtue at all if the substantive institutional rules are unjust. Rawls's answer is that it often is: "even where laws and institutions are unjust, it is often better that they should be consistently applied. In this way those subject to them at least know what is demanded and they can try to protect themselves accordingly; whereas there is even greater injustice if those already disadvantaged are also arbitrarily treated in particular cases when the rules would give them some security" (*TJ* 51). There are limits to this argument, however. It is not hard to imagine laws that are so unjust and exploitative that justice requires defiance whenever possible. It is difficult to

Formal justice / 289

identify when this point has been reached, however. "In general, all that can be said is that the strength of the claims of formal justice, of obedience to system, clearly depends upon the substantive justice of institutions and the possibilities of their reform" (*TJ* 52). Following Lon Fuller, Rawls speculates (but does not commit himself to) the proposition that "substantive and formal justice tend to go together and therefore at least grossly unjust institutions are never, or at any rate rarely, impartially and consistently administered" (*TJ* 52). Even if this speculation is correct, it doesn't help much in identifying the principles of substantive justice.

Jon Mandle

SEE ALSO:

Justice, concept of
Law, system of
Procedural justice
Publicity
Rule of law

77.

THE FOUR-STAGE SEQUENCE

THE FOUR-STAGE sequence (*TJ* 171–176) is the procedure through which Rawls's conception of social justice is made progressively determinate, so as to be applied to the specific circumstances of a given society.

Justice as fairness is based on the idea that the appropriate principles of justice are those which would be agreed to in a situation that is itself fair (*TJ* 11). In the first stage of the sequence, the basic features of such a situation are conceived: the parties are to choose principles of justice in the original position, namely under (1) conditions of freedom and equality, and (2) the veil of ignorance, which prevents each party from knowing, among other things, her place in society, natural talents, conception of the good, and specific features of the society in question. Rawls argues that the parties, so situated, would select the two principles of justice.

The first stage of the sequence, namely the original position proper, constitutes the kernel of justice as fairness as we know it. However, the principles devised in it are not sufficiently determinate to yield recommendations for a specific society. In order to know which institutions and policies will best serve the principles of justice, we must tailor their general content to the particular conditions of a given society. For that to be possible, more information must feed into the deliberative process. Thus, whereas the condition of freedom and equality holds throughout the process, the veil of ignorance is gradually thinned (or lifted), so as to enable the parties to work out the institutional implications of the two principles. The entire process, however, must unfold within public reason – that is to say, the parties justify proposals to one another using premises and standards that all citizens in a pluralistic society may reasonably endorse, rather than controversial views about what is ultimately true or of value. Moreover, in

The four-stage sequence / 291

each of the consecutive stages, the parties are differently motivated than in the original position, in that they try to figure out how best to honor already accepted principles rather than to advance their own interests in primary goods.

At the second stage, the parties must agree on a constitutional framework for the basic structure of their society. The content of the constitution roughly corresponds to the area covered by the first principle. To achieve this goal, the parties remain ignorant about themselves, but acquire some knowledge about their own society. It is not sufficient for them to be acquainted with general sociological notions; they must also know what history their own society has undergone so far; what level of economic development the country has reached, as well as which natural resources it is endowed with; and what its general political culture and tendencies are. This knowledge is essential to establishing whether basic liberties will best be protected, for instance, through a presidential as opposed to a parliamentary democracy; through judicial review as opposed to significant discretion of the legislature over fundamental rights; through a centralized as opposed to a federal state. Rawls's remarks on public funding of elections, restrictions on private campaign contributions, and equal access to the media as instruments to guarantee the fair value of political liberties can be read as an application of the second stage to the United States (*PL* 324–331).

At the third stage, the parties move on to the legislative level, which mainly deals with the second principle. This way of proceeding is based on two grounds: first, the priority of the first principle over the second is mirrored in the priority of the second stage over the third, and of constitutional constraints over legislation; second, violations of equal liberties are likely to be less controversial than the injustice of social and economic policies, and hence a constitutional protection is appropriate for the former but not for the latter. At the third stage, the parties gain full knowledge of the socioeconomic structure of their society, and deliberate about which economic and welfare system (including education, health care, property, contract, inheritance, taxation, and labour regulation) will best protect fair equality of opportunity and the difference principles. Rawls's rejection of the capitalist welfare state in favor of property-owning democracy or liberal socialism can be read as belonging to third-stage deliberation (*JF* 137–140).

Rawls does not specify which information is concealed in the second stage but must be made available in the third; we can imagine, however, that information regarding, for instance, the number of unskilled workers within a society or its class cleavages will be part of it. It is worth noting that Rawls sees the four-stage sequence as part of ideal theory. An interesting open question, however, is whether and at what stage, in the progressive lifting of the veil of ignorance, the parties should become aware of nonideal circumstances (such as levels of racism, sexism, or corruption) within their own society. It would seem that the information to be disclosed at the third stage would have to include knowledge of the baggage of injustice that a society carries (both in historical and in structural terms).

At the final stage all information, including knowledge about specific individuals, is disclosed, so as to enable us to apply the previously agreed laws and policies to particular cases.

Miriam Ronzoni

SEE ALSO:

> *Constitution and constitutional essentials*
> *The original position*
> *Property-owning democracy*
> *Public reason*
> *Two principles of justice (in justice as fairness)*

78.

FREEDOM

THE CONCEPT OF freedom (or liberty – he doesn't distinguish the two) is central to Rawls's theory of justice at a number of levels. On the first page of *A Theory of Justice*, anticipating the priority that he gives to his first principle of justice over his second, as well as his critique of utilitarianism, Rawls asserts that "justice denies that the loss of freedom for some is made right by a greater good shared by others" (*TJ* 3). At the start of *Political Liberalism*, he orients his project by noting the apparent conflict between the ideals of freedom and equality (*PL* 4), and later he claims that "the point" of developing justice as fairness is to try to resolve this "impasse in our recent political history" (*PL* 300). He also notes the dispute concerning the proper understanding of liberty itself by pointing to the conflict

> between the tradition associated with Locke, which gives greater weight to what Constant called 'the liberties of the moderns,' freedom of thought and conscience, certain basic rights of the person and of property, and the rule of law, and the tradition associated with Rousseau, which gives greater weight to what Constant called 'the liberties of the ancients,' the equal political liberties and the values of public life. (*PL* 4–5; cf. *JF* 2)

In "Justice as Fairness," the 1958 article that introduced the two principles of justice that Rawls would develop and defend throughout his career, he states the first principle this way: "each person participating in a practice, or affected by it, has an equal right to the most extensive liberty compatible with a like liberty for all" (*CP* 48). (Deflecting claims to originality, he notes that "if the principle of equal liberty is commonly associated with Kant...it may be claimed that it can also be found in J. S. Mill's *On Liberty* and elsewhere, and in many other liberal writers" (*CP* 48–49 n.2).) In the first edition of *A Theory of Justice*, he closely follows this formulation of this principle, stating: "each person is to have an equal right to the most extensive basic liberty compatible with a similar liberty for others" (*TJ*, original edition, 60). In discussing the content of this first principle, Rawls attempts "to bypass the dispute about the meaning of liberty that has so often troubled this topic" (*TJ*, original edition, 201). The dispute between defenders of negative liberty and defenders of positive liberty, he suggests, is best understood not as a disagreement about definitions, but rather one concerning "the relative values of the several liberties when they come into conflict" (*TJ*, original edition, 201). Rawls proposes that "liberty can always be explained by a reference to three items: the agents who are free, the restrictions or limitations which they are free from, and what it is that they are free to do or not to do" (*TJ*, original edition, 202). He illustrates this with the example of liberty of conscience: "individuals have this liberty when they are free to pursue their moral, philosophical, or religious interests without legal restrictions requiring them to engage or not to engage in any particular form of religious or other practice, and when other men have a legal duty not to interfere" (*TJ*, original edition, 202–203).

Rawls was well aware of the traditional Marxist charge that so-called bourgeois liberal rights are merely formally equal and are undermined by material inequality (*LHPP* 321). In reply, he insists that "poverty and ignorance, and a lack of means generally" do not, by themselves, undermine liberty. Instead, they affect "the worth of liberty, the value to individuals of the rights that the first principle defines" (*TJ* 179). The first principle guarantees that "Freedom as equal liberty is the same for all" (*TJ* 179). Political institutions must offer the same permissions and prohibitions for everyone. The first principle does not, however, guarantee that everyone will be able equally to take advantage of these permissions and opportunities. The worth of liberty is given by the institutionally determined share of resources that one can reasonably expect to be attached to one's social position. Although some inequalities in the worth of liberty may be allowed, they will be constrained by the difference principle. (Indeed, the worth of the *political* liberties is constrained even more by the requirement of "fair value.") This illustrates the importance of recognizing how the two principles work together. "Taking the two principles together, the basic structure is to be arranged to maximize the worth to the least advantaged of the complete scheme of equal liberty shared by all. This defines the end of social justice" (*TJ* 179).

In a review of *A Theory of Justice*, first published in 1973, H. L. A. Hart noted that sometimes Rawls formulated his first principle in terms of liberty (as quoted above), but other times in terms of "basic liberties," for example: "Each person is to have an equal right to the most extensive total system of equal basic liberties compatible with a similar system of liberty for all" (*TJ*, original edition, 302). Often, as with the example of liberty of conscience above, he focused on specific basic liberties, rather than liberty as such. But when it came to assessing the fulfillment of the first principle, a single measure of liberty seemed to be required: "the basic liberties must be assessed as a whole, as one system . . . While it is by and large true that a greater liberty is preferable, this holds primarily for the system of liberty as a whole, and not for each particular liberty" (*TJ*, original edition, 203). It seemed important to have a single overall measure of the extent of liberty because Rawls recognized that "when the liberties are left unrestricted they collide with one another" (*TJ*, original edition, 203). The parties to the hypothetical constitutional convention, as part of the four-stage sequence, would need some way of resolving these conflicts, and Rawls seemed to suggest that this could be done by combining the liberties into a single measure of "liberty" which then could be maximized. Hart (1989) argued that this was inadequate.

Rawls acknowledged the criticism and revised his theory accordingly. As he put it in "The Basic Liberties and Their Priority," first delivered in 1981, and subsequently incorporated into *Political Liberalism*, "No priority is assigned to liberty as such, as if the exercise of something called 'liberty' has a preeminent value and is the main if not the sole end of political and social justice" (*PL* 291–292). Instead, the basic liberties were to be identified based on their necessity for the "adequate development and the full and informed exercise of" the two moral powers (the capacity for a conception of the good and the capacity for a sense of justice). Necessary trade-offs among the basic liberties were to be made with reference to these capacities, but there is no assumption that there is any single dimension of "liberty" to be maximized. (*PL* 332) In the revised edition of *A Theory of Justice*, Rawls took steps to clarify this point. Thus, he revised the initial statement of the two principles so that instead of referring to "the most extensive basic liberty," it instead referred to "the most extensive scheme of equal basic liberties compatible with a similar scheme of liberties for others" (*TJ* 53). However, these revisions did not eliminate all traces of the earlier view, and the revised edition continues to refer to "the principle of equal liberty" (e.g. 38) and to the "priority of liberty" (e.g. the title of §39), among much else. In the "Preface for the Revised Edition," he notes that on this point, "the account in the revised text, although considerably improved, is still not fully satisfactory. A better version is found in a later essay of 1982 entitled 'The Basic Liberties and Their Priority'" (*TJ* xii).

By tying the basic liberties to the two moral powers, Rawls not only provides a criterion for identifying the basic liberties, he also presents a path for integrating them into a single scheme by assessing their relative significance and resolving conflicts among them. He illustrates this with an extensive discussion of freedom of speech (*PL* 340–368). The connection to the two moral powers also allows Rawls to clarify the argument for the priority of the first principle over the second. Briefly: citizens must have the two moral powers above a certain minimal threshold in order to be fully cooperating members of society. Citizens have two "higher-order" interests in developing and exercising these two moral powers above that level. Because of the vital importance of full and free participation in such a cooperative scheme, "these interests are viewed as basic and hence as normally regulative and effective" (*PL* 74). And since the basic liberties are necessary in order to develop and protect the two moral powers, the parties in the original position will give priority to protecting the basic liberties over potential gains among other primary goods, such as wealth and income. Note that the liberties associated with individual autonomy (the "liberties of the moderns") and the liberties associated with public autonomy (the "liberties of the ancients") both have their source in protecting the higher-order interests of moral persons. Thus, neither has priority over the other, and they are "both co-original and of equal weight" (*PL* 412).

In *A Theory of Justice*, Rawls identifies as "moral persons" those that have the two moral powers (although he did not yet call them that) to an adequate degree. And he held that all moral persons "are entitled to equal justice" (*TJ* 442). In other words, "the capacity for moral personality [i.e., the two moral powers] is a sufficient condition for being entitled to equal justice" (*TJ* 442). In *Political Liberalism*, the two moral powers also underwrite the claim that citizens are considered free in three senses. (The shift from moral person to citizen corresponds to the shift to a political conception of justice.)

First, for purposes of political justice, citizens are not inevitably tied to any particular conception of the good. Rather, "they are seen as capable of revising and changing this conception on reasonable and rational grounds, and they may do this if they so desire" (*PL* 30). For some nonpolitical purposes, a radical change in one's values may properly be thought of as a change in one's identity, but for political purposes one's basic rights and duties and social standing are unaffected. Rawls makes no assumptions concerning the grounds or perspective from which such a change may be made. The point is simply that a just basic structure will not prohibit citizens from exercising this moral power.

Citizens view themselves as free in a second sense: "they regard themselves as self-authenticating sources of valid claims" (*PL* 32). As long as their conception of the good is reasonable and does not conflict with the principles of justice themselves, they are entitled to a fair share of social resources with which to pursue their ends. They need not offer public justifications for the value that they attach to their ends. For purposes of political justice, their simple assertion that they value them is sufficient, and as long as their ends are permissible, there is no further evaluation to be made from a public political point of view (although, of course, further assessment is perfectly appropriate within the institutions and associations of civil society).

Since the principles of justice put limits on permissible conceptions of the good, citizens, third, are also viewed as "capable of taking responsibility for their ends" (*PL* 33). This means that they must revise their conception of the good if it conflicts with the requirements of justice and adjust their ends in light of the resources that the principles of justice will enable them to claim. Their share of resources is not determined by the strength or intensity of their desires or preferences since they are viewed as responsible for these. This does not mean that all of our preferences are the result of our own deliberate choice or that our upbringing or other factors do not have profound influences on the values that we come to endorse. But for purposes of political justice, citizens should not be viewed as "passive carriers of desires" (*CP* 369). Instead, regardless of the actual etiology of one's values, political justice holds citizens responsible for their conception of the good.

Since justice as fairness models citizens as having the two moral powers, it treats them as free in the above three senses and as equally entitled to justice. This aligns it with other members of a tradition that Rawls identifies as "the liberalism of freedom" (*LHMP* 330). In his *Lectures on the History of Political Philosophy* and *Lectures on the History of Moral Philosophy*, Rawls discusses how various members of this tradition interpret the freedom of individuals. When Locke discusses freedom, for example, it is connected to what Rawls would identify as our first moral power (to set and pursue a conception of the good). Locke's state of nature is a state of freedom "because all are at liberty to order their actions and to dispose of their possessions and persons as they see fit, within the limits set by the law of nature. It is not necessary that they ask the permission of anyone else, nor are they dependent on another's will" (*LHPP* 115).

Rousseau moves us beyond this by offering three different senses of freedom. When we enter into the social contract, we give up our natural freedom, "the right to anything we want and can get, limited only by the force of the individual" (*LHPP* 220). In exchange, we gain both civil and moral freedom. Civil freedom, as Rawls interprets it, is simply the freedom that citizens enjoy "to pursue their aims within the limits laid down by the general will" (*LHPP* 235). This is an advance over natural freedom since interactions among private wills are now limited by principles of justice and right rather than mere force. The general will also creates moral freedom, which "consists in obeying the law one has prescribed for oneself" (*LHPP* 235). This requires "the form of deliberative reason appropriate to the situation at hand," and this capacity can only be developed and exercised in a (reasonably) just society guided by the general will (*LHPP* 237). "With this capacity of reason fully developed, we have free will: we are in a position to understand and to be guided by the most appropriate reasons" (*LHPP* 243).

Kant, as Rawls reads him, builds on Rousseau's understanding of free will. Specifically, Kant draws a tight connection between the moral law of the categorical imperative and the idea of freedom as self-legislation. In Kant, the categorical imperative is a law of freedom that is a development of Rousseau's thought that "to be driven by appetite alone is slavery, and obedience to the law one has prescribed for oneself is liberty" (*LHMP* 204). It is through our awareness of the moral law that we recognize ourselves to be free (*LHMP* 202; cf. 269, 297). And in contrast to Leibniz's compatibilism, this freedom excludes the possibility of predetermination (*LHMP* 280–281). Such "absolute spontaneity" is, ultimately, "the spontaneity of pure reason, so in the case of freedom in the moral sphere, it is the absolute spontaneity of our pure practical reason" (*LHMP* 280, cf. 318).

It is worth noting that although Rawls distinguishes and discusses three ideas of freedom in Kant – "the idea of acting under the idea of freedom, the idea of practical freedom, and the idea of transcendental freedom" (*LHMP* 285ff.) – he does not discuss what Kant calls "outer freedom," and which he places at the foundation of his *Doctrine of Right* (Kant 1996 [1797], 165 [Ak.406–407]). Outer freedom, for Kant, is not concerned with independence from causal determinism or the selection of the maxims on which one acts or the ends that one pursues. Instead, it is simply a matter of "independence from being constrained by another's choice" (*Metaphysics of Morals*, 1996 [1797], 30 [Ak.237]). There is a striking parallel between Rawls's understanding of the freedom that citizens have to set their own ends without the need to offer public justification and Kant's understanding of outer freedom. Yet the similarity goes unremarked and unexplored in Rawls's work.

In contrast, when it comes to discussing Mill's "Principle of Liberty," the issue is manifestly one of "outer freedom" – the concern "is not the philosophical problem of freedom of the will, but that of civil or social liberty" (*LHPP*

284). Generally, and strikingly, Rawls holds that "the content of Mill's principles of political and social justice is very close to the content of the two principles of justice as fairness" (*LHPP* 267). Notably, in light of the above discussion, he interprets Mill's principle of liberty "as covering certain enumerated liberties...given by a list and not by a definition of liberty in general, or as such" (*LHPP* 288). Equally important, the Liberty Principle is "a principle of public reason – a political principle to guide the public's discussion in a democratic society" (*LHPP* 289). It excludes "certain kinds of reasons from being taken into account in legislation, or in guiding the moral coercion of public opinion (as a social sanction)" (*LHPP* 291). On the other hand, of course, Rawls notes that Mill's "Principle of Liberty is not a first or supreme principle: it is subordinate to the Principle of Utility and to be justified in terms of it" (*LHPP* 289). In *A Theory of Justice*, Rawls notes that on the basis of utilitarianism Mill is able to give "forceful arguments and under some circumstances anyway they might justify many if not most of the equal liberties." Still: "The liberties of equal citizenship are insecure when founded upon teleological principles. The argument for them relies upon precarious calculations as well as controversial and uncertain premises" (*TJ* 185).

Jon Mandle

SEE ALSO:

Basic liberties
Freedom of speech
Hart, H. L. A.
Kant, Immanuel
Leibniz, G. W.
Lexical priority: liberty, opportunity, wealth
Locke, John
Mill, John Stuart
Moral persons
Rousseau, Jean-Jacques
Two principles of justice (in justice as fairness)

79.

FREEDOM OF SPEECH

FREEDOM OF SPEECH occupies a central place in Rawls's theory of justice. Like other liberal theorists, Rawls assigns great importance to the protection of freedom of speech. But unlike some liberals, he does not ground the value of freedom of speech in the purported value of liberty per se and he distinguishes between different kinds of speech with a view to determining the appropriate kind of protection different categories of speech should receive. Also in contrast to liberals who adopt a Millian approach in which the regulation of speech is grounded solely in the harm principle, Rawls analyzes the value of free speech and the grounds on which it may be regulated via an account of the moral powers of free and equal citizens. Political speech, artistic and literary expression, along with freedom of scientific and other forms of intellectual inquiry are amongst the basic liberties that have a special status in Rawls's theory. Under Rawls's first principle of justice "each person has the same indefeasible claim to a fully adequate scheme of equal basic liberties, which scheme is compatible with the same scheme of liberties for all" (*JF* 42). Protection of the basic liberties has lexical priority over pursuit of either of the other dimensions of Rawls's second principle of justice. Those kinds of speech that are considered basic liberties cannot be restricted in the name of pursuing fair equality of opportunity or the difference principle. Instead, protected varieties of free speech may be limited only in order to give adequate recognition to other, potentially conflicting, basic liberties. Like all the basic liberties, rights to freedom of speech are not absolute rights. All of the basic "liberties are to be adjusted to give one coherent scheme" that is "secured equally for all citizens" (*PL* 295). Only considerations grounded in the basic liberties themselves and the moral powers they serve are relevant to the adjustment of the overall scheme of liberties.

Rawls's strategy for distinguishing basic liberties from nonbasic liberties and hence for identifying those categories of free speech that enjoy special constitutional protection rests on the two moral powers that are essential to his conception of citizens as free and equal persons. The adjustment of the contours of the basic liberties to generate a coherent scheme also proceeds via consideration of the relation between liberties and the moral powers. The moral powers are: (1) the capacity for a conception of the good and (2) the sense of justice. The former is the capacity "to form, to revise, and rationally to pursue a determinate conception of the good" (*PL* 312). The latter is the capacity "to understand, to apply, and to act from the public conception of justice which characterizes the fair terms of social cooperation" (*PL* 19). Basic liberties are those liberties that play a particularly important role in the full and informed exercise and development of the moral powers. Since political, scientific, and artistic forms of expression are intimately connected to the exercise and development of the moral powers, free speech in these areas is amongst the basic liberties. Protecting free speech in these categories of expression is valuable in relation to the capacity for a conception of the good in part because it helps people with similar conceptions of the good to identify one another and to share ideas relevant to the implementation of valued projects and commitments. It also facilitates the dissemination of information and ideas that are relevant to reflective formation or revision of a conception of the good. The possibility of open debate, discussion, and deliberation about political issues concerning the policies and institutional arrangements of a just democratic polity is intimately linked to the exercise and development of the sense of justice. Persons cannot develop and exercise their sense of justice without unfettered access to the moral and political convictions and opinions of their fellow citizens. Thus strong protection of free political speech is extremely important for Rawls.

In the categories of speech that are most linked to the exercise and development of the moral powers, Rawls opposes restrictions on the content of permissible speech. In general, speech that is closely linked to informed and free examination of religious, moral, philosophical or political doctrines has special value. In these matters, whether a doctrine or opinion is false, implausible or offensive is irrelevant to determining whether there is a right to express it or to have access to it. However, even in these protected categories free speech rights are subject to regulation of the sort necessary both to the meaningful exercise of free speech and to the reduction of public disturbances that can accompany some forms of speech. Thus free speech is reasonably *regulated* but not restricted by the enforcement of rules of order at public events. Similarly, familiar time, manner, and place regulations whose purpose is to manage the nuisance caused by some forms of speech are acceptable providing they do not unduly encumber opportunities for expressing or accessing protected speech at other venues or at different times etc. Rawls also accepts content-based restrictions on some, less valuable, kinds of speech. Libel, defamation of private persons, and some uses of "fighting words" are not protected and can be prohibited. Also although Rawls insists that political speech advocating political subversion or revolution is protected speech, incitement to imminent violence or lawless use of force is not. Content-based limitations of political speech are only tolerable in an extreme constitutional crisis where the temporary suspension of basic liberties is necessary to the preservation of democratic institutions and processes themselves.

Kinds of speech that have some value but which are more distantly related to the exercise and development of the moral powers are not protected as basic liberties. Here the precise character of free speech rights is determined by considerations related to fair equality of opportunity and the difference principle. The main example Rawls discusses under this heading is commercial speech. Advertising plays an important role in providing citizens with potentially valuable information about goods, services, and opportunities. Dissemination of such information is crucial to ensuring that citizens enjoy fair equality of opportunity to pursue careers and offices. Moreover, accurate and reliable information about the prices and qualities of goods and services contributes to economic efficiency. However, false and misleading advertising or advertising that is primarily aimed at influencing consumer preferences through manipulative marketing techniques (e.g. empty slogans or enticing images) makes no contribution to the development or exercise of the moral powers and can be socially wasteful. Commercial speech may, therefore, be highly regulated both with respect to its form and content. Laws prohibiting false or misleading advertising claims as well as laws sharply restricting manipulative techniques used in commercial speech are legitimate.

Rawls draws a distinction between liberty and the worth of liberty that has important implications for his treatment of political speech. The first principle of justice secures for all persons equal basic liberties but this does not mean that the worth – i.e. the value or usefulness – of liberties will be the same for all persons. For instance, the share of income persons have can influence the value persons can derive from exercising the basic liberties. Those with high incomes will be better placed than those with low incomes to achieve their ends. The worth of political speech for most people is greatly diminished if the opportunity to express views and to influence debate is largely determined by wealth and power. In the context of democratic political processes, significant differences in the worth of political liberties can undermine the equal political standing of citizens that justice requires. In order to avoid the charge that liberalism secures only formal

Freedom of speech / 303

protection of political liberty, Rawls argues that the basic liberties must be regulated so as to secure the *fair value* of the political liberties. This means that citizens, irrespective of their economic standing or class background, should have an equal opportunity to pursue and hold public office and to participate on equal terms with other citizens in democratic debate, discussion and deliberation. Guaranteeing the fair value of political liberty does not justify any restrictions on the content of political speech but it does provide a basis for regulating access to and control over the media through which political debate and discussion takes place. Rawls endorses strict limits on how much individuals and groups can spend on political advertising and campaigning. He was sharply critical of the US Supreme Court decision in *Buckley* v. *Valeo* (1976), which greatly relaxed campaign finance rules and treated any concern for the fair value of political liberty as alien to first amendment jurisprudence. He certainly would have been equally critical of more recent decisions such as *Citizens United* v. *Federal Election Commission* (2010), which continued to erode campaign finance rules.

Some important controversies about the appropriate contours of free speech are not explicitly addressed by Rawls. He does not discuss obscenity, pornography, hate speech, the free speech rights of children and adolescents, or special issues raised by new technologies (e.g. the internet) that have radically changed the way in which information can be shared, stored, and accessed. Given the subtlety of Rawls's approach and the complex judgments about the relation between liberty and the moral powers on which it depends, it is not possible to sketch simple answers to how these matters should be resolved. But it is clear that Rawls's theory has the resources to offer an analysis of such issues that differs significantly from other liberal approaches that either favor undifferentiated protection of speech or that appeal only to considerations of harm in fixing limits on free speech.

Colin Macleod

SEE ALSO:

Basic liberties
Freedom
Lexical priority: liberty, opportunity, wealth
Liberty, equal worth of

80.

FREEMAN, SAMUEL

SAMUEL FREEMAN (b. 1950) is an American political and legal philosopher. After obtaining a J.D. from the University of North Carolina at Chapel Hill, Freeman clerked for Justice Dan K. Moore at the North Carolina Supreme Court in 1977–1978 and again for Judge Dickson Phillips at the US Court of Appeals, 4th Circuit, in 1979. While in law school, Freeman had read Rawls's *A Theory of Justice* and in this he found a political philosophy that was original, persuasive, and that represented his beliefs about social justice. After he read *A Theory of Justice*, Freeman decided that his future should be in political philosophy. And so, in 1979, he left the legal profession to enter the graduate program in philosophy at Harvard University.

In 1985 Freeman graduated from Harvard with the dissertation "Contractarianism and Fundamental Rights (Democracy, Judicial Review, Persons)," written under the supervision of Rawls and Burton Dreben. Influenced also by Scanlon's work, Freeman was at the time interested primarily in the contractarian justification of basic rights, but Rawls insisted that Freeman pursued the reconciliation of democratic ideals and judicial review. Rawls's insistence was vindicated when Freeman's article "Constitutional Democracy and the Legitimacy of Judicial Review" – a shortened and revised version of chapter 3 of his dissertation – was awarded the APA Berger Prize in 1993.

Freeman has dedicated much of his career to explaining, defending, and elaborating Rawls's philosophy. Freeman persuaded Rawls that he should publish his collected papers as well as his lectures on the history of political philosophy, and, when Rawls agreed, Freeman edited these for publication. Examples of Freeman's explanatory work are *Rawls* (Freeman 2007b) and "John Rawls – An Overview" in the *Cambridge Companion to Rawls*, which he also edited (Freeman

2003a). In addition to explicating Rawls's philosophy, Freeman has defended it by clarifying ambiguities and elaborating on aspects of Rawls's philosophy that are not fully dealt with in Rawls's writings. Examples of this type of work include explaining the place and significance of the natural and social lotteries in Rawls's thought (and why Rawls is not a luck-egalitarian), explaining the development in Rawls's ideas about public reason, stability, congruence, and political legitimacy, and elaborating Rawls's position regarding international justice. Finally, Freeman has extended Rawls's philosophy to fields of inquiry that Rawls did not write about. Examples include the aforementioned discussion of the relation between democracy and judicial review, an extended analysis of the differences between Rawlsian liberalism and libertarianism, and an investigation into the relation between the right and the good in social contract theory (some of these works are included in Freeman 2007a).

Freeman currently works on three projects. First, a book-length discussion of the differences between and comparative merits of classical liberalism, libertarianism, and high liberalism. This discussion aims to show how justice as fairness, the variant of high liberalism offered by Rawls, is a better fit for the ideas and values of liberal constitutional democracy than the other liberal traditions. Second, a book that explains and defends the theory of distributive justice offered by justice as fairness. And, third, a book on social contract doctrine that further explains and defends the type of justification that establishes justice as fairness as the best conception of justice for constitutional liberal democracies.

Jeppe von Platz

SEE ALSO:

Libertarianism
Luck egalitarianism
Property-owning democracy
Public reason
Supreme Court and judicial review

81.

FUNDAMENTAL IDEAS (IN JUSTICE AS FAIRNESS)

JUSTICE AS FAIRNESS involves six fundamental ideas. They are laid out in a sequence in *Justice as Fairness: A Restatement* (part 1; see also *PL* lecture 1). The first is the organizing idea, which the following five make more determinate by addressing important questions (*JF* 24–25). The ideas are worked out on the basis of a reflection on aspects of the public political culture of a democratic society (*JF* 5).

(1) The central, organizing idea is that of *society as a fair system of cooperation over time from one generation to the next*. Social cooperation has at least three features: it is guided by publicly recognized rules and procedures, it includes terms of cooperation that are fair (they can reasonably be accepted by its participants and involve reciprocity or mutuality), and it tracks each participant's rational advantage or good (*JF* 6). The terms of social cooperation (the fundamental rights, liberties, opportunities, and allocation of benefits and burdens it involves) are specified by the principles of justice (*JF* 7).

(2) What would result when the first idea is fully realized? The result would be a *well-ordered society*, a society effectively regulated by the principles of justice (*JF* 8–9).

(3) What do the principles of justice apply to, exactly? They apply primarily to *the basic structure of society*, to "the way in which the main political and social institutions of society fit together into one system of social cooperation, and the way they assign basic rights and duties and regulate the division of advantages that arises from social cooperation over time" (*JF* 10). The basic structure includes, for example, a society's constitution, its economic structure, and the family in some form.

Fundamental ideas (in justice as fairness) / 307

(4) How are the fair terms of cooperation (the principles of justice) to be specified? In justice as fairness, they are presented as the focus of a hypothetical agreement, a social contract, between free and equal citizens reached under fair conditions. The *original position* is a device of representation through which such an agreement is envisaged. Its several features (such as the veil of ignorance) guarantee conditions that situate free and equal persons fairly and impose appropriate restrictions on the reasons used in assessing principles (*JF* 14–18).

(5) How are the citizens participating in social cooperation regarded? They are *free and equal persons*. They have to the requisite minimum degree the two moral powers that enable them to be full cooperators in a well-ordered society: a capacity for a sense of justice and a capacity for a conception of the good (*JF* 18–24).

(6) How is a conception of justice, as a political conception, to be justified in a democratic society characterized by reasonable pluralism? It should be the subject of *public justification* (*JF* 26–28). Through public justification, citizens justify to one another their political judgments on the basis of grounds they can all reasonably endorse as free and equal, regardless of their deeper, different, and often opposing moral, religious or philosophical comprehensive doctrines. The idea of public justification is further developed through the ideas of *reflective equilibrium*, *overlapping consensus*, and *public reason*.

Pablo Gilabert

SEE ALSO:

Basic structure of society
Cooperation and coordination
Moral person
The original position
Overlapping consensus
Public reason
Reflective equilibrium
Well-ordered society

G

82.

GAMES

GAMES APPEAR IN a variety of contexts within Rawls's thought: as examples of practices in his early essay, "Two Concepts of Rules"; as contrasting with nonvoluntary systems of cooperation, and so governed by norms of fairness rather than justice, in "Justice as Fairness"; as examples of social unions in part III of *A Theory of Justice*; and in the guise of game theory in the development of and argument from the "original position" in part I of *Theory*. This entry will briefly summarize each usage and then suggest what they might have to do with one another.

In "Two Concepts of Rules" (1955), Rawls introduces the idea of a "practice": "the specification of a new form of activity" (*CP* 36) which is defined by a set of rules that are logically prior to the particular actions within it. Rawls illustrates the idea of a practice with the game of baseball (37). The rules of baseball not only regulate but make possible a series of activities like striking out or stealing a base. Rawls introduces the idea of a practice to distinguish two sorts of justification: the justification of a practice as a whole and the justification of an action within a practice.

In "Justice as Fairness" Rawls discusses the justice of practices, and argues that fundamental to our concept of justice is the idea of fairness: both justice and fairness involve practices whose rules are ones the participants could propose to one another for mutual acceptance under conditions where no one has authority over the others and they regard themselves as determining together what the rules will be. This means that if a practice is just or fair, then I have no complaint against the practice itself when I fare badly under it. The claims that others raise that lead to my situation are claims I acknowledge as legitimate. Rawls differentiates justice and fairness by claiming that fairness applies to voluntary practices (like games) whereas justice applies to practices in which we must participate. Once again, an idea of justice is illustrated with an analysis of games.

In the third part of *A Theory of Justice*, Rawls introduces the idea of "social unions" in the course of his argument that individual citizens of a well-ordered society can find their sense of justice to be good. In a social union, participants have at least some shared final ends. Through the pursuit of those ends, they realize goods that are not merely instrumental. Interestingly enough, Rawls illustrates the idea of a social union with the example of competitive games. In a competitive game, Rawls says, the players, despite competing with each other to win, share a final end in having a good play of the game. A good play of a game is, he says, a "collective achievement" that allows the players to take pleasure in the very same thing (*TJ* 461).

Game theory is a branch of rational choice theory that deals specifically with situations where the choices of a number of different agents intertwine, so that the choices some players make affect the outcomes of other players' choices. Rational agents deciding together how to divide up a cooperative surplus find themselves in the kind of situation game theory is designed to analyze, and so social contract theory seems like a perfect place to use game theory within political philosophy. Although Rawls does invoke the formal trappings of rational choice theory in his discussion of the original position, he offers some skeptical remarks about the direct applicability of game theory for addressing questions of justice (see *CP* 58 n.11; *TJ* 21 n.10). The chief problem, Rawls argues, is that the outcome of a game can only represent a fair position if the game itself is fair, and so merely using game theory to work out the outcome of a situation is insufficient to determine whether that outcome is just or fair. Moreover, invoking the idea of a practice, he argues that the choice faced by the parties in the original position is not the choice between different outcomes, but between different games or sets of rules: it is a choice of which practice to adopt, not of which strategy to adopt within the practice. With those caveats in place, however, Rawls thinks game theory can help us understand why the parties in the original position would choose the two principles of justice.

In light of the foregoing discussion, we can see one reason why this is so. The set-up of the original position assures that it is a fair game that will produce rules for a practice that members of a society can also regard as fair (or just). Since the outcome of the original position is itself a practice, it will afford individuals within it further intrinsic goods if it also establishes a social union. Among the chief goods such a social union can provide is the social analogue of a good play of the game. The parties thus have reasons to choose a practice (rules determining a basic structure) that increases the likelihood of good plays of the game. Games which provide the best opportunities for good plays are not only formally fair, but designed to be maximally competitive, not in the sense of setting up opposing sides, but in the sense of being evenly matched. Thus, although Rawls does not put his argument in these terms, one can then think of the two principles of justice as establishing such a maximally competitive social game, and this is one of the reasons the parties should choose them.

Anthony Simon Laden

SEE ALSO:

Basic structure of society
The original position
Rational choice theory
Rules (two concepts of)
Social union

83.

GOODNESS AS RATIONALITY

JOHN RAWLS INTRODUCES goodness as rationality as his formal account of a person's good within justice as fairness. This formal account holds for both the so-called "thin theory" of the good that Rawls uses in setting up the original position and the full theory of the good applicable to citizens in a well-ordered society. The account holds that a person's good is given by the plan of life he or she would arrive at under ideal conditions of deliberation. Rawls defines goodness over three stages. At each stage, the thought is that we can, without altering truth values, substitute talk of the properties that it is rational to want in an object of a certain type for talk of the goodness of objects of that type with those properties. The first stage of definition says that "A is a good X if and only if A has the properties... which it is rational to want in an X, given what X's are used for, or expected to do, and the like" (*TJ* 350–351). Next, "A is a good X for K (where K is some person) if and only if A has the properties which it is rational for K to want in an X, given K's circumstances, abilities, and plan of life, and therefore in view of what he intends to do with an X" (*TJ* 351). The first stage, then, defines the goodness of some object in terms of the properties it is rational to want in that object, given the purposes for which objects of its kind are typically used. The next stage relativizes the idea of the good to a particular person's wants and ends. For example, a hammer that is good for my purposes may have properties that are not good for hammers to have in general, because of my specialized or peculiar purposes. Moving to the third stage, note that the objective value of an object is undercut if the end for which it is suited is itself not rational. Therefore we need assurance that our purposes, our wants and ends, are themselves rational. The third stage of the definition of the good adds this requirement to the second.

Goodness as rationality / 315

For Rawls, our wants and ends are rational if they are part of a plan of life which is rational. A plan of life, in turn, is rational "if and only if, (1) it is one of the plans that is consistent with the principles of rational choice when these are applied to all the relevant features of his situation, and (2) it is that plan among those meeting this condition which would be chosen by him with full deliberative rationality" (*TJ* 359). Full deliberative rationality includes "full awareness of the relevant facts," an absence of errors of reasoning, and a complete understanding of the consequences of choosing from among various possible aims. This is a plan of life in that it takes into account not only one's current situation, but also one's aims and conditions at every stage of life. The idea is to arrive at an overall system of ends that regulate the continuing structure of one's life and that define what count as goods in relation to most effectively realizing this overall structure of aims.

A final component of goodness as rationality is what Rawls calls the Aristotelian principle. The Aristotelian principle brings into the account an empirical but general view of human motivation. It says, "other things equal, human beings enjoy the exercise of their realized capacities... and this enjoyment increases the more the capacity is realized, or the greater its complexity" (*TJ* 374). It is substantive, in contrast to the formal elements of the account given in the three stages of definition above.

Taken simply as a formal account, without any substance other than that provided by the Aristotelian principle, goodness as rationality, as set forth above, constitutes a "thin theory" of the good. It is a thin theory of the good in that it is specified prior to and independent of any reference to principles of right. A full theory of the good is not so specified and thus presupposes principles of right. Rawls uses this thin theory within justice as fairness to set up the original position, for example, by accounting for primary goods and the interests and motivations of agents in the original position. A theory of the good is needed because in choosing the principles of justice from the original position, the parties must be understood as having a good that they will pursue – this is their motivation for seeking an agreement within the original position. The parties also need to be able to make interpersonal comparisons between social positions created by proposed principles of justice, and this is the role served by an index of primary goods. Though the account of primary goods changes importantly from *TJ* to *PL*, it remains grounded in the thin theory of the good or the purely formal account of goodness as rationality.

A *thin* theory of the good is needed because of the priority of right within justice as fairness. The task in the original position is to choose principles of justice, and so the account of the good to be used cannot itself rely on or include a conception of justice on pain of circularity. Moreover, the theory cannot assume some full and substantive conception of final ends at which justice aims, because agents in the original position represent parties (you and me) who often reasonably disagree when it comes to a full theory of the good. This requirement accounts for the largely formal nature of the thin theory of the good or goodness as rationality. Of course, as a formal account, goodness as rationality applies also to, but does not exhaust, the full theory of the good.

In justice as fairness, both Rawls's account of justice and his account of the good involve reasoning from within hypothetical choice situations. The account of justice makes use of the original position, while goodness as rationality requires reasoning under ideal conditions of deliberation to arrive at one's rational plan of life. But the different purposes of the choice situations result in marked differences between them. For example, the original position imposes a veil of ignorance while full deliberative rationality requires full information. Perhaps the most significant difference is that the choice from the original position is followed all the way through to a set of principles, while the choice from full deliberative rationality of a rational plan is not. Justice as fairness requires a substantive account of justice, but the choice of one's good may be left within justice as fairness as a merely formal account because justice as fairness does not need to, nor could it, provide any particular individual with their own conception of the good.

Finally, the thin theory of the good, or the formal account of goodness as rationality, plays a role in Rawls's "congruence argument" for the stability of a society well-ordered by the principles of justice as fairness. Rawls recognizes that it would be trivial to demonstrate congruence between the demands of justice and the full or complete conceptions of the good citizens affirm in a society well-ordered by justice as fairness, for citizens will naturally be socialized into full conceptions of the good congruent with justice as fairness. To demonstrate the stability of a society well-ordered by the principles of justice as fairness, Rawls seeks to show that the demands of justice, as specified by the principles of justice as fairness, are congruent with the good of citizens as seen from the point of view of the thin theory of the good, or the purely formal idea of goodness as rationality. While his congruence or stability argument does depend on principles of moral psychology and development not at work in the original position argument, it is, in principle, an argument that agents in the original position

Goodness as rationality / 317

should endorse, for it addresses itself to the thin rather than the full theory of the good.

Pete Murray

SEE ALSO:

Conception of the good
Counting principles
Deliberative rationality
Plan of life
Thin and full theories of good

84.

GUILT AND SHAME

G UILT AND SHAME are unpleasant moral feelings that persons experience on particular occasions. Moral feelings, which may be pleasant or unpleasant, are a normal part of human life. Moral feelings are episodic, being triggered by particular events. Moral attitudes and sentiments, in contrast to feelings, are not episodic; they are deeper and more entrenched features of our affective nature. While episodic, moral feelings, like guilt and shame, express and constitute evidence of less transient moral and natural sentiments and attitudes, for without these deeper and more entrenched dimensions of our affective nature, our moral feelings would not be triggered by the events that give rise to them. In his account of the stability of a society organized on the principles of justice as fairness, Rawls endeavors to show, inter alia, that those living within such a society will develop moral feelings, attitudes, and sentiments inclining them toward justice and toward remedial action in the case of injustice.

Our affective nature includes both moral and natural feelings, attitudes, and sentiments. These are distinguished by the fact that an adequate explanation of the former, but not the latter, necessarily requires appeal to moral principles, concepts or ideals. Moral feelings are often associated with certain linguistic expressions, behaviors, and physical sensations (e.g. feeling hot or flushed). But these signs do not constitute the moral feeling and an explanation of any moral feeling is incomplete if it refers only to these signs and triggering events. An adequate explanation must make appeal to appropriate moral principles, concepts or ideals. Indeed, sometimes an adequate explanation of a moral feeling is just that a person says that she has it and that her having it makes sense in light of appropriate moral principles, concepts, or ideals.

What distinguishes one moral feeling from another, and so guilt from shame, is the content and nature of the appeal to moral principles, concepts, or ideals necessary to its explanation. Feelings of guilt and shame may be triggered by one and the same action and may have signs that overlap or prove difficult to distinguish. Yet they remain distinct insofar as the appeals to moral notions in their respective explanations differ. In general, to explain guilt one must appeal to a standard of right or obligation and thus to a wrong done (the triggering event) to others, and to explain shame one must appeal to an ideal or conception of the good with which one's failure to adhere (the triggering event) compromises one's sense of self-worth (*TJ* 391, 421, 425).

Every moral theory must account for guilt and shame, since these are normal parts of human experience. But different moral theories may account for them in somewhat different ways, depending on how they understand the relationship between, and the principles or ideals of, the right and the good. Further, as internalized by and regulative within persons, different moral theories, or different conceptions of justice and ideals of a good life may lead persons to experience and understand guilt and shame in slightly different ways. Of course, persons living under institutions publicly ordered in accord with the principles of justice as fairness will affirm many different conceptions or ideals of a good life and so understand their self-worth in different ways. But they will all, Rawls argues, acquire a sense of justice informed by justice as fairness and come to affirm their acting on this sense of justice as at least congruent with their diverse conceptions or ideals of a good life or thus their self-worth. Thus, persons engaged in substantial injustice will properly feel not only guilt but also shame. They will experience their conduct as not only a violation of what they owe to others but also as a failure to live up to an ideal essential to their self-worth, to the self-understanding of themselves as persons. Since living with others as free equals on publicly and mutually justifiable terms is part of this ideal or self-understanding, persons engaged in substantial injustice will properly feel shame in being not worthy of the dignity of human persons. Here Rawls's account of the shame properly felt by those engaged in substantial injustice accords with the accounts given by Rousseau and Kant (*TJ* 225).

Episodic moral feelings like guilt and shame presuppose not only deeper and more enduring moral sentiments such as a sense of justice, but also natural feelings, attitudes, and sentiments such as love and affection, trust and friendship, and devotion to institutions and traditions, the explanation of which need not make reference to moral principles, concepts, or ideals. Indeed, Rawls argues that our liability to moral feelings like guilt and shame is the normal result of our natural development. Under ordinary conditions, events constitutive of our natural development trigger the acquisition of natural feelings, attitudes, and sentiments, and these in turn, again given ordinary conditions, give rise to the moral attitudes and sentiments that, when engaged by particular events, generate our episodic moral feelings.

This development begins with the love and trust that emerge in the family (in whatever form it takes). According to what Rawls characterizes as the first psychological law of moral development, a child (infant, toddler) will naturally love her parents so long as they manifestly love her, respond unconditionally to her pain and needs, and so on. So loving her parents, upon whom she is fully dependent, a child will regard her parents' commands to her as authoritative and will feel (a primitive or rudimentary form of) guilt and/or shame, what we might call authority guilt and/or shame, upon failing to comply with them. These (primitive or rudimentary) moral feelings are continuous with and the normal outgrowth of the natural love and affection that (very young) children feel for their parents or caregivers in accord (under ordinary conditions) with the first psychological law. The absence in an (otherwise normal) child of primitive or rudimentary feelings of guilt and/or shame upon noncompliance with parental commands suggests the absence of parental love and care.

As children grow and age within the family, they experience the family as a more complex and cooperative form of association. Typically they will also begin to participate in other complex, cooperative associations outside the family. Within each of these they come to understand how structured cooperation can advance the good of each person engaged in it and how its so doing may depend upon different persons occupying and fulfilling different roles. Here the love and trust that begins in the family is extended and deepened by virtue of the operation of a second psychological law, namely that when we see others doing their part in a cooperative association from which we benefit, we develop natural feelings of friendship and trust toward them. These natural feelings then lead us to the moral feelings of guilt and/or shame, what we might call association guilt and/or shame, when we fail to do our part in the shared association, letting others down and revealing ourselves to be less than a good father, sister, teammate, etc. This is a more complex form of guilt and/or shame than that to which the (very young) child is liable in the family. But as with the latter, its absence suggests the absence of certain natural feelings, here ties of friendship and trust.

Over time, persons engaged in structured cooperation with others may come to understand their activity as properly regulated not simply by a catalog of job or role descriptions, but rather by general principles governing their various cooperative undertakings as a whole. As they come to understand these principles and the relations between persons they support, they will develop, according to a third psychological law operative once the first two laws are already in play, an allegiance to these principles and the institutions and practices they regulate. This allegiance engenders in them a sense of justice and leads to feelings of what we might call principle guilt and/or shame for unjust conduct. These feelings are triggered by unjust conduct irrespective of whether the conduct wrongs persons with whom one has natural relations of love and affection or friendship and trust. At this point, Rawls argues, persons are able to feel guilt and/or shame "in the strict sense," that is, in the sense that the feelings arise from unjust conduct irrespective of other contingencies (*TJ* 415). Of course, when contingent relations and natural feelings of love and affection or friendship and trust are in play, feelings of principle guilt and/or shame will typically be stronger than they would otherwise be. This indicates, Rawls suggests, that injustices done to those with whom we have special ties or relations are worse, ceteris paribus, than those done to strangers, even though wrongs done to strangers are still wrongs and properly give rise to feelings of principle guilt and/or shame (*TJ* 416).

While guilt and shame are moral rather than natural feelings, they are "natural" in the sense that given ordinary human conditions (biology, environment, interaction, etc.) human beings normally develop a liability to them, first in a primitive or rudimentary form, but finally "in the strict sense." There is no way to be free of this liability without forsaking the natural feelings of love and affection, trust and friendship, and allegiance to institutions and practices that naturally develop in persons, first within the family and finally in any society within which persons cooperate for their common good.

David A. Reidy

SEE ALSO:

Moral education
Moral person
Moral psychology
Moral sentiments
Self-respect
Sense of justice

H

85.

HAPPINESS

RAWLS HOLDS THAT a person is happy "when he is in the way of a successful execution (more or less) of a rational plan of life drawn up under (more or less) favorable conditions, and he is reasonably confident that his intentions can be carried through." When our rational plans are going reasonably well and our more important aims are being fulfilled and we're with reason optimistic that our good fortune will continue, we are happy (*TJ* 480). Happiness, then, is dependent in part on luck and circumstance. But it is a matter of objective facts. It is not enough merely to believe that one is successfully executing a rational plan; one must in fact be doing so. It is not enough merely to believe that one's plan is rational; it must in fact be so and be so in light of the objective circumstances of one's condition. And it is not enough merely to believe that one will likely continue successfully to execute one's plan; the facts must support that belief (*TJ* 481).

Happiness so understood fulfills some of the criteria traditionally attached to it. For example, it is a self-contained and self-sufficient end. But it would be a mistake to think that the happy person must or should be pursuing happiness. Happiness is just the objective state, welcome to be sure, that she is in when her rational plan is fulfilled and she is with good reason confident that it will continue to be fulfilled. It is her rational plan, her consistent, coherent, and not unrealistic system of final ends, that she is primarily pursuing. Her rational plan is not simply a means to her happiness, as if her happiness were her dominant end. At most her happiness is perhaps an inclusive end, something she aims at in addition to aiming at all the final ends constitutive of her rational plan and so ingredient in her happiness. But ordinarily happiness is simply the state one is in when one successfully pursues a rational plan with a forward-looking confidence.

Happiness approaches blessedness when a person enjoys favorable circumstances and good luck and is able to realize a wide range of final ends over the course of her life.

As a conception of justice, justice as fairness aims at neither the maximization nor the equalization of happiness. Instead it aims at a social world – the institutions of a basic social structure and the various resources and opportunities they attach to particular social positions – within which individuals may pursue and realize their own happiness, adjusting their final ends as needed to what they may reasonably expect in terms of resources and opportunities from social institutions and accepting without resentment the contingencies of luck and circumstance as they endeavor to execute successfully their life plans. In this way, individuals are responsible for their own happiness within justice as fairness. But this needs to be understood properly. For, within justice as fairness, each individual will include among her final ends realizing with compatriots the collective good of a just and stable pluralist democracy. And insofar as all together do their parts to successfully execute this element of the rational life plan of each, each contributes something important to the happiness of others.

David A. Reidy

SEE ALSO:

Conception of the good
Dominant end theories
Plan of life
Self-interest

86.

HARSANYI, JOHN C.

JOHN C. HARSANYI is a Hungarian-American game theorist (1920–2000). Prior to *TJ*, Harsanyi (1953) appeals to rational choice in a hypothetical situation similar to Rawls's original position in order to justify a principle that governs the basic structure of society. He contends that average utilitarianism would be rationally chosen. Harsanyi (1955) attempts to establish average utilitarianism through two theorems. The Aggregation Theorem holds that if (1) individual and social preferences satisfy the expected utility axioms and are represented by the von Neumann-Morgenstern utility function and (2) a Pareto principle is satisfied, then the social utility is a weighted sum of individual utilities. This theorem allows for different weights to individual utilities. The Impartial Observer Theorem introduces a hypothetical observer who is sympathetic to, but impartial amongst, individual preferences. Given that this impartial observer does not know who will occupy a particular actual position, he would judge that there is an equal chance of being any member of society. As such, the Impartial Observer Theorem holds that the weight given to each individual's utilities must be 1/n in an n-person society. From these two theorems, Harsanyi concludes that it is rational to prefer the principle that would maximize average expected utility.

To this type of general argument for average utilitarianism, Rawls raises three objections. First, the heuristic basis for average utilitarianism – the principle of insufficient reason – is unsound (*TJ* 145–149). According to this principle, if there is no ground for assigning probabilities to different outcomes, it is rational to believe that all possible outcomes are equally probable. Rawls rejects this principle as the heuristic basis for parties choosing the basic structure of society. He argues that the parties would care for a satisfactory minimum and therefore prefer to avoid the risk of falling below the satisfactory minimum level rather than maximize their expected utility. Second, average utilitarianism fails to guarantee a satisfactory minimum to the parties because it may justify serious infractions of liberty or a loss to the worse-off social group for the sake of greater average utility (*TJ* 135). The third objection is closely related to the second. Since average utilitarianism fails to guarantee a satisfactory minimum, the parties would find it hard to accept average. On the other hand, Rawls's principles of justice guarantee a satisfactory minimum, and therefore better contribute to psychological stability, self-respect, and the strains of commitment (*TJ* 153–160).

On the other hand, Harsanyi claims that (1) Rawls's maximin rule is too extreme because it only focuses on the worst-off social group and ignores other groups, (2) it is irrational because the parties are supposed to have an extreme risk-averse attitude towards uncertainty, and (3) it is unstable because the non-worst-off social groups would find it difficult to accept the maximin rule.

Iwao Hirose

SEE ALSO:

> *Maximin rule of choice*
> *The original position*
> *Rational choice theory*
> *Utilitarianism*

87.

HART, H. L. A.

H. L. A. HART (1907–1992) was lecturer in philosophy, Professor of Jurisprudence (1952–1969), and Principal of Brasenose College, Oxford. His writings range widely over legal theory, and touch on many important areas in political philosophy as well. He is widely credited with reestablishing analytic jurisprudence as an important area of study with his book *The Concept of Law* (second edition 1994). Hart's importance for Rawls falls into three main areas. First, through his influence on the young Rawls, who spent the 1952–1953 academic year at Oxford on a Fulbright, shortly after having finished his dissertation at Princeton University. Rawls attended Hart's lectures on the philosophy of law, and was greatly influenced by them. (See Freeman 2007b, 3.) (As the influence of this time is diffuse rather than specific, I shall not specifically further discuss it.) Secondly, Rawls attributes many important ideas in *A Theory of Justice* to Hart. Finally, and most substantively, Hart's criticism of Rawls's First Principle of Justice, as presented in *A Theory of Justice*, led Rawls to significantly revise and clarify it in his later works. In turn, Rawls's influence on Hart is apparent in Hart's work at many places, perhaps most clearly in Hart's work on punishment, where his program of distinguishing the justificatory aim of punishment from the proper distributive principle has clear parallels with, and draws on, Rawls's discussion of punishment in his early paper, "Two Concepts of Rules." (See Hart 1968, esp. 8–13.) The remainder of this entry details Hart's clearest and most important points of influence on Rawls.

Hart's influence on Rawls is felt at several points in *A Theory of Justice* (and the papers leading up to it) where Rawls makes use of ideas developed by Hart. These include the important distinction between concepts and conceptions (*TJ* 5; Hart 1994, 160–163; note that Rawls consistently cites the first edition of

The Concept of Law, and that the pagination is slightly different in the second, now more common edition, making cross-referencing somewhat more difficult. I cite the second edition); the distinction between obligations arising under a fair legal and social system and "natural obligations" (*TJ* 96–7; Hart 1955, 1958); the rule of law and "natural justice" (*TJ* 210; Hart 1994 160, 206); the role of punishment in a just state (*TJ* 277; Hart 1994, 39); and the "circumstances of justice" (*TJ* 109; Hart 1994, 193–200). Finally, though this point lacks specific textual support, we might see Rawls in *TJ* as adapting and modifying Hart's notion of the "internal point of view" towards law (Hart 1994, 89) On Hart's account, only officials must take up the internal point of view towards law (1994, 116–117). We might understand one aspect of Rawls's project as working out how, in a democracy, all citizens are "officials" in the relevant sense, and then trying to work out what the rule of recognition would be for such a society. The extent of Rawls's debt to Hart is not completely clear in any of these cases, and in some, perhaps most notably in the case of the "circumstances of justice," other influences, such as Hume, are also prominent and arguably more important. That being the case, Hart's influence on Rawls is apparent and important in many places leading up to and culminating in *A Theory of Justice*.

The most important and far-reaching influence of Hart on Rawls, however, stems from Hart's criticism of Rawls's first principle of justice and the account of liberty found in it. In his paper, "Rawls on Liberty and its Priority" (Hart 1989), Hart notes what Rawls came to accept as fundamental difficulties in his original presentation of the first principle of justice and the argument for its priority. Hart here notes that Rawls's presentation of the first principle of justice in (the first edition of) *A Theory of Justice* has two significant problems. As presented at the time, the first principle read, "Each person is to have an equal right to the most extensive total system of equal basic liberties compatible with a similar system of liberty for all" (*TJ*, original edition, 302). Hart points out, first, that the idea of the "extent" of a system of basic liberties is difficult, if not impossible, to make sense of in all but the least interesting and unimportant cases. (Hart 1989, 233–239) Defending a choice between systems of liberties on the basis of it providing the "most extensive" total system is therefore not feasible. Hart also argues that the motivation of the parties in the original position to give the strong priority to the basic liberties that they do is not clear enough to do the work Rawls requires of it (Hart 1989, 240–244).

Rawls recast the first principle in order to meet these objections, first in the foreign language editions of *A Theory of Justice* (changes later incorporated in the revised edition; see *TJ* xii), and more fully and satisfactorily in *Political Liberalism*.

The first principle now reads, "Each person has an equal right to a fully adequate scheme of equal basic liberties which is compatible with a similar scheme for all" (*PL* 291). This eliminates the problematic idea of measuring the "greatest extent" of liberties and clarifies that Rawls is interested in a scheme of basic liberties, not "liberty" as a distinctive value (Hart 1989, 234–237). Finally, Rawls, in *Political Liberalism*, clarifies that account of the priority of the basic liberties in light of Hart's criticism, showing it to rest on a liberal political conception of the person as a free and equal citizen (*PL* 296). The basic liberties are then specified not according to the "rational advantage" of the parties in the original position, but rather by what is necessary for the development of the two moral powers (*PL* 302). Here we see how Hart's criticism of certain aspects of *A Theory of Justice* played an important role in the development of Rawls's views into the form found in *Political Liberalism*.

Matt Lister

SEE ALSO:

Fairness, principle of
Freedom
Lexical priority: liberty, opportunity, wealth
Rules (two concepts of)
System of law

88.

HEALTH AND HEALTH CARE

RAWLS DEVELOPS HIS account of justice as fairness in *A Theory of Justice* with a widely recognized theoretical simplification that abstracts from the variation among people caused by differences in health states and duration of life. By hypothesis, his contractors are fully functional over a normal lifespan; disease, disability, and death as we know them are not issues that such contractors must grapple with. Instead, these fully normal contractors are to select fair terms of cooperation for whatever society in which they emerge. He repeats this simplification in *Political Liberalism* (20) when he states the fundamental ideas in his view. How the theory developed in *TJ* should be extended to address significant illness, disability, and premature death, is not an issue addressed in *TJ* itself.

Two Nobel economists challenged Rawls about this omission early on. In his review of *TJ*, Kenneth Arrow (1973, 251) complained that a theory that could not tell us who was worse off, a rich but sick person or a poor but well one, had a serious problem. A few years later, Sen (1980, 215–219) argued that a person with a significant disability could not convert a given amount of primary social goods into as many things that he can do or be as someone without such a disability, and so Rawls's concern about distribution is focused on the wrong space. The target of justice should be capabilities, the things people can actually do or be, not primary social goods.

Other commentators thought that justice as fairness should be modified slightly to address issues of the distribution of health care. Some thought we should add health care as a primary social good; others thought we should use the difference principle to address needs for health care. One approach to which Rawls (*PL* 184 n.1) is sympathetic in his later work sees health care (and health) as important because of its impact on opportunity (Daniels 1985, 32–35).

Health and health care / 333

In *PL* (184) Rawls says that the needs of people who have functional limitations as a result of illness or accident can be addressed by a legislature that knows the prevalence of these misfortunes and their costs. The key idea is to develop institutions that aim to restore people to full functioning, keeping people as close to his initial simplifying assumption as possible. In *JF* Rawls adds: The provision of medical care, say through some form of social insurance, should not be seen as a way

> merely to supplement the income of the least advantaged when they cannot cover the costs of the medical care they may prefer. To the contrary: as already emphasized, provision for medical care, as with primary goods generally, is to meet the needs and requirements of citizens as free and equal. Such care *falls under the general means necessary to underwrite fair equality of opportunity and our capacity to take advantage of our basic rights and liberties,* and thus to be normal and fully cooperating members of society over a complete life. (*JF* 174, emphasis added)

Rawls is primarily concerned in *PL* and *JF* with the provision of medical care. But, the rationale he gives in *JF* for providing appropriate medical care to all applies more broadly to traditional public health measures and to the social determinants of health, about which he may have known little. Working out the details of these extensions is not something Rawls did, but they can be plausibly developed.

Consider first preventive or curative personal medical care. As Rawls suggests (*PL* 184), legislators must design a system that balances the cost of providing preventive and curative care with the other tasks of government. This should not create a bottomless pit into which all resources are poured, for doing that would make it impossible to carry out the other requirements of justice. Health and health care are important goods but they are not the only important goods. Rawls, however, says nothing about how to set reasonable limits to the services provided – though some other ideas he had are helpful in thinking about that problem (to which we return shortly).

The rationale Rawls endorses for providing appropriate medical care to all applies to traditional public health measures as well. Keeping people functioning normally means society must provide all with a healthy environment, in which the regulation of air, water, food, and living and working conditions provide reasonable attention to protecting health and safety. Traditional public health measures thus aim to protect people against both infectious diseases and chronic illness through overt measures and through public education such as health promotion.

We might lump together medical services and traditional public health as aspects of health care (Daniels 1985, 2), but there is another tier of policy concerning the distributions of various goods that have a large impact on population health. There is robust social epidemiological evidence that the distribution of education, income, and wealth, as well as exclusionary policies focused on race, ethnicity, gender, and religion also have a vast impact on population health: the richer and better-educated one is (the higher one's socioeconomic status or SES), the longer and healthier one's life. (This is referred to as the SES gradient of health.) The broad rationale Rawls gives in *JF* (174) could apply to the distribution of the goods that are involved in SES, making all of social justice an instance of health policy.

Rawls need not turn all of social justice into health policy, however. His principles of justice as fairness turn out – in ways he could not have anticipated – to distribute the social determinants of health in a way that would flatten the socioeconomic gradient of health significantly (Daniels, Kennedy, and Kawachi 2000, 17–20). This serendipitous result means that the conception of justice that was developed in abstraction from considerations of health (all contractors function normally over a normal lifespan) produces a distribution of important goods that lead to better population health and a more equal distribution of it as well. In effect, justice as fairness is good for our health (Daniels 2008a, 4).

Rawls emphasized that a legislature would have to balance what it spent in protecting population health with its other obligations. This implies that not every health need may be met; since meeting health needs is only one requirement of justice among others, resources for health will be limited. Still, we are obliged to be fair about how we do meet health needs, so how can we meet health needs fairly when we cannot meet them all?

Two of Rawls's ideas suggest a way to approach this issue, the idea of procedural justice and the idea of democratic deliberation. We might think of combining these ideas into a process that can advise legislatures about how to meet health needs fairly when all needs cannot be met. Suppose that broader principles of justice, such as the principle assuring fair equality of opportunity, do not tell us how to make resource allocations to health care services when all the allocations open to us promote opportunity in reasonable ways. For example, suppose we are considering whether to fund a prenatal care outreach program or a screening program for coronary artery disease. Reasonable people may disagree about what should get priority. The disagreement may result from the fact that we lack consensus on ethical principles adequate to resolving the dispute. We might then think that we need a process that we can agree is a fair way to arrive at a decision, and we would take our cue from Rawls's discussion of procedural justice and say that the outcome of such a fair process will count as fair (Daniels and Sabin 2008, 43–66).

We may, however, also think that argument and reasoning is relevant to achieving a fair outcome – that this is not a case where we want to avoid giving reasons and appeal to a lottery. We may want to assure people that ethical reasons are taken into account, along with relevant evidence about effectiveness and cost. In this case we may insist on a process that emphasizes deliberation. We may want a transparent process that involves an appropriate range of stakeholders seeking reasons they can agree are relevant to the problem, and we may insist that decisions are revisable in light of new evidence and arguments. In this way we may combine Rawls's defense of procedural justice with his defense of democratic deliberation as a way of improving the legitimacy and fairness of decisions about health care limits (Daniels and Sabin 2008, 34–36, 44–45).

Norman Daniels

SEE ALSO:

Capabilities
Daniels, Norman
Equal opportunity, democratic interpretation
Fair equality of opportunity
Justice as fairness
Procedural justice
Public reason

89.

HEDONISM

THERE ARE THREE broad types of hedonism in the philosophical literature. Psychological hedonism is a thesis about human motivation. It claims
that humans are exclusively driven by the attainment of pleasure and the
avoidance of pain (usually, their own). This is an empirical thesis: a claim about
how humans are. The other two types of hedonism are normative: they are concerned with what is good or valuable. Axiological hedonism is a thesis about the
nature of the good in general. It claims that pleasure is the only thing that is
intrinsically good (i.e. good for its own sake, rather than as a means to other
goods). As one of its most famous defenders, Jeremy Bentham, wrote in 1789:
"Now, pleasure is in itself a good: nay, even setting aside immunity from pain,
the only good: pain is in itself an evil; and, indeed, without exception, the only
evil." Prudential hedonism, by contrast, is a thesis about the nature of individual welfare. It claims that well-being consists in the presence of pleasure and the
absence of pain. The best life for an individual, as far as her own self-interest
is concerned, is the one that has the greatest balance of pleasure over pain. It is
possible to be a prudential hedonist without being an axiological hedonist, since
one might claim that, while welfare is constituted by pleasure, things other than
welfare – say, freedom, beauty or friendship – are intrinsically good. However,
many philosophers, including classical utilitarians such as Bentham, have been
psychological, axiological, and prudential hedonists all at once.

Hedonists of each of the above types can be further distinguished according to their view about the nature of pleasure. Traditionally, two chief positions on that question have been prevalent. The first, sensation hedonism, claims
that pleasure is a particular type of physical sensation present in all pleasurable
experiences. The second, attitudinal hedonism, claims that pleasure is a positive

affective response that a subject has toward an experience. What makes an experience pleasant, that is, is not any quality intrinsic to that experience, but instead the favorable reaction that the person enjoying the experience has to it. Because it is difficult to identify a single common sensation shared by the diverse array of experiences that people find pleasurable (eating ice cream; falling in love; reading Rawls), most philosophers prefer some version of attitudinal hedonism to sensation hedonism.

Rawls is not a hedonist in any of the above senses. His remarks on hedonism in part III of *TJ* (486–491) are designed to highlight the distinctive features of his own contrasting account of the good and to criticize the normative versions of hedonism in favor of that account. Rawls approaches the topic from an unusual angle. He claims that the reason that many people are drawn to each of the above types of hedonism – perhaps without knowing it – is that they are attracted to what Rawls terms "the dominant end conception of deliberation" (*TJ* 486). According to that conception, the only rational way for a person to decide how to live is to first identify a single ultimate goal and then ensure that all of her other lesser aims in life are directed toward achieving that goal. Rationality requires a single ultimate aim, since if we have multiple irreducible aims we will end up with conflicts between them that cannot be resolved through the use of reason. Rawls argues that many people who find this conception of rational deliberation plausible end up selecting pleasure as their dominant end, since it alone seems to be able to provide the sort of all-encompassing, flexible, and attractive goal that they are seeking. If we add a few further natural assumptions, psychological, axiological, and prudential hedonism then swiftly follow.

However, Rawls argues, this motivation fails to support hedonism for three reasons. First, pleasure is in fact much too narrow a candidate for a dominant end. We all care about a huge variety of things other than pleasure. Robert Nozick famously made a similar point by asking us to imagine an "experience machine" that is designed to produce the most pleasurable experiences imaginable. Most of us, Nozick argued, would not want to be attached to such a machine for life – because we care about being, acting on and connecting to things, not just experiencing them (Nozick 1974, 44–45). Second, although hedonists claim that exclusively pursuing pleasure provides a determinate and relatively simple method of decision-making, Rawls argues that this is false. Given that pleasurable experiences differ dramatically in quality, intensity, and duration, and given that pleasure must somehow be weighed up against the pain that sometimes accompanies it, "the problem of a plurality of ends arises all over again within the class of subjective feelings" (*TJ* 488). It is in practice difficult to make even crude estimates about how best to maximize even a single agent's pleasure. Finally, the dominant end conception of rationality that motivates hedonism is itself flawed. According to Rawls, a rational plan of life for each person is one that would be chosen by him or her "with full awareness of the relevant facts and after a careful consideration of the consequences" (*TJ* 359) and that also satisfies certain straightforward formal principles of rational choice (*TJ* 361–362). Although such a plan of life may at times produce conflicts between incompatible aims, this is a fact of life and not a sign of irrationality. If this is right, rationality does not require us to pursue any single dominant end, let alone pleasure, and what Rawls sees as the chief motivation for hedonism is undercut.

Hedonists will, of course, fight back. They will claim that while we may appear to pursue or value many things other than pleasure, in fact the appeal of those things can be fully explained by the pleasure that they produce. They will argue that we are averse to entering the experience machine precisely because we fear that it will not produce enough pleasure – perhaps because we are familiar with "the paradox of hedonism," according to which pleasure is most effectively pursued indirectly. And they will insist that hedonism is intuitively appealing in itself and does not depend for its support on a controversial account of rationality. Because many other concerns about hedonism remain to be addressed, the debate over its merits is sure to continue, whether or not these responses to Rawls's criticisms succeed.

Helena de Bres

SEE ALSO:

> *Deliberative rationality*
> *Dominant end theories*
> *Goodness as rationality*
> *Happiness*
> *Plan of life*
> *Utilitarianism*

90.

HEGEL, G. W. F.

MANY STILL TODAY consider John Rawls a straightforward Kantian and thus the degree to which his theory has been influenced by the thought of G. W. F. Hegel (1770–1831) goes largely unnoticed. Numerous communitarian thinkers (e.g. Alasdair MacIntyre, Charles Taylor and Michael Sandel) have criticized Rawls for his "individualism" and lack of an "adequate conception of community"– much in the manner Hegel criticized his predecessor Kant. Not only does *A Theory of Justice* have strong parallels to Hegel's *Philosophy of Right* (1991 [1821]), however, but Rawls fully accepts a number of Hegel's central criticisms of Kant. The former cites Hegel (and the British Idealist F. G. H. Bradley) numerous times in *A Theory of Justice*, and he lectured on Hegel at Harvard in the 1960s and again in the 1990s. So what is his theory's relation to Hegel?

Rejecting the need to ground political philosophy in a metaphysical system (such as Hegel does with his monism, talk of one world spirit or *Geist*, etc.), Rawls considers his theory "political not metaphysical" – a point emphasized in his later work (*CP* 388ff.). He denies that political philosophy needs any grounding in a comprehensive metaphysics for such systems generally *underdetermine* practical positions in political philosophy (*CP* 404 n.22); the materialist Hobbes and the idealist Hegel, after all, both end up defending monarchy. The aim of "justice as fairness" is far more modest; it is to provide a conception of justice that may serve as a public basis for the justification of modern democratic institutions under conditions of pluralism and be supported by (at least) a "reasonable overlapping consensus" (*CP* 421ff.).

Once this crucial difference between the two thinkers is granted, however, one finds numerous important areas in which Rawls sides with Hegel *against*

Kant. Three such areas will be touched upon here: the view of political philosophy as historical "reconciliation," the conception of the person as fundamentally "social," and the rejection of a moral cosmopolitanism typically associated with Kant.

In general, Rawls considers Hegel a "moderately progressive reform-minded liberal" and representative of the liberalism of freedom (*LHMP* 349): both descriptions apply to his own theory as well as to Kant's. However, like Hegel's *Philosophy of Right*, *A Theory of Justice* is not strictly speaking an ethics at all, but already "political." That is, for Kant the categorical imperative (at the heart of our common moral sense) provides an eternal moral standard by which we can determine individual right action, and Kant's later political philosophy (and his notion of civil society) is constructed in light of this fundamental ahistorical moral norm. In the thought of both Hegel and Rawls, by contrast, the task of political philosophy begins by identifying the major political conflicts of the present historical age, and from there attempts to "reconcile by reason" or reach a "reflective equilibrium": to comprehend and help resolve the deepest cultural conflicts of the modern period (Hegel 1991 [1821], 11ff.; *PL* 8–9). Hegel views the central conflict as that between the claims of ancient communal life and the modern principle of subjective freedom, whereas Rawls believes an "impasse" has been reached in our "post-Reformational political culture" between the claims of liberty (in the tradition of Locke and Mill) on the one hand, and those of equality (represented by Rousseau and Marx) on the other (*PL* 4–5; *CP* 391ff.). Hegel's solution rests in his notion of a modern rational state grounded in *Sittlichkeit*: in the ensemble of social institutions and life forms that make universal individual freedom both possible and actual. Rawls's resolution consists in a well-ordered "basic structure" (the background system of social, economic and political institutions) regulated by his two principles of justice. Both thinkers seek to formulate – not an eternal moral norm but – the underlying animating principles of the modern state.

The emphasis by both on conflict resolution, as well as on the foundational role of historical social institutions in political philosophy, leads to similarities in their respective notions of the person. In contrast to the Kantian individual, whose transcendental reason and autonomy is typically defined *in opposition* to the material and sociohistorical conditions in which it finds itself, both Rawls's political person and Hegel's politico-legal individual (depicted in his section *Abstract Right*) are the product of a long historical process (*LHMP* 366; Hegel 1991 [1821], 87–88). Individual freedom entails for both, not the exercise of some supersensible freedom, nor merely the capacity to follow universal rules and choose between de facto alternatives, but the positing of particular goals and life plans in material and social existence: in "expressing" (*entäussern*) a self-conception in an external publicly recognized sphere (Hegel 1991 [1821], 39; *TJ* 224). This requires, however, a background of reciprocal recognition and institutional acceptance by other reasonable selves. For Rawls, as for Hegel, the person is conceived as "fundamentally social." Only in active cooperation with similar selves, writes Rawls, can the person develop and realize his distinctive abilities (*TJ* 460 n.4). (Of course, Rawls rejects the idea that this social individual is ultimately but an accident of one substantive world spirit or *Geist* – see *LHMP* 369ff.)

Finally, in his last major work on international relations, Rawls explicitly rejects the moral cosmopolitan position (*LP* 119): a position insisting on the moral equality of all reasoning beings and which leads Kant to assert the necessity of a republican civil constitution for all states (*Perpetual Peace*, First Definitive Article – Kant 1983 [1795]). By contrast, Rawls's concern in *The Law of Peoples* shifts from the well-being of individuals and the global "worst off" (he does acknowledge a minimal set of human rights) to the justice of *whole societies* both liberal and "decent" (*LP* 119–120). In decent societies, those minimally maintaining "a just consultation hierarchy" (an idea Rawls attributes to Hegel, *PL* 64ff.), the moral freedom and equality of all persons may even legitimately be *denied*: a group such as women, for instance, may be considered morally inferior and granted lesser rights so long as their interests are "taken into consideration" by a meaningful consultation procedure (*LP* 71–73). Rawls's position on international justice thereby, however, moves surprisingly close to treating "a people" (a more or less just, politically organized group) as the *primary* moral unit similar to Hegel's *Geist*. One might even conclude that Rawls's thinking – as it develops over the decades – moves closer and closer to the Hegelian position: to the utter chagrin of those who side with the spirit of Kant.

Sibyl A. Schwarzenbach

SEE ALSO:

Cosmopolitanism
Decent societies
Kant, Immanuel
Moral person
Reflective equilibrium
Social union

91.

HIGHER-ORDER INTERESTS

RAWLS'S THEORY OF justice is supposed to tell us how to fairly assign the benefits and burdens of social cooperation. To answer this question one must first develop a metric for determining whether and how much different individuals benefit from different sets of social arrangements: a metric of advantage. This metric will serve as a public basis that all members of society can appeal to for evaluating whether some people are being unfairly advantaged over others.

Rawls suggests that because it is to play this public role the metric of advantage must meet some important constraints. One constraint is that it needs to be relatively easy to evaluate how someone is doing according to the metric. For instance, Rawls rejects using simply a person's happiness as the basis for evaluating advantage because it would be too hard to work out whether one individual was happier than another and thus there would be too much disagreement to reach public consensus on whether there was unfairness.

Another important constraint is that the metric must not be biased toward any particular conception of what makes for a good life. Different members of society have very different views about what it takes to live well but they are all going to be expected to use the same public criterion for evaluating advantage. Thus, the metric must be suitable for a "pluralistic society," where there is disagreement about the nature of the good life. If we are to show respect for these people with their different views we need to adopt a metric that doesn't rest on a view of the good life that some people endorse but others reject. This constraint is part of what is required to accept the use of "public reason" in political decision making, a central part of Rawls's "political liberalism."

Higher-order interests / 343

Rawls's discussion of "higher-order interests" is part of his argument for his own preferred metric of advantage: the distribution of primary goods. Rawls proposes that a liberal society should focus on the satisfaction of particular interests, what Rawls calls our "higher-order interests." There are three such interests. First, there is the interest in developing and using the capacity for a sense of justice. A capacity for a sense of justice is a capacity to come up with one's own view about what constitutes a fair division of benefits and burden in one's society. Second, there is the interest in developing and using the capacity to form a conception of the good. A "conception of the good" is a view about what constitutes a successful life. Unlike the sense of justice, it concerns just what is best for an individual, not how relations between people should be structured. To exercise one's capacity to form a conception of the good is to think about what the best way to live is and, especially, to decide how to lead one's own life. Third, there is the capacity to effectively advance one's conception of the good. Having formed a view about how best to live, people should make plans about how to lead their lives in light of this view. They have an interest in being successful in their pursuit of these plans.

Now, the satisfaction of higher-order interests is not itself an appropriate metric for public measurement of benefits because it does not satisfy the first constraint mentioned earlier: that the metric needs to be easy to apply. Unlike the metric of happiness, this metric does not seem to require invasive assessments of exactly what any individual's mental states are like. But it still seems hard to apply: the three higher-order interests are quite abstract, so there might be disagreement about how exactly to apply them. To solve this problem Rawls suggests that in practice we should rely on a more concrete list of "primary goods" to judge advantage: we should look at what particular liberties, resources, and so on individuals have. Access to these primary goods will be a good proxy, he thinks, for satisfaction of the higher-order interests and relatively easy to publicly monitor.

What about the second constraint: that the metric not be biased toward any particular conception of the good? Rawls gives us two kinds of argument for the claim that his metric is neutral between different conceptions of the good. The first argument is that all persons, irrespective of their particular conception of the good, have the three higher-order interests and thus need primary goods. If everyone has these interests, then, the argument goes, promoting them will not favor any particular conception of the good. This argument seems relatively successful when we think about the third "higher-order interest" – the interest in successfully pursuing a conception of the good. People with different conceptions of the good all make plans and surely they all have an interest in fulfilling those plans, whatever they may be. And so focusing on this interest doesn't seem to privilege any particular conception. But the argument is less obviously successful when we consider the other higher-order interests, in developing and using a capacity for a sense of justice and a capacity to form a conception of the good. On some views about the good life – an Aristotelian view for instance – making judgments about justice and acting on them is essential to living well, but on other views about the good life making these judgments is much less important.

The second argument for the neutrality of his metric concerns the grounds for this metric. A fundamental moral idea in liberal democracies is that political authority must be exercised in a way that treats all citizens as free and equal. Treating them in this way, Rawls claims, requires us to give fundamental importance to certain interests, in particular the three higher-order interests. Very briefly, here is why. One thing required to treat citizens as free and equal is that we treat them as worthy participants in political decision-making. For instance, many campaigns for equality have emphasized that certain groups, such as women and African Americans, are worthy participants in politics. This is one reason why voting is considered a central right in liberal democracies. Thus, Rawls suggests that we must give central importance to each citizen's interest in forming a view about justice and acting on it – their "sense of justice" is fundamental.

Another central part of treating citizens as free and equal is treating them as capable of making up their own minds about what is of central importance in life. For instance, in liberal democracies we give great weight to freedom of conscience to ensure that no individual is punished for forming a point of view and to freedom of speech to ensure that individuals have an opportunity to hear different points of view. This is an important part of what it is to recognize citizens as free and Rawls thinks it justifies giving central importance to their capacity to form a "conception of the good" for themselves.

Finally, treating citizens as equals requires that we respect the views about the good life that they decide on and thus treat their plans as important. This means that we must act to promote their opportunity to carry out those plans by ensuring that they have the means to do so. Thus, we must give importance to each citizen's capacity to advance their own conception of the good.

Thus, the basic moral idea that citizens should be treated as free and equal in political decision-making can be used to justify focusing on the three high-order interests and thus using the primary goods as a public measure of advantage. Now, that basic moral idea, that citizens should be treated as free and equal, is one that can be endorsed by people with different views about the good life. It

Higher-order interests / 345

does not rest on any particular conception of the good for its justification. So, we can appeal to that basic moral idea without being biased towards any particular conception of the good. Thus, Rawls concludes that his metric is not objectionably biased, because it can be justified on grounds that are independent of any particular conception of the good.

Adam Hosein

SEE ALSO:

Citizen
Moral person
Political liberalism, justice as fairness as
Primary goods, social
Public reason

92.

HOBBES, THOMAS

R AWLS WAS SO struck by what he called the overwhelming and dramatic effect on our thought and feeling of reading Hobbes's *Leviathan* that he deemed it the greatest single work of political thought in the English language (*LHPP* 23). He did so despite his view that "Hobbes's substantive theory can't be, *in general*, correct; since *constitutional democratic* institutions that violate his conditions for the Sovereign *have actually* existed and have not been noticeably less stable and orderly regimes than the kind of absolutism that Hobbes favored" (*LHPP* 85). Rawls attributed Hobbes's error in thinking that a system of divided government limited by a constitution must be unstable, to Hobbes's exclusion of "reasonable desires" to act from principles of fairness/reciprocity and of reasonable self-restraint from his political account of human psychology. As far as political questions are concerned, Hobbes took such reasonable desires to be too weak or unreliable to secure a stable society, preferring instead to rely exclusively on a common set of rational desires (*LHPP* 88). But, in Rawls's view, reasonable self-restraint and fairness are necessary for sustaining the sort of social cooperation on which constitutional democracy depends. Study of Hobbes helps us to see the importance of these reasonable notions and to think about how the social contract view might be recast to make room for them.

On Rawls's interpretation, Hobbes's social contract was intended to provide a point of view for showing that everyone has an overriding and fundamental interest in supporting an effective sovereign when one exists, by showing that the state of nature is an ever present possibility of disabling warfare. His argument to that conclusion rested, Rawls wrote, on "quite plausible assumptions about the normal conditions of human life…Hobbes's psychological and other assumptions need not be strictly true of all human conduct…On the interpretation proposed, Hobbes's secular moral system is meant as a political doctrine; and as such, it is appropriate that it stress certain aspects of human life" (*LHPP* 50–51). It is worth noticing that this interpretation of Hobbes as offering a "political doctrine" akin to Rawls's "justice as fairness," as it is presented in *Political Liberalism*, is exceedingly unusual. Rawls recognized Hobbes as having a complex and fairly realistic conception of human psychology: he was not a psychological egoist, but adopted a presumption of predominant self-focus for the purpose of his political doctrine; he recognized that some are motivated by the desire to be just and noble and to act justly for its own sake, but these "generous natures" are too rare to be relied on; people may have and care deeply about their religious interests, but these cannot serve as the basis for a stable political society (*LHPP* 45–48). In part because Hobbes attempted to develop a "political doctrine" or "secular moral system" grounded only in the most basic common interests of citizens/subjects, apart from their religious views or specific conceptions of a good life, Rawls wondered whether Hobbes may have been "the first political liberal." (Rawls asked me to investigate this question in the early 1990s. The result appears in Lloyd 1998.)

Hobbes's laws of nature, the summary formulation of which is not to do to another what we would not have done to us, are reasonable principles, rationally justified, according to Rawls. He terms them "articles of civic concord" and they "define a family of *reasonable* principles so far as their content and role discern, the *general* compliance with which is *rational* for each and every person" (*LHPP* 64). Because the laws of nature are justified as assertoric hypothetical imperatives by appeal to each individual's end of self-preservation, Rawls thinks that Hobbes has no place in his theory for what we would call moral obligation or moral right. Hobbesian people do have principle-dependent, and not just object-dependent, desires; but these are all defined by the principles of rational choice (e.g. taking effective means) rather than by the principles of reasonable conduct (e.g. reciprocity). As we saw earlier, Rawls views the reasonable principles of mutuality and reasonable self-restraint as necessary to the social cooperation on which constitutional democracy relies. It is thus not surprising that Hobbes saw that political form of "mixed and limited" regime as unstable.

The role of the Hobbesian sovereign is, on Rawls's view, to stabilize a condition in which everyone normally and regularly adheres to the laws of nature (which produce social harmony) by providing each with assurance that others will do so as well. Rawls credits Hobbes as being one of the first theorists to clearly understand that there are situations in which it is rational to want a coercive sanction to be imposed on ourselves, even though we are all willing to do what we are supposed to do, so long as others do so also (*LHPP* 79). A sovereign is created through a process of authorization, in which people agree with one another to let a third party (the sovereign) use their rights as it judges best to secure peace and the common defense.

Rawls imagines the content of the social contract Hobbes has in mind (expanding on Hobbes's pithy remarks) as a covenant to authorize the same person or body as their sole political representative in perpetuity, and grant it all necessary powers (as enumerated by Hobbes), and to agree neither to release one another nor to seek release from one another from the covenant, and to submit to the sovereign's judgment as to whether it is properly exercising that authority (*LHPP* 81–82). The motive for entering the social contract is to secure the means of secure and commodious living.

Hobbes's interest for Rawls was more than just as an exemplar of a fully formed political theory in the social contract tradition, or an original political liberalism. Rawls held that it is useful to think of British modern moral and political philosophy as beginning with Hobbes and with the reaction to him. Christian orthodoxy, including Cudworth, Clarke, and Butler, rejected the entire idea that political authority could rest on a social contract, as well as Hobbes's supposed atheism, materialism, determinism, relativism, and subjectivism. Utilitarian critics such as Hume, Bentham, Hutcheson, and Smith rejected Hobbes's supposed egoism and subjectivism, substituting their own objective principle of utility both as a moral principle and as a ground for justifying political authority and obligation. Although Rawls thought orthodox critics had largely misinterpreted Hobbes's views, Hobbes's impact was clearly seismic: "his system of thought was something in regard to which one *had* to decide where one stood" (*LHPP* 26).

S. A. Lloyd

SEE ALSO:

Desires
Moral psychology
The reasonable and the rational
Social contract
Sovereignty
Utilitarianism

93.

HUMAN RIGHTS

THE NOTION OF human rights plays an important role in Rawls's *The Law of Peoples*. Respecting human rights is not only a core principle of political justice and legitimacy, it also assists in determining which people are well-ordered and when sanctions or even military intervention might be permissible.

To understand Rawls's position on human rights, we should note some key ideas that compose crucial elements of his account. In *LP*, §10, Rawls outlines what he takes to be the role human rights play in the Law of Peoples:

> Human rights are a class of rights that play a special role in a reasonable Law of Peoples: they restrict the justifying reasons for war and its conduct, and they specify limits to a regime's internal autonomy. In this way they reflect the two basic and historically profound changes in how the powers of sovereignty have been conceived since World War II. First, war is no longer an admissible means of government policy and is justified only in self-defense, or in grave cases of intervention to protect human rights. And second, a government's internal autonomy is now limited. (*LP* 79)

Human rights set necessary but not sufficient standards for decent domestic political and social institutions. In setting these standards, human rights limit admissible domestic law of all societies and help determine which peoples are in good standing in the Society of Peoples. Furthermore, fulfillment of human rights is sufficient to exclude justified and forceful intervention by other peoples.

Human rights, as Rawls understands them, are "universal" in that they apply to all societies, whether or not these societies recognize them. Liberal states do not have to tolerate those states that do not recognize human rights, namely outlaw states (*LP* §10.3). They have good reason to put limits on toleration here since outlaw states are aggressive and dangerous, so all peoples are more secure if such states change, even if they are forced to change by the international community.

Rawls argues that the foreign policy of "well-ordered peoples" (those that are liberal or decent) should be governed by eight principles, which constitute his Law of Peoples. These are principles acknowledging peoples' independence, their equality, that they have a right to self-defense, that they have duties of non-intervention, to observe treaties, to honor a particular set of human rights, to conduct themselves appropriately in war, and to assist other peoples living in unfavorable conditions. These principles do not include distinctively liberal rights, fair equality of opportunity, or egalitarian distributive principles, but they do include a core set of human rights that all well-ordered people have good reason to recognize and to uphold. Human rights, therefore, play an important role in defining principles of justice that all well-ordered peoples have reason to endorse.

Another important area in which discussion of human rights plays a key role is in covering the criteria for which peoples count as decent. Decent peoples must meet various criteria to qualify as decent, such as not having aggressive aims. The second criterion for eligibility explicitly involves a commitment to human rights. Rawls says that a decent people's system of law

> in accordance with its common good idea of justice ... secures for all members of the people what have come to be called human rights. A social system that violates these rights cannot specify a decent scheme of political and social cooperation. A slave society lacks a decent system of law, as its slave economy is driven by a scheme of commands imposed by force. It lacks the idea of social cooperation. (*LP* 65)

Rawls then offers a set of illustrations of the rights that must be satisfied and here he includes the right to life (by which he means the right to the means of subsistence and security); the right to liberty (which includes freedom from slavery and the right to enough liberty of conscience to ensure freedom of religion and thought); the right to own some personal property; and the right to formal equality as expressed by the rules of natural justice (by which he means that like cases should be treated similarly). It is important to draw attention to the fact that Rawls here offers only an indicative and partial list, as many commentators take him to be offering an exhaustive treatment of the human rights that must be honored, but this is not the case. (The elaborations and discussions in the footnotes of §8.2 help clarify his position.)

Rawls argues that liberal and decent peoples have a "duty of civility to offer other peoples public reasons appropriate to the Society of Peoples for their actions" (*LP* 59). The idea of public reason plays an important part in the argument offered for the Law of Peoples, and these public reasons must refer to shared principles, norms, and the like. This shared set of norms and principles helps stabilize a mutually respectful peace. Appealing to human rights constitutes one such relevant shared norm. Indeed, part of our shared norms are that human rights are "a special class of urgent rights" whose violation is condemned by both reasonable liberal peoples and decent peoples. This class of urgent rights would include those necessary for any common good idea of justice and therefore this makes them not especially liberal or Western ideas. Liberal and decent peoples can agree to this set of human rights for their own reasons.

Critics frequently remark that Rawls appears to endorse an overly concise list of human rights. Should well-ordered peoples not embrace several of the rights he seems to neglect, such as freedom of expression, association, political participation, and nondiscrimination? Much has been said in attempting to defend Rawls's perceived abbreviated list of human rights. Two approaches are standardly used: one revolves around a concern with wide acceptability and the other draws attention to the way violations of human rights can function to legitimate coercion in Rawls's account. According to the first line of defense, Rawls is concerned with how one might justify a list of human rights in the face of a wide range of views about conceptions of valuable lives in the international community. He wants to ensure his account can avoid the charge of parochialism. The idea is that a list of rights containing only the most essential of human entitlements would gain the relevant international consensus and therefore circumvent accusations that such a list could be endorsed by only a slim set of the world's nations. According to the other common line of defense, attention is drawn to the status of violations of human rights in justifying coercion in the international order. On this account, failure to comply with human rights on the concise list he offers would constitute legitimate grounds for considering the possibility of external intervention, including military intervention. It is this particular view of the function of human rights that accounts for the minimalist approach to human rights that Rawls adopts. Intervention in the affairs of a sovereign people is such a weighty matter that we should reserve space on the list of human rights for only those rights for which non-compliance could adequately justify considering the full force of international interventive measures. It is sometimes suggested that this explains why certain rights, such as the right to belong to a trade union or free speech, are not included.

A prominent defender of Rawls's views on human rights, David Reidy, argues that Rawls's endorsed list of human rights is much fuller than his critics seem to appreciate. In the commonly identified passages in which Rawls presents his list, Rawls offers only an incomplete sketch of what he has in mind. David Reidy notes that most readers think Rawls's list is excessively minimalist, but he draws attention to the fact that Rawls begins his list with the words "Among the human rights are..." and therefore leaves open the possibility that what he presents is not an exhaustive treatment (Reidy 2006a, 2006b). Indeed, there is much other textual evidence that Rawls endorses a wider set of human rights than the set commonly attributed to him. For instance, Reidy suggests that Rawls may affirm a wider range of rights such as nondiscrimination and democratic rights if they turn out to be "empirically necessary" (*LP* 173) to other basic rights.

Another noteworthy attempt to defend Rawls's limited list of human rights is made by Samuel Freeman (2006a), who draws attention to Rawls's own arguments on this matter. Rawls says: "What have come to be called human rights are recognized as necessary conditions of any system of social cooperation. When they are regularly violated, we have command by force, a slave system, and no cooperation of any kind" (*LP* 68). For Rawls, social cooperation involves reciprocity and an idea of fair terms of cooperation. The minimum reasonable terms of cooperation are respect for those rights he includes on his basic list. Freeman points out that however central the right to vote or run for office are to democratic societies, they are not necessary for social cooperation. Indeed, considered historically, most people have not enjoyed democratic rights, and even where democratic rights are upheld these rights often willingly go unexercised.

So, in conclusion, there are good reasons to find compelling Rawls's view that any decent political system must secure for its members certain minimum protections if it is to be a system of social cooperation. The minimum reasonable terms of cooperation include the items on the well-known short list, though they would include others as well, including Universal Declaration of Human Rights Articles 3–18. (*LP* 80 n.23) Furthermore, when we consider the ways in which

Human rights / 353

failure to respect central human rights might be grounds for coercive intervention, the firm limits placed on the core rights seems eminently reasonable. (See Mandle 2006; Reidy 2006a, 2006b.)

Gillian Brock

SEE ALSO:

Beitz, Charles
Buchanan, Allen
Decent societies
Just war theory
Law of Peoples
Legitimacy
Outlaw states
Rights, moral and legal

94.

HUME, DAVID

DAVID HUME (1711–1776) was a Scottish philosopher, historian, and economist. Although Rawls treats Hume primarily as an early utilitarian and critic of contractarianism, he incorporates certain elements of Hume's theory of justice into his own. In addition to references in *A Theory of Justice* and other works, Rawls devotes five chapters to Hume in his *Lectures on the History of Moral Philosophy* and two lectures in his *Lectures on the History of Political Philosophy*.

Hume's understanding of justice is more narrowly focused than Rawls's, since it is largely concerned with "the regulation of economic production and competition between members of civil society, as they pursue their economic interests" (*LHPP* 178–179). He treats justice as an "artificial virtue" since the principles of justice are conventionally established to serve the general interest of society. Rawls identifies four essential features in this account. First, the focus is on "a system of general institutional rules" as opposed to individual transactions (*LHPP* 181). Second, the rules are publicly recognized. Third, the rules are "inflexibly followed," even if departures on individual occasions would appear more beneficial. (This is compatible with "certain kinds of exceptions (e.g. to prevent imminent disaster)" (*LHPP* 181–182). Fourth, "the disposition to be just is a quality of character to adhere to these rules with the appropriate degree of inflexibility, *provided that others* in society have a manifest intention likewise to comply with them" (*LHPP* 182). Rawls accepts or adapts all of these points in his own theory: his principles focus on the rules of a practice or institutional structure; they are publicly recognized; they subordinate and limit the pursuit of individual goods; and they are founded on and exhibit a commitment to reciprocity.

In *A Theory of Justice*, Rawls describes the "circumstances of justice" as "the normal conditions under which human cooperation is both possible and necessary" (*TJ* 109), and he notes that his account "largely follows that of Hume" (*TJ* 109 n.3; cf. *LHMP* 58–59). Rawls distinguishes objective from subjective circumstances "which make human cooperation both possible and necessary." The objective circumstances include such things as "many individuals coexist together at the same time on a definite geographical territory" and "moderate scarcity." This implies that "Natural and other resources are not so abundant that schemes of cooperation become superfluous, nor are conditions so harsh that fruitful ventures must inevitably break down" (*TJ* 109–110). The subjective circumstances include the requirement that individuals "have roughly similar needs and interests, so that mutually advantageous cooperation among them is possible," but also that they have different conceptions of the good that lead them to make conflicting demands for social resources (*TJ* 110).

Hume was a critic of social contract theory, specifically arguing against John Locke's view. He makes a number of objections, including: that parents cannot bind their descendants to a government or authority; that most existing governments were formed on the basis of force and violence; and that tacit consent cannot be inferred when individuals do not have the resources, knowledge, and genuine option to leave (*LHPP* 167–168). Furthermore, even if a social contract *were* the basis of government authority, we would then want to know why we should honor such a contract. Hume's answer would be to point out that fidelity to contracts is itself an artificial virtue that can only be grounded in the benefits accruing to all from general compliance. In other words, something like the principle of utility underlies the artificial virtues, and therefore "when asked for the grounds of our allegiance to government, instead of taking the extra step of appealing to the principle of fidelity to a presumed contract, why not appeal directly to the principle of utility? Nothing is gained by way of a philosophical justification by founding the duty of allegiance on the duty of fidelity" (*LHPP* 169). It should be noted that Rawls's interpretation, which closely ties Hume to the utilitarian tradition, is controversial.

Rawls, however, thinks that Locke and Hume are asking importantly different questions. Whereas Locke is "like a *constitutional lawyer* working within the system of law defined by the Fundamental Law of nature... Hume's view is that of a *naturalist* observing and studying the phenomena of human institutions and practices, and the role of moral concepts, judgments, and sentiments, in supporting these institutions and practices, and in regulating human conduct" (*LHPP* 164). As Rawls sees it, Locke is working out the implications of a system of law – the law of nature – while Hume investigates how such a system informs human behavior or societies. This different orientation means that Hume never confronts "the really substantive issue of importance": "whether Locke's criterion of agreement beginning from a state of equal right, and his own criteria of general advantage, are going to lead to the same form of regimes as being legitimate" (*LHPP* 172).

Rawls emphasizes the naturalism in both Hume's moral philosophy and in his account of reason, which is not "an account of rational deliberation understood as normative," but describes "how, psychologically, we do deliberate" (*LHMP* 38). If a theory of practical reason is one that identifies principles that guide or check our deliberations (*LHMP* 45), then in the *Treatise* (Hume 1978 [1738]), at least, "Hume's view lacks a conception of practical reason and psychologizes moral deliberation by relying on laws of association and of the emotions, and invoking the strengths of desires and their influence" (*LHMP* 69). In a note, Rawls continues: "A moral doctrine that affirms the idea of practical reason may object to Hume's view for just this reason, in much the way Frege objected to psychologism in logic" (*LHMP* 69 n.2).

Hume's moral theory invokes the idea or perspective of a "judicious spectator" to correct the partiality and variability that our sympathy naturally shows. As Rawls interprets it, this is necessary in order to explain the fact that we largely agree with one another in our moral judgments. However, this correction "is made in our *judgments*" rather than in our sentiments, which are the basis of action (*LHMP* 93–94). The fact that we share judgments about morality does not imply that we are equally motivated to act accordingly, for recognizing what morality requires and being motivated so to act are quite different for Hume. Rawls suggests that the account of the judicious spectator "might become, if pressed, a conception of practical reason," even if that is not what Hume intended (*LHMP* 96–97). This could form the basis of a classical utilitarian conception of morality along the lines of Bentham or Sidgwick, although, once again, this connection is certainly not accepted by all interpreters of Hume.

Finally, Rawls suggests that Hume's moral psychology relies only on "object-dependent desires" as opposed to "principle-dependent desires." In the case of the former, we can describe the object of the desire "*without* the use of any moral conceptions, or reasonable or rational principles," while the latter require reference to either rational or reasonable principles (*LHMP* 46–47). The limited focus on object-dependent desires makes Hume's claim that reason alone cannot be the source of motivation appear more plausible than it is. Rational intuitionists, such as Richard Clark, could reply to Hume's critique by acknowledging that "bare knowledge of morality alone does not move us, but that knowledge, given our nature as rational beings, generates in us a principle-dependent desire...to act accordingly" (*LHMP* 80). By itself, this is not much more than asserting and labelling a desire generated by reason. To make such a claim plausible, one would have to "lay out how these principles connect with human beings' needs, aims, and purposes; it should say why, for example, oppression and tyranny, murder and torture, injustice and degradation and the rest, are wrongs, and not only wrongs but great wrongs" (*LHMP* 80–81). One could read Rawls himself as taking up this challenge in justice as fairness.

Jon Mandle

SEE ALSO:

Basic structure of society
Circumstances of justice
Desires
Intuitionism
Locke, John
Obligations
Reciprocity
Social contract
Utilitarianism

I

95.

IDEAL AND NONIDEAL THEORY

RAWLS FIRST SET out his conception of ideal theory in *A Theory of Justice*. Ideal theory asks "what a perfectly just society would be like" as well as which principles of justice "would regulate a well-ordered society." In such a society "Everyone is presumed to act justly and to do his part in upholding just institutions" (*TJ* 8). Consequently, ideal theory is concerned with "strict compliance as opposed to partial compliance theory." The rationale for this approach, according to Rawls, is that starting with ideal theory provides the basis for a "deeper understanding" of justice and a "more systematic grasp" of the problems of nonideal theory such as "the theory of punishment, the doctrine of just war, and the justification of the various ways of opposing unjust regimes..." (*TJ* 8). Nonideal theory fleshes out the principles that ideal theory has produced and considers how they "might be achieved, or worked toward, usually in gradual steps" (*TJ* 246). Nonideal theory is not much developed in *A Theory of Justice*. At the end of part II Rawls wrote that "for the most part I have tried to develop an ideal conception, only occasionally commenting on the various cases of nonideal theory" (*TJ* 391).

Ideal and nonideal theory are *sequenced* in the sense that nonideal theory will be better able to make progress once ideal theory has succeeded. There is nothing unusual in this sort of sequencing. Both theorists and practitioners often divide complex problems into several parts and work on those parts in sequenced stages and with different teams. For example, in designing an office tower the outer shell is often sketched before structural and interior layout work begins.

Rawls used sequenced stages of deliberation again in elaborating the content of the two principles of justice within ideal theory. He suggested a "four-stage sequence" that begins with the original position, moves to the "constitutional convention" where the primary standard is the first principle of equal liberty, proceeds next to the "legislative stage" where the primary standard is the second principle of justice, and finally gets to the application stage in which rules are applied "to particular cases by judges and administrators" and are used by citizens generally (*TJ* 195–200). As deliberation progresses through these stages the veil of ignorance is gradually lifted and by the application stage "everyone has complete access to all the facts" (*JF* 48).

The distinction between ideal and nonideal theory also plays a large role in Rawls's last book, *The Law of Peoples*, in which Rawls sketched a just international order – a "realistic utopia." He did this by advocating and elaborating eight principles for the fair and mutually respectful cooperation of countries (or "peoples"). These include requirements such as observing treaties, nonintervention, and honoring international human rights (*LP* 37). Ideal theory occupies the first two sections of the book (*LP* 3–88). It provides the normative "aim" which nonideal theory attempts to realize in "the highly nonideal conditions of our world with its great injustices and widespread social evils" (*LP* 89). By postponing consideration of noncompliance and unfavorable circumstances, ideal international normative theory is able to identify the principles or "laws" which liberal and "decent" peoples can reasonably accept as fair terms for their life together on Earth.

The section of *The Law of Peoples* on nonideal theory (*LP* 89–120) divides international problems into those resulting from noncompliance (conditions in which outlaw states "refuse to comply with a reasonable Law of Peoples") and those resulting from unfavorable conditions – ones that make "achieving a well-ordered regime ... difficult if not impossible" (*LP* 5). Rawls referred to countries living under unfavorable conditions as "burdened societies." They lack "the political and cultural traditions, the human capital and know-how, and, often, the material and technological resources needed to be well-ordered" (*LP* 105–106). The section on noncompliance mainly considers when and how war may be conducted against aggressive states, and the section on burdened societies discusses duties of international assistance and distributive justice.

"Ideal theory" has at least two senses. One is for the theory to be a theory of what would be ideal – as when a theory advocates a demanding aspiration such as eliminating poverty or ending war. Another is seen when a theory is deliberately simplified or makes use of idealizations in order to enable us to "focus on certain main questions free from distracting details" (*PL* 12). The first sense applies to Rawls's idea of a "realistic utopia." Rawls held that "Political philosophy is reasonably utopian when it extends what are ordinarily thought of as the limits of practical political possibility" (*LP* 6). The second sense, however, is the one that best applies to the assumption of full compliance. Ideal theory's assumption of full compliance has the advantage of making it much easier (for us, and for the parties in the original position) to predict the consequences of adopting a rule or principle of justice. Without that assumption we have to estimate how many people will violate the principle and try to predict how that will deflect outcomes.

Idealizations and simplifications are common in theoretical work (see McMullin 1985). They involve deliberately (1) taking a relevant factor out of the theory even though it is known to be present, sometimes present, or possibly present, and/or (2) representing a relevant factor in a way that is counterfactual. Since a theorist may not know whether a factor is present and decide to proceed on the assumption that it is not, idealizations need not be intentionally contrary to known facts. Rawls's assumption of full compliance, however, is consciously counterfactual. Other simplifications that Rawls uses in his theorizing include: (1) the parties in the original position decide on the basis of the very limited information permitted by the veil of ignorance; (2) a narrow list of basic goods provides the exclusive basis for decision in the original position; (3) the assumption that the parties exhibit mutually disinterested rationality and thus are neither envious nor altruistic; (5) a very limited range of theoretical alternatives is available for choice in the original position; and (6) the society for which principles are being chosen is a "closed system isolated from other societies" (*TJ* 8). As Thomas Nagel suggested, such a list may lead one to wonder "why the results of a decision taken under these highly specific and rather peculiar conditions should confirm the justice of the principles chosen" (Nagel 1975, 2).

After idealizations within a theory have played their role in generating predictions or other results they generally need to be adjusted or discharged. True, or at least truer, assumptions should be brought back into deliberation. For example, if one's economic theory assumed zero transaction costs in order to generate certain results, that assumption must be shown to make little difference or else replaced with a more realistic estimate when the theory is applied.

The assumption of full compliance is counterfactual everywhere in the contemporary world. Limiting the application of Rawls's theory of justice to societies with full compliance would mean that the theory applies nowhere on earth. Further, partial compliance cannot be discharged on the grounds that it makes little difference which principles of justice we choose. Rawls himself requires that principles of justice be able to gain sustainable commitment from citizens. A better possibility for Rawls is to suggest, optimistically, that compliance will progressively improve as citizens grow up and are socialized under more just institutions.

The moral psychology sketched in chapter 8 of *A Theory of Justice* suggests exactly this. Sadly, however, this way of discharging the idealization of full compliance is of no help at the earliest and most difficult stages of nonideal theory, namely when one has to apply (or adapt) the principles of justice to countries as they currently are (that is, when no improvements in actual compliance with the requirements of justice have as yet occurred).

A. J. Simmons emphasizes the "strongly transitional" dimension of nonideal theory. He notes that "nonideal theory requires that we pursue policies that are not only morally permissible, but also politically possible and likely to be effective." He suggests that "likely to be effective" should be understood not only in terms of eliminating present injustice, but also in terms of not creating conditions that stand in the way of further moves towards greater justice. "A particular policy might...be a good bet for remedying a particular injustice...while at the same time being a policy that retarded, stalled, or set back efforts to achieve overall justice" (Simmons 2010, 21).

Unsurprisingly, Rawls's insistence that ideal normative theory should come before nonideal theory has generated considerable criticism from political philosophers who resist idealizations that are hard to discharge, who doubt that better knowledge of the requirements of justice can be provided by abstract theory, and who prefer more critically engaged forms of scholarship. (See Nagel 1975, Sen 2009, and Schmidtz 2011. For responses to these sorts of criticisms see O'Neill 1988 and Simmons 2010.)

James W. Nickel

SEE ALSO:

> *Circumstances of justice*
> *Four-stage sequence*
> *Law of Peoples*
> *The original position*
> *Realistic utopia*
> *Well-ordered society*

96.

INDIVIDUALISM

RAWLS'S THEORY OF justice is individualistic in one sense, but, according to him, not in another. The sense in which it is individualistic can be gleaned from the passage in which Rawls writes that although "it is customary to think of utilitarianism as individualistic...utilitarianism is not individualistic" because it does not "take seriously the plurality and distinctness of individuals" (*TJ* 29). The principle of utility directs us to evaluate a government policy by considering only whether it would result in the greatest aggregate sum of utility. Parties in the original position would therefore choose the principle of utility to govern their society only if they assume that a big loss to one person is compensated for by small gains to many people. But to assume this, Rawls argues, is to apply the principle of rational choice for one person to all of society, which fails to take seriously the separateness of persons. Parties in the original position, according to Rawls, do not assume this. Rather they rank systems of principles by considering whether the best possible outcome for them under a system (for example, the outcome of being super rich) is good enough to justify accepting the worst possible outcome under this system (for example, the outcome of being terribly poor), or whether they should choose another system which has a less desirable best possible outcome (being well off but not super rich) but also a more desirable worst possible outcome (having relatively modest means but not being poor). This method of ranking is individualistic in requiring one-to-one comparisons of the situations of individuals under different systems of principles. If someone will fare poorly under a system, parties in the original position will reject this system unless someone will fare as badly or worse under every other feasible alternative, even if the first system will produce the most welfare in the aggregate.

The principles of justice that Rawls argues that parties in the original position would choose are individualistic in another sense, too: they guarantee to each person the highest possible minimum index of primary goods, which guarantees that each person will have an adequate opportunity to lead a good life, which utilitarianism does not do. Rawls, however, denies that his view is individualistic in a different sense. Thomas Nagel argued in his review of *TJ* that the argument from the original position "contains a strong individualistic bias" because parties in the original position choose between conceptions of justice on the basis of which will maximize their minimum index of primary goods and because, according to Nagel, the goods that Rawls identifies as primary are of greater value to those who have individualistic conceptions of the good (Nagel 1975, 9). A conception of the good is individualistic in the sense relevant here if it is possible to succeed in living according to it without a community committed to the same conception. Rawls denies that his conception of justice is biased toward conceptions of the good that are individualistic in this sense. Parties in the original position are assumed to have "higher-order interests" in the full development and exercise of their two moral powers, the capacity for a sense of justice and a capacity for a conception of the good. A social good is identified as "primary" if it is necessary for the full development and exercise of these two moral powers. Parties in the original position therefore want a larger share of primary goods rather than a smaller share. But they are not assumed to have individualistic conceptions of the good, and a social good is not identified as primary on the ground that it is especially useful in pursuing conceptions of the good that are individualistic in this sense.

Furthermore, to those who endorse nonindividualistic conceptions of the good – those who can live successfully according to their conceptions of the good only in a community of people who share the same conception – Rawls's conception of justice guarantees the liberty necessary to do so: freedom of conscience and freedom of association. For these reasons, Rawls argues, his theory does not have an individualistic bias. Rawls also points out that his conception of justice is not justified as promoting the Millian value of individuality. As understood by Mill, individuality is uniqueness in personality, character, ability, tastes, or way of life. Mill believed that individuality in this sense is both a constitutive part of full human development and an essential means to it. Rawls characterizes his conception of justice as a *political* conception of justice, and distinguishes his *political* liberalism from the *comprehensive* liberalism of Mill. Mill argued that social institutions should be arranged so as to promote individuality, but Rawls does not endorse this view or defend his conception of justice in this way.

Peter de Marneffe

SEE ALSO:

Communitarianism
Higher-order interests
Liberalism as comprehensive doctrine
Mill, John Stuart
The original position
Primary goods, social
Reasonable pluralism
Utilitarianism

97.

INSTITUTIONS

RAWLS'S ACCOUNT OF institutions has features that are inspired both by Hart's work on law as a social practice (Hart 1994) and by Searle's account of speech acts (Searle 1969). He understands institutions as being "public systems of rules which define offices and positions with their rights and duties, powers and immunities" (*TJ* 47). Such rules define certain kinds of actions as permissible, mandatory, or forbidden, and envisage sanctions when violations occur. In this sense, the game of football is an institution just as much as the American Congress. We can refer to an institution as an abstract object, by describing its rules; said institution then exists, following Hart, when a set of agents actually perform the appropriate actions foreseen by its rules, and mutually understand one another's conduct as compliance with those rules. This mutual knowledge and publicity are necessary features of institutions. For example, for two people to play the game of chess, it is not sufficient that they happen to perform the actions that the game prescribes. Additionally, each of them must also (1) know what the rules of chess are; (2) understand herself and the other player as being engaged in the game of chess according to those rules; (3) know that the other player also has the same knowledge and understanding; and (4) know that the other player knows that she knows this. Institutions, in order to exist, must not only be upheld, but must also be known to be upheld. In this way, the publicity requirement ensures that the participants in an institution know which constraints on one another's conduct they can expect from one another. This is essential as Rawls envisages (especially social) institutions as being mainly frameworks for cooperation under broad rules of reciprocity, rather than mere systems of coordination. For Rawls a society is just when it can be correctly described as a system of fair cooperation over time under institutional rules of the right kind (more on this below).

Another important feature of institutions is, following Searle, the fact that they are characterized both by constitutive rules (which establish rights and duties) and the set of possible strategies that their participants can pursue within them, or incentives that the constitutive rules generate. When we design institutions, what matters most are their constitutive rules, but we must also pay attention to the types of conduct that the system of rules overall encourages. Ideally, a good institution should have constitutive rules that are both intrinsically sound and designed in such a way so as to encourage conduct which promotes the very same ends for which the institution is conceived. For instance, a democratic institution should both have democratic constitutive rules and be designed so as to discourage its members (say, the delegates of a representative body) from behaving in ways that undermine its democratic purpose.

Institutions play a central role in Rawls's work for a number of reasons. First of all, Rawls assigns a certain explanatory and normative primacy to them. Institutions are primary from an explanatory point of view because they affect their members and largely influence the kind of persons that they are and/or want to be (*PL* 269–271). They are primary from a normative point of view because most individual duties and obligations can be defined only against the background of an institutional setting. The content of obligations, in particular, is defined by the rules of an institution which sets the requirements that their participants must comply with; obligations fall upon us, therefore, not qua abstract moral agents, but qua participants in an institution with specific roles and offices. In making this point, Rawls partly embraces Bradley's claim that "the individual is a bare abstraction" (Bradley 1927; *TJ* 95).

Second, properly functioning (social and political) institutions are important because they realize formal justice (*TJ* 50–52). Formal justice is realized when the rule of law is successfully implemented, alike cases are treated alike, and unlike ones unlike. Formal justice is consistent with deep substantive injustice; yet, by raising and fulfilling regular and reliable expectations, it constitutes a valuable shield against significant kinds of injustice, especially with regard to the arbitrary abuse of power for private or tyrannical purposes.

Third, institutions constitute, for Rawls, the very subject of social justice. More specifically, the subject of social justice is the basic structure of society, namely "the way in which the major social institutions distribute rights and duties and determine the division of advantages from social cooperation" (*TJ* 6). The basic structure is so central because of how pervasive, profound, and omnipresent its effect is, and because, by distributing rights, duties, and social positions, it generates inescapable inequalities, which affect people's initial chances in life and therefore stand in need of a justification. The basic structure, however, is distinct from each and every institution which is part of it. In particular, it is not necessary for each institution to be designed according to the principles of justice that the basic structure overall must realize (*TJ* 50). An institution might be unjust without necessarily making the social system it belongs to unjust as a result – one (apparent) injustice might compensate another in a wider scheme. Conversely, a social system might be unjust without any of its constitutive parts being unjust – say, when an institution raises a justified expectation that another one systematically frustrates.

Finally, by defining the background rules against which people act, (social and political) institutions make sure that individuals can interact with one another on free and fair terms (*PL* 265–269). Individuals, Rawls argues, can interact without any malign intent, and yet inevitably come to agreements that (say, by impoverishing third parties or their future selves) alter their mutual standing in such a way that "the conditions for free and fair agreements no longer hold" (*PL* 266). Institutions make sure that this does not happen, by constantly correcting the background conditions against which people interact and thus maintaining background justice.

Miriam Ronzoni

SEE ALSO:

Basic structure of society
Cohen, G. A.
Cooperation and coordination
Obligations
Political obligations
Rules (two concepts of)

98.

INTUITIONISM

R AWLS'S USE OF the term "intuitionism" is to be distinguished from intuitionism as it is traditionally understood. As traditionally understood, intuitionism refers to moral views whose principles, norms, precepts, and so on are self-evident, apprehended directly, or knowable (or justifiable) independently of inference. (These are claims associated with philosophers G. E. Moore and W. D. Ross.) However, as Rawls uses the term, intuitionism, though compatible with these epistemic commitments, does not require them. Rawls instead uses the term to refer to the *structure* of a moral view, not its epistemic commitments. That structure is characterized by two or more irreducible first principles without any priority rules for weighing them against one another. That structure differs from both utilitarianism (which contains one such principle and a priority rule) and justice as fairness (which contains more than one such principle and a priority rule).

As Rawls uses the term, intuitionism refers to a moral view that includes two or more irreducible first principles without any priority rules for weighing them against one another. Instead, when the need arises for weighing them, we are to appeal to intuition – our judgment of which way of balancing them seems best upon reflection. Rawls gives the example of a view that uses principles of efficiency and equality to determine a just distribution of wealth. Given two societies that produce the same amount of wealth, the more just society will be the one that distributes its wealth more equally to its members. Similarly, given two societies that contain the same degree of inequality in wealth among their members, the more just society will be the more efficient one – the one that produces more wealth. However, given two societies in which one is more efficient but less equal than the other, a view such as this provides us with no explicit priority rule to determine which one is more just. What we must do, in such cases, is appeal to intuition in order to determine whether efficiency or equality possesses more weight. The more just society will depend on the (proper) outcome of that weighting.

As Rawls views things, the main rivals in moral theory, prior to *A Theory of Justice*, were intuitionism and utilitarianism. According to utilitarianism, the more just society is the one that produces the greatest happiness for the greatest number. Unlike intuitionism, utilitarianism includes just one irreducible first principle (the greatest happiness principle). This principle is its sole and ultimate standard. All other norms (insofar as they are justified) are justified by reference to this principle – they are *derivative* norms. When derivative norms conflict, however, we weigh them, not by appealing to intuition, as intuitionism maintains, but by determining which one, if honored, will produce the greatest total amount of happiness. For example, given two societies in which one is more efficient but less equal than the other, the more just society, according to utilitarianism, is the one that produces the greatest total amount of happiness. In giving us an explicit priority rule for ranking the claims of efficiency and equality, utilitarianism avoids the appeal to intuition.

Rawls believes that both intuitionism and utilitarianism are defective: intuitionism because it leaves us unable to resolve conflicts of intuitions, utilitarianism because its resolutions violate our most firmly held intuitions. Accordingly, in *A Theory of Justice* he develops and defends an alternative, which he calls *justice as fairness*. Like intuitionism but unlike utilitarianism, justice as fairness consists of two or more irreducible first principles. But like utilitarianism and unlike intuitionism, justice as fairness provides an explicit priority rule for ranking its principles – it does not appeal to intuition. That priority rule ranks the first principle ahead of the second principle. In cases where they conflict, the first principle always controls; no trade-offs are allowed between the two. Rawls describes this as a case of *lexical priority*: the first principle is lexically prior to the second. According to the first principle, each person is to have the most extensive liberty compatible with a like liberty for all. According to the second principle, all positions and offices in society must be equally open to all of its members, and inequalities in wealth and income must work to everyone's advantage, in particular to the advantage of the least well-off members of society. Hence, the lexical priority of the first principle to the second implies that no sacrifices in liberty are permitted for the sake of achieving greater amounts of wealth and income.

Intuitionism / 373

Given two societies, then – one having a higher amount of wealth and income than the other (though distributed as the second principle requires), but lacking either its extent or its equal distribution of liberty (as the first principle requires) – the more just society, according to justice as fairness, is the second.

Chris Naticchia

SEE ALSO:

Least-advantaged position
Lexical priority: liberty, opportunity, wealth
Rational intuitionism
Utilitarianism

J

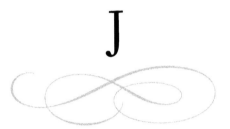

99.

JUST WAR THEORY

RAWLS CHARACTERIZES JUST war theory as part of the nonideal component of a reasonable Law of Peoples. Specifically, it serves to guide well-ordered peoples in their interactions with what Rawls labels outlaw states. Such states, or the regimes that rule them, fail to honor the human rights of individuals belonging to other societies by launching aggressive wars against them, or they fail to respect the human rights of (some of) the members of their own society by adopting policies that egregiously violate those rights, or both. Indeed, Rawls defines human rights in terms of the special role they play in a reasonable Law of Peoples, namely specifying those cases in which well-ordered (or at least human rights respecting) peoples may resort to war, and the constraints under which they must wage it.

As Rawls describes them, outlaw states believe that the advancement of the state's rational interest in, for example, economic gain, the acquisition of territory, or the attainment of power, suffice to justify the resort to war. Well-ordered states, in contrast, acknowledge the constraints that the reasonable places on the rational by submitting to a reasonable Law of Peoples that sanctions war in only two cases: the defense of a human rights respecting society against aggression, and forceful intervention to protect those individuals whose own state egregiously violates their human rights. In other words, a reasonable Law of Peoples condones waging war only if it targets an outlaw state.

Consider, first, Rawls's treatment of the right to wage war in self-defense. Only those societies that honor both their own members' human rights and those of individuals belonging to other peoples possess such a right. It follows that outlaw states have no right to wage war, even in self-defense. Respect for human rights is not only a necessary condition for possession of a right to wage war in self-defense, however; it is also sufficient. As Rawls explicitly notes, this entails that even a benevolent absolutism, meaning a regime that respects human rights but that denies those it rules a meaningful say in political decisions, may resort to force to preserve itself (*LP* 92).

As the attribution of a right of self-defense to a benevolent absolutism indicates, Rawls does not include a right to political participation among those human rights specified by a reasonable Law of Peoples. It follows that neither the promotion of democracy nor the less than fully equal form of political participation Rawls labels a decent consultation hierarchy provides a just cause for war. Rawls also rules out the use of force to bring about the adoption of a liberal political order. He does so not only in the case of decent societies and benevolent absolutisms, both of which respect human rights, but even in the case of burdened societies, meaning ones that fail to honor some of their members' human rights due to historical, social, and economic conditions that militate against the creation of well-ordered society. Where a regime that does not confront such conditions adopts a policy that violates (some of) its subjects' human rights, Rawls does sanction forceful intervention, but only on two conditions: first, that the violations are egregious, and second, that the use of various nonviolent strategies such as economic sanctions have failed to persuade the regime in question to desist from such behavior.

Possession of a just cause does not suffice to render just a war waged by a human rights-respecting state; rather, Rawls maintains that such a state must also adhere to several principles that limit how it may fight. One of these requires that the state conduct itself in a manner conducive to a just and lasting peace. As Rawls remarks, "the way a war is fought and the deeds done in ending it live on in the historical memory of societies and may or may not set the stage for future war" (*LP* 96). Ironically, the example Rawls offers of a state's failure to limit its pursuit of victory in war as required by the aforementioned principle, namely the United States' decision during World War II to eschew a negotiated surrender on the part of Japan in favor of the demand that the Japanese surrender unconditionally, is not one in which that failure undermined a just and lasting peace. The origins of World War II in Europe better illustrate the principle Rawls invokes, as they clearly owe much to the failure of the British and French to conduct themselves in a manner conducive to a just and lasting peace at the conclusion of World War I.

A second principle that limits the means a human rights-respecting state may adopt even when waging a just war requires that it discriminate between the outlaw state's leaders and officials, its soldiers (or, more broadly, combatants), and its civilians. Those in the last category, Rawls maintains, ought not to be directly attacked, meaning that they may not be the intentional target of an act of war. The reason for this prohibition is that civilians lack responsibility for the outlaw state's violations of human rights (i.e. its aggressive war or its egregiously rights-violating domestic conduct). Given the institutional arrangement of an outlaw state, its civilian population lacks the capacity to organize and launch a war; moreover, since they are "often kept in ignorance and swayed by state propaganda," civilian members of an outlaw state lack the ability to judge whether their state is justified in going to war. Neither of these conditions obtains in the case of an outlaw state's leaders and (high-ranking?) officials, or the "elites who control and staff the state apparatus" (*LP* 95). They do bear responsibility for the human rights violations that justify war, and therefore Rawls brands them as criminals. Unfortunately Rawls does not clarify what their status as criminals entails for their liability to attack. One possibility is that given the severity of their ongoing criminal conduct, for which they bear full responsibility, an outlaw state's leaders, officials, and elites are legitimate targets of war, even if, unlike an outlaw state's combatants, they do not pose a direct threat of harm to anyone. Whether Rawls would endorse such a view is impossible to say.

With regret, Rawls condones attacks against an outlaw state's combatants, but only on the grounds that they pose an unjust threat to others' human rights that cannot be resisted by another means. High-ranking officers aside, Rawls maintains that an outlaw state's combatants bear no responsibility for their unjust acts, since they "are often conscripted and in other ways forced into war, they are coercively indoctrinated in martial virtue, and their patriotism is often cruelly exploited" (*LP* 95). Though Rawls does not explicitly draw the inference, it seems likely that the principle that those fighting on behalf of a human rights-respecting state aim for a just and lasting peace constrains attacks even against legitimate targets. For example, one plausible implication of such a principle is that just combatants seek to harm as few of those fighting on behalf of an outlaw state as is consistent with achieving victory – or, to put the point in the language of the just war tradition, that their attacks be proportionate. Yet another silence in Rawls's all too brief discussion of the just conduct of war concerns the question of whether combatants pose a threat, and so are liable to attack, at all times, and the many vexing issues that arise if that question is answered in the negative. Still, Rawls's distinction between an outlaw state's leaders and senior officials, who bear responsibility for human rights violations, and that state's combatants, who do not, does have one clear implication: should a well-ordered state defeat an outlaw one, it may justifiably punish any surviving outlaw leaders and senior officials, but not any of the combatants who fought on behalf of the outlaw state.

Rawls maintains that the prohibition on acts of war that target civilians lapses in the case of a supreme emergency, such as the situation the British faced in their fight against the Nazis from the French surrender in June 1940 to the German surrender at Stalingrad in February 1943. The British were justified in deliberately bombing German civilians during this period only because a Nazi victory would have "portended incalculable moral and political evil for civilized life everywhere" (*LP* 99). Specifically, a Nazi victory would have led to the replacement of political relationships of equality grounded in mutual respect and toleration with hierarchical ones based on terror, force, enslavement, and extermination. Even then, however, British attacks on German cities would have been justified only if they were necessary to forestall defeat, and contributed substantially to that end (and, ultimately, to the defeat of the Nazis). Thus Allied attacks against German cities after February 1943, such as the fire-bombing of Dresden in 1945, were clearly unjustified, since no reasonable person could maintain that they were necessary to forestall a Nazi victory. Rawls also asserts that the United States never faced a supreme emergency in its war with Japan, presumably because it never faced the prospect of being comprehensively defeated by the Japanese if it limited itself to attacking only legitimate targets of war. It follows that the United States acted unjustly in dropping atomic bombs on Hiroshima and Nagasaki. Rawls does defend well-ordered states' possession of nuclear weapons, however, on the grounds that "some nuclear weapons need to be retained to keep those [outlaw] states at bay and to make sure they do not obtain and use those weapons against liberal or decent peoples" (*LP* 9).

If it is to wage war a human rights-respecting state must have a military, and to that end Rawls defends such a state's employment of conscription. Indeed, he suggests that insofar as a state's use of conscription entails that it will be more likely to refrain from waging unjust wars than would otherwise be the case, that alone justifies the use of conscription despite the considerable infringement it places on individual liberty. (Though, as a matter of ideal theory, Rawls defends the democratic peace hypothesis on the grounds that it follows from democratic states enjoying stability for the right reasons, he notes that given the myriad ways in which actual democratic states diverge from the ideal, they will frequently intervene in weaker states, including some whose political institutions exhibit certain democratic features. Rawls's claim vis-à-vis conscription's pacifying tendency gains its relevance in this nonideal context.) Yet Rawls also appears to endorse selective conscientious objection; that is, the view that the state ought to accommodate a combatant's refusal to participate in a particular war because he or she believes it to be unjust in its ends, or the means taken to achieve them, or both. Though not strictly a contradiction, these two positions do seem to be in some tension with one another. As for conscientious objection to war per se, while Rawls acknowledges that at some particular point in history pacifism may be warranted because a just war is not a realistic option at that time, he rejects absolute pacifism as "unworldly" and "bound to remain a sectarian doctrine"; that is, not a possible component of an overlapping consensus among free and equal people.

David Lefkowitz

SEE ALSO:

Human rights
Ideal and nonideal theory
Law of Peoples
Outlaw states

100.

JUSTICE AND INTERPERSONAL COMPARISON

ALTHOUGH ANY THEORY of distributive justice always requires some sort of interpersonal comparison, the possibility of interpersonal comparison remains one of the fundamental problems in theories of distributive justice, including Rawls's difference principle. The problem of interpersonal comparison concerns the question of whether we can compare the state of one person with that of another (Hammond 1991).

In economics, there is a deep and abiding skepticism about interpersonal comparisons. Many economists base their theories on individual preferences. But it is widely thought that there is no scientific basis to compare a person's mental states with another's, and that interpersonal comparisons cannot be done without including some normative judgments. Skeptics argue that, for economics to be a branch of science, it must eliminate any normative elements and thus avoid interpersonal comparisons. Economists instead appeal to a Pareto principle (e.g. the weak Pareto principle holds that if every person in society strictly prefers a state of affairs x to y, x is socially preferred to y) to construct a collective decision-making rule. However, Pareto principles are silent about distributional justice.

Rawls thinks that there is no need for interpersonal comparisons of overall well-being. His theory of justice only requires some basis for interpersonal comparison of what is relevant from the point of view of justice. This is why Rawls appeals to the notion of primary "social" goods. Rawls claims that the notion of primary social goods offers "the most feasible way to establish a publicly recognized objective measure, that is, a common measure that reasonable persons can accept" (*TJ* 81). According to Rawls, if primary social goods are used as the informational basis of distributive judgments, the problem of interpersonal comparison does not arise.

There are two basic forms of interpersonal comparisons. The first is interpersonal-level comparison of utility level (ICUL). According to ICUL, we can meaningfully say that the utility of one person is higher than the utility of another. The second is interpersonal comparisons of utility differences (ICUD). According to ICUD, we can meaningfully say that the difference in a person's utility between two states is greater than that of another person between the same two states. In other words, given ICUD, we can compare the gains and losses for the two persons. If ICUL and ICUD are assumed, we have full interpersonal comparison. Utilitarianism must assume at least ICUD. On the other hand, Rawls's difference principle only requires ICUL of primary social goods.

Kenneth Arrow, however, points out that Rawls's primary social goods cannot avoid the problem of interpersonal comparisons. Imagine that two persons have the same amount of primary social goods, but one person is perfectly healthy and the other is a hemophiliac, who requires $40,000 each year for coagulant therapy to maintain a normal level of functioning. According to Arrow, Rawls must judge that there is no relevant inequality between two persons from the point of view of justice. Arrow disagrees. He claims that the hemophiliac is worse off than the person with perfect health. Equality of primary social goods thus fails to capture the normatively relevant difference between these two persons. Arrow claims that Rawls would have to add health to the list of primary social goods. But then there must be a trade-off between health and other primary goods, such as wealth and income. The rate of trade-off may well be different from one person to another. Thus, insofar as there is more than one primary good, there is a problem in determining the relative importance among primary social goods. However, the relative importance of primary social goods may well vary from one person to another. Unless Rawls establish the same relative importance of goods across different individuals, Rawls's notion of primary social goods will encounter the problem of interpersonal comparison, which undermines the theoretical basis of his theory of distributive justice.

Similarly, Amartya Sen considers a case where a person with a disability can have more primary social goods than a person with no disability, but less capability and achievements due to the handicap. He argues that what people can do with goods depends on gender, age, disability, environment, and many other factors, and that primary social goods are insensitive to the diversity in people's ability to achieve what they value. Therefore, Sen claims that primary social goods are not the appropriate basis of interpersonal comparison and distributive justice. It is the capability to function, Sen (1992) argues, that is the appropriate basis from the point of view of justice. But Rawls does not support Sen's capability approach.

Rawls first introduces a distinction between a political conception of justice and a comprehensive moral doctrine, and then argues that his theory of justice is confined to a political conception of justice, which can allow for interpersonal variation of ends, with each person having his own comprehensive view of the good. Rawls then points out that the notion of the capability to function identifies the common ends specified by any particular comprehensive moral doctrine. Rawls thus claims that the capability approach goes against the ideal of political liberalism.

Iwao Hirose

SEE ALSO:

Capabilities
Difference principle
Primary goods, social
Sen, Amartya
Social choice theory
Utility

101.

JUSTICE, CONCEPT OF

THE CONCEPT OF justice is not the same as a conception of justice. This distinction is suggested by Rawls in the early stages of his work (see, for instance, *CP* 47–48 and 73–74) and is stated, in a clearer way, right at the beginning of *TJ*. As he writes: "Those who hold different conceptions of justice can, then, still agree that *institutions are just when no arbitrary distinctions are made between persons in the assigning of basic rights and when rules determine a proper balance between the competing claims to the advantages of social life*" (*TJ* 5, emphasis added). The part of the quotation in italics is the definition of the concept of justice.

This definition of the concept is formulated in the framework of a discussion on the role of justice. Rawls starts from the idea that society is a system of cooperation for the mutual advantage of its members. He further recognizes that both identity and conflict of interests arise in this system. Principles of justice are, thus, required in order to assign benefits and burdens, or rights and duties, to the members of society. The concept of justice illustrates this point by stressing that the role of justice is to establish the most adequate equilibrium ("proper balance") between the claims to the advantages of social life, excluding from the outset nonjustifiable discriminations between people ("no arbitrary distinctions"). However, what counts as "proper balance" and "arbitrary distinctions" is something that the concept cannot indicate and it must be substantiated by a conception of justice (such as the two principles of "justice as fairness").

The concept of justice states the common points which different conceptions share, along the lines of the distinction introduced by H. L. A. Hart between "the notion of justice" and "the applications of justice," both in matters of distribution and compensation. Hart's notion of justice is the idea that "individuals are entitled in respect to each other to a certain relative position of equality or inequality."

385

Justice, then, means to "treat like cases alike" and "different cases differently" (Hart 1994, 164). In matters of distribution, this arguably amounts to rejecting "arbitrary distinctions," but also to establishing a "proper balance" of benefits and burdens, as in Rawls's definition of the concept.

Rawls mentions Hart's contribution in a footnote (*TJ* 5 n.1), but he does not seem to realize that Hart's is, in fact, another version of Chaïm Perelman's distinction between "the formal or abstract formula of justice" and "the concrete formulas of justice." As in Rawls's concept and Hart's notion of justice, Perelman's "formal or abstract formula" discards arbitrary discrimination because it states that "beings of the same and essential category must be treated in the same way" and it also invites the specification of the adequate balance in that treatment, which is to be specified by "the concrete formulas," or conceptions, of justice (Perelman 1963, 16; the original text of these quotation, in French, is from 1945).

Rawls sees the concept of justice as not resolving any important question. The concept is very formal and Rawls is more interested in the development and justification of his two principles of justice in lexicographic order. Nevertheless, it may be the case that the concept does settle more than Rawls explicitly admits. First, it conveys a general idea of equality, which does not imply strict equality, linked to the refusal of "arbitrary distinctions" in the "assigning of basic rights," and also to the requirement of a "proper balance" between competing social claims. This general idea of equality is characteristic of modern concepts of justice – it is present in both Hart's and Perelman's – but it cannot be generalized to any such concept in the history of philosophy. Second, the concept of justice in Rawls also conveys the idea that the primary objects of justice are *institutions*, with their public rules and related practices, not individuals or social contexts in general. This means that, according to Rawls, if the main institutions of society and the way they work together for the distribution of benefits and burdens – what he calls "the basic structure of society" – are just, then the society is just, whatever the individual outcomes. This institutional and procedural account of justice is distinguishably Rawlsian and, thus, it is difficult to argue that, by stating this view, the concept of justice does not really settle any important point.

On another key, the significance of Rawls's distinction between the concept and the conception of justice may increase once one takes into consideration the question of disagreement. In view of that, Ronald Dworkin attributes to the concept/conception distinction an important role, as part of his own attempt to argue for the existence of genuine theoretical disagreements about the law (mainly against positivism, which considers empirical disagreements only).

Justice, concept of / 387

Dworkin believes that justice is an institution – i.e. a socially shared practice with its embedded rules – that we interpret. When one moves from the pre-interpretive stage to a conceptual stage, one captures the plateau from which conflicting arguments about justice proceed. This plateau is equivalent to the concept. However, Dworkin acknowledges that there may be many plateaus and that, in any case, a further interpretive stage is needed, establishing what the practice of justice requires. The latter interpretive stage amounts to the production of different conceptions of justice (see Dworkin 1986, ch. 2). The concept of justice, as defined by Rawls, cannot settle the dispute among the conceptions, but it may establish a common framework of discussion for at least some of those conceptions.

João Cardoso Rosas

SEE ALSO:

Basic structure of society
Distributive justice
Dworkin, Ronald
Formal justice
Institutions
Moral theory
Natural duty of justice
Procedural justice
Two principles of justice (in justice as fairness)

102.

JUSTIFICATION: FREESTANDING/POLITICAL

MOST POLITICAL PHILOSOPHERS believe that in justifying a conception of justice, we may draw on any claims that seem both true and relevant in establishing which principles ought to regulate the distribution of rights, goods, and other things that are properly the subject of a theory of justice. In particular, claims about human flourishing or the good life, as well as metaphysical arguments and controversial philosophical theories, might play an important role in justifying the correct theory of justice.

In *Political Liberalism*, John Rawls challenges this assumption. He argues that we must find a way to justify a theory of justice that does not appeal to controversial ideas from religion, morality, or philosophy – ideas that will always be the subject of reasonable disagreement. Instead he proposes that we ought to construct a conception of justice that is "political." Political conceptions have three main characteristics (*PL* 11–15).

First, the scope of a political conception is limited to the rules and norms regulating "the basic structure of society" – that is, society's main political, social, and economic institutions. A political conception is still a moral conception – it contains moral ideas and values – but it is not a "comprehensive" moral theory or doctrine in that it does not include "all recognized values and virtues within one rather precisely articulated system" (*PL* 13), with the aim of providing guidance for most aspects of human life. In particular, a political conception does not regulate (except indirectly) the many institutions and forms of life (e.g. churches and private associations) that exist in civil society or what Rawls calls the "background culture" (*PL* 14).

Second, a political conception is "freestanding." This means that it is neither derived from, nor presented as part of, some broader comprehensive doctrine or conception of the good life (*PL* 12). A conception of justice is thus freestanding when one does not need to accept, or have knowledge of, any particular religious, moral, or philosophical theory in order to understand and potentially endorse the political conception. A freestanding conception thereby avoids making any controversial claims about morality, religion, or philosophy, over which reasonable people are assumed to disagree. Restricting the scope of a political conception to the rules and norms governing the basic structure is meant to facilitate this objective. By being freestanding, a political conception can also ideally fit as a constituent part, or "module," within any reasonable person's wider comprehensive doctrine.

Finally, a political conception is developed by reference to certain fundamental ideas that are implicit in the public political culture of a constitutional democracy (*PL* 13). The point is to take certain abstract political ideas that it is assumed reasonable people could all accept, and from these abstract ideas develop a reasonably detailed and systematic theory of justice. The fundamental organizing idea that Rawls uses to develop his own theory is that of society as a fair system of social cooperation between free and equal citizens (*PL* 14–22).

Developing a political and freestanding justification for a conception of justice is the essential first stage in Rawls's political liberalism. This first stage provides what Rawls calls the "pro tanto" justification for a conception of justice, but "full justification" and "public justification" are only achieved when each reasonable person has determined that the political conception fits as a constituent module within his or her own comprehensive doctrine, and the fact of this achievement is public knowledge (*PL* 386–392).

Jonathan Quong

SEE ALSO:

Comprehensive doctrine
Fundamental ideas (in justice as fairness)
Overlapping consensus
Political conception of justice
Political liberalism, justice as fairness as

103.

JUSTIFICATION VS. PROOF

N THE FINAL section of *A Theory of Justice*, John Rawls contrasts justification and proof. He says:

> Justification is argument addressed to those who disagree with us, or to ourselves when we are of two minds. It presumes a clash of views between persons or within one person, and seeks to convince others, or ourselves, of the reasonableness of the principles upon which our claims and judgments are founded. Being designed to reconcile by reason, justification proceeds from what all parties to the discussion hold in common. Ideally, to justify a conception of justice to someone is to give him a proof of its principles from premises we both accept, these principles in turn having consequences that match our considered judgments. Thus mere proof is not justification. A proof simply displays logical relations between propositions. But proofs become justification once the starting points are mutually recognized, or the conclusions so comprehensive and compelling as to persuade us of the soundness of the conception expressed by their premises. (*TJ* 508)

We can draw several conclusions from this passage. For Rawls, justification is not simply about understanding logical implications or inferences. A proposition may be a logical implication of some set of premises, but realizing this is not itself a form of justification. Justification is about giving oneself or others sufficient reasons to believe some proposition. Of course, often the best way to provide someone with sufficient reasons to believe some proposition is to show that it is a logical implication of some other beliefs we already accept, and this may be why Rawls says that, ideally, to justify a conception of justice to some-one is to give him a proof. But there are other ways to provide someone with sufficient reasons for belief, for example, showing that a theory's conclusions are "comprehensive and compelling." Proofs are thus one way, but not the only way, to pursue justification.

There is a further difference between proof and justification. Justification, Rawls says, is the use of reason to resolve a disagreement or a clash of views. Justification is thus always addressed *to* someone: a real or imagined interlocutor with whom we disagree. To be successful, a justification must provide all parties to the disagreement with reasons they believe are sufficient to accept a given view. This is why Rawls says that, ideally, justification ought to proceed from premises *both* parties accept. It would not be a valid justification if I were to persuade you to believe ϕ by giving you a proof of ϕ derived from premises that you accept, but which I believe are false. In this case I would have persuaded you to believe ϕ, but not justified it to you, since I would not have offered you reasons in support of ϕ that I believe are sound. This is another way in which justification differs from proof. Proofs involve only one viewpoint or set of assumptions, from which further conclusions can then be derived. Justification, on the other hand, is a process by which opposed viewpoints are reconciled by reason – the previously opposed views come together in agreement regarding the reasons that support a given proposition or theory. Rawls's political philosophy is governed by this idea of justification: using reason to reconcile our deepest political disputes by constructing a conception of social justice that all free and equal citizens have sufficient reasons to endorse.

Jonathan Quong

SEE ALSO:

Justification: freestanding/political
Practical reason
Reconciliation

K

104.

KANT, IMMANUEL

MMANUEL KANT (1724–1804) is widely acknowledged to be Rawls's most important philosophical influence. There is no hope of doing justice to Kant's philosophical arguments in this short space; we will have to be content to list the features of Kant's practical philosophy which have been most influential for Rawls.

A crucial claim of Kant (and Rawls) is that moral and political philosophy constitutes an autonomous, specifically practical branch of inquiry, essentially independent of theoretical claims about the nature of things, both scientific and metaphysical. For Kant, ordinary moral consciousness already understands itself as bound by unconditional duties, by claims about what we ought to do, independent of empirical facts about what anyone does or the way the world is. Moral philosophy is then the clarification of the conceptual presuppositions of this commitment to unconditional duty, a clarification which aims to show that our moral beliefs are coherent. In Rawls, the analogous claim is that the citizens of constitutional democracies already possess a sense of justice which then merely needs to be clarified in reflective equilibrium to produce an ordered set of principles that can serve as the basis of political justification in a well-ordered society.

For Kant, the chief conceptual presupposition of moral consciousness is the self-understanding of agents as autonomous, as capable of acting on principles they have legislated for themselves. This autonomy has both a negative and a positive side. Negatively, autonomous agents are capable of setting aside any external and potentially opposing incentives to do what is morally required; their negative freedom is thus a condition of their being morally responsible. Positively, autonomous agents are capable of understanding moral principles as rationally required; their positive freedom is thus the expression of their understanding of themselves as practically rational. To these negative and positive aspects of autonomy correspond two Kantian projects of philosophical clarification and defense. First, showing that we are negatively free involves showing we are justified in thinking of ourselves as independent of causal determination. Kant's justification, unfolded at great length in the *Critique of Pure Reason*, claims that the idea of causal determination is itself a presupposition of theoretical inquiry, not an independent fact about the world that can itself be given a fully rational defense. That claim opens space for the denial of causal determination of our agency; negative freedom becomes the equally plausible presupposition of a different sort of rationality in the practical realm. Second, showing that morality is the form of positive freedom involves showing that moral (and political) principles can be derived simply from the idea of ourselves as free and rational. Kant's project of a *Metaphysics of Morals* (Kant 1996 [1796]), together with the *Groundwork* (Kant 1997a [1785]) to the later text, are essentially arguments of this form.

Rawls largely ignores (or takes for granted) the first of Kant's two philosophical projects, the metaphysical defense of the compatibility of countercausal freedom with scientific naturalism. But the second of Kant's philosophical projects, the derivation of practical principles from the idea of agents as free and rational, animates Rawls's work in an especially deep way.

In *TJ*, Rawls suggests that his account is broadly Kantian in the way the original position is designed to operationalize a moral criticism of utilitarianism. Because the parties in the original position do not know what social position they will occupy, they cannot choose a principle of justice that trades off their individual goods for the greater goods of others, as the principle of average utility might allow. The original position is thus a procedural form of Kant's principle that persons are ends in themselves, who are not to be used as mere means to the ends of others. For Kant it is autonomy that makes persons ends in themselves. In *TJ*, Rawls argues that an understanding of citizens as autonomous is optional for adherents of justice as fairness. He writes that his theory can be given a "Kantian interpretation," under which the choices of the parties in the original position can be understood as the choices of free and rational agents. Rawlsian citizens can be seen as having legislated principles of justice for themselves; in this sense, they can be understood as autonomous. But this understanding is not presented as essential to justice as fairness.

Perhaps the Rawls of *TJ* regards Kantian autonomy as too metaphysically loaded, or his own procedural account as not metaphysically loaded enough to count as Kantian. In any case, Rawls's views change sharply with the argument of "Kantian Constructivism in Moral Theory" (1980), which not only characterizes justice as fairness as a form of "Kantian constructivism," but specifically interprets this constructivism, and Kant's own practical philosophy more generally, as implying a less metaphysically loaded account of autonomy.

Constructivism, for Rawls, is a view on which practical principles are understood to be justified because they have been chosen according to a suitably defined procedure. What defines the procedure as suitable is its ability to solve a practical problem. For the Rawls of "Kantian Constructivism," the relevant practical problem is the conflict between different understandings of freedom and equality in modern liberal democracies. Rawls then explains his own theory of justice as providing a resolution to this conflict by understanding principles of justice as the objects of the choice of free and equal citizens, regarded only as free and equal. Citizens are free in the sense of having their own conceptions of the good, and equal in the sense of being able to regulate their pursuit of the good in terms of principles of justice that are equally binding on all citizens. To the extent that Rawls's favored principles of justice allow citizens to exercise their moral powers as free and equal persons, those principles can be understood as self-legislated.

In *PL*, Rawls explains this self-legislation as a form of specifically political autonomy. The practical problem that Rawls's constructivism is intended to solve is the political problem of finding a public basis for coercive legislation under conditions of reasonable pluralism. This is political constructivism, which Rawls distinguishes from Kant's moral constructivism. But this distinction does not alter the sense in which Rawlsian citizens are autonomous, legislating principles of justice for themselves as free and equal. The distinction affects only the way the conception of persons as free and equal is or is not understood to be true. Rawls's political constructivism says only that this conception of ourselves is appropriate to the political circumstances of modern pluralism. Kant's moral constructivism, however, takes the further step of arguing that this conception of ourselves is true, or more precisely, that it is fully rational in the terms of a modern scientific outlook that cannot itself be understood as fully rational without the understanding of ourselves as autonomous.

Larry Krasnoff

SEE ALSO:

Autonomy, moral
Autonomy, political
Constructivism: Kantian/political
Kantian interpretation
Moral person
Political liberalism, justice as fairness as
Practical reason
Utilitarianism

105.

KANTIAN INTERPRETATION

N TJ §40, RAWLS claims that his theory of justice can be given a Kantian interpretation. This formulation refers more to the justification than to the content of the theory. In an earlier but quite clearly separate discussion (*TJ* 29), Rawls points out that the content of his theory, the argument for the two principles of justice, expresses a version of Kant's principle that persons are to be treated not as mere means, but also as ends in themselves. Utilitarianism, Rawls argues, violates this Kantian principle by allowing the happiness of a minority to be traded off for the greater happiness of a greater number. The principle of utility could not be chosen by the parties in the original position, since they cannot rule out that they will occupy the position of the minority. Here the substantively Kantian, anti-utilitarian content of the theory is dictated by the specific constraints of the original position. How these constraints themselves are to be justified is a separate and deeper question, and it is this question that the Kantian interpretation is meant to address.

According to *TJ* §40, the original position can be understood as a procedural interpretation of Kant's idea of autonomy. Rawls notes that the central idea of Kant's moral philosophy is that "moral principles are the object of rational choice" (*TJ* 221). The parties in the original position are of course understood as making a rational choice of the two principles of justice under conditions of uncertainty. In an early critical article, Oliver Johnson objected to Rawls's appeal to a Kantian interpretation, arguing that because parties in the original position are clearly trying to advance their own interests, their choices are, in Kant's terms, heteronomous rather than autonomous (Johnson 1974). In an influential reply, Stephen Darwall responded that the relevant autonomous choice is not that of the parties in the original position, but that of the citizens of a

399

well-ordered society to conform to the principles that would be chosen in the original position (Darwall 1976). This reading seems to match Rawls's emphasis in *TJ* §40.

> Of course, the choice of the parties in the original position is subject to the restrictions of that situation. But when we knowingly act on the principles of justice in the ordinary course of events, we deliberately assume the limitations of the original position. One reason for doing this, for persons who can do so and want to, is to give expression to one's nature. (*TJ* 222)

For Rawls, it is the idea of expressing our nature as free and rational beings that is central to Kant's claim that moral action is autonomous. As Sidgwick objected to Kant, if we are really free to legislate for ourselves, we would seem to be able to choose any principle of action, moral or not (Sidgwick 1888). But not every principle of action, Rawls explains (*TJ* 224–225), expresses our identities as free. "Kant held, I believe, that a person is acting autonomously when the principles of his action are chosen by him as the most adequate possible expression of his nature as a free and rational being" (*TJ* 222). For justice as fairness, the corresponding claim is that the original position is a procedural interpretation of autonomy, because the choices of the parties express their natures as free and equal persons who can rationally choose principles of justice for themselves.

How does this claim deepen the justification of justice as fairness? The answer depends on one's view of the claim that the constraints of the original position express our considered moral judgments about justice in a democratic society, as clarified in reflective equilibrium. If one accepts this claim, then the Kantian interpretation is dispensable, not necessary to the justification of Rawls's theory. On the other hand, as Darwall argues (1976, 164–165), if one is skeptical about what can fairly be claimed about "our considered judgments," then the Kantian interpretation might seem an appealing way to "imbed a theory of justice in a theory of practical reason." If we can say that the constraints of the original position are grounded in our natures as rational beings, then those constraints would seem to have a deeper rational justification than could be provided by a contestable sociological generalization about our shared moral beliefs. That claim, however, presumes that there is some convincing way of understanding the Kantian claim about our natures as rational beings. To a significant extent, the discussion of justice as fairness since *TJ*, in both Rawls's own writing and that of his interpreters, has been dominated by the question of just how much (or how little) the theory needs a Kantian interpretation if it is to be understood as justified. Does Rawls's later talk of Kantian constructivism suggest that the theory is ultimately about free and equal persons choosing principles for themselves? Or does his even later talk of a merely political liberalism suggest that the theory ultimately rests on historical and sociological claims about the nature and possibility of political agreement under conditions of modern pluralism? Just what sort of Kantian claims about practical reason does Rawls need?

As this way of framing things already suggests, much of the debate about the justification of Rawls's theory of justice has assumed an opposition between a Kantian and hence more strongly metaphysical appeal to practical rationality and a less Kantian and hence more pragmatic or purely political appeal to the shared convictions of modern liberal democracies. In "Kantian Constructivism" and after, however, Rawls has consistently resisted this kind of opposition. That is, he has consistently maintained that a more purely Kantian account of persons as free and equal has an essential connection to an emphasis on the social role of morality in general, and political justice in particular. Even in his original account of the Kantian interpretation in *TJ*, Rawls was already insisting on this connection, and he was already aware that more traditional interpreters of Kant would find it puzzling. "It might appear that Kant meant his doctrine to apply to all rational beings as such and therefore to God and the angels as well. Men's social situation in the world may seem to have no role in his theory in determining the first principles of justice. I do not believe that Kant held this view, but I cannot discuss this question here" (*TJ*, original edition, 257). Though this passage is deliberately elliptical, it is clear that Rawls is here rejecting the idea that Kantian autonomy should be understood in any sort of metaphysical sense, as the solitary, timeless choice of a purely rational being. Instead Kantian autonomy can and should be understood as essentially connected to the historical and political circumstances of the modern world – which Rawls consistently describes as characterized by a plurality of competing conceptions of the good. The Kantian conception of persons as free and equal can itself be derived from this historical characterization: we are all equally free to adopt, revise, and pursue our own conceptions of the good. And the autonomous choice of principles of justice can be understood as a way of achieving social order that does not violate our freedom and equality: we legislate the principles of justice for ourselves, presuming nothing more than the conception of ourselves as free and equal. The specifically political constructivism of *PL* continues to characterize liberal citizens as (politically) autonomous, because it is precisely the principled response to conditions

of modern pluralism which can and should be given a "Kantian interpretation."
(See Krasnoff 2014.)

Larry Krasnoff

SEE ALSO:

Autonomy, moral
Congruence
Constructivism: Kantian/political
Kant, Immanuel
The original position

106.

KING, MARTIN LUTHER, JR.

MARTIN LUTHER KING, Jr. (1929–1968) was a famous American pastor and prominent civil rights era leader. King arguably had a larger role in promoting racial equality in the United States than anyone in the twentieth century. He was also well known for his nonviolent methods of political protest and his "I Have a Dream" speech which articulated a vision of racial equality that continues to evoke powerful emotional responses. King was, by all accounts, a deeply religious man. King's writings demonstrate that his Christian commitments suffused his thoughts and drove his actions. More significantly for Rawls, King advocated racial equality on explicitly Christian grounds, though he sometimes spoke in terms of more "political values" embodied in the constitution.

King makes a brief appearance in *TJ* in a footnote on civil disobedience (*TJ* 320 n.19). But in *PL*, King becomes cause for concern. In *PL*, Rawls famously sought an overlapping consensus on a political conception of justice. Included in the political conception are "guidelines of public reason" that citizens of a well-ordered society will follow in order to maintain their society's allegiance to its overlapping consensus. Initially Rawls thought that the guidelines included a principle that restricted the appeal to comprehensive values and reasons when constitutional essentials were at stake, the purely ethical duty of civility. He was inclined to what he called the "exclusive view" which holds that "on fundamental political matters, reasons given explicitly in terms of comprehensive doctrines are never to be introduced into public reason. The public reasons such a doctrine supports may, of course, be given but not the supporting doctrine itself" (*PL* 247). However, Martin Luther King's use of comprehensive reasons to produce an overlapping consensus on racial equality worried Rawls, since the exclusive view seemed to render King's advocacy inappropriate. As a result, Rawls moved to the "inclusive view" which allows "citizens, in certain situations, to present what they regard as the basis of political values rooted in their comprehensive doctrine, provided they do this in ways that strengthen the ideal of public reason itself" (*PL* 247).

Eventually Rawls became unsatisfied with the inclusive view and turned to embrace the "wide view" in "The Idea of Public Reason Revisited." The wide view is a "proviso" which holds that "Reasonable comprehensive doctrines, religious or nonreligious, may be introduced in public political discussion at any time, provided that in due course proper political reasons – and not reasons given solely by comprehensive doctrines – are presented that are sufficient to support whatever the comprehensive doctrines introduced are said to support" (*CP* 783–784). Rawls notes that while King may not have been thinking of the proviso, he believes that "had they [King and the abolitionists] known and accepted the idea of public reason, they would have" accepted it (*CP* 786). To put it simply, Martin Luther King, Jr.'s political methods pushed Rawls toward an increasingly inclusive view of the place of comprehensive (especially religious) reasons and values in public life.

Kevin Vallier

SEE ALSO:

Civil disobedience
Overlapping consensus
Public reason
Race

107.

KOHLBERG, LAWRENCE

L AWRENCE KOHLBERG (1927–1987) was an American developmental psychologist. Kohlberg's research focused mainly on moral development in children and adults, but also on links between moral reasoning and democratic communities. Kohlberg is best known for his stage theory of moral development.

Kohlberg posited six stages of moral development, paired to form three levels: pre-conventional, conventional, and post-conventional. Different levels represent qualitatively distinct ways of reasoning about moral problems. Higher stages incorporate elements of lower stages, but focus on new, more worthy moral considerations (judged from the individual's perspective). Full moral development requires moving from "nonreversible" moral judgments – judgments self-interestedly biased by awareness of social or situational position – to "reversible" ones – judgments that could be accepted from the perspective of any role-player in some moral dilemma. However, few adults reach the highest stages: less than one-fourth reach stage 5, and very few reach stage 6. Moral development can be encouraged through education.

At the lowest, pre-conventional level, children respond to cultural notions of right and wrong, but interpret them in terms of physical or hedonistic consequences. At stage 1, children seek to avoid punishment. At stage 2, children understand right and wrong in terms of instrumental satisfaction of their own needs, and sometimes the needs of others. Notions of reciprocity, fairness, and equality emerge, but are interpreted physically and pragmatically.

At the conventional level, individuals value meeting the conventional expectations of family and community, regardless of individual consequences. Stage 3 individuals seek to please others and gain approval, while stage 4 individuals seek to maintain social order through authority and rules.

At the post-conventional level, individuals define values and principles independent of the authority of, or the individual's identification with, others who hold them. Stage 5 individuals take a social-contract orientation toward social rules, seeing them in terms of rights critically evaluated and agreed upon by all, and choose procedural means of settling disagreements. However, the rules are accepted in part because they maximize the welfare of all, so they may be modified for reasons of social utility. This gives stage 5 a rule-utilitarian cast.

Stage 6 individuals understand right and wrong in terms of universal, abstract, and self-chosen ethical principles. This post-conventional orientation focuses on universal principles of justice, reciprocity, equality, and dignity. Utilitarian considerations are abandoned because they conflict with stage 6 values.

Kohlberg made many references to Rawls's theory of justice in his work. In his clearest statements, he claims that Rawls's theory offers an explication and vindication of post-conventional stage 6. Kohlberg attributes the convergence of his and Rawls's theories to their common roots in the theories of Kant and Piaget.

Rawls draws on Kohlberg's work (and the work of others) in part III of *A Theory of Justice*, where he describes moral development as it might occur in a well-ordered society structured by justice as fairness (*TJ* 404–434). Rawls distinguishes moralities of authority, of association, and of principles. He says his morality of association parallels Kohlberg's stages 3 to 5, but also notes that there are several differences between their views (*TJ* 404). Rawls regards his theory of justice as superior to others, but warns that this cannot be demonstrated through psychological research.

Kohlberg's theory has been criticized as male-biased, perhaps most notably by Carol Gilligan, who argues that women reason differently than men about moral problems. Kohlberg's theory has also been challenged as culturally biased.

Walter J. Riker

SEE ALSO:

Care
Moral psychology
Moral sentiments
Sense of justice
Stability

108.

KYMLICKA, WILL

WILL KYMLICKA (b. 1962) is a Canadian philosopher and author of influential writings on Rawls and his critics. Kymlicka's main critique of Rawls is connected with the issue of multiculturalism. According to Kymlicka, Rawls assumes that the political community is homogeneous from a cultural point of view. In other words, Rawls does not address the fact that many of the states in which we live are multinational for historical reasons and/or polyethnic as a consequence of immigration. Kymlicka attempts to correct this neglect in Rawls through an argument that leads to a liberal-egalitarian defence of multicultural rights, which remains, by and large, Rawlsian. This argument is theoretically set out in *Liberalism, Community and Culture* (Kymlicka 1989) and it is fleshed out with empirical details in *Multicultural Citizenship* (Kymlicka 1995) and in subsequent books.

Kymlicka's starting point is Rawls's conception of basic liberties. These liberties are not an end in themselves. They are instrumental to the various conceptions of the good that individuals may endorse. Where do these conceptions of the good come from? According to Kymlicka, they come from the "cultural community," or "societal culture," to which individuals are bound in their process of socialization. Therefore, societal cultures are the "context of choice" for the exercise of basic liberties. For Kymlicka, societal cultures may be internally plural and dynamic. Nevertheless, they are distinguished from each other and people create particular attachments to their societal culture (quite often through the sharing of the same language). Being fundamental for individuals as the context for the exercise of their basic liberties, Kymlicka concludes, the societal culture of each individual should be considered a "social primary good."

Now in many political states national and/or ethnic minority societal cultures are weakened and even at risk because they face the pressure of the cultural majority. Kymlicka sees a problem here for liberal-egalitarians since those individuals who belong to minority cultures do not have their cultural context for the exercise of basic liberties equally secure when compared with the context of members of the majority. This point leads to the justification of multicultural rights: these are the rights whose function is to protect the context of choice for members of cultural minorities.

Because his main concern is the equal value of basic liberties, Kymlicka is very keen on emphasizing that multicultural rights should be seen as "external protections" of the societal culture of minorities, not as "internal restrictions" of their members' liberty. Kymlicka believes that multicultural rights for national minorities (such as self-government rights) and also for immigrant minorities (in this case, polyethnic rights dealing with the protection of language, religious practices, etc.) are a fundamental aspect of a just society in the Rawlsian sense, in spite of the absence of the topic in Rawls's own writings.

On another key, Kymlicka also criticizes Rawls's shift to "political liberalism" by claiming that an effective defence of liberalism cannot avoid appealing to the value of autonomy as "rational revisability" (see Kymlicka 2002, 228–244).

João Cardoso Rosas

SEE ALSO:

Autonomy, moral
Communitarianism
Conception of the good
Political liberalism, justice as fairness as
Primary goods, social

L

109.

LAW OF PEOPLES

IN THE LAW OF PEOPLES Rawls is concerned with the justice and peaceful coexistence of well-ordered societies as members of a society of peoples. Well-ordered peoples, importantly, have institutions of self-government or of consultation in their internal governance. For Rawls, well-ordered peoples include reasonable liberal peoples and decent peoples, which, although they are not liberal, are not aggressive, recognize human rights, and have a legitimate political and legal order. A key part of this project is to argue for the principles which well-ordered peoples can agree on to guide their conduct in the international domain. Rawls argues that the Law of Peoples he endorses is a realistic utopia. It is realistic because it takes account of many real conditions, such as the fact that not all peoples of the world do or can reasonably be made to endorse liberal principles. The eight core principles that constitute the Law of Peoples can, by contrast, be endorsed by all well-ordered peoples, or at least they have no reason to reject them.

Rawls's argument occurs in several stages. First, he concerns himself only with liberal peoples and the principles they would have reason to endorse. He employs a second original position to derive his Law of Peoples for liberal peoples. In the first original position, the parties select principles to regulate the basic structure of society. After the principles governing domestic society have been derived, Rawls moves to the international level. At this stage, the second original position is employed to derive the foreign policy that liberal peoples would choose. The representatives of peoples are subject to an appropriate veil of ignorance for the situation. For instance, they do not know the size of the territory or population, its relative strength, or its level of economic development.

Rawls argues that the second original position would yield the following eight principles:

1. Peoples are free and independent, and their freedom and independence are to be respected by other peoples.
2. Peoples are to observe treaties and undertakings.
3. Peoples are equal and are parties to the agreements that bind them.
4. Peoples are to observe a duty of nonintervention.
5. Peoples have the right to self-defense but no right to instigate war for reasons other than self-defense.
6. Peoples are to honor human rights.
7. Peoples are to observe certain specified restrictions in the conduct of war.
8. Peoples have a duty to assist other peoples living under unfavorable conditions that prevent their having a just or decent political and social regime. (*LP* 37)

In addition to the eight principles, Rawls believes that three organizations would also be chosen: one aimed at securing fair trade among peoples; one that enables people to borrow from a cooperative banking institution; and one that plays a similar role to that of the United Nations, which he refers to as a "Confederation of Peoples" (*LP* 42).

Having shown that liberal peoples have reason to select the eight principles and three organizations, Rawls argues that decent peoples similarly have reason to endorse them as well. He illustrates this with the case of a hypothetical decent people, Kazanistan, an idealized Islamic people. In Kazanistan, human rights are recognized, but only Muslims are eligible for positions of political authority and have influence in important political matters, though other religions are tolerated and encouraged to pursue a flourishing cultural life. Rawls believes Kazanistan can be admitted to the society of well-ordered peoples. Liberal societies should tolerate states such as Kazanistan. Indeed, Rawls believes that "something like Kazanistan is the best we can realistically – and coherently – hope for" (*LP* 78).

Rawls's toleration of nonliberal but decent people is often criticized by cosmopolitans. It is also sometimes maintained that another important area of difference between cosmopolitans and Rawls concerns our duties of assistance. According to Rawls, some societies "lack the political and cultural traditions, the human capital and know-how, and, often, the material and technological resources needed to be well-ordered" (*LP* 106). Well-ordered peoples have a duty to assist such societies to become part of the society of well-ordered peoples. The aim of assistance is to "help burdened societies to be able to manage their own affairs reasonably and rationally and eventually to become members of the society of well-ordered peoples" (*LP* 111). After this target is achieved, additional assistance is not required by the duty of assistance, even though the society may still be "relatively poor" (*LP* 111). The aim is to realize and preserve just (or decent) domestic institutions that are self-sustaining, and once that is achieved, the duty of assistance is discharged. According to Rawls, the political culture of a burdened society is all-important to the levels of prosperity experienced in particular societies: wealth owes its origin and maintenance to the philosophical culture of the society rather than (say) to its stock of resources. Rawls says:

> I believe that the causes of the wealth of a people and the forms it takes lie in their political culture and in the religious, philosophical, and moral traditions that support the basic structure of their political and social institutions, as well as in the industriousness and cooperative talents of its members, all supported by their political virtues. (*LP* 108)

Rawls does engage directly with central claims made by some (though by no means all) cosmopolitans, who maintain that the principles of justice that applied in *A Theory of Justice*, particularly the difference principle, should apply globally. He takes up Charles Beitz's claim that since a global system of cooperation already exists between states, a global difference principle should apply across states as well. Rawls argues against this for a couple of reasons, but notably, as we have just seen, because he believes that wealth owes its origin and maintenance primarily to the political culture of the society. Furthermore, any global principle of distributive justice we endorse must have a target and a cut-off point, which is identified as the level at which the requirements of political autonomy can be secured. So a global difference principle is the wrong focus for our duties. In addition, an ongoing commitment to a global difference principle would not preserve the right incentives for peoples' taking responsibility for their own well-being, and well-ordered peoples would endorse a system of principles that would do so.

Some commonly advanced critical responses to *The Law of Peoples* include the following. (1) The background picture that Rawls invokes incorporates outmoded views of relations between states, peoples, and individuals of the world. According to some critics, Rawls presupposes that states are (sufficiently) independent of one another, so that each society can be held responsible for the well-being of its citizens. Furthermore, as we have seen, Rawls holds that differences in levels of wealth and prosperity are largely attributable to differences in political culture and the virtuous nature of its citizens. Critics point out, however, that Rawls ignores both the extent to which unfavorable conditions may result from factors external to the society and the fact that there are many morally relevant connections among states, notably that they are situated in a global economic order that perpetuates the interests of wealthy, developed states with little regard for the interests of poor, developing ones. Those who live in the affluent, developed world cannot thus morally insulate themselves from the misery of the worst off in the world, since they are complicit in ongoing global poverty. Thomas Pogge is a prominent advocate of such a view. (2) Critics also note substantial tension in the reasoning Rawls offers for our interest in socioeconomic equality at the domestic level and our apparent disinterest in this at the international level, claiming that the reasons for our interest in equality at the domestic level apply as well to the global. (3) Some critics hold that the notion of a people is not sufficiently clear or important to do the work Rawls thinks it can do. If we take a people to be constituted by commonalities such as shared language, culture, history, or ethnicity, then peoples often do not correspond well to official state borders. National territories are not typically comprised of a single people, nor is it clear that individuals belong to one and only one people. (4) Rawls argues for a respectful relationship among states (as representatives of peoples). Indeed, he argues that liberal democratic regimes have an obligation to deal with nonliberal decent regimes as equals and not to endeavor to impose their liberal values on them. Some argue that Rawls may take cultural pluralism too far, at the expense of the requirements of the domestic toleration of individuals. Decent societies may well contain individuals who hold liberal ideas or dissent from the dominant values. Rawls's account incorporates the wrong kind of toleration for such societies at the expense of liberal values. (5) Rawls aims at a realistic utopia, but critics charge that the result is neither sufficiently realistic nor utopian. In failing to take account of all the relevant realities, such as interdependence or domination in the global arena, he has not captured all the salient realities, and so his Law of Peoples is not "workable" and is unlikely to sustain ongoing cooperative political arrangements and relations between peoples. Furthermore, the view is not very utopian in that the ideals used are too tame to constitute much of an advance over the status quo. In his bow to realism, Rawls has tried to ensure that the Law of Peoples results in stability, yet the Law of Peoples he endorses might be quite unstable because it involves tolerance of unjust regimes, which are potentially much less stable than just ones.

Many philosophers have tried to defend Rawls against such criticisms. Several lines of defense have been attempted. It is often pointed out that critics have failed to appreciate some background assumptions that orient the Law of Peoples, such as what the goal of a Law of Peoples should be. As Samuel Freeman emphasizes, the Law of Peoples addresses the key question: what should the foreign policy of liberal peoples be? In particular, how should liberal peoples relate to nonliberal peoples? Should they tolerate and cooperate with nonliberal peoples, or should they try to convert nonliberal peoples to liberal ones? What are the limits of what liberal peoples should tolerate with respect to nonliberal peoples? To address these questions, Rawls needs to distinguish the concept of a decent society from a fully just one (in the liberal democratic sense), with the idea of a decent society playing the role of a theoretical construct. While liberal peoples should tolerate decent peoples, this is not the case with outlaw regimes. It is not reasonable to expect all decent societies to conform to all the norms of a constitutional democracy as a requirement of peacefully coexisting and cooperating with them. If we reject Rawls's way of addressing the issues, it appears the only alternative would be a standing threat to intervene coercively in other states' affairs, which seems unattractive and destabilizing. According to Freeman, this stance does not entail that citizens of liberal states must refrain from criticizing illiberal societies (*LP* 84). However, there is a key difference between liberal citizens engaging in criticism and their "government's hostile criticisms, sanctions, and other forms of coercive intervention. The Law of Peoples says that liberal peoples, as peoples represented by their governments have a duty to cooperate with, and not seek to undermine, decent non-liberal societies" (Freeman 2007b, 432).

If Rawls's aim is to establish the conditions for a peaceful and stable world order, respect for legitimate governments must play a key role. The notion of a legitimate government of a decent people is therefore central to the project. Moreover, defenders, such as Rex Martin, argue that we can find space to accommodate duties to change unsavory features of the global order by examining the duty of assistance in more detail. Martin argues that this duty entails a requirement to assist burdened societies to become self-supporting in a variety of ways including economically. On this account, we can include rather large duties to reform the existing global order in ways that work against the goal of helping burdened societies achieve political autonomy. Some defenders, such as Leif Wenar, argue that Rawls's morality of states is more plausible than rival cosmopolitan theories. The reason Rawls adopts the starting point of peoples rather than individual persons is that Rawls must construct his Law of Peoples from generally acceptable ideas from the public political culture, since no comprehensive doctrine can provide the content of the basic international structure. The global public political culture, according to Wenar, is primarily international, not interpersonal. If we consider the central ideas that regulate the institutions of global society these are primarily concerned with proper relations among nations rather persons, as we find exemplified in organizations such as the World Trade Organization and United Nations. A lively debate between critics and defenders on these and other points concerning Rawls's Law of Peoples continues.

Gillian Brock

SEE ALSO:

> *Burdened societies*
> *Cosmopolitanism*
> *Decent societies*
> *Duty of assistance*
> *Human rights*
> *Just war theory*
> *Liberal people*
> *Outlaw states*
> *Society of Peoples*
> *Toleration*
> *Well-ordered society*

110.

LAW, SYSTEM OF

"A LEGAL SYSTEM IS a coercive order of public rules addressed to rational persons for the purpose of regulating their conduct and providing the framework for their social cooperation" (*TJ* 207). Of course, in any society there may be a number of systems of public rules regulating conduct and framing various cooperative undertakings. A legal system is distinct from these in several respects. A legal system is comprehensive in a way that other systems of public rules, typically subordinated to a legal system, are not. The legal system defines the basic institutional structure within which the activities governed by other systems of public rules take place (*TJ* 207). In the paradigm case a legal system has a territorially bounded core, namely a state, in a way that other systems of public rules need not. Of course, jurisdiction may extend in particular cases beyond this territorially bounded core, as when a state asserts its legal jurisdiction over some extraterritorial activity of its nationals. And there may be legal systems, e.g. international law, without a territorially bounded core in the form of a state (though in fact much and arguably the core of international law is bounded by the territories of the several states the voluntary undertakings of which give rise to it). Further, the authority of a legal system is typically final within the territorial boundaries of its jurisdiction. The authority of other systems of public rules is constrained by law. Finally, while many systems of public rules may be coercively enforced to some degree or other, they may be so only at the discretion of the legal system to which they are subordinate, and it will in turn typically claim or reserve exclusively for itself the most serious forms of coercion. Its claim to the exclusive use of these forms of coercion reflects the fact that among the interests it serves are some of the most fundamental of human interests, which is not necessarily true for other systems of public rules.

417

In his classic *The Concept of Law*, H. L. A. Hart famously claimed that essential to a legal system is a union of primary rules (defining required and impermissible behaviors and the sanctions for noncompliance therewith) and secondary rules (establishing various powers, offices, statuses and so on, including those related to making, applying, and enforcing the law). Hart further claimed, perhaps even more famously, that essential to every legal system is a particular kind of secondary rule, not itself a legal rule but rather a social rule, implicit in and regulative of the practice of legal officials, those who claim and exercise the authority to make, apply, and enforce the law. This social secondary rule Hart dubbed the rule of recognition. It is the rule followed by those, legal officials, who claim and exercise the authority to make, apply, and enforce the law. Not itself a legal rule, it expresses the supreme criterion of legal validity at work within their shared activity or practice of making, applying, and enforcing law, and so underwrites the existence and unity of the legal system to which that shared activity or practice gives rise. While this shared activity or practice gives rise to a legal system, and while some elements of it will be given official legal recognition within the legal system to which it gives rise, there is necessarily an extra- or pre-legal social or political aspect of the activity or practice. A legal official cannot possess the *legal* authority to constitute herself as the legal official that she is. For every legal system, then, its supreme criterion of legal validity, and so the very possibility of its existence, arises out of rule-following behavior that is not itself fully legal but has rather an ineliminable extra- or pre-legal social or political dimension.

Rawls does not explicitly address these Hartian claims. But it is surely not too much of a stretch, especially given Rawls's interactions with Hart during the time Hart worked up his views on the nature of law, to think of Rawls as having the following thought. In a constitutional democracy, the supreme criterion of legal validity underwriting the unity and making possible the existence of the legal system is not to be extracted from the rule-governed and rule-following shared activity or practice of legislators, judges and/or executives as legal officials. For in a constitutional democracy, the most basic or fundamental office is that of citizenship. Indeed, it is that office that constitutes the bridge between the extra- or pre-legal social or political domain of persons free and equal and the legal domain of democratic citizenship with its various legal rights, responsibilities, powers, and immunities. It is through an extra- or pre-legal rule-governed and rule-following shared social and political activity or practice that persons constitute themselves as democratic citizens, legally recognized, and it is as democratic citizens, legally recognized, that they then in turn hold and exercise the most basic or fundamental office within the legal system of a constitutional democracy. It is, then, to this rule-governed and rule-following shared social or political activity or practice, that by which persons constitute themselves as democratic citizens, legally recognized, that one must look in order to identify the social rule of recognition, and so the supreme criterion of legal validity, underwriting the existence and unity of the legal system in any constitutional democracy.

As Rawls notes, in a constitutional democracy, even one like the United States with judicial review ensuring that a Court is the highest *judicial* interpreter of, and so has the last judicial word on, the written Constitution (as fundamental or higher law), the Constitution (as fundamental or higher law) is in the final analysis not what the Court says it is but is rather what *the people acting constitutionally* (claiming and exercising their legal authority as democratic citizens) allow the Court to say it is (*PL* 237). In any constitutional democracy, then, even one with judicial review, it is the people who by constituting themselves and acting as democratic citizens, legally recognized, serve as final interpreter of and get the last word with respect to their Constitution (as the fundamental or higher law governing their legal system). Rawls proposes his principles of justice, then, as an account of the rule-governed and rule-following behavior of free and equal persons engaged in the practice of constituting themselves and acting legally as democratic citizens but keen to understand and perfect their shared activity or practice in this regard. He offers them a proposed rule of recognition which in their extra- or pre-legal shared social and political activity or practice they might not only follow but also self-consciously and publicly affirm and internalize as regulative ideal. In this way it is not implausible to read Rawls's work as situated squarely at the intersections of social and political philosophy, on the one hand, and legal philosophy, on the other.

David A. Reidy

SEE ALSO:

Formal justice
Hart, H. L. A.
Legitimacy
Political obligation
Rule of law
Supreme Court and judicial review

111.

LEAST-ADVANTAGED POSITION

THE LEAST-ADVANTAGED position is a technical phrase meant to identify a structurally defined place in an order of distribution. It is from the perspective of this structurally defined place that choices are made between alternative economic structures in accordance with the difference principle. It is important to note that Rawls is concerned with the least-advantaged *representative* person, not the actually least-advantaged person in a given society. In more technical language, Rawls says that the least-advantaged position is identified by description and not by rigid designation. Therefore, justice is owed to actual persons by virtue of their place in a defined structure and not because of who they are independently of that place or anyone's compassion or pity for their plight.

The least advantaged are those members of society who comprise the "income class with the lowest expectations" (*JF* 59). They are disadvantaged by their family or class origins as well as by possibly inferior natural endowments and by bad fortune. Rawls sets aside psychological and physical handicaps as criteria for membership in the least-advantaged group, assuming that, in the ideal case, all citizens are full participants in society.

Rawls's account of justice as fairness requires that the least-advantaged social position is identified. It enables judgments to be made about how the basic structure of society affects the life prospects of the least well-off citizens. In a well-ordered society that conforms to the two principles of justice the least-advantaged group are better off than they would be under a realizable alternative social arrangement. Taking up the point of view of the least-advantaged representative person, and arguing that this is the appropriate view for assessing the justness of society, is one of the essential features of Rawlsian philosophy.

Least-advantaged position / 421

In the original position the contractors, employing the maximin rule, take on the point of view of the least-advantaged representative person. This tells them how proposed principles of justice affect citizens' life prospects. The difference principle is the result of adopting this point of view and so the assessment of the justness of a basic structure is made from the perspective of the least-advantaged position. As Rawls says, "The difference principle selects one representative for a special role" (*TJ* 83). According to the difference principle, gains by the most advantaged can only be justified if the circumstances of the least-advantaged group are also bettered. For example, Rawls argues that unequal shares of the material primary goods (income and wealth) can be justified from the point of view of the least-advantaged person if this representative person gains in her share of these goods, even though others have more. If we assume with Rawls that from the general point of view, having a greater share of the material primary goods is acceptable, then a scheme in which the least-advantaged group gains a larger share of such goods is also acceptable, even if this share is unequal. The operation of the principles of justice on the basic structure may not work in the interests of particular disadvantaged persons, yet should serve the interests of the group to which that person belongs.

Paul Voice

SEE ALSO:

Basic structure of society
Difference principle
Maximin rule of choice
The original position
Primary goods, social

112.

LEGITIMACY

POLITICAL LEGITIMACY DOES not figure in Rawls's early work, notably in *A Theory of Justice*. In *Theory* he does make use of the broader idea of "legitimate expectations" that citizens come to have when they participate in a social practice, but his main concern is to specify the principles of justice to which the basic structure of society, including the structure of political authority, must conform. Not surprisingly, legitimacy is a major theme of his later work, in which he develops his account of political liberalism. Legitimacy figures in two principal ways: one is the idea of "legitimate law," and the other is the "principle of legitimacy," or what he sometimes calls the "liberal (or democratic) principle of legitimacy." Both of these uses are related to the conventional notion of a legitimate authority as having the right to exercise political power to make a law or decide policy, with those subject to that authority having at least a presumptive obligation to obey. For Rawls, legitimate law results from a properly constituted political process, and "is politically (morally) binding on [one] as a citizen and is to be accepted as such" (*CP* 578). Such a properly constituted process must accord with the principle of legitimacy.

The principle of legitimacy arises directly from the defining problem of political liberalism, which is to explain how a society can be well-ordered by a conception of justice when its citizens adhere to conflicting comprehensive doctrines, each of which may give rise to its own conception of justice. Political liberalism solves that problem by proposing a political conception of justice that all reasonable citizens may accept because it is not based upon the concepts or principles of any particular comprehensive doctrine. Rather, it draws upon widely accepted ideas in the public political culture of a democratic society – notably the idea of a society as a fair system of cooperation among free and equal citizens. Citizenship in a democratic society is, first, an involuntary relationship. Although it is sometimes possible for people to emigrate from the society of their birth, this possibility is so limited that for purposes of assessing the justice of social arrangements we should treat the basic structure as one that "we enter only by birth and exit only by death" (*CP* 577; cf. *JF* 93–94). A person's continued membership in society cannot be construed as giving consent to the principles on which it is organized, and so cannot legitimate the basic structure of that society. Second, the "fundamental political relation of citizenship" is "a relation of free and equal citizens who exercise ultimate political power as a collective body" (*CP* 577). How, we must ask, can citizens "be bound to honor the structure of their constitutional democratic regime and abide by the statutes and laws enacted under it," especially when they do not share a comprehensive doctrine that could answer that question (*CP* 577–578)? Another way of putting this question is to ask how "are citizens[,] who share equally in ultimate political power[,] to exercise that power so that each can reasonably justify his or her political decisions to everyone?" (*CP* 578).

To justify the exercise of political power to other, equal citizens, we must acknowledge what Rawls calls "the criterion of reciprocity." As he puts it:

> The criterion of reciprocity requires that when those terms are proposed as the most reasonable terms of fair cooperation, those proposing them must also think it at least reasonable for others to accept them, as free and equal citizens, and not as dominated or manipulated, or under the pressure of inferior political or social position. (*CP* 578)

The criterion of reciprocity leads directly to the principle of legitimacy. Rawls offers a number of formulations of this principle, all of which embody the same basic ideas, but among which there are interesting variations. One formulation, focusing on what we might call the subjective orientation of those who exercise power – their beliefs and values – holds that "Our exercise of political power is proper only when we sincerely believe that the reasons we would offer for our political actions – were we to state them as government officials – are sufficient, and we also reasonably think that other citizens might also reasonably accept those reasons" (*CP* 578). Another formulation, focusing on the procedures through which power is exercised, holds that "political power is legitimate only when it is exercised in accordance with a constitution (written or unwritten) the essentials of which all citizens, as reasonable and rational, can endorse in light of their common human reason" (*JF* 41). Rawls adds that the principle also applies to "legislative questions that concern or border on these essentials, or are highly divisive" (*JF* 41).

Reasons that can be accepted by all must be "public reasons," reasons not rooted solely in any particular comprehensive doctrine, since it would be unreasonable to think that other citizens "might...reasonably accept" values and principles that are based on doctrines they do not share. Public reason must therefore be rooted in a political conception of justice. In addition, public reason must also include an account of "the principles of reasoning and the rules of evidence in the light of which citizens are to decide whether the principles of justice apply, when and how far they are satisfied, and which laws and policies best fulfill them in existing social conditions" (*JF* 89). The principle of legitimacy, Rawls argues, is "the most appropriate and perhaps the only way to specify" the guidelines of reasoning that are a necessary component of public reason, without which the political conception of justice would "not provide a basis of political legitimacy" (*JF* 90). The values of public reason "reflect an ideal of citizenship" in which one is willing to decide fundamental questions in ways that other citizens can recognize as reasonable. Such citizens acknowledge a "duty of civility," which requires that we "reason within the limits set by the principle of legitimacy" when deciding "constitutional essentials and questions of basic justice" (*JF* 92).

It is crucial to stress that the application of the principle of legitimacy is limited to these constitutional essentials and questions of basic justice. On other issues Rawls argues that "it is often more reasonable to go beyond the political conception and the values its principles express, and to invoke nonpolitical values that such a view does not include" (*PL* 230). Rawls's idea of political legitimacy, then, might be described as having a dualistic structure. Where "essential matters are at stake," issues are to be decided solely on the basis of "publicly acceptable reasons," which "means that our reasons should fall under the political values expressed by a political conception of justice" and thus must conform to the principle of legitimacy. By contrast, ordinary legislative issues normally "do not concern these matters," including "tax legislation" and "laws regulating property," and "voting funds for museums and the arts," where "the restrictions imposed by public reason do not apply..., or, if they do, at least not in the same way or so stringently" (*JF* 91). Thus, constitutional essentials and fundamental questions of justice are directly subject to the principle of legitimacy – they must be based on public reason, and public reason alone. But other legislation and public policy are only indirectly subject to the principle of legitimacy. Laws and policies must be adopted through constitutional procedures that satisfy the principle of legitimacy, but they do not themselves have to pass such a stringent test. They may be based on nonpublic reasons, although it is desirable that ordinary legislation also conform to the principle of legitimacy when possible.

Rawls does not offer a full discussion of the difference between "essentials" and ordinary policy, and one might wonder whether this distinction can be maintained. Ordinary laws involve the exercise of political power and are coercively enforced, so why should they not be justifiable on the basis of public reason? Why is it "more reasonable" to settle these issues on the basis of nonpublic values? After all, nonpublic values are not used to justify "essentials" precisely because they are not "reasonable" in that they do not satisfy the criterion of reciprocity. It might seem natural to think, therefore, that the scope of the principle of legitimacy should include not only the processes through which "legitimate law" is created, but also the content of "legitimate law," so that the laws themselves are "reasonable" in the sense that they satisfy the criterion of reciprocity.

A full discussion of this question is beyond the scope of this entry, but the question points to important differences between justice and legitimacy, and more particularly between the ideas of legitimate law and the principle of legitimacy. The principles of justice govern the basic structure of society, requiring that the institutions of the basic structure be organized, and their interactions governed, in such a way that the principles of justice are satisfied as much as possible. Obviously, then, the structure of the political system through which the institutions of the basic structure are regulated, and which itself is part of the basic structure, must satisfy the principle of legitimacy. And, equally obvious, laws and policies enacted by the legislature or pursued by the executive must not violate the rights established by the political conception of justice. But restricting the scope of political decision-making to matters that can be decided on the basis of public reason is not reasonable, and so would not satisfy the principle of legitimacy.

First, such a restriction would unfairly burden those citizens whose nonpublic values and objectives could not be adequately pursued through individual or voluntary efforts. Consider, for example, the objective of historical preservation, such as maintaining the character of a district for esthetic reasons, or because of the historical interest of the structures involved, or to sustain awareness of the traditions and ways of life of the community. It would be difficult to promote such nonpublic values through purely voluntary means, since they are collective or public goods, in the sense that people often could not be excluded from their benefits and thus would have an incentive to free-ride on the efforts of others. Similar issues arise for other values such as certain kinds of wilderness preservation, environmental protections, or maintaining a cultural legacy. To restrict the legitimate purposes of law and policy to political values would make it impossible for citizens to realize some of their other objectives, even when they could do so without violating the basic rights protected by a reasonable political conception of justice. One might argue that these policies involve an infringement of liberty, and therefore would violate basic rights unless they could be justified in terms of public reason. But Rawls argues that there is no general right to liberty. As he explains, at least in justice as fairness "no priority is assigned to liberty as such, as if the exercise of something called 'liberty' had a preeminent value and were the main, if not the sole, end of political and social justice" (*JF* 44).

The second reason is that many questions of policy are too complex, involve significant areas of uncertainty, or raise controversial scientific (including social scientific) issues that cannot be settled in terms of "the principles of reasoning and the rules of evidence" that constitute the guidelines of inquiry that are part of public reason. In such cases, then, citizens and their representatives would have no choice in their deliberations but to rely upon methods of reasoning that go beyond public reason, thus reaching decisions that would not themselves satisfy the principle of legitimacy. So long as these decisions do not involve essentials, they would be legitimate provided that they are made in accordance with a constitution that satisfies the principle of legitimacy.

Considerations such as these explain why "legitimacy is a weaker idea than justice and imposes weaker constraints on what can be done." In the cases just surveyed, "democratic decisions and laws are legitimate, not because they are just but because they are legitimately enacted" through a proper procedure. Rawls hastens to add that "the constitution specifying the procedure be sufficiently just, even though not perfectly just." In short, "legitimacy allows for an indeterminate range of injustice that justice might not permit" (*PL* 428). This speaks to the "practical role" of political philosophy, which is to at least narrow the differences among conflicting positions "so that cooperation on a footing of mutual respect among citizens can still be maintained" (*JF* 2). To fulfill this role political philosophy must not rest upon idealizations that make its proposals unworkable.

J. Donald Moon

SEE ALSO:

Basic structure of society
Constitution and constitutional essentials
Democracy
Duty of civility
Liberal conception of justice
Political conception of justice
Political obligation
Public reason
Reasonable pluralism
Reciprocity

113.

LEGITIMATE EXPECTATIONS

ONE OF THE most radical features of Rawls's conception of justice as fairness is that it fundamentally rejects the widespread and perennial view that justice is centrally about giving people what they morally deserve (at least where what individuals morally deserve is viewed as being identifiable prior to standards of justice). In his discussion of "Legitimate Expectations and Moral Desert" (*TJ* 273–277), Rawls allows that "[t]here is a tendency for common sense to suppose that income and wealth, and the good things in life generally, should be distributed according to moral desert," but makes clear that "justice as fairness rejects this conception" (*TJ* 273). He states unambiguously that "the principles of justice that regulate the basic structure and specify the duties and obligations of individuals do not mention moral desert, and there is no tendency for distributive shares to correspond to it" (*TJ* 273). Rawls thereby takes himself to be departing from one central tradition in philosophical understandings of the relationship between justice, desert and virtue, stretching from W. D. Ross back to Leibniz (at *TJ* 273 n.11, Rawls refers to Ross 1930 and Leibniz 1951 [1697]), even though he nevertheless thinks that his account of the relative priority of justice and desert need not be in tension with the central features of Aristotle's view of justice (*TJ* 9–10).

As a replacement or successor notion to the idea of desert, Rawls instead advances a conception of legitimate expectations. The central idea of legitimate expectations is that "as persons and groups take part in just arrangements, they acquire claims on one another defined by the publicly recognized rules. Having done various things encouraged by the existing arrangements, they now have certain rights, and just distributive shares honor those claims" (*TJ* 273). To give an example, if we assume that Wilt Chamberlain goes to work at the basketball

Legitimate expectations / 429

arena in a society with a just basic structure, and which therefore has a particular schedule of income taxation that has been promulgated clearly and publicly in advance, then Chamberlain has a legitimate expectation to receive his full post-tax income, even if that post-tax income is an extremely high one which thereby creates significant economic inequalities in that society. Action by the state to engage in the *post hoc* confiscation of any part of those high earnings, even if pursued in the name of promoting greater political equality, would illegitimately and unjustly confound Chamberlain's legitimate expectations to be treated in a transparent manner by the laws of his society. Respecting legitimate expectations means that governments must avoid the "continual interference with particular individual transactions" (*JF* 52 n.18) that Nozick mistakenly believed justice as fairness would involve (see Nozick 1974).

Significantly, though, Chamberlain's legitimate claim to a particular income level is not morally *deserved*, either in the specific sense of rewarding moral virtue, or in the more general sense of satisfying any standard of entitlement that might be defined prior to the rules of the just basic structure itself. (Rawls distinguishes these two senses from each other at *TJ* 276.) Rather, Chamberlain's legitimate expectations are defined by the rules of the interlocking institutions of the basic structure, which have been designed to secure background justice (*JF* 50–52). Rather than responding to any commonsensical moral precept of rewarding the virtue or talent or effort of any specific individual, these institutions instead aim at realizing the two principles of justice holistically, at the level of society (*TJ* 267–271). There is therefore a close connection between a conception of legitimate expectations defined with reference to the operation of just institutions and Rawls's parallel idea of pure procedural justice, whereby "no attempt is made to define the just distribution of goods and services on the basis of information about the preferences and claims of particular individuals" (*TJ* 267).

Rawls can thus endorse the Aristotelian dictum that justice involves giving each his due (*TJ* 10, 275–276), but only when the standard for what each is due is defined by the institutional scheme of a just society itself, and avowedly not when such a standard seeks to incorporate an individualized standard of moral desert or any other "prejustitial" measure of individual entitlement (*JF* 72; cf. Scheffler 2001). Legitimate expectations can thus be said to stand in a rather complicated and potentially ambiguous relationship to traditional ideas of desert. In one sense, Rawls's idea of legitimate expectations is founded on the stark denial of desert-based approaches to justice. Indeed, in his later work, Rawls added to his reasons for rejecting any prejustitial standard of entitlement, insofar as he saw any appeal to such a standard as a violation of *political* liberalism, given the fact of reasonable pluralism, and the reality of pervasive disagreements among reasonable citizens regarding standards of moral worth (or regarding any other putative prejustitial desert-base) (*JF* 73).

Nevertheless, in a different sense, we can instead view the idea of legitimate expectations as vindicating the idea of desert in a revised form: that is, in a form suitable for incorporation into the public morality of a just, pluralistic society. As Rawls puts it, "there are many ways to specify deservingness depending on the public rules in question together with the ends and purposes they are meant to serve" (*JF* 74). Thus, an idea of rewarding the deserving remains but, instead of hoping to index individuals' rewards to morally (or metaphysically) controversial, or unknowable, or impracticable, standards of individual virtue or worth, as in the superseded understanding of desert, legitimate expectations give us a notion of desert fit for public use. Conscientiousness, effort and hard work are likely to find their reward under a just basic structure, but the justification for this alignment will be in terms of shared standards of justice, and there will be no attempt to outrun the ability of real institutions to deliver such alignments in a fine-grained manner.

Martin O'Neill

SEE ALSO:

> *Aristotle*
> *Desert*
> *Distributive justice*
> *Libertarianism*
> *Luck egalitarianism*
> *Precepts of justice*
> *Reasonable pluralism*

114.

LEIBNIZ, G. W.

OTTFRIED WILHELM LEIBNIZ (1646–1716) was a prolific and influential German philosopher and mathematician. Rawls devotes two lectures in his *Lectures on the History of Moral Philosophy* to Leibniz, largely in connection to his more extensive discussion of Kant, since Leibniz was, as Rawls observes, "the dominant figure in Germany in philosophy in Kant's time" (*LHMP* 105). Rawls holds that Leibniz "fully accepted an orthodox Christian view" but "he confronted and mastered – indeed, contributed to – the new science of his day, making use of it in his philosophical theology" (*LHMP* 106). A central part of this philosophical theology was to show that Christian faith "is fully compatible with reasonable belief" (*LHMP* 107).

Leibniz famously held that the world is the best of all possible worlds. This follows from his beliefs that God is the absolutely perfect being and the creator of the world. God created the most perfect world that he was capable of creating. And because he has the perfections of omnipotence and omniscience – he is "able to create any possible world…and [knows] all these worlds (their content and possible history), down to the last detail, and [knows] which world is best and why" (*LHMP* 112) – the best world of which he is capable of creating is the best possible world. Because there are multiple, irreducible perfections, the best possible world is the one which realizes "the most fitting balance of the various perfections. It is not found by seeing which one maximizes the fulfillment of any one principle (or value) taken by itself." Furthermore, "The most perfect balance of perfections rests with God's intuitive judgment. We can't say much about it" (*LHMP* 110). Thus, Leibniz's substantive view is a form of pluralism (or "intuitionism" as Rawls uses the term in *TJ*).

Leibniz's perfectionism is also a form of what Rawls calls "rational intuitionism": "the principles of perfection that specify the best of all possible worlds are eternal truths: they rest on and lie in the divine reason. These truths are superior to and prior to the divine will" (*LHMP* 110). The key contrast, for Rawls, is with Kant's moral constructivism, which holds that "the so-called independent order of values does not constitute itself but is constituted by the activity, actual or ideal, of practical (human) reason itself" (*PL* 99). Because Leibniz's perfections are prior to and independent of the operation of practical reason (both human and divine), from Kant's point of view it is a form of heteronomy: "Heteronomy obtains not only when first principles are fixed by the special psychological constitution of human nature, as in Hume, but also when they are fixed by an order of universals or concepts grasped by rational intuition, as in Plato's realm of forms or in Leibniz's hierarchy of perfections" (*CP* 345).

Finally, Leibniz is a determinist and a compatibilist. While God knows all of our actions before they occur, we remain free since the sources or principles of our actions remain within us, and "there is no possible way that our deliberations and conduct can be foreseen or predicted by natural science or social thought, however much we may know" (*LHMP* 128). Because God's foreknowledge is inaccessible to us, it is irrelevant to our practical deliberations. Thus, Leibniz introduces a crucial difference between prediction and deliberation, which Kant would develop further. Yet, it is worth emphasizing that in the *Critique of Practical Reason*, Kant singles out Leibniz's understanding of freedom as being "at bottom...nothing better than the freedom of a turnspit, which, when once it is wound up, also accomplishes its movements of itself" (Kant 1997b [1788], 82 [Ak.5:97]).

Jon Mandle

SEE ALSO:

Constructivism
Intuitionism
Kant, Immanuel
Practical reason
Rational intuitionism

115.

LEISURE

I N HIS ORIGINAL specification of the goods governed by the difference principle, Rawls made no reference to leisure. As R. A. Musgrave pointed out, however, this omission leads to problems of both horizontal and vertical equity (Musgrave 1974, 629–632). To illustrate the first: if a skilled laborer working twenty hours per week makes the same income as an unskilled laborer working sixty hours per week, the difference principle would seemingly not concern itself with their inequality in leisure. Yet, to illustrate the second, if two individuals have identical earning capacities but different incomes because one chooses to surf all day off Malibu while the other works, the difference principle would seemingly favor the surfer.

Both worries are overstated. The difference principle applies not to specific individuals, but rather to groups (*TJ* 56). Although Rawls tended toward identifying the least advantaged as those individuals with less than half the median income and wealth (*TJ* 84; *JF* 59), he also suggested the possibility of identifying the least advantaged either by social position, such as unskilled laborers, or as those who are disadvantaged in family or class origins, natural endowments, and luck (*TJ* 83–84). This choice affects the likelihood of the Malibu surfer being among the least advantaged. Moreover, comparisons are to be made in terms of the lifetime expectations of representative individuals, not actual earnings (*TJ* 56). Finally, leisure considerations might already be effectively included, if, for example, differences in leisure lead to inequalities in the social bases of self-respect.

Even with these emendations, however, the problem is not entirely eliminated. In response, Musgrave proposed – albeit only in theory – a lump sum tax, under which individuals would be taxed according to their ability to earn, regardless of their actual earnings (Musgrave 1974, 630–631). Although Rawls rejected Musgrave's proposal, he acknowledged that "there might be good reasons" for including leisure among the goods governed by the difference principle (*CP* 253). Including leisure – "twenty-four hours less a standard working day" – in the index would require Malibu surfers to support themselves (*PL* 181–182).

Extending the list of primary goods to include leisure would have practical consequences for the basic income debate, the choice of tax base (e.g., hourly versus total earnings), the need for an employer of last resort, and, depending on how leisure is defined, gender equity for unpaid labor. Restricting the extension to leisure, however, might be problematic. The reasons for including leisure would seem to require also including labor burdens, even though, in contrast to leisure time, labor burdens are unlikely to pass Rawls's public checkability test (Cohen 2008, 99, 368–369).

Despite its theoretical and practical significance, the leisure question remains unresolved. Although Rawls frequently referred to the *possibility* of including leisure (e.g. *JF* 179; *PL* 181–182), he never fully committed himself.

Kristi A. Olson

SEE ALSO:

Cohen, G. A.
Difference principle
Least-advantaged position
Luck egalitarianism
Primary goods, social
Reciprocity
Taxation

116.

LEXICAL PRIORITY: LIBERTY, OPPORTUNITY, WEALTH

ONE OF THE purposes of Rawls's theory of justice was to provide a systematic but nonutilitarian alternative to the intuitive balancing of competing values that characterizes ordinary moral thinking. Pre-theoretical reflection on justice typically involves a number of different "common sense precepts," such as that people ought to be rewarded according to effort, contribution, or need (*TJ* 268). These "maxims of justice" frequently conflict, raising the problem of how they are to be weighted or prioritized. "Intuitionism" is Rawls's term for the view that there is no "explicit" or "constructive" method for establishing general priority rules or assigning weights (*TJ* 30), and that we must simply "strike a balance by intuition" in each specific situation. Rawls thought that we should try to avoid direct appeals to intuition in disputes about justice, for if we have no procedure for determining the weights we assign to competing considerations, "the means of rational discourse have come to an end" (*TJ* 37). One of the great attractions of utilitarianism, for Rawls, was that it tried to solve "the priority problem" without relying on intuition (*TJ* 36; Scheffler 2003a, 427). Rawls sought a theory of justice that was systematic, like utilitarianism, but that did not reduce all considerations to the one criterion of utility. His theory therefore had to establish definite priority relations among its different principles.

The priority of liberty refers to the fact that the first principle of justice is prior to the second; Rawls refers to this as "the first priority rule" (*TJ* 220, 266). Rawls also affirms the priority of the second principle over considerations of efficiency or aggregate welfare; this is "the second priority rule" (*TJ* 266). Within the second principle, fair equality of opportunity is prior to the difference principle. Thus Rawls's "special conception" of justice (*TJ* 77) establishes a hierarchy of considerations relevant to the design of social institutions: equal basic liberties, fair equality of opportunity, difference principle, efficiency/welfare.

The specific kind of priority Rawls sought to defend was "serial" or "lexical" priority. In an alphabetical ordering, AZZZ...comes before BAAA...; no matter how many Z's and A's we add, words are ordered according to their first letter, and only if the first letter is the same do we then consider the second letter. Similarly, social orders are ranked according to whether or how close they come to satisfying the first principle, and only if two orders do equally well by this criterion do we then rank according to the second principle. For example, an inequality might raise the economic position of the worst off as required by the second principle but still not be permissible if it undermined equal political liberty, which is covered by the first principle. There would in this instance be no question of having to compare the size of the benefit to the least well off with the size of the political inequality, and in particular no question of having to count how many people would gain economically and how many people would be disadvantaged politically. Lexical ordering avoids balancing different principles; instead, it assigns absolute weight to the prior principle.

The meaning of the priority of liberty depends on exactly how the first principle is specified. In "Justice as Fairness," the first principle guaranteed "an equal right to the most extensive liberty compatible with a like liberty for all" (*CP* 48). In *Theory*, the first principle was formulated in terms of a list of equal basic liberties, but still with the stipulation this system be the most extensive system compatible with a like system for all (*TJ* 220, 266). In *Political Liberalism*, "most extensive" was replaced with "fully adequate" (*PL* 332). If the principle covers only basic liberties and need only be adequate for the development and exercise of the two moral powers (rather than as extensive as possible), it is plausible that the principle enjoys lexical priority over other considerations. In this more limited form, however, the principle is not as liberal as other possible liberty principles, e.g. Mill's harm principle, since gambling, prostitution, drug use, and suicide, are not *basic* liberties, and could therefore justifiably be limited by any public reasons, not just by the need to prevent people from harming each other (Freeman 2007b, 78).

Rawls recognized that lexical priority seems too extreme (*TJ* 38, 55). A lexical order could not be "strictly correct" but was only "an illuminating approximation under certain special though significant conditions" (*TJ* 40, 55, 132, 267). He also understood that it could hold only for principles that "have limited application and establish definite requirements," otherwise the satisfaction of later principles would always come at the expense of the earlier principle. For example, if the principle of utility came first, all further criteria would be "otiose,"

Lexical priority: liberty, opportunity, wealth / 437

because virtually any choice about institutional design will have some impact on expected utility (*TJ* 38). Also, the priority of liberty applies first in the context of ideal theory, where we assume strict compliance with principles of justice and favorable technological, social, and economic conditions (*TJ* 215). Rawls admits that this priority will not hold when social conditions do not permit the effective realization of basic liberties (*TJ* 55, 132). In these circumstances we revert to the "general conception" of justice: "all social values...are to be distributed equally unless an unequal distribution of any, or all, of these values is to everyone's advantage" (*TJ* 54). Even in these unfavorable conditions, however, the priority of liberty serves as a goal that orients efforts to achieve greater justice. Basic rights can be limited or denied, Rawls says, only in so far as these restrictions are "necessary to prepare the way for a time when they [these restrictions] are no longer justified," to "change the conditions of civilization so that in due course these liberties can be enjoyed" (*TJ* 132, 217, 475). For example, suppose that a primitive society were incapable of fully realizing certain important liberties, such as equal political liberty. It does not follow that it would be right to discount political liberty entirely, and simply seek to maximize the economic position of the least well off. Limitations on political liberty would be justified only as necessary for social and economic development that would eventually make the effective realization of political liberty possible. Thus, while the principles for ideal conditions do not apply directly in nonideal conditions, they are still relevant in nonideal conditions because they guide us in the identification of more and less serious injustices, and in establishing priorities for efforts at reform (*TJ* 216).

Rawls discusses two main cases of justifiable deviations from equal liberty. A particular liberty may be for everyone less extensive than it might be, if this limitation represents a gain for liberty on balance, considering the whole scheme of liberties (*TJ* 214–215). For example, freedom of conscience will be limited by the need for public order and security, since such order is an "enabling" condition for the enjoyment of other liberties (*TJ* 187). The right of participation may also be limited by a bill of rights or other familiar constitutional devices if "the less extensive freedom of participation is sufficiently outweighed by the greater security and extent of the other liberties" (*TJ* 201). Liberties may not be limited for the sake of economic wealth, even gains for the least well off, but only for the sake of liberty itself. Secondly, a particular liberty may be unequal, as for example when some people's votes are weighted more heavily than others, if this inequality is justified from the perspective of those with less liberty. The argument would have to be that in the social conditions in question, unequal weighting of votes is beneficial for the overall freedom of those whose votes count less (*TJ* 217).

Rawls gave two general reasons for the priority of liberty (*TJ* 475–476). First, the parties to the original position seek to advance particular conceptions of the good. Although they do not know what these conceptions are, they know that they may be religious in nature. Not knowing whether or not their view will end up being in the majority, they will not be willing to permit the dominant doctrine to suppress minority views, which could put themselves in the situation of having to renounce or repudiate what they take to be overriding obligations (*TJ* 181). As they have to make an agreement by which they would be willing to abide in all eventualities, the parties must consider the strains of commitment, and so not propose principles that they might not be willing to comply with (*TJ* 153–154). Second, the parties to the original position have a "highest-order interest in how their other interests, including even their fundamental ones, are shaped and regulated by social institutions" (*TJ* 475). The parties conceive of themselves as free persons in the sense that they want to ensure that they can revise and alter their final ends, should they see fit to do so. Of course, realizing these higher-order interests requires that one's basic material needs be met, but once basic needs can be met, the higher-order interests are regulative (*TJ* 476).

One problem with the priority of liberty is that the basic liberties need to be specified. For example, does freedom of speech include commercial advertising? If so, it would be forbidden to regulate advertising except for the sake of free speech itself, or other basic liberties, even if, for example, false advertising threatened public health. In the revised edition of *Theory*, Rawls distinguished central and noncentral applications of a liberty (*TJ* 54). The central range of application of a liberty refers to those cases in which the liberty is essential to realize the moral powers. Thus political discussion would receive full protection, under freedom of speech, but commercial advertising would not (Freeman 2007b, 70).

A second problem with the lexical priority of the equal basic liberties concerns the issue of limited application / definite requirements (*TJ* 38). When it is assumed that everyone complies with social rules, there is no gap between rights on paper and actual freedoms. Under conditions of partial compliance, however, people's enjoyments of their liberties will be more or less secure depending on how much government spends on their protection (Pogge 1995, 256–257; Farrelly 2007, 850–854, citing Holmes and Sunstein 1999). Unless Rawls specifies a security threshold for each liberty, virtually every policy choice will affect basic liberties, and so have to be decided on the basis of the first principle, again making further principles otiose. Any such threshold is bound to be locally arbitrary, however, making it implausible that up to that point additional security is our sole concern, while beyond that point additional security matters not at all (Pogge

1995, 256). Thus some conclude that Rawls's theory does not help us make decisions about how to allocate scarce social resources in nonideal conditions, e.g. how much to spend on protecting people's right to vote or their physical security versus how much to spend on health care or national defense (Farrelly 2007, 854). However, the fact that we must decide how much to spend on reducing the probability of rights violations and that we cannot fix a precise threshold at which such spending switches from our first priority to a matter of indifference should not lead us to conclude that we should engage in utilitarian balancing, allowing qualitatively lesser gains for the many to outweigh the more urgent interests of a few. One of the main consequences of lexical priority is that it limits the aggregation of different values across persons. One person's freedom of conscience is not to be sacrificed for the sake of greater wealth for n others, no matter the size of n. If all principles simply receive a weight, then at some point the greater interests of one person under one principle will be outweighed by the lesser interests of other persons under another principle, because for some value of n it will be more important to satisfy the secondary principle. Assuming that we want to restrict such aggregation, the challenge for Rawlsians is to refine rather than to reject the idea of lexical priority.

Andrew Lister

SEE ALSO:

Basic liberties
Basic needs, principle of
Freedom
Intuitionism
Liberty, equal worth of
Precepts of justice
Two principles of justice (in justice as fairness)
Utilitarianism

117.

LIBERAL CONCEPTION OF JUSTICE

IBERAL CONCEPTIONS OF justice form a particular class of *political* conceptions of justice and should not be confused with liberal comprehensive views, which do not limit their positions to the domain of the political (*PL* xlvi). Political conceptions are those articulated as freestanding from the controversial claims of comprehensive doctrines, limited in focus to the political domain, and expounded using the shared, intuitive ideas from a democracy's political culture (*PL* 11–15, 376, 452–453). According to Rawls, it is from among a family of reasonable, liberal political conceptions of justice that the most reasonable conception of political justice for a democratic regime will be found – one that can meet with an overlapping consensus of citizens' reasonable comprehensive doctrines (*PL* 156–157, 167–168).

Liberal political conceptions of justice have three major defining features (*PL* xlvi–xlvii, 6, 156–157, 223, 375, 450–451; *LHPP* 12). First, they articulate a list of fundamental rights, specifying freedoms and opportunities familiar to citizens of modern democratic societies: freedoms of speech, thought, conscience, press, movement, and assembly; rights of personal integrity (e.g. freedom from serfdom and slavery); political liberties (e.g. the right to vote and opportunities to run for office); and rights associated with the rule of law (e.g. rights to due process and a fair trial) (*PL* 291, 334–335; *JF* 44; *LHPP* 12). Second, liberal conceptions of justice must accord *special priority* to this framework of rights vis-à-vis other, sometimes competing, values, in part by holding these rights up as democratic constitutional essentials (*PL* 227–230, 363–368; *JF* 46–50). These liberties are granted an absolute precedence: they cannot be outweighed by other goods such as the value of promoting the greatest public welfare or perfectionist ideals of society or citizenry (*PL* 294–295). Third, liberal conceptions articulate

440

measures to assure all citizens, regardless of socioeconomic status, suitable, general-purpose resources (*primary goods* or something suitably like them (*PL* 176–190)) to effectively and thoughtfully exercise the freedoms and opportunities accorded by their basic rights. A reasonable, liberal provision of such general-purpose resources would require society's basic socioeconomic and political institutions to prevent excessive levels of socioeconomic inequality (*PL* lv).

Different liberal conceptions of justice proceed from different understandings of these conditions, leading to their differing content (*PL* xlvi–xlvii, 6, 450–452). Rawls's account of political justice, *justice as fairness*, is a liberal conception of justice. He takes it to be "the most reasonable [such] conception" since it best interprets and fulfills the aforementioned three features, in his view (*PL* xlvi). Still, in any democratic society various liberal conceptions of justice rival each other in political debates, and Rawls admits that reasonable people can disagree with his view about which is most reasonable (*PL* xlvi–xlvii). Despite the plurality of liberal, conceptions of justice, Rawls takes it that liberal views all share in the virtue of "removing from the political agenda the most divisive issues, serious contention about which must undermine the bases of social cooperation," in their protection, prioritization, and enabling of basic liberties (*PL* 157). Still, not every liberal political conception of justice will necessarily be *reasonable*, but rather only those "that [meet] the criterion of reciprocity and [recognize] the burdens of judgment" (*PL* xlvi–xlvii, 446–447, 450). If, for instance, a liberal, political conception did not recognize that "there are different and incompatible liberal political conceptions" (*PL* xlvii) and thus did not accord reasonable, rival conceptions a place within public reason, it would fail to meet these standards and thus not be reasonable.

Micah Lewin

SEE ALSO:

Basic liberties
Lexical priority: liberty, opportunity, wealth
Overlapping consensus
Political conception of justice
Primary goods, social
Public reason
Reciprocity

118.

LIBERAL PEOPLE

R AWLS'S "PEOPLES" ARE artificial corporate moral persons or group
agents (*LP* 23–30). They are "well-ordered," which means the members
of a people govern themselves politically through a public conception of
justice (*LP* 4, 19, 64–67). A liberal people governs itself through a liberal political conception of justice, which assigns basic rights, liberties, and opportunities
to all individuals, gives these rights, liberties, and opportunities special priority
over perfectionist claims or claims of the general good, and guarantees for all
citizens the primary goods necessary for effective use of their freedoms (*LP* 14).
There are many liberal conceptions, since the ideas at their core – citizens as free
and equal persons who form a society that is a fair scheme of cooperation – can
be interpreted in different ways (*LP* 11, 14). Rawls's generic liberalism is fleshed
out in particular cases through actual democratic processes. The United States,
the United Kingdom, France, and Germany are all examples of liberal peoples,
despite their political differences (e.g. presidential versus parliamentary government, different taxation and redistribution schemes, France's ban on burqas,
Germany's ban on Holocaust denial).

Liberal peoples alone are represented in Rawls's second original position (*LP*
32–35, 70). They choose principles of international cooperation for a society of
liberal peoples regarded as free equals. (Rawls sets up a third original position
for decent peoples (*LP* 70).) Fairness is modeled by the symmetrical positions
of the representatives of liberal peoples in the original position. The representatives choose principles according to the fundamental interests of democratic
societies, i.e. preserving independence and self-respect as a people, and securing

the freedom and safety of all members of the people. A veil of ignorance prevents representatives from knowing, e.g. the size of the territory or population of the people they represent, its relative strength, or its level of natural resources or economic development. The representatives do know the people has enough to sustain a constitutional democracy. The representatives select Rawls's eight principles (*LP* 37).

Liberal peoples are tolerant of nonliberal, decent peoples (*LP* 59–62). Rawls draws a parallel between a liberal society's tolerance for different ways of life among its citizens and its tolerance for different ways of life expressed by different conceptions of justice in some nonliberal societies. This tolerance, in each case, is conditioned upon the presence of certain features. In the domestic case, tolerance is limited to doctrines that can be pursued compatibly with a liberal conception of justice and its public reason. In the international case, liberal tolerance is limited to societies whose nonliberal commitments are compatible with affirming certain minimal conditions of right and justice at home, as well as the Law of Peoples itself.

Liberal tolerance forbids sanctions meant to force political changes, and includes treating decent peoples as equals in good standing (*LP* 59–62). The Law of Peoples leaves room for self-determination. If liberal peoples were to insist that all peoples be liberal, they would deny respect to nonliberal peoples. This would be wrong, because decent peoples meet many basic conditions of right and justice. Further, such disrespect might stifle development and change, rather than encouraging it. Hence, liberal peoples must regard all peoples as having equal and good standing, and must offer appropriately public reasons for their actions.

One puzzling aspect of Rawls's liberal peoples is their refusal to insist on more fully liberal principles of global justice in the second original position. After all, their goal in this situation is to choose principles of international cooperation for a society of liberal peoples. The answer may be that liberal peoples recognize a state of corporate moral agency in their historical pasts that existed before they became fully liberal peoples. For instance, the US would surely have claimed for itself a significant right to self-determination, even before blacks and women were afforded many of the rights held by white men. By selecting principles of international cooperation centered on this pre-liberal stage of corporate agency, liberal peoples preserve maximal self-determination rights for all corporate persons. This intuitive notion of nonliberal corporate personhood is given normative substance through Rawls's "common good idea of justice," an idea which plays a central role in demonstrating that decent peoples are genuine schemes of social cooperation.

Walter J. Riker

SEE ALSO:

Law of Peoples
Legitimacy
Liberal conception of justice
Peoples

119.

LIBERALISM AS COMPREHENSIVE DOCTRINE

A VARIETY OF COMPREHENSIVE doctrine, comprehensive liberalism is a philosophical position, complete with an ordering of values, that supports liberal political principles; Kant and Mill are Rawls's main exemplars of it (*CP* 409). Like other comprehensive doctrines, as opposed to "merely political" ones like Rawls's, such theories present their political elements as entailed by more general moral, religious, or metaphysical considerations. Since liberal principles are embedded within broader, deeper theories that make claims of epistemic correctness, they are thought to be emphatically true, and opposed doctrines to be false. Moreover, they represent relatively cohesive worldviews that cover matters (in particular, interpersonal ethics) beyond the scope of Rawls's theory, which is more narrowly focused on the institutions and principles of the basic structure of society. Kant's and Mill's comprehensive liberalisms, according to Rawls, have two major components. First, they base the primacy of rights and liberties on the notion that the value of either autonomy (Kant) or individualism (Mill) is preeminent (*CP* 409–412). Second, since these values do not dictate individuals' ways of life, emphasizing instead the importance of freely choosing such things for themselves, comprehensive liberals accept the existence of a multiplicity of rationally desirable human goods that correspond to different ways of life. Hence, they reject classical and Christian doctrines according to which political order is secured through widespread acceptance of a more unitary or exclusive conception of the good life, and thus endorse some principle of toleration or neutrality vis-à-vis different comprehensive doctrines.

Comprehensive liberalism has an ambivalent place in Rawls's thought. He clearly has an affinity for Kant and Mill, often making the point that doctrines such as theirs could occupy a prominent place in an overlapping consensus based

445

on justice as fairness, as they represent plausible ways of connecting the principles of justice to broader beliefs and values. Rawls is equally clear, however, that these doctrines cannot themselves be the basis of such a consensus, since they view liberal principles as entailed by the central importance of autonomy or individualism to human life. This excludes reasonable citizens (especially religious ones) who are prepared to accept fair terms of social cooperation, but do not view the validity of liberal principles as rooted in secular, Enlightenment values, as Kant and Mill do. Comprehensive liberalism amounts to another "secular doctrine" that cannot serve as a basis for social unity in societies characterized by the fact of pluralism (*CP* 409). Rawls comes to view *Theory* as itself being a "partially comprehensive doctrine" (*JF* 186–187; *PL* xviii), due largely to the fact that it expects adherence to the principles of justice to be based on the argument that justice is a part of the human good presented in part III of *Theory*, an expectation that Rawls later takes to be at odds with the fact of reasonable pluralism (*PL* xlii). Hence Rawls's later political liberalism aims to stay "on the surface, philosophically speaking" (*CP* 395), by basing its conceptions on a freestanding notion of reasonableness, rather than some deeper account of value (*PL* 376).

Todd Hedrick

SEE ALSO:

> *Autonomy, moral*
> *Comprehensive doctrine*
> *Conceptions of the good*
> *Individualism*
> *Kant, Immanuel*
> *Mill, John Stuart*
> *Political liberalisms, family of*

120.

LIBERALISM, COMPREHENSIVE VS. POLITICAL

COMPREHENSIVE LIBERALISM, FOR Rawls, refers to *comprehensive doctrines* with distinctly *liberal* content. Taking these two elements in turn, comprehensive doctrines are more or less complete worldviews, whether religious, philosophical, moral, or metaphysical. Comprehensive views include "conceptions of what is of value in human life, and ideals of human character, as well as ideals of friendship and of familial and associational relationships, and much else that informs our conduct" – including "nonpolitical conduct" – "and in the limit...our life as a whole" (*PL* 13). And by *liberal*, Rawls is referring to a historical tradition of moral, political, and philosophical thought, whose constituent views share in some distinctive features of their understandings of morality, its psychology and epistemology, and associated ideals of government and politics. Historically, Rawls understands the liberal tradition to originate in the aftermath of the Reformation where the resulting religious pluralism and religious wars led to discussions of and struggles for tolerance and liberties of thought and conscience. This tradition extends up to the present day, through the revolutionary, constitutional, and democratic taming of monarchical authority by rising middle classes, and the extension of majority rule and suffrage eventually to working classes, women, and people of all ethnicities (*LHPP* 11; *PL*, xxii–xxx, xxxviii–xxxix, 159; *JF* 1, 192–193; *LHMM* 5–7).

As examples of comprehensive liberalisms, Rawls frequently invokes those of Kant and Mill. Moreover, in *A Theory of Justice*, Rawls's conception of justice, *justice as fairness*, might seem to be presented as part of an encompassing, comprehensively liberal, moral doctrine which he sometimes refers to as "rightness as fairness" (*TJ* 15, 95–96, part III; *JF* xvii, 186–187; *PL* xl). Rawls later makes

447

it clear that he views *justice as fairness* as a freestanding *political* liberalism – that is, as a reasonable, liberal, political conception of justice, which as *political*, limits this liberal view's scope to speaking only to the political domain rather than to more comprehensive matters outside this sphere (e.g. *CP* 389; *PL* xv, xli–xliii, l–li, 450–451; *JF* xvii). In fact, Rawls first invokes the notion of comprehensive liberalism in his writings, at least in part, as an elucidating contrast or foil to political liberalism and (liberal) political conceptions of justice (*CP* 408ff., 426ff.), and he continues to use it, in many instances, in such a way.

In liberal moral views, according to Rawls, practical and moral knowledge is available to common human reason (not just to a privileged few), the moral domain arises from aspects of human nature and social existence (not from aspects or commands of a deity), and persons are constituted so as to have in their natures sufficient motives to be moral and comply with duties and obligations (without the need for external sanctions from the state, religious authority, or deity) (*PL* xxvi–xxvii). Of course these views of moral psychology and epistemology may be restricted in application to a certain class or range of moral claims. For Rawls, the pertinent example is that of his *political* liberalism, whose focus is on a class of moral views that share in the aforementioned features, but only as restricted in application to the *political domain* – i.e. to *politically* moral values. Political liberalism "does not take a general position" on these claims but rather affirms them only "with respect to a political conception of justice for a democratic regime," leaving the question of their general status "to be answered in their own way by different comprehensive views" (*PL* xxvii).

Bound up with this distinctive, liberal moral epistemology and psychology is liberalism's special emphasis on the moral values of autonomy and individuality (e.g. *CP* 409f.; *PL* 98–99). And yet there are "great differences in scope and generality" between comprehensive liberalisms, like the historical examples of Kant's and Mill's liberalisms, and political liberalism when it comes to "foster[ing] the values of autonomy and individuality" (*PL* 199–200). While Mill's comprehensive liberalism places value "in a certain mode of life and reflection that critically examines our deepest ends and ideals" and Kant's comprehensive liberalism locates the source of value in acting from universalizable principles, categorical imperatives, that all "would acknowledge under conditions that best express their nature as free and equal rational beings," political liberalism only defends democratic citizens' political autonomy, or "the legal independence and assured political integrity of citizens and their sharing with other citizens equally in the exercise of political power" (*PL* xlii–xliii, 77–79; *TJ* 222, 452). The former views hold moral autonomy and individuality up "as ideals to govern much if not all of life" while the latter has a "different aim," restricted to the domain of the political, that requires "far less" be done: it asks merely that children's education properly informs them of their constitutional and civic rights, "prepare[s] them to be fully cooperating members of society...enable[s] them to be self-supporting," and encourages the development of political virtues to support the society's fair terms of social cooperation (*PL* 199–200; *JF* 156–157). Beyond such matters as these, political liberalism "does not seek to cultivate the distinctive virtues and values of the liberalisms of autonomy and individuality" (*PL* 200; *JF* 157).

With regard to political matters, comprehensive liberalisms generally see their political positions and "doctrines of free institutions" as largely resting on, rooted in, or continuous with their more general liberal, moral positions – whether they be their conceptions of free and equal persons, autonomy, individuality, etc. – as they apply to the political domain (e.g. *CP* 427, 408f.; *PL* xlii–xliii, 159, 169; *LHPP* 297–313, esp. 299ff.). Comprehensive and political liberalisms agree that the legitimacy of a liberal, state regime is tied to its social and political institutions being justifiable to the reason of all citizens, so that the justification for these institutions of their social world "must be, in principle, available to everyone, and so justifiable to all who live under them"; liberalisms thus intertwine with the views of the social contract tradition "and the idea that a legitimate political order rests on unanimous consent" (*LHPP* 13ff.). This means that comprehensive liberalisms, like political liberalisms, will sanction and warrant the principles of a just constitutional democracy (often as ideals) for the purposes of political governance. Comprehensive liberalisms largely, substantively align with the views of liberal, political conceptions of justice, which Rawls's political liberalism encompasses a reasonable family or class thereof; such liberal, political conceptions, although not themselves presented this way, can be seen, generally, by comprehensive liberalisms as consequences or, at least, workable approximations of what their wider, liberal moral views require (*PL* xxxvii, 159, 169–171). According to Rawls, liberal conceptions of justice, each (a) specify a list of fundamental rights, liberties, and opportunities familiar to citizens of constitutional democracies, (b) grant a special primacy to these rights as opposed to other, sometimes competing values, and (c) have measures in place to mutually assure suitable general-purpose resources to all citizens for effectively and intelligently exercising these fundamental rights (*PL* xlvi–xlvii, 6, 156–157, 223, 291–292, 375, 450–451; *LHPP*, 12). Comprehensive liberalisms generally agree with liberal political conceptions of justice in viewing these rights, their priority over other values, and the ensured availability to all of effective enabling measures for their use as morally required for the political domain: for the most part, they can readily view the features of a liberal, political conception of justice as the upshot or suitable estimation of their own, more comprehensive views and thus embed it within their wider, liberal moral doctrines (*PL* xxxvii, 159, 169–171). Rawls invokes Kant's and Mill's comprehensive liberalisms both as examples of reasonable comprehensive doctrines that can embed and endorse a reasonable, liberal political conception of justice (like *justice as fairness*) within their comprehensive views as part of a reasonable overlapping consensus within society (*PL* xxxvii–xxxix, 145–146, 159ff., 168–172; *JF* 33, 190–192, 194–195).

Still, comprehensive liberalisms may depart from the claims of liberal, political conceptions of justice in taking these liberal politically moral standards as having morally binding application beyond the domain of the political. For instance, a comprehensive liberalism might view these rights as having broad, moral application to and precedence over other values within private associations or family life, and not just applying to or holding precedence within the political domain. So while comprehensive liberalisms will largely agree with liberal, political conceptions of justice about (a)–(c) as they apply to the political domain, comprehensive liberalisms may well endorse some elements of (a)–(c) as holding beyond this domain. They may thus depart from the claims of liberal, political views about (a)–(c), as political conceptions of justice will not speak to – will neither affirm nor deny – (a)–(c), or any claims for that matter, insofar as these claims are applied beyond the political sphere. Political liberalisms, as liberal, *political* views, *take no stance* on such matters, remaining agnostic about them, as to take a stance – whether for or against – would itself be to move beyond the domain of the political (*PL* 10, 95, 126–128, 150, 377–378). There is no corresponding restriction on comprehensive liberalisms lending moral weight to claims beyond the political domain. Still, we can distinguish *politically reasonable* comprehensive liberalisms from a class of *politically unreasonable* comprehensive liberalisms that take further, liberal positions to not only be *morally* binding outside the political domain (e.g. (a)–(c) applied outside the political domain) but also hold them to be *politically* enforceable through the coercive and oppressive use of state-backed power and sanctions (*JF* 34, 183–184; *PL* 37). Rawls again mentions Kant's and Mill's comprehensive liberalisms as examples of comprehensive doctrines, that although liberal, would require state oppression if they were to try to force the unity of a single, moral worldview on their fellow citizens (*PL* 37; *JF* 34). Reasonable comprehensive liberalisms will not take such state-backed, coercive or oppressive measures to enforce their nonpolitical, moral beliefs on other

Liberalism, comprehensive vs. political / 451

citizens, and Kant's and Mill's comprehensive liberalisms may well be interpreted as reasonable in this way.

Micah Lewin

SEE ALSO:

Comprehensive doctrine
Kant, Immanuel
Liberal conception of justice
Mill, John Stuart
Political liberalism, justice as fairness as
Political liberalisms, family of

121.

LIBERTARIANISM

LIBERTARIANISM IS THE view that agents initially morally fully own themselves and have certain moral powers to acquire property rights in external things. It can be understood as a basic moral principle or as a derivative one. For example, it can be advocated as a natural rights doctrine (e.g. Nozick 1974) or defended on the basis of rule consequentialism (e.g. Epstein 1998; Shapiro 2007) or rule contractarianism (e.g. Narveson 1988; Lomasky 1987). For concreteness, I shall here interpret libertarianism as a natural rights doctrine. For a full discussion of libertarianism, see Vallentyne (2010). For critical discussion of Nozick's version of libertarianism, see Vallentyne (2011).

Although it has a long history (e.g. at least back to Locke 1960 [1689]), libertarianism was not widely discussed by political philosophers prior to Nozick (1974). Rawls, for example, does not explicitly discuss it at all in *TJ* and only briefly discusses it in *PL* (262–265). Nonetheless, Rawls's discussion of the entitlement to one's natural endowment is highly relevant to libertarianism's assertion of self-ownership, and we shall focus on that issue.

Philosophers, unfortunately, use "justice" to mean several different things. Rawls used this term to mean, roughly, the moral permissibility (rightness) of basic structures, or social institutions creating profound and unavoidable effects on individuals' lives (*TJ* 3–6, 93–98). By contrast, Nozick (1974, e.g. 52), and libertarians generally, tend to use "justice" to mean, roughly, infringes no one's rights. Thus, it's not clear that they are addressing the same topic.

Related to this, Rawls (e.g. *TJ* 4, 6, 10, 47) takes justice to apply only in contexts of social cooperation (e.g. coordination for reciprocal benefit guided by publicly recognized rules). (This, however, is in tension with his claim (*TJ* 251–258) that justice requires saving for the benefit of future generations.) By contrast, libertarians (e.g. Nozick 1974, 185–186) insist that (1) issues of justice arise in the

Libertarianism / 453

absence of cooperation (e.g. theft, murder), and (2) antecedent rights still have moral force in the context of cooperation. Many theories agree with (1), and most natural rights theories agree with (2).

The topic discussed by Rawls that is most central to libertarianism is his claim that the distribution of natural assets and starting social positions is a common (or collective) asset. In defending his interpretation of his two principles, he writes:

> [T]he initial distribution of assets for any period of time is strongly influenced by natural and social contingencies...Intuitively, the most obvious injustice of the system of natural liberty is that it permits distributive shares to be improperly influenced by these factors so arbitrary from a moral point of view. (*TJ* 62–63)

> [T]he difference principle represents, in effect, an agreement to regard the distribution of natural talents [and of starting places in society] as in some respects a common asset and to share in the greater social and economic benefits made possible by the complementarities of this distribution...No one deserves his greater natural capacity nor merits a more favorable starting place in society. (*TJ* 101–102)

Here, Rawls is rightly claiming that the *starting* positions of agents in society are not something that those agents can influence through their choices, and hence are not something for which they are agent-responsible or that they deserve in virtue of their past choices. Their starting positions are the result of their genetic endowment (natural talents), their fetal and childhood environment (for the development of those talents), and their initial socioeconomic position (wealth, social connections, etc.). Clearly, no one can rightly claim credit for her starting position. (In *JF* 55–57, Rawls also mentions luck during the lives of autonomous agents as a further social contingency.)

Let us agree that no one deserves, or is agent-responsible for, her starting position in society and examine whether this supports the claim that the income and wealth in society are common assets to be shared by all in some sense.

First, as Nozick (1974, 214) rightly claims, the fact that no one deserves her initial position does not entail that no one deserves the benefits of her choices to take advantage of her position (e.g. to develop or exercise her natural talents). No one deserves the cards she is dealt, but one may deserve credit for how well one plays those cards. Rawls holds, however, that:

The precept which seems intuitively to come the closest to reward moral desert is that of distribution according to effort, or perhaps better, conscientious effort. Once again, however, it seems clear that the effort a person is willing to make is influenced by his natural abilities and skills and the alternatives open to him...The better endowed are more likely, other things equal, to strive conscientiously, and there seems to be no way to discount for their greater good fortune. (*TJ* 274; cf. 89)

Rawls is certainly right that people's initial positions include choice-making and choice-implementing capacities and that individuals are not more deserving simply because they possess such better capacities. This clearly complicates the task of disentangling agent-responsibility from initial brute luck. Still, it is arguable that there is a basis for agent-responsibility and desert in how individuals exercise and develop the capacities with which they start. Luck egalitarians, for example, agree with Nozick that this cannot be ruled out so quickly. Obviously, however, the issue is complex and depends on crucial issues about free will and agent-responsibility.

In any case, Rawls and libertarians agree that justice is not based on any notion of institution-independent desert. Indeed, they agree that justice requires that individuals get that to which they are entitled (have a right) (*TJ* 88–89, 273–277). The disagreement is over what people's entitlements are. The most basic disagreement is that (natural right) libertarians hold that people's entitlements are not, except contingently, institution-dependent, whereas Rawls holds that they are largely institution-dependent. Roughly speaking, libertarians hold that one has well-defined entitlements in the absence of institutions (e.g. self-ownership and rights to resources one acquired in accordance with libertarian principles governing appropriation, transfer, and rectification), whereas Rawls holds that people are only entitled to whatever they may legitimately expect from just institutions. For libertarians, natural entitlements determine the justice of institutions, whereas, for Rawls, the justice of institutions determines entitlements.

It's worth noting, however, that even Rawls holds that there are certain entitlements that institutions must respect in order to be just:

To be sure, the more advantaged have a right to their natural assets, as does everyone else; this right is covered by the first principle under the basic liberty protecting the integrity of the person. And so the more advantaged are entitled to whatever they can acquire in accordance with the rules of a fair system of social cooperation. (*TJ* 89; not in the first edition; cf. *JF* 75–77)

Rawls agrees, that is, that individuals have a right, secured by the equal liberty principle, to control the exercise and development of their natural endowments. Institutions must respect this right in order to be just. This entitlement, known as *control self-ownership*, is part of what libertarians assert when they claim that agents initially fully own themselves. Full self-ownership, however, involves much more than control self-ownership. It also involves a full power to transfer (by sale, gift, rental, or loan) those rights to others (thereby giving others rights to control the use of one's person). Rawls, however, would presumably reject unrestricted powers of transfer of these rights, since it would give one person a kind of dominion over another (and can even involve voluntary enslavement). (See Freeman 2001 for discussion of this issue.)

Control self-ownership also does not include the right to any benefits from exercising one's rights of control. It will be instructive here to consider an argument scheme presented by Nozick (1974, 225–226) as an argument for his favored entitlement theory (libertarianism) and against Rawls:

1. People are entitled to their natural assets.
2. If people are entitled to something, they are entitled to whatever flows from it (via specified types of processes).
3. People's holdings flow from their natural assets [via the specified types of process].
   Therefore,
4. People are entitled to their holdings.
5. If people are entitled to something, then they ought to have it (and this overrides any presumption of equality there may be about holdings).

The crucial conclusion is 4. Conclusion 5 merely makes clear that the entitlement is conclusive and not merely *pro tanto*.

Conclusion 4 and the supporting Premise 3, however, are clearly too strong. The history of the world is the history of theft and violence. It is thus implausible that the holdings that people happen to have flow from their natural assets via the specified entitlement-generating types of process (Premise 3). It is therefore implausible that people are entitled to the holdings that they happen to have (Conclusion 4). Nozick, of course, was aware of this, and he must here have intended merely to give an argument for the claim that it is possible for people to be entitled to their holdings. For our purposes, then, we should drop Premise 3 and weaken Conclusion 4 to:

(4*) If peoples' holdings flow from their natural assets (via the specified types of process), then they are entitled to their holdings.

This is the core conclusion of the argument that is relevant to our purposes. Let us, then, examine the two supporting premises.

The first premise asserts an entitlement to one's natural assets. Nozick presumably understands natural assets as one's internal endowment when one first becomes an autonomous agent (and not merely one's genetic endowment at conception). Entitlement to this endowment is thus a form of self-ownership (control ownership of one's person). As indicated above, Rawls would accept this premise if it merely asserts *control* self-ownership, but he would reject it if it asserts *full* self-ownership.

The second premise asserts that someone who is entitled to something is entitled to the results of applying specified processes to it. Nozick, of course, assumes that the specified processes are something like libertarian processes of appropriation, transfer, and rectification. Rawls would, of course, reject the second premise so specified. If, however, the specified processes consist of *complying with the just institutions of society*, then Rawls could agree that one is entitled to their results that flow from these processes.

In conclusion, Rawls agrees with libertarianism that autonomous agents are self-owners in the weak sense of control ownership (although he wouldn't use those words). The main disagreement concerns entitlements to the benefits that flow from the exercise of that ownership. Rawls denies that there are institution-independent entitlements governing appropriation, transfer, and rectification. One's entitlements are merely whatever just institutions say they are.

Peter Vallentyne

SEE ALSO:

Basic liberties
Desert
Freedom
Locke, John
The market
Nozick, Robert
Priority of the right over the good
Property-owning democracy
Right: concept of and formal constraints of

122.

LIBERTY, EQUAL WORTH OF

RAWLS DISTINGUISHES BETWEEN *liberty* and the *worth* of liberty. We need to separate out, he suggests, what it is for liberty to be protected in a society and what the value is to a citizen in that society of having liberty protected. This distinction plays a central role in Rawls's thinking about the values of freedom and equality.

It is commonly thought, and many theorists have argued, that the important values of liberty and equality can conflict and that we must often choose which one to promote. (See, for instance, Isaiah Berlin's discussion of liberty and equality in *Four Essays on Liberty* (1969).) A central thesis of *A Theory of Justice* is that liberty and equality can be reconciled and Rawls's distinction between liberty and its "worth" is crucial to establishing this thesis (*TJ* 179). Securing liberty and promoting equality are not competing goals that have to be traded against one another, Rawls claims. Rather, laws that secure liberty and laws that promote equality work together to secure some other important goals.

Rawls defines liberty as "the complete system of the liberties of equal citizens" (*TJ* 179). Liberty, on this view, consists of the various specific freedoms guaranteed equally to all by the first principle of justice, including freedom of speech, conscience, religion, and so on. Each of these freedoms ensures that people are able to do certain things without interference from the government or from private actors. For instance, freedom of speech ensures that people are able to engage in acts of, say, artistic expression without the government censoring them or private agents coercing them to stop.

Rawls asks us to consider why it is valuable to citizens to have these freedoms protected. How does it benefit me that expression, religious practices, and so on are protected from interference? Part of what makes it worthwhile to live in a society with these freedoms, he suggests, is that they enable me to form plans and to carry them out. For instance, without freedom of speech I would not be able to hear the views of others about how to lead my life and use those views to form my life plans. And I would not be able to carry out certain plans, such as plans that involve making a controversial sculpture or publishing unpopular political views.

Now, suppose that I want to make my controversial sculpture or publish my unpopular political views. To be successful I will need to live in a society where the basic liberties are protected. But other things will be needed too. One thing that would help is having resources. Without resources I will not have the clay to construct my sculpture or to buy ad space for my political arguments. And the more resources I have, the better able I will be to do these things.

Similarly, having freedom of religion would prevent the government from making a law that prohibits me from building my mosque and would stop private actors from punishing me if I try to build it. But to actually build the mosque I would need resources to buy the bricks, tiles, ink, and so on. The more resources I have, the more able I will be to do these things also.

More generally, it seems that the extent to which I am able to carry out plans – be they religious, moral, artistic or political – depends upon the resources that I have. And we saw earlier that having the various basic liberties protected is useful to me in so far as it helps me form and pursue plans. So, it seems that how useful it is to me to have the basic liberties protected depends on the resources that I have. The more resources I have to pursue plans, the more useful it will be to be able to form them and be free from interference when I try to carry them out. In this way Rawls distinguishes between liberty, the protection of the basic liberties or freedoms, and the worth of liberty, the extent to which having those liberties is useful to me. Rawls's principles require that every citizen have equal liberties but they also regulate the worth of those liberties.

First, special emphasis is put on ensuring that political liberties, including voting and running for office, are given their "fair value": ensuring this fair value is, along with ensuring equal liberty for all, given lexical priority. Those who are similarly motivated and similarly able must have a similar chance at political influence. This ensures that in a democratic society all individuals have a fair opportunity to exercise political power, rather than there being simply rule by the rich or the well connected.

Second, Rawls's principles put significant constraints on inequality in the worth of other liberties. If we just had equal liberties for all there could still be significant inequalities of wealth and thus significant inequality in the worth of those liberties. Rawls's "Equality of Opportunity Principle" and "Difference Principle" put significant constraints on inequalities of wealth. The first requires us to eradicate any inequalities except those due to natural talent or greater motivation and the second requires that any remaining inequalities work to the advantage of the least well off. By ensuring that the distribution of wealth is fair these principles also ensure that the worth to each individual of her liberties is fair. We can now see why Rawls thinks that securing liberty and promoting equality serve a common ultimate goal. Both Rawls's principles governing liberties and those which are solely concerned with distribution serve the common goal of ensuring that every member of society has liberty of fair worth.

Adam Hosein

SEE ALSO:

Basic liberties
Democracy
Difference principle
Fair equality of opportunity
Freedom
Freedom of speech
Liberty of conscience

123.

LIBERTY OF CONSCIENCE

LIBERTY OF CONSCIENCE plays two roles throughout Rawls's work. First, it is among the most important basic liberties that Rawls endorses in *A Theory of Justice*, *Justice as Fairness*, *Political Liberalism*, and *Law of Peoples*. Second, and more broadly, the idea liberty of conscience helps to explain the aim of Rawls's entire philosophical project. Let us explore these two roles in turn.

Liberty of conscience is one of the first liberties Rawls defends as part of his first principle of justice, for "each person is to have an equal right to the most extensive scheme of equal basic liberties compatible with a similar scheme of liberties for others" (*TJ* 53). One of these maximally extensive liberties is liberty of conscience. Because liberty of conscience is one of our "fixed points" among considered judgments, any good theory of justice must account for it (*TJ* 181). The argument for liberty of conscience in *TJ* §33 runs roughly as follows: behind the veil of ignorance, the parties are unaware of their conception of the good. Accordingly, they are unaware of their moral and religious views (*TJ* 181). Rawls also argues that parties do not know which religions are present in their society or which religions are in the majority or minority (*TJ* 181). Therefore, the parties, knowing how important their conceptions of the good might be to them, cannot take the chance that their religion will come out on top if principles of justice favor a particular religion (*TJ* 181). Consequently, the parties will guarantee liberty of conscience up to the point where it produces public disorder: "liberty of conscience is to be limited only when there is a reasonable expectation that not doing so will damage the public order which the government should maintain" (*TJ* 186; also see *JF* 104). Like other liberties, liberty of conscience is insecurely protected by "teleological principles" like the principle of utility, for it might obligate governments to limit religious liberty when it is thought to produce bad consequences (*TJ* 185). Religious toleration must also be based on justice, not pragmatism (*TJ* 188). Rawls concludes in §34 that parties to the original position will enshrine liberty of conscience in their constitution at the second stage of the four-stage sequence, that is, the constitutional stage. At this stage the idea of a confessional state is rejected (*TJ* 186). Rawls also addresses liberty of conscience for the intolerant. He believes that while the intolerant have no right to complain when their liberty of conscience is restricted, parties will refrain from accepting restrictions on their liberty of conscience (*TJ* 193) but only so long as they do not excessively threaten inherent stability (*TJ* 192).

Toward the end of part II of *TJ*, Rawls argues that principles of conscientious refusal and civil disobedience both flow from liberty of conscience. §55 addresses the theory of civil disobedience, though Rawls discusses the matter in the context of natural duties and obligations. §56 explains that conscientious refusal – "non-compliance with a more or less direct legal injunction or administrative order" – can be justified according to liberty of conscience (*TJ* 323). For instance, Rawls concludes that liberty of conscience makes conscription hard to justify (*TJ* 333). But here too liberty of conscience cannot be absolute if it is to protect liberty equally for all.

In both *Justice as Fairness* and *Political Liberalism*, Rawls argues that liberty of conscience is required to develop the two moral powers (*JF* 45; *PL* 310–312):

> equal political liberties and freedom of thought enable citizens to develop and to exercise these powers in judging the justice of the basic structure of society and its social policies; and second, that liberties of conscience and freedom of association enable citizens to develop and exercise their moral powers in forming and revising and in rationally pursuing…their conceptions of the good. (*JF* 45)

The two moral powers are required in order to produce stability, publicity and other goods to implement a theory of justice.

Rawls leaves the defense of liberty of conscience relatively unchanged in *Justice as Fairness* and *Political Liberalism* (see *JF* 104–102; *PL* 310–311), though he adds a number of details to his account and applies liberty of conscience to more specific subjects. First, in *Justice as Fairness*, Rawls argues that liberty of conscience does not apply within organizations like churches, such that churches can exclude whomever they like (*JF* 164) and also that liberty of conscience helps to restrain ideology (*JF* 122). In *Political Liberalism*, Rawls argues that the burdens of judgment help ground liberty of conscience (*PL* xlvii). Rawls emphasizes that the right to err in religious matters is required to develop the two moral powers and a conception of the good (*PL* 313). He also argues that liberty of conscience is essential to the process of full justification. Liberty of conscience is required in order for each reasonable person to figure out how to integrate the political conception into her comprehensive doctrine. If she had no such liberty, it is not clear whether she would truly be left to herself to work out the integration of the political conception within her own worldview (*PL* 140). Since Rawls makes much of the distinction between political conceptions of justice and reasonable comprehensive doctrines, we should expect some revision of the derivation of the basic liberties. However, Rawls maintains that the ground of liberty of conscience is still worked out within the political conception even if citizens must integrate it into their comprehensive doctrines themselves (*PL* 151). For many reasons, Rawls includes liberty of conscience as a constitutional essential (*PL* 166) and notes that the right of liberty of conscience must be known as a right, that is, it must be public knowledge (*PL* 199). Rawls also argues that the limitations of liberty of conscience must be derived from the nature of liberty itself. In other words, liberty of conscience is "self-limiting" (*PL* 341).

Rawls provides an illuminating summary of three grounds of liberty of conscience in *Political Liberalism*. The first ground takes the fact that conceptions of the good are "given and firmly rooted" for granted, along with the fact that there are "a plurality of such conceptions, each...non-negotiable" (*PL* 314). For this reason, the parties guarantee near absolute liberty of conscience to protect their views. The last two grounds note that conceptions of the good are not given but "seen as subject to revision with deliberative reason, which is part of the capacity for a conception of the good. But since the full and informed exercise of this capacity requires the social conditions secured by liberty of conscience, these grounds support the same conclusion as the first" (*PL* 315). Again, liberty of conscience is required to develop one's conception of the good.

Worthy of note is the place of liberty of conscience in *Law of Peoples*. Rawls argues that liberty of conscience is a basic human right (*LP* 65). However, Rawls allows that some societies can be (somewhat) restrictive of liberty of conscience, such as a decent consultation hierarchy. They must still have some limited liberty of thought and conscience but he notes that these regimes are not therefore "fully reasonable" (*LP* 74). This leaves somewhat unclear how nonliberal societies violate human rights in restricting liberty of conscience, since reasonableness is turned into a continuum concept. Rawls wants to walk the line between making absolute liberty of conscience a human right and permitting the clear injustice of excessively limiting it.

Liberty of conscience / 463

The second role of liberty of conscience throughout Rawls's work arises as part of the narrative explaining what motivates the alterations to Rawls's theory of justice explained in *Justice as Fairness* and more fully developed in *Political Liberalism*. In both books, Rawls discusses the formation of liberty of conscience after the Reformation. He points out that liberty of conscience was the original liberal liberty and that it arose unintentionally. Freedom of religion was the consequence of the *modus vivendi* that arose among warring Catholic and Protestant sects. However, over time, liberty of conscience came to be accepted as a basic freedom, valuable for its own sake. The challenge of the Reformation was that the warring sects both had doctrines with a "transcendent element not admitting of compromise" (*PL* xxvi). The political consequence of this was either war that leads to exhaustion or convergence on an overlapping consensus. Rawls spends a lot of time developing this narrative which suggests that it is vital for motivating his later work. He even claims that political liberalism can be understood as the application of "the principle of toleration to philosophy itself" (*PL* 10).

Kevin Vallier

SEE ALSO:

Basic liberties
Burdens of judgment
Freedom
Higher-order interests
Human rights
Lexical priority: liberty, opportunity, wealth
Political conception of justice
Religion

124.

LOCKE, JOHN

RAWLS WAS A great admirer of John Locke (1632–1704). He admired Locke the thinker as one of the seminal figures in the social contract tradition. But Rawls admired Locke the person perhaps even more. At various points Rawls called him a truly great person. He commended Locke for his loyalty to the Earl of Shaftesbury, and especially for the "enormous risks to his life" he took in defense of constitutional government against royal absolutism. Locke, as Rawls tellingly put it, "had the courage to put his head where his mouth was" (*LHPP* 140).

Philosophically, Locke's main influence on Rawls concerns the issue of legitimacy. Rawls took Locke to have identified with remarkable clarity the source of this problem: the fact that people are morally symmetrically positioned. In his *Two Treatises of Government* (Locke 1960 [1689]), Locke argued that all individuals are naturally free and equal, and that this means that no one has natural authority over anyone else. This gives rise to the problem of legitimacy. How can government, claiming precisely such authority, be justified?

Rawls also agreed with Locke about the major outlines of how this problem is to be solved. Both adopted a social contract approach. If political society can be seen as the result of a contract between all its members, then the terms of interaction that it imposes on them can be seen as agreed upon. Such agreement would render the exercise of political power importantly self-imposed and thus compatible with the status of all as free and equal. Rawls and Locke thus shared a vision of a fully legitimate society as one in which citizens are facing laws that they can regard as self-imposed. One concrete implication of this is that, for both Rawls (most explicitly in *Political Liberalism*) and Locke (most explicitly in

A Letter Concerning Toleration (Locke 2010 [1689])), political authority must remain confined to what is of genuinely public concern. Religious matters, and other views about the good life, as such are thus categorically ruled out of the court of politics.

Rawls's most explicit discussion of Locke is found in the *Lectures on the History of Political Philosophy*. Rawls there ascribes to Locke a distinction between two questions: (i) what are the conditions under which a regime is legitimate? And (ii) what are the conditions under which a regime's subjects have political obligations? Rawls suggested that Locke considered a regime legitimate if and only if an idealized history can be constructed in which rational and morally motivated subjects could have agreed to that regime. This standard for legitimacy is most visible in Locke's objection to royal absolutism: such rule is illegitimate because no rational person could have consented to it. But a regime's legitimacy is only a necessary condition for subjects to have political obligations. Here Rawls saw the role of express consent in Locke's thought. On Rawls's interpretation of Locke, people have political obligations if and only if they expressly consent to a legitimate regime (*LHPP* 124–135). It is worth mentioning that this is a somewhat controversial reading of Locke, whom many consider to have accepted identical conditions for legitimacy and political obligation.

Whichever of these interpretations of Locke is correct, however, it is clear that Rawls deeply disagreed with Locke on a number of points. For one, Rawls considered the standard of legitimacy that he ascribed to Locke too permissive. This, Rawls argued, was due to Locke's mistaken construal of the choice-situation in which parties agree to the social contract. According to Rawls, we should consider the social contract as agreed upon not in an historical, but in a nonhistorical hypothetical choice-situation, such as the original position (*LHPP* 131). His reason was that rational and morally motivated people could have agreed to all sorts of regimes, even in an idealized history, and this includes regimes that should not be accepted as legitimate. All it takes are sufficiently adverse circumstances, as there may well have been.

Similarly, Rawls objected to Locke's acceptance as part of the background of the social contract that people can have morally valid private property rights in land, goods, and their labor. For Locke, the desire to see these rights protected forms an important part of the rationale of the parties to the contract to agree to submit to government. Rawls objected that recognizing such property rights prior to the signing of the social contract could unduly skew people's respective bargaining positions and thus, again, lead to unacceptable agreements. For those with (sufficient) property might be in such a strong position as to be able to secure for themselves significantly advantaged terms, including special political privileges. Since no such arrangement could be legitimate, Rawls concluded, no prior property rights are to be recognized by the parties to the social contract (*LHPP* 150–155).

Finally, what may be Rawls's deepest disagreement with Locke became more pronounced in some of his later writings. This concerns the nature of justification capable of solving the problem of legitimacy. According to Rawls, "Locke's conception of natural law provides us with an example of an independent order of moral and political values by reference to which our political judgments of justice and the common good are to be assessed." By contrast, Rawls required justification to be public in the sense that reasons should be provided that could be endorsed by all reasonable citizens (*PL* 136–137). Thus, "Locke's view contains a conception of justification distinct from the conception of public justification in justice as fairness as a form of political liberalism" (*LHPP* 112).

This disagreement can perhaps be understood in light of Rawls's and Locke's respective views of what can be expected from the human exercise of reason. Rawls thought the deepest questions of religion, philosophy, morality, and the good life are all very complex and difficult to answer. People will conscientiously answer them differently in light of their personal history, experiences, commitments, and so on. It is a fact of our world, then, that reasonable people will end up disagreeing about these issues. For Locke, while moral disagreement about particular issues may indeed be inevitable, the fundamental rule of morality, the Law of Nature, can be clearly and univocally known by the use of reason to "all who will but consult it" (Locke 1960 [1689], §6; 1997 [1663–1664]).

For Locke, then, the question of legitimacy is ultimately answered by reference to the Law of Nature (Locke 2010 [1689], 49). But for Rawls, since reasonable persons will disagree about even such fundamentals, this would not do. The problem of legitimacy is how to square government with the moral status of all as free and equal. People enjoy this moral status to an important degree, for Rawls, in light of their two moral powers. But since the exercise of these moral powers leads to reasonable disagreement, the only justification that takes seriously the moral status of all as free and equal will be justification that survives this reasonable disagreement. Thus, Rawls took public justification of a regime's constitutional essentials to all citizens to be a necessary condition of its legitimacy (*PL* 136–137). Absent that, reasonable persons might still not be able to regard their society's laws as self-imposed. As a result, for Rawls, a society based on Locke's views cannot achieve legitimacy (*CP* 531–532).

Bas van der Vossen

SEE ALSO:

Comprehensive doctrine
Constitution and constitutional essentials
Legitimacy
The original position
Political obligation
Social contract

125.

LOVE

OVE PLAYS AN important role in Rawls's early thinking about justice. First, the idea of love is crucial in *A Theory of Justice* to his account of how citizens come to acquire a sense of justice and the accompanying moral psychology that is essential for its development. Second, Rawls uses the concept of love as an analogy with the concept of justice to explain why citizens would accept the possible liabilities and losses of acting justly. Third, he discusses the idea of the love of mankind in his criticism of classical utilitarianism. Finally, Christian love is the topic of Rawls's posthumously published undergraduate senior thesis.

In the third part of *A Theory of Justice* Rawls moves on from the task of justifying the principles of justice to the difficult question of the motivation citizens have to take these principles as their own and to abide by their requirements. While Rawls later abandons the theory of congruence between the good of citizens and the requirements of justice that he develops in this part of *A Theory of Justice*, he retains the moral psychology that he elaborates in these pages. Rawls assumes at the outset of his theory that citizens have a sense of justice, understood as a moral feeling or sentiment that motivates them to abide by their rationally chosen principles of justice. A sense of justice is developed in three stages and love plays its crucial role in the first stage. These are stages of childhood during which moral feelings, necessary for democratic citizenship, are developed. In his somewhat speculative discussion of the first stage Rawls assumes the truth of a psychological law that a child, initially motivated by rational self-love, will come to genuinely love her parents when they "manifestly love" their child, and in loving their child they affirm the child's sense of worth. In these circumstances the capacity to love others develops as a consequence of being the recipient of unconditional parental love. The reciprocity between self-love and the love of others suggests another conceptual reciprocity between the rational and reasonable that Rawls explicitly developed in later work.

Rawls defines love by saying that it is "the desire to advance the other person's good as this person's rational self-love would require" (*TJ* 166). In this stage, where the relationship between parent and child is hierarchical, the moral dimension of love appears in the form of "authority guilt." The feeling of guilt arises when there is a violation of love and the trust that accompanies love. Rawls states that where there is no authority guilt this would show that love is absent. Thus, the clearly moral sentiment of guilt is a necessary condition for the presence of love. Furthermore, authority guilt gives rise to the desire to repair the love relationship through confession on the part of the violator and forgiveness on the part of the transgressed. This then is the first stage in the development of a sense of justice. The subsequent stages following the morality of authority are the morality of association and the morality of principles. Together these stages combine to result in a citizen's capacity to be motivated by the reasons of justice. The capacity to love is therefore at the base of our moral sentiments and necessary for a sense of justice.

Alongside this argument on the moral feelings is a suggestive analogy Rawls draws between love and justice. He points to the unavoidable "liabilities" that confront the person who loves. He says that love makes a person a "hostage to misfortune" and is liable to be "ruinous." The point of these remarks is not to express pessimism about love but to emphasize the case that love, like justice, is not merely a matter of rational choice but rather a commitment that has uncertain consequences. Love cannot be a matter of rational calculation and remain love. Rawls says, "there is no such thing as loving while being ready to consider whether to love" (*TJ* 502). Likewise, justice cannot be a matter of rational calculation, a mere *modus vivendi* in the language of his later work. Thus, to act justly is to take on a commitment and to bear the outcomes, good as well as bad, that follow.

Rawls mentions the love of mankind in several passages in *A Theory of Justice*. In his critical discussion of classical utilitarianism he contrasts two understandings of what the love of mankind might mean. One understanding is a general benevolence toward mankind as a whole. Rawls rejects this understanding by arguing that where people's interests conflict the attitude of general benevolence is "at sea" unless it combines and amalgamates all interests into a single register, as classical utilitarianism does. Rawls famously rejects this move arguing instead for the separateness of persons and concludes that a love of mankind, properly respectful of the distinctiveness of individuals, would incorporate the two principles of justice arrived at in the original position. Rawls goes on to say that the love of mankind while continuous with a sense of justice is not identical with it. The love of mankind is more comprehensive and "prompts acts of supererogation" that a sense of justice does not.

Feminist critics have taken issue with a variety of claims Rawls makes about the place of the family in his account of justice. Of particular relevance here is Rawls's claim that although the family, in some form, is one of the basic institutions of society it should not be directly governed by the two principles of justice. Instead Rawls proposes that in the end we must trust the "natural affection and goodwill of parents" (*JF* 165) to ensure that family members are treated justly. This is not to say that the state cannot intervene should violations occur, but that the default is to allow the natural capacities for love and trust to govern relations between family members.

Finally, Rawls's recently published Princeton senior undergraduate thesis contains an extensive discussion of the concept of Christian love (*BIMSF*). This work examines the notion of *agape*, focusing largely on the work of the theologian Anders Nygren. The text is suggestive of links between Rawls's youthful discussion of Christian love as spontaneous, unmotivated, and bereft of rational explanation, and his use of the idea of love in *A Theory of Justice*.

Paul Voice

SEE ALSO:

> *Congruence*
> *Feminism*
> *Guilt and shame*
> *Moral psychology*
> *Moral sentiments*
> *Religion*
> *Sense of justice*

126.

LUCK EGALITARIANISM

THE TERM *luck egalitarianism* was originally coined by Elizabeth Anderson in her "What Is the Point of Equality?" (1999). Luck egalitarianism, she writes, is "the view that the fundamental aim of equality is to compensate people for undeserved bad luck – being born with poor native endowments, bad parents, and disagreeable personalities, suffering from accidents and illness, and so forth." As a result, luck egalitarianism is focused on eliminating "the impact of brute luck from human affairs" (Anderson 1999, 288). More generally, the focus on *involuntary* inequalities is the commitment of authors Anderson described as luck egalitarian: principally G. A. Cohen and Ronald Dworkin, but also Richard Arneson, Eric Rakowski, as well as John Roemer (a list to which we might add Larry Temkin). *Involuntary* inequalities are those that do not appropriately reflect the choices of those who suffer them. A distinction is thus established between inequalities which are a result of choices agents are responsible for and inequalities which are the result of bad brute luck. Justice demands that the impact on people of the latter form of inequalities be eliminated, or at least lessened. Luck egalitarians believe that equality is one of our essential political values; and a proper understanding of this value states that it is bad that some, through no fault or choice of theirs, are worse off than others. (Contrast the Rawlsian claim that inequalities are unjust if they do not benefit the least well off.)

Initially used by Anderson to bundle together a number of egalitarian authors whose views she wished to criticize for their emphasis "on correcting a supposed cosmic injustice," the term *luck egalitarianism* is not embraced by all of the authors she grouped under this label. G. A. Cohen is happy to borrow the term luck egalitarianism to describe his view, namely that "accidental inequality is unjust" (Cohen 2008, 8). However, the same is not true of Ronald

Dworkin, even though the critics of luck egalitarianism consider that Dworkin's, no less than Cohen's views, are definitional of luck egalitarianism. See, in particular Anderson, but also Samuel Scheffler's "What is Egalitarianism?" (2003b); Dworkin denies that he is a luck egalitarian in his "Equality, Luck and Hierarchy," (Dworkin 2003).

In addition to their relation to the label, authors characterized as luck egalitarians have many other fundamental disagreements. Which inequalities are to be considered involuntary is an object of dispute among them. Moreover, there isn't even concordance on the claim that "the purpose of egalitarianism is to *eliminate* involuntary inequalities" (Cohen 1989, 916). Again, Ronald Dworkin, for one, would deny that this is the goal of his egalitarianism. This is illustrated by Cohen's and Dworkin's respective attitudes to expensive tastes. Welfare deficits which result from *unchosen* expensive tastes are treated on a par with handicaps by Cohen and other luck egalitarians; whereas Dworkin refuses to subsidize expensive tastes, whether chosen or not. It seems intuitively unfair, he presses, to impose the cost of one's preferences on others. Arguably, this attitude to expensive tastes aligns Dworkin more with Rawls's refusal to accommodate expensive tastes in the distribution of primary goods than with pure luck egalitarians. Be that as it may, the crucial point is that for the form of luck egalitarianism represented by Dworkin, justice does not require the removal or reduction of *all* types of involuntary inequalities. Alternatively, if Cohen provides the canonical definition of luck egalitarianism with the cited formula that "accidental inequality is unjust," then authors such as Dworkin are not strictly speaking luck egalitarians.

Is there still a recognizable family of views here? If there is, it is to be identified by the focus on brute luck, and not by what is taken to follow in terms of compensation, nor by the definition of injustice. Dworkin stands as one of the main proponents of an egalitarianism focused on choice and luck in virtue of his now canonical distinction between inequalities that are traceable to "brute luck" and those which are the result of "option luck," where the latter are risks we choose to undertake and are responsible for. Equality, for Dworkin, consists in equal opportunity to insure against bad luck, rather than in an ideal state of affairs in which brute inequality has been eliminated. What justice requires, in his view, is not that brute luck (inequalities deriving from unchosen circumstances) be eliminated or compensated for, but rather that people be given the equal opportunity to insure, and so provide in advance, against them. Through equal opportunities for insurance against bad luck, we transform many inequalities into *option* luck, that is: differentials that are the upshot of a *chosen* gamble (Dworkin 1981, 293; and 2000, 76). This distinction between option luck and brute luck, between how deliberate gambles turn out and how risks which are not deliberate gambles fall out, might be considered the essential definitional element of luck egalitarianism. Thus Cohen famously claims that Dworkin "has, in effect, performed for egalitarianism the considerable service of incorporating within it the most powerful idea in the arsenal of the antiegalitarian right: the idea of choice and responsibility" (Cohen 1989, 933). And this focus on the distinction between brute and option luck, in turn, explains why Dworkin should be classified by many as a core luck egalitarian, despite his explicit rejections of the label.

Luck egalitarianism might thus be considered to be no more than a loosely bundled family of views. Its common core, nonetheless, can be defined as the ambition to delineate a responsibility- and choice-based form of egalitarianism. Luck egalitarians hold that it is objectionable, at least to some extent, for some to be worse off than others through no fault, or choice, of their own. If one person is worse off than another through no fault or choice of her own, luck egalitarians consider that the situation is unfair, and hence that the inequality between the two people is objectionable. This focus on the value of fairness seems well summarized by Larry Temkin's claim that egalitarians "generally believe that it is bad for some to be worse off than others through no fault or choice of their own. The connection between equality and comparative fairness explains both the importance, and limits, of the 'no fault or choice' clause" (Temkin 2003, 62). The emphasis on equality, fairness, and the fate of the least well off all seems to echo core Rawlsian concerns. At the same time, luck egalitarians are all critical of Rawlsian egalitarianism.

There are two ways in which luck egalitarianism relates critically to Rawls. (a) On the one hand, it is seen by its proponents as a superior form of egalitarianism, free of what is considered problematic in Rawls's theory, namely the insensitivity of the difference principle to the distinction between inequalities which are created by voluntary choices and those which are the result of bad brute luck. (b) On the other hand, Rawls's focus on fairness and on "inequalities which are arbitrary from a moral point of view" is often presented as a commitment to eliminating arbitrary inequalities. According to this second reading, Rawls endorses one of the core elements of luck egalitarianism: justice demands that we even out the effects of brute luck. Is luck egalitarianism a rival theory, or a more coherent Rawlsian doctrine? As we shall see, luck egalitarians make both claims.

In *Anarchy, State, and Utopia*, Nozick accuses Rawls of arguing for economic egalitarianism by overemphasizing social contingencies and natural chance, and underestimating the centrality and importance of individual responsibility and autonomy. Luck egalitarians may seem to echo and endorse this criticism. Recall that Rawls's difference principle stipulates that social and economic inequalities are just if they are to the greatest benefit of the least-advantaged members of society. In so stipulating the difference principle, Rawls does not introduce a distinction between inequalities deriving from choices people have voluntarily made, and social and economic inequalities which derive from *unchosen* features of those who are disadvantaged relative to others.

Picking up and expanding on Nozick's criticism, luck egalitarians complain:

(i) that the difference principle inappropriately rewards those who are responsible for their deficit in primary goods, e.g. those able-bodied who choose not to work, or to work less hard than others, and

(ii) that the index of primary goods used in the difference principle is insensitive to, and fails to compensate for, disadvantages some suffer relative to others through no fault of their own. That is, Rawls accepts as just a distribution in which some are disadvantaged through brute luck, e.g. because they are handicapped or severely ill.

If the focus is on these two complaints, then luck egalitarianism aims at defining an *alternative*, more robust, form of egalitarianism by accommodating such concerns with responsibility for the outcome of one's choices, and with deficits which are the effects of bad brute luck.

The second manner in which luck egalitarianism could be related to Rawls's work contrasts with this first line of criticism. From this second viewpoint, the core concern of luck egalitarianism with involuntary inequalities is continuous with Rawls's insistence on fairness and his focus on inequalities which are "morally arbitrary." The question luck egalitarians raise is how to reconcile the Rawlsian emphasis on arbitrary inequalities with the exact formulation of Rawlsian egalitarian principles of justice. Luck egalitarianism seeks to offer such a reconciliation. By demanding that no one be disadvantaged, or advantaged, by arbitrary factors they aim to define an egalitarianism truer to the focus on fairness, and so more Rawlsian than Rawls, so to speak. More precisely, there are two supposed inconsistencies, internal to Rawlsian theory, that luck egalitarianism aims at resolving:

(i) On the one hand, the difference principle is, as mentioned, insensitive to the choice/luck distinction. However, Rawls seems to make use precisely of this distinction when he argues that the system of natural liberty unjustly allows "natural and social contingencies" to have a strong impact on distribution:

Luck egalitarianism / 475

"[I]ntuitively, the most obvious injustice [of that system] is that it permits distributive shares to be improperly influenced by these factors so *arbitrary from a moral point of view*" (*TJ* 62–63).

(ii) On the other hand, Rawls stresses the "capacity to take responsibility for our ends" and considers it unjust to give a greater share of primary goods to those with expensive taste: "[I]t is regarded as *unfair* that [those with less expensive taste] should have less in order to spare others from the consequences of their lack of foresight and self-discipline" ("Social Unity and Primary Goods", *CP* 369–370). This treatment of expensive tastes is famously read by G. A. Cohen through luck egalitarian lenses thus: "People with expensive tastes could have chosen otherwise, and if and when they press compensation, others are entitled to insist that they themselves bear the cost 'of their lack of foresight or self-discipline'" (Cohen 1989, 913).

One can respond to both the internal and external criticisms of Rawls here. A proper understanding of the exegetical points does not lead beyond Rawls to the luck egalitarian position. And luck egalitarianism is neither a convincing alternative to Rawls, nor a plausible elaboration of the intuitions which ground political egalitarian movements.

First, luck egalitarians are mistaken to think that they can best Rawls at his own game. How can Rawls's principles, and in particular the difference principle, be made consistent with what Rawls himself says about moral arbitrariness, and about natural talents, expensive tastes, and self-discipline? Does Rawls rely on premises regarding choice and luck, which the formulation of his principles then contradicts? To these questions, Rawlsians briskly retort that Rawls's arguments support his own principles rather than luck egalitarianism. "[T]he best explanation of the fact that Rawls's theory of justice does not respect the distinction between choice and circumstances," Scheffler writes, "is that Rawls is not attempting to respect it. He simply does not regard the distinction as having the kind of fundamental importance that it has for luck egalitarians" (Scheffler 2003b, 7; see also Scanlon 2006).

Let us note that Rawls clearly denies that inequalities which are the result of genetic and social luck are unjust, or that they ought to be eliminated: "The natural distribution is neither just nor unjust; nor is it unjust that persons are born into society at some particular position. These are simply natural facts. What is just or unjust is the way that institutions deal with these facts" (*TJ* 87). He thus distinguishes between his theory and what he calls "a principle of redress," that is "the [luck egalitarian] principle that undeserved inequalities call for redress"

(*TJ* 100). Rawls further explains that "the difference principle is not of course the principle of redress. It does not require society to try to even out handicaps as if all were expected to compete on a fair basis in the same race" (*TJ* 101).

Why, then, does Rawls emphasize the "moral arbitrariness" of facts such as natural endowments and social factors? Justice, for Rawls, may not demand the elimination of all effects of bad brute luck; nevertheless, he stresses that a society which systematically disadvantages some of its members on the basis of morally arbitrary factors, such as their natural endowments or the social environment in which they are born, *is* unjust. This type of morally arbitrary discrimination can happen through overt exclusion, but also simply because contingent social factors happen to favor an ethnic, gender, or social group in the distribution of resources. A just society, according to Rawls, addresses these injustices at the outset, by redistributing to ensure for all fair and favorable background conditions.

The priority of fair background conditions and the role of our institutions in insuring that they are in place is thus what lies behind the Rawlsian emphasis on the moral arbitrariness of certain factors. It constitutes an explanation and defence of the difference principle. To those who claim that they did nothing but work hard without violating anybody's rights, or that they competed in conditions of formal equality of opportunity for positions which required certain talents, and so ought to reap the rewards of their efforts, Rawls responds that "the kind of limits and provisos that in Locke's view apply to separate transactions of individuals and associations in the state of nature are not stringent enough to ensure that fair background conditions are maintained" (*JF* 53).

A just society for Rawls is not one that meets luck egalitarian requirements, but rather one in which each person is given the opportunities to develop their abilities, and can do so with the guarantee of fair equality of opportunities with others similarly talented and inclined. (See Freeman 2007b, 98, 449.) What matters is not that the consequences of bad brute luck be as far as possible eliminated, nor that life chances be evened out (which, among other things, would require the abolition of the family: see *TJ* 448 and Munoz-Dardé 1998), nor a fortiori that our expensive tastes, however acquired, be satisfied in the same measure as those of others. What matters is that all have enough resources to satisfy their interest in pursuing a good life.

In sum, then, there is no internal tension of the sort identified by luck egalitarians in the Rawlsian account. Nor, *pace* luck egalitarians, is there any need to reincorporate individual responsibility into that story. In brief, all individuals have two types of responsibilities: first to contribute to maintaining favorable

Luck egalitarianism / 477

background social circumstances; second, to make a sensible use of their share of primary goods, without imposing unreasonable demands on others.

Leaving their connection to Rawlsian principles aside, are luck egalitarians truer to our intuitive ideals of equality than Rawls? There is no compelling case for this. By comparison with a view focused on compensating people for undeserved bad luck, Rawlsian egalitarianism is more theoretically ambitious. Instead of the main emphasis on choice and luck, it aims at finding room for the multiple values which a well-ordered society must attend to: respect for persons, needs, opportunities, fairness, solidarity, and so on. Politically, its perspective on individual responsibility aims at providing a feasible utopia. It does not ask society to aim at the compensation of all disadvantages that derive from unchosen features, all accidental inequalities (something that cannot be fully delivered anyway). Nor does it have the sometimes implausibly harsh consequence that people should bear the full price of their choices, and be denied compensation for disadvantages that result from these choices. The Rawlsian account constitutes a multifaceted theoretical take on the political ideal of equality. In line with that ideal, it explains and motivates the need to eliminate many types of unjust inequalities. Moreover, a Rawlsian society is prepared to repair inequalities which are not purely the result of brute luck. Contrary to the contentions by luck egalitarians, a Rawlsian society measures up entirely to the standards of political egalitarianism in its distributional and social policies. Indeed, once one reflects on the concerns of political egalitarianism, a Rawlsian society arguably gets closer to their ends than any society guided by luck egalitarian policies would.

Véronique Munoz-Dardé

SEE ALSO:

Arneson, Richard
Cohen, G. A.
Desert
Difference principle
Dworkin, Ronald
Fair equality of opportunity
Primary goods, social
Redress, principle of

M

127.

THE MARKET

Rawls followed Hume in thinking that the rules of property and contract were institutional rules – social practices involving rules of conduct justified as a system, assuming general compliance (Hume 1978 [1738]). Rawls thus describes markets as one of the "major social institutions" that comprise the "basic structure of society" (*TJ* 6, 48). There are good reasons for having markets, but they are reasons that justify our collective choice of this institutional system. The market is not simply the consequence of interaction within the scope of individuals' natural moral rights, as argued by libertarians.

It might seem natural to suppose that the market is justified by the idea that people's relationships should be based on free agreement (*PL* 265); I shouldn't have to buy your product or sell you my labor unless we both agree to the transaction. This principle presupposes an account of the circumstances under which a transaction will count as genuinely voluntary, and fairly arrived at. While the necessary conditions may be in place at time 1, the accumulated results of many agreements may alter people's opportunities so that later the conditions for free and fair agreement are absent. It is impossible to forestall this possibility by putting additional requirements on individual transactions because the effects of any one agreement on "background justice" (*PL* 266) will normally make up only a small part of a long-term process. The institutions that make up the basic structure of society must therefore be designed to maintain the social conditions necessary for free and fair agreement to be possible. For example, without a social minimum (the responsibility of the "transfer branch"; *TJ* 244), some people might find themselves in situations in which they had no choice but to accept dangerous or degrading work. Only with the necessary background institutions in place can we say that the results of agreements are fair no matter what they are, as per the idea of "pure procedural justice" (*TJ* 243, 73–78).

Rawls assumed that all regimes would make use of the market for distributing consumer goods, i.e. individuals or households would be allowed to make their own decisions about what to purchase. The major divide in the twentieth century was over the role of the market in allocating resources across different productive tasks. Command systems attempt to impose central control on production and investment, whereas market systems allow prices to determine output of commodities and allocation of resources. Market systems need not involve private ownership of the means of production, however. Rawls thought that at least in principle the function of allocating resources to different productive activities could be separated from the function of distributing income to individuals, permitting market socialism to benefit from the efficiency of the market without its tendency toward inequality and class domination (*TJ* 241–242). Rawls claimed that either market socialism or what he called "property-owning democracy" could be compatible with his own two principles, depending on the empirical circumstances of the society in question. The distinctive feature of a property-owning democracy, as compared to welfare-state capitalism, is that it includes measures designed to ensure that property is widely distributed, so that economic inequalities do not undermine the fair value of political liberty and fair equality of opportunity, which might be the case for inequalities satisfying the difference principle by itself. These measures (such as inheritance tax and perhaps progressive income tax) would be the responsibility of the "distribution branch" (*TJ* 245). The fact that an ideal property-owning system is feasible does not imply that actual societies that involve free markets and private property are just "or even tolerable" (*TJ* 242).

The separation Rawls speaks of between the allocative and distributive function of prices is not complete, however. In either market socialism or property-owning democracy, individual shares of income and wealth will to some extent depend upon the choices people make within the existing system of rules – for example, about how much to work, how much to save, what to purchase, and so on. Distributive justice therefore cannot characterize allocations of goods across specific persons, but only the system of rules within which they interact. Following the idea of pure procedural justice, when just institutions are in place, the distribution that results from the choices individuals make is just whatever it is. Yet justice in institutions is defined in terms of the distribution of income and wealth across the social positions a system makes available.

The market / 483

Rawls identified two main virtues of the market. First, at least given the necessary background institutions, it is consistent with equal liberty and fair opportunity, in that people have free choice of occupation (*TJ* 241). When markets are competitive, economic power is decentralized; individual households and firms can make their own decisions independently, without coercively enforced central direction. Second, perfectly competitive markets are Pareto efficient, and even imperfect markets are more efficient than the alternative of central planning (*TJ* 240). In contrast, even a well-designed legislature is never guaranteed to attain its objective (justice). Rawls notes that despite some similarities, "the ideal market process and the ideal legislative procedure are different in crucial respects" (*TJ* 316). One contrast is that while an ideal market is a "perfect" procedure with respect to efficiency, democracy is at best an imperfect procedure for justice (*TJ* 316). Another fundamental contrast is that while market actors are assumed to be "advancing their ends as the rules allow, and any judgment they make is from their own point of view" (*TJ* 316), political actors adopt a shared, public point of view from which to make their judgments concerning justice. "There seems to be no way of allowing them to take a narrow or group-interested standpoint of then regulating the process so that it leads to a just outcome" (*TJ* 317).

Rawls explicitly rejected justifications of the market based on reward for individual merit. While his rejection of desert would come in for criticism by David Miller, Michael Sandel, and others, Rawls saw himself as building upon widely recognized truths about the functioning of market economies. Proponents of laissez-faire had defended the market on the grounds that the principle of reward according to marginal productivity was fair, not only useful in directing resources to their most efficient uses. Rawls followed the Chicago economist Frank Knight in denying that marginal productivity had any intrinsic ethical importance. The theory in question was that a competitive market tends to place productive resources where they can make the greatest possible addition to the total social dividend, "and tends to reward every participant in production by giving it the increase in the social dividend which its cooperation makes possible" (Knight 1923, 588). Knight accepted that this principle explained the actual distribution of income, in an approximately competitive market, but he denied that it constituted a sound ethical ideal. Productive contribution is not a measure of desert, Knight argued, because individual contribution includes the contribution of all of the tools or resources a person owns, and because prices depend on scarcity in relation to preferences given an ever-changing technological environment, which no one can predict with any accuracy (Knight 1923, 596–599). Rawls summarized these points by saying that the extent of one's contribution depends on supply and demand, and that a person's moral worth doesn't vary according to how many other people offer similar skills or happen to want what he can produce. "No one supposes that when someone's abilities are less in demand or have deteriorated (as in the case of singers) his moral deservingness undergoes a similar shift. All of this is perfectly obvious and has long been agreed to" (*TJ* 274). Knight's denial that the marginal productivity theory of distribution constitutes an ethical standard of desert would be taken up by his student Milton Friedman. Like Knight, Friedman recognized the important role that luck had to play in the market. "Most differences of status or position can be regarded as the product of chance at a far enough remove"; even the qualities of being hard-working and thrifty owe much to one's genetic makeup (Friedman 1962, 166). Of the principle guiding distribution of income in a market society – "to each according to what he and the instruments he owns produces" – Friedman said that "it cannot in and of itself be regarded as an ethical principle ... [but] must be regarded as instrumental or a corollary of some other principle such as freedom" (Friedman 1962, 161, 165). Friedrich Hayek reached similar conclusions about the incompability of distribution according to merit with the free market (Hayek 1960, 93–99). The principles chosen in the original position would license a market economy (duly circumscribed and embedded). Therefore, justice does not require distribution according to individual desert.

Rawls was aware that socialists criticized the market on a number of grounds: that it was degrading, since it involved people treating each other purely as means to their own ends; that it involved a lack of autonomy, since its results were not consciously willed and chosen; and more generally that it did not represent true emancipation, which would do away with the conditions that set people at odds with one another (*TJ* 248–249). Rawls's answer to the first objection was to concede that the market was not ideal, from the point of view of human relations, but to maintain that given the right surrounding institutions its imperfections were tolerable. It is crucial to recall that the results of market transactions are only just, according to Rawls, if the necessary background institutions are in place, e.g. equal basic liberties including fair value of political liberty, state-enforced equality of opportunity in economic activities, a government-guaranteed social minimum involving family allowances and special payments for sickness (*TJ* 243), macroeconomic measures designed to ensure reasonably full employment (*TJ* 244), public schools or subsidies for private schools (*TJ* 243, 245), and limits on inheritance and bequest (*TJ* 245), among others things. Rawls's answer to the autonomy objection was that a society's choice to rely on the market could be "perfectly reasoned and free," in the sense that the society could view its adoption of market institutions (duly circumscribed) as a choice correctly guided by principles of justice, rather than simply as a fatality, a fact of nature. Finally, Rawls conceded that property-owning democracy did not realize true emancipation, as envisaged by Marxists. However, he claimed that these critics envisaged a society that had transcended the circumstances of justice. Individuals may not be narrowly selfish, but there will always be conflicting interests over the design of social institutions and the division of the benefits of cooperation. "[A] society in which all can achieve their complete good, or in which there are no conflicting demands and the wants of all fit together without coercion into a harmonious plan of activity, is a society in a certain sense beyond justice" (*TJ* 249).

Andrew Lister

SEE ALSO:

Branches of government
Desert
Difference principle
The economy
Fair equality of opportunity
Legitimate expectations
Liberty, equal worth of
Procedural justice
Property-owning democracy

128.

MARX, KARL

A LTHOUGH RAWLS DOESN'T engage Marxism in his writings he does speak of Marx (1818–1883), and while Rawls certainly rejects much of what Marx (and later Marxists) claim, now that we have access to his *Lectures on the History of Political Philosophy*, published in 2007, we know that he had a high respect for Marx as a theorist and seems to have agreed with much of Marx's general labor theory of value (or, more accurately, Marx's theory of surplus labor or surplus social product), as well as with his theories of the nature of class societies, exploitation, and ideology. (However, this does not include Marx's *specific* labor theory of value which claims that prices in equilibrium market conditions are determined by the socially necessary labor time presently required to produce them.) (See Cohen 1979, 23–29, 433–436; Peffer 1990.)

Rawls writes that Marx

> turned to economics to clarify and to deepen his ideas only after he was about 28 years old. It is testimony to his marvelous gifts that he succeeded in becoming one of the great 19th-century figures of that subject, to be ranked along with Ricardo and [J. S.] Mill, Walras and Marshall. He was a self-taught, isolated scholar...Given the circumstances of Marx's life, his achievement as an economic theorist and political sociologist of capitalism is extraordinary and heroic. (*LHPP* 319)

> It may be thought that with the recent collapse of the Soviet Union, Marx's socialist philosophy and economics are of no significance today. I believe this would be a serious mistake for two reasons at least. The first reason is that while central command socialism, such as reigned in the Soviet

Union, is discredited – indeed, it was never a plausible doctrine – the same is not true of liberal [market] socialism... The other reason for viewing Marx's socialist thought as significant is that laissez-faire capitalism has grave drawbacks, and these should be noted and reformed in fundamental ways. Liberal socialism, as well as other views [e.g. justice as fairness and property-owning democracy], can help clear our minds as to how these changes are best done. (*LHPP* 323)

In its most general sense Rawls means by "liberal socialism" a democratic, politically liberal, constitutional government conjoined to an economy that has extensive markets for both production and consumer goods but in which the preponderance of large-scale enterprises are publicly owned (in one sense or another). Following John Roemer at this point, though, Rawls adds to his characterization of liberal socialism that the enterprises can be "worker-owned... or, in part, also public-owned through stock shares, and managed by elected or firm-chosen managers" (*LHPP* 323) and also that it is characterized by "A property system establishing a widespread and a more or less even distribution of the means of production and natural resources" (*LHPP* 323). Arguably, these latter two properties are much too specific since there are many proposed variations of liberal socialism and not all of them have these properties.

Before examining what Rawls writes more specifically about Marx's theories in *LHPP*, first consider what he writes about Marx in his earlier works. First, Rawls cites Marx as one of many theorists who point out the widely held view that the social institutions of a society form the kind of persons that people become in those societies (*TJ* 229; *JF* 121–122). Rawls also recruits both Marx and J. S. Mill as allies in arguing that specifying material income and wealth as a primary social good does not introduce an individualistic bias into Rawls's strategy of the original position as a means of justifying a theory of social justice for large-scale societies in the modern era. He claims that Marx and Mill both assert that material wealth – whether held by individuals or by communities as public goods – is essential for a good and just society (*CP* 273). Similarly, Rawls recruits both Marx and Mill as (supposed) supporters of the sociological theses that "primary goods are socially strategic" because "given a just distribution of primary goods, individuals and associations can protect themselves against the remaining institutional forms of injustice" (*CP* 276).

Second, along with Nietzsche and Freud, Marx puts forward considerations that may cast doubt on our common sense moral precepts and beliefs. Although Rawls doesn't specify what he has in mind here, presumably it is Marx's theory of ideology and other aspects of his thought that encouraged the Marxist "anti-moralism" view that Allen W. Wood, Richard Miller *et al.* promulgated in the 1980s and 90s.

In relation to his theory of ideology, Marx reminds us that we must always ask ourselves if a particular moral or political theory or perspective is just an ideological justification of the social status quo (*JF* 4 n.4, 29). This is required by Rawls's method of wide reflective equilibrium.

More specifically, Marx's theory of ideology attempts to account for the fact that people living in capitalist societies do not normally realize that it is a system of exploitation and domination in which surplus value – or, better, surplus labor or surplus social product – is systematically (and presumably unfairly) created by the working class but (disproportionally) expropriated by the capitalist class (and landlords). This is Marx's theory of capitalist exploitation (*TJ* 271–272 n.34; *LHMP* 100).

And whereas Hegel calls on us to understand and then accept (or become "reconciled to") the social status quo since it is "rational" from the point of view of the development of the *Weltgeist* (world spirit) at the level of human culture and civilization, Marx calls on us to understand a class society we may find ourselves in but then to change it (if it is not a "rational" or just society) (*LHMP* 336). This is memorialized in Marx's 11th thesis in his *Theses on Feuerbach* (1845, but not published until 1888): "Philosophers have so far only sought to understand the world; but the point is to change it."

This is connected to Marx's general critique of liberalism as an ideological cover for capitalism (*TJ* 249 n.18; *JF* 148). Marx also more specifically objects to capitalism on grounds that its civil and political liberties are merely formal (*JF* 176–178) and not of nearly equal worth to members of different classes. Rawls, of course, addresses this issue by demanding that at least the political liberties (and those related to due process) must be of approximately equal worth or have fair value, as well as be formally equal.

But Marx's second or "higher" state of communism is beyond the circumstances of justice – namely, moderate material scarcity and moderate egoism – in that it is specified by Marx to be characterized by super-material abundance and the transformation of human nature into much more altruistic, peaceful, cooperative, benevolent natures of all individuals (*TJ* 268 n.32). Therefore, traditional standards of justice do not apply to it. Marx claimed that the principle that would characterize such a society is "From each according to his ability; to each according to his needs" where by "needs" in this context Marx means anything and everything people need for their maximum self-realization or self-development. This is connected to Marx's theory of human flourishing which suggests that people would want to (and, in the higher stage of communism, would be able to) develop all or at least a great many of their natural talents and abilities to a very high degree. But no one can develop all of their natural talents and abilities to a high degree because all normal humans have indefinitely many natural talents and abilities and must choose which ones to spend time on to develop them (*TJ* 459–460 n.4; *JF* 157).

Rawls also claims that Marx's maxim concerning abilities and needs could be realized if Rawls's difference principle was supplemented by a head tax on people's natural talents and abilities (which normally translates into potential earning capacities in modern, mass societies) (*TJ* 459–460 n.4; *CP* 252). But this seems dubious given that Marx thought of this principle as only applying within societies that had transcended the circumstances of justice.

We know that Rawls paid attention to ongoing developments in Marxist (and neo-Marxist) theory. In the Editor's Preface to *LHPP* Samuel Freeman states that in his lectures of the early 1980s "Rawls endorsed the position (held by Allen Wood, among others) that Marx did not have a conception of justice…but he revises that position [in his later lectures on Marx] under the influence of G. A. Cohen and others" (*LHPP* x) to the view that "Marx did condemn capitalism. On the other hand, he did not see himself as doing so [because]…Marx's implicit comments about justice interpret the concept in a narrow way…" (*LHPP* 336).

Moreover, according to Freeman, "Rawls's interpretation of the Labor Theory of Value seeks to separate its outmoded economics from what he regards as its main aim. He construes it as a powerful response to the Marginal Productivity Theory of Just Distribution and other classical liberal and right-wing libertarian conceptions which regard pure ownership as making a tangible contribution to production" (*LHPP* x).

Rawls outlines the essential components of Marx's general (transhistorical) theory of surplus social product, classes, and exploitation and then specifically applies it to capitalist societies (with the addition of a thesis concerning the hidden nature of capitalist exploitation). "The societies Marx studied were ones he called class societies. These are societies in which the social surplus – the total product of surplus labor or unpaid labor – is appropriated by one class of persons in virtue of their position in the social system" (*LHPP* 323).

> Now it is a fact about class societies that the total value added is not shared solely by those who produce it, but large shares are also received by people who either perform no labor at all, or else their shares are far in excess of what their labor time would warrant…Marx thinks [this]…is hidden from view under capitalism; and so we need a theory, he thinks, of how

this happens in a system of personal independence in which contracts are agreed to between ostensibly free and equal economic agents. (*LHPP* 329)

The point of the labor theory of value is to penetrate beneath the surface appearances of the capitalist order and to enable us to keep track of the expenditures of labor time and to discern the various institutional devices by which surplus or unpaid labor is extracted from the working class and in what amounts. (*LHPP* 331)

[It] concerns the fundamental controversy about the nature of capitalist product. Contrary to the dominant neo-orthodox view, which stresses the parity of the claims of land, capital and labor, and therefore the parity of the claims of landlords, capitalists, and laborers, Marx puts forward the central and basic role of the working class under the capitalist mode of production as under previous such modes. The aim of the theory is to highlight the main features of capitalism as a mode of production that are hidden from view by the parity of the capitalists in market relations of exchange. All this is by way of providing what Marx thought was a truly scientific basis for condemning capitalism as a system of domination and exploitation. (*LHPP* 331)

Strangely, in contradiction to what he says in his lectures on Marx about these aspects of Marx's theory both before and after the following quote, Rawls also writes:

I do not think the labor theory of value is successful. Indeed, I think Marx's view can better be stated without using this theory at all. In saying this I accept the view of Marglin, and many other present-day Marxist economists, who do not regard the labor theory of value either as sound or as essential. Sometimes it is insufficient; at other times, even when sufficient, it is superfluous. (*LHPP* 331)

Apparently, Rawls takes this position on the basis that, interpreted as a *factual* statement, Marx's claim that labor is the only source of value (and surplus value) cannot be substantiated. Here he refers to Roemer's proof of the Generalized Commodity Exploitation Theorem which shows:

we can, if we like, attribute the total output [of an economy] to capital, or to land … In this case, land or capital, whichever we pick, produces more than is necessary to reproduce itself and so it yields a surplus. If, as factors of production, capital, land and labor are to be viewed as perfectly symmetrical, we can indeed do this. (*LHPP* 351)

Nevertheless, Rawls clearly agrees with Marx that *from a normative point of view* labor is *not* on par with land and capital.

[Marx] thinks that human labor is the sole factor of production that is relevant from a social point of view in considering the justice of economic institutions. This being so, pure profit, interest, and rent, as returns of pure ownership, are to be attributed to labor...Thus, I take Marx to say that when we step back from the various modes of production that have existed historically, and which will exist, we must of course recognize that capital and land are productive. But from the point of view of the members of society, as they might consider together these modes of production, the only relevant social resource is their combined labor. What concerns them is how social and economic institutions are to be organized so that they can cooperate on fair terms and use their combined labor effectively with the forces of nature in ways to be decided by society as a whole. (*LHPP* 351)

Therefore, for him pure economic rent of property ownership is unjust because it in effect denies just claims to access and use, and any system instituting such rent is a system of domination and exploitation. And this is why he describes capitalists' appropriation of the product of surplus labor by such terms as robbery and embezzlement, forced labor and theft. (*LHPP* 352)

It is this fundamental insight that leads Rawls throughout his work to insist that there is no natural (fundamental moral) right to either the private or public ownership of large-scale productive property and that this question can only be decided by ascertaining which set of property relations will best meet the principles of justice in particular historical circumstances. In this context, Rawls believes it important to distinguish between the "allocative and distributive roles of prices...In capitalism these prices do have a distributive role, and it is this role that characterizes...pure ownership" (*LHPP* 350). On the other hand, "prices under socialism do not correspond to income paid to private persons. Instead, the prices imputed to natural resources and collective assets have no distributional role" (*LHPP* 350). Thus, it is arguable that although Rawls chooses not to use Marx's terminology in his works, he does not fundamentally disagree with Marx's theory of surplus labor and exploitation, even though he presumably had fundamental disagreements on much else in Marx and the Marxist tradition.

Rodney G. Peffer

SEE ALSO:

Cohen, G. A.
The economy
Hegel, G. W. F.
Liberal conception of justice
The market
Property-owning democracy
Socialism

129.

MAXIMIN RULE OF CHOICE

MAXIMIN IS A rule for making choices under conditions of uncertainty (or risk), that is, when one must select from a range of options, each one of which may result in various outcomes. Maximin says that one should identify the worst possible outcome for each option, and then select the option for which the worst outcome is least bad. It thus represents an extremely risk-averse or pessimistic standard of choice. Rawls recognizes that it is "clearly...not, in general, a suitable guide for choices under uncertainty" (*TJ* 133). However, he argues that because of the highly unusual features of the original position, it can be "useful as a heuristic device" (*TJ* 132) to think of the parties there selecting principles of justice on that basis.

Although it is sometimes assumed that Rawls simply stipulates that the parties would accept maximin reasoning, this is not the case. As he pointed out in a 1974 article, such a stipulation "would indeed have been no argument at all" (*CP* 247). There are three main features of the original position that push the parties toward a very risk-averse choice, represented by maximin reasoning. First, the veil of ignorance prevents the parties from assigning probabilities to the various possible outcomes. They have no basis for estimating the likelihood that they will find themselves in each of the various social positions when the veil is lifted. Indeed, because they are choosing fundamental principles of justice and not institutional arrangements directly, they do not have much of a basis for determining what the various social positions will be, let alone the likelihood that they will occupy any one in particular. Second, the parties are much more concerned with ensuring that certain basic interests are satisfied than they are with the prospects of additional gains above this level. Finally, the worst outcomes of some of their possible choices fall below this minimal level. That is, some of the conceptions that they might choose fail to ensure the protection of their basic interests.

The basic interests at stake involve the development and protection of the two moral powers – the capacity for a sense of justice and the capacity for a conception of the good sense of justice – together with ensuring a share of resources necessary to protect basic needs. The protection of these "higher-order interests" at the level necessary to be a fully participating member in a scheme of social cooperation takes absolute precedence over any possible gains above that level. Rawls argues that ensuring an equal scheme of basic liberties is necessary, either directly or indirectly, for protecting these interests. Therefore the parties would reject any conception that fails to, or might fail to protect the basic liberties, no matter what other advantages it might have, for example, by increasing the prospects for a high level of material well-being. Similarly, they would reject any conception that fails to ensure a share of resources necessary to be a fully participating member of society. Even if in many or most circumstances utilitarianism would tend to support basic liberties and a minimal share of resources for all, such support is contingent and based on highly complex and uncertain calculations. The possibility that they might be left without adequate protection or resources – the worst case scenario under utilitarianism – is enough to lead the parties to reject it and accept the two principles instead.

Another way to make the point is to say that the parties must make their agreement in good faith, with the sincere expectation that they will be able to act in accordance with the principles no matter where they find themselves when the veil is lifted. However, they cannot reasonably be expected to comply with principles that might require them to sacrifice their fundamental interests and capacity to participate fully in society. The "strains of commitment" in complying with such principles would be too great.

There is a structural similarity between maximin and the difference principle since each requires us to focus on the least-advantaged position or outcome. (While maximin is a strategy for choice under uncertainty, the difference principle is a standard for evaluating social institutions.) This may have led to the widespread assumption that Rawls relies on maximin reasoning to support the difference principle. This is not the case, however (*JF* 43 n.3, 94–95). The higher order interests are protected not by the difference principle but by the first principle and the guarantee of material resources to satisfy our basic needs. As Rawls uses the term, a "liberal political conception" of justice specifies certain basic rights, liberties, and opportunities; assigns special priority to these rights, liberties, and opportunities; and ensures adequate resources to make effective use of these rights and opportunities (*PL* 6). Justice as fairness is one such conception, but there are others, including the mixed conception that accepts the first principle of justice, and fair equality of opportunity, but substitutes for the difference principle utilitarianism constrained by a minimal floor. While the "maximin argument" shows the superiority of a liberal conception over utilitarianism, by itself it cannot show that any one of the liberal conceptions is superior to the others. There may be differences in the strains of commitment associated with the different liberal conceptions, but none will be so great that the parties could not select it in good faith. The grounds of comparison and choice among the liberal conceptions, and therefore, the defense of the difference principle, must be found elsewhere.

Jon Mandle

SEE ALSO:

Basic liberties
Difference principle
Higher-order interests
Liberal conception of justice
Mixed conceptions of justice
Moral person
The original position
Social minimum
Strains of commitment

130.

MIGRATION

MIGRATION IN RAWLS'S political philosophy is notable primarily because of its absence. During the late twentieth and early twenty-first centuries, issues of migration became prominent, both in political practice and in activist response to that practice. Rawls's work, however, contains very few explicit discussions of the issue of migration. Nevertheless, Rawls's work has been enormously influential in analyses of the justice of immigration, and an account of justice in immigration can also be found in some scattered remarks in Rawls's *The Law of Peoples*.

Rawls's domestic political philosophy assumes that migration does not exist; he assumes that an individual enters society at birth, and exits only at death (*TJ* 152; *PL* 12, 40). Rawls is, here, making a simplifying assumption, one that is justified with reference to his focus on justice in the basic structure of a particular society; he is not making the statement that migration in fact does not exist, nor that it does not stand in need of analysis from the standpoint of justice. Nevertheless, this is a striking assumption. Throughout his domestic work on political justice, he consistently ignores the issue of migration – with one small exception, when he argues that a just political community cannot prohibit emigration (*PL* 277). The issue of immigration, however, is ignored entirely.

This does not mean, however, that Rawls has not been influential in discussions of immigration. Early cosmopolitan interpreters of Rawls argued that Rawls had misinterpreted his own theory; Rawls should have applied his original position, and the two principles of justice that emerged, to the world as a whole, taken as a single basic structure for purposes of political justice. These cosmopolitans often focused on international distributive justice, but the consequence of such views for migration should be obvious. If Rawls was prepared to condemn restrictions on mobility within the domestic political society as unjust, he should have been similarly willing to condemn restrictions on mobility internationally. The right to move across national borders, on this account, was a simple implication of Rawls's first principle of liberty, once the proper scope of Rawls's principles was understood (Carens 1987). Alternatively, free movement could be justified with reference to the patterns of distributive justice it created. Rawls's difference principle was likely to demand significant reorganization of global institutions and rules; if our current patterns of exclusion had the effect of making the worst off less wealthy than they might be, then we had good reason to reject the institutions that created these results (Carens 1992).

Rawls rejected the cosmopolitan reading of his views; in *The Law of Peoples*, he developed an alternative approach to international distributive justice. This approach would have considerably more moderate implications for questions of immigration than would those of his cosmopolitan interpreters. The Law of Peoples is concerned primarily with the freedom and equality of peoples, rather than with individual persons. As such, the self-determination of peoples takes a primary role within Rawls's theory of international justice; the Society of Peoples is set up to ensure that each of its members is able to exercise its own powers of self-determination, without being unjustly coerced or dominated by others.

The analysis leads Rawls to acknowledge that there can be no general right to immigrate to the country one wishes to join; the self-determination of that society precludes it from having an obligation to admit all interested outsiders. Rawls makes this general case more specific, by tying it to two duties held by political communities: to care for a particular territory, and to protect and embody a particular political culture. In the first case, Rawls argues, a particular people is obliged to take care in perpetuity of a particular place – a fact which immediately demands a distinction between insider and outsider as regards that place (*LP* 8). In the second case, Rawls argues that a society includes a particular history, a particular political culture, and a moral nature that make it permissible for that society to refuse to admit unwanted outsiders (*LP* 111). Both of these, Rawls suggests, show that the centrality of self-determination makes any supposed general right to immigration implausible.

Rawls argues, further, that the "problem of immigration" results primarily from injustices that will not occur within the Society of Peoples: persecution of minorities; political oppression and famine resulting from this oppression; and population pressure in the home country. In the ideal case, immigration simply ceases to be a problem (*LP* 9). This suggests that, in the ideal case, Rawls believes each well-ordered state can simply refuse any unwanted immigrant. This impression is supported by Rawls's brief remark that the duty of assistance might include some constraints on the right to exclude outsiders (*LP* 39 n.48). Rawls does not develop this idea in any depth, but two things are worth noting. The first is that this remark only applies, as above, to cases involving nonideal circumstances; whatever migration rights are imagined would last only until the target of the duty of assistance is reached. The second is that nothing here even goes so far as to demand rights to immigration. If immigration entails the right to cross borders permanently – to make a home in a new society – it might be the case that Rawls would not defend a right to immigration even in a nonideal case; people can be protected by any number of more temporary border-crossings than full immigration status.

Rawls's mature picture of immigration, then, is much more restrictive than that painted by his cosmopolitan interpreters. Critics of Rawls's own analysis have tended to focus on his insistence that a "realistic utopia" could include several states, each of which utterly refused to allow outsiders to resettle within their borders. This, some commentators have argued, is a somewhat impoverished vision of the human needs and interests that have led people to seek to cross national borders (Benhabib 2004). Critics have also focused on his insistence that the protection of a culture and a place are sufficient reason to refuse admission to needy outsiders. Rawls's view, however, remains more a sketch than anything more substantive, and might be developed into a useful and attractive alternative to cosmopolitan views.

Michael Blake

SEE ALSO:

> *Basic structure of society*
> *Cosmopolitanism*
> *Law of Peoples*
> *Peoples*

131.

MILL, JOHN STUART

THANKS TO THE publication of *Lectures on the History of Political Philosophy*, we now have a much better understanding of Rawls's views on John Stuart Mill (1806–1873) and this strengthens the suggestion that Mill has always occupied a very special place in Rawls's thinking. Rawls sees Mill as supporting versions of utilitarianism and liberalism that are congenial to his own thinking and that have even inspired the development of justice as fairness and helped sharpen its arguments. Nonetheless, we must conclude that there are real limits to the rapprochement.

It is clear that, for Rawls, Mill is at a distance from the classical utilitarian doctrines of Bentham, Edgeworth, and Sidgwick ("the BES line" *LHPP* 375), even if he shares with Sidgwick a criticism of intuitionism and believes, like him, "that at some point we must have a single principle to straighten out and to systematize our judgments" (*TJ* 36). Even if Mill's perfectionism has been understood as a form of intuitionism, Rawls sees him as searching for first principles and an answer to the "priority problem" (*LHPP* 269).

More importantly for Rawls, Mill anticipates the classical distinction between act- and rule-utilitarianism and reckons that the principle of utility applies to "rules" and institutions as "practices" (*CP* 33–40) rather than solely to particular acts (*CP* 45–46). Rawls stresses that for Mill, in contrast to Bentham, political institutions constitute the basic framework of social life, "the very groundwork of our existence (Mill, *Utilitarianism*, v §25)" (*PL* 139; *JF* 189), a formula that anticipates Rawls's social ontology and the importance of the "basic structure of society" (*TJ* 6).

Mill thought that what is fundamental is not the consequences of particular laws taken one by one (although these are not, of course, unimportant), but the main institutions of society as a whole, as one system, as these are shaped by the legal order, and the kind of national character (Mill's term) that the institutions so shaped encourage. He was concerned to specify the idea of utility in line with the permanent interests of man as a progressive being so that the principle of utility would underwrite a social world congenial to human good. Similar reasoning characterizes the second argument for the two principles: the well-ordered society that realizes these two principles is a highly satisfactory social world because it encourages a political character that, by taking basic rights and liberties as settled once and for all, sustains the political virtues of social cooperation. (*JF* 119)

This is the reason why

we can think of Mill's 'principles of the modern world' (*Subjection of Women*, IV §2) as principles of political and social justice for the basic structure of society...necessary to protect the rights of individuals against the possible oppression of modern democratic majorities...and as very close to the content of the two principles of justice as fairness. (*LHPP* 267)

Moreover, Rawls insists that Mill's defense of average utilitarianism is much closer to his own principles of justice as fairness (*TJ* 140). He uses a utility function that is different from, but compatible with his own argument.

In specifying the rights of justice, there is no apparent reference to aggregate social well-being. When Mill identifies the essentials of human well-being or the elements of the groundwork of our existence, he does not do so via the idea of maximizing utility. He looks to individuals' basic needs and to what constitutes the very framework of their existence. (*LHPP* 277)

Rawls suggests that one way of reading Mill is to say that he uses a utility function that is possibly nonutilitarian, that is, which can be understood not in terms of subjective preference satisfaction, but of basic human needs and interests (*LHPP* 269 n.6). Finally, as a perfectionist, Mill, in contrast to Bentham's famous statement that all pleasures are equal, establishes a hierarchy of pleasures and pursuits that has inspired Rawls's use of a lexical ordering of principles (*TJ* 38).

The problem is, then, for Rawls "how does it happen that an apparently utilitarian view leads to the same substantive content as justice as fairness?"

(*LHPP* 267). Is Mill's conception of utility able to explain how it is that "equal rights are necessarily compatible with the greater social utility" (*LHPP* 278) and that "the political and social institutions that realize the principles of the modern world...are necessary to maximize social utility" (*LHPP* 280)? The question is raised in an early paper where Rawls is still utilitarian and tries to answer Mill's difficulties. He notes (*CP* 45) that in *A System of Logic* (VI, 12 §2), Mill distinguishes clearly between the two concepts of rules, rules as "generalizations from the decisions of individuals" (*CP* 36) and rules as "logically prior to particular cases" (*CP* 36), what Rawls calls the "practice conception of rules." Such a distinction should prevent the utilitarian principle from "accepting the infliction of suffering on innocent persons if it is for the good of society" (*CP* 25) because "a practice necessarily involves the abdication of full liberty to act on utilitarian and prudential grounds" (*CP* 36). Mill seems to be aware of this, as, for him, "having a right does not depend on the balance of utilities of particular cases, but rather on the rules of justice and their utility" (*LHPP* 275). "Yet, Mill also says that, if he is asked why we ought legally to protect the rights of justice, he can give no other reason than utility" (*LHPP* 277). This very failure is explored in "Two Concepts of Rules" and led Rawls eventually to abandon rule-utilitarianism and to build his own alternative defense of rights on the conception of persons not as satisfaction maximizers, but as free and equal moral human beings, which is central in democratic institutions and values.

In his mature work, Rawls clarifies his debt to Mill's "liberalism of freedom" (*LHMP* 330 and *LP* 127) as a source for his first principle of justice and for the defense of liberty of conscience. "As Mill would say (*On Liberty* II §5 and 2–9), we may seek to make our conception of the good our own; we are not content to accept it ready-made from our society or social peers" (*PL* 313). He follows Mill's famous distinction between higher and lower pleasures in the sense that, for a rational agent, interests and pleasures are not simply aggregated, but ranked in a plan of life (*TJ* §63). "The persons in the original position are moved by a certain hierarchy of interests...and, as Mill supposed, the higher-order interests become more intense and reveal their prior place" (*TJ* 476 and n.13). He sees a source for his Aristotelian principle in Mill's *Utilitarianism* as it "characterizes human beings as importantly moved not only by the pressure of bodily needs, but also by the desire to do things enjoyed simply for their own sakes" (*TJ* 374 n.20, 379).

Rawls is also inspired by Mill's moral psychology, in particular Mill's "principle of living in unity with others" (*LHPP* 280–283) as a principle of reciprocity (*TJ* 439), and stresses "the value of publicly shared common ends and of the state for the liberalism of freedom of Kant and Mill" (*LHMP* 366). Like Mill and

Humboldt, Rawls believes that "a well-ordered society is a social union of social unions" and that "a democratic society well-ordered by the two principles of justice can be for each citizen a far more comprehensive good than the determinate good of individuals when left to their own devices or limited to smaller associations. Participation in this more comprehensive good can greatly enlarge and sustain each person's determinate good" (*PL* 320; *TJ* §79).

Finally, there is a distinctive influence of Mill's later texts on socialism on Rawls, his critique of free markets and capitalism and his analysis of the stationary state of the economy. Rawls, for instance, insists that: "the difference principle does not require continual economic growth and is compatible with Mill's idea of a society in a just stationary state where real capital accumulation is zero" (*PL* 7 n.5). Even if feminism and the family do not attract enough attention in *TJ*, Rawls still recognizes Mill's enormous influence in adding these concerns to the list of questions of justice and rights (*JF* 166).

However, in Rawls's later work, the references to Mill are more sparse and he is only presented as an example of "comprehensive liberalism," serving as a contrast for Rawls's own political liberalism. Mill's liberalism is unable to serve as a basis for an overlapping consensus on justice because his doctrine of individuality along with the Greek ideal of self-development and the Christian ideal of self-government is perfectionist and incompatible with the "fact of pluralism" in modern societies (*PL* 199). Rawls claims that Mill is a paradoxical illustration, given his defense of liberty, of the dangers of "a society united on a reasonable form of utilitarianism or on the reasonable liberalisms of Kant or Mill, that would likewise require the sanctions of state power to remain so" (*PL* 37). Rawls calls this "the fact of oppression." "Even societies where everyone affirms the same reasonable liberal doctrine cannot long endure without state intervention" (*PL* 37 n.39).

Still, in Rawls's last work, *The Law of Peoples*, the influence of Mill's social ontology on the conception of international justice resurfaces, which is not surprising, given that for Rawls as for Mill, the primary subject of justice is not individual situations, but the basic structure of society. In the case of international justice, the subject matter is not the individual, as for cosmopolitan thinkers, but peoples. Peoples for both Mill and Rawls are more than collections of individuals. Besides their common political institutions, "citizens are united by what Mill called "common sympathies," says Rawls, mentioning Mill's *Considerations on Representative Government*, 1861, chapter XVI (*LP* 23 n.17). "I think of the idea of nation as distinct from the idea of government or state, and I interpret it as referring to a pattern of cultural values of the kind described by Mill" (*LP* 25 n.20).

Nonetheless, there are limits to any rapprochement between Rawls and Mill. One should note that the Millian concept of individuality plays no role in *TJ*, where it is replaced by the Kantian concept of autonomy as liberalism's main value. As an egalitarian, Rawls clashes with Mill's conception of self-development, even if Rawls's conception of society as a "social union of social unions" could appear close to the Humboldtian ideal that Mill adopts, that "only in a social union is the individual complete" (*TJ* 459 and n.4). However, Rawls adds the egalitarian proviso that "it is important not to confuse the idea of social union with the high value put upon human diversity and individuality as found in Mill's *On Liberty*" and that "in the limiting case where the powers of each are similar, the group achieves, by a coordination of activities among peers, the same totality of capacities latent in each" (*TJ* 459–460 n.4).

Finally, Rawls's conception of political and moral theory is at odds with Mill's doctrine which relies too much on the natural facts of human psychology in a way that runs the risk of naturalism, that weakens its conclusions and that, on the whole, is too optimistic, unable, in the end, to provide a suitable basis for ordering the various precepts of justice when they conflict (*LHPP* 269, 300).

Catherine Audard

SEE ALSO:

Family
Feminism
Intuitionism
Liberalism, comprehensive vs. political
Liberty of conscience
Peoples
Perfectionism
Precepts of justice
Reciprocity
Sense of justice
Sidgwick, Henry
Social union
Utilitarianism

132.

MIXED CONCEPTIONS OF JUSTICE

R AWLS CALLS A conception of justice a *mixed conception* when it combines his first principle, the principle of equal liberties, with a principle of distributive justice other than his second principle, such as average utility (*TJ* 107 and §49).

Mixed conceptions help clarify the justification of principles from the original position. Introduced briefly in *TJ*, the argument involving mixed conceptions is emphasized in the revised edition. In the preface to the 1999 edition, Rawls expresses regrets not to have presented the argument from the original position for the two principles of justice by way of a comparison with a mixed conception:

> It would have been better to present [the argument] in terms of two comparisons. In the first parties would decide between the two principles of justice, taken as a unit, and the principle of (average) utility as the sole principle of justice. In the second comparison, the parties would decide between the two principles of justice and those same principles but for one important change: the principle of (average) utility is substituted for the difference principle. (The two principles after this substitution I called a *mixed conception*, and here it is understood that the principle of utility is to be applied subject to the constraints of the prior principles: the principle of the equal liberties and the principle of fair equality of opportunity.) (*TJ* xiv, emphasis added)

In contrasting this mixed conception with justice as fairness, Rawls is able to separate out arguments for the equal basic liberties and their priority, and

Mixed conceptions of justice / 505

for fair equality of opportunity, from the argument for the difference principle. Rawls considers that the arguments for the equal basic liberties and their priority are very strong, and would be established by a first comparison between his two principles and an unconstrained principle of average utility as the sole principle of justice. (The principle of average utility says that the institutions of the basic structure are to be arranged so as to maximize the average welfare of the members of society.) The parties assume that they have an interest in the fulfillment of their moral and religious conceptions. The two principles protect the basic rights and liberties and provide an adequate complement of the primary goods to exercise and enjoy those freedoms. To agree to the principle of average utility might jeopardize those rights and liberties, in particular for minorities. Therefore the parties would not take this kind of risk. Furthermore, the basic liberties protect fundamental interests that have a special significance: thus the priority of the first principle over the second.

By contrast, Rawls considers that a second comparison, focused on advantages of the difference principle, involves more delicate considerations. In this second comparison Rawls's two principles of justice are contrasted with the same principles with one change: the principle of average utility combined with a social minimum is substituted for the difference principle. This *mixed conception* is the *principle of restricted utility*. The basic structure maximizes average utility, but under two constraints: first equal basic liberties and fair equality of opportunities are guaranteed, and second a suitable social minimum is also introduced. The social minimum is intended to meet essential human needs; its incorporation in the mixed conception makes the principle of restricted utility a particularly robust alternative to the two principles of justice. Rawls concedes that his two principles and a principle of restricted utility might not be very far apart if we restrict ourselves to the social policies which would result from the principles. In particular, the least well off are assured not only against denial of liberties or opportunities, but also against serious losses of well-being. Still, this might not be sufficient for the worst off to feel "that they are a part of political society" (*JF* 127). Therefore, the crucial consideration which weighs in favour of the difference principle over the principle of restricted utility is the Ralwsian idea of society as a fair system of cooperation. In a society arranged as a fair system of cooperation between citizens, a principle of reciprocity whereby those who are better off are not better off *to the detriment* of those who are worse off is superior to a maximizing principle such as average utility however constrained. This suggests that behind the veil of ignorance the parties would endorse the difference principle. That is: they would choose a principle whereby those who gain more do so on terms acceptable to those who gain the least. (Besides reciprocity, Rawls argues that other considerations such as publicity and stability also tell in favor of the difference principle over restricted utility; see *JF* 119ff.)

Why is it so important for Rawls to make the comparison between his principles and the mixed conception of restricted utility? First, because it allows us to understand more deeply the contrast between the utilitarian's conception of society as a system arranged to produce most good over all of its members and the Rawlsian idea of society as a fair system of cooperation. Second, because this comparison between a mixed conception and Rawls's two principles highlights that the argument for the difference principle does not rest, *pace* what Arrow, Harsanyi, and many others had thought, on aversion to risk, but rather on *reciprocity* between citizens regarded as free and equal.

Véronique Munoz-Dardé

SEE ALSO:

Arrow, Kenneth
Difference principle
Harsanyi, John
Maximin rule of choice
The original position
Perfectionism
Publicity
Social minimum
Two principles of justice (in justice as fairness)
Utilitarianism
Utility

133.

MORAL EDUCATION

As PART OF his wider discussion of the problem of the stability of the theory of justice as fairness, Rawls examines various aspects of the moral education of citizens. In considering this issue, he is concerned to show that a society that is effectively regulated by the two principles of justice is likely to persist over time. A necessary condition for such persistence is that the society continues to produce the right kind of support for its institutions in each new generation. Rawls argues that, given certain general features of human psychology, it is very likely that children who grow up surrounded by just institutions will develop a sense of justice – that is, a complex set of moral dispositions that favor compliance with the requirements of justice. Different social institutions will contribute at different times and in overlapping ways to the acquisition of a mature sense of justice, in both intentional and unintentional ways.

In *A Theory of Justice*, Rawls sketches a speculative account of moral learning and the underlying psychological processes that make it possible (*TJ* 397–419). This account of moral learning includes elements from a variety of psychological theories. But its main inspiration comes from the particular theories developed by Jean Piaget and Lawrence Kohlberg. These theories hold that moral development goes through a sequence of stages that require increasing cognitive development. Rawls agrees with this general framework. In his view early moral education takes place primarily in the context of the family. Assuming that the family is just, and that parents are loving and supportive, children will naturally come to love and trust their parents and develop a disposition to respect and obey their guidelines. Rawls calls this early stage of moral learning the morality of authority. It does not presuppose any understanding of the wider schemes within which parental precepts or norms are justified.

As children mature, they participate in different kinds of associations that require social cooperation. In families, at school, or when playing games with their peers, children learn to take on different roles and to adopt different points of view, and they become aware of the benefits that come from their cooperative interactions with others. This allows them to develop feelings of friendship and trust toward those who cooperate with them. In this way, they learn about different social roles and the different duties that are attached to them. Aided by friendly feelings toward other participants, they acquire a desire to do their part in these just cooperative arrangements. Rawls calls this intermediate stage of moral learning the morality of association.

Rawls argues that the morality of association, in its most complex and demanding form, comes when children have grown up and see themselves as citizens. Assuming that one's society is just, seeing oneself in this way will involve seeing other citizens as equal participants in a fair system of social cooperation. The young adult who is capable of adopting this point of view will already have acquired an understanding of the principles of justice that underlie such a system. This understanding ushers in the third and final stage of moral development. Once a person with such an understanding realizes that the principles of justice promote her good and the good of others she cares about, she may ultimately acquire a standing desire to act according to the principles of justice themselves, even in situations in which feelings of friendship for others are absent. Rawls calls this final stage the morality of principle.

Although Rawls holds that a primary role of the family is to ensure the moral development of children (*JF* 163), this is consistent with the idea that schools also play a necessary role in the development of a sense of justice in children. An appreciation of this role for schools seems to underlie Rawls's brief remarks, in *Political Liberalism* and in *Justice as Fairness* (*PL* 199–200; *JF* 156–157) regarding the moral and political education that the state can legitimately require schools to provide. After all, if families – together with associations of civil society – were expected to impart all the knowledge, abilities, and dispositions that are essential for citizens to have a mature sense of justice, there would be no need to require that these educational contents be taught in schools as well. Since teaching such matters in schools is compulsory, Rawls stresses that the content must be justified in political terms – terms that are acceptable to reasonable citizens. Otherwise such an educational policy would not be legitimate.

Schools teach a wide range of facts that children will need to know in order to be competent in navigating the social world in which they will live as adults. These facts include such things as the history and characteristics of their particular society and the structure of its political system. Schools offer a more diverse environment than families do, and this means that they can help children become aware of the variety of conceptions of the good that exist in contemporary societies, and of the existence of reasonable disagreements about them. Schools also help future citizens gain a deeper understanding of the functioning of society as a system of cooperation. Rawls points out that schools should try to impart knowledge of citizens' constitutional and civic rights, and that they should cultivate political virtues such as reasonableness, fairness, civility, and mutual respect. He explains that the state's concern with the education of children lies in their role as future citizens and the need for them to participate on fair terms in a variety of social, economic, and political institutions.

Rawls is at pains to contrast the educational requirements derived from his own political liberal theory with those of other liberal theories that are based on comprehensive ideals of the good life. In contrast with the theories of Immanuel Kant and John Stuart Mill, he argues that his own theory does not support the promotion of any specific comprehensive ideals. Kant and Mill, on the other hand, endorse comprehensive ideals of personal autonomy and individuality. Contrary to such theories, Rawls's theory of justice does not directly recommend educational practices that are designed to promote a critical examination of the conceptions of the good life that children tend to inherit from their families. Instead, the educational aims Rawls advocates include such things as providing knowledge about one's rights and responsibilities and developing the political virtues characteristic of reasonable citizens. It is true that Rawls also includes some minimal capacity to revise one's conception of the good. But he defends the cultivation of such a capacity in schools on the basis of public reasons that are widely shared.

Rawls admits that an education that tries to promote the kind of political values he advocates may sometimes have effects similar to those of the sort of education defended by advocates of comprehensive liberal theories. For example, it may happen that after learning about their right to religious freedom, about the existence of reasonable disagreements about religious truths, and about the value of tolerance for other citizens' views, some children will feel compelled to revise the beliefs they inherited from their families. In response, Rawls argues that the reasonable educational requirements of his theory must be accepted, even if the impact on certain reasonable conceptions of the good may sometimes be regrettable. He also stresses that there are important differences in scope and generality between political liberal theories and comprehensive liberal theories.

Rawls's comparison of the educational requirements of his theory with those of liberal comprehensive theories has been the subject of a good deal of debate. Some scholars have sided with Rawls and held that political liberalism has more modest educational implications than other liberal theories. They argue that the fact that these educational implications are justified in terms of public reasons is a significant difference, since it ensures their acceptability by reasonable citizens (Costa 2011, 56–71). But many others have argued that an education designed to promote the political virtues and reasonability is indistinguishable in practice from an education inspired by more comprehensive liberal ideals. And they make the further point that this practical similarity makes the distinction hard to defend (Callan 1997, 12–42). A third position that has surfaced in this debate is that, given the level of abstraction at which many liberal theories are pitched, it is possible to apply the same theory in more than one way, generating different educational implications (Gutmann 1995).

One important consideration relevant to debates about the kind of moral and political education that schools should provide has to do with whether or not one can expect other social institutions to transmit the relevant political values. If other institutions could be relied upon to play this educational role, just institutions might be sustained over time without schools being required to comply with very demanding requirements in the arena of moral and political education. Rawls's somewhat modest description of the education schools should provide may therefore be explained by his confidence in the broad educational effects of the public political culture. This suggestion seems plausible in light of his argument that when the primary political and legal institutions embody the principles of justice then the functioning of these institutions will have an educational role. That is, by becoming acquainted with the functioning of just political and legal institutions and the public deliberations that take place within them, citizens will learn to appreciate the core political values that underlie their practices. This appreciation is supported by the human tendency to reciprocity. That is, when people are treated fairly, they tend to behave fairly in return.

Among the entities that play an educational role, one might include those associations that form much of the background nonpolitical culture: associations such as churches, clubs, civic associations, and the media (Reidy 1996). These associations certainly can encourage compliance with the principles of justice and the cultivation of the political virtues. In fact, a good deal of moral and political education is informally imparted in a wide variety of social contexts. However, associations – as well as families – can sometimes emphasize a particular comprehensive doctrine. This would not be problematic if the comprehensive doctrine in question included the principles of justice as a "module," so that the teaching of the doctrine would include them. But such congruence cannot always be guaranteed. This generates a certain amount of tension between granting different social groups the freedom to educate their members according to their comprehensive views, and the need to reproduce a widespread adherence to the principles of justice in each new generation. For example, parents may wish to pass on a religious view that prescribes very rigid gender roles. Such a view conflicts with the requirements of fair equality of opportunity for women, since girls educated according to such a comprehensive view are likely to have restricted opportunities later in life. Moreover, widespread acceptance of such a view would affect the opportunities of women in that particular society in general. Rawls hopes that this tension can be resolved without seriously restricting the educational preferences of parents, and his hope is underwritten by a faith that schools and shared legal and political institutions will have significant educational effects. This tension has been the source of a wide debate about the limits of the educational authority of parents and the state. Some theorists argue that liberal democratic societies should respect the diversity of comprehensive views held by citizens and strive to accommodate parental requests as much as possible (Galston 1995). Others worry that such accommodations fail to respect the rights of children, and may undermine the acceptance of liberal political values among future generations (Macedo 1995).

Victoria Costa

SEE ALSO:

Autonomy, moral
Comprehensive doctrine
Family
Kohlberg, Lawrence
Moral person
Moral psychology
Neutrality
Sense of justice
Stability

134.

MORAL PERSON

RAWLS PROPOSES JUSTICE as fairness, his favored liberal theory of justice, as the best account of institutional or distributive justice for any modern liberal democratic society. He addresses his arguments primarily to readers already committed to the ideals implicit in such a society. In order to orient himself and his audience in advance of making his arguments, Rawls characterizes such a society in terms of three fundamental ideas. Each is normative and so also an ideal. These are the idea(l)s of (i) fair social cooperation among (ii) moral persons as free and equal within (iii) a well-ordered basic institutional structure. These are among the most basic idea(l)s undergirding Rawls's arguments for justice as fairness. The original position organizes them into a heuristic that those committed to determining and realizing institutional or distributive justice for a modern liberal democracy might use to organize and check their deliberation and judgment and guide their political activity.

While abstract and in need of further specification and interpretation, the three fundamental idea(l)s that Rawls takes as his point of departure are already specifications or interpretations of still more abstract idea(l)s familiar from the history of moral and political thought. For example, the idea(l) of *fair* social cooperation is a specification or interpretation of the more general and long familiar idea(l) of society as a cooperative undertaking for the common good. And the idea(l) of moral persons as free and equal is a specification or interpretation of persons as responsible participants in social life. Rawls assumes that the three fundamental idea(l)s are expressed by the public political culture of a liberal democratic society and are common ground among those committed to such a society but divided over pressing political issues of constitutional design, basic justice, and public policy. He does not claim, however, that they are expressed by the public political cultures of or common ground among members of *all* societies. For example, he acknowledges in *The Law of Peoples* that there may be societies, perhaps even well-ordered societies, the members of which affirm and the public political cultures of which express alternative specifications of the abstract idea(l)s of society as a cooperative venture and of persons as responsible participants in social life. Among the topics addressed in that book are how liberal democratic societies are to interact with such societies.

But Rawls's two central books, *A Theory of Justice* and *Political Liberalism*, are addressed to issues of domestic institutional and distributive justice as they arise in liberal democratic societies. Accordingly, Rawls begins with the three fundamental normative ideas set out above and then endeavors to flesh them out in more detail, so that they might be put to effective use in his arguments, without compromising their status as common ground for his target audience. Judging that he missed this mark to some degree in *A Theory of Justice*, Rawls revised his account of these ideas in *Political Liberalism*, taking care to cut them free of any doctrinal moral, metaphysical, or religious content that might prove controversial among citizens committed to core liberal democratic ideals. For example, whereas in *TJ* he tended to speak of moral persons as free equals without distinguishing between the purely political and institutional dimensions of this idea and its many other dimensions as articulated and understood within one or another comprehensive moral, religious, and philosophical doctrine, in *PL* he focused solely or nearly solely on the political and institutional dimensions of moral persons *qua citizens*.

By the latter part of the eighteenth century, the general idea of the moral person as free and equal appears prominently in moral and political philosophy, for example in the work of Rousseau and Kant and in the philosophy of idealism. Roughly the idea is of human beings as equally capable of fully taking part in social cooperation and honoring its various ties and relationships over a complete life and who therefore possess a common moral standing reciprocally recognized as calling for justice among them. For the purposes of moral or political philosophy, Rawls takes this familiar but relatively indeterminate idea as something like the general concept of the moral person. He then develops this general concept into a more determinate conception which he takes, like the general concept itself, to be noncontroversial within and part of the public political culture of any modern liberal democratic society. The general concept of the moral person as responsible participant in social life should be distinguished from other concepts, for example, of the self as knower, or as substance, or as the persisting carrier of psychological states. These concepts, familiar from epistemology and metaphysics, are prima facie distinct from the idea of the moral person as a responsible participant in social life. So too are many of the ideas of the person used by the natural and social sciences. Rawls maintains that we are unlikely to make headway clarifying any of these ideas if we initially lump them all together and examine them apart from the specific inquiries and discourses in which they are used. Of course, we will in due course need to determine whether our best conceptions of each of these ideas of what it is to be a person or self can cohere with one another.

For the purposes of theorizing justice, moral persons are, in the first and paradigmatic instance, natural human beings possessed of two basic capacities and inclinations. The first of these is the capacity and inclination to intelligently form, revise, and pursue a conception of their good. Rawls characterizes this capacity and inclination as rationality. That moral persons are so capable and inclined is shown by their identifying effective means to their ends, setting and organizing their ends, revising their ends in light of new information or significant changes in circumstance, and so on. Human beings routinely unable or without any inclination to do these things are defective or undeveloped as moral persons. To be sure, no human being is perfectly rational all the time. Occasional lapses, while properly criticized, are to be expected.

The second capacity and inclination possessed by human beings who are moral persons is to seek and honor fair terms of social cooperation with others as responsible participants in social life and to subordinate the rational pursuit of their own good to the terms of fair social cooperation. Rawls characterizes this second capacity and inclination as reasonableness. As reasonable, moral persons rationally advance their own good only on terms that others as reasonable could publicly accept and honor.

Reasonableness itself can be analyzed in terms of three elements. To be reasonable, a human being must first be capable of and inclined to reciprocally recognize and respond to others as responsible participants in a common social life organized as a genuine scheme of cooperation. Human beings evidence their possession of this element of reasonableness by acknowledging and honoring certain natural duties – for example, to aid others in need when they can do so without significant risk to themselves or their own good – and certain obligations acquired through their participation in social life – for example, as workers, office holders, compatriots, and so on. Their liability to moral feelings of guilt, shame, resentment, and indignation upon the violation of these natural duties and social obligations also evidences their possession of this first element of reasonableness. Those unwilling or unable to acknowledge and honor, or to feel guilt, shame, resentment or indignation upon the violation of, natural duties and social obligations are defective or undeveloped as moral persons (*CP* 62–63). They lack the most basic element of reasonableness without which well-ordered social cooperation is not possible: a willingness to recognize and respond to others as persons and to do their part within cooperative ventures aimed at the common good. To be sure, fully unreasonable persons might be rational. But as merely rational, they would be unfit for social life and incapable of genuine cooperation. If human beings were only rational, interaction would never be more than a means to each individual's own ends, friendships and other intimate relations would be out of reach, and there would be no path to advancing the common good together through joint action save through the force of some external agent coordinating their conduct.

Second, to be reasonable, a human being must also be capable of and inclined to organizing her cooperation with others, at least with respect to the basic institutional structure of their shared social life, only on public terms mutually intelligible and reciprocally acceptable to all. As reasonable, persons do not take the basic institutional structure of their common social life or their obligations and responsibilities within it as fixed or given or beyond criticism, revision, or reform. Rather, they are able and inclined to cast and bring these in line with public terms that all can understand and together freely affirm without manipulation, coercion, duress, or deception. And they reciprocally recognize one another as so able and inclined. This second element of reasonableness, which extends but goes beyond the first and is not obviously part of the public political culture of all societies, recognizes that moral persons are not simply responsible *participants in* social life but are also responsible *authors of* (at least) the institutional structure of their society. This second element of reasonableness is essential within modern liberal democracies to the idea(l) of moral persons, or of moral persons qua citizens.

In *TJ*, Rawls tended to characterize reasonableness in terms of the two just mentioned and jointly necessary elements. In *PL* he explicitly adds a third necessary element of reasonableness the status of which *TJ* had left unclear. This third element is the capacity and inclination of persons already possessed of the prior two elements to recognize and accept the consequences of the fact that it is unrealistic to expect or require any agreement reached on fair terms of cooperation to extend much beyond political principles governing constitutional essentials and matters of basic justice. That is, it is unrealistic, at least for political purposes, to expect or require for social cooperation at the level of basic institutions agreement on anything like a comprehensive worldview, whether moral, religious or philosophical in nature. As reasonable, moral persons recognize that in a free society, and surely a modern liberal democracy must be a free society, they will forever disagree over comprehensive worldviews, and the reason for this is not that some of them are too stupid or vicious to participate responsibly in social life. When citizens publicly and freely reason together they face collectively certain burdens of judgment that stand as insurmountable obstacles to a reasoned public consensus over comprehensive worldviews. These burdens are familiar: many concepts central to moral, religious, and philosophical thinking are vague and can be specified in many plausible ways; the evidence bearing on many questions central to moral, religious, and philosophical thinking is often complex or inadequate and thus often supports more than one conclusion; no two individuals have the exact same experience of or perspective on the world; and so on. As reasonable, moral persons recognize these burdens and accept their consequences for the free public exercise of reason in political life. When it comes to fair terms of social cooperation, they neither hope for nor expect agreement on more than some general and generically liberal political principles of justice governing constitutional essentials and matters of basic justice and justified in terms of widely shared political values and common sense truths. Of course, they may work within the democratic process to advance their preferred generically liberal political conception of justice. But they recognize and accept the fact that a general social consensus over any particular member of the family is unlikely to arise or endure, and so they accept the legitimacy of democratic processes as a social mechanism for selecting among candidates generically liberal conceptions of political justice. Of course, none of this suggests that as reasonable, moral persons will not work within the many voluntary associations of civil society to generate and maintain consensus with other like-minded individuals over this or that comprehensive worldview. But they will do so cognizant of the fact that it is unreasonable to expect or require agreement on terms of social cooperation, at least at the level of basic institutions, justified exclusively in terms of the comprehensive worldview they affirm with other like-minded individuals.

The capacities and inclinations that Rawls identifies as the rational and the reasonable jointly constitute moral personality. Both are necessary and neither can be derived from the other. In particular, the reasonable cannot be derived from rationality alone. Of course, a reasonable person necessarily is capable of rationality, of forming, revising, and pursuing a conception of her own good; there would otherwise be no point in her cooperating with others. But while a rational human being will ordinarily aim at certain ends that cannot be secured apart from reasonable relations with others, the capacity for and inclination to reasonableness cannot be reduced to or explained solely in terms of the rational. Under ordinary conditions, as persons mature and develop they tend reciprocally to recognize, respect, and care for others who manifestly recognize, respect, and care for them. Through this shared impulse to reciprocity, manifest at all stages of human life, human beings collectively constitute one another as moral persons, both rational and reasonable. Human nature permits the reasonable, but the reasonable generates itself by answering itself in kind (*JF* 196).

The freedom and equality of moral persons is established by their rationality and reasonableness. While human beings may possess and/or actualize these capacities to varying degrees, in the normal course of things they all possess and actualize them to the minimum degree required for responsible participation in social life in a liberal democracy and so institutional recognition and treatment as a moral person or citizen. In this sense, all human beings are equal as moral persons and are equally eligible or suited for citizenship in a liberal democracy. Rawls cites three elements of the freedom of moral persons. First, the equal public political standing of moral persons, or of citizens, is independent of any particular conception of the good or schedule of final ends. Moral persons or citizens are free to adjust their ends without losing their public status as equal moral persons. Second, moral persons or citizens understand themselves and are publicly understood by others to be capable of and responsible for adjusting their ends to fit with mutually intelligible and reciprocally acceptable public terms of social cooperation with others. They are not slaves to their desires. Third, moral persons or citizens affirm one another and are publicly recognized as self-authenticating sources of valid claims; they need do no more than be ready and willing to be reasonable in their dealings with others in order to validate their claims when it comes to settling on fair terms of social cooperation (*PL* 72).

By explaining the status of moral persons or citizens as free and equal in terms of their natural capacities for rationality and reasonableness, Rawls is explicitly avoiding appeals to human dignity, intrinsic worth, or a basic imperative to respect persons. To be sure, Rawls does not deny human dignity or intrinsic worth. But these are vague and controversial notions that themselves call for explanation and cannot explain the status of moral persons or citizens as free and equal. Likewise, Rawls affirms a natural duty to respect moral persons, but the duty does not itself explain what a moral person is or why they are owed respect (*TJ* 446–447).

The status of moral persons or citizens as free and equal is distinct from and prior to the various perfections of moral character that fall under the heading of value generally. These will figure prominently in any explanation of the moral worth of a particular person. A courageous person has a character of greater moral worth than a cowardly person. A just and benevolent person has a character of greater moral worth than an equally just but not at all benevolent person. While these perfections of character are relevant to judgments of the moral worth of character, they are not relevant to and do not explain the status of moral persons as free and equal and they do not undermine the commitment to *equal* justice for all citizens (*TJ* 274–275, 289, 381–384).

In order to put the idea of moral persons to work in an argument for fair terms of social cooperation within a well-ordered liberal democracy, Rawls must give some content to the self-authenticated valid moral claims moral persons have. Every moral person will have a valid moral claim to a fair share of socially produced means to the pursuit of her rational and reasonable ends, whatever they happen to be. And every moral person will have a valid moral claim to basic social institutions that enable her to develop and exercise her two basic moral capacities, to be rational and to be reasonable. And finally, every moral person will have a valid moral claim to the institutional and social bases of her self-respect as a moral person, free and equal with others. Putting these together, we may say that every moral person has a valid moral claim to a social world (the basic elements of which – liberties, opportunities for various social positions, wealth and income, etc. – Rawls refers to as "primary goods") within which she may develop and express herself as a free and equal moral person with others. Rawls organizes his argument from the original position so that it models these valid moral claims of free and equal moral persons or citizens. These claims may be taken as an account of the objective social needs common to all moral persons or citizens.

Rational and reasonable natural human beings constitute the paradigm case of moral persons, but they do not exhaust the category. Natural human persons may organize themselves through institutions and practices so that they are collectively and corporately able to have and exercise not only a bare capacity for agency but a capacity for rational and reasonable agency. Thus, on Rawls's view, it is possible for teams, churches, nation states, and other associations to constitute (corporate and artificial) moral persons (*CP* 193–194). As rational and reasonable, moral persons of these other sorts will also seek to cooperate on public terms that are mutually intelligible and publicly acceptable to all. So, nation states constituted as moral persons will seek to cooperate with one another internationally on such terms. And this sets the problem, for Rawls, of international justice, at least as it arises for liberal democracies committed to the idea of the moral person as rational and reasonable. Of course, one must treat with care these extensions of the idea of moral persons. For example, the self-authenticated valid moral claims

Moral person / 519

of nation states, or as Rawls refers to them, peoples, as moral persons will differ from those of natural human beings as moral persons. And the moral psychology of nation states or peoples as moral persons will differ in various ways from that of natural human beings as moral persons.

Finally, while it is *sufficient* for natural human beings to be owed justice that they be rational and reasonable and so be moral persons, Rawls typically neither asserts nor denies that being rational and reasonable or being a moral person is *necessary* to being owed justice (*TJ* 446). He thereby sets to the side the question of whether severely and permanently disabled natural human beings or nonhuman animals are sources of self-authenticating valid moral claims or are otherwise owed justice.

David A. Reidy

SEE ALSO:

> *Citizen*
> *Conception of the good*
> *Desires*
> *Fundamental ideas (in justice as fairness)*
> *Moral education*
> *Moral psychology*
> *Political liberalism, justice as fairness as*
> *The reasonable and the rational*
> *Reciprocity*
> *Sense of justice*

135.

MORAL PSYCHOLOGY

MORAL PSYCHOLOGY AIMS at understanding the moral experience of persons – moral feelings, attitudes, and sentiments – and the patterns of moral deliberation, judgment, and motivation with which they are associated. And it aims at understanding this experience, a normal part of human life, as distinctively moral and not simply as general psychological experience or as neural activity in the brain. A person's psychological experience is distinctively moral when it cannot be identified or explained without reference to moral concepts, principles or values. So, for example, a person's experience of guilt is distinctively moral because the feeling of guilt can be neither identified nor explained as guilt without appeal to principles of right and notions of wrongdoing. On the other hand, a person's experience of fear is not distinctively moral because the feeling of fear can often be identified and explained without appeals to moral concepts, principles, or values. Finally, it is primarily for the sake of addressing particular issues within moral and political philosophy, not natural or social sciences, that moral psychology aims at understanding the moral experience of persons as distinctively moral.

Because moral psychology aims at explaining its target phenomena as distinctively moral and so necessarily appeals to moral concepts, principles, or values, and because it is primarily for the sake of addressing issues in moral and political philosophy, rather than natural or social sciences, that it aims at explaining its target phenomena, there is a normative dimension to moral psychology absent from empirical psychology more generally. Of course, empirical psychology may aim at explaining and understanding moral psychological experience, too. But it aims to explain and understand psychological experiences neutrally,

Moral psychology / 521

without itself endorsing any moral principles or values, and in a manner continuous with natural and social sciences. So, for example, insofar as empirical psychology aims at explaining and understanding feelings of guilt, it will draw no categorical distinction between moral feelings, such as guilt, and nonmoral feelings, such as fear, and will aim, without appealing to moral concepts, principles or values, at the same sort of explanation and understanding of each.

As the foregoing suggests, moral psychology is not, at least for Rawls, a subfield of empirical psychology. It is not empirical psychology extended to psychological moral experience. Of course, both empirical and moral psychology aim at self-understanding. But moral psychology aims at self-understanding from a point of view shaped by and thus in terms of moral concepts and commitments. Though not a subfield of empirical psychology, moral psychology is, nevertheless, informed and constrained by empirical psychology. It must offer an account of moral psychological experience that is consistent with the best explanations and understandings provided by empirical psychology.

There is an important sense in which the totality of Rawls's moral and political philosophy belongs to moral psychology. For example, Rawls sometimes described his theory of justice as a normative theory of the moral sentiment often referred to as the "sense of justice." Moral psychology includes normative theories of the moral sentiments (*TJ* 44). It explains and helps us to understand our sense of justice as a proper part of our moral nature and to assess its proper functioning. But notwithstanding the ways in which the bulk of his work might be thought of as part of moral psychology, discussions of Rawls and moral psychology most often focus on the ways in which he explicitly appeals to and draws on specific claims of moral psychology *within* his work, and in particular within his theory of justice.

The main instances of Rawls explicitly appealing to and drawing on specific claims of moral psychology within his theory of justice are two. Both occur in his argument for the stability of a society well-ordered by the principles of justice as fairness. In part III of *A Theory of Justice*, after having articulated and argued for his two principles of justice and sketched the institutions of a basic social structure faithful to them, Rawls first argues that persons born and raised within such a social structure will naturally acquire the moral sentiment of a sense of justice shaped and informed by justice as fairness. He then argues that this sense of justice will be sufficiently well rooted in their overall psychological makeup to move them voluntarily to comply with the demands of justice to a degree sufficient for social stability without excessive policing, indoctrination, manipulation, and so on. In setting out this first step of his stability argument, he draws from moral psychology and relies upon a particular theory of moral development. He then argues, in the second step of his stability argument, that persons will experience and understand their coming to have and act on this sense of justice as part of their rational good, as something they would rationally desire even from a point of view as yet unshaped and uninformed by their moral commitments, especially their commitment to justice as fairness. Having and acting on the sense of justice cultivated in a society well-ordered by justice as fairness belongs to the "thin theory of the good," to use Rawls's phrase. In setting out this second step of his stability argument, Rawls draws a number of premises from moral psychology, including the Aristotelian principle, to establish the rationality of principle- and conception-dependent desires to act from and in accord with the effectively regulative sense of justice naturally acquired by growing up within a society that institutionally embodies justice as fairness. He concludes that his theory of justice sets out an account of the moral sentiment of the sense of justice for which persons are naturally fit and that is, in a non-question-begging way, congruent with their good.

After the publication of *TJ*, Rawls realized that he made some unreasonable assumptions in the stability argument he made there. He unreasonably assumed that the sense of justice acquired by all persons born and raised within a society well-ordered by justice as fairness would be, and would be understood and experienced by them to be, broadly Kantian in nature. And he unreasonably assumed the rationality for all persons of principle- and conception-dependent desires to act from and in accord with this broadly Kantian sense of justice. In short, he unreasonably assumed that persons would all come to experience, understand, and affirm the goodness of their sense of justice in broadly Kantian terms. This assumption is unreasonable because in a free society, and a society well-ordered by justice as fairness would be a free society, persons are likely to remain reasonably divided over comprehensive moral, religious, and philosophical doctrines and so are unlikely all to experience, understand, and affirm the goodness of their sense of justice in broadly Kantian terms. To be sure, they are likely to acquire a shared sense of justice and to recognize and affirm the rationality of principle- and conception-dependent desires to act from and accord with it, but it will be a more narrowly circumscribed sense of political justice not tied exclusively to any one broader moral, philosophical, or religious outlook, Kantian or otherwise, and the principle- and conception-dependent desires will be tied to the principles and ideals of liberal democratic citizenship, not Kantian personhood. In *Political Liberalism*, Rawls sets out to show that this more narrowly circumscribed and free-standing sense of political justice is sufficient for social stability free of excessive

Moral psychology / 523

policing, indoctrination, manipulation, and so on. Doing so did not require any substantial revision to his account of moral development in *TJ* beyond allowing that in a free society well-ordered by justice as fairness persons will not all naturally develop a sense of justice fairly characterized as broadly Kantian but will instead all naturally develop a more narrowly circumscribed and freestanding sense of political justice. But it did require revision to the account of how acting from and in accord with this sense of justice belonged to the thin theory of the good by satisfying principle- and conception-dependent desires rational for all persons to have irrespective of their broader moral, religious or philosophical commitments (*PL* 81–87). And this required explication of the political good, implicit in *Theory* but not given much attention there, of political legitimacy.

Before setting out the elements of the moral psychology Rawls appeals to and draws from in *TJ* and *PL*, three points should be noted. First, Rawls's stability arguments explicitly appeal to and draw on not only moral psychology but general empirical psychology as well. For example, envy is, like fear, a natural, not a moral, feeling. Because it is, if widespread among persons and strongly felt, corrosive of social stability, Rawls must establish that a society well-ordered by justice as fairness will not generate levels of envy sufficient to create instability. Rawls offers two lines of argument. The first is that a society well-ordered by justice as fairness will not trigger high levels of envy (or other destructive feelings or attitudes) and so will avoid their destabilizing effects. While this argument appeals to and draws on claims from general empirical psychology, it makes no necessary appeal to moral psychology. The second line of argument is that it is reasonable to think that the sense of justice, as a stable moral sentiment, engendered in persons born and raised in a society well-ordered by justice as fairness will prove sufficient to keep in check any destabilizing tendencies that might be thought to flow from the isolated and low levels of envy that may arise in any human society, even one well-ordered by justice as fairness. This argument appeals to and draws on claims from not only general empirical psychology but moral psychology as well.

Rawls sometimes characterizes the psychology of natural feelings and attitudes such as high levels of envy or aversion to risk as "special psychologies" (*TJ* 464–465). These features of human psychology, real empirical possibilities, require special attention when arguing for the stability of a theory of justice because of their destabilizing or destructive potential. However, it is important to note – and this is the second point – that while these possibilities must be addressed when it comes to assessing the stability of justice as fairness, the parties in the original position are not themselves liable to these feelings or attitudes. Rawls sets these special psychologies to the side when setting up the original position and characterizing the psychology of the parties in it. Thus, the psychology – if that word can be used – of the parties in the original position should not be taken as indicating or expressing a general empirical account of human psychology.

Nor should it be construed as indicating or expressing the moral psychology appealed to and drawn on in justice as fairness. This is the third point. To be sure, the original position argument, including the veil of ignorance and so on, does embody and express certain general commitments of moral psychology. For example, it models and expresses a normative conception of persons as both rational and reasonable. But the parties in the original position, their circumstances and task, and the veil of ignorance are all set out without any appeal to a theory of moral development or of the rationality of principle- and conception-dependent desires to act from and in accord with the sense of justice. Of course, the parties in the original position know that they represent persons or citizens who will have a sense of justice. And they know that in the same way that there is no point to agreeing to principles that those they represent could not understand or apply, given noncontroversial facts about the limits of human intelligence and so on, there is also no point to agreeing to principles – for example, principles requiring heroic self-sacrifice or saintly benevolence of all citizens – that those they represent could not honor, given the noncontroversial facts of empirical psychology. The parties aim to agree on principles for which strains of commitment will not be so great, no matter the eventual social position or share of wealth and income of the party they represent, as to render their agreement pointless (*TJ* 126, 153–154). But the psychology – again, if that word can be used – of the parties in the original position is not itself drawn from and does not express any commitments within moral psychology, though it does draw upon and express certain commitments about rational choice.

Rawls's stability argument aims to show that it is not unreasonable to anticipate a reflectively endorsed allegiance to fair social cooperation taking hold, as a high priority final end, of compatriots within a society institutionally embodying justice as fairness. The argument begins with an account of the moral development of persons as rational and reasonable – from the first stages of moral development in infants and children to the final stages in, presumably, young adults. What drives development at each stage is a tendency to reciprocity deeply embedded in human nature (*TJ* 433). At each stage, when activated by certain natural feelings, attitudes, and sentiments this tendency to reciprocity generates moral growth, enriching the domain of reasonable moral judgments and giving rise to new moral feelings, attitudes, and sentiments.

Moral psychology / 525

In the first stages the infant and then child naturally comes to love and trust her parents who she experiences as responding unconditionally to her needs. Because she loves and trusts her parents, she desires their good and thus wishes not to disappoint or displease them. And so she comes herself to understand and experience their directions or commands as normative; she desires to comply for the sake not only of her own good but that of her parents as well. Noncompliance leaves her liable to primitive feelings of guilt and shame. These first stages of moral development Rawls characterizes as the morality of authority.

These are followed by intermediate stages Rawls characterizes as the morality of association. In these stages the growing child comes to participate in various cooperative activities within and beyond the family unit. In so doing, she sees that others advance the common good and so her own good by fulfilling their role-specific responsibilities and this leads her to care for and trust them and to desire to advance in turn their good, as part of the common good, by fulfilling her role-specific responsibilities in return. She comes to understand and experience social roles as normative; she desires to comply for the sake not only of her own good but that of those with whom she cooperates as well. With this development, she becomes liable to new, more fully developed moral feelings and develops new, more complex moral attitudes and sentiments.

The final stages of moral development Rawls dubs the morality of principle. In these the now grown child or young adult comes to understand and experience her cooperative interaction with others as rooted in and expressive of certain principles that contribute to her good and so draw her allegiance independent of her affectionate feelings for those she cooperates with. Of course she still has those affectionate feelings for particular family member, friends, and colleagues. But she also now identifies with various moral principles, the most basic of which she recognizes as underwriting any and all forms of human cooperation. As she sees others similarly drawn to these principles, she comes to feel a kind of love and trust for any being similarly drawn to them, irrespective of her immediate affectionate relations. She acquires a general love of humankind and desires to honor the moral principles both for their own sake and as an expression of this general love of humankind. She finds herself liable to fully developed moral feelings of guilt or shame when she fails to honor these principles and, assuming appropriate social conditions, a sense of justice, as a mature moral sentiment, will arise in her.

To have a sense of justice, as a mature moral sentiment, is to be reliably moved to act from and in accord with general principles of fair cooperation with others, provided they do the same in return. Rawls's account of moral development is aimed at showing that it is reasonable to suppose that persons living in a society governed by justice as fairness will naturally acquire a sense of justice the content of which is consonant with justice as fairness. But this account of moral development does not establish that they will reflectively embrace their acquisition of this moral sentiment, or their susceptibility to the natural feelings, attitudes and sentiments out of which this moral sentiment develops, as part of their good. To establish this, Rawls argues that they will find it rational to have the desires associated with this moral sentiment. Notwithstanding certain alterations from *TJ* to *PL*, Rawls's core claim is that these desires, to act in accord with certain principles of justice and to realize a certain conception of oneself, whether as a person in broadly Kantian terms (*TJ*) or as a citizen in freestanding politically liberal terms (*PL*), are rational, because their fulfillment is experienced as good even from a point of view as yet unshaped by a sense of justice. Their fulfillment secures certain weighty goods, involves the development and exercise of complex capacities and so fulfills the Aristotelian principle, and permits for each individual a kind of vicarious realization of or identification with a wider range of good lives led than it is possible for any one person to live herself. By cooperating with others and realizing a conception of herself as not only rational but also reasonable, she is able to participate in the fulfillment by others of desires that it would not be irrational for her to have and act on but that she must forego if she is to act on the rational desires that she in fact acts on. Her reasonableness, including her sense of justice, enables her to realize a wider range of goods than she would otherwise be able to realize, including a number of distinctively political goods such as political legitimacy and civic friendship. This is not to say that her reasonableness or her sense of justice is reducible to or originates from her rationality or the fulfillment of her rational desires. It is just to say that she will regard her reasonable social nature, once it has fully developed and taken root in her, as part of her own good, indeed as a weighty and forceful part of her own good.

A key theme in Rawls's overall stability argument is that institutions faithful to justice as fairness will not tend to produce alienated, resentful, envious, unhappy persons but will instead tend to produce satisfied persons secure in their self-respect and oriented toward a meaningful and enjoyable life. His arguments for this general claim often depend on various claims of general empirical psychology, for example that fair inequalities will not engender envy or damage self-respect. While these are empirical claims, they are not claims that can be understood or tested without reference to moral concepts, principles, or ideals.

While most of Rawls's use of and contributions to moral psychology center on his theory of justice, he hoped eventually to, but never in fact did, extend his work in moral psychology to the moral feelings, attitudes, and sentiments, and related judgments, principle- and conception-dependent desires, and social institutions and practices, associated with the supererogatory moralities of exceptional self-discipline (e.g. the reliable disposition to do what justice requires even at great risk to or sacrifice of one's own good) and benevolence (e.g. the reliable disposition to advance the good of others or the common good even when not required to do so by justice) (*TJ* 419). One might think of these inquiries as complementing his inquiry into the moral psychology of the citizen with that of the hero and the saint.

David A. Reidy

SEE ALSO:

> *Aristotelian principle*
> *Desires*
> *Envy*
> *Kohlberg, Lawrence*
> *Moral education*
> *Moral sentiments*
> *Political liberalism, justice as fairness as*
> *Reciprocity*
> *Sense of justice*
> *Stability*

136.

MORAL SENTIMENTS

ENTIMENTS ARE ORDERED families of governing dispositions to feel and act in particular ways in response to particular circumstances. A person's sentiments constitute an essential part of her enduring character. Sentiments may be natural or moral. The key difference is that to understand and explain the latter, but not the former, one must appeal to moral concepts, principles, or ideals. So, for example, a person who has a sense of justice necessarily has a moral sentiment, whereas a person who has a deep and abiding love for her child might have only a natural sentiment. Of course, many sentiments are complex, comprised of both natural and moral elements. Indeed, the love of others is often such a complex sentiment.

Like sentiments, attitudes are also structured dispositions to feel and act in particular ways that may be natural or moral and simple or complex. But attitudes are not as regulative, enduring, or profound within a person's character as sentiments. Feelings, which again may be natural or moral and simple or complex, are what a person's sentiments or attitudes lead her to experience on particular occasions and in particular circumstances. Unlike attitudes and sentiments, they are episodic. Feelings, which are identical with neither the sensations nor the behaviors that often accompany and serve as indicators of them, express the underlying sentiments or attitudes that give rise to them.

These sentiments or attitudes may not only give rise to a number of feelings in response to a particular situation, they may interact so as to give these feelings a distinctive force. For example, if a friend or loved one wrongly suffers harm, we may feel both grief and indignation. As a natural feeling, grief indicates that we have a natural attitude or sentiment of affection. As a moral feeling, indignation indicates that we have a sense of justice, a moral sentiment. These underlying

Moral sentiments / 529

attitudes and sentiments may interact so that we feel a pronounced indignation when a friend or loved one wrongly suffers harm as compared to when a stranger wrongly suffers harm; our natural affection interacts with our sense of justice and magnifies our feeling of indignation.

Sentiments, natural and moral, play an important role in Rawls's argument for the stability of a society the basic structure of which is faithful to his two principles of justice as fairness. While the argument is complex, Rawls's key points are (1) that under ordinary circumstances citizens growing up in such a society will develop a character marked not by divisive attitudes or sentiments such as generalized envy or jealousy or distrust (especially as directed to particular social positions) but rather by the moral sentiment of a sense of justice understandable and explainable in terms of the concepts, principles and ideals of justice as fairness, (2) that this moral sentiment will naturally develop out of natural feelings, attitudes and sentiments reliably generated under normal conditions, (3) that it will effectively regulate their conduct to a degree sufficient to render social institutions stable in the right way (without excessive policing, coercion, deception, etc.), and (4) that citizens will experience and understand their coming to have and act from and in accord with this sense of justice as part of or congruent with their rational good.

Rawls's attention to the sense of justice as a moral sentiment is not limited to his stability argument, however. His argument for his two principles of justice as fairness begins from certain considered judgments of political morality, assumed to be noncontroversial among citizens living under conditions of modern constitutional democracy and thus taken as provisionally fixed and calling for explication and justification. These judgments constitute evidence, albeit incomplete and indeterminate, of these citizens' (Rawls's, yours, my) sense of justice. By identifying a conception of justice that explicates and justifies these judgments in a mutually intelligible and acceptable way, Rawls aims, inter alia, to advance citizens' reflective self-understanding of their (his, your, my) sense of justice. It is no accident, then, that he describes justice as fairness as a theory, or part of a theory, of the moral sentiments, not least the sense of justice (*TJ* 44). Since a theory of moral sentiments belongs to moral psychology, justice as fairness belongs to moral psychology. Of course, it belongs also to political philosophy. In contrast to the empirical psychology of natural sentiments, attitudes, or feelings, a moral psychology of the moral sentiments, attitudes, and feelings necessarily draws on moral and/or political philosophy for the moral concepts, principles, and ideals needed to explain and justify these aspects of a person's character. As an exercise in political philosophy, justice as fairness contributes a distinctive set of concepts, principles, and ideals to moral psychology.

Moral sentiments, including the sense of justice, are acquired over time and develop out of natural feelings and attitudes. Rawls describes a three-stage process of development. In the first stage, which Rawls describes as a morality of authority, a child comes naturally to love and trust her parents who respond to her needs and promote her good and upon whom she is dependent. This natural love and trust generates in the child a disposition to comply with parental commands and so secure the approval and admiration of her parents. Failure to comply generates in the child moral feelings of guilt for the violation of a parental command and shame for acting in a manner unworthy of parental approval and admiration. These rudimentary or primitive moral feelings indicate the emergence in the child of elementary moral attitudes or sentiments associated with duty, obligation, right and wrong, justice, and so on, and these proto-attitudes or sentiments dispose the child to act in ways that advance her parents' as well as her own good. In the second stage, which Rawls describes as the morality of association, the child, now presumably older, comes to understand and experience the family (and other cooperative undertakings, such as a sports team) as an association organized around defined roles and aimed at the common good of all members. When others live up to their roles, the child comes naturally to love and trust the association's other members, and these natural feelings lead her to be disposed to live up to her own role and to feel guilt and shame if she fails to do so. These feelings indicate the presence of more but not yet fully developed moral attitudes or sentiments associated with duty, obligation, right and wrong, justice, and so on. In the third and final stage, which Rawls describes as the morality of principle, the now mature individual comes to understand the associations and social institutions she participates in as governed by principles which she understands and experiences as serving the good of all. Accordingly, these principles draw her allegiance and she is disposed to act in accord with and from them, provided others are disposed to do the same. She experiences the moral feelings of guilt and shame when she violates them. And she feels indignation and resentment when others violate them, even if their conduct in no way involves her or any person for whom she has natural affection. She finally experiences guilt, shame, indignation, and related moral feelings "in the strict sense," for her liability to these feelings is no longer predicated on any contingent relationships or natural affections. On Rawls's view, her liability to these feelings now indicates her possession of a sense of justice as a fully developed moral sentiment. Of course, the shape of any person's sense of justice will depend on

Moral sentiments / 531

the concepts, principles, and ideals the violation of which gives rise to feelings of guilt, shame, indignation, and so on. And similarly for other moral sentiments and the moral feelings to which they give rise on particular occasions. But the identification of the concepts, principles and ideals that determine the shape of our moral sentiments is, on Rawls's view, something we are able to do only by interpreting ourselves with the aim of arriving at a reflective self-understanding capable of publicly underwriting wide, full, and general reflective equilibrium. Of course, such a self-understanding may not be forthcoming for all our moral sentiments given the plurality of reasonable comprehensive doctrines citizens bound together by justice as fairness as their shared sense of justice are likely to affirm. Still, what is true of the sense of justice will be true of the other moral sentiments as well: while nature makes our moral sentiments possible (and under ordinary conditions inevitable), their precise nature depends in many ways on us.

As the previous developmental account makes clear, Rawls argues that familiar *moral* feelings, attitudes, and sentiments develop out of our *natural* feelings, attitudes, and sentiments, at least under ordinary conditions. Thus, the absence of the former indicates an absence of the latter. An individual without moral feelings, attitudes, or sentiments would be an individual without natural feelings, attitudes, or sentiments essential to humanity. To put it otherwise, under ordinary conditions human beings naturally develop into persons with moral feelings, attitudes, and sentiments. And as they endeavor reflectively to understand those feelings, attitudes, and sentiments, and to bring the structure of their social world into line with them, they play an active role in shaping their own character as persons and so giving more determinate content to their humanity.

Rawls understandably devotes considerable attention to the moral sentiment of the sense of justice, but he recognizes a number of other moral sentiments in need of theorizing: for example, benevolence or the love of mankind, humility, empathy and courage, magnanimity, self-control (*TJ* 419). These he thinks we can more easily understand once we have an adequate theory of our sense of justice. For example, a person who is reliably disposed to do more for the common good than fulfill her obligations and natural duties, spelled out by her sense of justice, displays the moral sentiment of benevolence or love of mankind. A person with this sentiment has a supererogatory virtue. And a person who is reliably disposed to fulfill her obligations and natural duties, as spelled out by her sense of justice, with ease and grace regardless of the costs or challenges, displays the moral sentiments of courage and self-control. She too has a supererogatory virtue. To understand these moral sentiments, we need to theorize the concepts, principles, and ideals of the saint and hero. But for Rawls, we must first theorize the concepts, principles, and ideals of justice, for we cannot have the moral sentiments of the saint or hero if we do not have the moral sentiment essential to citizenship or membership within social life.

David A. Reidy

SEE ALSO:

Guilt and shame
Moral education
Moral psychology
Sense of justice
Stability

137.

MORAL THEORY

RAWLS DISTINGUISHES SHARPLY between moral philosophy and moral theory. The distinction is first elaborated in "The Independence of Moral Theory" (1975). Moral theory is concerned with what Rawls calls "substantive moral conceptions." It subjects these conceptions to philosophical scrutiny to test for rational coherence and their applicability to existing social conditions. While moral theory is an important part of moral philosophy, the latter has a much wider scope that includes epistemological, conceptual, and metaphysical issues as they pertain to morality. The main point of the distinction is to argue that progress can be made in moral theory quite independently of whether advances are achieved in these other areas of inquiry. The target of Rawls's claim is philosophers who think that epistemological, conceptual, and metaphysical questions need to be answered prior to any advances in our moral understanding. In the history of philosophy, at different times, one of these areas has been assumed to be the foundation of philosophical inquiry that subordinates other philosophical investigations, and subordinates moral inquiry in particular. On the contrary, Rawls thinks that substantial progress in our moral thinking is possible, and moreover that justice as fairness is an example of how this can be achieved.

A moral conception is a moral view that is more or less structured and which engages in a practical way with our moral psychology. These structures address problems of the good, what is right, and issues concerning the moral worth of persons. While Rawls assumes we all have such a view and that these individual views can be a source of philosophical reflection, our intellectual tradition supplies us with a number of highly articulated moral conceptions. Rawls offers the following as examples: utilitarianism, intuitionism, Kantianism, and

533

perfectionism. He adds his own conception, Kantian constructivism, to this list.

Moral theory examines these conceptions for both internal coherence and how they engage with our historically, socially, and psychologically specific circumstances. In addition, moral conceptions can be compared and contrasted to determine a relative ranking of conceptions. It is important to note that the point of moral theory is not merely to describe these different conceptions and note their differences, but rather to aim at selecting the philosophically best conception. The point is to achieve reflective equilibrium in our moral thinking. Thus, Rawls says that the philosophical task of moral theory is to "perfect" moral conceptions. This method of philosophical investigation into morality Rawls attributes to Sidgwick, although he differs substantially from Sidgwick in his conclusions.

Rawls argues that epistemological questions concerning the truth or falsehood of a moral conception should be "bracketed" when we engage in moral theory. This is not to say that the notion of moral truth of a conception is not important to the moral theorist, but that whether or not the conception itself is true is a question that is not addressed at this level of moral inquiry. Rawls is not here expressing skepticism about the possibility of moral truth. Rather he is setting aside this difficult and philosophically controversial issue to focus on the coherence of a moral conception. There is, therefore, no assumption that a single moral conception corresponds with the moral truth since it is possible, as Rawls insists, that there is a plurality of moral conceptions that are coherent and plausible for our circumstances. So it might be reasonable to accept a rationally coherent and socially and psychologically plausible moral conception without affirming its truth. This stance should be distinguished from Rawls's views in his own favored moral conception, Kantian constructivism, in which he argues for an account of objectivity that eschews the notion of moral truth and replaces it with an idea of the reasonable. At the level of moral conceptions the issue of moral truth is set aside. Within the moral conception of Kantian constructivism the place of moral truth is denied.

Moral theory is also independent of the philosophy of language. The idea that linguistic analysis is the key to philosophical progress was important in early twentieth-century philosophy. Rawls denies, however, that our philosophical understanding of morality is much advanced by focusing merely on the meaning of moral terms. He does acknowledge that some contributions in this area have been useful, but argues that looking only at the linguistic characteristics of moral language is too narrow and restricted and yields only formal requirements rather than substantial progress in moral theory. More particularly, he shows that different moral conceptions will fill in the formal requirements of moral language in different ways. Therefore, attending only to the formal requirements does not enable us to make the kinds of philosophical distinctions between moral conceptions that it is the job of moral theory to make. Furthermore, there are other considerations when assessing moral conceptions, such as their relation to our moral psychology, that go well beyond what a conceptual analysis of language can provide. Overall, relying on the theory of meaning to answer moral questions is too restrictive according to Rawls.

Finally, moral theory need not await answers to the traditional metaphysical problems in the philosophy of mind, such as the nature of personal identity. Rawls says the accounts of personal identity offered in the philosophical literature can be accommodated by the traditional moral conceptions. Moral conceptions develop a normative view of the self, an ideal of moral personhood, but these ideals are compatible with the metaphysical specification of personal identity. Moreover, different moral conceptions will emphasize different aspects of the self, its development, and its relation to the good and the right. So what distinguishes moral conceptions from one another is not adherence to different metaphysical views on personal identity but rather differences of emphasis and attention in their account of the self. Rawls illustrates this point by contrasting utilitarian and Kantian notions of moral personality. The latter, he argues, requires a much stronger degree of psychological connectedness than utilitarianism because Kantian theories place more stress on the ideas of responsibility and autonomy. What is in dispute between utilitarianism and Kantianism is a moral ideal, not a metaphysical question concerning whether or not psychological connectedness is the correct criterion of personal identity.

The argument marks out two connected but conceptually distinct territories. On the one hand there is moral theory that scrutinizes, compares, and perfects moral conceptions as well as arguing for the best of these conceptions. On the other hand there is moral philosophy which is engaged in creating and elaborating particular moral conceptions. One might think of John Stuart Mill as engaged in moral philosophy insofar as he articulates a particular account of the good, the right, and a person's moral worth alongside particular ideas about the justification of moral judgments and so forth. However, when we take Rawls's advice and attend to the task of moral theory we look at utilitarianism as a moral conception, assess its coherence and compare its philosophical worth against other moral conceptions. Additionally, and for Rawls this is important, we also assess a moral conception in the light of our social needs and our moral psychology. The aim of moral theory is thus both narrow and wide reflective equilibrium – not just internal rational coherence but also a fuller social, political, and psychological coherence. The aim of moral philosophy is broader and engages moral questions on a much wider front thereby incorporating (and perhaps adding to) our knowledge in areas of epistemology, language, and metaphysics. For example, moral philosophy will have something to say about objectivity that depends on a certain view of the relation of truth to moral judgments. A moral conception will call on and incorporate a particular account of objectivity and moral theory will critically assess and compare this account with alternatives. Rawls believes this division of philosophical labor allows for practical progress in our moral thinking.

While Rawls focuses on the distinct role and tasks of moral theory it is important to keep in view that this is one part of the wider aims of moral philosophy. Moral conceptions are candidates for citizens' allegiance. In this role questions concerning how they engage with a citizen's broader epistemological and metaphysical commitments are relevant and so these larger philosophical issues are unbracketed. The task of moral theory in seeking internal coherence aims at narrow reflective equilibrium whereas the larger question of the general acceptance of a moral conception requires public justification and aims at wide reflective equilibrium. As we will see below, in his later work Rawls is clear that in a pluralistic democratic society no single moral conception is likely to gain the allegiance of all or most citizens.

Aside from the role of moral theory and its distinction from moral philosophy and independence from the rest of philosophical inquiry, Rawls also argues for a particular position within moral theory. He argues in favor of a constructivist moral conception in general and a Kantian constructivist conception in particular. He argues that these are superior to the alternative traditional moral conceptions and they fit with justice as fairness as it is argued for in *A Theory of Justice*. Briefly stated, a constructivist moral conception lays out a procedure that connects a particular view of persons and society with principles of justice. The original position is an example of such a procedure. What makes Kantian constructivism Kantian is that, first, Rawls adopts the view that autonomy is an essential feature of a moral ideal of the self. Second, he offers a Kantian-inspired view of moral objectivity. This view denies that moral judgments can be true in the same sense that, say, scientific or mathematical judgments can be true. Instead,

Moral theory / 537

our moral judgments are practical rather than theoretical and so are more or less reasonable rather than true or false. Rawls thus understands his defense of the two principles of justice in *A Theory of Justice* as an application of a Kantian constructivist moral conception which, as an exercise in moral theory, he takes to be superior to alternative available moral conceptions.

It is important to note that in *Political Liberalism*, published more than a decade after Rawls first set out his views on moral theory and Kantian constructivism, he abandons the Kantian constructivist moral conception as the proper justification for justice as fairness. He argues that Kantian constructivism is a comprehensive view and thus unsuited to the task of providing the basis for an overlapping consensus in a pluralistic society. It is comprehensive in part because it advocates a Kantian view of the self which is not a view that could be widely agreed to in a democratic society with a diversity of moral ideals of the self. In *Political Liberalism* he argues instead for political constructivism, which is not a fully comprehensive moral conception but a narrower view that is focused only on constructing principles of justice for modern democratic societies. The elements that enter into the construction are only those that could achieve widespread support among democratic citizens.

Rawls's discussion of moral theory, therefore, drops from view once he adopts the political perspective in his later work. It does, however, lurk in the background insofar as citizens' comprehensive doctrines, their moral, religious, and metaphysical beliefs, must contain, as an essential part, a moral conception. A citizen's moral conception, whatever it is and however coherent and articulate it is, plays an important role in the argument for political liberalism. The overlapping consensus that provides the stability that political liberalism is designed to achieve has to be grounded in the various moral beliefs citizens espouse. If the overlapping consensus is not grounded in a moral conception, then the consensus would be a mere *modus vivendi* agreement and for this reason unstable. Instead citizens are supposed to affirm the two principles for moral reasons, albeit, different moral reasons. The fact that the principles of justice are grounded in the moral beliefs and attitudes of citizens is what secures the legitimacy and stability of the two principles of justice in a pluralistic democratic society.

In summary, it is important to distinguish clearly between the meta-ethical argument that divides moral theory from moral philosophy and which argues for its independence from the findings of other branches of philosophy, and the moral argument for a particular moral conception, namely, Kantian constructivism. And, further, it is important to distinguish the latter from political constructivism, and finally to recognize the role that the idea of a moral conception plays in political liberalism.

Paul Voice

SEE ALSO:

Constructivism: Kantian/political
Objectivity
Political liberalism, justice as fairness as
Reflective equilibrium
Sidgwick, Henry

138.

MORAL WORTH OF PERSONS

ORAL WORTH IS a kind of goodness that is predicated of persons. Rawls claims that after the good and the right, moral worth is the third main concept of ethics and develops it as part of his conception of goodness as rationality. According to this, a good or morally worthy person is someone who has to a higher degree than the average the broadly based features of moral character that it is rational for members of a well-ordered society to want in one another (*TJ* 383–384). Such broadly based features are the moral virtues.

In extending the conception of goodness as rationality to persons Rawls does not assume that a person as such has some definite role or function in light of which we might say that someone is good as a person because he has the properties that it is rational to want for performing such a role. Nor does he start from a basic role of persons (or a set of most important roles), such as that of citizen, in order to identify the properties that it is rational for persons to want in one another. Instead, he surmises that "there may exist properties which it is rational to want in persons when they are viewed with respect to almost any of their social roles" (*TJ* 382). The idea of a well-ordered society provides the point of view from which the "broadly based" properties are to be identified. In such a society, it is rational for its members to want others to act upon the principles of right and justice and to have the corresponding moral virtues; in particular, it is rational for them to want others to have a sense of justice. Though this perspective does not single out the role of citizenship, the former includes the latter. Since the extension is possible through the use of the principles of right and justice, the concept of moral worth belongs to the full theory of the good. A morally good or worthy person, on this view, is someone who has to a higher degree than average the moral virtues as determined by the principles of right and justice. Since in a well-ordered society all its members have the appropriate sense of justice, everyone has the same moral worth (*TJ* 274–275).

Since the concept of moral worth presupposes the principles of right and justice, the former cannot provide a first principle of distributive justice. This is why the conception of justice as a reward to virtue would not be chosen in the original position: legitimate expectations cannot be determined by rewarding people according to moral virtue because part of moral virtue consists precisely in satisfying, or at least not interfering with, people's legitimate expectations as determined by the principles of justice.

Beginning with "The Priority of Right and Ideas of the Good" (1988), the concept of moral worth is importantly revised in order to make it compatible with a political conception of justice. Though political liberalism may "affirm the superiority of certain forms of moral character and encourage certain moral virtues," these must be specifically political, which means that they "characterize the ideal of a good citizen of a democratic state" only and do not depend on any particular comprehensive doctrine. As Rawls puts it in the *Restatement*, this is a partial conception of moral worth (*JF*142).

Faviola Rivera-Castro

SEE ALSO:

Desert
Goodness as rationality
Sense of Justice
Thin and full theories of good

N

139.

NAGEL, THOMAS

THOMAS NAGEL (born 1937), Professor of Philosophy and Law at New York University, is one of Rawls's most important philosophical interlocutors and the author of a number of influential papers about Rawls's political philosophy (e.g. Nagel 1975, 2003). His most significant engagement with Rawls's ideas is in *Equality and Partiality* (Nagel 1991). In that book, Nagel uses his central distinction between objective and subjective ways of conceiving of the world to address the feasibility of Rawls's egalitarianism. Liberalism must leave us with enough personal space to realize the "subjective" values of our own lives. There is, however, a complementary objective discipline to ethical and political thought, namely, the impersonal demands of others as mediated via political institutions. Influenced by G. A. Cohen's claim that Rawls's egalitarianism focuses on the institutions of the basic structure of society to the exclusion of personal choice, Nagel seeks to ameliorate the conflict between personal values and the impersonal demands of equality (see Cohen 2008). The latter are realized in an institutional scheme; we aim, by contrast, to give subjective values sufficient free play within the scope of the personal, beyond those institutions.

Nagel is, however, pessimistic as to whether there is a satisfactory resolution of this tension between the personal and the institutional, because of our commitment to a free market. Market motivations will see individual support for just institutions eroded, and generate pressure toward an expedient society that accepts substantial inequality in return for efficiency and prosperity. Nagel argues that while our goal should be a Rawlsian egalitarianism that rests on a "general suspicion of inequalities owing to class or talent," that does not seem realistic taking people's psychologies as they are (Nagel 1991, 121). Our most feasible egalitarianism, then, falls short of Rawls's view. It will combine equal basic liberties and equality of opportunity with a decent social minimum. Any more radical changes of individual motive require a transformatory change within the personal comparable to that envisaged in Cohen's "ethos of justice." Nagel is pessimistic as to whether this development is feasible. He concludes that we cannot devise any theoretically satisfactory reconciliation of the demands of the personal and the impersonal within politics.

Nagel's overall appraisal of the feasibility of Rawlsian egalitarianism is negative: we are confronted by an insuperable practical paradox when we try to reconcile the subject and the objective in this domain. However, his arguments also ground a limited optimism: welfare state capitalist societies are the most feasible arrangement that can currently be justified, taking people's psychologies as they are. It is noteworthy that in his own discussion Nagel does not engage with Rawls's account in *Justice as Fairness* of the choice between fundamental economic systems. Rawls there rejects residual welfare-state capitalism and argues that the only two economic systems that can realize his principle of reciprocity are a property-owning democracy or liberal market socialism.

Where Nagel does more to engage with the institutional dimensions of a just society is in his book on justice and taxation co-authored with Liam Murphy, *The Myth of Ownership* (Murphy and Nagel 2002). The argument of this book proceeds from a fundamentally Rawlsian starting point, whereby the justice of systems of taxation is to be assessed simply as one aspect of the justice of the overall basic structure of society. Murphy and Nagel show that, once we understand the tax rules of a society to be a constitutive element of its basic structure, traditional measures of tax justice, such as "horizontal equity" and "vertical equity," must be understood as confused, as they depend on giving an illegitimate normative standing to notional pre-tax holdings.

Complementary to Nagel's engagement with Rawls's work on domestic justice is an influential paper on global distributive justice that defends a statist approach with affinities with Rawls's own in *The Law of Peoples* (Nagel 2005). The basis of Nagel's own position is a Hobbesian claim that justice between members of a given political community depends on an enabling role that can be played only by the legal order of a sovereign nation state. This role underwrites a system of sanctions that underpin stable expectations and the mutual assurance that every citizen will comply with just institutions. The duty of justice between citizens of a single state is an associative obligation (Nagel 2005, 120–121). Nagel's institutional focus places him on the same side as Rawls in the ongoing dispute between statists and cosmopolitans about global justice.

Alan Thomas and Martin O'Neill

SEE ALSO:

Basic structure of society
Law of Peoples
Self-interest
Taxation
Two principles of justice (in justice as fairness)

140.

NASH POINT

IN EXPLAINING BOTH the meaning of the difference principle and its choice by the parties in the original position, Rawls treats it as the solution to what is often called a bargaining game. He then contrasts the solution represented by the difference principle with other proposed solutions, in particular that of classical utilitarianism (what he calls the Bentham point) and that proposed by John Nash, the Nash point (*JF* 62–63).

In a bargaining game, players must divide up a pay-off between them, which they forfeit if they cannot agree. The size of the pay-off can be dependent on the agreement reached. Bargaining games capture essential features of social cooperation that raise the problem of distributive justice in the first place: social cooperation produces a surplus, but the size of the surplus is dependent on the rules governing the cooperation including how the surplus is to be divided.

In a bargaining game, any agreement that distributes all of the surplus will be what is called a Nash equilibrium: once adopted, there is no way for any player to improve her outcome by unilaterally changing her actions. The question is then which equilibrium point should be chosen. The difference principle can be thought of as a rule for choosing an outcome to the bargaining game. It says to choose the outcome that maximizes the pay-off to the worst off. Classical utilitarianism also yields a principle for choosing an outcome: it says, choose the outcome that maximizes the sum of the pay-offs, understood as utilities.

The Nash solution lies between these two positions. It says to choose the point that maximizes the product of the utility gains of the players. This differs from the utilitarian solution in two important ways.

First, it maximizes the product, rather than the sum of the utility gains. This puts a certain egalitarian pressure on the choice that is not present in the classical

546

utilitarian solution. For a given total utility, the distribution that maximizes the product of the utilities is an equal one. Nevertheless, it allows for distributions in which, compared to the schemes that satisfy the difference principle, the better off profit at the expense of the worst off, and so it violates the idea of reciprocity.

Second, it focuses on utility gains, not the total utility of each player. Gains here are measured against what is called the disagreement point: the result if the players fail to come to an agreement and so do not create a cooperative surplus. This makes the Nash point dependent on the relative strength of the players going into the game, and so gives weight to their threat advantage. Rawls cites Amartya Sen and others who criticize the Nash solution on these grounds, remarking that "to each according to his threat advantage is not a conception of justice" (*TJ* 116 and n.10).

Anthony Simon Laden

SEE ALSO:

Difference principle
The original position
Rational choice theory
Utilitarianism

141.

NATURAL DUTIES

THE NATURAL DUTIES are those that are binding on individuals without the performance of previous voluntary acts. Among them, Rawls mentions the duties of mutual aid, mutual respect, not to harm or injure another, and not to cause unnecessary suffering. From the standpoint of a theory of justice, the duty of justice is the fundamental requirement for individuals (*TJ* 296). These duties are "natural" because they are owed to persons generally regardless of any institutional relationship, and their content is not defined by the rules of institutions or of social practices. Rawls contrasts them with "obligations," which are grounded on the principles of fairness. Obligations, in this sense, are defined by the rules of just (or fair) institutions or practices, they arise as a result of voluntary acts, and they are owed to definite individuals. The natural duty of justice has two parts: "it requires us to support and to comply with just institutions that exist and apply to us"; it "also constrains us to further just arrangements not yet established" (*TJ* 99). According to this, everyone has a natural duty to do his or her part in a social scheme in which the basic structure is just or "as just as it is reasonable to expect in the circumstances" (*TJ* 99). Thus, the duty of justice has an important role in making social cooperation stable (*TJ* 293).

The natural duties are the content of principles for individuals, as opposed to the principles for institutions, such as the principles of justice as fairness, which apply to the institutions of the basic structure. In *TJ* Rawls maintains that any theory of justice must include, along with principles for institutions, principles for individuals as well as principles for the law of nations because they are part of a complete theory of right. He also claims that all such principles are chosen in the original position. Principles for the basic structure are to be chosen first, followed by principles for individuals and those for the law of nations. The reason

Natural duties / 549

he offers for this "definite sequence" is that obligations presuppose principles for social institutions, and some natural duties, such as the duty of justice, do so as well. This ordering, which is indicative of the social nature of the duty of justice (*TJ* 95), greatly simplifies the choice of principles for individuals because they are to be chosen such that they cohere with the principles of justice as fairness. This last point excludes from the start any serious consideration of the principle of utility as the standard for principles for individuals. The choice of the utility principle in this context "would lead to an incoherent conception of right" that would provide individuals with incompatible criteria for determining how to act in institutional contexts.

Rawls's discussion of the natural duties and of the reasons why the parties in the original position would choose them is not systematic or complete. However, he describes the reasons for the choice of the duties of justice, mutual respect, and mutual aid. Considerations of publicity and stability are central to the choice of the duty of justice. He argues that, in light of the parties' interest in securing the stability of just institutions and of the assurance problem, they do best by making the requirement to comply with just institutions binding regardless of one's voluntary acts. The "assurance problem" is that of assuring the participants in a cooperative scheme that everyone does his part since "each person's willingness to contribute is contingent upon the contribution of others" (*TJ* 238). In order to maintain public confidence that the common agreement is being carried out, it is best for the parties to choose the natural duty of justice instead of an obligation to comply with just institutions. This natural duty is also superior to a principle of utility in terms of simplicity and clarity (*TJ* 296).

The duty of respect requires that we "show a person the respect which is due to him as a moral being, that is, as a being with a sense of justice and a conception of the good" (*TJ* 297). Mutual respect is shown "in our willingness to see the situation of others from their point of view, from the perspective of their conception of their good; and in our being prepared to give reasons for our actions whenever the interests of others are materially affected" (*TJ* 297). Considerations of publicity are central in the choice of this duty in the original position. The parties "know that in society they need to be assured by the esteem of their associates" (*TJ* 297). For this reason, the public knowledge that the duty of mutual aid is honored is of great value to everyone. Similar considerations enter into the choice of the duty of mutual aid: the public knowledge that it is honored greatly improves "the quality of everyday life" (*TJ* 298).

It could be thought that the contractarian basis of the principles of natural duty might be incompatible with the claim that they apply to individuals without any previous voluntary acts because such an application seems to presuppose a voluntary act of consent. But this is not correct, as Rawls explicitly points out. All principles of right are the outcome of a hypothetical agreement in the original position, but this is independent from the conditions under which they are binding for specific agents. In the case of the principle of fairness, the reason why obligations depend upon voluntary acts does not follow from its contractarian basis, but is part of the content of the principle itself. The same holds, mutatis mutandis, for the principles of natural duty.

Rawls divides the natural duties into positive (such as the duty to help others) and negative (such as the duty not to be cruel to others), and claims that the latter have more weight than the former. This point is relevant for answering questions of priority, and though he claims that priority rules must be adopted in the original position, he does not pursue this issue.

Faviola Rivera-Castro

SEE ALSO:

Fairness, principle of
Natural duty of justice
Obligations
Reciprocity
Sense of justice
Stability

142.

NATURAL DUTY OF JUSTICE

IN A THEORY OF JUSTICE Rawls distinguishes "natural duties" from obligations: natural duties are incumbent upon each of us unconditionally, whereas obligations are voluntarily incurred. He also distinguishes natural duties from duties that are attached to institutional offices or other social positions. Natural duties are moral requirements. As the institutions and social positions to which institutional and social duties attach may be morally defensible or indefensible, they do not necessarily possess any moral force (*TJ* 98f.).

Rawls acknowledges a diverse set of natural duties, including "the duty of helping another when he is in need or jeopardy ...; the duty not to harm or injure another; ... the duty not to cause unnecessary suffering" and the duty of mutual respect (*TJ* 98, 297). Within the context of a theory of justice, however, the most important natural duty requires us "to comply with and do our share in just institutions when they exist and apply to us" and "to assist in the establishment of just arrangements when they do not exist" (*TJ* 293f.).

Rawls holds that the parties in the "original position" would endorse this natural duty of justice as "the easiest and most direct way" "to secure the stability of just institutions" (*TJ* 295). By contrast, the principle of fairness, which in effect supplements the duty of justice for those who "gain political office" and "take advantage of the opportunities offered by the constitutional system," provides less support for just institutions (*TJ* 302f.). This represents a departure from his earlier position, which was that mere receipt of benefits from mutually beneficial and just social arrangements grounds a moral obligation of obedience to law (*CP* 117–128).

As Rawls conceives it, the natural duty of justice calls for obedience to law within nearly just societies. "When the basic structure of society is reasonably just, as estimated by what the current state of things allows, we are to recognize unjust laws as binding provided that they do not exceed certain limits of injustice" (*TJ* 308).

Because the duty to obey can be overridden, principled disobedience can sometimes be justified (*TJ* 309). More importantly, the duty to obey does not always obtain. Rawls remarks that "the duty to comply is problematic for permanent minorities that have suffered from injustice for many years. And certainly we are not required to acquiesce in the denial of our own and others' basic liberties" (*TJ* 312). A duty of justice that would be endorsed in the original position could not support a duty to comply with arrangements that violate the basic principles of justice so significantly.

Rawls appends a wide escape clause to the second part of the duty of justice. He says, in effect, that we are not bound to promote just institutions unless that "can be done at little cost to ourselves." However, one might have supposed that, the greater the injustice, the greater the sacrifice that morality might call on us to risk.

Rawls does not pursue such themes further, for his main concern is to lay the groundwork for a theory of civil disobedience, at least one that applies in a nearly just society in which the duty of justice grounds a moral requirement of obedience to law (*TJ* 319–343).

David Lyons

SEE ALSO:

Basic structure of society
Civil disobedience
Fairness, principle of
Natural duties
The original position
Political obligation
Sense of justice
Stability

143.

NATURAL TALENTS

A PERSON'S "NATURAL TALENTS," as Rawls uses the term, are roughly the set of abilities that they were "born with" that affect their success in life. Our opportunities to succeed in life have a number of sources. The sources that are purely genetic are our natural talents. For instance, genetic dispositions to be successful at sport, to do math, to maintain good health, and so on all affect a person's chance of success and thus are natural talents in this broad sense. Whether these dispositions are manifested depends on the social conditions someone is born into. For instance, whether someone actually becomes good at sports will depend on whether they are suitably nurtured, trained, and so on.

Rawls considers whether it is just for these natural talents to affect an individual's success in life. The mere fact that some people are born with greater natural talents than others, Rawls claims, is neither just nor unjust. But it is unjust, Rawls argues, if social and political institutions inappropriately favor those who have greater natural talents with greater material advantages (hence referred to as just "advantages") (*TJ* 87).

One reason why we cannot use differences of natural talents as a basis for assigning advantages is that, as I noted earlier, natural talents are mere genetic *potentials* to be successful at certain tasks, if particular social conditions obtain. How much value we are willing to place on a particular natural talent depends on the ways in which that disposition is likely to be manifested given the social conditions we live in. For instance, we care about the disposition to be good at sport because we happen to live in a society where that disposition tends to be nurtured and where there are various social structures, such as organized, commercial sports teams, which make it useful. But when we are considering questions of social justice we are deciding how to design these background conditions, so we can't take it for granted that they are going to be as they currently are. So we can't assign values to particular natural talents, for the purposes of assessing questions of social justice, without already assuming, unacceptably, that a particular conception of social justice will be implemented.

As well as thinking that natural talents are an unworkable basis for assigning advantages, Rawls thinks that it is *unjust* for people to benefit more from social and political arrangements just because of their natural talents, unless those inequalities work to the advantage of the least well off in society. To understand Rawls's argument for why people should not benefit more from social and political arrangements just because they have greater natural talents (unless this helps the least well off) it is helpful to consider other ways in which advantages could be assigned. For instance, we could arrange society so that better jobs are legally restricted to men, advantaging everyone who is born male. Or we could institute a "free market" economy with no such legal restrictions, which would work to the advantage of people born into high social classes and with scarce natural talents.

Common views about justice disagree about which of these ways of assigning advantages are acceptable. For instance, libertarians would reject legal restrictions on which jobs women can occupy but are untroubled by inequalities which track differences of natural talents and social class. By contrast, people who believe in equality of opportunity or "meritocracy," what Rawls calls "liberal equality," think that both inequalities due to formal legal restrictions on jobs and inequalities due to social class are unjust but are not troubled by inequalities due to differences of natural talent (*TJ* 63).

Rawls argues that there is no moral difference between these different types of inequality in a society. It is unjust if any of these inequalities exist (unless they work to the advantage of the least well off). The reason for this, Rawls tell us, is that all of these inequalities involve some people gaining advantages over others just because they possess characteristics that are "arbitrary from a moral perspective" (*TJ* 64). His argument is that it is *unfair* if society is organized in such as way that it advantages people on an arbitrary basis.

Why does Rawls think these advantages are assigned on an arbitrary basis, and thus unfair? We can distinguish two different (perhaps overlapping) suggestions in his thought. The first suggestion is this would be unfair because people only have the relevant characteristics due to *luck* (Rawls calls it "fortune"), or

Natural talents / 555

factors beyond people's control (*TJ* 65). For instance, it is clearly simply good luck to be born a man rather than a woman. It is obviously not within someone's control to determine their own sex at birth and so it seems unfair to favor them just because of their happening to be born one sex rather than another. Similarly, Rawls says, we have no control over the social class we are born into or the natural talents we are born with. So if some people do better than others because they are born with more favorable natural talents or in a higher social class then advantages are being distributed in accordance with luck and this again is unfair.

The other, second, line of argument for thinking that all of these inequalities are unfair is less focused on the role of luck. On this second line of argument we should first ask what the proper basis is for a society to favor someone with advantages. The appropriate basis for favoring someone is their meeting the requirement of being a contributing member of society by upholding its political institutions, following its laws and so on (*TJ* 13–14). But none of the factors we have discussed affect someone's abilities to contribute in these ways. For instance, people born into different social classes are all able to follow the law and so on. Thus, it is arbitrary and thus unfair if social and political institutions favor someone just because they are born into a higher social class.

Rawls designs his "original position" thought experiment with these considerations in mind. Because he views natural talents as an inappropriate basis for allocating advantages in a society, he requires that knowledge of natural talents be put behind the "veil of ignorance": parties to the agreement in the original position are not aware of what natural talents they possess or will possess. In this way he ensures that none of the parties to the agreement will choose principles that favor them because of their natural talents and thus that the principles of justice do not grant unfair advantages on the basis of natural talent.

Now, egalitarians are sometimes accused of being hostile to inequalities in the distribution of natural talents, perhaps even committed to trying to eradicate the talents themselves. We've seen that Rawls thinks superior natural talents do not create entitlements to advantage. But that doesn't mean he thinks inequalities of natural talent are to be regretted. In fact, Rawls suggests that we view those inequalities as, in some respects, a "collective" or "common asset" (*TJ* 87–88, 92). The idea is that society as a whole can benefit from the fact that people have different, and sometimes superior, genetic abilities. By creating a society in which some of those dispositions can be manifested we enable people to produce greater advantages and can reasonably demand that those advantages accrue not only to themselves but also to society as a whole.

Adam Hosein

SEE ALSO:

Desert
Difference principle
Equal opportunity, democratic interpretation
Fair equality of opportunity
Liberal conception of justice
Libertarianism
Luck egalitarianism
The original position

144.

NEUTRALITY

LIBERALISM IS COMMONLY associated with the principle that democratic governments should remain neutral on the question of what the best kind of life is. Rawls's theory of justice is commonly thought to be committed to this kind of neutrality in virtue of the veil of ignorance, which plays an important role in his argument from the original position. The veil of ignorance prevents parties in the original position from knowing their own conceptions of a good life, which means that the justification of Rawls's principles of justice does not presuppose the truth of any such conception. In this sense his theory of justice is neutral toward different conceptions of a good life, and a government regulated by his conception of justice is therefore neutral in this sense too. How are parties in the original position supposed to choose between principles if they do not know their conceptions of a good life? Rawls supposes that parties in the original position have "higher-order interests" in developing and exercising their two moral powers fully, the capacity for a sense of justice and the capacity for a conception of the good. He supposes that in virtue of these interests they will choose a liberal conception of justice that guarantees an equal right to the basic liberties, because the basic liberties are social conditions necessary for the full development and exercise of the two moral powers. But, he maintains, to suppose that parties in the original position have these higher-order interests in the development of their moral powers is not to assume the truth of any comprehensive moral, religious, or philosophical doctrine, thus preserving the neutrality of the argument from the original position.

Although Rawls is commonly thought to be committed to neutrality in virtue of the argument from the original position, he does not explicitly endorse neutrality until *PL*, where he endorses the principle "that the state is not to do anything intended to favor or promote any particular comprehensive [religious, philosophical, or moral] doctrine rather than another, or to give greater assistance to those who pursue it" (*PL* 193). According to Rawls, this principle is satisfied by a state in virtue of being effectively regulated by his two principles of justice. Note that Rawls is advocating neutrality of intent here, and not neutrality of effect. Some conceptions of a good life will be easier to live by than others and some will gain more adherents in any society, including any society that is regulated by Rawls's conception of justice. Rawls recognizes this and does not maintain that neutrality of effect, or equality of impact, is feasible or desirable. He maintains instead that although some conceptions of the good life will be easier to live by and some will gain more adherents than others in a society regulated by his conception of justice, the intent of a society in being so regulated is to establish justice, not to advance any particular comprehensive doctrine.

Rawls's claim that a state satisfies neutrality of intent in being effectively regulated by his conception of justice is nonetheless puzzling. Although his conception of justice includes the priority of basic liberty – which permits the government to limit basic liberties only for the sake of basic liberties, and never to promote a particular religious view, or to promote human excellence or perfection according to a particular conception, or to maximize pleasure – the priority of liberty seems to permit the government to limit nonbasic liberties for these reasons, and so seems to allow the government to intend to favor some comprehensive doctrines in this way. Also puzzling is Rawls's claim (*PL* 193 n.25) that his principle of neutrality of intent is the same principle of neutrality that Dworkin endorses in "Liberalism" (Dworkin 1985). Dworkin's principle, as originally stated, is that "political decisions must be, so far as is possible, independent of any particular conception of the good life, or of what gives value to life" (Dworkin 1985, 191). There is no mention of intent here. Moreover, Dworkin's principle is ambiguous between a justificatory interpretation and a motivational interpretation. On a justificatory interpretation, political decisions must be justifiable without presupposing that any particular conception of the good life or of what gives value to life is true. If a political decision can be justified only on the assumption that a particular contested conception of the good life (or set of such conceptions) is true, then the government is not permitted to make it. On a motivational interpretation, the government is not permitted to make a decision that is motivated by the belief that a particular contested conception of the good life is true or by the desire to advance this conception. If a political decision will be made only because government officials believe that a particular contested conception of the good life (or set of such conceptions) is true or only because they wish to advance some such conception, then the government is not permitted to make this decision.

This ambiguity is relevant to Rawls's claim of neutrality because even if the state is effectively regulated by Rawls's conception of justice, this does not guarantee that no government official will be motivated by the belief that some contested conception of the good life is true or by a desire to advance some such conception. If Rawls's conception of justice is generally accepted for the reasons that he gives for it, which do not presuppose the truth of any particular comprehensive doctrine, and a basic structure is effectively regulated by this conception of justice because it is generally accepted for these reasons, then the basic structure, including the state, is not intended to favor or promote any particular comprehensive doctrine. It does not follow, however, that government officials within this basic structure will never make a political decision intended to favor or promote such a doctrine. To illustrate, even if the difference principle can be justified without assuming the truth of any comprehensive religious doctrine, a majority of government officials might be motivated to adopt policies that bring the distribution of wealth in line with the difference principle by their desire to promote Christianity. Rawls's claim therefore appears to be mistaken that the principle of neutrality that he identifies "is satisfied in virtue of the features of a political conception expressing the priority of right" (*PL* 193). It is true, as Rawls goes on to write, that "so long as the basic structure is regulated by such a view [a liberal, political conception of justice], its institutions are not intended to favor any comprehensive doctrine." But it does not follow that the state does nothing intended to favor or promote such a doctrine, because a state action might be intended by its human agents to do this, even in a society that is regulated by a liberal, political conception of justice.

In addition to his endorsement of neutrality of intent in *PL*, Rawls is thought to be committed to neutrality also because he argues there for a duty of civility, which permits us to take only those positions on important matters of justice that can be justified by public reason and because it is assumed that public reasons are neutral reasons. The duty of civility permits government officials, and all of us when acting in our official capacity as citizens, by voting for example, to support policies that bear on constitutional essentials, such as basic liberties, or on other matters of basic justice, such as meeting citizens' basic material needs, only if we sincerely believe that these positions can be justified by a conception of justice that is both liberal and political in nature. A conception of justice is *liberal* if it recognizes an equal right to basic liberties; it assigns basic liberty priority over other social values; and it ensures that each citizen has the material means necessary to make effective use of their basic liberties (*PL* 223). A conception of justice is *political* if it applies only to the basic structure of society, and is not proposed to govern all of life; it does not presuppose the truth of any particular comprehensive doctrine; and it is developed as an interpretation of political ideas implicit in the public culture of a modern, democratic society (*PL* 223). A public reason, then, is one that is identified as sufficient to justify a government policy by some conception of justice of this kind, when its principles are applied by using valid methods of factual inquiry. Because the validity of a public reason does not depend upon the truth of any particular comprehensive doctrine, public reasons are, in this sense, neutral reasons, and the duty of civility is, in this sense, a principle of neutrality. However, the duty of civility does not require strict government neutrality as this is ordinarily understood. Consider, for the sake of illustration, the inscription of "In God We Trust" on US currency. Suppose, for the sake of argument, that this policy does not restrict any basic liberty. Then it is possible to construct a liberal, political conception of justice – one that satisfies Rawls's six criteria – that identifies the fact that most people find this inscription inspiring and comforting as a sufficient reason for it. This policy is clearly nonneutral, however, in favoring belief in God over nonbelief.

Peter de Marneffe

SEE ALSO:

Communitarianism
Duty of civility
Dworkin, Ronald
Liberal conception of justice
Moral person
Political liberalisms, family of
Primary goods, social
Public reason
Reasonable pluralism

145.

NOZICK, ROBERT

I N MANY WAYS Robert Nozick's (1938–2002) objections to Rawls revisit a classical issue in liberal theory, namely the reconciliation of exclusive private property rights with redistribution in response to poverty. Before focusing on their disagreement about redistributive justice, it is useful to note a couple of important agreements between the two. Both Rawls (in *A Theory of Justice*) and Nozick (*State, Anarchy, and Utopia*) considered utilitarian theories to be the dominant political theories of their day, and both thought that, nevertheless, utilitarianism fails as a liberal theory of justice. Rawls expresses this point by saying that utilitarianism does not "take seriously the distinction between persons" (*TJ* 24), whereas Nozick expresses it by saying that utilitarianism fails to take the liberal principle of "self-ownership" seriously. The main problem, they agree, issues from utilitarianism's focus on the aggregate sum of values as well as how these values are distributed in a society at any given time. This focus, Rawls and Nozick argue, makes utilitarianism incapable of protecting each person's right to be free (not enslaved) or to be the one who has sole, exclusive coercive authority with regard to herself and her own powers and means. Both thinkers also explicitly view the contract tradition, especially Lockean and Kantian approaches, as more suited to developing contemporary liberal theories of justice (see *TJ* 10 n.4; Nozick 1974, 3–20). Nozick's various objections to Rawls may be summarized as a charge that Rawls fails to stay true to their shared liberal aspirations. Nozick argues that although Rawls's theory of justice as fairness is "undeniably [a] great advance over utilitarianism," it still encounters the same types of problems (Nozick 1974, 230, cf. 172). Also Rawls's theory, Nozick argues at length, fails to take seriously enough the distinction between persons or each person's right to self-ownership. The main culprit is seen to be Rawls's "difference principle" and the way in which it involves giving some (the least advantaged) coercive access to or "(partial) ownership" of others (the less disadvantaged), ownership of their persons, powers, and means (Nozick 1974, 172). In what follows, I outline the core elements in Nozick's criticism of Rawls before indicating some possible Rawlsian responses to Nozick, including Rawls's own responses in *Political Liberalism*.

A central thesis defended by Nozick in his 1974 *Anarchy, State, and Utopia* is that there is no coercive right – no right of justice – to material goods beyond what one can create through one's labor on a fair share of the world's resources. This fair share is identifiable by means of a version of a Lockean "enough-and-as-good proviso." Nozick's version of the proviso uses the original value of material goods (their value in their natural state or before anyone had created value from them) as the baseline for calculating each person's fair share of resources. Hence, each person has a right or is entitled to access 1/nth of the original value of all the natural resources in the world, where "n" refers to the sum of persons in the world. Such access may be provided directly to natural goods or through compensation for the lack of direct access, such as through employment within the context of money-based economies (Nozick 1974, 174–182). Each person is entitled to all the values or means she creates with her fair share of resources and to all the values she can obtain through trade with other persons. Nozick thinks that liberalism requires such a theory of acquisition since exclusive property rights are necessary to secure a person's freedom to set and pursue ends of their own. Consequently, a liberal theory of justice cannot justify anything beyond a fair starting point with regard to material resources. Any attempt to do more is inconsistent with liberal theory's commitment to individuals' right to self-ownership or freedom – to have sole, exclusive coercive authority over their own persons, powers, and means. It follows, Nozick also argues, that we cannot predict or require a particular pattern or distribution of resources in a just society. Any distribution of resources beyond an original fair share of resources ("justice in acquisition") will depend on the actual or historical facts describing how persons have created more values, including by trade, from their original fair share ("justice in transfer") (Nozick 1974, 150–174). Resulting is a conception of justice often called "right-wing libertarian," according to which the state must be "minimal." Because the state is seen as a voluntary enterprise that simply does better (more prudent and efficient) what individuals have a right to do on their own, and because individuals only have a right to access the value of an original fair share of resources, it is impossible to justify any more extensive state redistribution to alleviate inequality as such.

The above reasoning, Nozick argues, can be applied to show the incorrectness of most so-called "left-wing" theories, including liberal and libertarian versions thereof. These theories seek to justify the redistribution of goods in response to need as such or simply to decrease inequality or poverty in society. Such moves seek, Nozick argues, to enforce a certain "pattern" or "end-result" as determined by some "nonhistorical" principle of distribution, which is seen as a fundamentally illiberal move. Any theory that defends coercive redistribution beyond giving everyone a fair starting point with regard to material resources ends up defending principles of slavery, not freedom. Likewise, Nozick argues, because Rawls defends the difference principle – and especially its demand that "social and economic inequalities are to be arranged so that they are ... reasonably expected to be to everyone's advantage" (*TJ* 53) – his theory fails as a liberal theory of justice. The difference principle is inconsistent with the parameters set by a theory of freedom; it fails to take the distinction between persons sufficiently seriously, since it entails that there will be continuous coercive redistribution insofar as it is necessary to ensure that the distribution of goods is advantageous to all. Nozick maintains that Rawls's notion of redistribution is to take from those who have more in order to give to those who have less, which disrespects the distinction between persons by using the rich as a mere means for the poor, or by enslaving the rich to the poor, or by giving the poor (partial) ownership in the rich. According to Nozick, the only way to justify the coercive redistribution the difference principle involves requires thinking of it as a very different kind of principle altogether. Instead of a general principle of justice for all liberal societies, it must be seen as a principle of rectification to address great historical wrongdoings in a particular society's past (Nozick 1974, 231).

Rawlsian and Rawls's own responses to Nozick's criticisms (and others similar) naturally attack some of Nozick's needed assumptions for the success of the arguments. A possible line of defense is to argue within libertarian (including Lockean) parameters. For example, one may simply maintain that Rawls's difference principle can be seen as a better solution to the problem of acquisition than Nozick's version of the "enough-and-as-good" principle, at least under historical conditions of modern, property-owning democracies. (Whether or not Rawls's later version of the difference principle, which requires maximization of the prospective benefit for the least advantaged, also can be seen as such a Lockean-type principle of acquisition is an open question.) Another, possibly complementary defense involves appealing to how Rawls's basic, procedural approach to justice implies that the difference principle is neither an "end-result" nor a "non-historical" principle, but a dynamic principle that is sensitive to particular histories of societies. In *Political Liberalism*, Rawls himself employs a different strategy by appealing to "Kantian social contract theory" (*PL* 265), rather than taking the libertarian route. Rawls challenges Nozick's libertarian assumptions that the state is a voluntary enterprise (simply a more prudent and efficient way to realize individuals' rights). His account of justice, rather, is not an account of individuals' rights, but of the liberal state's rights ("public law") or the citizens' fundamental rights in relation to the basic structure of their public legal-political institutions (*PL* 265; cf. *PL* 262–274).

Helga Varden

SEE ALSO:

Cohen, G. A.
Difference principle
Distributive justice
Kant, Immanuel
Libertarianism
Locke, John
Procedural justice
Property-owning democracy
Social minimum
Socialism

146.

NUSSBAUM, MARTHA

MARTHA NUSSBAUM (b. 1947) is an American philosopher and public intellectual. Having received a Ph.D. in Classical Philology at Harvard University, her academic positions have included posts at Harvard, where she was a colleague of John Rawls; Brown University; and the University of Chicago. Nussbaum is both an ardent defender of Rawls's work and a searching critic of his theories.

Much of Nussbaum's work centers on the articulation of an approach to moral and political questions known as the "capabilities approach." Originally developed as an alternative to the use of Gross Domestic Product as a comparative index of the quality of life in developing countries, this approach sets forth a list of functional capabilities the development of which to at least a minimal threshold level is central to living a life worthy of human dignity. This list, which Nussbaum emphasizes is open to revision, includes life; bodily health; bodily integrity; senses, imagination, and thought; emotions; practical reason; affiliation; concern for and living with other species; play; and control over one's environment (both political and material) (Nussbaum 2011, 33–34).

Nussbaum also employs the capabilities approach as a partial theory of social justice. Like Rawls, she locates her approach squarely within the liberal tradition. The approach emphasizes that each individual is to be regarded as an end. Nussbaum also categorizes the capabilities approach as a form of political liberalism, and this entails the promotion and empowerment of all of the capabilities as a matter of political justice. She holds that it must at least be plausible to regard the list of capabilities and the associated political principles as subjects of public deliberation and overlapping consensus among people of differing comprehensive doctrines. It is this respect for reasonable disagreement that causes Nussbaum not to develop the capabilities approach into a comprehensive theory of the quality of life or social justice (Nussbaum 2011, 75–76).

The capabilities approach, however, also involves significant criticisms of Rawls's views (Nussbaum 2006). Nussbaum's view of dignity has more in common with Aristotle's ethics of flourishing than Rawls's affinity toward a Kantian respect for practical reason. Each of the capabilities is an aspect of the striving that commands our awe and respect, and each entails claims of justice. Thus, for Nussbaum, persons with disabilities and even many nonhuman animals display multiple capabilities, and the claims related to these are squarely questions of political justice. Rawls's social contract view, however, cannot regard them as such. Similarly, Nussbaum argues that Rawls's extension of the social contract tradition in *The Law of Peoples* is not able to accommodate the assignment of priority to the development of the capabilities and, accordingly, is inadequate as a minimal account of international justice.

A long-standing theme in Nussbaum's work is to extend liberal principles in service of feminist concerns, while showing earlier lapses as not intrinsic to liberalism itself. She argues, e.g., that it is inadequate to assume that heads of households will altruistically promote the interests of women in a social contracting situation (Nussbaum 1999, 65). Instead, she advocates that the family must be named explicitly as a part of the basic structure of society and analyzed according to its profound role in shaping the possibilities open to each member, yet without losing respect for the depth of conscience involved in individuals' choices regarding their roles in a family (Nussbaum 2000, 270–283).

Other major, related topics of Nussbaum's work include her sustained philosophical attention to the emotions, law and education. Nussbaum defends a view of the emotions as having cognitive content and responding to perceptions of value, though not always in a trustworthy or reliable way (Nussbaum 2001). This ties the emotions directly to the capacity of practical reason and renders them of central importance to political theory. Thus, Nussbaum has examined extensively problems of grounding law in such negative emotions as disgust and shame (Nussbaum 2004; 2010a). Similarly, Nussbaum holds that education is central to the full development of human capabilities and that education through the arts and humanities, in particular, are important to the cultivation of the imagination and emotions as important capacities for practical reasoning and democratic citizenship (Nussbaum 1997, 2010b).

Alan W. Grose

SEE ALSO:

Capabilities
Family
Feminism
Overlapping consensus
Political conception of justice
Primary goods, social

O

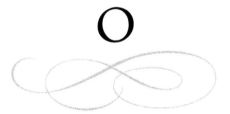

147.

OBJECTIVITY

RAWLS WAS CONCERNED with the conditions underlying the objectivity of moral and political judgment from the very beginning of his philosophical career. His first published essay, "Outline of a Decision Procedure for Ethics," represents a first attempt at delineating the conditions that must be satisfied both by the competent judge and by the judgments that she reaches if they are to be deemed objective.

Despite changes in emphasis and restrictions of scope (by the time of his final writings, he makes it clear that he is interested exclusively in *political* objectivity), certain themes remain as constants throughout Rawls's writings on objectivity. The first of these themes is that objectivity emerges from the taking up by moral and political judges of a certain standpoint. That standpoint is elaborated through the exclusion of those kinds of particularities that might incline otherwise competent judges to partiality. The original position, the situation of choice from which principles of justice are chosen, embodies this set of constraints. To quote Rawls in *A Theory of Justice*, "its stipulations express the restrictions on arguments that force us to consider the choice of principles unencumbered by the singularities of the circumstances in which we find ourselves" (*TJ* 516).

A second aspect of Rawls's conception of objectivity that has remained unchanged is that he views it and the process of reasoning that is carried out on the basis of it as eminently practical. The goal of Rawls's theory as a whole, and of his operationalization of objectivity in particular, is not to survey eternal moral truths, but rather to "reconcile by reason" (*TJ* 580) those persons who find themselves locked in "disagreement over the just form of basic institutions within a democratic society under modern conditions" (*CP* 305–306).

A third recurrent theme in Rawls's account of objectivity is that it is a resolutely nonepistemic notion. That is, the point of the adoption of the objective perspective embodied in the original position is not to place us in a privileged perspective from which to ascertain independently existing moral or political facts. Rawls's is a Kantian conception of objectivity, one that places a great deal of importance on the autonomy of the subject. That autonomy would be compromised were the relationship of the will to purportedly independent "moral facts" to be one of mere assent. The objectivity of the original position thus does not lie in its affording us epistemic access to moral truths, but rather in constituting a standpoint from which suitably situated persons conceived of as free and equal can construct principles of justice.

A fourth important idea emerges from the foregoing differentiation of Rawls's conception of objectivity from that which characterizes positions such as rational intuitionism. It is that Rawls's conception is inextricably linked to a certain conception of the person. The objectivity of the judgments yielded by the original position depends upon their being representable as those that would be arrived at by agents conceived of as free and equal. They are free, first, in that they view themselves as capable of having, but also of revising, a conception of the good and, second, in that they view themselves as being entitled to make claims on the basis of that conception, provided that that conception is not contrary to principles of justice. The Rawlsian moral subject which serves as the basis for the construction of principles of justice is thus both rational (in that she has a conception of the good) and reasonable (in that she accepts the primacy of justice as posing constraints upon her conception of the good), and equal (in that she views all of her fellow citizens as "equally worthy of being represented in any procedure of construction that is to determine the principles of justice that are to regulate the basic institutions of their society" (*CP* 333)). In the original position, rationality is embodied in the principles of rational choice on the basis of which parties reason, and reasonableness is captured by the constraints that prevent them from reasoning on the basis of morally arbitrary particularity. Equality flows from the latter constraints, in that all subjects are represented in the same way.

The introduction of a conception of the person conceived of as free and equal in the manner just described may seem ad hoc in the context of a theory of objectivity. That it is not can be appreciated by adverting to the second of the points made above, namely, that the purpose of the theory within which the conception of objectivity is lodged is to reconcile citizens of democratic societies by reason. To do so requires proceeding "from what all parties to the discussion

Objectivity / 573

hold in common" (*TJ* 580). The conception of citizens as free and equal fulfills this function in the context of a free and democratic society.

A fifth aspect of Rawls's conception of objectivity that is in my view important to highlight is that, for Rawls, objectivity does not entail certainty. Reasoning from an objective standpoint means for Rawls that we place ourselves in a position that will allow us to arrive at uncoerced, principled agreement with those with whom we disagree. The taking up of this perspective in other words does not determine a result. Rather, the objectivity that Rawls places at the heart of his practical project "can establish but a loose framework for deliberation which must rely very considerably on our powers of reflection and judgment" (*CP* 347).

That objectivity is compatible with uncertainty is made clearest by the time Rawls develops the doctrine of the "burdens of judgment" in *Political Liberalism*. The burdens of judgment are defined by Rawls as those factors that can lead people who have disciplined their reasoning by taking on the constraints of an objective point of view nonetheless to disagree (*PL* 54–58).

Finally, it is worth pointing out something that is evident from the way in which Rawlsian objectivity has been characterized here. On Rawls's account, objectivity is not a foundational justificatory notion. Moral and (especially) political objectivity for Rawls is constructed on the basis of ideas that are latent in the common sense of citizens of a liberal democracy. Its appropriateness depends upon its fitting into a coherentist justificatory structure in which it is part of a larger web of convictions and moral beliefs at different levels of generality. Wide reflective equilibrium, rather than objectivity, is the most important notion in Rawls's overall theory of justification.

Daniel Weinstock

SEE ALSO:

Burdens of judgment
Constructivism: Kantian/political
Moral person
The original position
Practical reason
Rational intuitionism
Reflective equilibrium

148.

OBLIGATIONS

FTER THE PARTIES in the original position agree on principles for the basic structure of society, they set themselves the task of identifying principles for individuals (*TJ* 93–101). Among such principles, some are permissions, whereas others are requirements (*TJ* 94). Permissions indicate which acts we are at liberty to do or not do, and further subdivide into indifferent acts, whose performance (or lack thereof) is insignificant from a moral point of view; and supererogatory acts, which are not morally mandated but whose performance is nevertheless commendable. Requirements are mandatory, and can be either obligations or duties.

Following Brandt (1964) and Hart (1958), Rawls conceives of an obligation as a requirement to take, or refrain from taking, some course of action, which differs from a duty on a number of grounds (*TJ* 97). First, obligations are either voluntarily undertaken or incurred in some way that tracks our agency, such as by making a promise, signing a contract, or damaging someone else's property whilst using it. Second, the content of obligations is defined by the rules of an institution or practice which set requirements that their participants or members must comply with. Therefore, obligations derive from playing specific roles within social practices or institutions and fall on us upon joining these practices or institutions either explicitly or implicitly (such as by signing a contract, running for public office, or driving a car). Finally, obligations are owed to specific individuals in virtue of our interaction or cooperation with them within those institutions and practices. Duties, on the other hand, fall on us independently of what we commit to do, which role we cover, or which action we have previously undertaken; their content is not identified by institutions or practices; and they often have either unspecified or universal addressees. I have, for instance, a general duty to tell the truth simply in virtue of being a moral agent, rather than as a result of undertaking a certain course of action; the content of the duty is not specified by any rule-governed social practice; and I owe it, other things being equal, to all other human beings. Instead, when I drive a car, I incur obligations that I did not previously have towards pedestrians and fellow drivers (such as abiding by the highway code and having a valid driving license and insurance); the content of such obligations is clearly derived from the rules of the social practice of driving; and the addressees of the obligation are specified by that very practice (the person waiting at the pedestrian crossing or the owner of the car I accidentally drive into).

Obligations, then, are requirements which presuppose rule-governed practices and institutions, and therefore principles for such social forms. This is mirrored in the order in which the principles are chosen. Indeed, the dependence of obligations on institutions is the reason why all principles for individuals are chosen, for the sake of simplicity, *after* the principles for the basic structure – even if the content of duties, for instance, do not depend on institutions. Duties can also be related to institutions, albeit in a different way from obligations. The natural duty of justice, for instance, mandates the support of just institutions, although it falls upon all moral agents, and its content and addressees are not defined by the rules of a specific institution (indeed, it can also mandate work toward the establishment of not yet existing institutions). Indeed, this is the main reason why many scholars believe that the natural duty of justice cannot provide an adequate account of political obligation, since it cannot ground loyalty to any specific state.

In light of this institutional understanding of obligations, Rawls argues that all obligations can be interpreted as a specification of the principle of fairness. The principle of fairness mandates that a person comply with the rules of an institution that specifically applies to her when the following conditions are met: first, the institution is reasonably just; second, one has already taken advantage of, or explicitly accepted, the benefits which the institution generates. This applies to cases such as the driving example we have previously discussed, the practice of making contracts, and to individuals who hold specific offices in social and political instititutions. It does not apply, however, to ordinary citizens in virtue of their being members of a specific society. Given how obligations are distinguished from duties, claiming that the requirement to obey the law of one's state is an obligation would mean subscribing to a transactional theory of political obligation, according to which the latter arises through a morally relevant transaction among fellow citizens or between a citizen and her state, such as by consenting to its coercive apparatus or benefitting from the cooperative venture it establishes. The very principle of fairness is often used to justify political obligation in this way (Hart 1955; Klosko 1987). Rawls argues, instead, that there is no general obligation to obey the law of one's state on the part of ordinary citizens (as opposed to those who hold specific offices), because it is not clear what the relevant binding act could be in their case. As already mentioned, however, each person has a natural duty to support just institutions that exist and apply to us, and to further not yet existing just social arrangements, when this can be done at a reasonable cost.

The obligation to keep promises, instead, can be interpreted as an instantiation of the principle of fair play, in spite of appearances (*TJ* 303–306). First of all, promising is an institution defined by a system of rules (Searle 1969). Second, the obligation to keep a promise only arises if and when the practice of promising itself can be interpreted as being just. Third, the social practice of promising generates the benefits of regular expectations, cooperation, and trust, which one accepts by the very act of making a promise.

Miriam Ronzoni

SEE ALSO:

Fairness, principle of
Hart, H. L. A.
Institutions
Legitimate expectations
Natural duties
Political obligation

149.

OKIN, SUSAN MOLLER

SUSAN MOLLER OKIN (1946–2004) was a feminist political philosopher and political theorist. Her *Justice, Gender and the Family* (1989) sought both to critique Rawls's theory of justice, and to demonstrate that this theory might provide a valuable critical stance from which to criticize contemporary gender norms, especially as those norms affected equality within the family. Okin critiqued Rawls's construction of his theory; his assumption that the parties to the original position were the heads of households, for example, was criticized as concealing relationships of power within the household that should be taken as relevant from the standpoint of justice. Rawls's tools, though, were taken to have tremendous feminist potential. In particular, his recognition that the family was itself an important part of the basic structure of society, and that it had a role to play in socializing children with an appropriate sense of social justice, were both important insights that could be the starting point for feminist analyses of family life. Okin argued that feminist political philosophy could apply the methods and concepts introduced by Rawls – including the concepts of the original position and the veil of ignorance – to produce a radical argument for the injustice of our gender norms.

Okin was, accordingly, a critic of the direction of Rawls's thought after the publication of *A Theory of Justice*. Rawls was increasingly willing to place limitations on the range of applicability of his theory; by the time of *Political Liberalism*, he believed that the two principles of justice he defended were only applicable in the context of the political deliberations of a constitutional democracy. The values inherent in his liberal project, moreover, were now taken as the subject of an overlapping consensus, rather than as foundational commitments about how individuals ought to be treated. Okin regarded both sorts of limitations as betraying the transformative power of Rawlsian ideas. To restrict the ideas of the original position and the veil of ignorance to the overtly political deliberations of a particular form of government was to ignore the fact that women faced oppression and marginalization in other contexts. Similarly, to insist that liberal values could be validly insisted upon only in certain public and political contexts, was to remove the possibility of justice-based critique in the family and personal relationships Okin was concerned with. Although Rawls continued to describe the family as a basic social institution, Okin criticized Rawls as abandoning this commitment in his theory, by making justice within the family once again opaque from the standpoint of justice.

Okin's work, prior to her unexpected passing in 2004, expanded these themes into a general criticism of the modern liberal tendency to privilege toleration of difference over the concrete rights of women (*Is Multiculturalism Bad for Women?* 1999). While this work did not directly focus on Rawls's political liberalism, it is fair to think that many of the arguments developed here could function as criticisms not only of multicultural politics, but of Rawls's own stated analysis of how considerations of stability led him to revise the liberalism of *A Theory of Justice*. Okin's arguments might be taken to reject the idea that liberalism must avoid confronting the foundational moral beliefs of citizens even when they are sexist; her work as a whole can be taken as arguing that Rawls's true liberating potential would be revealed only by a Rawlsian method willing to criticize any form of unjustified hierarchy, whether or not that hierarchy was within the domain of the political.

Michael Blake

SEE ALSO:

Family
Feminism
Liberal conception of justice
The original position
Political conception of justice

150.

THE ORIGINAL POSITION

THE "ORIGINAL POSITION" is the name Rawls gives to the central formal device in his argument for the two principles of justice within the conception of justice he calls "justice as fairness." It is perhaps the most well-known part of Rawls's theory, and not surprisingly, the one over which there has been the most disagreement amongst his readers and commentators. This entry provides an overview of the original position's place within Rawls's overall project, discusses its various elements and their justification, and provides a summary of the argument from the original position to the two principles of justice.

Rawls aims to present a conception of justice that could serve as a more appropriate basis for a democratic society than utilitarianism. Such a conception must be able to be justified to our fellow citizens, and so must rest on an argument whose premises and presuppositions we share with them. Rawls came to describe one form of such argument as constructivist. The basic idea of a constructivist argument is that it models the main elements of a concept, a particular conception of which one is trying to defend. An argument is then made that the favored conception would be generated by the model, and so it follows from an interpretation of the basic concept that can be made good to one's fellow citizens. Within such an argument for justice as fairness, the original position is meant to model the main elements of a concept of justice. Since the argument is designed to work out a conception of justice that can serve as an appropriate basis for a democratic society, the concept of justice the original position is meant to model is in various ways shaped by this fact. The argument is thus designed to appeal to citizens of a democratic society who are trying to work out together a conception of democratic justice they can share. Although Rawls only developed the full articulation of this constructivist strategy in his writings after *A Theory of Justice* (from about 1980 on), the basic idea is present in his description of the original position as a "device of representation" in *TJ*. So understood, the original position is a device for representing to us and those with whom we are working out a conception of justice, how the elements of our concept of justice fit together.

Before looking at the details of the original position argument, it is important to be clear about the role it plays within Rawls's overall argument. Finding an appropriate moral basis for a conception of justice for a democratic society requires finding principles that all citizens can agree to, despite their differences. The agreement in the original position is not that agreement, however, as the parties are not, nor are they supposed to resemble, real people. The point of the original position is that it helps to convince actual citizens, like the readers of *A Theory of Justice*, that reasons they are willing to acknowledge, when combined in a perspicuous manner, favor the two principles of justice over utilitarianism. It thus helps to capture the basic insight of social contract theory, by imagining the principles of justice as a kind of agreement among appropriately situated parties (*TJ* 102). The argument from the original position has two main parts. First, Rawls argues that the various elements of the original position serve to model features of the concept of justice in a democratic society that we regard as important. Second, he argues that this model generates the two principles of justice by showing that the parties in the original position would choose the two principles of justice over various rival conceptions of justice including, most importantly, utilitarian conceptions.

The original position is set up as follows: a number of purely rational, mutually disinterested people come together to choose a set of principles of justice to govern a society. They are purely rational: they are moved only by their own advantage, and not by sympathy for others, moral commitments, or Rawls insists, envy. Each acts to advance the goals of a group of citizens in that society. In the original position, these representatives are symmetrically situated: they have the same knowledge, the same level of influence, the same opportunities to voice their views. Furthermore, the parties are behind what Rawls calls the "veil of ignorance." The veil of ignorance prevents the parties from knowing a number of otherwise relevant facts about the society for which they are choosing principles or the people they represent. They do not know, for example, the level of development of the society, or what place in the society those they represent occupy. They do not know their levels of income, education, status, or even their conceptions of the good. All they know are the following: that the circumstances of justice obtain in their society, that those they represent prefer more primary goods to fewer, as well as various basic laws about human psychology and motivation and economic and social theory.

The parties must choose principles of justice from a list that includes, among others, Rawls's two principles and utilitarian principles. The list is provided to them, as it were, by us, the theorist. In practice, what this means is that if anyone wants to advocate a different set of principles of justice but accepts the basic constructivist framework for making arguments about justice, she can add her preferred conception to the list and try to show it would be chosen by the parties. The parties must come to a unanimous and binding agreement about their choice. To do this, they proceed in two steps. First, they select what seem to them the best principles, given what they know, the constraints of their position, and their rationality. Since these principles are being chosen as if the choice was final, however, they also need to check whether those for whom they choose will be able to live under them. Thus, in the second step, they try to figure out, on the basis of their general knowledge of human psychology, whether these principles would be stable, whether actual people living under them would come to affirm these principles and willingly guide their conduct in accord with them. The chosen principles are only to be adopted if they would be stable, and so it is only after the two principles of justice are shown to be stable that the argument from the original position is complete (*TJ* 124, 465; *JF* 89). Showing that the two principles are stable turns out to give us, here and now, further grounds for agreeing to them, and so the discussion of stability completes not only the original position argument but also the argument of the book as a whole.

The various features of the original position capture the elements of the concept of justice for a democratic society. First, justice is "the virtue of practices where there are competing interests and where persons feel entitled to press their rights on each other" (*TJ* 112). We invoke considerations of justice when our interests conflict, and each feels some entitlement to press her case. Rawls models this by making the parties purely rational and mutually disinterested. Furthermore, principles of justice set out fair terms of cooperation. Fairness is ensured because the parties are symmetrically and equally situated. Finally, when deciding on principles of justice, it is not appropriate to favor one principle over another in virtue of what it does for me, even if I can offer more neutral reasons on its behalf. The veil of ignorance prevents the parties from making choices on the basis of such self-regarding reasons. Note that the original position models the rationality of citizens through the characterization of the parties, and the reasonableness of citizens through its structure. Rawls is not attempting to derive moral concepts from nonmoral premises.

Since the argument aims to help us reach reflective equilibrium, Rawls points out that the final specification of the original position can be refined to ensure that it produces the desired result (*TJ* 122). The force of the overall argument for justice as fairness turns not merely on the step from the specification of the original position to the choice made within it, but rather on helping us to see how the two principles of justice and the institutions they would endorse reflect our ideas of justice. We can thus change parts of the structure in order to bring out those connections more clearly, and the clarity of those connections will have an impact on how we reconcile our particular considered judgments with our more theoretical commitments.

There has been a great deal written on Rawls's argument that the parties in the original position would choose the two principles of justice, and Rawls himself substantially altered his presentation of the argument in his later writings (*JF* 80–134). Nevertheless, the basic ideas have not changed in his various reformulations, and so they will be treated here as if they were stable throughout his writing. Given that the parties are equally and symmetrically situated, we can imagine a natural first proposal being purely egalitarian principles. Since the parties aim to maximize primary goods but do not care about their relative level (they are mutually disinterested and free of envy), they would all also agree to a set of principles that allowed departures from equality when these benefitted everyone's share of primary goods.

At this point, however, we can imagine a kind of counterargument wherein one of the parties points out to the others that liberties and opportunity have a special place among the primary goods, and that while an unequal distribution of income and wealth that raised everyone's standard of living might be good for all, it is not so clearly the case that the same would hold for liberty or opportunity. First, it is harder to see how giving some greater liberty than others would have the effect of increasing the liberty of those with less. Second, the value of liberty is of a different sort than the value of income and wealth. The parties know that the people they represent have particular conceptions of the good, and that these may very well lead them to have ends that they would consider non-negotiable (*TJ* 131, 180). Rawls calls these "fundamental interests." Think, for instance, of someone with strong religious beliefs, who believes as a result of his faith that he must engage in certain religious practices. Such a person will not regard his ability to worship as he wishes as just another one of his goods that might be

The original position / 583

traded for something else. The parties thus have a reason to put additional stress on the protection of basic liberties. Such protection would also secure what Rawls calls "higher-order interests" which are interests we have as free citizens in how our other interests, including our "fundamental ones, are shaped and regulated by social institutions" (*TJ* 131). In other words, the protection of basic liberty allows us both to pursue the ends we regard as non-negotiable and to develop the capacities and have the social space to revise our ends should we choose to do so.

Similar arguments can be made for fair equality of opportunity. First, it is hard to see how extending opportunities for only some people on the basis of anything but their talents and willingness to work could serve to increase the opportunities for all. Second, having the same opportunities in life as one's fellow citizens is a mark of one's equal standing, and so it plays a role in securing the social bases of self-respect in a way that equality of income does not. Finally, abandoning fair equality of opportunity for mere formal equality of opportunity allows one's opportunity to be in large part determined by one's social background. Since one's social background is undeserved, allowing one's life chances to be significantly shaped by one's social background would be arbitrary from a moral point of view. And so we are left with a preliminary argument for the two principles of justice, where liberty and opportunity are given strong egalitarian protection and only those departures from equality in income and wealth that make the worst off as well off as they can be are allowed.

In addition, Rawls provides a somewhat more formal argument by way of showing that the two principles would be chosen over utilitarian principles. We can see the force of that argument stemming from a consideration of what Rawls calls the "strains of commitment" (*TJ* 153–154). The parties in the original position must choose principles of justice as if they were making an irrevocable choice for all eternity. They must thus consider whether or not the strains of that agreement on those they represent will be bearable or not should, after the veil is lifted, those people turn out to fare poorly in the society. If the strains of commitment will be too great, that is a compelling reason to reject the given principles.

A consideration of the strains of commitment provides strong reasons for the parties to choose the two principles over utilitarianism. First, utilitarianism does not place the same emphasis on the protection of equal basic liberties. Although many utilitarians argue that a system that protects basic liberties increases overall utility, the protection of liberties is secured in an indirect manner, and this leads to the possibility that under utilitarian principles of justice, some individuals could find their liberties curtailed to increase the total utility in the society. Given the potential importance and non-negotiability of the kinds of ends that liberties protect, the parties should reject any conception of justice that provides a less stringent protection of basic liberties than the two principles.

A similar argument can be made about the difference principle over a utilitarian distributive principle. Principles for a democratic society must be stable even when they are publicly recognized as providing the basis for the institutions of the basic structure. Rawls argues that principles that embody an idea of reciprocity and mutual respect are more likely to be stable than principles that fail to do so and thus require a greater degree of altruism and sympathetic sacrifice. To see this point, imagine two societies. In the first, the two principles of justice hold. In the second, the first principle holds, there is fair equality of opportunity, but further inequality is governed by a principle of utility: economic inequality is justified to the extent that it raises the total level of wealth in the society. Now imagine that someone in the worst-off group in each society asks her fellow citizens why she should accept her lot and regard the terms of social cooperation as fair. In the first society, the publicly available answer is that the inequalities satisfy the difference principle, and so although she is worse off than others in her society, a different social arrangement would mean that someone, perhaps her, perhaps someone else, would be even worse off than she is now. Such an answer is consistent with her fellow citizens saying to her that she is one of them, and they take her well-being seriously. They can thus answer her truthfully in a manner that respects her as a free and equal fellow citizen. Furthermore, she cannot publicly advocate in good faith an alternative arrangement that would improve her lot. By hypothesis, any such alternative would leave some other group even worse off than she is now, and it is not reasonable for her to demand that they accept such an arrangement.

What can be said to the person at the bottom of the utilitarian distribution? By hypothesis, she is worse off than the worst-off person in the first society. Why should she accept her status, given that under the two principles of justice, she would be better off and no one else would be worse off than she is now. In the utilitarian society, the publicly available answer is that her being badly off makes possible greater total utility in the society. That is, she is poorer than she needs to be in order that people who are already richer than she is can be even richer. Such an answer clearly fails to show her respect as a full equal as it says that society is willing to use her for other people's benefit. As a result, she is not likely to endorse the principles that guide her society; the strains on her commitment will be much greater. If then, we agree with Rawls that the elements of the original position capture the central features of our concept of justice in a democratic society, then we have reason to adopt the two principles over utilitarianism as our principles of justice.

Anthony Simon Laden

SEE ALSO:

> *Circumstances of justice*
> *Constructivism: Kantian/political*
> *Facts, general (in OP argument and as part of justification)*
> *The four-stage sequence*
> *Maximin principle of choice*
> *Mixed conceptions of justice*
> *Moral person*
> *Neutrality*
> *Objectivity*
> *Strains of commitment*
> *Utilitarianism*

151.

OUTLAW STATES

OUTLAW STATES ARE one of four types of societies discussed in Rawls's *The Law of Peoples.* The discussion occurs within the context of nonideal theory, where one concern of justice is how to bring noncomplying societies into compliance (*LP* 89–90). Outlaw states fail to comply with principle 4 of the Law of Peoples, which states "a duty of non-intervention," and with principle 6, which requires societies "to honor human rights" (*LP* 37). Generally, Rawls distinguishes states from peoples by claiming that the former "as rational" are often "anxiously concerned with their power...and always guided by their basic interests" (*LP* 28). Outlaw states pursue their rational aims without limiting them by the reasonable constraints of the Law of Peoples. In contrast, "liberal peoples limit their basic interests as required by the reasonable" (*LP* 29).

Due to their noncompliance, outlaw states are not to be tolerated and respected as members of international society (*LP* 81). Various constraints of the Law of Peoples, such as the duty to honor treaties (*LP* 37), do not apply with respect to outlaw states. Liberal and decent societies may subject them to political and economic and sanction for their failure to honor human rights and if these violations are sufficiently grave military intervention may be justified (*LP* 81). Moreover, if liberal peoples and decent societies "sincerely and reasonably believe that their safety and security are seriously endangered" they may fight just wars against outlaw states that fail to observe the duty of nonintervention (*LP* 90–91). War against outlaw states, then, is justified only if the human rights violations occurring are very grave or if the outlaw states pose a reasonable threat to the safety and security of liberal and decent peoples.

In a just war against an outlaw state liberal and decent societies should observe a distinction between the outlaw state's leaders and officials and the civilians who are not among "those who organized and brought on the war" (*LP* 95). War is brought about "by the leaders and officials, assisted by other elites who control and staff the state apparatus. They are responsible; they willed the war, and, for doing that, they are criminal. But the civilian population, often kept in ignorance and swayed by state propaganda, is not responsible" (*LP* 95). Targeting civilians in outlaw states, except in conditions of supreme emergency, is forbidden (*LP* 95). Nonetheless, the existence of outlaw states may justify the possession of nuclear weapons by liberal and decent societies – even though their use would be presumptively wrong – in order to make sure that outlaw states "do not obtain and use those weapons against liberal or decent peoples" (*LP* 9). Statesmen in liberal and decent societies have a special duty to hold fast publicly to the distinction between the civilians and leaders of outlaw states during times of war (*LP* 100–101).

Darrel Moellendorf

SEE ALSO:

> *Human rights*
> *Ideal and nonideal theory*
> *Just war theory*
> *Law of Peoples*
> *Society of Peoples*
> *Toleration*

152.

OVERLAPPING CONSENSUS

N 1971 JOHN RAWLS published *A Theory of Justice*; over time, he appears to have become dissatisfied with the shape his theory had originally taken. The problem, Rawls says, is that he had initially assumed that the two principles of justice as fairness (the principle of equal basic rights and liberties and the principle of fair equality of opportunity paired with mutual benefit in outcomes and, in the ideal case, the greatest benefit of the least well-off income group) would become part of an overarching moral theory in any well-ordered society in which these principles were the public principles of justice. Such a society would be stable because everybody in it would continue to hold to the two principles in the light of this overarching moral theory, which contained those principles as an integral part. But such uniform acceptance of a moral theory, Rawls now says, is implausible. (For Rawls's own account of the problem, see *PL* xv–xviii; also *CP* 414 n.33.)

In Rawls's writings in the 1980s, he argues that there is going to be, in a continuing free and open society, an irreducible pluralism of reasonable comprehensive moral and religious and philosophical doctrines. Accordingly, a new idea, overlapping consensus, is called on to form the basis of stability in a well-ordered, pluralistic society. An overlapping consensus is said to hold in a society when individuals who adhere to different comprehensive doctrines can nonetheless agree on a political conception of justice for evaluating the shared basic institutional structure of their society.

Overlapping consensus is contrasted by Rawls with a *modus vivendi*. In a mere *modus vivendi*, certain principles and practices are accepted as a way for people to live together without constant fighting and disruption. Rawls's own example, of accepting religious toleration (in a time of deep intolerance), is one important

Overlapping consensus / 589

instance. Such acceptance by warring sects was indeed a mere *modus vivendi* because, where any one faith became dominant, through a dynastic change, for example, "the principle of toleration would no longer be followed" (see *PL* 146–148).

The agreement that exists in such a case is not wide (it concerns only a fairly narrow set of arrangements, covering primarily official toleration for several competing sects to profess their faith). It is not deep (in that the reasons offered for the desirability of these accepted arrangements do not go beyond the idea of establishing a *modus vivendi*). And it lacks a distinctive political focus: fellow co-inhabitants have no shared conception of a public political life – no animating reasons, widely accepted, that would take them beyond the status quo, beyond the *modus vivendi* itself. They have accepted that status quo simply out of fear of a worse alternative.

Rawls gives his preoccupation with assuring political stability in a pluralist or multicultural social environment its most complete elaboration in his second book, *Political Liberalism* (initially published in hardback in 1993, in paperback 1996). Rawls claims that his revised theory in this second book is specifically a *political* theory of justice; it is not a general or comprehensive critical moral theory. Rather, the most significant feature of Rawls's current, revised theory is that he takes the public political culture of a contemporary democratic society to be the deep background of the entire theory. For the leading ideas out of which the political conception of justice is to be constructed and by reference to which it is to be justified are said by Rawls to be implicit in that culture (*PL* 13).

Here political justification sets out from four "model conceptions" or "fundamental ideas" (*PL* lecture I). First is the idea of the person or citizen as free and equal and as having two distinctive capacities or moral powers and two corresponding "higher-order interests" (*PL* 74, 75) in the realization of these capacities. Thus, each person has, over that person's entire life, (i) an interest in being able to have, formulate, revise, promulgate, live according to, and advance one's particular determinate conception of the good and (ii) an interest in exercising one's "sense of justice" and being motivated by it, providing others do so as well. Next is the idea of society as "a fair system of cooperation over time, from one generation to the next"; here free and equal citizens work together for mutual (or reciprocal) benefit. Third is the idea of the well-ordered society and its basic institutional structure (see *JF* 8–9). And last is the idea of a linking or mediating conception which lays out the standards for discussion and decision-making to which fellow citizens could be expected to adhere in reaching a decision respecting the governing principles of political justice (principles for the basic structure of their well-ordered society, in which they could expect to live their entire lives). This fourth idea is linked with what Rawls called "the original position" in his earlier book (*TJ* chapter 3). Herein would be included such ideas as sharply limited information (the so-called veil of ignorance), publicity, unanimity. The function of this mediating conception is to help unify the other fundamental ideas into a single coherent whole from which one could then reason to certain principles and institutional arrangements.

Establishing terms for social cooperation for mutual benefit – principles for a fair distribution of certain primary goods (including such things as rights and liberties, opportunities, social and economic positions, income and wealth) – continues to be the main object of Rawls's conception of justice. In the new account, though, the principles that emerge as preferred (from among a small set of historically available candidate principles) are the principles that are best supported by the background *democratic* ideas, from within the nexus formed by the four "model conceptions."

Rawls thinks that those best-supported principles will be his own two principles of justice, understood now as *political* principles (see *PL* 5–6, for Rawls's current version of these principles). Or, to be precise, he thinks the preferred set will actually be a "family" of principles, among which are included the two he emphasizes. (See *PL* 7, 164, also 439.)

This "family" is constituted by the set of "generic" liberal principles. Generic liberalism, as Rawls conceives it, has three main features: (1) certain familiar rights, liberties, opportunities are to be singled out and specified and maintained; (2) a certain priority is to be given to these rights, etc. over against "the claims of the general good and of perfectionist values"; (3) measures to help citizens make effective use of these rights (etc.), by having an adequate base of income and wealth, are to be set in place. (See *PL* 6.) These generic liberal principles are well designed to specify an acceptable distribution of primary goods in the context of existing democratic "fundamental ideas."

The "political conception of justice," as Rawls calls it, is not limited to such principles alone. It also includes certain of the institutional arrangements that are required to put the principles into effect in a given society. These institutions – political, economic, social – are the sort of thing Rawls had in mind when he referred to the basic structure of a society.

Rawls's account of the political conception proceeds in two main stages (see *PL* 140). The first stage is the one we have focused on up to now. The main project here is to settle on that principle or set of principles for distributing primary goods which is optimally appropriate, given the fundamental democratic ideas from which we started. This first line of justification (justification from democratic ideas in a democratic context) is said by Rawls to be "freestanding," in the sense that it draws only on these background democratic ideas (*PL* 40). Such justification is independent (*PL* 144) and does not draw, in an essential way, on the ideas or values of any comprehensive moral or religious doctrine.

What Rawls calls overlapping consensus is a second stage in which the antecedently established "freestanding" justification is endorsed from the respective points of view of a variety of comprehensive ethical doctrines (such as Kant's moral theory or Mill's utilitarianism) and religious doctrines (such as contemporary Catholic Christianity). On this view, the political conception is a "module...that fits into and can be supported by various reasonable comprehensive doctrines that endure in the society regulated by it" (*PL* 12; also 145, 387). But it need not be *presented* by reference to such support initially; rather it is established completely independently of direct consideration of any and all such doctrines (hence Rawls's description of it as "freestanding"). At this second stage, we contemplate the support provided the political conception from *within* the respective confines of a variety of individual comprehensive views.

One question, much disputed in contemporary Rawls scholarship, concerns the main point of overlapping consensus: is it stability (as Rawls initially had suggested) or is it justification? Granted, one can *distinguish* these two emphases (on stability and on justification); but there's no need to separate them. They can have complementary and mutually supporting roles in Rawls's account.

Rawls thinks that an overlapping consensus presupposes and arises in concert with constitutional consensus (see *PL* lecture iv, §§3, 5–7). In the case envisioned, there is already an independent, widespread, and long-lived support by citizens for the public political conception – that is, for a family of liberal principles (see *PL* 164, 168). An overlapping consensus would arise, then, where the great bulk of citizens could also affirm, upon reflection and given experience, that the fundamental ideas and the governing principles and institutional essentials of the public political conception were compatible (or could be made so), in each of their respective cases, with the comprehensive moral and religious and philosophical doctrine(s) that they individually held (see *PL* 210).

The general run of citizens in that society don't regard the perspectives they individually have as *in*compatible, in general or in principle, with the overall public political conception there. It follows, for the *variety* of diverse perspectives that happen to be held by these citizens en masse, that these diverse views constitute (or can be regarded as constituting) an overlapping consensus on a family of liberal principles and on a given set of institutional essentials.

An overlapping consensus, like the public political conception on which it focuses, is directed to the basic framework, to the institutional essentials themselves; it does not require or imply an agreement on all matters of policy. Indeed, it is compatible with disagreement, even considerable disagreement, on such matters – on detailed pieces of legislation, say (see *CP* 604–607).

Such an overlapping consensus would, arguably, be stronger and more enduring were it to attach itself to a suitably broad, deep, focused public political conception, for example, to a family of liberal political conceptions (with justice as fairness among its members). None of this shows, of course, that an overlapping consensus *will* occur. It shows merely that such a consensus plausibly could occur, in the way Rawls envisioned (see *PL* xlv–xlvii).

A political conception, simply on its own, is always a consensus within and from public political reasons; in the case at hand, the reasons appropriate to a liberal democratic society. As such it lacks a certain dimension: it lacks moral credentials of the sort afforded by a comprehensive critical moral theory. What overlapping consensus adds, then, is that the political conception can be "affirmed on moral grounds" (*PL* 147).

Several different critical moral and religious doctrines can be drawn on, at a given time, in a liberal society. Each of them is controversial; no one of them is accepted by everybody. Insofar as we are concerned, then, with anything like a full *public* justification of the political conception, using accredited critical moral doctrines, we must accept that the only form a full public justification could take in a morally and religiously pluralistic society and still have authority outside a narrow circle of partisan sentiment would be as an overlapping consensus – with the public political conception as focal – of these various doctrines.

What citizens could do, as adherents of any one of these doctrinal lines (or even of none), is to note and register the fact of overlapping consensus. This fact is a *public* fact and general acknowledgment – common knowledge – of this fact is the form that overlapping consensus would take insofar as it was itself a matter of full public justification of the political conception. (See *PL* 385–394.)

What overlapping consensus supplies, which freestanding justification and constitutional consensus can't, is a distinctive set of comprehensive moral and religious reasons endorsing and thereby justifying, each for its own reasons, the liberal order (*PL* 134). An overlapping consensus is not a mere compromise, among the various relevant critical moral and religious doctrines. A mere compromise would be a tenuous solution, continually subject to renegotiation as the balance of powers and interests shifts (see *PL* 148, 161). By avoiding such constant renegotiation, or the continuing threat of defection, overlapping consensus reinforces the existing stability of a suitably broad, deep, and focused public political conception. Overlapping consensus provides, not simply stability, but "stability for the right reasons" (*PL* 394). Overlapping consensus addresses the questions of political stability and of normative justification in the context of a continuing pluralist or multicultural social environment.

Rex Martin

SEE ALSO:

Comprehensive doctrine
Constitutional consensus
Fundamental ideas (in justice as fairness)
Justification, freestanding/political
Political conception of justice
Realistic utopia
Reconciliation
Stability

Note: This entry draws on my chapter "Overlapping Consensus" in *A Companion to Rawls*, ed. Jon Mandle and David A. Reidy (Blackwell, 2014).

P

153.

PATERNALISM

THOUGH IT IS said that paternalism is inconsistent with liberalism, Rawls is one liberal who holds that some paternalistic actions are permissible. Although he does not define this term, he uses it in discussing coercive actions that are justified as benefitting those who are coerced against their present wishes (*TJ* 249). According to Rawls, parties in the original position will agree to permit some actions of this kind because they are motivated to choose principles that guarantee each person the primary social goods necessary to develop and exercise their moral powers fully, and because, due to immaturity, mental disability, or "irrational inclinations" (*TJ* 249), a person might act so as to lose these goods or to undermine in some other way the conditions necessary for the full development and exercise of their moral powers. Parties in the original position will therefore agree to principles that authorize others in some cases "to act in their behalf and to override their present wishes if necessary" (*TJ* 249). Paternalistic decisions, however, must be guided by a person's own settled preferences or, when this is unknown, by the theory of primary goods. Furthermore, "we must be able to argue that with the development or recovery of his rational powers the individual in question will accept our decision on his behalf and agree with us that we did the best thing for him" (*TJ* 249). So although some paternalistic actions are permissible – those that prevent a person from acting on a temporary lapse in judgment in a way that will result in the permanent loss of some important good – paternalistic actions are not permissible that prevent a mature, mentally sound person from acting on his settled convictions.

To illustrate, parties in the original position will presumably authorize the police to interfere with suicide attempts, because people are typically not thinking clearly when they try to kill themselves, and because with death one loses life, a necessary condition for the full development and exercise of one's moral powers, and with it all the primary social goods as well. However, parties in the original position will not authorize the government to issue a blanket legal prohibition of suicide. They do not acknowledge duties to self, and so do not acknowledge the kind of unconditional duty not to kill oneself that Kant defended. Moreover, the decision to kill oneself is sometimes based on sound reasoning from one's fundamental convictions, one's views about the value of life and what makes life worth living. So we could not plausibly argue in defense of a blanket prohibition that with the "recovery of his rational powers" everyone who wishes to kill himself will "accept our decision on his behalf and agree with us that we did the best thing for him."

Peter de Marneffe

SEE ALSO:

> *Conception of the good*
> *Liberal conception of justice*
> *Moral person*
> *Neutrality*
> *The original position*

154.

PEOPLES

A NY THEORY OF international justice must include an account of the agents between whom duties of justice apply. In Rawls's *LP* these agents are "peoples." The term is somewhat obscure. While Rawls gives no general definition, certain key features are evident: a people is an independent, territorially based, political community united by "common sympathies" (*LP* 23) and a shared sense of justice. Though the emphasis on common sympathies, formed partly by cultural, historical, and linguistic ties, might suggest that peoples are akin to nations or ethnic groups, Rawls clearly construes peoples as essentially politically organized in a way that these other collectivities are not. However, at the same time, he carefully distinguishes peoples from states, to avoid implying two features traditionally associated with the latter in international law: the right to wage war for national gain and the right to unlimited discretion regarding internal affairs (*LP* 25). Rawls also emphasizes that, unlike states as traditionally conceived, peoples are capable of having a moral character: ideally, they are concerned to cooperate on fair, mutually respectful terms with other peoples (*LP* 35).

Rawlsian peoples come in two types: liberal peoples and decent peoples (Rawls refers to them collectively as "well-ordered peoples"). Liberal peoples are ruled by a constitutional democratic government and their internal affairs are reasonably just. Decent peoples are not internally just, since they lack a constitutional democracy. However, they recognize and protect human rights, allow their members a significant role in political decision-making and are concerned to promote the common good as a matter of justice. Like liberal peoples, decent peoples are also committed to peaceful foreign relations. To this extent they are beyond reproach, where the foreign policy of liberal peoples is concerned.

Representatives of liberal and decent peoples are the parties to the pair of social contracts that generate the Law of Peoples. Rawls presents all well-ordered peoples as sharing a set of fundamental interests, which their representatives are concerned to further. These interests include the protection of their territory, the safety of their members, the preservation of their culture and the maintenance of their legitimate autonomy and self-respect as peoples. Peoples are assumed to have no interest in an indefinite increase in wealth nor in their economic position relative to that of other peoples.

Rawls also distinguishes three other types of domestic societies that are not parties to the contracts generating the Law of Peoples. Societies ruled by "benevolent absolutisms" are distinguished from decent peoples by their members' lack of any influence over government policy. "Burdened societies" lack the material, technological, cultural, and other conditions required to achieve a liberal or decent regime. These types of societies are not well-ordered, since they are neither just nor decent internally. By contrast, societies ruled by "outlaw states" fail to be well-ordered for both external and internal reasons: their regimes act aggressively toward other peoples; they may also violate the human rights of their own members. An ultimate aim of the Law of Peoples is to bring all of these societies into the set of well-ordered peoples.

Rawls's choice of peoples as the bearers and objects of global duties has significant moral implications and has generated extensive criticism. Some argue that Rawls's apparent claim that peoples are moral units in their own right, deserving of (conditional) equal respect, violates the core liberal idea that only individual persons can fill this role. Rawls's defenders counter that his position is in fact consistent with normative individualism: respect for individuals may require respect for the political groups that those individuals form. His account is also consistent with additional global duties that apply directly to individuals, rather than being filtered through peoples. Whether or not this reply is adequate, a theory of international justice that privileges the perspective of peoples does raise a second, related concern. This is the worry that respecting illiberal peoples will require liberals to stand by while the rights of those peoples' individual members are violated. Here, Rawls argues that the objection begs the question against his account, by assuming that only liberal peoples deserve toleration. If Rawls is right, decent peoples too deserve respect, even if they deny their members the full panoply of liberal rights (*LP* 82–83). Finally, some argue that a world composed of Rawlsian peoples is so unlike our contemporary world that a theory of justice centered on peoples fails to provide sufficient moral guidance. Contemporary states are populated by diverse, often warring, groups lacking solidarity and affinity; many individuals migrate from one state to another across their lifetimes; and cross-border interactions between individuals, multi-national corporations, non-governmental organizations and other non-state actors are far-reaching and morally consequential. Is Rawls's *LP* a theory for a "vanished Westphalian world" (Buchanan 2000)? Rawls acknowledges that his people-centered account involves simplification (*LP* 24–25) and does not provide answers to every question about international justice (*LP* 8–9). He intends it to strike the balance between realism and idealization that he claims is necessary as a starting point for moral reflection. Whether or not his theory succeeds on this front, it remains a key reference point in philosophical debates on global justice.

Helena de Bres

SEE ALSO:

Decent societies
Law of Peoples
Liberal people
Mill, John Stuart
Society of Peoples

155.

PERFECTIONISM

AWLS CHARACTERIZES PERFECTIONISM as both a general teleological ethical theory and as a controversial conception of justice. As a general teleological ethical theory, it directs "society to arrange institutions and to define the duties and obligations of individuals so as to maximize the achievement of excellence in art, science and culture" (*TJ* 285–286). A theory of this kind is sometimes attributed to Nietzsche. As a controversial conception of justice, perfectionism is a comprehensive doctrine that directs the state to favor some conceptions of the good over others and holds that "some persons have special claims because their greater gifts enable them to engage in the higher activities that realize perfectionist values" (*JF* 152). Rawls rejects perfectionism under both descriptions. He advances a number of arguments for doing so. To appreciate these arguments, an initial difficulty must be confronted. Rawls's characterizations of perfectionism are too narrow. They do not capture the full range of views that plausibly qualify as perfectionist. For example, construed as a general teleological ethical theory, perfectionism need not be identified with the promotion of specific goods, such as those realized in art and science. Many perfectionist writers have appealed to the value of self-development, or the development of human capacities and powers in general. This development can take place in many different spheres of human activity. Moreover, perfectionism, despite its name, need not take a maximizing form. Rather than aiming to maximize human achievements, a perfectionist theory could aim to secure an adequate level of achievement or self-development. Likewise, construed as a conception of justice, perfectionism need not hold that some are entitled to more because of their special gifts or talents. Instead, it might value the perfectionist achievements of each person equally. Egalitarian conceptions of perfectionist justice are available.

Rawls's flagship argument against perfectionism appeals to the design of the original position. The parties in the original position would not adopt perfectionist principles for much the same reason that they would not adopt other teleological principles. The parties do not share a conception of the good that would enable them to identify the kind of self-development or the types of human achievement that ought to be promoted in a well-ordered society. For this reason, political efforts to promote perfectionist values threaten to compromise the liberty of those who are not committed to these values. Much as utilitarian principles countenance reducing the liberty of some for the realization of greater overall utility, perfectionist principles countenance reducing the liberty of some for the sake of greater overall achievement.

However, as Rawls recognizes, this line of argument only applies to perfectionism in its pure form in which it is understood as the sole principle of political morality. Mixed or intuitionistic forms of perfectionism balance the principle of perfectionism against other ideals and principles. Thus, as Rawls allows, a perfectionist theory could be committed to the principle of equal liberty. On this theory, perfectionist values would be promoted subject to the constraint that they not unequally infringe the basic liberties of any citizen. It is also possible, although Rawls does not mention it, that a pure perfectionist theory could be committed to autonomy, understood itself as an element of perfection; and that the perfectionist value of autonomy could support a commitment to the principle of equal liberty.

Liberty-respecting perfectionist views, Rawls nonetheless insists, would be rejected as well by the parties in the original position. Since the parties are presumed to represent people who do not agree on perfectionist values, they cannot appeal to them in selecting principles of justice. It follows that, on Rawls's view, it would be unjust for citizens to use the coercive power of the state to favor some pursuits over others on the grounds that they are more excellent or have greater intrinsic value. In reply, it can be argued that the parties in the original position could agree on the general proposition that a well-ordered society should promote human achievement and excellence. In other words, they could agree to a principle of perfection abstractly stated. The content of perfectionist policies could then be determined at a later stage. Rawlsian justice, on this view, would permit, but not require, state promotion of perfectionist values. Against this, Rawls contends that political judgments about perfectionist values would likely be made on an arbitrary or ad hoc manner. When it comes to judgments about human perfection "we are likely to be influenced by subtle aesthetic preferences and personal feelings of propriety" (*TJ* 291). Thus Rawls appears to believe that since judgments of perfectionist value are often unreliable, they should not be relied on to justify coercive state action.

Does this mean that perfectionism has no place at all in Rawlsian politics? Not quite. In *TJ* Rawls allows that in a just society perfectionist values can be supported through an exchange branch of government. This branch would require government activities and the costs for funding them to be unanimously approved, or nearly so. In effect, the requirement of unanimity ensures that no citizen can use the power of the state to compel others to pay for unwanted benefits. More interestingly, in his later work, Rawls softens his resistance to perfectionist politics further. Perfectionist theories are ruled out as conceptions of justice, since they are comprehensive doctrines and therefore cannot be the object of an overlapping consensus in a modern democratic society. But Rawls allows that so long as the basic constitutional framework of a society is justified without reference to perfectionist values, then laws and policies enacted within that framework may permissibly advance these values. "Fundamental justice must be achieved first. After that a democratic electorate may devote large resources to grand projects in art and science if it so chooses" (*JF* 152).

It should also be noted that Rawls affirmed what he called the "Aristotelian principle." This principle states that "other things equal, human beings enjoy the exercise of their realized capacities (their innate or trained abilities), and the enjoyment increases the more the capacity is realized, or the greater its complexity" (*TJ* 374). As its content indicates, this principle provides support for the perfectionist idea that the development and exercise of our capacities and talents is a leading human good. The principle is not a perfectionist principle, since it merely purports to describe human motivation. But if it is accepted as true, then it implies that rational plans of life for human beings must make room for the perfectionist value of self-development. Rawls further claims that the self-development associated with the Aristotelian principle "ties in with the primary good of self-respect," which is, in turn, an essential element of the good for persons.

In *TJ* Rawls observes that the rejection of "the principle of perfection" might leave too little scope for ideal-regarding considerations within justice as fairness, and he acknowledges that we should remain open to the possibility that the consequences of rejecting perfectionism might prove on reflection to be unacceptable.

Perfectionism / 605

Thus, despite his general anti-perfectionist stance, Rawls's rejection of perfectionist politics was neither dogmatic nor uncompromising.

Steven Wall

SEE ALSO:

Aristotelian principle
Constitution and constitutional essentials
Liberal conception of justice
Neutrality
Self-respect

156.

PLAN OF LIFE

A PLAN OF LIFE is a person's long-term scheme of conduct and activities designed to permit, given reasonably favorable circumstances, the harmonious satisfaction of his interests, desires, and final ends. A rational plan of life encourages and secures the fulfillment of a person's more permanent and general aims, influences the formation of subsequent interests and desires, allows the exercise of his abilities, and "allows him to flourish, so far as circumstances permit" (*TJ* 376). Happiness consists in the successful execution of a rational plan of life.

Rawls's account of the rationality of plans of life articulates an ideal model that is central to both the justification of primary goods and the conception of stability in *TJ*. The account belongs to his conception of goodness as rationality. This ideal model is absent in later writings because it is neither compatible with, nor necessary for, a political conception of justice. Beginning in "Priority of Right and Ideas of the Good" he claims that goodness as rationality supposes that citizens have a rational plan of life "at least in an intuitive way," but there is no characterization of plans and their rationality (*CP* 451).

According to the account in *TJ*, a person's good is determined by the most rational plan of life, which is the plan that he would choose from "the maximal class of plans" on the basis of the principles of rational choice, the Aristotelian principle, and with full deliberative rationality (which requires full information). Since persons can only choose on the basis of the information available, their plans of life are only subjectively rational. Even assuming full deliberative rationality, however, there is indeterminacy in the rational choice among plans because of the multiplicity of aims. How to go about narrowing down such indeterminacy will depend on the relation of priority between the right and the good. On a

606

teleological theory, such as utilitarianism, in which the good is prior to the right, the alternative is to assess the multiple aims by their relation to a dominant aim that serves as the standard of comparison and of choice. Because of the priority of right in justice as fairness, by contrast, the principles of right and justice constrain the choice of a conception of the good. The problem with the dominant-end conception of deliberation is that it either "disfigures" the self by putting it to the service of one single end or drifts to hedonism as a method of choice, the weaknesses of which are well known. The advantage of the second alternative is that it allows for a unity of the self in which moral personality is its fundamental aspect (*TJ* 493). A moral person has a "fundamental preference" for "conditions that enable him to frame a mode of life that expresses his nature as a free and equal rational being as fully as circumstances permit" (*TJ* 491). By constraining the choice of a conception of the good within the limits set by the principles of right and justice, a moral person expresses such a nature. Rawls takes this to count in favor of the priority of right, which in justice as fairness accounts for the fact that the basic structure encourages and supports certain plans of life more than others.

Faviola Rivera-Castro

SEE ALSO:

Aristotelian principle
Conception of the good
Deliberative rationality
Dominant end theories
Goodness as rationality
Primary goods, social

157.

POGGE, THOMAS

THOMAS POGGE (b. 1953) is the Leitner Professor of Philosophy and International Affairs at Yale University. He wrote his dissertation at Harvard under the direction of Rawls, and became a close friend, as well as interpreter and critic of Rawls's work. Pogge is very prolific, and his work spans many areas of political philosophy, with an emphasis on issues of global justice.

Pogge's first book was *Realizing Rawls* (1989), in which he argues that Rawls's "focus on the basic structure, combined with the priority concern for the least advantaged, makes Rawls a radical thinker" (Pogge 1989, 9). In the first part, he offers an interpretation of justice as fairness that responds to critics Nozick and Sandel. In the second part, he provides a reconstruction and defense of the two principles of justice, while offering criticisms of his own. For example, he doubts that Rawls adequately justified his claim that the lexical priority of the first principle over the second necessarily provides guidance for the relative urgency of reforms in nonideal conditions, and he rejects Rawls's argument that the difference principle should not be formally incorporated into a just society's constitution. The third part of the book represents the first step of an ambitious project to extend justice as fairness to apply to the global order. Pogge rejects "the dogma of absolute sovereignty, the belief that a *juridical state* (as distinct from a lawless state of nature) presupposes an authority of last resort" (Pogge 1989, 216). Instead, he suggests a model analogous to federalism, in which authority is dispersed among different levels. (He explores this further in Pogge 1992.) And extending Rawls's institutional focus, he argues:

By ignoring the misery of the world's poorest populations, we are disregarding not merely our positive duty of mutual aid but our negative duty not to make others the victims of unjust institutions. As citizens of the developed nations, we have created and are perpetuating by use of our economic and military power a global institutional order under which tens of millions avoidably cannot meet their most fundamental needs for food and physical security. (Pogge 1989, 238)

As a concrete way partially to address this injustice, he suggests, but does not explore in detail, a proposal for "an international tax on the extraction of national mineral resources through which at least the distributional effects of the morally arbitrary geographical distribution of natural assets could be mitigated" (Pogge 1989, 205).

In 1993, Rawls published "The Law of Peoples" which, for the first time, articulated in detail his own view of how justice as fairness should be extended to govern the relations among societies. The next year, Pogge replied with "An Egalitarian Law of Peoples." He argues that the vastly different life prospects of individuals born in different countries is difficult to reconcile with justice because such differences "on the face of it, [are] no less morally arbitrary than differences in sex, in skin color, or in the affluence of one's parents" (Pogge 1994, 198). Against Rawls, he argues that "A plausible conception of global justice must be sensitive to international social and economic inequalities" (Pogge 1994, 196). Expanding on the arguments of the final part of *Realizing Rawls*, Pogge explores in more detail the idea of a "global resources tax, or GRT" (Pogge 1994, 200ff.), and argues that a proper understanding of the structure of the second (global) original position, would result in the parties endorsing the GRT (Pogge 1994, 208). (He would later call this a "global resource dividend" or GRD (Pogge 1998a).) The details of Pogge's concrete proposal aside, the question of whether global justice has an egalitarian distributive component would be a central point of debate in political philosophy ever since. In *The Law of Peoples* (Rawls's 1999 book, which revised and expanded the 1993 article of the same name), Rawls includes a duty of assistance that wealthy societies owe toward "burdened societies" to help them become well-ordered. Responding to Pogge directly, he holds that once a society becomes well-ordered, and human rights are secured, there is no requirement of egalitarian distributive justice at a global level. However, he suggests that if Pogge's proposal is interpreted primarily as focused on securing human rights, their principles "could be much the same, with largely practical matters of taxation and administration to distinguish between them" (*LP* 119).

World Poverty and Human Rights (incorporating previous work, first published in 2002, second edition in 2008) is perhaps Pogge's best-known book. There, he argues for an understanding of human rights in which they are conceived "primarily as claims on coercive social institutions and secondarily as claims against those who uphold such institutions" (Pogge 2008, 50–51). This allows him to bypass controversies concerning whether there are *positive* duties associated with social and economic rights. Instead, he focuses on "negative duties across the board. Human agents are not to collaborate in upholding a coercive institutional order that avoidably restricts the freedom of some so as to render their access to basic necessities insecure without compensating for their collaboration by protecting its victims or by working for its reform" (Pogge 2008, 76). He does not deny that there are such positive duties, nor that there are egalitarian requirements of distributive justice globally. He simply limits his discussion to the negative duty not to impose institutions that predictably and avoidably result in severe deprivation. And he argues that in a number of ways, such as the "international resource privilege," the "international borrowing privilege," and the structure of tariffs and subsidies countenanced by the World Trade Organization, the global institutional order does, in fact, contribute, predictably and avoidably, to the persistence of severe poverty in the world (Pogge 2008, 118–123, 145–150).

Pogge's scholarly work on global justice has been especially notable for integrating his theoretical concerns with proposals for concrete reforms. For example, in a number of papers (such as Pogge 2005, and Pogge 2012), he proposes a "health impact fund" as a way to provide incentives to pharmaceutical companies to develop and deploy medicines that will have the greatest effect on relieving the disease burden on the poor. He is currently president of the organizations Incentives for Global Health (IGH) and Academics Stand Against Poverty (ASAP).

Pogge's work has not been limited to issues of global justice. He has offered important interpretations of Kant (e.g. Pogge 1998b, 2002a), and well as discussions of luck egalitarianism (Pogge 2000) and the capabilities approach (Pogge 2002b). Finally, in 1994, he published *John Rawls* (in German), translated by Michelle Kosch in 2007 as *John Rawls: His Life and Theory of Justice*. This volume is notable not only for its overall interpretation of Rawls's theory, but also because it contains, in its first chapter, what is currently the most extensive published biography of Rawls.

Jon Mandle

SEE ALSO:

Cosmopolitanism
Kant, Immanuel
Law of Peoples
Nozick, Robert
Sandel, Michael
Two principles of justice (in justice as fairness)

158.

POLITICAL CONCEPTION OF JUSTICE

OR RAWLS, A *political conception of* justice is what is required to avoid serious conflict with democratic citizens' many reasonable comprehensive doctrines (religious, philosophical, and/or moral worldviews) so as to garner a stable overlapping consensus of their support through the conception's provision of politically moral principles and justifications (*PL* xl–xli, 143, 147–148). Jettisoning his earlier, unrealistic assumption from *TJ* that citizens share a set of comprehensively liberal values, Rawls acknowledges that a reasonable diversity of citizens' conflicting comprehensive views unregrettably characterizes free democratic societies' normal, enduring circumstances. Rawls revises the idea of a well-ordered society to show how, even under conditions of reasonable pluralism, a *political* conception of justice can still meet with proper and stable societal acceptance: namely, through a reasonable overlapping consensus (*PL* xxxv–xli). Political conceptions of justice have three major features (*PL* 11–15, 174–175, 223, 376, 452–453; *CP* 480): (1) they are freestanding from comprehensive doctrines in society; (2) they articulate a conception of distinctly political, moral values, pertaining specifically to the political domain; and (3) they are laid out with reference to certain basic, intuitive ideas implicit in a democratic society's public, political culture.

First, as *freestanding*, political conceptions are worked out *independently* of existing comprehensive doctrines in society and do not themselves offer one. They steer clear of disputed philosophical, religious, metaphysical, and epistemological claims making it possible to win the endorsement of all persons affirming one of the many reasonable comprehensive doctrines. Aside from what is implied or implicitly contained in its limited sphere, a freestanding, political conception does not recommend any determinate doctrine or philosophical program. Rather,

Political conception of justice / 613

a freestanding, political conception, on its own terms, "is neither presented as, nor … derived from" any comprehensive doctrine and can be "expounded apart from, or without reference to, any such wider [comprehensive] background" (*PL* 10, 12). A political conception of justice is neither tailored to fit into any specific comprehensive doctrines, nor is it worked out with an eye to actually existing comprehensive doctrines so as to strike a stable consensus or compromise between these specific, existing doctrines. This would be political in the wrong sense, in Rawls's view (*JF* 37, 188, 386; *PL* xlv). A political conception focuses on and formulates political values without "mentioning, independent nonpolitical values" (*JF* 182–183). As such, it is freestanding.

Next, rather than being the upshot of an independent, moral philosophy or religious code, a political conception *itself formulates* a species of significant politically moral values centered on "the domain of the political," or the sphere of matters characterized by two features of citizens' distinctive "political relationship" within a democratic, constitutional regime (*PL* xliii, 11–15, 135–137, 452–453; *JF* 182). First, politically moral content focuses solely on the *basic structure of society*, or the basic political and socioeconomic institutions within a society seen as a closed, nonvoluntary, multigenerational system of social cooperation. Persons can neither freely enter political society from a pre-political life nor leave it to a post-political one: it is entered into at birth and exited only in death. Second, the political relationship is characterized by the fact that even in such a constitutional democracy, "political power is … always coercive power" backed by the state's monopoly of enforcement through coercive force and sanctions (*JF* 182; *PL* 11, 135–136). In a constitutional democracy, this means that coercive political power is "the power of the public … the power of free and equal citizens as a collective body" imposed on citizens as individuals or as members of associations, some of whom might not accept the reasons that are said to justify the structure, particular laws, or specific actions of the society's political authority (*PL* 136; *JF* 182). The political relationship is involuntary, unlike membership in private associations, and inescapably coercive, unlike the (at least ideally) affectionate bonds of family life. So political conceptions of justice formulate moral values that are narrowly tailored to the specific domain of the political relationship of citizens in a democratic society: the involuntary relationship of free and equal citizens, who share in the collective exercise of ultimate, and inescapably coercive political power, with regard to the basic political and socioeconomic institutions of society (*PL* xliii). Importantly, political conceptions of justice will neither affirm nor deny claims grappling with issues beyond the political domain: as *political* views, they *take no stance* on such matters, refraining from speaking to them and remaining agnostic about them, since to take a position – whether positive or negative – would itself be to trespass the bounds of the political domain (*PL* 10, 95, 126–128, 150, 377–378).

Finally, a political conception is, as far as possible, laid out with reference to "fundamental intuitive ideas" implicit within the common political culture of a constitutional democracy (*CP* 480). The public political culture includes the democracy's political institutions, these institutions' commonly accepted, public traditions and histories of interpretation, and the democracy's shared, historic texts. Rawls takes this culture to incorporate a general tradition of democratic, political thought whose ideas are clear and relatively familiar to the "educated common sense of citizens generally" (*PL* 13–14). For Rawls, a political conception's "fundamental ideas" like "those of political society as a fair system of social cooperation, of citizens as reasonable and rational, and free and equal … all belong to the category of the political and are familiar from the public political culture of a democratic society" (*PL* 376). These ideas serve as a "fund of implicitly shared ideas and principles" that are particularly ripe to serve in a *freestanding*, political conception of justice since they are not the sole possession of any particular comprehensive doctrine(s), but rather of the society and the public as a whole via their shared, political culture (*PL* 14). That is why a political conception of justice is worked out and elaborated from, as far as it can, in terms of such ideas.

These three features enable a political conception to be the possible focus of an overlapping consensus of reasonable comprehensive doctrines, and thus enable Rawls to show how stable acceptance of a conception of justice for the right reasons is possible (*PL* xl–xli, 15, 143ff.; *JF* 32–33, 184ff.). By refraining, as it does, from taking deep, comprehensive positions that extend beyond the political sphere, a freestanding, political conception of justice can be understood as a module which can be fitted into reasonable persons' various, diverse comprehensive doctrines in different ways (*PL* 12). In tailoring itself to focus on the "political relationship," a political conception of justice articulates an important, but limited subset of *politically* moral values rather than wide-ranging, comprehensive values. Finally, in employing, as far as possible, commonly known and accepted ideas implicit in the public, political culture of modern constitutional democracies, a political conception of justice articulates its principles, arguments, and justifications in publicly shared terms. Thus, for Rawls, these three features of a *political conception of justice* – its (1) freestanding, (2) limited focus on political matters, (3) articulated in the publicly shared ideas of a democratic society – help it to meet with a reasonable overlapping consensus (*JF* 33), by steering it clear of treading on reasonable citizens' comprehensive worldviews and hopefully garnering their support through its articulation of shareable politically moral principles and justifications in terms of common, democratic ideas.

Micah Lewin

SEE ALSO:

Basic structure of society
Comprehensive doctrine
Culture, political vs. background
Fundamental ideas (in justice as fairness)
Overlapping consensus
Political liberalisms, family of
Stability

159.

POLITICAL LIBERALISM, JUSTICE AS FAIRNESS AS

RAWLS INTRODUCED THE phrase "political liberalism" to distinguish his own account of liberalism from what he called "comprehensive liberalism," which denotes a liberal theory of politics rooted in a "comprehensive doctrine," or a doctrine that is at least partially comprehensive. As Rawls explains, modern political thinkers "hoped to establish a basis of moral knowledge independent of ecclesiastical authority" that could be grasped by ordinary people, and that could be used "to develop the full range of concepts and principles in terms of which to characterize the requirements of moral life" (*PL* xxvi). In this type of theory, political principles are derived from the "basis of moral knowledge," suggesting that in this view political philosophy is "applied moral philosophy" (*JF* 14). Although Rawls does not explicitly mention it, many liberals such as J. S. Mill envisioned that the establishment of liberal forms of politics and related changes in the law and economic relationships would be accompanied by a cultural transformation, as society became increasingly secular and religious and other traditional sources of values and identity would atrophy. The widespread acceptance of liberal comprehensive doctrines, then, would support liberal political institutions.

The problem of basing an account of justice and political principles on a comprehensive doctrine, Rawls came to see, is that in a democratic society we can expect people to hold different comprehensive moral, religious, and philosophical doctrines, and so to accept different conceptions of justice rooted in those doctrines. He realized that the account of justice he had set out in *A Theory of Justice* required both a democratic polity *and* a consensus on the "comprehensive philosophical doctrine" (*PL* xvi) on which it is based, a combination that is "unrealistic" (*PL* xvii) because of the (reasonable) moral pluralism of democratic societies. That recognition required him to rethink his original theory of justice. Since it was not possible for a democratic society to be "well-ordered" by a conception of justice based on a comprehensive doctrine, Rawls proposed instead that the conception of justice for a democratic society – or any society marked by a plurality of reasonable comprehensive doctrines – must be a "political conception," one that is not based on any comprehensive doctrine. And this recognition brought a new question to the fore. Most sharply put, the question is, "How is it possible for those affirming a religious doctrine that is based on religious authority... also to hold a reasonable political conception that supports a just democratic regime?" (*PL* xxxix). Political liberalism is designed to answer that question.

Unlike comprehensive liberalism, political liberalism does not derive the principles of justice – the principles governing the basic structure of society – from a comprehensive doctrine, one that many reasonable citizens, particularly religious citizens, do not accept. Rather, it sees these principles as "freestanding," drawing on ideas and values that are widely shared in the public political culture of democratic societies, which adherents of conflicting comprehensive doctrines can and do accept. A political conception of justice is put forward not as "true," but as a set of principles that it is reasonable for people in a pluralist society to accept for the purpose of governing the basic political and economic institutions of their society. Rawls argues that citizens adhering to different comprehensive doctrines can endorse a freestanding conception of justice because it would not be based on any comprehensive doctrine, nor would it call any comprehensive doctrine into question. It is important to note that in drawing on the ideas found in a common political culture Rawls does not use these ideas as "foundations" or as definitive for political reflection, but as sources of values and principles that can be criticized and refined in the process of developing a political conception of justice.

One of these widely shared ideas is that of society as a fair system of cooperation among free and equal citizens, organized by "publicly recognized rules and procedures which those cooperating accept as appropriate to regulate their conduct" (*JF* 5). These publicly recognized rules and procedures constitute the "basic structure" of society, that is, "the way in which the main political and social institutions of society fit together into one system of cooperation, and the way they assign basic rights and duties and regulate the division of advantages that arises from social cooperation over time" (*JF* 10). When citizens share a conception of justice that endorses the publicly recognized rules and procedures of the basic structure, which includes but is not limited to the political system and its use of coercive power, the society meets a necessary condition of being well-ordered.

Coming to share a political conception of justice involves three critical steps. First, we assume that citizens are "reasonable" in that they accept the "criterion of reciprocity." That is to say, they are "reasonable" when "they are prepared to offer one another fair terms of cooperation according to what they consider the most reasonable conception of political justice" (*CP* 578). Specifically, when one proposes such terms to others, one must "think it at least reasonable for others to accept them, as free and equal citizens, and not as dominated or manipulated, or under the pressure of inferior political or social positions" (*CP* 578).

Second, we assume citizens to be "reasonable" in that they acknowledge the existence of "reasonable disagreement," or "disagreement between reasonable persons," due to what Rawls calls the "burdens of judgment" (*PL* 55). The burdens of judgment include such factors as the difficulty and complexity of the evidence that bears on an issue, the relative weight of different considerations, the difficulties of interpreting and applying relevant concepts, and so forth (*PL* 54–58). These factors explain why "it is not to be expected that conscientious persons with full powers of reason, even after free discussion, will all arrive at the same conclusion" (*PL* 58). Thus, reasonable citizens will acknowledge that "a public and shared basis of justification that applies to comprehensive doctrines is lacking in the public culture of a democratic society." For that reason they recognize "limits on what can be reasonably justified to others, and so they endorse some form of liberty of conscience and freedom of thought." Specifically, in recognizing the burdens of judgment, or reasonable pluralism, they agree that it "is unreasonable ... to use political power ... to repress comprehensive views that are not unreasonable" (*PL* 61).

Third, citizens share "a conception of democratic citizenship" as "a relation of free and equal citizens who exercise ultimate political power as a collective body" (*CP* 577). Being reasonable in the two senses explained above, they therefore endorse a conception of political legitimacy that holds that our "exercise of political power is proper only when we sincerely believe that the reasons we would offer for our political actions ... are sufficient, and we also reasonably think that other citizens might also reasonably accept those reasons" (*CP* 578). In short, at least on issues involving "constitutional essentials, or basic questions of justice" (*PL* 137) exercises of political power must be based on public reason, not on other considerations, where the content of public reason is a political conception of justice. This is not to say that nonpublic reasons may not be put forward in discussions of "essentials." Rawls endorses what he calls the "wide view of the public political culture" under which reasons rooted in a comprehensive doctrine may, and for some purposes should, be offered, "provided that in due course proper political reasons... are presented that are sufficient to support whatever the comprehensive doctrines introduced are said to support" (*CP* 591).

Political liberalism encompasses a family of liberal – but political – conceptions of justice, all of which put forward principles governing the basic structure of society that are reasonable in that all citizens who wish to live cooperatively with others, and who acknowledge reasonable disagreement about comprehensive doctrines, have reason to accept them. Any liberal political conception of justice meets three substantive "conditions" (*PL* xlviii n.18): first, it specifies "certain basic rights, liberties and opportunities" that citizens must enjoy; second, it assigns "special priority to those rights, liberties, and opportunities, especially with respect to claims of the general good and of perfectionist values"; and third, it includes "measures assuring to all citizens adequate all-purpose means to make effective use of their liberties and opportunities" (*PL* 6). Rawls lists Habermas's "discourse conception of legitimacy" and "Catholic views of the common good and solidarity when they are expressed in terms of political values" (*CP* 582–583) as forms of political liberalism. Although there are "many variant liberalisms," Rawls argues that his own theory – justice as fairness – is "the most reasonable because it best satisfies these conditions" (*PL* xlix), but he also insists that political liberalism is open to other political conceptions of justice, and that "new variations may be proposed from time to time and older ones may cease to be represented," allowing "the claims of groups or interests arising from social change... to gain their appropriate political voice" (*CP* 583). Citizens of a well-ordered democratic society, then, will not necessarily share a single conception of political justice, so long as they accept some member of the family of liberal conceptions of justice.

A political conception of justice applies to what Rawls calls "a special domain of the political" (*PL* 137), which comprises the basic structure of society, and the use of political power, or "coercive power backed by the government's use of sanctions" (*PL* 135–136). The political domain is limited – it does not include voluntary or associational life, or personal relationships, for example.

The political domain does not correspond to traditional views of the distinction between the public and private spheres, which frequently see the "public" or the political sphere as comprising the state with its "monopoly of the legitimate use of physical force," to use Weber's famous phrase. Rawls's political domain includes specifically "political" institutions, but also the other major institutions that comprise the basic structure of society, including "the legally recognized forms of property, and the structure of the economy...as well as the family" (*JF* 10). He conceives of the political domain in this broad way "because the effects of the basic structure on citizens' aims, aspirations, and character, as well as on their opportunities and their ability to take advantage of them, are pervasive and present from the beginning of life" (*JF* 10); a narrower concept of the political would be inadequate to secure "background justice from one generation to the next" (*JF* 54).

Rawls's conception of the political domain is also different from traditional views in that its boundaries are not viewed as in some sense "prepolitical" – as rooted in nature, or practical reason or some other source, and functioning as a constraint on legitimate political authority. Rather, a political conception of justice provides "a framework of thought" that enables us to determine how its boundaries should be adjusted "to different social circumstances" (*JF* 12). Although we start with a "loose characterization" of the scope of the political domain, we decide its scope politically, through a deliberative process governed by political values.

Fundamental questions regarding the structure of the political domain – the basic structure including the political system – must be decided by political values, that is, a political conception of justice that satisfies the criterion of reciprocity, and so can be regarded by all citizens as "reasonable, even if barely so" (*CP* 578). Political values, then, exclude nonpolitical values, such as those rooted in one's comprehensive doctrine, since appealing to such values violates the criterion of reciprocity – I cannot reasonably expect you to accept a proposed norm if the norm is based only on a comprehensive doctrine that we do not share. Citizens have a duty of civility, a duty to decide fundamental questions exclusively in terms of political values.

In Rawls's view it is important that a political conception of justice be developed in a systematic way if it is to be "freestanding," and thus to pose no doctrinal bar to being adopted by adherents of comprehensive doctrines. Rawls's political liberalism differs from those responses to reasonable moral pluralism that allow a more or less unlimited range of reasons to be offered in

Political liberalism, justice as fairness as / 621

justification of principles of justice, and rely on some processes of deliberation or contestation to generate at least temporary agreements about important constitutional matters. A disadvantage of such approaches is that they keep basic rights and liberties on the political agenda, rather than removing them from day-to-day contestation, thus "raising the stakes of political controversy" and increasing "the insecurity and hostility of public life" (*PL* 161). But, even more important, such apparently more inclusive conceptions are, in Rawls's view, defective because they allow fundamental decisions to be made on the basis of values that are not shared, rather than on the basis of political values alone, thus violating the principle of legitimacy: such decisions cannot be justified to all reasonable citizens in a society marked by reasonable pluralism.

A society well-ordered by a family of liberal political conception of justice is one in which all citizens accept a liberal conception of justice that satisfies the three conditions set out above, but they do not do so for the same reasons. Because of the plurality of comprehensive doctrines held by citizens, "they affirm the political conception from within different and opposing comprehensive doctrines and so, in part at least, for different reasons" (*JF* 32). Such a society is marked by an "overlapping consensus" of reasonable comprehensive doctrines. Each citizen, then, affirms the political conception of justice from within her own comprehensive doctrine, as "theorems," Rawls suggests, of her larger view (*JF* 35). Of course, many citizens do not have fully worked-out comprehensive views, and so they may "affirm [the political conception] on its own" because they "appreciate the public good it accomplishes in a democratic society" (*JF* 193). The emergence of an overlapping consensus is a dynamic process, which may begin with a "consensus only on constitutional principles" (*PL* 149) rather than on a full political conception of justice. As citizens cooperate with each other on the basis of a constitutional consensus, they may gain "increasing trust and confidence in one another," and come to affirm the political conception of justice itself (*PL* 158–168), adjusting their comprehensive views to more fully incorporate the political values.

In summary, we can say that political liberalism is a form of liberalism because it endorses principles that liberals have always espoused, such as limited government and the freedom and equality of citizens, summarized by the three conditions of political liberalism set out above. What makes it political is the account it provides of those principles. Political liberalism offers a different way of justifying or grounding liberal principles, one that is compatible with adherence to nonliberal comprehensive doctrines.

J. Donald Moon

SEE ALSO:

Autonomy, political
Basic structure of society
Burdens of judgment
Comprehensive doctrine
Democracy
Duty of civility
Legitimacy
Liberalism, comprehensive vs. political
Overlapping consensus
Political conception of justice
Political liberalisms, family of
Public reason
Reasonable pluralism
Reciprocity
Truth

160.

POLITICAL LIBERALISMS, FAMILY OF

R AWLS'S IDEA OF political liberalism centers on a family of reasonable, liberal political conceptions of justice, the common problems they address, and the shared features of their solutions. Rawls understands this family to harbor the most reasonable conception of political justice for a pluralistic democracy (*PL* 156–157); to include his offering for this title, *justice as fairness*, as a central and prototypical member (*PL* xlvi–xlvii, 167–168, 226, 451 n.27); to specify the "focal class" of conceptions capable of meeting with a reasonable overlapping consensus in such a society (*PL* 167–168); and to furnish the content of democracy's public reason (*PL* xlvii–xlviii, 226, 450). This family of *reasonable, liberal, political* conceptions of justice is delimited by the intersection of these very notions: (1) *political* conceptions of justice; (2) *liberal* conceptions of justice; and (3) *reasonable* ones at that.

(1) Members of this family count as *political* conceptions of justice by adhering to the following three strictures: steering clear and being articulated independently of the contentious claims of comprehensive doctrines (i.e. wide-ranging religious, philosophical, metaphysical, and/or moral worldviews); retaining focus squarely on "the domain of the political," or the province of matters centered around the involuntary and inescapably coercive political relationship of citizens with respect to their society's basic structure of socioeconomic and political institutions; and formulating their positions using the shared, intuitive ideas of the democracy's public, political culture (*PL* 11–15, 174–175, 376, 452–453). Although Rawls sometimes refers to the members of this family as various *liberalisms*, he is referring to *political* liberalism and its constituent reasonable, liberal *political* conceptions of justice rather than *comprehensively* liberal views (*PL* xxiv–xxvii, xlvi, 303, 374 n.1; *LHPP* 11–12). Political liberalism operates in the narrow

623

domain of the political without delving farther afield, into a wider, comprehensive moral, religious, or philosophical issues. While the general nature of morality or human agency might be discussed by comprehensively liberal philosophies, these topics are not per se subjects of discussion for political liberalism. Insofar as similar topics are addressed by politically liberal conceptions, they have, in comparison to comprehensive views, tailored roles within an extensionally limited scope. In political liberalism, while these discussions are still moral in content, they can be taken only to address, independently of particular worldviews, the specifically *political* relationship of citizens with regard to the basic institutional structure of their democratic society, using ideas implicit in the common, political culture (*PL* xxvi–xxvii, 11–15, 125, 174–175, 376, 452–453). For example, rather than presenting a comprehensive view of *persons* as moral agents, political liberalisms articulate a freestanding, political notion of persons – free and equal *citizens* – and their *politically* moral powers and duties (*PL* xxvi–xxvii, xliii, 18–20, esp. 18 n.20, 66–68).

Political conceptions, as such, will neither affirm nor deny claims that deal with or touch on matters beyond the political domain: they remain agnostic about these claims, *taking no stance* on them, as to take a position – whether pro or con – would itself involve overstepping the bounds of the political domain (*PL* 10, 95, 126–128, 150, 377–378). Political liberalism generally accomplishes this by refraining from taking a stance on the claims or positions of comprehensive doctrines, which is possible insofar as such doctrines do not speak to the political domain. Yet when a comprehensive doctrine itself presents, *within the domain of the political*, politically unreasonable claims about matters of basic justice or constitutional essentials, a politically liberal conception of justice will have no choice but to take an opposed stance, deeming the doctrines' positions unreasonable. Still, political liberalism strives to avoid speaking to even the purported grounds of such a comprehensive view's political claims to the extent these fall outside or extend beyond the political domain (*PL* 138, 150–154). Instead, political liberalism can remain within the domain of the political simply by insisting that adherents of this comprehensive view be politically reasonable and treat others with reciprocity regarding matters of basic justice or constitutional essentials within the public political forum and the voting booth. Living up to these standards requires that these adherents not simply or primarily "invoke the grounding reasons of their comprehensive views" for their political positions about such fundamental matters: rather, these believers must hold that sufficient, freestanding, *political* justifications that best express "the ordering of *political* values they sincerely think the most reasonable" (as formulated within a complete, politically liberal conception of justice) and that they honestly believe their free and equal

Political liberalisms, family of / 625

fellows could at least accept as reasonable can be provided in due course (*PL* liii, 442–447, 453–455, 462–463, emphasis added).

Political liberalism's focus on *political* conceptions of justice comes in response to the overarching problem it addresses: articulating conceptions of political justice for a constitutional democracy that a plurality of citizens' diverse, reasonable comprehensive doctrines may freely and stably accept, in part based on the conception's own politically moral reasons (*PL* xxxvi–xli, xlv, 143–148, 490). Political liberalism faces this problem because, in acknowledging that a reasonable pluralism of citizens' comprehensive views unregrettably characterizes free democracies' enduring circumstances, Rawls revokes as unrealistic his assumption from *TJ* that citizens share a comprehensively liberal set of values, and reworks his idea of a well-ordered society in order to show how a shared conception of political justice can still be steadfastly accepted in such a society for the right reasons (*PL* xxxv–xli, 140–144). He does this, first, by reconceiving his theory of *justice as fairness* and the related family of political liberalisms into explicitly *political* conceptions of justice (*PL* xli) and, second, by introducing the integral, correlated idea – shared amongst political liberalisms – of *reasonable overlapping consensus*, which characterizes how politically moral and steady acceptance of a conception of justice with its political values by reasonable citizens may be achieved (*PL* xxxvi, xl–xli, xlv, 143–144, 147–148, 208). A political conception's freestanding content that is limited to the political domain and articulated with ideas common to the democratic political culture leads to shareable politically-moral principles and justifications that avoid conflicts with reasonable comprehensive doctrines; this enables the political conception to freely garner these doctrines' support, thereby allowing it to meet with proper and stable allegiance through overlapping consensus (*JF* 32–33,184ff.; *PL* xxxviii–xxxix, 143ff.).

(2) Members of political liberalism's focal class count as *liberal*, political conceptions of justice insofar as they (a) articulate a list of basic rights, liberties, and opportunities common to constitutional democracies, (b) accord a special priority to these rights as opposed to other values, and (c) mutually assure all citizens suitable general-purpose resources for effectively and intelligently exercising these rights (*PL* xlvi–xlvii, 6, 156–157, 223, 291–292, 375, 450–451; *LHPP* 12). Liberal political conceptions do not just propagate and prioritize the value of liberty in the abstract, but rather refer to a historically or analytically drawn up *list* of basic rights and liberties (*PL* 291–292; *JF* 44–45; *LHPP* 12–13). The list must at least include freedoms of speech, thought, conscience, association, and personal integrity, political rights to participation, and rights enshrined in the rule of law (*PL* 228, 291–293, 334–335; *JF* 44–48; *LHPP* 12).

For Rawls, (b) means that the listed liberties have "an absolute weight" compared to other values and cannot be overruled by such considerations as what is required for a social ideal or for the greatest public welfare (*PL* 294–295). Basic liberties are to be protected as "constitutional essentials" while less urgent matters of basic justice can be left to democratic legislatures (*PL* 227–230, 363–368; *JF* 46–50). Still, these liberties can be regulated and interpretively adjusted so that they can fit together into "one coherent scheme" (*PL* 294–296). Prioritizing a list of basic liberties vis-à-vis other values does not preclude political liberalism from providing a political conception of the goodness of political society (*PL* 202–204), or from promoting a number of *politically moral* virtues, all of which can be shared amongst reasonable comprehensive doctrines (*PL* 192–195).

Reasonably providing for (c) means that political liberalisms (as opposed to libertarianisms (*PL* lvi, 262–271, 324–331; *LHPP* 12–13)) must require societies to prevent burdensome levels of inequality through requirements placed on their scheme of basic institutions. This requires (something like) institutions allowing democratic officials independence from entrenched socioeconomic interests and providing citizens with the information requisite to think through public policy (e.g. publicly financed campaigns), some decent social minimum of welfare (*PL* 228–229; *JF* 47–48), "society as employer of last resort," and basic health care guaranteed to citizens (*PL* lv–lvii). Indeed, politically liberal conceptions of justice must provide substantive principles of justice to serve as ideals for the maintenance of a just background of society's basic institutional structure (*PL* 281–285, 451), because while particular interactions among persons taken in isolation might seem unobjectionable, such interactions might actually be less than free and fair when viewed against a background of unjust conditions in society's basic structure (*PL* 266–269).

(3) Liberal, political conceptions count as *reasonable* if they (d) meet "the criterion of reciprocity" and (e) properly recognize and respond to "the burdens of judgment" (the complications of reasoning that are reasonable disagreements' wellsprings (*PL* 54–58, 375; *JF* 35–37; *CP* 476–477)) and their consequences (*PL* xlvii, 446–447, 450). These criteria likewise specify the defining features of reasonable citizens, the idea of whom provides Rawls's primary characterization of reasonableness (*PL* 394–395). In fact, common to all political liberalisms are fundamental ideas of free and equal, reasonable and rational citizens, and society as a fair system of social cooperation over time, with different interpretations of these ideas yielding different political liberalisms (*PL* 167–168, 226, 450–451).

Living up to (d) requires that liberal political conceptions, first, be put forward as the most reasonable, fair terms of social cooperation that free and equal fellow citizens could reasonably accept and mutually abide by without coercion,

Political liberalisms, family of / 627

winning stable "support by addressing each citizen's reason" with its arguments while allowing room for other reasonable proposals of the like (*JF* 6–7; *PL* 49–50, 142–143, 375, 446–447). Second, (d) requires that such conceptions only legitimize democratic constitutions, legislation, and government action when it can be honestly and reasonably believed that sufficient reasons that all free and equal citizens can reasonably accept have been offered for the incorporated matters of constitutional essentials and basic justice (*PL* 137, 217, 446–447). Adherence to (e) requires that liberal political conceptions acknowledge and tolerate both a reasonable pluralism of worldviews in society and also "different and incompatible liberal political conceptions" that are nonetheless reasonable (*PL* xlvii, 375; *JF* 35–37). Properly acknowledging the former requires securing freedoms of thought and conscience (*PL* xlvii, 60ff., 395) and offering a freestanding, *political* conception capable of garnering an overlapping consensus of reasonable worldviews (*JF* 36–37). Properly acknowledging the latter – in accord with (d) as well as (e) – requires allowing the whole class of political liberalisms to provide the content of a democratic society's public reason with the principles of justice and guidelines of inquiry they specify. "Political liberalism applies the principle of toleration to philosophy itself" (*PL* 10) through its constituent conceptions making room not only for the reasonable pluralism of comprehensive views in society but also for incompatible, though reasonable, alternative political liberalisms in the content of public reason (*PL* xlvii–xlviii, l–li, 226, 450–451).

Micah Lewin

SEE ALSO:

Basic structure of society
Burdens of judgment
Comprehensive doctrine
Liberal conception of justice
Liberalism, comprehensive vs. political
Overlapping consensus
Political conception of justice
Public reason
The reasonable and the rational
Reasonable pluralism
Reciprocity

161.

POLITICAL OBLIGATION

QUESTIONS OF POLITICAL obligation concern people's duties to obey the law. Rawls's first sustained discussion of this subject was in his 1964 article, "Legal Obligation and the Duty of Fair Play." In this piece, Rawls assumes that in acceptably just modern societies, there is a moral obligation to obey the law, which rests on some general moral principle (*CP* 117). The principle to which Rawls appeals is the principle of fair play.

This principle was first clearly formulated by H. L. A. Hart in 1955 (Hart 1955, 185–186). Rawls's formulation is as follows:

> Suppose there is a mutually beneficial and just scheme of social cooperation, and that the advantages it yields can only be obtained if everyone, or nearly everyone, cooperates. Suppose further that cooperation requires a certain sacrifice from each person [...] Suppose finally that the benefits produced by cooperation are, up to a certain point, free [...] Under these conditions a person who has accepted the benefits of the scheme is bound by a duty of fair play to do his part and not to take advantage of the free benefit by not cooperating. (*CP* 122)

The moral basis of the principle is mutuality of restrictions. Under specified conditions, if members of a cooperative scheme make sacrifices in order to produce benefits that are also received by non-cooperators, the latter may have obligations to make similar sacrifices. As Rawls later says, "We are not to gain from the cooperative labors of others without doing our fair share" (*TJ* 96).

According to Rawls's formulation, fair play obligations are incurred only if one *accepts* the benefits provided by a cooperative scheme (*CP* 122). At first sight,

628

this "acceptance condition" may appear justified. If a group of neighbors holds a pot luck supper, in which all participants supply dishes, if Adam partakes of the dinner, he too should bring a dish. Not to do so would take advantage of the other participants. In this case, Adam is unfair only if he voluntarily attends the supper and partakes of the dishes. Rawls's reasoning seems to be along similar lines. But the difficulty with this condition is that major benefits provided by government – e.g. defense, law and order, a clean environment – are public goods. Because they are received more or less regardless of how recipients behave in regard to them, they cannot be accepted in the usual sense.

This problem led Rawls to abandon the principle of fairness as a basis for political obligation. In *A Theory of Justice*, he argues that the principle binds only office holders and other people who have taken special advantage of the system. But it does not establish obligations for average citizens (*TJ* 97–98). In order to establish a basis for binding all members of society, Rawls turns to a natural duty of justice.

According to Rawls, the natural duties of justice are moral principles that apply directly to individuals, unlike the principles of justice, which apply to institutions. But like the principles of justice, natural duties are justified by being chosen in the original position. For instance, a duty of mutual aid, i.e. a duty to help another person who is in need or distress, would be chosen because the likely benefits of such a principle outweigh its costs (*TJ* 298). To answer questions of political obligation, Rawls invokes a natural duty "to comply with and to do our share in just institutions when they exist and apply to us" (*TJ* 293; cf. 99). Rawls does not view requirements established by natural duties as obligations. According to his use of the term, obligations must be self-imposed, based on acts such as promising or accepting benefits, performed by the obligee. But, unlike the principle of fair play, this natural duty binds all inhabitants of society, whether or not they have accepted benefits provided by government.

Although not developed in detail, Rawls's view of political obligation has had considerable influence. A significant literature on natural duty approaches to political obligation has emerged (e.g. Waldron 1993; Simmons and Wellman 2005). But while Rawls argues for his position using the device of the original position, scholars generally discuss the political duty as an intuitively clear principle in its own right.

In spite of the favorable attention it has received, Rawls's position is subject to criticism. First, his rejection of the principle of fair play has been questioned (Klosko 1994a). As indicated, the problem he identifies is the need to accept benefits. But from the point of view of the original position, it is difficult to justify this requirement. If all members of society require certain benefits and these are provided by general cooperation throughout society, everyone who receives the benefits should be required to cooperate, regardless of whether or not they have accepted the benefits. Requiring that benefits be accepted makes no sense in regard to benefits that, by their very nature, cannot be accepted.

An important criticism of Rawls's natural duty argument turns on a requirement of "particularity." As discussed especially by A. John Simmons, a theory of political obligation should explain the close ties people have to their own states (Simmons 1979). But on Rawls's position it is difficult to explain why, if Denmark and many other states have just institutions, we should support and comply with those of our own state rather than of these other countries. Rawls appears to have a response. He says that we are to support the state that "applies" to us. But he does not explain what this means. As argued by Simmons, clear ways for a state to "apply" to Adam include his consenting to or receiving benefits from it (1979, chapter 6). If this is what Rawls has in mind, the problem, then, is that relationships with one's state such as these appear to be able to generate obligations to obey its laws on their own, without reference to the natural duty. Recent years have seen significant discussion of both the possibilities and problems of a natural duty theory of political obligation.

George Klosko

SEE ALSO:

> *Fairness, principle of*
> *Natural duties*
> *Natural duty of justice*
> *Obligations*

162.

POLITICAL VIRTUES

N POLITICAL LIBERALISM the political virtues are understood as the attitudes, dispositions, and other qualities of character that would characterize good citizens of a just and stable liberal-democratic constitutional regime. Citizenship is a formal status, referring to various legal privileges, immunities, and responsibilities. The political virtues refer to good or exemplary citizenship, and so they correspond to "the ideal of a good citizen of a democratic state – a role specified by its political institutions" (*PL* 195). With their connection to this role and their inclusion in a political conception of justice, the political virtues presuppose the distinction between comprehensive doctrine and the domain of the political, i.e. the more narrowly defined set of liberal-democratic values, ideas, and ideals that make political liberalism possible.

References to the political virtues are sometimes accompanied by different examples, but the principal virtues include toleration, reasonableness, mutual respect, a sense of fairness, a spirit of compromise, and a readiness to meet others halfway (*PL* 122, 157, 163, 194; *CP* 439–444, 460). These are the characteristics associated with the willingness to cooperate with others on publicly acceptable terms (*PL* 163). The refusal to engage in resistance or revolution – what one might see as a form of civic moderation – is also said to be a political virtue, at least in those regimes that rise to the standard of being "moderately well-governed" (*PL* 347). Rawls even refers at times to the sense of justice as among the political virtues, though his more standard formulation is to describe the capacity for a sense of justice as a basic moral power (*PL* 402).

While *A Theory of Justice* describes virtue in terms of "sentiments and habitual attitudes" leading to right action, the nature of the virtues is not explored in great detail in *Political Liberalism* (*TJ* 383). Yet several passages are instructive. That certain qualities of character are political virtues counts as a fact relevant to our practical reasoning (*PL* 121). But according to Rawls's political constructivism, facts concerning the nature of the virtues are ultimately "facts about the possibilities of construction" (*PL* 123). That is, a feature of a person's character – e.g. that he or she is disposed to those attitudes and actions that would be called tolerant in the relevant circumstances – is understood to be a political virtue in accordance with a constructivist procedure through which principles of justice are developed. By organizing and connecting facts about human character, this procedure establishes certain political virtues as part of a political conception of justice and as worth encouraging politically (*PL* 123–125; cf. 147).

A second point, and one that is in keeping with traditional accounts of the virtues stressing habituation and activity, is that the political virtues are the result of regular practice. They are "built up slowly over time" and must be "constantly renewed by being reaffirmed and acted from in the present" (*PL* 157 n.23). As a form of political capital, these virtues are sustained not only by well-ordered institutions but also by the relations of mutual trust and reassurance among citizens who recognize their institutions as just.

The political virtues are a basic good that citizens would hope to find realized in one another. In this sense they resemble the moral virtues that are described in *TJ* as "broadly based properties," i.e. those properties that members of society have reason to want in one another (*PL* 208 n.41; *TJ* 382). Yet the virtues set forth in political liberalism cannot simply be a special case of the excellences and other characteristics that are required or recommended by a comprehensive moral doctrine. The political virtues are in principle distinct from comprehensive moral virtues as well as from the virtues of family life, friendship, interpersonal relations, churches, and other associations of civil society. Of course, a quality of character like a sense of fairness may be both a political and a nonpolitical virtue, depending on the reasons one has for valuing it in different contexts (*PL* 195 n.29).

An important question about the virtues is the extent to which they may be promoted by the state through education and other social policy. Perfectionist political theories that are based on an objective ethical account of the good life can easily answer this question in the affirmative: the state may permissibly encourage those virtues that contribute to the human good. With his defense of state neutrality, construed as neutrality of aim, Rawls rejects the perfectionist approach, refusing moreover to endorse liberal versions of perfectionism grounded in the ideals of individuality or autonomy. The politically liberal state should not aim to favor or promote a particular comprehensive moral doctrine, not even a secular liberal doctrine. Nor should it provide greater support to those who have adopted such a worldview (*PL* 193).

This does not mean, however, that the state must refrain from promoting the *political virtues*. After all, those virtues are not tied to a particular comprehensive doctrine but rather to the very preconditions for sustaining social cooperation over time. Social policy that intends to strengthen political virtue is thus consistent with neutrality. For example, educational policy may aim to foster civic knowledge, prepare independent and cooperating citizens, and encourage the political virtues (*PL* 199). It may turn out that such policies have the effect indirectly of strengthening other ideals and virtues that fit most easily with a liberal comprehensive doctrine and that are contrary to the ways of life pursued by religious groups or cultural minorities. For Rawls this fact alone is not a sufficient objection to the goal of encouraging a politically virtuous citizenry.

Among the political virtues, reasonableness deserves special mention, given the important role played by the *reasonable* in political liberalism. Applied to persons, reasonableness primarily suggests both a willingness to seek and abide by fair terms of cooperation among free and equal citizens and a disposition to honor the burdens of judgment (*PL* 48–58). Hence to be reasonable is to accept and act on political liberalism's fundamental ideas of society and the person given the fact of reasonable pluralism. Reasonable persons also abide by the methods and standards of commonsense knowledge and mainstream science (*PL* 139). And they respect what Rawls calls the "precepts of reasonable discussion" by crediting others with good faith, expecting reasonable disagreement, and avoiding hasty or groundless accusations of bias, self-interest, or ideological delusion (*CP* 478–479).

Reasonableness and the other political virtues are thus essential to democratic political cooperation. While they cannot be categorized as "intrinsically more important than other values," due to the noncomprehensive standpoint of political liberalism, Rawls nevertheless observes that the political virtues are "very great virtues" that would normally outweigh other values that might come into conflict with them (*PL* 157).

James Boettcher

SEE ALSO:

> *Moral education*
> *Neutrality*
> *Perfectionism*
> *Political conception of justice*
> *The reasonable and the rational*
> *Stability*

163.

PRACTICAL REASON

P RACTICAL REASONS ARE reasons for action, while theoretical reasons
are reasons for belief. The former direct us to what is good to do, while
the latter direct us to what is true about the world. To make this standard
distinction is not yet to say anything about the nature of either practical or theoretical reasons, or about how they do or do not relate to one another. In *PL*
Rawls explains that his theory of justice is grounded in a distinctive view about
the nature and independence of practical reason, one which Rawls explicitly associates with Kant, and which Rawls calls constructivist.

Rawls contrasts this view with a kind of moral realism illustrated by rational
intuitionism (*PL* 91–94; see also *CP* 343–346). On this opposing view, practical
reasons, or at least moral reasons, are just a special case of theoretical reasons:
the moral good is an object of knowledge, "gained in part by a kind of perception or intuition, as well as organized by first principles found acceptable on due
reflection" (*PL* 92). By contrast, Rawls associates his own political constructivism
with the (Kantian) view that there are distinctly practical reasons which are not
grounded in theoretical knowledge.

> [T]he procedure of construction is based essentially on practical reason
> and not on theoretical reason. Following Kant's way of making the distinc-
> tion, we say: practical reason is concerned with the production of objects
> according to a conception of those objects – for example, the conception
> of a just constitutional regime taken as the aim of political endeavor –
> while theoretical reason is concerned with the knowledge of given objects.
> (*PL* 93)

This claim is complicated. Rawls is asserting not just that there are specifically practical reasons, but also that the nature of those reasons comes from the nature of practical activity itself. To be an agent, a practical subject, is to act to carry out an intention: to have a "conception" of what is good to do in one's mind, and then causally to realize or "produce" the object of that conception through one's own efforts. It is quite possible to hold that the content of practical reasons comes from considerations outside the nature of agency itself, and that our agency is simply an instrument that we use to bring about external goals. For instance, a familiar view claims that practical reasons are grounded in an agent's desires, and that our agency is always directed to the objects of those desires. On this view, there are practical reasons, but their rationality has nothing to do with the structure of agency itself. Rawls, following Kant, is rejecting this kind of view. In the above passage, Rawls claims that practical reasons themselves derive from the nature of practical activity, from "the production of objects according to a conception of those objects." That is, practical rationality is to be found in the fit between the objects that we conceive and those that we produce. In the case of Rawls's political liberalism, the relevant conception is "the conception of a just constitutional regime taken as the aim of political endeavor." Rawls's positive theory of justice is practically rational, a source of valid political reasons, insofar as that theory is produced – or, in Rawls's preferred term, constructed – from the very idea of a just constitutional regime. Political constructivism holds that valid (and hence rational) political claims are those that can be derived from the idea of a just political regime through a recognizable procedure of construction.

This procedure, once again, is specifically practical: it is one in which agents choose for themselves, on the basis of conceptions that they endorse. A just constitutional regime is one that all citizens, conceived as free and equal, agree to endorse. Now one might hold that what makes a political order good, and thus serves as the basis for agreement, is that it achieves certain good political ends, which can be specified independently of the derivative goodness of our agreeing on the political means to achieving those ends. This is the kind of (theoretical) view that Rawls is rejecting, in which independently good ends can be identified outside the choice of a political conception. Rawls marks this point with his distinction between the reasonable and the rational. Individuals, Rawls notes, may have their own particular reasons for action, which make practical sense for them but which others should not necessarily be expected to accept as justifying. In that case, we describe the demand that others conform to those putative reasons for action as unreasonable. To be reasonable, then, is to be willing to propose terms of action that others can be expected to accept. Notice that the reasonable is not defined here in terms of any specific reasons that anyone can or should accept. Reasonableness is a feature of persons, and that feature is those persons' commitment to securing the agreement of all others. The reasonable is thus independent of the rational, of the specific practical reasons that would justify particular ends. Nonetheless Rawls proposes that the reasonable can and must have political priority: the bare idea of reasonable political agreement suffices to determine the content of a just political regime. To show this is so, we begin with the idea of political citizens as free and equal: as agents who hold potentially different conceptions of the good, and who are equally capable of regulating their mutual pursuit of their conceptions of the good in terms of principles of justice that are equally binding on them all. We then ask what principles of justice those free and equal citizens, using only the ideas of themselves as free and equal, would impose on themselves. If Rawls's positive theory of justice is correct, it is because the answering of this question is modeled by the choice of the parties in the original position for the two principles of justice. Because they ultimately follow from the bare idea of a political agreement between free and equal citizens, the two principles of justice are said to be reasonable.

The original position is a constructive procedure because it is one in which agents take a given conception (in this case, the idea of reasonable political agreement) and use it to produce a more definite object (in this case, the specific content of reasonable political principles). In the procedure of construction, no values are deployed that are external to the original conception (in this case, again, the idea of reasonable political agreement). Rawlsian political principles are thus understood as sources of practical (in this case, political) reasons not because they match some externally good reality, but because of the fit between the conception of reasonable political agreement and Rawls's favored principles of justice, a fit that is modeled in the choices of the parties in the original position. The rationality of the principles of justice remains specifically and fully practical, because at no point does Rawls say that they, or the purely political values they express, are true in any independent sense. All Rawls says is that his principles of justice can be shown (practically, in the choices of free and equal citizens) to express the value of reasonable political agreement.

As for why reasonable political agreement should have the supreme political value Rawls says it should have, Rawls's argument is, again, specifically practical. Politics requires the compliance of citizens with laws and institutions. Rawls emphasizes that under conditions of reasonable pluralism, which he thinks characterize the exercise of practical reason in the modern world, it is not possible to secure public agreement on claims about the meaning and purpose of human life. There are simply too many such claims that individuals might come to understand as rational, as practically justified for themselves. Given this fact, citizens cannot reasonably be expected to comply freely with laws and institutions that depend on such potentially controversial claims. We can expect free public compliance only with laws and institutions that can be endorsed by any reasonable citizen, regardless of his or her conception of the good, and regardless of the comprehensive doctrine that he or she uses to justify that conception of the good. In this sense, there is a practical, political motivation for fixing on the idea of reasonable political agreement, and reasoning politically from this idea alone. But as to why this practical, political motivation should be rationally sufficient, why we should give it the priority that Rawls asks us to give it in our political lives, that is a question that political liberalism cannot answer on its own. To do so would be to make claims about the role of politics in a good human life, and thus to exceed the boundaries of a merely political liberalism. But there is no reason for political liberalism to answer this question, because the various comprehensive doctrines held by different liberal citizens, as themselves exercises of practical reason, are perfectly capable of answering the question in their own comprehensive terms. If they can all endorse a merely political liberalism for their own, potentially different comprehensive reasons, then there exists a practical agreement, an overlapping consensus, around the idea of a merely political liberalism.

On Rawls's account of practical reason, if such an overlapping consensus obtains, then political liberalism is fully justified. This is so because the idea of an overlapping consensus, like the argument for the two principles of justice themselves, is derived solely from the conception of a reasonable political agreement. In each case, we "produce" the relevant idea from the "conception" alone. The two principles of justice express just what free and equal citizens, holding different comprehensive doctrines, can agree to impose on themselves, collectively, reasoning together. The idea of an overlapping consensus expresses just what free and equal citizens, holding different comprehensive doctrines, can agree to impose on themselves, individually, reasoning separately. It is the fit between these arguments, the way they derive equally from the idea of free and equal citizens, and converge from different directions on the same conclusions,

Practical reason / 639

that constitutes the specifically practical justification of Rawls's political liberalism.

Larry Krasnoff

SEE ALSO:

Constructivism: Kantian/political
Deliberative rationality
Kant, Immanuel
The original position
Political conception of justice
Rational intuitionism
The reasonable and the rational
Sense of justice

164.

PRECEPTS OF JUSTICE

A S RAWLS DEFINES it, "intuitionism" is the doctrine that holds that there is "a plurality of first principles which may conflict to give contrary directives in particular cases," and that there is "no explicit method, no priority rules, for weighing these principles against one another: we are simply to strike a balance by intuition, by what seems to us most nearly right" (*TJ* 30). Our pre-philosophical moral sense is intuitionistic, as we rely on "groups of rather specific precepts, each group applying to a particular problem of justice" (*TJ* 31). We use these various common-sense precepts intuitively to determine things like a fair wage, just taxation, and appropriate punishments. Justice as fairness holds that since an intuitionistic theory does not assign weights to its various precepts, it is "but half a conception" (*TJ* 37). On the other hand, because justice as fairness aims to describe our moral sense in reflective equilibrium, and because the various precepts are intuitively plausible, Rawls wants to explain how justice as fairness captures their plausibility, even if none can properly be elevated to the position of the sole standard of justice.

For example, two common precepts concerning the justice of wages are, first, that each individual should be paid according to her contribution, and second, that each should be paid according to her effort. While each of these precepts has some plausibility, they often conflict, and it is not obvious how these conflicts should be resolved or combined into a unified account of just wages. Mill argued that the conflict between these precepts could only be resolved by subordinating them to utilitarianism as the ultimate moral standard. Rawls argues,

Precepts of justice / 641

of course, that they are to be explained by reference to his two principles of justice. One problem that he notes with utilitarianism as the public criterion for assigning weights to the various precepts is that its demands on information are so overwhelming that virtually any weights could be viewed as plausible or reasonable. Because justice as fairness treats distributive justice as a matter of pure procedural justice, it reserves a significant role for market relations. In a reasonably competitive market, we can think of these precepts as identifying "features of jobs that are significant on either the demand or the supply side of the market, or both" (*TJ* 269). The precept that workers should be paid according to their contribution reflects the fact that "A firm's demand for workers is determined by the marginal productivity of labor ... Experience and training, natural ability and special know-how, tend to earn a premium" (*TJ* 269). At the same time, "jobs which involve uncertain or unstable employment, or which are performed under hazardous and unpleasantly strenuous conditions, tend to receive more pay ... From this circumstance arise such precepts as to each according to his effort, or the risks he bears, and so on" (*TJ* 269). Thus, while there is no need to invoke these precepts explicitly, justice as fairness captures part of what is attractive about each.

While both Mill's utilitarianism and justice as fairness can recognize these same precepts of justice, they play different roles in the two theories and, in effect, receive different weights. This highlights the fact that market systems will generate very different outcomes depending on what background conditions are in place and whether they are maintained. "When the family of background institutions is governed by distinct conceptions, the market forces to which firms and workers have to adjust will not be the same" (*TJ* 270). For example, a society committed to fair equality of opportunity will likely generate market outcomes that are more egalitarian than one that has no such commitment. In effect, it will give less weight to the precept of rewarding training and education (since these are available to everyone) and give more weight to the precept of rewarding effort. It follows that

> There is no presumption ... that following the precept of contribution leads to a just outcome unless the underlying market forces, and the availability of opportunities which they reflect, are appropriately regulated. And this implies, as we have seen, that the basic structure as a whole is just. There is no way, then, to give a proper weight to the precepts of justice

except by instituting the surrounding arrangements required by the principles of justice. (*TJ* 271)

Jon Mandle

SEE ALSO:

Distributive justice
Intuitionism
Lexical priority
The market
Mill, John Stuart
Two principles of justice (in justice as fairness)

165.

PRIMARY GOODS, SOCIAL

AWLS'S THEORY OF justice concerns the scope of required equalities and permitted inequalities engendered by the basic social structure of a society: the distributive justice of "the way in which the major social institutions fit together into one system, and how they assign fundamental rights and duties and shape the division of advantages that arises through social cooperation" (PL 258). Within this basic structure individuals act so as to secure an actual allocation of determinate goods to each participant. Arguments concerning this subject require an index of benefits and burdens that allows publicly accessible interpersonal comparisons of citizens' well-being, in the relevant sense, among representative members of various social groups: "the idea is to find a practicable public basis of interpersonal comparisons in terms of objective features of citizens' social circumstances open to view" (CP 454–455).

Rawls's answer is to focus on how the basic structure of society distributes *social primary goods*. These arise out of institutions – that is, legal powers and immunities:

(a) First, the basic liberties as given by a list, for example: freedom of thought and liberty of conscience; freedom of association; and the freedom defined by the liberty and integrity of the person, as well as by the rule of law; and finally the political liberties; (b) Second, freedom of movement and choice of occupation against a background of diverse opportunities; (c) Third, powers and prerogatives of offices and positions of responsibility, particularly those in the main political and economic institutions; (d) Fourth, income and wealth; and (e) Finally, the social bases of self-respect. (CP 362–363)

This list is not claimed to be exhaustive; Rawls was, for example, prepared to include such goods as leisure (*CP* 253).

Each of Rawls's two principles of justice regulate different social primary goods: the first principle of liberty regulates the first set of social primary goods; the principle of fair equality of opportunity the second and third; and the difference principle addresses the fourth. The fifth – "social bases of self-respect" – merits separate attention below.

Why does Rawls identify these goods as the appropriate "metric" for principles of distributive justice for the basic structure of society? Social primary goods satisfy several demanding conditions imposed on the metric for interpersonal comparisons suitable for principles to assess this particular subject of *TJ*. (A) The metric must allow for *interval comparisons* to compare departures from equality. (B) The metric must be under societal control by the basic structure. (C) The metric should be *publicly observable*, not least to avoid hazards of self-reporting mental states. (D) The metric must accommodate the social fact that the basic structure shapes citizens' *malleable* preferences profoundly, thus rendering preference satisfaction *simpliciter* unsatisfactory as a metric. (E) The principles of justice for this particular subject must be justifiable under *pluralism*, that is: to citizens who have drastically different substantive conceptions of the good. Any such "thick" theory of the good is therefore unsuitable as a basis for identifying the metric.

In response to these conditions, Rawls argues that social primary goods are rational to want on the basis of a "thin" theory of the good. They are rational to desire regardless of what else one wants, in order to develop and promote three "higher-order interests" that even under pluralism count as bases for individuals' claims on social institutions: First, a ("reasonable") interest in developing their capacity to be reasonable in the sense of having a sense of justice. Second, a ("rational") interest in developing their capacity to form, revise and pursue a conception of their good; and third, a ("rational") interest in advancing this conception – i.e. actually realizing one's determinate conception of the good (*TJ* 19, 46).

The social primary goods are claimed to be background conditions and/or all-purpose social means that contribute to securing and promoting these three interests. Social primary goods answer the question: what would a citizen who is engaged in political cooperation rationally desire from that cooperation – simply as such a cooperating citizen? For purposes of arguments about principles of distributive justice, individuals are thus assumed to prefer more social primary goods rather than less (*TJ* 142). They are rights and benefits which the basic structure regulates; and they allow interpersonal comparison at least of an ordinal kind (person A has more of social primary goods 1 than does person B), and allows some interval comparisons (the gain in income and wealth for person A between distribution 1 and 2 is larger than the loss in this social primary good for person B). Moreover, social primary goods satisfy important publicity concerns, since they provide a transparent way to identify the distributive pattern engendered by a basic social structure without creating moral costs, e.g. in the form of incentives to misrepresent shares of such goods.

> ...an explanation of why it is rational for the parties to assess principles of justice in terms of primary goods is needed: (i) The basic liberties (freedom of thought and liberty of conscience, etc.) are the background institutions necessary for the development and exercise of the capacity to decide upon and revise, and rationally to pursue, a conception of the good. Similarly, these liberties allow for the development and exercise of the sense of right and justice under political and social conditions that are free. (ii) Freedom of movement and free choice of occupation against a background of diverse opportunities are required for the pursuit of final ends as well as to give effect to a decision to revise and change them, if one so desires. (iii) Powers and prerogatives of offices of responsibility are needed to give scope to various self-governing and social capacities of the self. (iv) Income and wealth, understood broadly as they must be, are all-purpose means (having an exchange value) for achieving directly or indirectly a wide range of ends, whatever they happen to be. (v) The social bases of self-respect are those aspects of basic institutions that are normally essential if citizens are to have a lively sense of their own worth as moral persons and to be able to realize their highest-order interests and advance their ends with self-confidence. (*CP* 366)

Many critics have questioned Rawls's focus on social primary goods, arguing instead for another "currency" (Cohen 1989) or "metric." Why limit the social primary goods in this way? For instance, why not include more specifics about each person's conception of the good – and thus details about a wider range of requisite goods under societal control? Why not include "natural primary goods" such as health, intelligence and imagination (*TJ* 54)? Three reasons follow from the specific features of the basic structure: pluralism about conceptions of the good; the need for a publicly accessible metric; and the malleability of social primary goods by the basic structure that is the subject of *TJ*.

Some criticize Rawls for "fetishizing" goods, instead of selecting an index or space that focuses directly on what goods do *for* people (Sen 1980, 366). The claimed flaws of social primary goods are illustrated by individuals with handicaps, who are less efficient in converting such goods to well-being or quality of life, e.g. in the form of capabilities, or a "basic minimum of truly human functioning" (Nussbaum 2006), or "midfare" – what the goods do for people (Cohen 1993).

Responses might pursue several strands: (a) Social primary goods are not meant to approximate what most individuals value, but are especially *constructed* for arguments about principles of distributive justice for the basic structure of a society characterized by pluralism about conceptions of the good. For instance, the social primary goods and the interests they further are specified not on the basis of any comprehensive conception of the good (*CP* 456). (b) *Basic* capabilities, e.g. to nutrition and basic health care, may be recognized even under pluralism (*PL* 183), and may take priority under circumstances of extreme scarcity. But social primary goods are intended as an index for the distribution of the remaining benefits and burdens in societies characterized by moderate affluence. (c) Social primary goods, more so than alternatives such as capabilities (e.g. as acknowledged by Nussbaum 2006, 75), allow for interpersonal comparability, and even determination of *equal* levels, which is required for the subject matter of *TJ* concerning the distributive justice of the basic social structure (Freeman 2006b, 220ff.).

Among the most perplexing issues concerning social primary goods is the "most important primary good" (*TJ* 440) "the social bases of self respect." Rawls explains this "in institutional terms supplemented by features of the public political culture such as the public recognition and acceptance of the principles of justice" (*CP* 454). Some critics (e.g. Young 1997) have been concerned that liberal theories of distributive justice cannot provide such social bases of self-respect, insofar as such theories cannot ensure that background cultures, institutional structures, and individuals' motivations are sufficiently free of racism, gendered injustice, and other forms of domination.

In response, Rawls's theory might firstly seem to avoid such charges insofar as its subject matter is precisely the institutions of the basic structure of society. However, critics have rebutted that important aspects, such as family roles and responsibilities, are excluded (Bojer 2003; Okin 2004). Second, *TJ* may be explicated to mean that this social primary good is largely supervenient on the satisfaction of the other social primary goods: this good is secured by a basic structure that publicly satisfies the two principles of justice.

Primary goods, social / 647

What more might be required? One interpretation may draw on Rawls's claim that "respect for persons is shown by treating them in ways that they can see to be justified" (*TJ* 513). The social bases of self-respect may thus consist in the existence of a public justification of the basic structure, in terms that express equal respect for all citizens. On this view, Rawls's theory of justice as fairness sought to help provide precisely this primary social good.

Andreas Follesdal

SEE ALSO:

Capabilities
Conception of the good
Higher-order interests
Leisure
Publicity
Self-respect
Thin and full theories of the good
Two principles of justice (in justice as fairness)
Utility

166.

THE PRIORITY OF THE RIGHT OVER THE GOOD

FOR RAWLS, THE priority of right signifies the ways in which justice as fairness (as a conception of right) constrains and regulates how ideas of the good are integrated into justice. He describes two meanings of the priority of right over the good, one general and one particular (*PL* 209). Each will be described in turn.

In its general meaning, the priority of right requires that any ideas of the good used in justice as fairness be political ideas. No specific, comprehensive or partial conceptions of the good can be relied upon in the conception of justice. In order to be political in the relevant way, a conception of justice must be capable of commanding an overlapping consensus. Thus, any ideas of the good that are used in justice as fairness must be capable of being endorsed from multiple points of view. Rawls identifies five such ideas of the good contained within justice as fairness (*PL* 176–206, *CP* 451–470): (1) goodness as rationality, (2) social primary goods as representing a "thin" theory of the good, (3) the idea of permissible comprehensive conceptions of the good, (4) the political virtues expected of citizens, and (5) the good of political society. In the discussion of these five goods that follows, it should become clear that Rawls thinks of the right and the good as complementary. Justice (as part of the right) puts certain limitations on the good, but depends upon political ideas of the good in order to be fully formulated.

According to goodness as rationality, a person's good is indicated by the rational plan of life she would form and pursue under conditions of full deliberative rationality (*TJ* 372). This idea of the good serves two functions: it helps to identify the currency of justice as those general things necessary for carrying out rational plans of life, and it helps to specify the motivation of the parties in the original position (*CP* 452). Once citizens are recognized as aiming at rational life

The priority of the right over the good / 649

plans, and in consideration of their desire to develop and exercise their two moral powers, the parties in the original position are motivated to secure the social primary goods as the currency of justice. These goods (rights and liberties, powers and opportunities, income and wealth, and the social bases of self-respect) are what citizens, in general, need to advance their conception of the good and their two moral powers. The social primary goods thus amount to a "thin" idea of the good that is incorporated into justice as fairness; it is a conception of goods that all citizens can endorse, qua citizens.

Once the social primary goods are settled, the argument from the original position can proceed to arrive at the two principles of justice. The two principles then help to show which conceptions of the good are permissible in a just society, as well as to identify the political virtues. First, Rawls describes permissible conceptions of the good as "subplan[s] of the larger comprehensive plan that regulates the community as a social union" (*TJ* 493). Some individuals' conceptions of the good will thus be prohibited from the political point of view, if they oppose justice (e.g. racist conceptions). Second, citizens can support those virtues of character essential to secure fair cooperation over time: civility, tolerance, reasonableness, and a sense of fairness. Justice as fairness recommends these virtues while remaining entirely political because no particular, comprehensive conception of the good need be presupposed in identifying these characteristics as valuable.

Lastly, citizens can accept the idea of a well-ordered society as a good, for themselves individually as well as collectively. As individuals, citizens experience the exercise of their moral powers as a good, and they recognize that a well-ordered society secures their fundamental needs as citizens. From the collective viewpoint, a good results from a well-ordered society's persisting over generations. People can identify this as an achievement just as members of an orchestra can appreciate the good of a piece of music they have collectively produced (*CP* 468).

The "particular meaning" of the priority of right is that the principles of justice limit citizens' permissible ways of life, and thus, circumscribe the claims they make on society to pursue their desired ends. The priority of right thus organizes the reasons offered in individual and social deliberation, such that the principles of justice have precedence over considerations that are in conflict with them. A just society "defines the scope within which individuals must develop their aims" (*TJ* 28) such that any claims made in the service of ends that transgress the principles "have no weight" (*PL* 209).

It is tempting to equate the priority of right (in this particular meaning) with the deontological nature of justice as fairness. Since the priority of right restricts permissible ways of life, one might think that it is simply asserting the deontological nature of justice as fairness; what can count as good is dependent upon the right, i.e. the principles of justice. But there is a distinction to be made here. The priority of right in its particular meaning is about the terms on which individual and social deliberation are to take place. It limits the kinds of considerations that count as legitimate reasons in deliberation to those that are responsive to the principles of justice (which, again, are deontological considerations). As Samuel Freeman has put it, "the 'priority' of the priority of right refers to the lexical ordering of principles of right and justice in individual and social deliberation" (Freeman 2007b, 63). Equating the priority of right with Rawls's deontologism, therefore, overlooks the specific deliberative requirements upon which the priority of right insists.

Jaime Ahlberg

SEE ALSO:

Conception of the good
Deontological and teleological theories
Dominant end theories
Goodness as rationality
Plan of life
The reasonable and the rational
Thin and full theories of the good

167.

PROCEDURAL JUSTICE

Rawls's principal account of the justice of procedures appears in §14 of *A Theory of Justice* (*TJ* 73–78). There Rawls distinguishes pure from impure procedural justice. In a case of impure procedural justice, the justice of a procedure is determined by the justice of the outcomes it produces; in a case of pure procedural justice, by contrast, the justice of the procedure confers justice on the outcomes it produces.

Among cases of impure procedural justice Rawls distinguishes cases of perfect impure procedural justice from cases of imperfect impure procedural justice. In a case of perfect impure procedural justice, it is possible to design a procedure that guarantees a just outcome. Rawls offers as an example the problem of cake division between two persons, where one-cuts-the-other-chooses ensures that each person receives at least half the cake by her own estimation. In a case of imperfect impure procedural justice, no procedure guarantees a just outcome. Rawls's example here is a criminal trial. The just outcome is for the guilty to be convicted and the not guilty to be acquitted, but there is no set of institutional procedures that enables this result always to be reached. Rawls's illustration of pure procedural justice is a lottery. In this case no particular outcome is just as such; one person might win fairly, or another. What makes an outcome just is that the procedure is fairly conducted, say by having each ticket accorded an equal chance of winning (*CP* 310–312; *PL* 148–150).

Rawls claims distributive justice is purely procedural. This distinguishes his theory from outcome-based forms of utilitarianism and egalitarianism. On Rawls's view distributive justice does not consist in the least-advantaged group possessing as many social primary goods as possible. Rather, distributive justice consists in having an institutional structure producing and distributing goods effectively and publicly regulated by a conception of justice where the least-advantaged group ought to receive as many social primary goods as possible. It is thus rational expectations about the outcomes of a distributive procedure which determines its justice, not actual outcomes (*CP* 421–433). The latter is an allocation of goods to individuals and associations, which Rawls denies is the locus of distributive justice, since social goods are cooperatively produced and distributive principles are chosen in abstraction from individuals' particular desires (*TJ* 75–77). This is a vital distinction. If an institutional structure is designed and accepted on a rational expectation that it satisfies justice as fairness, then on Rawls's view the outcomes this structure produces are just, whatever they may be. This is true even if an unforeseen event (an earthquake, say) occurs which, had it been anticipated, would have altered the design of that structure. This feature of Rawls's position also enables him to say there is no injustice if, after goods are produced and distributed, members of the least-advantaged group waste goods.

Rawls's conception of distributive justice as purely procedural is intimately connected to his conception of it as a "social process" theory (*JF* 51–55). A social process theory emphasizes operations of the "basic structure" of society, the set of institutions and conventions constituting a society's cooperation in producing and distributing goods. This institutional structure is the procedure that is subject to norms of distributive justice, and if properly organized it confers justice on its outcomes. Rawls characterizes the justice of the basic structure as "background" justice, since it is the backdrop against which individuals and associations make decisions. Of special interest are decisions made in elections and labor markets, since the outcomes of these institutions are so important to the distribution of social goods (*JF* 131). Rawls contends that we should see the outcomes of these institutions of the basic structure as just – regardless of which party wins an election, or of how prudent or foolish employees and employers are in their labor contracts – provided everyone participating in them has equal social standing and acts in a sincere spirit of cooperation. According to Rawls, this equal social standing consists in a basic structure publicly conforming to justice as fairness. Sometimes particular policies are incompatible with justice as fairness, and so are incompatible with equal social standing. Sometimes justice as fairness sets boundaries for policy but does not determine a particular policy; Rawls refers to this phenomenon as "quasi-pure" procedural justice (*TJ* 176). And even if procedures do not fully satisfy justice as fairness, Rawls maintains their outcomes should be accepted as legitimate so long as they reasonably approximate justice under the historical circumstances (*PL* 428–429). The institutions of the basic structure, including chiefly institutions of taxation and transfer, are thus assessed in the first instance not by their outcomes but by the social relationships they help constitute.

There is thus a superficial similarity between Rawls's position and a libertarian position, since each contends that justice is purely procedural and hence that the justice of a distributive outcome is a function of the justice of the transactions that produce it. These two positions are nonetheless radically distinct, for Rawls has a far more stringent understanding of the conditions under which a transaction is fair. On a typical libertarian view all that is required is the absence of coercion, but on Rawls's view background social conditions also matter (*PL* 262–265).

Relatedly, Rawls's purely procedural conception of distributive justice does not involve an understanding of democratic legitimacy where the procedures of majority rule operate without any substantive constraints on their legislative power. In contrast to this narrowly proceduralist majoritarianism, Rawls advocates a strong and substantive constitution (*TJ* 195–196, 311–318; *PL* 140–142, 179–181). His ground for this view is not that constitutionalism is less purely procedural than narrow majoritarianism, but rather that it better enables equal social standing. And on Rawls's understanding, this equality is the social background condition needed to ensure that the multifarious outcomes of voluntary transactions among individuals and associations are distributively just.

Jon Garthoff

SEE ALSO:

Allocative justice
Basic structure of society
Democracy
Distributive justice
Libertarianism

168.

PROMISING

RAWLS ADDRESSED THE question in moral philosophy of why we must keep our promises at various places in his work. Over the course of his intellectual career he defended different accounts of promising, which reflect broader shifts in his theoretical views. But they all share the feature of being "practice based" or "conventionalist": they rely on the existence of a social practice of promising as an essential part of the explanation for why you should keep your promises.

The social practice of promising is the existence of a general adherence to the rule "Do A whenever you utter the words 'I promise to do A.'" The existence of this practice is in the public interest. Because of this general adherence, it is possible for us to rely on people to A when they say that they promise to do so. And being able to rely on them in this way is very useful. When I know what other people are going to do I am in a better position to make my own plans.

The practice of promising also makes us better positioned to form stable cooperative relationships. Suppose that there is a project which, if completed, will benefit two different people but will only be completed if they both contribute to it. Neither person will be motivated to contribute to this project unless they can rely on the other person to do their part. By making promises to each other to do their part each person can rely on the other and thus the project can be completed, to their mutual benefit (*TJ* 304–305).

A utilitarian account of promising says that we should not break our promises because doing so will fail to promote aggregate happiness, or "utility." One way breaking a promise can do this is by harming the promisee. Assuming that she has relied on my promise, I will upset her plans if I break it. Also breaking a promise can damage the practice of promising itself. By lowering trust in

654

Promising / 655

people it can also reduce general adherence to the rule of keeping your promises. Since that practice benefits people, utilitarians think we should not damage it.

There is an obvious concern about this account. If the reason to keep our promises is to promote aggregate happiness, why shouldn't we break our promises whenever doing so will create slightly greater aggregate happiness than keeping it? In his early work, Rawls responds to this concern as follows. Where social practices exist we can distinguish between two different questions. First, there is the question of what justifies a particular agent's *actions*. We can answer this, Rawls says, by appealing to the rules of the practice they are engaged in. For instance, we can say that someone who utters, "I promise to do A," ought to do A because there is a rule that requires it. The rule requires them to do A even if not doing it would promote aggregate happiness. Second, there is the question of what justifies the *practice* itself as a whole; for instance, what explains why it is desirable for there to be a rule governing promising which everyone follows. Utilitarianism, Rawls suggested, should be seen as a theory of what justifies the practice of promising: its effects on aggregate happiness. But it is compatible with this theory, he claimed, that the actions of individual promisors are governed solely by the rules of the practice. Thus, utilitarians can agree that people shouldn't break their promises just in order to promote aggregate utility because the rules of the practice prohibit this (*CP* 29–46).

In his later work Rawls moved further away from the utilitarian account and relied on *fairness*. Promisors, Rawls says, voluntarily make use of the practice of promising. Because the practice exists, promisors are able to get others to rely on them to do A when they say "I promise to do A," and they make promises to create this reliance. But, when you voluntarily make use of a mutually advantageous social practice to further your ends, fairness demands that you follow its rules. In this case the rules demand that you keep your promise – that you do A having made a promise to do A. So fairness demands that you keep your promise (*TJ* 96, 303–305).

Adam Hosein

SEE ALSO:

Fairness, principle of
Obligations
Rules (two concepts of)
Utilitarianism

169.

PROPERTY-OWNING DEMOCRACY

CONTRARY TO MUCH common opinion, John Rawls has never been an advocate of welfare-state capitalism; or perhaps of any form of capitalism, given his definitions. Rather, as a matter of ideal theory, the only two kinds of modern societies that he believes to be compatible with his two principles of justice are a property-owning democracy – which he sometimes calls "private-property democracy" (*PL* 328, 364; *JF* 159) – and a liberal socialist regime that has extensive markets. He contrasts these three types of societies when he speaks of "[Marx's] criticisms of capitalism as a social system, criticisms that might seem ... to apply as well to property-owning democracy, or equally to liberal socialism" (*JF* 139).

It is necessary "to bring out the distinction between a property-owning democracy, which realizes all the main political values expressed by the two principles of justice, and a capitalist welfare state, which does not. We think of such a democracy as an alternative to capitalism" (*JF* 135–136). We must distinguish "between property-owning democracy and a capitalist welfare state [since] ... the latter conflicts with justice as fairness" (*JF* 8 n.7). "This leaves [only] ... property-owning democracy and liberal socialism [as types of modern societies whose] ideal descriptions include arrangements designed to satisfy the two principles of justice" (*JF* 138).

In the "Preface to the French Edition of *A Theory of Justice*" Rawls expresses regrets for his failure in *TJ* to "distinguish more sharply the idea of a property-owning democracy ... from the idea of a welfare state. These ideas are quite different, but since they both allow private property in productive assets, we may be misled into thinking them essentially the same" (*CP* 419). "They are not ... One

656

Property-owning democracy / 657

major difference is [that] the background institutions of property-owning democracy work to disperse the ownership of wealth and capital and thus to prevent a small part of society from controlling the economy, and indirectly, political life as well. By contrast welfare-state capitalism permits a small class to have a near monopoly of the means of production" (*JF* 139). "Property-owning democracy avoids this, not by the redistribution of income to those with less at the end of each period, so to speak, but rather by ensuring the widespread ownership of productive assets and human capital (that is, education and trained skills) at the beginning of each period…" (*JF* 139).

> In welfare-state capitalism the aim is that none should fall below a decent minimum standard of life, one in which their basic needs are met, and all should receive certain protections against accident and misfortune, for example, unemployment compensation and medical care [which is also a goal of property-owning democracy]. The redistribution of income serves this purpose when, at the end of each period, those who need assistance can be identified. (*JF* 139–140)

However, "such a system may allow large and inheritable inequalities of wealth incompatible with the fair value of political liberties…as well as large disparities of income that violate the difference principle. While some effort is made to secure fair equality of opportunity, it is either insufficient or else ineffective given the disparities of wealth and the political influence they permit" (*CP* 419). Moreover, "given the lack of background justice and inequalities in income and wealth there may develop a discouraged and depressed underclass many of whose members are chronically dependent on welfare. This underclass feels left out and dos not participate in the public political culture" (*JF* 140).

> By contrast, in a property-owning democracy…basic institutions must from the outset put in the hands of citizens generally, and not only of a few, the productive means to be fully cooperating members of a society. The emphasis falls on the steady dispersal over time of the ownership of capital and resources by the laws of inheritance and bequest, on fair equality of opportunity secured by provisions for education and training…as well as on institutions that support the fair value of the political liberties. (*CP* 419–420)

In fact, "To see the full force of the difference principle it should be taken in the context of property-owning democracy (or a liberal socialist regime) and not a welfare state" (*CP* 419–420).

> In property-owning democracy ... the aim is to realize in the basic institutions the idea of society as a fair system of cooperation between citizens regarded as free and equal. To do this, those institutions must, from the outset, put in the hands of citizens generally, and not only a few, sufficient productive means for them to be fully cooperating members of society on a footing of equality. Among these means is human as well as real capital, that is, knowledge and an understanding of institutions, educated abilities, and trained skills ... Under these conditions we hope that an underclass will not exist. (*JF* 140)

Unfortunately, Rawls never explains exactly what he has in mind by "sufficient productive means" or "the widespread ownership of productive assets," or how such a state of affairs could be maintained over time if individuals were free to buy and sell their productive assets or shares in productive assets (for example, corporate stocks and/or bonds). On the other hand, if individuals were not free to buy and sell their productive assets then the arrangement seems more like the social ownership of productive assets; that is, socialism.

While contrasting property-owning democracy with a liberal market socialist regime, he writes: "At the start I assume a property-owning democracy since this case is likely to be better known" (*TJ* 242). (Here he notes that this is the title of chapter 5 of Meade (1964), a work that much influenced Rawls's economic views.) He then notes that "this is not intended to prejudge the choice of regime [between this and liberal market socialism] in particular cases ... That there exists an ideal property-owning system that would be just does not imply that historical forms are just, of even tolerable. And, of course, the same is true of socialism" (*TJ* 242).

> We must ask whether a liberal socialist regime does significantly better in realizing the two principles. Should it do so, then the case for liberal socialism is made from the standpoint of justice as fairness. But we must be careful here not to compare the ideal of one conception with the actuality of the other, but rather to compare actuality with actuality, and in our particular historical circumstances. (*JF* 140)

Property-owning democracy / 659

"Both a property-owning democracy and a liberal socialist regime set up a constitutional framework for democratic politics, guarantee the basic liberties with the fair value of the political liberties and fair equality of opportunity, and regulate economic and social inequalities by a principle of mutuality, if not by the difference principle" (*JF* 138). "Justice as fairness does not decide between these regimes but tries to set out guidelines for how the decision can reasonably be approached" (*JF* 139).

> ...justice as fairness leaves open the question whether its principles are best realized by some form of property-owning democracy or by a liberal socialist regime. This question is left to be settled by historical conditions and the traditions, institutions, and social forces of each country...justice as fairness includes...no natural right of private property in the means of production (although it does include a right to personal property as necessary for citizens' independence and integrity), nor a natural right to worker-owned and managed firms. It offers instead a conception of justice in the light of which, given the particular circumstances of a country, those questions can be reasonably decided. (*CP* 420)

A "property-owning democracy tries to meet legitimate objections of the socialist tradition" (*JF* 177; cf. *LHPP* 321). In response to Marx's criticisms that individual liberties in capitalist societies only express and protect mutual egoism, Rawls argues that

> in a well designed property-owning democracy those rights and liberties, properly specified, suitably express and protect the higher-order interests of citizens as free and equal. And while a right to property in productive assets is permitted, that right is not a basic right but subject to the requirement that, in existing conditions, it is the most effective way to meet the principles of justice...[Moreover] the background institutions of a property-owning democracy, together with fair equality of opportunity and the difference principle, give adequate protection to the so-called positive liberties. (*JF* 177; cf. *LHPP* 321)

> Marx would raise another objection, namely, that our account of the institutions of property-owning democracy has not considered the importance of democracy in the workplace and in shaping the general course of the

economy. This is...a major difficulty. I shall not try to meet it except to recall that Mill's idea of worker-managed firms is fully compatible with property-owning democracy. (*JF* 178)

Rawls also specifies other features that a property–owning democracy (as well as any other just society) must have. For example, "the main institutions of property-owning democracy" include "(a) Provisions for securing the fair value of the political liberties...(b) So far as practicable, provisions for realizing fair equality of opportunity in education and training of various kinds. (c) A basic level of health-care provided for all..." (*JF* 176).

"A property-owning democracy [is, as any just society] a constitutional regime...one in which laws and statutes must be consistent with certain fundamental rights and liberties, for example, those covered by the first principle of justice. There [are, unlike in purely procedural democracies]...constitutional limits on legislation" (*JF* 145). Moreover, electoral politics may require

> public financing of elections and restrictions on campaign contributions, the assurance of more even access to public media; and certain regulations of freedom of speech and of the press (but not restrictions affecting the content of speech)...In adjusting these basic liberties one aim is to enable legislators and political parties to be independent of large concentrations of private economic and social power in a private-property democracy and of government control and bureaucratic power in a liberal socialist regime. (*JF* 149–150)

> ...property-owning democracy aims for full equality of women...If a basic...cause of women's inequality is their greater share in the bearing, nurturing, and caring for children in the traditional division of labor within the family, steps need to be taken either to equalize their share or to compensate them for it. (*JF* 167)

Besides a just savings tax being adopted, bequest and inheritance are also regulated with "the principle of progressive taxation...applied at the receiver's end....[and] income taxation might be avoided altogether and a proportional expenditure tax adopted instead, that is, a tax on consumption at a constant marginal rate" (*JF* 161). (In Krouse and McPherson (1988), the authors argue that Rawls undervalues the redistributive function of progressive income taxes and social transfers.)

Property-owning democracy / 661

A feature of the difference principle is that it does not require contin-ual economic growth over generations to maximize upward indefinitely the expectations of the least advantaged measured in terms of income and wealth...We certainly do not want to rule out Mill's idea of a society in a just stationary state where (real) capital accumulation may cease. A property-owning democracy should allow for this possibility. (*JF* 159)

This may be considered an especially important point given the relation between ever greater economic growth and environmental degradation and destruction, although justice as fairness may judge economic growth in less well-developed countries to be justified and necessary, as well as redistribution within such soci-eties and between wealthier and poorer societies.

Rodney G. Peffer

SEE ALSO:

The economy
Libertarianism
The market
Marx, Karl
Socialism
Two principles of justice (in justice as fairness)

170.

PUBLIC CHOICE THEORY

P UBLIC CHOICE THEORY is an approach to political science that employs assumptions and models common in economics. It analyzes politicians and other political actors as (largely) self-interested agents. Public choice economics arose in response to the work of economist Duncan Black but was made famous by James Buchanan and Gordon Tullock in their well-known *The Calculus of Consent: Logical Foundations of Constitutional Democracy* (1962). Early in his career, Rawls communicated with Buchanan on a number of matters. Rawls always considered himself an admirer of Buchanan's work (for the text of the Rawls–Buchanan correspondence and commentary, see Peart and Levy 2008, 395–415).

Nonetheless, Rawls thought that the insights of public choice did not apply to the selection of principles of justice. Instead, if public choice analysis was sound, it was relevant only to the implementation of justice in the second "constitutional stage" of Rawls's four-stage sequence. In his 1963 article, "Constitutional Liberty and the Concept of Justice," Rawls distinguishes his approach from Buchanan and Tullock's because "they are mainly concerned with that part of constitutions having to do with legislative procedure..." (*CP* 74 n.1). Rawls argues in *TJ* that Buchanan and Tullock misunderstand the conditions of constitutional choice. On Rawls's view, "[t]he idea of the four-stage sequence is a part of a moral theory... the aim is to characterize a just constitution and not to ascertain which sort of constitution would be adopted, or acquiesced in, under more or less realistic (though simplified) assumptions about political life, much less on individualistic assumptions of the kind characteristic of economic theory" (*TJ* 173 n.2). Here Rawls denies that public choice economics applies directly to his second-stage. Instead, he sees the Buchanan–Tullock conception of constitutional choice as amoralist and excessively individualistic.

While Rawls initially thought that Buchanan and Tullock had merely constructed a theory of constitutional choice, he later realizes that their conception of constitutional choice relies on an objectionable conception of justice. If so, we can make better sense of Rawls's remarks on public choice in *JF* when he claims that the "first comparison" between his two principles and the principle of average utility is essential in replying to "recent libertarian" and "explicitly contractarian" views of Buchanan, Robert Nozick, and David Gauthier (*JF* 97). Rawls seems to hold that the public choice approach to constitutional choice requires substantive moral assumptions. For instance, he claims that in Buchanan's work, among others, "citizens' basic rights, liberties, and opportunities, as secured by the basic structure, depend on contingencies of history, and social circumstance and native endowment, in ways excluded by justice as fairness" (*JF* 16 n.16). Thus, Rawls's mature position on Buchanan and Tullock's conception of justice is that it relies on unjust initial endowments and an overly individualistic conception of social life.

While Rawls rejects Buchanan and Tullock's conception of justice so tightly associated with public choice, he could still hold that public choice economics provides important resources for completing the second-stage of constitutional choice, even if the practice of public choice involves normative presuppositions that Rawls rejects.

Kevin Vallier

SEE ALSO:

Libertarianism
Maximin rule of choice
The original position
Rational choice theory
Social choice theory

171.

PUBLIC POLITICAL CULTURE

I N POLITICAL LIBERALISM Rawls aims to show that it is possible for citizens with otherwise diverse beliefs and commitments to nevertheless converge on a conception of justice that can be used as a public regulative ideal. Given the fact of reasonable pluralism, a conception of justice can be broadly acceptable in this way only if it disavows reliance on comprehensive doctrines and is, instead, rooted in the ideas and principles of a democratic community's public sphere. These ideas and principles constitute the public political culture.

As Rawls explains, we start "by looking to the public culture itself as the shared fund of implicitly recognized basic ideas and principles" (*PL* 8). The hope is to connect these ideas and principles together in a way that allows citizens to reach reflective equilibrium. Principles constructed in this way would be ones that "all citizens, whatever their religious view, can endorse" (*PL* 10). So, it is by rooting the conception of justice in ideas from the public political culture that an overlapping consensus is made possible. The public political culture includes:

> The political institutions of a constitutional regime and the public traditions of their interpretation (including those of the judiciary), as well as historic texts and documents that are common knowledge...In a democratic society there is a tradition of democratic thought...seen as a fund of implicitly shared ideas and principles. (*PL* 14)

More specifically, the values embedded in the public political culture of the United States include:

Public political culture / 665

those mentioned in the preamble to the United States Constitution: a more perfect union, justice, domestic tranquility, the common defense, the general welfare, and the blessings of liberty for ourselves and our posterity. (*LP* 144)

However, because these ideas are very general and the public political culture "may be of two minds at a very deep level" a political conception of justice "must find a way of organizing familiar ideas and principles … in a somewhat different way than before" (*PL* 9).

Rawls attempts to do this by developing a conception of justice rooted in three ideas fundamental to the public political culture:

1. The idea of society as a "fair system of cooperation over time, from one generation to the next";
2. The idea of citizens as "free and equal persons"; and
3. The idea of a well-ordered society as a society "effectively regulated by a political conception of justice" (*PL* 14).

The original position is to be understood as a mechanism that helps us to collect together these fundamental ideas and connect them to favored principles of justice. Thus, the public political culture is important as the fund of shared ideas in a democratic society that provides a mutually agreeable basis from which a political conception of justice can be constructed. So, it is the broad acceptability of the ideas of the public political culture that makes possible a conception of justice that can be accepted by reasonable citizens who nevertheless subscribe to different comprehensive doctrines.

Ryan Prevnick

SEE ALSO:

Culture: political vs. background
Democracy
Duty of civility
Overlapping consensus
Political liberalism
Publicity

172.

PUBLIC REASON

"**P**UBLIC REASON" IS the name that Rawls gives to the shared form of reasoning that the citizens of a pluralist democratic society should use when deciding constitutional essentials and questions of basic justice. Public reason not only makes the realization of the ideal of fair social cooperation amongst free and equal citizens possible in pluralist societies; according to Rawls, it should be understood as "part of the idea of democracy itself" (*PL* 441). By employing public reason when deciding fundamental political questions, citizens relate to one another as equal co-sovereigns and ensure the legitimacy of their shared exercise of political power. Political power in an adequately just liberal society, Rawls writes, "is ultimately ... the power of free and equal citizens as a collective body" (*PL* 136; cf. xliv, 445). In order to exercise political power in a genuinely shared manner, citizens need to provide mutually acceptable justifications for that exercise. The terms of public reason provide such mutually acceptable justifications. In addition to being co-sovereigns, citizens also are related to the institutions of their society's "basic structure" as subjects, as they cannot exempt themselves from the demands of those institutions. The institutions of the basic structure determine the shape of citizens' freedom by specifying and protecting their basic liberties, distributing opportunities and resources, and so forth. Because citizens are conceived of as free and equal, such determinations need to be justifiable to them. Once again, the terms of public reason provide such justifications.

The idea of public reason is an integral part of Rawls's overall account of political legitimacy:

> the criterion of reciprocity [says]: our exercise of political power is proper only when we sincerely believe that the reasons we would offer for our

Public reason / 667

> political actions may reasonably be accepted by other citizens as a justifi-
> cation of those actions. This criterion applies on two levels: one is to the
> constitutional structure itself, and the other is to particular statutes and
> laws enacted in accordance with that structure. (*PL* xliv)

Rawls refers to this idea as the "liberal principle of legitimacy" (*PL* xliv, 137). Political decisions concerning "constitutional essentials" and "matters of basic justice" made by means of public reason satisfy the liberal principle of legitimacy, and consequently have normative authority for citizens (*PL* 19). This is because such terms are acceptable to all reasonable citizens, even though they adhere to different comprehensive doctrines. Although the terms of public reason are acceptable to all reasonable citizens, individuals may reach different conclusions concerning which decisions have the greatest support of public reason. It is to be expected that individuals will give different weights to these considerations. As Rawls says, "this is the normal case: unanimity of views is not to be expected" (*PL* 479). Even when they disagree with a decision, though, individuals can rec-ognize it to be legitimate when it is supported by public reasons.

Because of the integral role of public reason in realizing the ideal of fair social cooperation amongst free and equal citizens in a pluralist society, Rawls holds that citizens have a moral (nonenforceable) duty to employ public reason when justifying to each other their decisions regarding constitutional essentials and matters of basic justice. This is the "duty of civility" (*PL* 444–445). Insofar as citizens fulfill their duty of civility, they realize the "ideal of public reason" (*PL* 444). And while all citizens are subject to the duty of civility, Rawls holds that it is especially demanding with respect to public officials.

The duty of civility applies to public officials within what Rawls calls the "public political forum." This forum is where fundamental political issues are debated and authoritative decisions regarding them are made. It consists of three parts: "the discourse of judges in their decisions, especially of the judges of a supreme court; the discourse of government officials, especially chief executives and legislators; and finally, the discourse of candidates for public office and their campaign managers" (*PL* 443). Since public officials help determine (or, in the case of candidates, aspire to determine) the ways in which political power is exer-cised – through their shaping, implementation, and interpretation of laws – their respect for the equal status of other citizens requires that they justify that exer-cise in terms of public reason. If a public official violates her duty of civility, say, by deciding a matter of basic justice on grounds that presuppose the truth of her particular comprehensive doctrine, those citizens who do not endorse that doctrine are not treated as equals. Citizens who are not public officials fulfill their duty of civility by holding public officials to the idea of public reason when evaluating their performance within the public political forum, especially when voting (*PL* 444–445).

The public political forum is distinct from what Rawls calls the "background culture" of society. The duty of civility applies only to decisions concerning constitutional essentials and matters of basic justice within the public political forum. The background culture of society, which is "the culture of civil society," is not subject to this duty (*PL* 443; cf. 443–444 n.13). Citizens may employ any form of nonpublic reasoning, including drawing upon the beliefs and values of their respective comprehensive doctrines, when expressing their views or debating issues within the background culture. Activities and deliberations within the background culture do not directly determine the exercise of political power.

Furthermore, within the public political forum, Rawls suggests that when it comes to deciding legislative questions not concerned with constitutional essentials or matters of basic social justice – what we might think of as "ordinary legislation" – "the restrictions of public reason may not apply ...; or if they do, not in the same way, or so strictly" (*PL* 215). However, insofar as ordinary legislation also involves the exercise of political power, it would seem natural to regard such legislation as properly subject to the duty of civility. And indeed, in relation to ordinary legislation, Rawls notes, "it is usually highly desirable to settle political questions by invoking the values of public reason." But he goes on to remark, "this may not always be so" (*PL* 215). One consideration that may help explain Rawls's hesitancy to apply the duty of civility to ordinary legislation is that the terms of public reason are drawn from the political conceptions of justice endorsed by reasonable citizens, and such conceptions focus primarily on questions regarding constitutional essentials and matters of basic justice. In any case, Rawls does not explore this question further, noting simply: "my aim is to consider first the strongest case where the political questions concern the most fundamental matters" (*PL* 215).

Rawls distinguishes different accounts of the limits on the kinds of reasons that citizens may employ in compliance with their duty of civility. It should be emphasized that all of these are accounts of what kinds of reasons *should* properly count in deliberations within the public political forum. There is never a suggestion that there should be legal limits placed upon public speech (as noted earlier, the duty of civility is a nonenforceable moral duty). Rawls reports that he was "At first inclined to...the 'exclusive view'" according to which "on fundamental political matters, reasons given explicitly in terms of comprehensive doctrines are never to be introduced into public reason" (*PL* 247, and n.36). After all, no one comprehensive doctrine is shared by all citizens, so reasons given in terms of a particular comprehensive doctrine will not be shared by all citizens. Rawls decided that this interpretation was too restrictive, however, and in the first edition of *Political Liberalism*, endorsed what he called "the inclusive view." Essentially, the inclusive view started with the exclusive view, but allowed the introduction of full comprehensive doctrines (and their reasons) when doing so would "[encourage] citizens to honor the ideal of public reason and [secure] its social conditions in the longer run in a well-ordered society" (*PL* 248). Rawls illustrates this idea with several examples, including "the abolitionists who argued against the antebellum South that its institution of slavery was contrary to God's law" (*PL* 249). Such invocations clearly depended on a particular (reasonable) comprehensive doctrine, but the abolitionists "did not go against the ideal of public reason ... [because] the comprehensive reasons they appealed to were required to give sufficient strength to the political conception to be subsequently realized" (*PL* 251).

With the publication of the paperback edition of *Political Liberalism*, and in "The Idea of Public Reason Revisited," Rawls revised his account to make it even less restrictive. In his final formulation of the idea of public reason, Rawls endorses what he calls a "wide view of public political culture" (*PL* 462). According to this view, reasons drawn from citizens' various comprehensive doctrines can be introduced within the public political forum, so long as in doing so what Rawls calls "the proviso" is satisfied. The proviso is described as follows:

> [R]easonable comprehensive doctrines, religious or non-religious, may be introduced in public political discussion at any time, provided that in due course proper political reasons – and not reasons given solely by comprehensive doctrines – are presented that are sufficient to support whatever the comprehensive doctrines introduced are said to support. (*PL* 462)

Thus reasons drawn from citizens' comprehensive doctrines are not barred from the public political forum; satisfying the proviso is sufficient for the fulfillment of the duty of civility. Moreover, compared to the inclusive view, the wide view does not require that citizens try to assess the likely long-term effects of the introduction of their (reasonable) comprehensive doctrines into public political discussion, as long as the proviso is satisfied.

Why does Rawls endorse the wide view of public political culture? One function of public reason is to foster trust amongst citizens through their use of mutually acceptable justifications when deciding fundamental political questions (*PL* 249, 464–465). Indeed, in places Rawls characterizes the political relation that obtains amongst citizens who share a commitment to public reason as "one of civic friendship" (*PL* 447; cf. li). The wide view of public political culture can encourage relations of trust and civic friendship amongst adherents of different comprehensive doctrines by allowing citizens to clarify the ways in which their respective comprehensive doctrines support the reasonable political conceptions of justice that they endorse; doing so can help assure citizens who endorse other comprehensive doctrines of their enduring commitment to the idea of public reason (*PL* 463–464). Nonetheless, comprehensive doctrines can play no *justificatory* role with respect to decisions concerning constitutional essentials and matters of basic justice, as only public reason justifications can satisfy the liberal principle of legitimacy.

The idea of public reason concerns the *kinds* of justifications that ought to be deployed when deciding fundamental political questions. It may be the case, though, that a political question can be decided in more than one way by means of public reason. Indeed, if citizens endorse more than one reasonable political conception of justice, it is quite likely that they will disagree over how best to answer certain fundamental political questions, despite their shared commitment to the criterion of reciprocity. Even amongst adherents of the same conception of justice, citizens may interpret how best to apply that conception's principles in their society in somewhat different ways. (Consider, for instance, Rawls's claim that the "social systems" of "property-owning democracy" and "liberal (democratic) socialism" both are capable of realizing the principles of his conception of "justice as fairness" (*JF* part IV). Citizens equally committed to the principles of justice as fairness may advocate different kinds of institutions and laws, such as different property regimes, for realizing its two principles in their society.) Rawls maintains that public reason is part of a broader idea of "deliberative democracy" (*PL* 448), according to which political decisions are made by means of deliberation amongst free and equal citizens who share political power. What is essential for the fulfillment of the duty of civility is that citizens justify their positions in terms of public reason, not that they arrive at the same answers to all fundamental political questions.

In a footnote in *Political Liberalism*, Rawls illustrates the operation of public reason by discussing "the troubled question of abortion" (*PL* 243 n.32). He notes that there are at least three important political values at stake: "the due respect for human life, the ordered reproduction of political society over time, including the family in some form, and finally the equality of women as equal citizens." He then asserts: "I believe any reasonable balance of these three values will give a woman a duly qualified right to decide whether or not to end her pregnancy during the first trimester. The reason for this is that at this early stage of pregnancy the political value of the equality of women is overriding, and this right is required to give it substance and force." In the introduction to the paperback edition, Rawls clarified that his purpose was not to resolve the abortion debate, but rather to illustrate how public reason must recognize and attempt to balance various political values. In this matter and others, it might initially seem as though the only relevant considerations would be tied to particular comprehensive doctrines, especially religious doctrines. On the contrary, there are multiple political values recognized by public reason that are at stake and that must be balanced somehow. And as noted above, even when restricting themselves to the political values recognized by public reason, reasonable citizens may balance them in different ways. In the case of such a "stand-off between different political conceptions...citizens must simply vote on the question" (*PL* liii).

According to Rawlsian political liberalism, then, a society characterized by reasonable pluralism in which fundamental political decisions are made by means of public reason is a society in which the exercise of political power is legitimate, and in which the ideal of fair social cooperation amongst free and equal citizens is realized. The idea of public reason, though, applies not only to deliberations regarding the exercise of political power *within* pluralist liberal societies; it applies as well to the global domain (*LP* §17). Liberal peoples and non-liberal but "decent" peoples are to employ public reason when justifying their foreign policy decisions to one another. (There is no commitment to the criterion of reciprocity in peoples' relations with what Rawls calls "outlaw states," just as there is no commitment to this criterion in reasonable citizens' relations with "unreasonable" citizens within liberal societies.) However, since the political conception of justice that is to regulate relations between peoples – what Rawls calls the "Law of Peoples" (*LP* 37) – differs significantly from the reasonable political conceptions of justice endorsed by citizens within liberal societies, the content of public reason within the global domain also differs significantly from the content of public reason within liberal societies. Citizens within liberal societies employ one form of public reason when determining how to exercise political power vis-à-vis their respective basic structures; peoples employ a different form of public reason in their relations with other peoples. Despite the differences between the reasonable political conceptions of justice that provide the terms of public reason within liberal societies and the Law of Peoples that provides the terms of public reason within the global domain, both kinds of public reason share certain underlying normative features: namely, a recognition of the fact of reasonable pluralism, and a commitment to satisfying the criterion of reciprocity when justifying the exercise of political power.

Blain Neufeld

SEE ALSO:

> *Basic structure of society*
> *Duty of civility*
> *Law of Peoples*
> *Moral person*
> *Neutrality*
> *Political liberalism, justice as fairness as*
> *Practical reason*
> *Reasonable pluralism*
> *The reasonable and the rational*
> *Reciprocity*

173.

PUBLICITY

ACCORDING TO JOHN RAWLS, publicity considerations constrain a theory of distributive justice in multiple ways. The most fundamental way follows immediately from his understanding of society as a "cooperative venture for mutual advantage" (*TJ* 4; *JF* 5–8). Since Rawls has in mind a relatively robust form of cooperation – mere coordination of action among mutually disinterested parties does not suffice – this conception of social justice brings with it a need for mutual understanding among persons about the terms on which they are cooperating. This mutual understanding is possible only if everyone understands the conception of justice governing their joint activity, as well as what justifies this conception. This in turn requires that this conception be publicly known and articulated. It is in this sense that Rawls claims that publicity is a "formal condition" on a conception of right. By this expression Rawls does not mean that the concept of rightness or of justice entails that a conception of rightness or of justice is publicly known. He means rather that the problem to which a conception of distributive justice is addressed – namely, constituting societal cooperation – can be solved by that conception only on the supposition that it is publicly known (*TJ* 112–115).

This is also why Rawls claims that, to be adequate, a conception of justice must be stable under conditions of free thought and association; and in Rawls's view, publicity is an essential constituent of this stability. His arguments for justice as fairness in *A Theory of Justice* depend on this conception being more stable than its rivals, including especially forms of utilitarianism (*TJ* 436–437; *JF* 119–126). In his expansion and amendment of his views in *Political Liberalism*, Rawls revises this standard of assessment for conceptions of justice to apply under conditions

673

of reasonable pluralism (*PL* 140–144). To explain fully the role of publicity in Rawls's theory, then, it is necessary first to elaborate his understanding of stability.

Rawls's notion of stability is an instance of the same notion used in physics, biology, economics, and other systems theories (*TJ* 399–401). It is a property of equilibrium states, where an equilibrium state is one which does not change unless acted on from without. An equilibrium state is unstable if influences from outside the system can easily move the system away from this equilibrium; it is stable if it tends to restore itself to this state despite external influences. The analog to an equilibrium state in Rawls's theory is a "well-ordered society." In a well-ordered society (i) everyone accepts the same conception of justice, and knows that everyone accepts the same conception of justice; (ii) the society conforms to that conception of justice, and everyone knows it so conforms; and (iii) everyone has a normally effective sense of justice, which is to say they understand their conception of justice and conform to it out of their own endorsement of it (*TJ* 397–399; *JF* 8–9).

Well-orderedness is not always to be desired – a society well-ordered around a decent hierarchical conception of justice might be improved by externally caused disorder. But Rawls's thought is that a well-ordered society does not change unless acted on from without, since in a well-ordered society everyone approves of the status quo of the society's system of justice and lives up to the demands of this system. On Rawls's approach the stability test for a conception of justice is whether, once a society is well-ordered around that conception, it would maintain that equilibrium despite significant external influences.

One external influence with the potential to disrupt well-orderedness is technological innovation in the production of goods, for example the advent of personal computing or the internet. Another we might label "cultural drift"; this consists in religions and lifestyles gaining and losing adherents, which may affect people's understandings of justice. But third and most important is that Rawls views succeeding generations as external to the status quo of a system of distributive justice. This is why the crux of the issue of stability is whether a conception of justice "generates sufficient support for itself," where this obtains to the extent humans raised within a society well-ordered by a conception would "acquire a sufficiently strong and effective sense of justice so that they normally comply with just arrangements" (*JF* 181). If a conception of justice self-perpetuates in this way from one generation to the next while preserving freedom of thought and association, then that conception of justice is stable for the right reasons and so is preferred over less stable rivals. (This also explains Rawls's use of the term "ideal theory"; the notion of ideality here is akin to that of the ideal gas law in

Publicity / 675

physics, in that it articulates a putatively stable equilibrium state under relevantly idealized conditions.)

This stability requirement explains Rawls's interest in human cognitive development. In the 1960s he co-developed a theory of human moral development with his Harvard colleague psychologist Lawrence Kohlberg. According to this theory humans tend to develop an effective sense of justice to the extent they are treated justly (*TJ* 414–419, 429–434). On this account it is crucial not only that society satisfy demands like justice as fairness but also that it is seen to do so, since only then do people tend to develop their senses of justice and hence perpetuate a well-ordered society. This is why, on Rawls's position, publicity is an essential constituent of stability and hence of justice (*CP* 292–294).

It is also why for Rawls the main problem of justice is not to keep people in line who are looking to manipulate institutions to their advantage. The main problem is instead assurance: how to get people to be disposed to be fair to others on the condition that others are fair in return, and how to get people so disposed to want to live up to the demands of justice (*TJ* 237–238). Once again this problem is solved only when people can appreciate that they have been treated fairly. Which is to say: it is solved when people are publicly treated fairly (*PL* 66–68).

This publicity constraint is central in Rawls's elaboration and defense of his theory. It is crucial to Rawls's case that his principles of justice are superior to what he calls the "principle of restricted utility," which is the principle of average utility subject to a constraint that Rawlsian constitutional essentials – such as access to equal and adequate political liberty and adequate opportunities and material resources – be provided to everyone. Since the principle of restricted utility guarantees the constitutional essentials, it is not vulnerable to the objection, so telling against other forms of utilitarianism, that it fails to rule out slavery or other violations of political and economic liberty. Rawls treats this principle as the most plausible alternative to justice as fairness. And ultimately Rawls rests his case for his conception of justice largely on grounds of publicity, claiming it is too difficult to tell how well the principle of restricted utility is satisfied and hence that it is too difficult to expect people to develop a normally effective sense of justice in a society governed by that principle (*JF* 126–130).

Two facts are insufficiently public on restricted utilitarian accounts of justice: the point at which adequate opportunities and material resources are provided, which is where the principle of average utility kicks in, and the point beyond this when the restricted principle of average utility is maximally satisfied. The former fact is insufficiently public because there is no clear fact about what constitutes adequate provision. (Rawls's theory need not identify this point because any society satisfying his conception of justice provides opportunities and material resources to the least-advantaged group in society at least as well as any other.) The latter fact is insufficiently public because the currency of utilitarian justice is characteristically desire-satisfaction, and relative satisfaction of desire is notoriously difficult to discern, measure, and compare among individuals. (Rawls's theory does not have this problem because his currency – social primary goods – is publicly discernible by definition. Indeed he chooses this metric in part because its public discernibility enables it to play the educational role he and Kohlberg claim it must.)

A second and related application of the publicity constraint is in Rawls's response to the capabilities theories of Amartya Sen (1987, 1992, 1993) and Martha Nussbaum (1993, 2000). Sen and Nussbaum charge Rawls with insensitivity to people's differential abilities to convert social primary goods into well-being, citing disability as an example of a condition that entitles a person to a greater share of social primary goods. They instead propose "capabilities" as part of an alternative metric not vulnerable to this objection; capabilities in this technical sense are abilities to convert resources like social primary goods to well-being.

Rawls's response to this charge consists mainly in an appeal to publicity constraints. He is sympathetic to the concerns Sen and Nussbaum raise, but thinks a theory should respond to them only so far as is compatible with public accessibility of how well a conception of justice is satisfied. By Rawls's lights, capabilities are not sufficiently public; well-being is somewhat inscrutable, and abilities to convert resources into well-being inherit that inscrutability. According to this response it is fine – indeed even required – that a conception of justice responds to the existence of diminished capabilities, for example by providing ramps and elevators for use by the physically impaired. Similarly, medical conditions that make it impossible to engage in most forms of work might entitle a person to enhanced job training or unemployment insurance. But what Rawls will insist on, insofar as issues of distributive justice are at stake, is that the disability in question be publicly accessible and publicly remediable. This does not proceed from skeptical concerns about the seriousness of other disabilities; it is simply a consequence of the educational role he believes a conception of justice must play (*JF* 168–170).

Thirdly and finally, the notion of publicity is central to the development of Rawls's theory into political liberalism in his later work. In that later work Rawls develops his idea of public reason, which includes the idea already discussed that conceptions of justice must be publicly known, along with the further idea that the forms of reasoning by which people engage one another in political discourse must be publicly intelligible. This second claim is elaborated into Rawls's claim that there is an "ideal of public reason," a duty to be self-imposed by citizens, judges, and public officials (*PL* 223–254; *CP* 581–588). This duty consists in restricting oneself to publicly accessible considerations, to the extent feasible, when helping to implement a system of distributive justice. This means not advancing considerations drawn from a particular doctrine about life or value which might be unintelligible as having force by those who do not endorse that doctrine, and it means seeking whenever possible to formulate arguments and policies about justice using ideas and terms drawn from a shared public political culture. A willingness to abide by this publicity constraint is for citizens a criterion of reasonableness, as Rawls understands this notion. There is a feasibility constraint on this criterion, since the public needs resources rich enough to articulate and defend a conception of justice. But Rawls maintains that notwithstanding this caveat the ideal of public reason has widespread implications for civic conduct, for on his view the resources available in a public political culture typically suffice to specify completely one or more conceptions of distributive justice. Hence on his view it is typically obligatory for citizens to self-impose the ideal of public reason.

Jon Garthoff

SEE ALSO:

> *Capabilities*
> *Cooperation and coordination*
> *Moral psychology*
> *Primary goods, social*
> *Public reason*
> *Sense of justice*
> *Stability*
> *Well-ordered society*

R

174.

RACE

A RACE IS A discrete, biologically defined group, no members of which belong to another such group. Members of a race are identified by shared physical characteristics, such as skin color, hair texture, and facial features. Philosophers of science disagree about whether racial categories are biologically significant. People who falsely believe in the moral significance of races, called racists, believe that races are ranked in order of superiority and inferiority based on shared moral and intellectual characteristics that are represented by the shared physical characteristics. They also believe that the shared physical, moral, and intellectual characteristics of a race are inherited from one generation to the next.

Whether or not racial categories are biologically significant, in justice as fairness race plays no role in the public or moral identity of a person. One's public identity depends exclusively on one's capacity to have a conception of the good and one's status as a self-authenticating source of valid claims, which are not affected by race. One's moral identity depends exclusively on one's affirmation of the value of political justice and the associations and commitments one makes and withdraws voluntarily. Since membership in a race is involuntary, it plays no role in moral identity. And since race is irrelevant to both public and moral identity, races are morally arbitrary collections of persons.

Because race is morally insignificant, it plays little or no role in determining what makes a society just, at least when addressed from the point of view of ideal theory. The veil of ignorance conceals from the parties in the original position their own social status, including their membership in any race that may be considered superior or inferior by racists in their society; the particular circumstances of their society, including whether the society's members belong to one or more races; their membership in one generation of a society rather than another, such as a generation before or after the abolition of racial slavery; and their own particular conceptions of the good, including whether their conceptions of the good include commitments to racial hatred or racial solidarity. The parties in the original position do, however, know the general basis of social organization and the laws of human psychology, which would involve some knowledge of how humans interact with groups they consider relevantly different from themselves.

Since the principles of justice are selected from a perspective that views race as morally insignificant, the principles can condemn as unjust certain forms of differential treatment based on race. The first principle of justice can condemn as unjust the denial of basic civil or political liberties on the basis of race. The second principle of justice can condemn as unjust any race-based distribution of the following primary goods that would absolutely disadvantage the least advantaged group: freedom of movement; free choice of occupation from among a diversity of opportunities; powers and prerogatives of office and positions of responsibility; income and wealth; and the ability to pursue a rational plan of life in the association of others with whom one shares mutual respect and whose company one enjoys.

Kevin M. Graham

SEE ALSO:

> *Fair equality of opportunity*
> *Ideal and nonideal theory*
> *King, Martin Luther, Jr.*
> *Least-advantaged position*
> *The original position*
> *Primary goods, social*

175.

RATIONAL CHOICE THEORY

R ATIONAL CHOICE THEORY (RCT) concerns the formal structure of the choices of individuals and the preference ordering behind their choices. It identifies a set of basic properties that rational individuals are supposed to satisfy. The most basic properties of rational preferences are reflexivity, transitivity, and completeness. If the choices include risk, the independence of irrelevant alternatives is thought to be one additional basic property. Many economists believe that these properties not only help us to explain and predict individuals' behaviors but also have normative force in their own right.

RCT plays a fundamental role in *TJ* as Rawls contends that parties in the original position would unanimously choose his principles of justice through rational choice. In fact, he refers to the literature of rational choice throughout *TJ*. At the beginning of *TJ* (12), Rawls claims that "the concept of rationality must be interpreted as far as possible in the narrow sense, standard in economic theory, of taking the most effective means to given ends," and that "one must try to avoid introducing into it any controversial ethical elements." However, he does add several substantive qualifications. First, the rational parties aim to maximize the expectations of primary goods, regardless of their rational plan of life. Second, the rational parties are mutually disinterested and not moved by envy. Third, in considering their rational life plan, the rational parties accept the Aristotelian principle, according to which people enjoy the exercise of their developed capacities, and this enjoyment increases as the capacity gets more developed. These three qualifications do not appear in standard RCT. Rawls adds substantive qualifications and assumptions to the standard RCT because, according to him, the parties in the original position are supposed to not only be rational in a formal sense, but also in their choice situation to represent citizens who have a capacity for reasonableness and a sense of justice.

Arguably, Rawls's most controversial decision-theoretic claim is that the rational parties in the original position would choose the difference principle. The decision-theoretic ground for the difference principle is the maximin rule. Many rational choice theorists believe that the maximin rule is too extreme and irrational. John C. Harsanyi, for example, appeals to rational choice in a hypothetical situation, where people's actual situation is unknown, and claims that average utilitarianism would be rationally adopted. Rawls agrees that the maximin rule is not appropriate as a general method for choice under uncertainty. However, Rawls maintains that relying on the maximin rule is rational when irreversibly choosing the basic structure of society from the original position.

Iwao Hirose

SEE ALSO:

Arrow, Kenneth
Harsanyi, John C.
Maximin rule of choice
The original position
Practical reason
Social choice theory

176.

RATIONAL INTUITIONISM

RATIONAL INTUITIONISM (not to be confused with "intuitionism") is a meta-ethical view that, starting with his Dewey Lectures in 1980, Rawls consistently contrasts with constructivism. Rawls notes that there have been variations on the doctrine, "but in one form or another it dominated moral philosophy from Plato and Aristotle onward until it was challenged by Hobbes and Hume, and, I believe, in a very different way by Kant." He further associates it with "in the English tradition by Clarke and Price, Sidgwick and Moore, and [it was] formulated in its minimum essentials by W. D. Ross. With qualifications, it was accepted by Leibniz and Wolff in the guise of perfectionism, and Kant knows of it in this form" (*CP* 343). Obviously, the idea of rational intuitionism is compatible with many different theories of the content of morality.

In *Political Liberalism*, Rawls identifies four features characteristic of rational intuitionism. First, and most importantly, it holds that "moral first principles and judgments, when correct, are true statements about an independent order of moral values; moreover, this order does not depend on, nor is it to be explained by, the activity of any actual (human) minds, including the activity of reason" (*PL* 91). Second, our knowledge of these principles and judgments is the result of exercising our theoretical (as opposed to practical) reason. Third, rational intuitionism is able to rely on a "sparse conception of the person" (*PL* 92). Although forms of it may rely on a richer conception of the person, all that is required is to understand the self as a knower that is capable of being motivated to act on the moral principles that it recognizes for their own sake. Finally, "rational intuitionism conceives of truth in a traditional way by viewing moral judgments as true when they are both about and accurate to the independent order of moral values. Otherwise they are false" (*PL* 92). In his initial formulation of rational intuitionism in the Dewey Lectures, Rawls held that it is also committed to the first principles of morality being "self-evident propositions" (*CP* 343). However, when he returned to the issue in the context of discussing Kant's moral philosophy in 1989, and then continuing through *Political Liberalism*, he dropped this requirement: "although intuitionists have often held first principles to be self-evident, this feature is not essential" (*CP* 511).

Political constructivism differs on each of these four points. It represents principles of political justice not as being true of an independent order of moral values, but rather as "the outcome of a procedure of construction." This construction "is based essentially on practical reason." It relies on a more complex conception of person and society: persons are viewed not simply as intuiting or perceiving the realm of value, but as "belonging to political society understood as a fair system of cooperation from one generation to the next" and as possessing "the two moral powers." And finally, rather than relying on the idea of truth as a standard of correctness and objectivity, it relies on the idea of reasonableness: it does not "use (or deny) the concept of truth; nor does it question that concept, nor could it say that the concept of truth and its idea of the reasonable are the same" (*PL* 93–94).

It is well understood, Rawls believes, that Kant rejects moral theories based on empirical desires as forms of heteronomy, but it is perhaps less clear that he would also reject rational intuitionism as heteronomous. "Yet it suffices for heteronomy that these [first] principles [of morality] obtain in virtue of relations among objects the nature of which is not affected or determined by the conception of the person. Kant's idea of autonomy requires that there exist no such order of given objects determining the first principles of right and justice among free and equal moral persons" (*CP* 345). The Kantian doctrine of autonomy requires that moral principles be generated by a procedure that is "suitably founded on practical reason, or, more exactly, on notions which characterize persons as reasonable and rational and which are incorporated into the ways in which, as such persons, they represent to themselves their free and equal moral personality" (*CP* 346). This, in turn, explains why constructivism relies on a more robust conception of the person.

In *Political Liberalism*, Rawls contrasts rational intuitionism not only with "Kant's moral constructivism" but also with "political constructivism." All three, he holds, have their own understanding of objectivity. Rational intuitionism holds that a moral judgment is correct when it is true of an independent realm of values that is "prior to the criteria of reasonableness and rationality as well as prior to the appropriate conception of persons as autonomous and responsible, and free and

Rational intuitionism / 687

equal members of a moral community. Indeed, it is that order that settles what those reasonable and rational criteria are, and how autonomy and responsibility are to be conceived" (*CP* 515). Kant's moral constructivism, in contrast, asserts that "moral objectivity is to be understood in terms of a suitably constructed social point of view that all can accept. Apart from the procedure of constructing the principles of justice, there are no moral facts" (*CP* 307). Political constructivism has its own understanding of objectivity suitable to its more limited purpose. Like Kant's moral constructivism, it treats the principles of justice as the result of a suitably defined procedure. But unlike Kant's moral constructivism, it does *not* say that "the procedure of construction makes, or produces, the order of moral values ... Political constructivism neither denies nor asserts this" (*PL* 95). This allows political constructivism to be compatible with rational intuitionism. "The difference is that rational intuitionism would add that a reasonable judgment is true, or probably true (depending on the strength of the reasons), of an independent order of values. Political constructivism would neither assert nor deny that" (*PL* 113).

Jon Mandle

SEE ALSO:

> *Autonomy, moral*
> *Constructivism: Kantian/political*
> *Intuitionism*
> *Kant, Immanuel*
> *Objectivity*
> *Political liberalism, justice as fairness as*
> *Practical reason*

177.

REALISTIC UTOPIA

THE PHRASE "REALISTIC UTOPIA" is used by Rawls in his later work to contrast his view with conceptions, which are "utopian in the pejorative sense" or "unrealistic" (*JF* 188). This is the case, for instance, of his own "unrealistic" "idea of a well-ordered society by justice as fairness" and of "the account of stability in Part III of *TJ*" (*PL* xix). On the other hand, Rawls rejects mere political realism and, quoting Rousseau, wants to "take men as they are and laws as they might be" (*LP* 7; *LHPP* 193, 207).

The expression has three main occurrences. First, it applies to political philosophy and its ambitions as Rawls sees them (*JF* 4–5; *LHPP* 10–11; *PL* 45). Second, and more importantly, it applies to the possibility of reaching an overlapping consensus on a public conception of justice (*PL* 133–172; *JF* §58). Third, it applies to the possibility of a reasonably just Society of Peoples (*LP* 127).

Political philosophy is "realistically utopian" (*JF* 4–5; *LP* 4 and §§1, 5–6, 7–11, 124) in the sense that it should try "not to withdraw from society and the world" (*PL* 45), but to reconcile us with our social world (*LP* 124; *JF* 3–4), to strike a balance between ideals and facts, between "the real and the rational," to use Hegel's phrase (*JF* 3).

However, for a constructivist such as Rawls, the "facts" are never a mere given and "the limits of the possible are not given by the actual, for we can to a greater or lesser extent change political and social institutions, and much else" (*JF* 5; *PL* 46). Assuming political institutions to be human constructs is crucial to transforming and contesting the status quo and making progress toward, say, the "liberal ideal" of a just constitutional regime (*JF* 190). Political philosophy has to be realistic in that it takes into account "historical conditions, conditions allowed by the laws and tendencies of the social world" (*JF* 4), what Rawls calls the "political circumstances of justice" (*TJ* §§22; cf. *JF* 4, 33, 197), but also the "ideals and principles" of a democratic culture (*JF* 4), its "familiar fundamental intuitive ideas" (*JF* 5–6). In other words, a realistically utopian political philosophy requires both *descriptive* and *normative* accuracy and should never stop "probing the limits of practicable political possibility" (*JF* 5).

These two demands justify the methodology adopted by Rawls, the recourse to an "ideal or strict compliance theory" (*TJ* 7–8; *JF* 13), to "idealizations" or "abstract conceptions" (*PL* 44) similar to Weberian "ideal-types," which should not be confused with utopian and "unrealistic" constructs.

The value of political philosophy is also to explain "how it is possible for there to exist over time a just and stable society of free and equal citizens" (*PL* 4). Stability in such a context would require a consensus. But of what kind? A unanimous consensus such as the one suggested in *TJ* would be unrealistic in view of the deep divisions and conflicts that characterize democratic societies. The "fact of reasonable pluralism" is a permanent feature of democratic societies (*PL* xix; *JF* 3–4, 40, 84). "A free democratic society well ordered by any comprehensive doctrine, religious or secular, is surely utopian in the pejorative sense. Achieving it would in any case require the oppressive use of power" (*JF* 187–188), which is incompatible with the liberal ideal. Does that mean that only a mere compromise or some sort of *modus vivendi* can be hoped for? In that case, stability would last no longer than the balance of powers, to "stability for the wrong reasons" (*PL* 435–490; *JF* 37, §58).

An alternative and "realistically utopian" source of stability is "the idea of an overlapping consensus introduced to make the idea of a well-ordered society more realistic and to adjust it to the historical and social conditions of democratic societies, which include the fact of reasonable pluralism" (*JF* 32). "While in a well-ordered society, all citizens affirm the same political conception of justice, we do not assume they do so for the same reasons, all the way down" (*JF* 32). "In this way, justice as fairness is realistically utopian" (*JF* 13). "It probes the limits of the realistically practicable, that is, how far in our world (given its laws and tendencies) a democratic regime can attain complete realization of its appropriate political values – democratic perfection, if you like . . . it should also provide some guidance in thinking about nonideal theory, and so about difficult cases of how to deal with existing injustices" (*JF* 13).

In line with the idea of an overlapping consensus among citizens, Rawls sketches the conditions of possibility of an international consensus among peoples, of a reasonably just Society of Peoples (*LP* 29–30, 124, 127), which he calls "a realistic utopia" (*LP* 4, 5–6, 11–12). A just or quasi-just society of peoples is a realistic hope, first, if it abandons "the cosmopolitan ideal of global justice for all persons" (*LP* 82) that leads it "to shape all not yet liberal societies in a liberal direction, until eventually (in the ideal case) all societies are liberal" (*LP* 82). Instead it recognizes the existence of a real world of sovereign states, the majority of which are far from democratic. Second, Rawls accepts that cultural and religious diversity among peoples cannot be eliminated and that not all peoples will become liberal and democratic. "Decent" but nonliberal peoples exist that accept a "common good," not a liberal, conception of justice (*LP* 71) and a measure of liberty of conscience (*LP* 74–75), that recognize certain human rights, but not the full list (*LP* 61), and have a decent consultation hierarchy (*LP* 61). Third, he claims that peoples, not individuals, are the objects of international justice, which may limit the defense of individuals against discriminations and persecutions by their own governments. Fourth, our duty of assistance should be limited, with a cut-off point, as a way of respecting peoples' autonomy and choices (*LP* 106–113). Finally, he thinks it impossible to consider a global difference principle, because the inequalities of resources among various peoples cannot be assimilated to the social inequalities among members of a specific society. A public justification of justice is only relevant within the limits of a society united by a common political culture.

The utopian element of a Society of Peoples is, for Rawls, the hope that "once political injustice has been eliminated by following just (or at least decent) social policies and establishing just (or at least decent) basic institutions . . . all peoples may belong as members in good standing to a reasonable Society of Peoples" (*LP* 126). Peace among democratic or decent peoples will prevail as a realistic possibility. The aim of political philosophy "in the tradition of the late writings of Kant (*Perpetual Peace*)" (*LP* 126) is "to reconcile us to our social world" and to show that a just Society of Peoples is *possible*. Kant spoke of a "foedus pacificum," of democratic peace as a realistic utopia (*LP* 21, 54), Hegel of historical developments, and Rawls of "a possibility which is not a mere logical possibility, but one that connects with the deep tendencies and inclinations of our social world" (*LP* 128). "By showing how the social world may realize the features of a realistic utopia, political philosophy provides a long-term goal of political endeavor, and in working toward it gives meaning to what we can do today" (*LP* 128). If this is impossible, then, "one might ask with Kant whether it is worthwhile for

Realistic utopia / 691

human beings to live on the earth" (*LP* 128). Rawls's liberalism is a liberalism of hope.

Catherine Audard

SEE ALSO:

Cosmopolitanism
Ideal and nonideal theory
Law of Peoples
Overlapping consensus
Reasonable hope
Reasonable pluralism
Reconciliation
Rousseau, Jean-Jacques
Society of Peoples

178.

THE REASONABLE AND THE RATIONAL

BEGINNING WITH THE Dewey Lectures ("Kantian Constructivism in Moral Theory" (1980) in *CP*), Rawls distinguishes between the reasonable and the rational. The reasonable is a particular form of practical rationality, but it is not always easy to understand what distinguishes it from the rational. At times it seems that the reasonable is the broader category: Rawls explains that a course of action may be rational in the sense of being in a person's narrow interest, but nonetheless unreasonable because unacceptable to others (*LHMP* 164). At other times, however, it seems that the rational is the broader category: especially in *PL*, the principles of justice are said to be merely reasonable, not rationally justified in some deeper sense. How can we make sense of these distinctions?

In *TJ*, Rawls writes that his contractarian theory of justice "conveys the idea that principles of justice may be conceived as principles that would be chosen by rational persons, and that in this way conceptions of justice may be explained and justified. The theory of justice is a part, perhaps the most significant part, of the theory of rational choice" (*TJ* 3, 16). This striking claim was soon subject to severe criticism, and Rawls eventually abandoned it (*PL* 53 n.7). Even in *TJ*, it is clear that Rawls is operating with more than one conception of rationality, and much of his later work is devoted to clarifying their differences.

In the passage from *TJ*, Rawls is pointing out that his theory of justice represents principles of justice as the objects of the choices of the parties in the original position, who are conceived as merely trying to advance their own interests under conditions of uncertainty. The parties reason in the instrumental and strategic manner presumed in game theory, maximizing the chances that they will realize their ends. In one sense, this explains why the principles of justice can be rationally justified: because we can all understand why they would be chosen in the original position. Rawlsian citizens can rationally justify their political claims, because they can appeal to a common decision procedure with determinate outcomes. But in another sense, the principles of justice have yet to be justified at all, because we have not yet explained why we should accept this particular decision procedure as the appropriate method for justifying our political claims. As for why we should identify with the hypothetical choices of the artificial agents in the original position, Rawls's answer is clearly *not* that doing so advances our narrowly strategic interests as individual, natural persons. In this sense, the critics were exactly right to point out that Rawls's theory of justice is not simply a part of the theory of rational choice. To justify the design of the original position, Rawls reaches beyond the theory of rational choice to an argument from reflective equilibrium, claiming that our acceptance of the constraints of the original position coheres with our moral interests and our moral psychology. If we say that much of *TJ* is devoted to the rational justification of the choice of the original position as the rational framework for political justification, then it is clear that we are using the term "rational" in two different senses. The particular, political use of strategic rationality is justified not as itself strategically rational, but because that particular use is rational in a broader sense. In his later work, beginning with the Dewey Lectures, the term that Rawls uses for rationality in this broader sense is "the reasonable."

The reasonable, Rawls explains, is "a conception of the *fair terms of cooperation*, that is, terms each person may reasonably be expected to accept, provided that everyone likewise accepts them. Fair terms of cooperation articulate an idea of mutuality and cooperation: all who cooperate must benefit, or share in common burdens, in some appropriate fashion as judged by a suitable benchmark of comparison" (*CP* 316). This definition may appear puzzlingly circular. The reasonable is defined as referring primarily to fair terms of cooperation (as in "reasonable political principles"), but those fair terms are in turn defined with reference to the reasonable itself (reasonable political principles are thus principles that "each person may reasonably be expected to accept"). To avoid vicious circularity, we need to understand the reasonable as being primarily a quality of persons (*PL* 48; *JF* 6), although one directed specifically toward principles of mutual cooperation. A reasonable person is a person who sincerely desires to identify, propose, and act on principles that all other such persons could likewise accept (*PL* 49; *JF* 6–7). Reasonable political principles are then just principles that reasonable people could all accept. "Reasonable persons, we say, are not moved by the general good as such but desire for its own sake a social world in which they, as free and equal, can cooperate with others on terms all can accept. They insist that reciprocity should hold within that world so that each benefits along with others" (*PL* 50).

With this understanding of the reasonable in hand, Rawls can reformulate the sense in which his principles of justice can be said to be justified. The principles are justified because they are rationally chosen through an appropriate decision procedure, and that decision procedure is appropriate because it is reasonable, because its constraints express the willingness to find principles of justice that all can accept. Each person has a particular conception of the good that he or she will be trying to advance, but if each person is conceived as ignorant of what that conception will be, then each person can rationally choose only those principles of justice that will equally support each person in advancing their particular conception. In this sense, Rawls writes, the reasonable "presupposes and subordinates" the rational (*CP* 317). To be reasonable is to accept that each person has a conception of the good that they will be (rationally) trying to advance. But to be reasonable is also to accept that one is entitled to advance one's own conception of the good only within terms of cooperation that others can accept as equally advancing their own conceptions of the good.

Because the reasonable presupposes and subordinates the rational, we can see that the real justificatory work of the theory is done not by the rational choice of the parties in the original position, but by the broader concept of the reasonable, which expresses the value of that rational choice. If there is a further question about whether the theory is truly justified, that question concerns the justification of the idea of the reasonable itself. Here we are not asking about the basic goodness of the reasonable; Rawls takes it for granted that the willingness to propose fair terms of cooperation counts as a virtue. The further question is whether and why this virtue should serve as the sole basis for political justification. In the passage quoted above, Rawls tells us that reasonable persons are not moved by "the general good as such"; instead they have an independent desire to propose fair terms of cooperation for free and equal persons. The idea of such fair terms of cooperation, as we have seen, then dictates the specification of the parties in the original position, whose rational choices in turn dictate the principles of justice. On its own, the idea of the reasonable seems to suggest mere political cooperativeness; it says nothing, in itself, about what the terms of political cooperation should be. On Rawls's view, however, the content of justice is constructed, via the original position, from the bare idea of the reasonable. The question is why we should allow this recognizable but thin virtue, this one example of "the general good as such," to serve as the sole political virtue.

The reasonable and the rational / 695

Rawls's answer to this question is his political liberalism. Recall that the idea of the reasonable presupposes that of the rational, because the reasonable proposes that each person, as free and equal, has a particular conception of the good that he or she is trying to advance. In the choice situation of the original position, we understand the advancement of such conceptions in a narrow, instrumental way, precisely because we are ignorant of the particular content of any such conception. But the reality of the various conceptions of the good is more complex and more diverse. Insofar as persons are rational, they are not simply pursuing efficient means to already given ends; they are selecting valuable ends according to specific criteria. But in the modern world, argues Rawls, under conditions of reasonable pluralism, we come to understand the complexity and diversity of specific conceptions of the good as "the normal result of the exercise of human reason within the framework of the free institutions of a constitutional democratic regime" (*PL* xvi). There is a plurality of conceptions of the good because these conceptions are derived from a plurality of comprehensive doctrines, exercises of practical reasoning which seek to order and justify claims about the nature of the good. Under conditions of reasonable pluralism, there is no agreement about the nature of the good, because there is no agreement on the ways in which we can and should reason about it.

Two consequences follow. The first is that the thought that our political principles should be reasonable, that they should be potentially acceptable to all individuals, no matter what comprehensive doctrine they hold, is not directed simply at achieving a particular virtue or a kind of practical advantage. Rather, this thought is a demand of practical reason itself, in the even broader sense of practical reason demonstrated in the workings of the various comprehensive doctrines. Because comprehensive doctrines are exercises of practical reason, sincere and disciplined attempts to explain the meaning and purpose of human life, their failure to come to agreement under conditions of modern pluralism is a fact about what practical reason can and cannot do. Given this fact, a demand for political agreement on principles that could not be shown to be reasonable would be in conflict with practical reason itself. And since political principles always demand compliance, it follows from the nature of practical reason that political principles must be reasonable.

The second consequence of the fact of reasonable pluralism is that our agreement to merely reasonable political principles can no longer be understood as fully justified within Rawls's own theory of justice. Throughout all of his work, Rawls insists that part of the justification of his theory of justice is an argument that the principles of justice are stable, where this means showing why individuals have good reason to comply with what has been shown to be just. Even in *TJ*, even before Rawls had explicitly formulated the idea of the reasonable, he was already asking why individuals have good reason to act on reasonable political principles, given the full range of their values. In *TJ*, this question was answered by a sprawling argument in moral psychology, which seeks to show that a commitment to reasonable political principles is a natural and coherent part of the psychology of agents in a well-ordered society. In his later work, however, Rawls becomes convinced that this kind of generalization about the psychology of agents threatens to be in conflict with the fact of reasonable pluralism, under which we come to understand the agency of individuals as essentially connected to their various comprehensive doctrines, which speak diversely to the nature and purpose of human life. In that sense, it is the individual comprehensive doctrines that must speak to the question of whether individuals have good reason to act on merely reasonable political principles. The final stage of the justification of Rawls's political liberalism is thus his proposal for an overlapping consensus, in which different reasonable comprehensive doctrines justify a commitment to merely reasonable political justification in their own ways, as determined by their particular comprehensive claims. If overlapping consensus obtains, Rawls argues, political liberalism is fully justified, because all individuals understand themselves as having (different sorts of) reasons for rationally justifying their political claims from the bare idea of the reasonable.

Ultimately, then, Rawls invokes rationality in three different senses. There is first the rational in the narrow or instrumental sense, the sense in which the parties in the original position have reason to choose the two principles of justice. This is the sense of rationality that Rawlsian citizens will invoke when they justify their political claims to one another, taking the values of political liberalism for granted. But this sense of rationality is different from the rationality of liberal political values, which are meant to be expressed in the constraints of the original position itself. These constraints are justified because they express the idea of the reasonable, the desire to justify political principles on terms that all can equally accept. The reasonable subordinates the rational, in the sense that we should rationally justify our political claims only in reasonable terms. Finally, there is the third sense of rationality expressed in the justification of the political use of the idea of the reasonable itself. This is the deeper sense of rationality at work in the various comprehensive doctrines. Their failure to come to agreement about the nature and purpose of human life is what justifies the idea of the reasonable as the necessary condition of political justification under conditions

The reasonable and the rational / 697

of reasonable pluralism. And their efforts to integrate the idea of the reasonable into their accounts of the nature and purpose of human life can generate an overlapping consensus around the reasonable as also a sufficient condition of political justification.

Larry Krasnoff

SEE ALSO:

Citizen
Constructivism: Kantian/political
Cooperation and coordination
Moral person
The original position
Political conception of justice
Practical reason
Reasonable pluralism
Reciprocity

179.

REASONABLE HOPE

RAWLS INTRODUCES THE idea of reasonable hope in *The Law of Peoples*. He links this idea to the notion of a realistic utopia. Briefly stated, a realistic utopia is a conception of a stable and just constitutional regime that conforms to known laws of nature and the real limitations of people, and that incorporates political ideals that inform the institutional arrangements of a just society. The features of a realistic utopia are realistic insofar as they conform to constraints imposed by reality on institutions and people, and it is utopian insofar as its ideals set a standard for what is to count as a just regime. Rawls states that the proper object of hope is the realization of a realistic utopia in both the domestic and the international case. In the domestic case one can reasonably hope for a constitutional regime in which the functioning of the major institutions are largely aligned with principles of justice that are the outcome of an overlapping consensus among reasonable citizens. In the international case the hope is for a society of peoples that abides by international law along the lines Rawls sets out in his eight principles in *The Law of Peoples*. In both of these cases the hope is for societies that have stable institutions and that therefore generate their own support across generations.

The introduction of the idea of reasonable hope as a distinct idea helps address the criticism that Rawls's principles of justice both require too much of citizens and are politically impracticable. However, Rawls is very much concerned with people "taken as they are" and with the practical realization of his ideas. Overall, the idea of reasonable hope reflects an attitude toward political philosophy as a whole that is made clear in Rawls's later works. This attitude rejects demands in political philosophy for universal and ahistorical truths and

Reasonable hope / 699

understands the problem of justice as a practical rather than a purely epistemological problem. According to Rawls then, political philosophy should be pragmatic in its philosophical ambitions without being skeptical. The attitude that corresponds with this pragmatic political philosophy is one of hope bounded by what is reasonable given who we are, what we can expect of ourselves, and the constraints of our circumstances. Therefore, to hope for a realistic utopia is not to aim for or expect perfection in our political arrangements. This would be unreasonable given the limitations imposed by our history, our circumstances, and our nature as people. While Rawls cautions us to be realistic in this sense, the idea of hope also serves as a caution against political pessimism. It is reasonable to hope within the confines of what is possible and it is also reasonable to hope for and thus imagine a society that is more just than the one we now inhabit. Reasonable hope navigates between political despair and the political impotency, or possible fanaticism, of detached utopian dreams. It also offers us a normative perspective on our present unjust societies.

The achievement of a realistic utopia would mark the end of tyranny, war, oppression, and other politically induced calamities. Rawls defines a good human nature as being capable of realizing a realistic utopia and human goodness as acting and hoping for its realization. Much is at stake in citizens acquiring reasonable hope and acting on it as Rawls states that in its absence "the wrongful, evil, and demonic conduct of others destroys us too and seals their victory" (*LP* 22).

Paul Voice

SEE ALSO:

Law of Peoples
Moral theory
Realistic utopia

180.

REASONABLE PLURALISM

REASONABLE PLURALISM IS a thesis about the operation of human reason under conditions of liberty. A diversity of irreconcilable but reasonable religious, philosophical, and moral doctrines is "the inevitable long-run result of the powers of human reason at work within the background of enduring free institutions" (*PL*4; cf. 36, 135). The precursor of this idea in *A Theory of Justice* is the assumption that among the circumstances of justice is doctrinal diversity that does not spring simply from moral faults such as selfishness or negligence (*TJ* 110, 112; compare *PL* 36–37, 55). Reasonable pluralism gives rise to the practical and moral problem to which political liberalism is a response: "how is it possible for there to exist over time a just and stable society of free and equal citizens, who remain profoundly divided by reasonable religious, philosophical and moral doctrines?" (*PL* 4). This doctrinal diversity is the consequence of the burdens of judgment, which are the obstacles to agreement between reasonable persons: empirical complexity, diversity of relevant values, conceptual vagueness, etc. (*PL* 54–58). Reasonable pluralism helps justify the claim that the exercise of political power must be publicly justifiable, an idea that finds expression in the "liberal principle of legitimacy" (*PL* xlvi, 217), the "criterion of reciprocity" (*PL* xlvi, li, 446–447), and the ideal of "public reason" (*PL* l, 226). Although from some points of view reasonable pluralism may seem unfortunate, Rawls insists that it is not a disaster, because if the theory of political liberalism is correct reasonable pluralism does not make it impossible to have a stable, approximately just society (*PL* xxvi, 37, 144). Thus we can be reconciled with this fixed point of the (modern) human condition, and not lose hope that over time we will make progress towards justice (*LP* 124–128).

A reasonable doctrine is one to which a reasonable person can stably adhere, after due reflection and deliberation, without putting into question the person's reasonableness. A reasonable person is, at a minimum, someone willing and able to reason in good faith with others, and to be guided by the results of these deliberations (cf. Larmore 1996, 168); the burdens of judgment are the obstacles to agreement between persons who are reasonable in this sense. Rawls also says that reasonable persons recognize the burdens of judgment and accept the idea of society as a fair scheme of cooperation between free and equal persons (*PL* 48–54). One might question whether all persons willing and able to reason with others would after deliberation recognize the burdens of judgment and accept that society should be understood as a fair scheme of cooperation. If not, we might say that the fully reasonable are a subset of the minimally reasonable, although Rawls himself does not draw this distinction. Reasonable pluralism is not, however, the optimistic thesis that fully reasonable persons will not disagree much. Since "the most intractable struggles...are for the highest things," it is remarkable that just cooperation is possible at all, for people "so deeply opposed in these ways" (*PL* 4).

Reasonable pluralism is not the thesis of value pluralism associated with Isaiah Berlin. Whether genuine ultimate values are irreducibly diverse, conflicting and/or incommensurable is one of the philosophical questions about which we should expect that reasonable persons will disagree (Larmore 1996, 152–174). Reasonable pluralism is also not a skeptical thesis (*PL* 63). Perhaps in the ideal speech situation, in the long run, reasonable deliberation would converge on a particular comprehensive doctrine, but real people do not have the luxury of deliberation unconstrained by pressures of time and the need to decide. We can express the thesis in such a way as to avoid the charge of skepticism by saying that for a broad range of religious, philosophical, and moral questions, sincere, well-intentioned and at least minimally competent deliberation does not generate convergence of views quickly enough for it ever to be the case that all of the reasonable citizens of a democratic society would ever espouse substantially the same doctrine.

One controversy about reasonable pluralism is whether it applies to the right as well as the good. Reasonable people do disagree about justice, precisely because they espouse different comprehensive doctrines, which have different implications for the rights and duties we owe each other as a matter of justice. Here, however, we are using the term "reasonable" in its minimal sense, denoting willingness and ability to reason with others, not its full sense, which includes recognition of the burdens of judgment and acceptance of society as a fair scheme of cooperation. Disagreement about justice by people who are reasonable in this sense will necessarily be disagreement limited by these shared commitments (Quong 2005). While fully reasonable disagreement about the good must also be limited by those shared commitments, there may not be very many aspects of human flourishing that all fully reasonable people agree about. The asymmetry between the right and the good is thus a function of the fact that reasonableness is defined in terms of ideas that have a more direct connection with questions of justice than with questions of human flourishing. This definitional asymmetry is not arbitrary, but a product of the fact that we need to live together under common laws and institutions, despite our many religious and philosophical disagreements, and so are led to the idea of society as a fair scheme of cooperation between persons who for public purposes will be conceived of as free and equal citizens.

A further worry about reasonable pluralism is that the thesis itself might be controversial amongst reasonable persons. If we expect the premises of political justification to be beyond reasonable rejection, reasonable pluralism might exclude itself, making Rawls's later political theory self-defeating (Wenar 1995, 41–48; Raz 1998, 30; Wall 2002; Reidy 2007). The response to this objection should be to admit that reasonable pluralism may be controversial amongst minimally reasonable persons, but to insist that acceptance of the burdens of judgment and reasonable pluralism is properly a criterion of reasonableness in the full sense. Why should I care about acceptability to points of view that do not care about acceptability to others? Common acceptance of the criterion of reciprocity establishes a relation of civic friendship (*PL* li). One can't have this relation with people who reject the basic ideas of political liberalism and public justifiability, making it pointless to include their points of view in the set of qualified perspectives acceptability to whom defines public justification. Counting a view as unreasonable does not, however, imply that we must name and shame those who adhere to it, nor that we should refuse to engage them in respectful debate. If one simply wants to exclude unreasonable views from debate, one has no need of the principle of public justification, whose distinctive deliberative function is to allow citizens to claim that particular reasons are not legitimate grounds for public decision-making despite *not* being unreasonable.

Andrew Lister

SEE ALSO:

Burdens of judgment
Comprehensive doctrine
Legitimacy
Political conception of justice
Public reason
Reciprocity

181.

RECIPROCITY

THE IDEA OF reciprocity has always been central to Rawls's thinking about justice. In *A Theory of Justice* he writes that reciprocity is "implicit in the notion of a well-ordered society" (*TJ* 13). But in his later work it plays an explicitly foundational role. Indeed, that work is based on the "fundamental idea...of society as a fair system of cooperation over time, from one generation to the next" (*PL* 14), and reciprocity is integral to that idea because "Fair terms of cooperation specify an idea of reciprocity: all who are engaged in cooperation and who do their part as the rules and procedure require, are to benefit in an appropriate way as assessed by a suitable benchmark of comparison" (*PL* 16). Reciprocity differs from pure altruism, in which one is motivated simply "by the general good," and "mutual advantage," under which everyone's interests are advanced relative to a merely existing situation or baseline. In a relationship of reciprocity, by contrast to mutual advantage, "everyone benefits judged with respect to an appropriate benchmark of equality" (*PL* 17).

The defining problem of political liberalism is to explain how a society can be well-ordered by a conception of justice when its citizens adhere to conflicting comprehensive doctrines, each of which may give rise to its own conception of justice. It solves that problem by proposing a political conception of justice that all reasonable citizens may accept because it is not based upon the concepts or principles of any particular comprehensive doctrine. "Reasonable citizens" or people, Rawls argues, accept the "criterion of reciprocity." That is to say, when they view "one another as free and equal in a system of social cooperation over generations, they are prepared to offer one another fair terms of cooperation according to what they consider the most reasonable conception of political justice" (*CP* 578). The "criterion of reciprocity" holds that when one proposes such terms to others, one must "think it at least reasonable for others to accept them, as free and equal citizens, and not as dominated or manipulated, or under the pressure of inferior political or social positions" (*CP* 578).

The criterion of reciprocity leads directly to the liberal principle of legitimacy and the related idea of public reason. One formulation, focusing on what we might call the subjective orientation of those who exercise power – their beliefs and values – holds that "Our exercise of political power is proper only when we sincerely believe that the reasons we would offer for our political actions – were we to state them as government officials – are sufficient, and we also reasonably think that other citizens might also reasonably accept those reasons" (*CP* 578). Reasons that all can accept are "public reasons," and Rawls adds that "the role of the criterion of reciprocity as expressed in public reason . . . is to specify the nature of the political relation in a constitutional democratic regime as one of civic friendship" (*CP* 578). In all of these ways reciprocity is one of the fundamental building blocks of Rawls's political conception of justice.

Reciprocity also figures as a key concept within Rawls's account of justice – particularly in the argument for the difference principle, and in his account of the stability of justice as fairness. Rawls's argument for the two principles of justice is framed as a comparison of the two principles, on the one hand, and other conceptions of justice, mainly utilitarianism, on the other. In *Justice as Fairness* he considers a variant of utilitarianism, or a principle of restricted utility, which is "the principle of [increasing or maximizing] average utility, combined with a suitable social minimum" (*JF* 126), as an alternative to the difference principle. One of the principal grounds for accepting the difference principle is that it satisfies a condition of reciprocity, namely that "those who are better off at any [given level of income and wealth] are not better off to the detriment of those who are worse off at that point" (*JF* 124). That is to say, the difference principle satisfies a condition of reciprocity since it forbids one party (the more advantaged) to gain at the expense of the other party (the disadvantaged): all gains must be reciprocal. Further, because the difference principle regulates the basic structure of society, and does not apply directly to the division of primary goods (in this case income and wealth), it incorporates "a deeper idea of reciprocity," namely "that social institutions are not to take advantage of contingencies of native endowment, or of initial social position, or of good or bad luck over the course of life, except in ways that benefit everyone," and so "represents a fair undertaking between the citizens seen as free and equal with respect to those inevitable contingencies" (*JF* 124).

The difference principle does call for a certain self-restraint on the part of the more advantaged, since by hypothesis they may be able to attain a higher material standard in a society governed by the principle of restricted utility. But, he argues, those who accept the idea of society as a fair system of cooperation will also believe that the principle of distribution that applies to society "should contain an appropriate idea of reciprocity," and thus have "reason to accept" the difference principle (*JF* 125–126). Moreover, the advantaged should be "mindful of the deeper idea of reciprocity, implicit in the difference principle" (*JF* 126). Recognizing that they are fortunate to have benefitted from such contingencies as superior native endowments, and are even further benefitted by being able to secure a greater share of primary goods, they should be willing to accept that these further benefits are conditional on improving "the situation of others" (*JF* 126). By contrast, the principle of maximizing average utility, even combined with a social minimum, "asks more of the less advantaged that the difference principle asks of the more advantaged" (*JF* 127), since their additional gains are possible only at the expense of those already disadvantaged.

Reciprocity is also essential to Rawls's account of how a political conception of justice can become "a stable overlapping consensus" (*JF* 195). This account turns on what he calls "a reasonable moral psychology," in which "the idea of reciprocity appears both as a principle giving its content and as a disposition to answer in kind" (*JF* 195–196). Rawls sets out "three psychological laws" or tendencies, describing how our desires or final ends are transformed when we come to recognize "the manner in which institutions and the actions of others affect our good" (*TJ* 432). These laws hold that "we acquire attachments to persons and institutions according to how we perceive our good to be affected by them," where the "basic idea is one of reciprocity, a tendency to answer in kind." Thus, reciprocity is "a deep psychological fact" (*TJ* 433) as well as a moral principle, the one reinforcing the other. A basic structure governed by justice as fairness with its criterion of reciprocity will "heighten the operation of the [psychological] reciprocity principle" by obviously enhancing one's good, leading in turn "to a closer affiliation with persons and institutions by way of an answer in kind" (*TJ* 437). In this way, people growing up and living under institutions that conform to a political conception of justice such as justice as fairness will tend to develop a sense of justice that will lead them to support those institutions, and in that way enhance the stability of that conception of justice.

J. Donald Moon

SEE ALSO:

Advantage, mutual vs. reciprocal
Basic structure of society
Cooperation and coordination
Democracy
Duty of civility
Legitimacy
Public reason
The reasonable and the rational
Reasonable pluralism
Stability
Well-ordered society

182.

RECONCILIATION

RECONCILIATION IS AMONG four functions Rawls enumerates that political philosophy can play as a part of public political culture, with Hegel's *Philosophy of Right* as its main historical exemplar (*LHPP* 10; *JF* 3). Rawls notes that the German word for reconciliation, *Versöhnung*, has a specialized meaning that Hegel distinguishes from a colloquial synonym like *Ergebenheit* (resignation) (*LHMP* 331). A political project centered around the latter might aim to show that, given the human condition or our historical predicament, our political institutions are as good as can be expected, even though they may seem seriously deficient. By contrast, a reconciliatory project attempts to show that although our social world may seem accidental or arbitrary, its institutions actually reflect the work of reason. By this, Hegel means that the institutional pillars of modern society – family, civil society, the constitutional state – are necessary for freedom (*LHMP* 336–340).

There is a question as to the extent to which Rawls's own political philosophy can be understood as a reconciliatory program. Although compared to figures like Kant and Mill, Rawls's references to Hegel are infrequent, the case can be made that the extent is significant. This is particularly true of Rawls's later work. *TJ* represents what Rawls, in his later view, calls a "partially comprehensive doctrine" (*JF* 186–187; *PL* xviii) insofar as it argues that the well-ordered society is stable by virtue of its members sharing certain beliefs about justice constituting the human good. In his self-critical reflections, Rawls comes to regard this as unrealistic in light of the fact of pluralism. In his subsequent conception of the overlapping consensus, a set of liberal principles of justice is agreed to by the citizens for a variety of reasons internal to their different comprehensive doctrines. It becomes an important task for Rawls to show this does not amount to a significant diminishment of the vision from *TJ*. Hence, it is crucial to realize that stabilizing a conception of justice through an overlapping consensus is not "simply a matter of avoiding futility" (*PL* 142) – it is not a compromise. Rather a plurality of reasonable comprehensive doctrines is a product of "free institutions," the stability of the overlapping consensus is publicly supported by moral reasons acceptable to all, i.e. "stability for the right reasons" (*PL* xlii), and is renewed through the citizens' own public use of reason. A more unitary consensus would not be normatively superior and so should not be pined over – we should recognize the overlapping consensus and the institutions of a pluralistic democracy as the work of reason under free institutions, and so reconciled, not resigned, to them. Reconciliation's importance for Rawls is therefore to a certain extent psychological, and related to Kant's ideas of reasonable hope and "philosophy as defense": to call a well-ordered society a "realistic utopia" is to indicate the social world is not implacably opposed to the aspirations and values embodied in the notion of reasonableness, but rather that it is at least possible for our world to be a product of it.

Todd Hedrick

SEE ALSO:

> *Hegel, G. W. F*
> *Overlapping consensus*
> *Realistic utopia*
> *Reasonable hope*
> *Reasonable pluralism*
> *Stability*

183.

REDRESS, PRINCIPLE OF

THE PRINCIPLE OF redress is "the principle that undeserved inequalities call for redress" (*TJ* 86). Consider the case of people who are born with debilitating handicaps or with a melancholy disposition. Since these people do not deserve to be less well off than others, they are entitled to compensation for their handicaps or dispositions under the principle of redress. Consider next the case of people who are born with great intelligence or beauty. Since these people do not deserve to be better off than others, it is appropriate to penalize them for their natural good fortune under the principle of redress. In one formulation or another, the principle of redress is accepted by all those who are identified as luck egalitarians. Rawls does not accept the principle of redress, but he does claim that the difference principle gives some weight to it. He does not accept the principle of redress because he does not think that justice applies to the distribution of natural primary goods, such as intelligence or beauty. The fact that some have more and others have less of these goods is neither just nor unjust. For Rawls, justice is a matter of how the basic structure of a society determines distributions of social primary goods, not natural primary goods. Yet, as mentioned, Rawls does claim that the difference principle gives some weight to the principle of redress. Like this latter principle, it holds that people do not deserve their good fortune in the distribution of natural talents and so they cannot make a desert-based claim that they are entitled to the social primary goods that flow from the exercise of these talents.

Does Rawls also think that it is unjust if natural contingencies, like differences in intelligence and beauty, allow those who are naturally favored to have greater shares of social primary goods like income and wealth? He writes that "intuitively, the most obvious injustice of the system of natural liberty is that it permits distributive shares to be improperly influenced by these factors that are so arbitrary from a moral point of view" (*TJ* 63). This statement has suggested to some commentators that Rawls must have had luck egalitarian intuitions. He must have thought that it is unjust for social institutions to allow those who are naturally lucky to use their good fortune to secure a larger share of social primary goods. At least part of the content of justice, he must have thought, is the injunction to neutralize the effects of natural contingencies. But it is unlikely that Rawls held such a view, for it would discredit the difference principle. The difference principle allows morally arbitrary factors, such as undeserved good fortune, to influence the distribution of income and wealth. Contrary to the principle of redress, it holds that just institutions may permit those with undeserved natural talents, not only to benefit from them without penalty, but also to have more income and wealth than those who are naturally less fortunate. This is permitted so long as the additional advantages enjoyed by the naturally talented redound to the benefit of the least-advantaged class.

Steven Wall

SEE ALSO:

Desert
Difference principle
Luck egalitarianism
Natural talents
The original position

184.

REFLECTIVE EQUILIBRIUM

JOHN RAWLS INTRODUCED the term "reflective equilibrium" in *TJ* (18), but he there insisted that the concept derives from earlier discussions of the justification of inductive logic, citing Nelson Goodman (1955, 65–68). We can ask, for instance, whether a particular inductive rule is a justifiable one, but our only basis for answering that question, Goodman argued, is to consider whether our practice of induction, broadly understood, includes that inductive rule. By analogy, we will have to judge whether specific principles of justice are acceptable by seeing if they fit well with our most deeply held specific judgments about what is just. Viewed most generally, a "reflective equilibrium" is the end point of a deliberative process in which we reflect on and revise our beliefs about an area of inquiry, moral or nonmoral. The inquiry might be as specific as the moral question, "What is the right thing to do in this case?" or the logical question, "Is this the correct inference to make?" Alternatively, the inquiry might be much more general, asking which theory or account of justice or right action we should accept, or which principles of inductive reasoning we should use. We can also refer to the process or method itself as the "method of reflective equilibrium."

In ethics, the method of reflective equilibrium consists in working back and forth among our considered moral judgments about particular instances or cases, the principles or rules that we believe govern them, and the theoretical considerations that we believe bear on accepting these considered judgments, principles, or rules, revising any of these elements wherever necessary in order to achieve an acceptable coherence among them (this characterizes wide as opposed to narrow reflective equilibrium (see *CP* 289; Daniels 1996, 21–26)). Sometimes, Rawls refers to our "convictions" instead of our considered moral judgments. A more familiar term in the philosophical literature is "moral intuitions," and this term, often used by a number of Rawls's critics, may carry with it a more specific epistemological meaning. In what follows, "considered moral judgments" seems appropriate since it better adheres to Rawls's usage, but this usage is not meant to preclude referring to moral intuitions instead. Whatever the terminology, in Rawls's view no type of moral belief is viewed as foundational, though we may have great confidence in some of them, which we tentatively can view as "fixed points." Although some of our considered moral judgments (or intuitions) are hard to abandon or revise, in principle all are revisable in reflective equilibrium (*CP* 289). Here Rawls disagrees with some theorists who treat their moral intuitions as bedrock while not explaining why intuitions should be credited with that status.

The method succeeds and we achieve reflective equilibrium when we arrive at an acceptable coherence among these beliefs. An acceptable coherence requires that our beliefs not only be consistent with each other (a weak requirement), but also that some of these beliefs provide support or provide a best explanation for others. In a reflective equilibrium, some of our beliefs are shown to cohere best with other things we believe; the claim is that these beliefs are therefore justified in light of them.

As Rawls's work evolved, reflective equilibrium as a form of justification evolved as well. Rawls realized that narrow reflective equilibrium, which seeks coherence between judgments about cases and principles, could not play the role of justification in *TJ* that he had intended for reflective equilibrium, and he contrasted it with wide reflective equilibrium which includes beliefs about a broader range of theoretical concerns and provides more of a basis for critical pressure to revise beliefs (*CP* 289; *PL* 384 n. 16). As his work evolved, he abandoned the idea that a shared wide reflective equilibrium is what justifies justice as fairness; instead he realized he must show how wide reflective equilibrium can be reconciled with the idea of an overlapping consensus, the central idea in the claim that justice is political. Despite this evolution in these ideas about justification, reflective equilibrium retains its coherentist nature and continues to include moral judgments (or intuitions). Reflective equilibrium thus invites challenges by advocates of other ethical theories that are skeptical about moral intuitions and by philosophers working from other epistemological perspectives. Nevertheless, the method of reflective equilibrium has achieved wide use in various fields. We take up this evolution, these challenges, and these uses in turn.

Rawls (*TJ* 18) insists that the principles of justice as fairness chosen as a solution to the rational choice problem posed in the original position must meet a further condition of adequacy. They must also be in reflective equilibrium with our considered judgments about justice. This adequacy condition might seem to be the requirement that the choice problem yields principles of justice, rather than some other kind of principle. That is, we end up in the right ballpark for the game we want to play. Why think the condition is part of a claim about justification?

In later work, Rawls explicitly contrasts narrow and wide reflective equilibrium and embraces that terminology, remarking that the latter notion is the philosophically more important one. He does in *TJ* note the substance of the contrast (*TJ* 43), but he later affirms that only wide reflective equilibrium carries the justificatory force that is of interest to him (*CP* 289; *PL* 384 n.16; *JF* 30–31). A narrow reflective equilibrium between principles chosen in the original position and our considered moral judgments about justice might have sufficed to show us the principles chosen were indeed principles of justice, but Rawls wanted more. Only a wide reflective equilibrium could at once bring into coherence background views about persons (the claims about their moral powers) and the role of justice in a well-ordered society, the features of the construction of the original position itself, and some elements of the arguments for the principles. Such a wide reflective equilibrium could bring to bear critical forces that assure us all the elements of the equilibrium are revisable and we are getting the best support possible for each component. Rawls came in this way to develop the idea of reflective equilibrium in a way that let it play the justificatory role he wanted it to play. The idea is that there is convergence on a particular wide reflective equilibrium that justifies the principles and the constructivist approach to the social contract in *TJ*.

Rawls's view of justification has yet a third component: not only must principles of justice be chosen in the original position and must that whole account achieve a wide reflective equilibrium, but also they must produce acceptable "strains of commitment" (*TJ* 126, 153–154) and yield a stable (and therefore feasible) conception that people can adhere to over time (*TJ* 398). Rawls came to believe that under conditions of liberty, as assured by his first principle of justice, the "burdens of judgment" would lead people to form different comprehensive views – views that might combine some philosophical and religious views (*PL* 54–58). If we then ask whether a conception of justice is stable (feasible), we have to show it is one that is compatible with these different reasonable comprehensive views. But then it cannot be a conception that presupposes one or another of these comprehensive views. Rawls's solution to this problem is to say that there is an overlapping consensus on the main ideas of justice, so that each reasonable comprehensive view includes the elements of that overlapping consensus, and that proponents of each such comprehensive view can point to a wide reflective equilibrium which provides a justification for them of the elements of the overlapping consensus. Rawls refers to this appeal to reflective equilibrium as "full reflective equilibrium" (*PL* 384 n.16, 384ff.) In this way Rawls preserves the justificatory role of wide reflective equilibrium while showing how he can also address the feasibility problem. What is sacrificed is the idea that convergence on a specific wide reflective equilibrium underlies the stable conception of justice that reasonable people can agree to.

Objections to the reflective equilibrium as a form of justification in ethics are of three types: to the use of considered moral judgments or intuitions at all; to the kinds of beliefs appealed to; and to the coherentist account of justification.

The first type is represented by the standard utilitarian objection to allowing moral intuitions to play a role in constructing or criticizing ethical theories. Some utilitarians complain that such judgments are riddled with historical contingencies, including various biases, and they should not therefore be given weight in ethical reasoning. Thus Richard Hare (1973a, 144–147) and Richard Brandt (1979, 20), two prominent twentieth-century utilitarians, complained that making coherent a set of "fictions" still leaves us with a fiction. Brandt (1990, 260–261) reaffirms that such judgments lack "evidential force," even if increasing coherence among them is persuasive to some people.

The objection reminds us that eighteenth-century moral theorists who thought they could intuit what was right through a moral faculty at least told a story about what underlies their confidence in their judgments, namely that people possess a "moral faculty" that perceives moral facts or truths. (Some important twentieth-century moral theorists give full weight to certain moral intuitions without providing an account of the source of their credibility (McMahan 2000, 3–4; Kamm 1993, 5–9; Cohen 2008, 4–6).) The objection also suggests there is a disanalogy between moral intuitions and perceptual judgments: some epistemologists try to explain the reliability of the latter through a causal theory of knowledge, but such an explanation is more problematic for moral judgments. Accordingly, proponents of reflective equilibrium must accept the task of explaining the initial credibility of moral intuitions or reject the claim that they face that burden of proof. Arguably, Rawls would have rejected the claim the burden of proof falls on him, perhaps because his approach is both pragmatic and contractarian, so that justification must build on points of agreement in our beliefs.

The second line of objection is an implication of G. A. Cohen's controversial meta-ethical claim that facts play no role in clarifying what justice requires.

Specifically, Cohen (2008, 243 n.19) suggests that only a narrow reflective equilibrium containing only notions of value focused on justice could be used to clarify what justice requires. A wide reflective equilibrium that contains moral notions other than justice as well as various kinds of facts, such as those about human nature or behavior, would take us out of the domain of justice and into the different arena of rules for regulating institutions. In effect, Cohen rejects the use of the sort of wide reflective equilibrium that Rawls invokes both in his early and late work because it contains too broad a set of beliefs to help us understand what justice itself requires.

A third line of objection derives from more general concerns in epistemology. One such challenge comes from the claim that we cannot readily distinguish a coherentist account of justification from a coherentist account of truth, and the latter is implausible (Sayre-McCord 1996). Such objections might readily combine with Hare's original charge that Rawls "rigged" the construction of the original position to get the conclusions he wanted or the charge that a coherent set of fictions is still a fiction. Yet the separation of an account of justification from a notion of moral truth is important to Rawls, especially in his later work. Even if one might have been tempted to think that convergence on the unique wide reflective equilibrium that provided justification for the principles of justice as fairness meant that these principles were moral truths, that view is less tempting in the later Rawls. The "burdens of judgment" mean that there are many reasonable comprehensive moral and religious views. Consequently, for those who believe such views, justification of the overlapping consensus they share must derive from the different wide reflective equilibria that those believers would appeal to. Other complaints about reflective equilibrium suggest that we should not accept a method as justificatory if it embodies unfortunate contingencies: some claim that people will arrive at different equilibria depending on what their starting points are, and these may be based on mere historical accidents; others say this kind of contingency shows the conservatism of the approach; others argue that sometimes appropriate change results from some form of conversion experience, which adds to the contingency of the components of an equilibrium.

Despite these lines of objection, reflective equilibrium has become a widely used account of justification within various areas of ethics, including bioethics and other areas of applied ethics, and it continues to be evaluated in other contexts, such as the justification of induction, as well. Wide reflective equilibrium shows us the complex structure of justification in ethics and political philosophy, revealing many connections among our component beliefs. At the same time, there are many different types of ethical analysis and normative inquiry. Arguably, the breadth of the approach has much to do with its appeal.

Norman Daniels

SEE ALSO:

Burdens of judgment
Cohen, G. A.
Comprehensive doctrine
Constructivism: Kantian/political
The original position
Overlapping consensus
Political conception of justice
Public reason

185.

RELIGION

S A PRINCETON undergraduate in 1942 Rawls wrote a long theological thesis on the topics of sin and faith. At that point in his life he was an
orthodox Episcopalian who entertained the thought of entering the seminary. His traditional religious beliefs changed, however, in response to several
incidents that occurred to him as a soldier in World War II. These all surrounded
the theodicy problem. Nonetheless, Rawls seems to have remained a Kantian
fideist (someone who believes in a God of some sort, but not as a result of rational argument) for the rest of his life, as a posthumously published 1997 essay
titled "On My Religion" indicates. Rawls was not the product of a secular background (see *BIMSF*, especially 261–264; also *LHMP* 291).

Despite appearances, there is much in the very early Rawls that prefigures
the political philosophy for which he was to later become famous. For example,
sin is a thoroughly social phenomenon in that it is defined as that which repudi-
ates or destroys community. Likewise, faith is defined as that which constitutes
and integrates community. And the thesis that human beings are made in the
image of God is interpreted not so much in terms of the presence of rationality
in human beings, but rather in terms of human beings being uniquely capable
of entering into community. As a result of these concepts of sin, faith, and *imago
Dei*, the very early Rawls thought that religion and ethics could not be separated
(*BIMSF* 113, 116, 193, 205, 207, 214, 219).

The less than adequate features of traditional Christianity that Rawls noticed
in the war led him to study in detail the history of religious intolerance, as well
as the rise of political liberalism, which was meant to respond to the disastrous
effects of the wars of religion in the early modern period. In addition to Locke's
famous "Open Letter Concerning Toleration," Rawls was heavily influenced by

a little-known work by the sixtenth-century Catholic thinker Jean Bodin, "Colloquium of the Seven." Bodin saw toleration not only in political terms, but as the expression of true Christianity. The seven speakers at an imaginary banquet represented different religious traditions, but they were happy to abandon attempts to refute each other's religious beliefs (*BIMSF* 264–265; also *LHPP* 311).

The deeply religious temperament in Rawls surfaces in his philosophy in many ways. Political philosophy itself involves a reasonable faith that a just society is possible, otherwise one might wonder whether it is worthwhile for human beings to live on this earth. Further, Rawls also aims to establish that human nature is good in the sense that it is capable of justice, which entails a rejection (à la Rousseau) of original sin (*LP* 128; cf. *CP* 448; *LHPP* 205–209). And Rawls concludes *TJ* by appeal to a view of our social world *sub specie aeternitatis*, which is also an indication of what Thomas Nagel would call his religious temperament, although it should be noted that this view is one within history, not beyond it (*TJ* 514; cf. *BIMSF* 5–6).

The most extended treatment of the role of religion in politics is in *PL*, where Rawls contrasts the Homeric religion of the ancient Greeks with Christianity. Specifically, the Reformation fragmented the religious unity of the Middle Ages by creating a situation of religious pluralism. This led to problems as rival versions of authoritative and salvationist religion vied for control of the populations of Europe. Luther and Calvin turned out to be as dogmatic and intolerant as the Catholic Church had been. This led to the question: how is a just society possible among those of different faiths? Political liberalism arose in the sixteenth and seventeenth centuries as a response to this very question (*PL* xxiii–xxvi, 303; cf. *JF*, 192; *LHMP* 3, 6–14).

Rawls seems to identify a view as religious if it involves a conception of the world as a whole that presents it as in certain respects holy or worthy of devotion (*LHMP* 160). But in *PL* Rawls tends to refer to comprehensive doctrines rather than to religions. A comprehensive doctrine involves a general conception of what is of value in human life. Contemporary society is characterized by a plurality of comprehensive doctrines, both religious and nonreligious, but this situation need not be seen as disastrous due to the conceptual and practical progress brought about by political liberalism. A just society does not depend on agreement on a common comprehensive doctrine. This is because the problem of political justice does not depend on a resolution of the problem of *the* highest good. Political liberalism starts with the realization of the depth and breadth of irreconcilable differences regarding which comprehensive doctrine, if any, is the true one (*PL* xvii–xxviii).

Rawls makes explicit in *PL* what was only implicit in *TJ*: political liberalism is not the same thing as comprehensive liberalism. The latter is a comprehensive doctrine that arose in the Enlightenment period in figures like Kant as a secular replacement for traditional Christian comprehensive doctrines, whereas the former has no such aspirations. Political liberalism is not a comprehensive doctrine, but a framework within which those who affirm uncompromisingly different comprehensive doctrines can live together in a just society (*PL* xxix–xxx, xl, li–lii; cf. *LHMP* 14–16).

One comprehensive doctrine can retain power in a condition of pluralism only by way of an oppressive use of state violence. This was true in the Catholic Church's use of the Inquisition and it would be equally true if a nonreligious comprehensive doctrine were seen as normative in the political sphere. Plato, Aristotle, St. Augustine, St. Thomas Aquinas, Luther, and Calvin all thought that there was only one comprehensive doctrine that was true and that a just society consisted in getting those who knew *the* good into power and to punish those who worked against the good. On this basis, toleration of reasonable differences among comprehensive doctrines was actually a vice. In political liberalism, by contrast, citizens are expected to have two views: a political conception of justice and a view of the good life. The latter should at least be consistent with the former; indeed it is wider than the former. Rawls's justice as fairness intentionally stays on the surface so as to sidestep deep and divisive problems surrounding the nature and content of the good (*PL* 37, 134, 138; cf. *TJ* 189–191; *JF* 34, 187; *CP* 329, 360, 391–395, 453, 475, 490).

A stable society is one in which there is not a mere *modus vivendi*, where adherents to different comprehensive doctrines would impose their will on each other if they could, but an overlapping consensus among adherents to different comprehensive doctrines. That is, reasonable religious believers can wholeheartedly affirm politically liberal principles in their own ways. Except for certain forms of fundamentalism, all of the major historical religions, including Islam, are capable of being reasonable comprehensive doctrines. Granted, some religious comprehensive doctrines provide limit cases regarding what can be tolerated in a just society, but if children in such religious traditions are educated in the democratic virtues and values then there is a good chance that such religious comprehensive doctrines can be brought within the sweep of politically liberal institutions. Religious comprehensive doctrines should not try to do too much in the political arena in a condition of pluralism; and democratic political institutions should not try to do too much at the associational level of religious institutions. The doctrine *extra ecclesia nulla salus* (outside the church there is no salvation) may or may not be true, but it should not have any political force (*PL* 148, 170, 195–199; cf. *JF* 164, 183; *CP* 411–412, 426, 433–434, 483, 590, 597).

The only comprehensive doctrines that run afoul of public reason are those that cannot support a reasonable balance of political values. Some, but not all, opponents to abortion on religious grounds do this. This does not mean that religious believers cannot bring their comprehensive doctrines to bear on public policies, but it does mean that they must meet the demands of "the proviso" that they translate their comprehensive doctrine into terms that any reasonable person could understand and could possibly accept. That is, difficult problems are not settled in advance against religious believers, as Rawls argues in his treatment of the debate between Patrick Henry and James Madison over religious freedom. Further, the demands of this proviso are placed on the shoulders of defenders of nonreligious comprehensive doctrines as well. This proviso is historically indexed, however, in that Lincoln's introduction of religious language into his speeches may have met the demands of public reason in his day, when religious pluralism was not recognized to include those with no faith at all (*PL* li–liii, 243–245, 254; cf. *CP* 280, 462, 586–587, 595, 601–613).

As before, much of Rawls's later thoughts on religion are implicit in *TJ*. Religious intolerance would never be chosen behind a veil of ignorance. However, an "omnicompetent laicist state" would also be rejected. Neither having religious beliefs nor conversion (a theme that goes back to *BIMSF*) nor apostasy should be seen as crimes. In *TJ* Rawls is neither skeptical toward nor indifferent regarding religion in that, although the right is prior to the good, the good is nonetheless a necessary feature of the moral life, in general, and a just society, in particular. Parties behind the veil of ignorance know that they will have *some* interests that concern religion, but which ones? That is, the priority of the right to the good does not mean that political values necessarily outweigh transcendent ones. Indeed, the importance of religious beliefs, including their role in constituting personal identity, plays a key role in the argument for the priority of liberty. However, strength of religious conviction does not trump justice (*TJ* 17, 181, 186, 188, 288; cf. *PL* 31–32, 109; *JF*, 23, 37; *CP* 17, 87, 91–92, 372, 405).

Further, it should be noted that Rawls's difference principle shows a noticeable similarity to the preferential option for the poor found in various religious traditions. Rather than a "trickle down" approach, he defends a "suffuse upwards" approach wherein a key feature of a just society is to make sure that everyone's basic needs are met and that any inegalitarian distribution of wealth be to everyone's advantage, especially to those who are least advantaged. This helps us to understand how Rawls could respond to certain religious ethicists who might be bothered by what appears to be the secondary place of love in Rawls's philosophy. The mutually disinterested agents of construction found in the original position *when constrained by* the veil of ignorance produce a conception of justice that is very close to what would result if a just society were planned by purely loving agents (*TJ* 57–73, 128–129, 167–168, 205).

Rawls defends the right of conscientious refusal, which is typically based on religious reasons, as in Christian pacifist opposition to conscription. But this defense is based on political rather than religious reasons. Likewise, the principles of justice, in general, should be freestanding, not in the sense that they could exist alone apart from any additional philosophical or metaphysical support, but in the sense that the principles of justice can be inserted into or embedded in several different comprehensive doctrines so long as they are reasonable. Religious belief need not be irrational or unreasonable, even if some versions of religious dominant ends are indeed mad (*TJ* 323–324, 331, 338, 398, 485–486, 492; cf. *PL* 374–375, 393; *JF* 151; *CP* 388).

These considerations regarding religion *in* society obtain as well in international justice *among* societies. Here Rawls makes some concessions to societies that are "decent" (in the sense that they do not commit grave human rights violations and they are nonaggressive), but who have a "consultation hierarchy" that is dominated by one religion, as in the mythical Kazanistan described in *LP*. Although such societies only dimly approximate justice, the fact that they are decent requires us to try, as far as possible, to bring them into the law of peoples. One wants to ensure that they, and thus their religious traditions, may develop in their own way and in their own terms, provided basic human rights and relations of international right are secure. There is no a priori reason to think that our history from the late Middle Ages to the present will necessarily be their history. Further, when international law breaks down Rawls defends a theory of just war that has several similarities to the traditional Catholic view, but without any appeal to the dominance of one comprehensive doctrine (*LP* 16, 21–22, 65, 69, 74–78, 103–105, 126; cf. *CP* 537, 547).

Although "religion" does not even appear in the Index to *TJ*, it is a theme that runs throughout his writings from beginning to end. Rawls was concerned about the survival and flourishing of constitutional democracy in countries where the majority of people claim in some fashion to be religious. He vigorously denied that his political philosophy was a veiled argument for either religion or for secularism. In fact, he defends Tocqueville's idea that religion flourishes in the United States *precisely because* of the separation of church and state. Both religion and democracy were on the way, in his estimation, in the effort to bring about a common good of common goods in that religions that once rejected toleration of reasonable differences as a virtue can come to accept it as such (*CP* 616–622; cf. 235, 256, 446, 582, 593–594; *JF* 198).

Daniel Dombrowski

SEE ALSO:

> *Aquinas, Thomas*
> *Catholicism*
> *Comprehensive doctrine*
> *Decent society*
> *Difference principle*
> *Liberty of conscience*
> *Political conception of justice*
> *Public reason*
> *Reasonable pluralism*

186.

RESPECT FOR PERSONS

ACCORDING TO RAWLS, "respect for persons...a recognition of their inherent worth and dignity...is manifest in the content [and ranking] of the principles to which we appeal" (*TJ* 513; cf. *TJ* 155, 158, 469–470, 477–478; *PL* 318–319). Citizens' civility also encompasses respect: "respect for persons is shown by treating them in ways that they can see to be justified" (*TJ* 513; cf. 297, 455). So does citizens' mutual reasonableness: "men [who] have a sense of justice...therefore respect one another" (*TJ* 513).

The *importance* of these expressions of respect lies downstream, Rawls suggests, from the "fundamental importance of self-respect" (*PL* 318). Self-respect is "perhaps the most important primary good" (*TJ* 386; *PL* 318–319), and "our self-respect...depends in part upon the respect shown to us by others" (*CP* 171; cf. *TJ* 155–156, 297, 477). This merely instrumental justification for respect for persons is unusual, but consistent with Rawls's constructivism. "The theory of justice provides a rendering of [ideas about Kantian respect and human dignity] but we cannot start out from them" (*TJ* 513).

Rawls calls this approach to respect Kantian (*CP* 171; *TJ* 225), but is it? Many commentators believe that what Rawls calls "self-respect" is actually self-esteem and so would require public principles that embody esteem, not Kantian respect. If respect should remain consonant with the worths of citizens' activities and accomplishments, then beyond a basic threshold of equality, it should be unequal – since these worths are clearly unequal (*TJ* 289). Indeed, demanding respect as a basis for others' self-respect recalls Hegel's, Mead's, Winnicot's, and Kohut's writing on the human need for recognition more than Kant's warnings that dignity commands awe and respect whether or not people need respect. Finally, what Rawlsian societies affirm is the worths of all citizens, not all persons.

723

Rawls mentions an additional way in which honoring principles elected in the original position forms a "substantive" and "visible" expression of Kantian respect for persons. "Treating persons always as ends and never as means only signifies at the very least dealing with them as required by those principles to which they would consent in an original position of equality. For in this situation men have equal representation as moral persons who regard themselves as ends" (*CP* 167–168; cf. *PL* 29ff.). In this formulation, respect for persons is not only a way to meet representatives' pleas for social bases of self-respect. It is what lends their pleas authority. It is why justice is constructed by choices behind a veil of ignorance. From that perspective, Rawls's theory does start out from a typical Kantian notion of equal respect.

Nir Eyal

SEE ALSO:

Basic liberties
Duty of civility
Kantian interpretation
Moral person
Reciprocity
Self-respect

187.

RIGHT: CONCEPT OF, AND FORMAL CONSTRAINTS OF

THE CONCEPT OF right is one of the three main concepts of practical reasoning; the other two are the concepts of value (the good) and moral worth (*TJ* 94). Contrary to teleological theories of justice, Rawls rejects that the concept of right can be defined in terms of any of the other two main concepts of practical reasoning. Instead Rawls follows the contractualist tradition and argues that the concept of right should be understood in terms of what appropriately situated and motivated parties would agree to. On this contractualist understanding of the concept of right, we can identify the best conception of right for a given subject by asking what principles would be agreed to by all parties in an appropriately defined initial situation (*CP* 59, 63, 222–223; *TJ* 95).

The concept of right divides according to the various domains of agency that are subjects of right, so that we can talk about the concept of right for individuals, for social systems and institutions, and for the law of nations. A special and fundamental subject of right is the basic structure of society. The concept of right for this special case is the concept of justice, the norm of proper balance between competing claims to the benefits and burdens of social cooperation. Utilitarians favor one set of principles for deciding how the competing claims to the benefits and burdens of social cooperation should be negotiated, libertarians another, perfectionists a third. Rawls argues that the principles of justice as fairness provide a superior interpretation.

The original position is Rawls's interpretation of what the appropriate initial situation is for the case of the basic structure of society, that is, for choosing the basic principles of justice. Since the choice of principles of justice that takes place in the original position is an interpretation of the concept of right for the basic structure, the choice of principles takes place within the formal constraints of the concept of right. These constraints are not a matter of semantics, but are elicited from the role that the principles of justice are to play – they spell out the basic conditions that principles of justice must satisfy to play their role of defining the rules for a fair distribution of the competing claims to the benefits and burdens of social cooperation.

Rawls identifies five distinct formal constraints of the concept of right, five conditions that candidate conceptions of justice must satisfy (*TJ* §23; *CP* 291–295; *JF* 85–87): generality, universality, order, finality, and publicity. First, the principles should be general, which entails that it must be possible to state them without the use of proper names, definite descriptions, or similar. Second, the principles should be universal in application, meaning that they must hold for all persons simply by virtue of their moral personality and that it must be possible for all moral persons to act on them. Third, the principles must order conflicting claims, so that they provide a principled basis for adjudicating the various claims that might arise. Fourth, the principles must be the final court of appeal when negotiating competing claims; when these principles have decided a matter, no other principles or arbitrary provisos can affect the order of competing claims: "reasoning successfully from these principles is conclusive" (*TJ* 116). Fifth, the principles must be publicly recognizable as first principles of justice, that is, it must be possible for all members to willingly accept and act upon them as if they were the outcome of a public agreement between them. All five conditions taken together provide a set of minimal requirements for conceptions of justice. Rawls summarizes the idea thus: "Taken together ... these conditions on conceptions of right come to this: a conception of right is a set of principles, general in form and universal in application, that is to be publicly recognized as a final court of appeal for ordering the conflicting claims of moral persons" (*TJ* 117).

The choice of principles that results from the original position is determined by the interests of the parties, the knowledge of the parties, and the list of principles of justice that the parties can choose from. Though Rawls indicates that the formal constraints of the concept of right primarily serve as conditions on the list of principles that the parties can choose from (*TJ* 112), a closer look reveals that the formal constraints also inform the reasoning of the parties.

The formal constraints of the concept of right bar varieties of egoism from appearing on the list of candidate conceptions of justice considered by the parties in the original position. Rawls generally distinguishes between three kinds of egoism (*TJ* 107): first-person dictatorship (all should serve my interest), free-rider egoism (everyone but I should act justly), and general egoism (everyone should advance his interests as he pleases). First-person dictatorship and free-rider egoism both fail by the generality condition. General egoism satisfies the generality condition, but fails by the ordering condition, since it rules out an impartial ranking of competing claims (*TJ* 117). Accordingly, no version of egoism is on the list of candidate conceptions of justice. This way of excluding egoism is Rawls's way of showing what is intuitively accepted already, namely that the "significance of egoism is not as an alternative conception of right but as a challenge to any such conception" (*TJ* 117).

The formal constraints of the concept of right also influence the deliberation of the parties once the list is settled. This influence is illustrated by the role of the publicity condition when the parties consider the comparative merits of justice as fairness and utilitarianism (e.g. *TJ* 154–159; *CP* 324–327; *JF* 120–122). Utilitarianism has a comparatively hard time satisfying the publicity condition and this counts as a reason against it, in part, because utilitarianism thereby has a hard time achieving the ideal of stability for the right reasons, in part, because the members of society won't achieve full autonomy if it is not transparent what principles of justice they are regulated by and why.

Jeppe von Platz

SEE ALSO:

Egoism
Justice, concept of
The original position
Perfectionism
Publicity
Utilitarianism

188.

RIGHTS, CONSTITUTIONAL

CONSTITUTIONAL RIGHTS COMPRISE a subset of legal rights. A right is a kind of guaranteed or warranted claim, attributed to a person or persons, respecting the conduct of others. The attribution is of a legal right if and insofar as a warrant for it is found in law. Where the warrant lodges in a publicly identifiable body of "higher" or "supreme" law, written or unwritten but in either case binding on everyday lawmakers and unalterable by everyday legislative procedures, it is a constitutional right.

Constitutional rights are required by Rawls's account of the possibility of the legitimacy of the force of law in a democratic state. Rawls holds that citizens can sometimes justifiably submit themselves and others to the coercion of laws they make democratically, but only subject to the condition that those laws can be seen to conform to the terms of "a constitution the essentials of which all [reasonable and rational] citizens may reasonably be expected to endorse" (*PL* 217). But since, by Rawls's argument, a constitution can normally meet that condition only by including – along with provisions for a determinate, democratic structure of government – a roster of "equal basic rights and liberties of citizenship that legislative majorities are to respect" (*PL* 227), it can be seen that a society cannot be well-ordered by Rawlsian standards unless constitutional rights compose a salient part of its political and legal practice.

In keeping with the list of "basic" liberties proclaimed by the first principle of justice as fairness (*PL* 291), the essential guarantees of a liberally legitimate constitutional-legal regime will include at least "the right to vote and to participate in politics, liberty of conscience, freedom of thought and association, and the protections of the rule of law" (*PL* 227), along with "the freedoms specified by the liberty and integrity of the person" (*PL* 291), apparently including occupational freedom (*PL* 308, 335) and control over "personal" property (*PL* 298). The first principle's specification of equal rights to a scheme of equal basic liberties furthermore apparently implies some form of anti-discrimination guarantee (short of a full-fledged guarantee of materially fair equality of opportunity) as a constitutional essential (*PL* 228).

Rawls issues no blanket proscription against constitutional rights additional to what those categories cover, but his argument does entail certain reservations against excess constitutionalization of rights. One sort of reservation arises from the need for relatively high transparency ("publicity") in constitutional law. Rawls argues that citizens who, in conditions of reasonable pluralism (and beset by burdens of judgment), cannot reasonably demand each other's outright concessions on disputed matters of the justice of concrete legislation (regarding, say, abortion or gay marriage), may nevertheless be justified in demanding each others' compliance with the political outcomes of visibly evident exercises, by citizens and officials, of public reason geared to the fulfillment of a relatively abstractly stated set of "essential" constitutional guarantees (*PL* 136–137, 216–217; *JF* 27–28). But then the population of constitutional guarantees must be kept thin enough that seemingly intractable conflicts among the members do not too often arise (*PL* 296–297). Along the same lines, constitutionalization should be restricted to those requirements of justice whose satisfaction (or not) "is more or less visible on the face of constitutional arrangements and how these can be seen to work in practice" (*PL* 229). Partly for this reason, and partly for what he sees as reasons of comparative urgency in the project of assuring a minimum of state legitimacy, Rawls quite controversially proposes to restrict the constitutional essentials (and correspondingly, it would seem, the constitutional rights) mainly to the basic liberties of the first principle, thus excluding fair equality of opportunity along with much of the rest of what is covered by the second principle. Those latter matters, Rawls says, are too wide open to intractable, reasonable disagreement to work well as a public measure of state legitimacy (*PL* 228–230). The exclusion appears to be subject to an exception for a constitutional guarantee of the fulfillment at all times of each person's "basic" material needs (*PL* 166, 228).

A second class of limits on excess constitutionalization arises from the first principle's demand, not for relentless pursuit of any one of the basic liberties taken apart from the others, but rather for commitment to a "scheme" of basic liberties (*PL* 291), aimed (as a whole) at equal assurance to each person of conditions conducive to the full and adequate development and exercise of the moral powers of the reasonable and the rational (*PL* 293, 334–335). Thus the first principle, while prohibiting trade-offs of basic liberties against any other social goals (*PL* 294–295), not only permits but positively requires legislative trimming of the scopes of the several basic liberties inevitably colliding in the course of social life, always in the pursuit of the scheme's full and equal adequacy for all. The exact scopes of the liberties named in the list must always be subject to continuing mutual adjustment by legislation, in the light of unfolding social conditions and experience, in the pursuit of that aim (*PL* 283, 298, 333, 338).

Two further consequences ensue, of possible interest to constitutional lawyers. First, Rawlsian constitutional rights are not rigid or "absolute," but rather are qualifiedly subject to legislative demarcation and modulation as described above (*PL* 295, 341). The Rawlsian test – adjustment as reasonably found to be required by the precept of the equal adequacy of the full scheme with regard to everyone's development and exercise of the moral powers – may be understood, then, as a specification of what comparative constitutional law studies know as the rule of "proportionality" as a limit on permissible legislative tinkering with constitutional rights. As a second consequence, it seems that Rawlsian constitutional rights cannot be restricted to so-called "vertical" cases in which the immediate perpetrators of alleged violations are state executive or administrative officials, but must extend to "horizontal" cases in which nonstate parties invoke the state's ordinary laws in defense of acts or demands that arguably infringe on basic liberties of others. Rawlsian justice would require that any ordinary laws on which any party thus relies must be subject to inspection for compliance with the Rawlsian proportionality test.

Frank I. Michelman

SEE ALSO:

> *Basic liberties*
> *Basic needs, principle of*
> *Constitution and constitutional essentials*
> *The four-stage sequence*
> *Freedom*
> *Legitimacy*
> *Public reason*
> *Rights, moral and legal*
> *Supreme Court and judicial review*

189.

RIGHTS, MORAL AND LEGAL

S OMEWHAT SURPRISINGLY, THERE is no index entry under "rights" in either *A Theory of Justice* or *Political Liberalism*. Part of the explanation is that many of the rights Rawls is committed to defending – including those to which he assigns a certain priority as "basic" rights – are often referred to simply as "liberties" (for which there are rather elaborate index entries). Consequently, his views about rights are often expressed obliquely, typically through the accounts he gives of the practical implications (for the shaping of institutions and practices) of the principles of "justice as fairness." Thus, most of the rights he regards as "basic" are identified and described when he itemizes the liberties protected by the equal liberty principle. "The basic liberties of citizens are, roughly speaking, political liberty (the right to vote and to be eligible for public office) together with freedom of speech and assembly; liberty of conscience and freedom of thought; freedom of the person along with the right to hold (personal) property; and freedom from arbitrary arrest and seizure as defined by the concept of the rule of law" (*TJ* 61). Other rights are linked to the opportunities secured under the auspices of the fair equality of opportunity principle, including (notably) rights to equality of educational and occupational opportunity. "(F)air equality of opportunity means a certain set of institutions that assures similar chances of education and culture for persons similarly motivated and keeps positions and offices open to all on the basis of qualities and efforts reasonably related to the relevant duties and tasks" (*TJ* 278, 83–90). Yet other rights are "covered" by the difference principle: individuals in a just society have rights to fair shares of the "social and economic advantages" secured and distributed under the auspices of this principle. "The intuitive idea is that the social order is not to establish and secure the more attractive prospects of those better off unless doing so is to the advantage of those less fortunate" (*TJ* 75, 75–78).

Perhaps because there is no concentrated attention to the notion of rights in his writings – and because, consequently, he nowhere offers a systematic account of the rights for which he thinks a justification can be mounted – Rawls doesn't invoke the distinction, which is familiar in many ordinary nonphilosophical contexts, between normatively neutral and expressly normative uses of the term "right." However, he seems always to use it in its expressly normative sense: he assumes that to say that someone has a right is to be committed to regarding it as defensible or justified other things being equal. It's always *moral* justification of a certain kind that Rawls has in mind, so it's safe to assume that the rights to which he gives recognition are always regarded as *moral* rights. Specifically "legal" rights are simply a subclass of moral rights – those moral rights for which legal protection and enforcement would be appropriate. (By contrast, when the term "right" is used in a normatively neutral way – which seems *not* to be one of the uses to which Rawls resorts – "legal rights" might have to be distinguished sharply from "moral rights" because questions about their existence are merely empirical questions about the laws that happen to be in force in particular jurisdictions, questions that can be answered without so much as asking whether the laws are morally defensible.)

As to what justifies statements about the existence of moral rights, it's clear that Rawls does not regard them as "self-vindicating" – as they would presumably have to be if they were thought to be "foundational" to a system of moral norms (a system of justice, for example). Rather, statements about rights are justified only if compelling reasons can be given in their support. The reasons, for Rawls, are of two kinds. The proximate reasons are institutional rules conferring the rights in question on identifiable individuals in given circumstances. However, since institutional rules must themselves be justified if they are to supply part of the basis for statements about the rights individuals have, the more fundamental reasons are provided by the principles that furnish the normative underpinning for defensible institutional rules. (I here make the simplifying assumption that rights are ascribable to individuals – ignoring questions about what Rawls might hold about the rights of groups, associations, corporations, or organizations.)

For a broad range of the rights the individuals of a given society might be said to have, Rawls claims that the institutional rules in which they are grounded must belong to the society's "basic structure" and the basic structure must satisfy, in turn, fundamental principles of justice. The members of a society have, for example, a right to freedom of speech because and so far as the rules that give content and shape to a society's most important institutions (those that constitute its "basic structure") include rules that protect this right *and* because these rules can be regarded as just.

The assumption that individual rights can only be shown to be defensible if they are derivable from the rules that give shape to a society's "basic structure" is itself in need both of clarification and of defense.

Clarification is needed because it has been maintained by some interpreters of Rawls that there is an unresolved ambiguity in his doctrine of the "basic structure." Sometimes, it is described as comprising only those institutional rules that are "legally coercive." "[T]he law defines the basic structure within which the pursuit of all other activities takes place" (*TJ* 236). This would imply that the only institutions that can be the source of individual rights are *legal* institutions and consequently that it is only *legal* rules (rules that are protected and enforced by the coercive machinery of a society's legal system) that can confer rights on individuals. On this view, the only rights individuals would have are legal rights – legal rights being understood, of course (as noted earlier), not as rights conferred by the laws that happen to exist in this or that jurisdiction regardless of whether the laws in question are just or unjust, but rather as the rights that would be secured for the members of a society by the enactment of *just* laws. On the other hand, a society's "basic structure" is sometimes understood by Rawls more broadly, as comprising all those institutions that have a fundamental impact on the lives lived by the members of a society. "The primary subject of justice . . . is the basic structure of society. The reason for this is that its effects are so profound and pervasive, and present from birth" (*TJ* 96). On this view, many institutional rules in the economic and political domains as well as many rules governing educational, cultural, and religious institutions qualify for inclusion in a society's "basic structure" and thus count, alongside legal rules, as furnishing part of the basis for statements about the rights of individual members.

Rawls's assumption that institutional rules of some sort (albeit rules that satisfy principles of justice) are crucial to the interpretation and defense of statements about the rights of individuals also stands in need of justification. Is it really the case, as G. A. Cohen has asked in his critique of the Rawlsian doctrine of "the basic structure as subject," that individuals can be seen, justifiably, to have a particular right *only* when there is some institutional rule under which the right is subsumable? Couldn't principles of justice be invoked *directly* in defense of certain statements about the rights of individuals, and thus *without* the mediation of institutional rules? Cohen thinks the answer to this question ought to be "yes," whether the "basic structure" is conceived (narrowly) as the "legally coercive" structure or (more permissively) as comprising all those institutions (legal and nonlegal) that have a pervasive impact on the lives of the members of society (Cohen 2000, chapter 8; and Cohen 2008, chapter 1).

Precisely because Rawls seems not to accept G. A. Cohen's view that principles of justice can have a direct application to the personal choices individuals make in certain situations, the justification for the rights that are defensibly ascribable to individuals is for Rawls a two-stage justification: the rights in question must have their source in institutional rules belonging to the society's basic structure and it must be possible to show that the basic structure is just.

There is a structural similarity, consequently, between the Rawlsian view of what justifies rights and the view favored by rule-utilitarians. Like Rawls, rule-utilitarians do not think that the rights defensibly ascribable to individuals can be foundational to a system of moral norms, and they agree too that it is defensible institutional rules that are the proximate source of individual rights, in that these rules are needed to specify the content of the rights in question and the circumstances in which they can be exercised. However, a different account is given of the (supra-institutional) moral principle that defensible right-conferring rules must satisfy. Instead of holding, with Rawls, that the rules must be subsumable under principles of justice, rule-utilitarians claim that it is (some version of) the principle of utility-maximization that supplies the ultimate ground of justified right-conferring rules.

It's because of this difference between their respective accounts of the structure of the arguments that have to be constructed in support of statements about the existence and content of the rights of individuals that Rawls is able to argue, in presenting his case against utilitarianism, that a merely utilitarian argument for the existence of rights provides an insufficiently secure basis for the stringency of moral rights. The right to freedom of expression, for example, is unacceptably vulnerable if its existence is contingent on the rules that confer the right being rules that happen to maximize social utility.

The rationale for the principles that determine the justice of institutional arrangements undergoes a significant change when, in *PL*, Rawls embraces an explicitly "political" conception of justice, thereby abandoning the "comprehensive" conception he defended in *TJ*. This shift generated some important changes in the view Rawls took of rival strategies for the justification of principles of justice, in that he was now prepared to allow for a good deal of disagreement about the ultimate moral or metaphysical or religious grounds on which defenders of rival justificatory strategies might endorse principles of justice. It was no longer necessary to try to determine the defensibility of these argumentative strategies.

It was necessary only for the strategies to be "reasonable" (*PL* 59–60). Moreover, Rawls's insistence that the sponsors of divergent "reasonable" strategies are nevertheless – remarkably, it might be thought – parties to a "consensus" about the *content* of principles of justice, makes it possible for him to claim that the very same principles he had articulated in *TJ* as principles of "justice as fairness" can now be represented as the principles constitutive of a "political" conception of justice. Since what Rawls has to say about the rights of individuals is a function of the justice of the institutional rules from which these rights are derivable – and since the shift, from the *TJ* account of justice to the *PL* view, involved a shift in the ultimate rationale for principles of justice without any modification of the content of the principles – the structure of the argument needed to justify individual rights remains broadly the same. Not only are the rights individuals can claim still rights conferred by the rules that govern the operation of social institutions of various kinds, but the rights in question can only be *justifiably* claimed if the institutional rules that are their proximate source themselves satisfy principles of justice.

A more dramatic shift in the content of an important part of Rawls's doctrine of rights occurred, however, when, in his last book, *The Law of Peoples*, he took up questions about human rights. In *LP*, Rawls rejects the view that liberal principles of justice – those embedded in his doctrine of "justice as fairness" – are needed for the justification of human rights. Liberal principles of justice are too demanding for many of the societies (or "peoples") whose peaceful coexistence a "Law of Peoples" is designed to facilitate. They are too demanding simply because membership on an equal basis in a "society of well-ordered peoples" – which is the sort of international society in which peaceful coexistence can reasonably be expected – cannot be made conditional on acceptance of *liberal* principles of justice: not all the peoples in a "society of well-ordered peoples" can be expected to be liberal societies. The nonliberal societies to whom full membership rights should be accorded under a suitably accommodating "Law of Peoples" are (what Rawls dubs) "decent" peoples, and decent peoples have institutional arrangements that satisfy a "common good" – rather than a "liberal" – conception of justice. While Rawls offers only a skeletal account of how precisely a "common good" approach is to be conceived, one of its distinguishing features is its sponsorship of a shorter list of human rights than might be defended by appeal to a "liberal" conception of justice. Since in *LP* Rawls also wants a people's right to nonintervention by other peoples to be conditional on its record of respect for the human rights of its members, the doctrine of human rights he embraces has to be consistent both with the "liberal" conception of justice favored by liberal societies and with the "common good" conception of justice favored by "decent" societies. This means that Rawls's doctrine of human rights in *LP* is a much narrower doctrine than he might have been expected to champion as a defender of liberal principles of justice. Among the important "liberal" rights that do not qualify as "human rights," consequently, are such rights as the right to (full) liberty of conscience and the right to participate on an equal basis in collective decision-making processes (*LP* 65, 78–81; Martin and Reidy 2006, part III).

Alistair Macleod

SEE ALSO:

Basic liberties
Basic structure of society
Civil disobedience
Cohen, G. A.
Decent societies
Human rights
Political conception of justice
The reasonable and the rational
Rights, constitutional

190.

RORTY, RICHARD

RICHARD RORTY (1931–2007) was an American philosopher and public intellectual. After earning a Ph.D. in philosophy from Yale University in 1956, Rorty secured professorships at Wellesley College and Princeton University. He spent twenty years in Princeton's Philosophy Department, and then took up the Kenan Professor of Humanities at the University of Virginia in 1982. In 1997, he moved to Stanford University's Comparative Literature department.

Rorty's earliest work is focused on standard topics in analytic philosophy, including meaning, reference, intentionality, and materialism. He was an early defender of a broadly Quinean naturalism and a Sellarsian eliminativism in the philosophy of mind. By the 1970s, however, Rorty's interests began to expand and he drew inspiration from Martin Heidegger, the later Wittgenstein, Jacques Derrida, and especially John Dewey. These shifts resulted in Rorty's highly influential 1979 book, *Philosophy and the Mirror of Nature*. Calling his view pragmatism, Rorty argues for a radical version of anti-foundationalism according to which all of the traditional aims of philosophy – including truth, rationality, knowledge, objectivity, and the accurate representation of reality – are rendered disposable. In place of these philosophical objectives, Rorty offers the pragmatized ideals of solidarity, empathy, shared hopes, unforced agreement, and social progress along social democratic lines. Rejecting the very idea of a philosophical foundation for these aims, Rorty unabashedly embraces "ethnocentrism." In fact, he endorses what he calls "ironism," claiming that it is the mark of a civilized person to be willing to stand unflinchingly for these ideals even after he or she realizes that they lack any philosophical grounding whatsoever.

Hence the radical nature of Rorty's anti-foundationalism comes to the fore. He does not deny that our practices *lack* the philosophical foundations that they should have; rather, he contends that the very idea of such foundations is to be dispensed with. In this, Rorty shares with his pragmatist predecessor John Dewey the metaphilosophical project of rejecting rather than trying to solve traditional philosophical problems. According to Rorty, philosophy is not a distinctive discipline with its own subject-matter, but rather a distinctive way of talking and writing.

In political philosophy, Rorty sees his ironic liberalism as allied with John Rawls's political liberalism. In his "The Priority of Democracy to Philosophy" (1991), Rorty reads Rawls's "political not metaphysical" version of justice as fairness as embracing anti-foundationalism. Rorty concedes that communitarian critics of liberalism (such as Michael Sandel and Charles Taylor) are correct to affirm a social and encumbered conception of the self, but he denies (and reads Rawls as denying) that liberalism needs to affirm any conception of the self at all. In Rorty's view, properly conceived liberalism is always "political not metaphysical" in that it denies that liberal democratic politics requires philosophical grounding of any kind. Indeed, Rorty contends that the dependence runs in the other direction – as liberal democrats, we should adopt a philosophy that suits our politics.

Robert B. Talisse

SEE ALSO:

Communitarianism
Democracy
Dewey, John
Political liberalism, justice as fairness as
Truth

191.

ROSS, W. D.

RAWLS TOOK VERY seriously the views of W. D. Ross (1877–1971), as representing two of the main traditions in moral and political philosophy that he sought to unsettle.

Pluralistic intuitionism is the normative view that there is a plurality of basic and conflicting values or principles that have to be weighed against one another on the basis of intuition to determine how we ought to act – Ross, for example, proposes seven prima facie duties that pick out features of acts that count for or against them but he also claims that there are no further principles, only bare intuitions, to help us decide what our duty is all things considered. Rawls regarded this view as the default position in moral and political theory because it captures core features of commonsense moral reasoning without oversimplifying the moral facts, so we ought to admit "the possibility that there is no way to get beyond a plurality of principles" (*TJ* 36). Yet he thinks that pluralistic intuitionism is "but half a conception" because "assignment of weights is an essential and not a minor part" of a moral and political theory (*TJ* 37). In addition to the philosophical drive for greater unity, Rawls thinks that a conception of justice is supposed to serve a social role in diminishing reasonable normative disagreement (*TJ* 79; *CP* 344). For example, the priority among different criteria of excellences is likely to be "unsettled and idiosyncratic" (*TJ* 290), the idea of a social minimum raises the question of how it is to be chosen given the many relevant reasons at stake (*TJ* 279); a conception of justice that seeks to promote well-being, liberty, and equality must address how they are to be weighed against one another (*CP* 348); and moral reasons about giving mutual aid and keeping promises must be reconciled (*TJ* 301). Although Rawls thinks normative theory cannot avoid appeals to intuitions, he claims that we should strive for greater structure, a task which Rawls takes up by arguing, for example, that justice takes absolute priority over efficiency and the liberty principle is lexically prior to the distributive one.

Ross also endorsed rational intuitionism, which is the meta-ethical view that there is an independent moral order that we know by intuition and that our beliefs about it in turn motivate us to act in virtue of our psychological nature as rational agents. Rawls contrasts this meta-ethical view with what he called "Kantian constructivism," which he distinguished both from Kant's own moral constructivism and from what he later calls "political constructivism." Kantian constructivism is the view that certain moral and political principles are reasonable because they are the result of a procedure of construction that emphasizes practical rather than theoretical reasoning and relies on a more robust conception of the person that is more closely connected with "human beings' needs, aims, and purposes" (*LHMP* 80; "Kantian Constructivism in Moral Theory" in *CP*). If justice as fairness is presented as part of Kantian constructivism, then it denies the rational intuitionist meta-ethical view Ross endorsed. But if justice as fairness is cast as a standalone political (not metaphysical) constructivism, which does not deny the truth of any meta-ethical view, then a rational intuitionist can join a reasonable overlapping consensus of reasonable comprehensive doctrines (*PL* 95).

There are other aspects of Ross's work that Rawls engaged with. He rejected Ross's claim, for example, that justice involves distributing happiness in accordance with merit (*TJ* 273; *CP* 24); he drew on Ross in formulating his conception of goodness as rationality (*TJ* 351), and he used Ross's objections to utilitarianism as examples of failing to distinguish between the justification of a practice and the justification of the actions falling under it (*CP* 29).

Adam Cureton

SEE ALSO:

> *Constructivism: Kantian/political*
> *Desert*
> *Goodness as rationality*
> *Intuitionism*
> *Precepts of justice*
> *Rational intuitionism*
> *Social minimum*
> *Utilitarianism*

192.

ROUSSEAU, JEAN-JACQUES

JEAN-JACQUES ROUSSEAU (1712–1778) occupies a prominent place in the *Lectures on the History of Political Philosophy*. Rawls there often refers to his own thought and to the ways in which it was shaped by his engagement with Rousseau. Indeed, the influence of Rousseau on Rawls is extensive and yet for the most part unappreciated by historians of political thought. There are two important and related ways in which Rawls's theory can be thought of as Rousseauian: (1) like Rousseau, Rawls believes that persons have a natural psychological need for recognition and for self-respect, that the denial of the former negates the possibility of the latter, and that these psychological needs are most effectively satisfied by egalitarian political institutions. And (2) like Rousseau, Rawls thinks that even the best-designed set of institutions must be supplemented by civic virtue; not the immersive patriotic virtue of the ancients, of course, but a modern, pluralism-compatible kind of virtue, the kind of virtue that conscientiously privileges the common good of the political community over the inevitable and ineradicable factional interests present within it.

(1) While Rawls is no doubt primarily concerned with matters of institutional design, justice as fairness is *also* importantly psychological. Like Rousseau, Rawls emphasizes the fundamental human proclivity to compare and he regards this psychological tendency as a fundamental consideration for justice (*TJ* §81). Human beings are fundamentally social creatures, desirous of the respect and recognition of their fellows; the *lack* of recognition – and the envy, resentment, and shame aroused by it – is both psychologically painful and destructive of mutually advantageous cooperation. "The individual who envies another,"

for example, "is prepared to do things that make them both worse off, if only the discrepancy between them is sufficiently reduced" (*TJ* 466). And so it is with the spite of society's advantaged members: "The spiteful man is willing to give up something to maintain the distance between himself and others" (*TJ* 468).

Rousseau and Rawls both trace the source of these destructive sentiments to inequalities of political status: perverse, anti-social forms of self-love are activated, and exacerbated, by institutional relations of hierarchy, domination, and exploitation (*TJ* 469). But Rousseau and Rawls are also united in the belief that the *cure* for destructive self-love is institutional. *This* is the heart of Rousseau's essential and enduring contribution to political theory: his view that in order to prevent the emergence of destructive psychological sentiments – and, conversely, to cultivate those salutary psychological dispositions conducive to mutually advantageous cooperation – our political institutions must treat us as equals at the highest level, i.e. at the level of citizenship (*TJ* 469, 477; *PL* 318; *LHPP* 234, 247–248). *To be a citizen is to be secure about one's place in society.* Hence Rousseau's advice to the Corsicans: "The fundamental law of your constitution must be equality."

It is in the same spirit that, in the *Social Contract*, Rousseau says, "because the force of things tends to destroy equality...the force of legislation should always tend to maintain it" (2011 [1762], 189). "This remark of Rousseau's," says Rawls in a revealing passage, "is an ancestor of the first reason why, in justice as fairness, the basic structure is taken as the first subject of justice" (*LHPP* 234). In other words, a central aim of the Rawlsian basic structure (following Rousseau) is to cultivate a pervasive spirit of equality despite the inevitable economic inequalities that will be present in any free society. Rawls and Rousseau share the belief that the necessary psychological support for egalitarian institutions exists as a part of our nature – *this* is what it means for man to be *naturally good* – but that part of our nature must be *activated*; it is a latent possibility, the emergence of which is dependent on political circumstance (*TJ* §72; *PL* §§II.8.1, IV.2.2, IV.7.3, V.6.3, VII.5; *LHPP* 199). For both Rousseau and Rawls, then, human nature is characterized, first, by its radical permissiveness but, second, by its compatibility with egalitarian political relations. We are, in other words, *perfectible*.

(2) "Public reason gives a view about voting on fundamental questions reminiscent of Rousseau's *Social Contract*. He saw voting as ideally expressing our opinion as to which of the alternatives best advances the common good" (*PL* 219–220;

cf. Rousseau 2011 [1762], 227–228). This will strike many as a strange remark. Doesn't Rousseau aim for a quasi-Platonic degree of psychic unity among citizens? Aren't debate and deliberation indicative of political decay for him? How can Rousseau be a model for Rawls here? After all, the starting premise of political liberalism is the fact of pluralism – the fact that the free community will be characterized by a radical heterogeneity of comprehensive beliefs. Such a community isn't a community at all, according to a Rousseauian way of thinking; such a community cannot be a home for justice.

Rawls rejects this standard interpretation of Rousseau. If the mark of the modern era is the existence of interests *separate from* the interest of the community – the interests one pursues in bourgeois civil society and in the domain of private religiosity – and if the possibility of a just and lasting political community depends on the institutional recognition of these private interests, then Rousseau *is* a philosopher of the modern era. Indeed, in the *Lectures* Rawls shows that Rousseau's psychology of citizenship is thoroughly modern: that he accepts a permanent but productive tension in the hearts of citizens between self- and the common interest (*LHPP* 218–219). In fact, this uniquely modern emergence of *self*-interest is a cause for celebration for Rousseau: it is precisely the ineluctability of self-interest that makes virtue possible, for one cannot privilege the good of the community over one's private good if the latter does not exist. This psychological tension is precisely what makes virtue – and freedom – possible (Rousseau 2011 [1762], 167, 172–173 n.38).

What Rousseau calls virtue, Rawls calls full autonomy. But the structure of both concepts is the same: full autonomy, says Rawls, is "realized in public life by affirming the political principle of justice . . . [full autonomy is] expressed by acting from the public principles of justice understood as specifying the fair terms of cooperation" (*PL* 77). This helps us to make better sense of the potentially mystifying passage at the beginning of section (2) above. For Rawls, abiding by the constraints of public reason is the essential expression of full autonomy: one has to learn to think and to speak with reference to the common good, not with exclusive reference to the sectarian tenets of one's private belief system. We may, instinctively, want to see our own comprehensive doctrine institutionalized in the basic structure – to the benefit of its holders, and to the detriment of all others – but full autonomy expresses our capacity for self-overcoming, our principled commitment to giving justice to all citizens regardless of the content of their private beliefs or the structure of their chosen ends (*LP* 1.2). *This* is what it means to *will* the general will, and *this* is the most needful thing for political stability in the plural milieu. Rawls learns these lessons from Rousseau.

Jeffrey Bercuson

SEE ALSO:

Autonomy, moral
Moral psychology
Realistic utopia
Reciprocity
Reconciliation
Sense of justice
Social contract

193.

RULE OF LAW

A LEGAL SYSTEM IS a coercively enforced system of public rules addressed to rational persons and aimed at regulating their conduct for the sake of their common good and so providing a framework for their social cooperation (*TJ* 207). At a minimum, the rule of law requires the regular and impartial administration of these rules. For example, like cases must be treated alike. This much is required by the very idea of a legal system as a system of public *rules*. When the "rules" are administered – interpreted and/or applied – in a manner stained by bribery, threats, prejudice, bias, and the like, those subject to them are regulated by something other than public *rules*.

In a sufficiently complex and long-enduring legal system, this minimum requirement of the rule of law, which Rawls dubs "justice as regularity," will constrain the discretion of legal officials in so-called "hard cases" for which there exists no applicable rule antecedently established either by legislation or by past judicial decisions. The reason for this is that, if it is to be decided in a regular and impartial fashion and so as a matter of law, the hard case must be decided in a manner sensitive to, at least consistent with, the framework, the distinctions, reasons, and so on, established by the existing rules. In a sufficiently complex and long-enduring legal system, then, the discretion of legal officials is almost always constrained in this way. This minimal rule of law requirement – no more than the regular and impartial administration of the rules – works to constrain at least a certain kind of injustice, namely that of coercing persons to comply with arbitrary commands rather than public rules (*TJ* 209).

This minimum requirement of the rule of law must be met if persons are to be regulated by something other than particular commands or other ad hoc social forces, the content of which they may or may not be able to anticipate. Without justice as regularity, persons cannot form and govern their conduct in light of stable public expectations. They cannot fix with any real certainty the potential costs and benefits of various courses of conduct. And so they cannot cooperate, at least not in any effective, enduring way. All they can do is guess or hope and react.

Suppose a system of public rules satisfies justice as regularity. Assuming it satisfies other requirements of a system of law, for example, that it is tied to a defined territory within which it subordinates most other systems of public rules, that it is reliably enforced, and so on, it may qualify, albeit perhaps only barely, as a legal system. But as a legal system it may still be imperfect. Of course, it may be imperfect because it is substantively unjust. The public rules, while administered in an impartial and regular fashion and sufficient to regulate the behavior of rational persons, advance their common good and underwrite their cooperation, may nevertheless fail fully to respect the rational persons it regulates as free and equal persons, may fall short of advancing their common good in the best way, or may underwrite cooperation (from which all benefit) but not fair cooperation (from which all fairly benefit). And if the substantive injustice is great enough, we may wonder whether what seemed at first to be a legal system, even if only barely, is in fact perhaps nothing more than a system of particular commands aimed at the good of the agent or agents issuing them.

But a legal system that meets the minimum rule of law requirement, or justice as regularity, may also be imperfect in other ways. It might require or forbid actions that persons could not reasonably be expected to perform or avoid, for example, forbidding actions in the past or requiring impossible actions. It might address itself not to a general population but rather only to particular properly named individuals. It might address itself to a general population but only for very brief periods of time. Or it might address itself to a general population but only in obscure or unclear language. Or it might address itself to a general population in an insufficiently public manner. Or it might fail to provide adequate procedures for the orderly and effective application and enforcement of the rules. In these and other ways it might fail to organize social behavior by providing a rational objective basis for legitimate expectations. A legal system might meet the minimum rule of law requirement, justice as regularity, then, and yet still suffer to some degree from one or more of these defects or imperfections, each of which is of a sort quite different from the sorts of defects or imperfections – for example, failing to respect persons as free equals – that make a legal system substantively unjust.

Reasoning from these various possible defects or imperfections of a legal system (simply as a legal system and apart from the substantive justice of its rules), Rawls identifies a family of familiar "precepts of justice associated with the rule of law," for example, "there is no offense without a law." Taken together these familiar precepts constitute a regulative ideal, the "principle of legality," to which legal systems, simply qua legal systems, properly aspire (*TJ* 207–209). With respect to the rule of law, then, justice as regularity establishes a mandatory minimum and the principle of legality sets an aspirational goal.

It is helpful to set Rawls's views on the rule of law in relation to those of H. L. A. Hart, Philip Soper, and Lon Fuller. Rawls refers to and draws from all three, but he does so only as needed, for his limited purposes, and with an eye toward remaining agnostic on many controversial issues in the philosophy of law. (See, e.g., *TJ* 210; *PL* 109 n.15; *LP* 66–67, 72.) So, for example, Rawls embraces Hart's ideas of justice as regularity and that no legal system is likely to endure for any length of time if it does not secure for at least a substantial portion of the population subject to it what Hart called a minimum necessary natural law content. But Rawls takes no position on Hart's view that, for example, the antebellum United States had a genuine legal system notwithstanding the fact that it was a slave-holding society. With respect to Soper, Rawls expresses sympathy for his view that there is no *prima facie* moral obligation to obey the law in the absence of a good faith effort by legal officials to advance the common good of those subject to the public rules they create, apply, and enforce. But Rawls expresses no view as to whether legal obligations simply as such – as distinct from a moral obligation, whether *prima* or *ultima facie*, to obey the law or to fulfill legal obligations – might survive in the absence of such an effort by legal officials. Finally, from Fuller, Rawls takes the distinction between a mandatory minimum required by the rule of law and an aspirational goal set by the rule of law. But Rawls does not address Fuller's view that because of tensions between some of its elements the aspirational goal can never be fully realized, even under the favorable conditions of ideal theory. To be sure, Rawls does allow that as a matter of nonideal or partial compliance theory, certain compromises to the rule of law ideal may be justified. For example, under nonideal conditions, a strict liability regime may be justified on some matters, notwithstanding the fact that strict liability runs counter to the rule of law precept of ought implies can. It may be justified if the loss of liberty involved in trespassing upon the rule of law precept of ought implies can is outweighed by gains in liberty elsewhere in the overall system of liberty, with special attention paid to those who gain the least liberty by reference to liberty, for given the lexical priority of the first principle, the only consideration that may justify a constraint on liberty is that of liberty itself. The rule of law may not be constrained or compromised for the sake of fair equality of opportunity, the difference principle, economic efficiency, perfectionist values, or corporate goods such as national defense (except in the most extreme cases where the nation's system of equal liberty is itself at risk).

Two final observations merit mention. First: it is often thought that implicit in the idea and/or ideal of the rule of law is a conception of legal reasoning as a distinct and to some significant degree autonomous form of reasoning. This raises, of course, important questions about the relationships between legal and moral reasoning, questions that have vexed philosophers of law for centuries. Rawls does not address these questions directly, but there can be little doubt, from his early paper "Two Concepts of Rules" on, that he would distinguish between legal reasoning and moral reasoning more generally, for the practices or institutions of law and morality are not one and the same, even if they are related in various ways. Of course, this does not mean that legal reasoning has no moral content. Rather, it means that legal reasoning is not simply the application of a more general or universal sort of moral reasoning to a particular context or institution. As with public political reason, which has moral content but is not simply the application of a more general or universal sort of moral reasoning to a particular context or institution, legal reasoning is a kind of moral reasoning without being simply an application of it to a particular subject. Indeed, as Rawls's later work on public reason makes clear, both public political reasoning and legal reasoning are distinct – by virtue of structural constraints tied to their institutional settings and essential publicity – from moral reasoning more generally and certainly moral reasoning as framed by comprehensive moral doctrines.

The second observation that merits mention concerns judicial review as practiced by the Supreme Court in the United States. Some claim that it is not only anti-democratic, because judges not subject to electoral politics assert the power to set aside democratically authorized legislation, but that it also violates the rule of law, since these judges are not themselves subject to legal constraint in the exercise of this power. Constitutionalism and judicial review are matters treated elsewhere in this volume, but it merits mentioning here that Rawls rejects these claims and in particular rejects the idea that judicial review as practiced by the Supreme Court in the United States is an affront to the rule of law. (See, e.g., *PL* 231–240.) Of course, in any given case it may be, as it would be if the Justices were to decide a case in a particular way only after receiving bribes to do so. But there is nothing in the practice itself that necessarily offends against the rule of law.

David A. Reidy

SEE ALSO:

Constitution and constitutional essentials
Formal justice
Hart, H. L. A.
Law, system of
Rights, constitutional
Supreme Court and judicial review

194.

RULES (TWO CONCEPTS OF)

JOHN RAWLS IS usually thought of as a stalwart critic of utilitarianism in all of its forms. It might therefore come as a surprise that Rawls devoted an entire early essay to providing utilitarianism with philosophical ammunition with which to deflect one of the most common objections to that theory, which is that, given certain empirical sets of circumstances, it can require morally quite counterintuitive behavior. As a theory which views the good-making properties of actions as residing solely in their consequences, and which views consequences in a purely aggregative way, utilitarianism can yield prescriptions that are startling in their distributive implications.

Utilitarianisms since John Stuart Mill have responded to this concern by claiming that the theory is best thought of as applying not to individual actions, but rather to rules. "Rule-utilitarianism" would have us focus not on the consequences of each particular instance of a kind of behavior X, but rather on a general practice of X-ing. Many counterintuitive consequences are thought to dissolve if the focus of the theory is changed in this manner. What may be justified in the individual case (lying, deceit, torture, etc.) ceases to be so justified when a general rule recommending this kind of behavior is envisaged.

Rule-utilitarianism has been viewed as inadequate by orthodox utilitarian such as J. J. C. Smart. They have accused rule-utilitarians of being "rule-fetishists," that is, of cleaving to rules even in individual cases in which the agent can plainly see that breaking the rule would best conduce to general utility.

In "Two Concepts of Rules" (1955 in *CP*), Rawls argues that the traditional rule-utilitarian appeal to rules, and the rule-fetishist objection, are premised on a faulty conception of rules, one which he wants to replace with a better alternative. This conception of rules is a "constitutive" rather than a "summary" one. To see the difference between these two construals, consider the two human practices that Rawls discusses in the beginning of his article: punishment and promising. Utilitarian embarrassments with respect to punishment are well known. If utilitarianism is a "forward-looking" theory, one that would justify all actions, including acts of punishment, on the basis of a calculation of the overall benefits that they will produce, there can be no general objection to the punishment of the innocent, if in particular cases it happens to be the case that it maximizes utility. The standard, backward-looking perspective that a theory of punishment such as retributivism instantiates, which looks to facts about the commission by the person being considered for punishment of the action for which punishment is being contemplated, has no place within the utilitarian scheme. The same is true of promising. A common-sense conception of promising would have it that we are obligated to do what we have promised to do in virtue of events in the past, namely whether we have in fact engaged in an act of promising. Pointing to the greater utility of going against one's promise in order to justify promise-breaking violates our intuitive sense of what promising requires, whereas utilitarianism would possibly require it in specific cases. What's more, appeals to "rule-utilitarianism" in either of these cases raises the problem that we have already briefly mooted, that of inviting the objection of rule-fetishism.

The way out of this conundrum is, on Rawls's view, that there are rules that summarize our accumulated wisdom about what it is best to do under specific sets of circumstances, and there are rules that *constitute practices*. Traditional utilitarian theories tend to uncritically support the summary view. Think of John Stuart Mill's idea that the long experience of humankind provides us with rules of thumb about what best conduces to the general welfare. Rules construed in this manner have a number of logical properties, of which the following are most important to understanding the difference with constitutive rules. First, the actions the justification of which is being considered can be specified independently of the rule itself. Second, the rule is eminently revisable, as new data emerge about whether the following of the rule does in fact conduce to the greater good. It is clear why rules construed in this manner fall foul of the rule-fetishism concern. Indeed, if the agent deliberating as to what the morally most justifiable action can "see through" to the consequences of her actions for the criterion that ultimately justifies her actions, why would she bother with rules at all, and in any case, why would she abide by the rule when it is clear that in a particular case the maximization of utility requires that it be violated?

Rules are constitutive when, contrary to what is the case in the summary construal, rules precede cases and when they are authoritative. Consider the institutions of punishment and of promising. A person who decides to punish anyone whose incarceration produces the best results (consider the falsely accused innocent man whose lynching would satisfy an angry mob) is, according to the constitutive conception of rules on offer here, simply not *punishing*. We punish when we do so according to the rules that constitute the practice of punishment (and Rawls assumes for the sake of argument that these have to do with retribution).

What's more, punishment involves not just something that some nebulous collective agent ("we") do. It involves the setting up of institutions which are charged with enforcing the rules. In the same way that referees and umpires are not just random individuals blowing whistles on the basis of some contestable reading of the rules, office-holders within institutional schemes occupy roles within practices that are authoritative. Those who think that there is some office-holder-independent standard on the basis of which actions within the practice can be evaluated are, simply, not engaged in the practice.

Rules construed in this manner allow the rule-utilitarian to defeat the rule-fetishist objection, since the person appealing to a utilitarian meta-rule that purportedly has authority over the rules that govern an area of behavior is simply not engaged in the rule-constituted practice.

Does the constitutive conception save utilitarianism? Arguably not. Consider the dilemma. For specific practices defined by constitutive rules to acquire their justification on utilitarian grounds, it has to be the case that these specific practices maximize utility relative to alternative ones. If that is the case, it is hard to see how, from a utilitarian perspective, the practice can be completely immunized from the concern with rule-fetishism. If, however, the connection with utility-maximization is looser (for example, the claim may simply be that the practice in a given area is preferable to no practice), then the link to utilitarianism is tenuous at best.

Daniel Weinstock

SEE ALSO:

> *Basic structure of society*
> *Games*
> *Mill, John Stuart*
> *Promising*
> *Utilitarianism*
> *Wittgenstein, Ludwig*

S

195.

SANDEL, MICHAEL

MICHAEL SANDEL (b. 1953) is an American political theorist and public intellectual. He earned his Ph.D. from Oxford University in 1981, where he was a Rhodes Scholar. He currently is Anne T. and Robert M. Bass Professor of Government at Harvard University, where he teaches a popular course on Justice that has become the subject of a PBS series, *Justice: What's the Right Thing to Do?*

Sandel focuses on the relationship between ethics and politics, and he is especially concerned with the question of whether a democratic state should aspire to be neutral with respect to moral controversies. Much of his work is critical of prevailing forms of liberalism, which contend that states must be neutral when it comes to controversies concerning the good life. Holding that such neutrality is chimerical and that the aspiration to it is socially perilous, Sandel advocates a communitarian form of civic republicanism according to which political participation and moral engagement with one's fellow citizens is an essential element of a good life. He sees the job of the democratic state to be that of inculcating among its citizens the virtues and attitudes appropriate to citizenship in self-governing communities.

Sandel's first book, *Liberalism and the Limits of Justice* (1982) is an extended criticism of liberalism aimed in particular at John Rawls's *A Theory of Justice*. Along with influential works by Charles Taylor, Alastair MacIntyre, and Michael Walzer, Sandel's book remains a definitive articulation of "the communitarian critique of liberalism." Taking Rawls's original position to capture the core liberal commitment to the priority of the right to the good, Sandel argues that liberalism as such presupposes a conception of the self according to which selves are always prior to, and thus detachable from, the moral ends they affirm. Sandel argues that in fact certain moral ends are *constitutive* of the self and thus not voluntary and not detachable; selves are, he claims, essentially *encumbered* with moral commitments. He contends that as selves are encumbered, there is no foundation for liberalism's distinction between the right and the good, and therefore no basis for liberal neutrality. Consequently, a politics that embraces a conception of the human good is inescapable; the question is which conception of the good our politics will promote.

In subsequent writings – including his *Democracy's Discontent* (1998) – Sandel has taken up the task of developing a civic republican political theory rooted in public virtue, the common good, and citizen moral engagement. In doing so, he has embraced a version of deliberative democracy and has rejected cosmopolitan visions of justice.

Some have held that Sandel's criticism of liberalism partially compelled Rawls's turn toward a *political* liberalism which reformulates justice as fairness as a freestanding conception; however, Rawls denied that Sandel's work had this impact, citing reasons internal to *A Theory of Justice* for the shift to political liberalism.

Robert B. Talisse

SEE ALSO:

> *Civil republicanism*
> *Communitarianism*
> *Individualism*
> *Liberal conception of justice*
> *Moral person*
> *Neutrality*
> *The original position*
> *Political conception of justice*
> *Unity of self*

196.

SCANLON, T. M.

T. M. SCANLON (b. 1940) presents a general theory of morality he calls *contractualism* (Scanlon 1998), and contrasts it with "philosophical utilitarianism" (Scanlon 2003, 129). Rawls writes in *TJ* that his aim is to "present a conception of justice which generalizes and carries to a higher level of abstraction the familiar idea of the social contract" (*TJ* 11), and also contrasts his view with utilitarianism. So it is not surprising that there are important similarities between the two views. Both hold that valid principles of morality are grounded on the (objective) interests of individuals. Both adopt an individualistic, nonaggregative, nonmaximizing, and hence nonutilitarian approach to dealing with conflicts between these interests. Both hold that valid principles are those that are, in some sense, acceptable to all. And both reject the Hobbesian view that what is right is a matter of what rationally self-interested individuals would or could agree to if thinking soundly about the best strategy for satisfying their preferences. When we turn to specifics, however, it is easier to list differences between the two views than similarities.

First, whereas Rawls determines what is right by asking what is permitted or required by principles that rationally self-interested individuals would agree to if they didn't know their positions in society, Scanlon determines what is right by asking what is permitted or required by principles that no one could reasonably reject. To determine whether S could reasonably reject a principle, we are not to consider whether it would be *rational* for S to reject this principle (even behind a veil of ignorance). We are to consider instead whether a reason for S to prefer

S's situation when S does not observe this principle, or when it is not observed by others, has greater (objective) weight than any reason for someone to prefer his situation when S does observe this principle, or when it is generally observed. When this is the case, S can reasonably reject this principle. Because the validity of principles is not determined by rational choice, but by the (objective) relative weight of personal reasons, it is not necessary for Scanlon to employ a device like the veil of ignorance.

Second, whereas Rawls supposes that parties in the original position are to choose among principles by the shares of "primary social goods" that they guarantee to each person, Scanlon does not restrict good reasons to reject principles to good reasons to want primary goods. Instead he allows as a good reason to reject a principle any good reason to prefer one's situation when one does not observe this principle or when it is not generally observed.

Third, whereas Rawls's argument from the original position seems to presuppose a pro tanto right to an equal distribution of resources, Scanlon's contractualism does not presuppose this. Fourth, and partly as a consequence, whereas Rawls holds that only inequalities that function to benefit the least advantaged are permissible, Scanlon does not hold this. Fifth, whereas Rawls offers his conception of justice as a political conception of justice, which does not presuppose the truth of any particular comprehensive moral, philosophical, or religious doctrine, Scanlon offers his conception as the truth about the nature of morality, at least that part of morality that concerns what we owe to each other. Finally, the goals of their theories are different. Whereas Rawls's primary goal is to identify the most reasonable conception of distributive justice for a modern, pluralistic, democratic society like ours, Scanlon's goals are more abstract: to understand what makes judgments of right and wrong true or false, what kind of theoretical reasoning justifies the belief that an action is right or wrong, and why it is so important that we do the right thing. In Scanlon's view, valuing each other properly as rational beings requires that we act only in ways that we can justify to each other, and, Scanlon supposes, we can justify an action to others, in the relevant sense, only if it is permitted by a principle they could not reasonably reject. Although Rawls probably agreed with this, he does not explicitly endorse this general view of morality or rely on it in presenting his theory. There are other differences between the two views, too, that are not directly related to their contractualism. For example, whereas Rawls follows Hume in defending a conventionalist account of the obligation to keep promises, Scanlon's account of promises does not make fundamental use of convention.

Peter de Marneffe

SEE ALSO:

Comprehensive doctrine
Individualism
Moral person
Promising
The reasonable and the rational
Reciprocity
Social contract

197.

SELF-INTEREST

A PERSON IS SELF-INTERESTED, in the narrow sense of selfish or egoistic, if her most fundamental ends are focused on herself, such as her own health, wealth, social position, influence, or prestige (*TJ* 111; *LHPP* 58; *JF* 62). Someone is self-interested in a broader sense if she regards her aims and aspirations, whether selfish or not, as "worthy of recognition" and "deserving satisfaction" (*TJ* 110). More specifically, Rawls proposes that the interests *of* a self, which are not necessarily interests *in* oneself, are not merely determined by her tastes and preferences or her pains and pleasures. Her interests are instead determined by her conception of the good, which is the consistent and coherent plan of life she would choose under favorable conditions, with full information after careful reflection (*TJ* 358).

Egoism is one conception of the good, but personal ties, affections, and concern for the interests of others are likely to figure in the rational life plans of most people. Indeed egoism, according to Rawls, is incompatible with friendship and mutual trust because these relationships presuppose caring about others for their own sake. Egoism is also inconsistent with resentment and guilt because these moral feelings presuppose acceptance of principles of right or justice, which are necessarily general and universal (*TJ* 427). Egoism in its various forms is not a moral doctrine either because it fails to satisfy these formal constraints of morality and justice.

The basic role of justice, according to Rawls, is to adjudicate conflicting claims that people press on behalf of their various interests. Parties in the original position know they have determinate conceptions of the good but they do not know the precise contents of their various ends. Without this information, Rawls claims it is rational for them to maximize their own share of primary goods

Self-interest / 761

without caring about the interests of one another. This puts them in a good position as citizens to pursue their own interests whatever they turn out to be. The parties would also choose retributive principles and individual duties and obligations because they know that even the best citizens will be tempted by self-interest to avoid doing their fair share, especially when they are not sure that others are doing their part. The public threat of sanctions, along with a natural duty to comply with just institutions whether or not one has voluntarily accepted their benefits, helps to stabilize just cooperative schemes in the face of self-interest (*TJ* 241, 295–296). And certain moral principles will make exceptions for cases in which otherwise fulfilling them would be particularly onerous (*TJ* 389–390). Principles of right and justice, according to Rawls, thus take into account the interests of persons, but once those standards are chosen, they always override self-interest should it ever conflict with morality and justice (*TJ* 117).

People who grow up against the background of just institutions, according to Rawls, are likely to develop a firm and overriding interest in accepting and complying with principles of justice. Just societies allow them to develop and realize their own capacities in concert with others as well as share in a wide variety of activities and values that they enjoy (*TJ* 500). For such people, justice and self-interest converge so that in acting justly they are also acting for their own good.

Adam Cureton

SEE ALSO:

Altruism
Desires
Egoism
Moral person
Moral psychology
Primary goods, social
Sense of justice
Social contract

198.

SELF-RESPECT

SELF-RESPECT IS an attitude grounded in the sense of one's own worth or value. In *TJ* self-respect is the most important primary good and Rawls explains this importance on the basis of the conception of goodness as rationality. According to this, self-respect has two aspects: first, it consists in the conviction that one's conception of the good or plan of life is worth carrying out; and second, it implies the confidence that one has the ability to pursue one's plan of life successfully (*TJ* 386). When self-respect is lacking, persons do not find the pursuit of their conceptions of the good fulfilling or satisfactory and may "sink into apathy and cynicism" (*TJ* 386). Given its importance, it is rational for persons to seek to secure self-respect, and consequently, it is also rational for the parties in the original position to avoid "at almost any cost" the social conditions that undermine it (*TJ* 386). Though Rawls identifies self-respect with self-esteem, in later writings he mentions that they are not the same, though the reasons for this are not entirely clear (*CP* 260).

The conditions that support the first aspect of self-respect are, on the one hand, having a rational plan of life that satisfies the Aristotelian principle, and, on the other, the appreciation of fellow associates, in the absence of which it is impossible to maintain the conviction that one's plan of life is worth carrying out. According to the Aristotelian principle, a person will be less confident about his own value when his plan of life does not allow for his abilities to be realized fully and to be "organized in ways of suitable complexity and refinement" (*TJ* 386–387). By the same token, others tend to value one's activities "only if what we do elicits their admiration and gives them pleasure" (*TJ* 387). Associative ties provide the required setting in which one's activities can be publicly affirmed by others and also offer support when one's confidence is weakening (*TJ* 387). Such ties strengthen the second aspect of self-respect (*TJ* 387). Rawls argues that the parties in the original position would accept the natural duty of mutual respect because self-respect depends upon the respect of others and is "reciprocally self-supporting" (*TJ* 156–157).

In *TJ* the interest of the parties in the original position to avoid the social conditions that undermine self-respect is decisive in the argument against utilitarianism. Likewise, the importance of securing the social basis of self-respect is crucial to the argument for the priority of liberty. Rawls holds that in a society governed by the principle of utility, persons would find it more difficult to be confident about their own worth, specially the least advantaged, because it is publicly known that inequalities are not arranged to the benefit of everyone (*TJ* 158). This suggests that in order to secure the social basis of self-respect, the parties in the original position would not accept inequalities that do not benefit everyone. However, Rawls makes the stronger assumption that the social basis of self-respect is to be distributed equally. According to this, in the absence of an equal distribution of such a social basis, the sense of self-worth of those who are disadvantaged would be undermined.

Rawls argues that in a well-ordered society, "self-respect is secured through the public affirmation of the status of equal citizenship for all" (*TJ* 478). This supports both aspects of self respect: on the one hand, he tells us that "in the public forum each person is treated with the respect due to a sovereign equal" (*TJ* 470), which supports the sense of one's own worth or value; on the other hand, the equal liberties allow for a plurality of associations that provide the needed associative ties, and this plurality also "tends to reduce the visibility, or at least the painful visibility of variations in men's prospects" (*TJ* 470). In arguing for the priority of liberty in *TJ*, it is crucial that inequalities in material prospects need not undermine self-respect. The reasons for this claim are the same he offers in favor of the difference principle; in particular, he argues that inequalities to the benefit of everyone should be acceptable to all assuming that nobody suffers from envy. He maintains that material inequalities would not undermine self-respect provided that the following two conditions hold: first, such inequalities are allowed only when they benefit the least advantaged; and second, the priority of liberty is firmly maintained, which is possible when the society has acquired a level of development such that inequalities in basic rights and liberties are not beneficial to everyone.

There are two important changes in later writings to the account offered in *TJ*. First, Rawls modifies the first aspect of self-respect in order to make it compatible with a political conception. Instead of the conception of goodness as rationality, the basis for the account of self-respect becomes the political conception of the person as citizen. Instead of focusing on the worthiness of one's conception of the good only, the first aspect now consists in "our self-confidence as a fully cooperating member of society rooted in the development and exercise of the two moral powers" (*PL* 319), which includes the development of one's capacity for a sense of justice. Second, in the *Restatement* he makes clear that the primary good is not self-respect as an attitude toward oneself but the social basis that helps to support it (*JF* 60). He recognizes that *Theory* is ambiguous on this point because it fails to distinguish between the two (*JF* 60n). He makes explicit that the social basis of self-respect includes equal basic rights and liberties, the fair value of the political liberties, fair equality of opportunity, and access to material means according to the difference principle. In the *Restatement* he also includes the basic right "to hold and to have the exclusive use of personal property" as well as the ability to exercise it effectively (*JF* 114).

Faviola Rivera-Castro

SEE ALSO:

Aristotelian principle
Envy
Goodness as rationality
Plan of life
Primary goods, social
Respect for persons
Utilitarianism

199.

SEN, AMARTYA

AMARTYA SEN (b. 1933) is an economist and philosopher whose work in social choice theory, development economics, and moral and political theory has been very influential. This entry focuses on Sen's discussion of Rawls's views. These are summarized in Sen's recent book *The Idea of Justice* (2009). Sen endorses several key features of Rawls's theory of justice, including its focus on fairness, its account of objectivity, its characterization of persons as rational and reasonable, its view of liberty as a separate value, its insistence on the importance of procedural fairness in addition to the achievement of certain social and economic outcomes, its particular attention to the plight of the worst off, and its effort to connect freedom with real opportunities (Sen 2009, 63–64).

However, Sen makes several criticisms. The three most important concern the metric of justice (2009, 234–235, 253–254, 261–263), the site of justice (2009, x–xi, 10, 18–27, 67–69, 85), and the aims and structure of theorizing about justice (2009, 9–18, 56–57, 97–102). First, Sen argues that Rawls's focus on social primary goods is insufficient for measuring and comparing peoples' quality of life. Specifically, the difference principle's focus on income and wealth faces a deficit common in "resourcist" views of justice. This is their blindness to the "conversion problem": given personal heterogeneities, diversities in physical environment, variations in social climate, and differences in relational (cultural) perspectives, different individuals can have quite different abilities to convert income and other primary goods into valuable forms of life. So when we answer the question "Equality of what?", referring to equality of resources will not necessarily track equal life-prospects. Sen recommends that instead of focusing on means such as primary goods, we focus on people's "capabilities," their real opportunities or substantive freedoms to do and be what they have reason to value. This broader focus would capture the sources of variation mentioned above. (Sen acknowledges, however, that the space of capabilities does not exhaust the metric of justice: personal liberty and procedural fairness, for example, are additional concerns, and are duly captured in the principles of Rawls's theory that complement the difference principle (2009, 297).)

Second, Sen claims that Rawls's primary focus on institutions is too narrow. We should not only assess the justice of institutional arrangements and rules, but also, simultaneously, illuminate the significance of people's real behavioral tendencies. If the ultimate normative concern is what kinds of lives people actually lead, the primary focus should be broadened to track "social realizations," the totality of what turns out to happen in a social context.

Third, Sen thinks that Rawls takes the crucial goal of theorizing about justice to be the identification of a perfectly just society. Against such a "transcendental approach" to justice, Sen defends a "comparative approach," according to which we should aim at making comparative assessments of feasible social scenarios in order to identify reforms that involve justice-enhancement, or injustice-reduction, even if the results fall short of perfect justice. Sen claims that transcendental theorizing is infeasible (e.g. even in the original position a unique set of principles would fail to be selected). He also argues that it is redundant: it is neither sufficient, nor necessary, nor even helpful, for the real task of comparing feasible political options. As an intuition pump, Sen suggests the analogous case in which we are comparing two paintings, one by Dali and another by Picasso. To decide which is better, knowing that the *Mona Lisa* is the perfect painting would be of no help.

Some additional criticisms leveled by Sen against Rawls's theory of justice are (i) that its ascription of total priority to liberty is too extreme (2009, 65, 299); (ii) that it wrongly focuses on "closed" rather than "open impartiality," ignoring the possibly illuminating judgments of agents who are not members of the focus group of a given social contract (2009, 123ff.); and (iii) that it narrowly focuses on requirements of mutually beneficial cooperation or reciprocity, ignoring the existence of unidirectional "obligations of effective power" in which agents who are more powerful than others have pro tanto reason to benefit them simply because doing so is feasible and would make the world more just (regardless of considerations of mutual benefit or reciprocity) (2009, 202–207).

Pablo Gilabert

SEE ALSO:

Basic structure of society
Capabilities
Ideal and nonideal theory
Primary goods, social
Social choice theory

200.

SENSE OF JUSTICE

N A THEORY OF JUSTICE, Rawls defines a "sense of justice" as a moral sentiment that involves "an effective desire to apply and to act from the principles of justice and so from the point of view of justice" (*TJ* 497). In a well-ordered society, this entails "an effective desire to comply with the existing rules and to give one another that to which they are entitled" (*TJ* 274–275). It also requires that we "do our part in maintaining these arrangements" and that we are willing "to work for (or at least not to oppose) the setting up of just institutions, and for the reform of existing ones when justice requires it...And this inclination goes beyond the support of those particular schemes that have affirmed our good" (*TJ* 415). This moral sentiment is essential for the stability of a well-ordered society, and its presence underwrites the equal status of citizens. Indeed, one way to understand the project of developing a theory of justice, as Rawls understands it, is as an attempt to characterize one's sense of justice in reflective equilibrium.

In order to think of a well-ordered society as "a fair system of cooperation over time, from one generation to the next" (*PL* 15), Rawls says, we must model its citizens as having two moral powers: a capacity for a sense of justice and a capacity for a conception of the good (*PL* 19). This is because cooperation, as opposed to mere coordination, is guided by "publicly recognized rules and procedures that those cooperating accept and regard as properly regulating their conduct" (*PL* 16). So individuals must be able "to understand, to apply, and to act from the public conception of justice which characterizes the fair terms of social cooperation" (*PL* 19). This is their sense of justice. Rawls associates this

Sense of justice / 769

first moral power – the capacity for a sense of justice – with being reasonable, and the second moral power – the capacity for a conception of the good – with being rational (*PL* 48–54). To cooperate fully in a fair scheme of cooperation, individuals must be both reasonable and rational: "Merely reasonable agents would have no ends of their own they wanted to advance by fair cooperation; merely rational agents lack a sense of justice and fail to recognize the independent validity of the claims of others" (*PL* 52). A basic point in Rawls's theory is that "there is no thought of deriving the reasonable from the rational" (*PL* 51). The sense of justice is not to be justified in terms of it serving the long-run self-interest of an individual, although it must be congruent with one's conception of the good, as explained below. Instead, individuals with a sense of justice value reciprocity with other moral persons. They "desire for its own sake a social world in which they, as free and equal, can cooperate with others on terms all can accept. They insist that reciprocity should hold within that world so that each benefits along with others" (*PL* 50). The two moral powers also provide the basis for the equality of citizens. Anyone who possesses the two moral powers to the degree necessary to be a fully cooperating member of society – and Rawls assumes that the vast majority of normal adults meet this minimal threshold – is entitled to equal justice (*TJ* 442; *PL* 19).

In a well-ordered society, the acquisition of a sense of justice is a normal process that occurs over time as a child matures. As parents (or other primary caregivers) manifest love and care for the child, the child comes to love them in return. "The child's love does not have a rational instrumental explanation: he does not love them as a means to achieve his initial self-interested ends" (*TJ* 406). Rather, he or she develops new ends. Although the child wants to please the parents and accepts their judgment, he or she also has desires that go beyond the limits that the parents establish. When the child transgresses, he or she will feel guilty (or what Rawls calls "authority guilt") (*TJ* 407). As the child matures and enters into more diverse relationships, he or she comes to recognize the benefits of cooperation in various associations. When the rules of the association are fair, and cooperative benefits emerge from each individual following the rules and playing their appropriate role, individuals will tend to acquire a desire to follow the rules and to act fairly. Again, on the occasions when one transgresses the rules of the association, one will feel guilty (what Rawls calls "association guilt") (*TJ* 412). Finally, as an individual reaches maturity, he or she recognizes that the basic structure of society is itself a cooperative scheme, even if there is no direct personal connection to the vast majority of participants.

"In due course we come to appreciate the ideal of just human cooperation" (*TJ* 415). Violations of this ideal are experienced as guilt, now in the strict sense (*TJ* 416).

There are three important points to emphasize about this account of the development of a sense of justice. First, at each of these stages there is a shift in our ends, not only a change in the means we take to our already existing ends (*TJ* 432). We come to desire to comply with the rules given by the adults who love us, the fair rules of our associations, and the principles of social justice, each for their own sake. Second, all three stages involve a certain interpretation of reciprocity – one acquires a desire to respond to loving, cooperative, or just behavior in kind. Third, although Rawls assumes that something like this path of development will be followed by the vast majority of individuals in a well-ordered society, and in that sense the acquisition of a sense of justice is natural, it is also true that the sense of justice is a moral, as opposed to a natural, sentiment. This means that our explanation of this sentiment "invokes a moral concept and its associated principles" (*TJ* 421).

Even if most individuals in a well-ordered society acquire a sense of justice in a way similar to that sketched above, it remains a question what reflective attitude they will take toward this desire. After all, each will have many other interests which may conflict with one's desire for justice on various occasions, and so it is possible that the sense of justice might appear to be an inauthentic or alien imposition on their true selves, or perhaps its promptings might appear to be "simply neurotic compulsions" (*TJ* 451). In *A Theory of Justice*, Rawls's "congruence argument" aims to show that this would not be the case. Individuals would come to affirm their sense of justice as authentic and congruent with their conception of the good: "being a good person (and in particular having an effective sense of justice) is indeed a good for that person" (*TJ* 505). Elements of this argument date back at least to his 1963 article, "The Sense of Justice," where he argued that without a sense of justice, persons "would be incapable of feeling resentment and indignation, and they would be without ties of friendship and mutual trust. They would lack certain essential elements of humanity" (*CP* 96). Notice that even if this argument is successful, there is no thought of reducing one's sense of justice to one's conception of the good. Rather, the argument *assumes* the acquisition of a sense of justice has taken place according to something like the path sketched above, and then asks whether there would be a reflective and stable affirmation of the desire for justice as valuable for its own sake.

Sense of justice / 771

Rawls came to believe that the complicated argument for congruence that he gave depended on assuming that everyone in a well-ordered society would come to share the same (partially) comprehensive doctrine. And this, he believed, was a mistake. In fact, in a well-ordered society, there would be a wide diversity of reasonable comprehensive doctrines. This meant that there could be no general argument, applicable to all of those doctrines, that would show how the sense of justice would relate to other nonpolitical values. It would have to be left to each reasonable comprehensive doctrine to affirm the sense of justice on its own terms. So, while there would be an overlapping consensus on the principles of justice as individuals came to acquire a shared sense of justice through something like the process sketched above, no general argument could establish congruence between these principles of justice and the various conceptions of the good that individuals affirm. When an overlapping consensus is in place, the shared sense of justice will normally trump competing concerns and interests. Yet, when hard cases emerge, it will remain up to each individual to decide how to order her natural duty of justice and the various obligations she has acquired in a well-ordered society with her other moral commitments drawn from her comprehensive doctrine.

The stability of a well-ordered society depends on the acquisition and affirmation of the sense of justice of "at least a substantial majority of its politically active citizens" (*PL* 38; cf. *TJ* 414). A society is stable in the relevant sense, not when it has unchanging institutions, but rather when its institutions remain just by changing and adapting as new circumstances arise (*TJ* 401). This tracking of the requirements of justice depends on the active involvement of individuals with a sense of justice. This is why the sense of justice requires not only compliance with just institutions but also the reform of existing institutions when justice requires it (*TJ* 415).

Finally, it is not only individuals in a well-ordered society who have a sense of justice. Rawls and his readers (he assumes) do so, as well. And one preliminary way to think of a moral theory is "as the attempt to describe our moral capacity; or, in the present case, one may regard a theory of justice as describing our sense of justice" (*TJ* 41). As we begin to construct our theory, we rely on our provisional fixed points and commonsense precepts. However, these will surely turn out to be inadequate as conflicts and gaps at various levels of generality emerge. Aiming to reconcile these, we attempt to move in the direction of reflective equilibrium. We expect the "struggle for reflective equilibrium" to continue "indefinitely" (*PL* 97). Still, a theory of justice can be defined as characterizing our sense of justice in this ideal position.

Jon Mandle

SEE ALSO:

Congruence
Cooperation and coordination
Desires
Family
Guilt and shame
Moral education
Moral person
Moral psychology
Moral sentiments
The reasonable and the rational
Reciprocity
Reflective equilibrium
Stability

201.

SIDGWICK, HENRY

THE BRITISH PHILOSOPHER Henry Sidgwick (1838–1900) has had a major influence on Rawls, especially on his methodology. "The *Methods of Ethics* is, I believe, the outstanding achievement in modern moral theory...the first truly academic work in moral theory, modern in both the method and spirit" (*CP* 341). In *LHPP*, Rawls dedicates four lectures to Sidgwick and he also wrote a "Foreword" for *Methods of Ethics* when it was last republished (1981, v–vi).

Rawls has borrowed heavily from Sidgwick's notion of the *methods of ethics*. "Sidgwick assumes that a rational method is one that can be applied to all rational (and reasonable) human beings to get the same result" (*LHPP* 381). Moral theory as an independent, impartial, and systematic inquiry should start, says Sidgwick, with "an examination at once expository and critical, of the different methods of obtaining reasoned convictions as to what ought to be done which are to be found – either explicit or implicit – in the moral consciousness of mankind generally" (Sidgwick 1981, V; and *LHPP* 381). Such comparison is the only way to reach a "reasoned and satisfactory justification" (*LHPP* 379) in a domain usually devoid of objectivity. The most significant moral conceptions in the philosophical tradition to be examined and compared are "egoistic hedonism, intuitionism and universal hedonism (the classical utilitarian doctrine)" (*LHPP* 378–379). There lies the inspiration for Rawls's own comparative method of justification: justice as fairness should be argued for on the basis of an impartial comparison between utilitarianism, perfectionism and intuitionism drawn by the parties in the original position and endorsed in reflective equilibrium (*TJ* 42).

Sidgwick's *epistemology* is also a strong inspiration for Rawls, who claims his allegiance to Sidgwick against contemporary linguistic moral philosophy and theory of meaning (*CP* 291). He writes:

> It is obviously impossible to develop a substantive theory of justice founded solely on truths of logic and definition. The analysis of moral concepts and the a priori is too slender a basis. Moral theory must be free to use contingent assumptions and general facts as it pleases. There is no other way to give an account of our considered judgments in reflective equilibrium. This is the conception adopted by most classical British writers through Sidgwick. I see no reason to depart from it. (*TJ* 44–45, 45 n.26; *CP* 290)

Sidgwick's major achievement, for Rawls, lies in the "sharpness and clarity" (*LHPP* 377; *CP* 349) of his formulation of the main problem for utilitarianism, that the concern for one's own happiness should involve an equal concern for the happiness of all as a duty, not as a feeling of sympathy, a problem left unresolved by Mill. Sidgwick wants to establish the utility principle as a universal duty on a par with Kant's categorical imperative (Sidgwick 1981, Preface to the sixth edition; *LHPP* 383). The principle of utility can only become a moral principle if it demonstrates against rational egoism that "the good of any one individual is of no more importance, from the point of view (if I may say so) of the Universe, than the good of any other" (Sidgwick 1981, 382 quoted in *TJ* 164 n.37). To achieve that result, Rawls says:

> Sidgwick thought that the notions of universal good and individual good are in essential respects similar. He held that just as the good of one person is constructed by comparison and integration of the different goods of each moment as they follow one another in time, so the universal good is constructed by the comparison and integration of the good of many different individuals. (*TJ* 259)

In spite of all these achievements, Rawls insists on numerous limitations in Sidgwick's doctrine. "First, Sidgwick gives relatively little attention to the conception of the person and the social role of morality as main parts of a moral doctrine" (*CP* 341). The reason lies in his focus on epistemological problems, on first principles and their truth (*CP* 342). However, another reason is that Sidgwick's rational "intuitionism requires but a sparse notion of the person, founded on the self as knower" (*CP* 346, 357). Like all classical utilitarians, he ends up "treating the person according to its capacities for pleasure and pain" (*LHPP* 399), as "a container-person" (*LHPP* 414).

Then, Sidgwick offers a substantive definition of the good in terms of "agreeable feelings or experiences" (*LHPP* 397) that, for Rawls, does not respect the agent's autonomy. Instead, for Rawls, "expected utility is understood to have no substantive content. That is, it does not mean expected pleasure or agreeable consciousness (Sidgwick), or satisfaction" (*JF* 99). Note, however that, in *TJ*, Rawls explains how he has "tried to fill in Sidgwick's notion of a person's good ... as determined by the plan of life we would adopt with full deliberative rationality if the future were accurately foreseen and realized in the imagination" (*TJ* 370). While Rawls endorses the idea that the plan of life adopted with full deliberative rationality serves as a criterion of a person's good, he doesn't actually offer a substantive account – he doesn't attempt to figure out what plan of life would actually be chosen by a person.

Third, Sidgwick fails "to recognize that Kant's doctrine (and perfectionism for that matter) is a distinctive method of ethics" (*CP* 342; *LHPP* 384) whereas he makes the mistake of treating egoistic hedonism or rational egoism as a moral doctrine (*CP* 342). The categorical imperative is for him "a purely formal principle or what he called the 'principle of equity': whatever is right for one person is right for similar persons in relevantly similar circumstances" (*CP* 342). "For Sidgwick, Kant's doctrine provides at best only the general or formal elements for a utilitarian or indeed for any other moral conception" (*TJ* 221 n.29). However, Rawls recognizes the validity of at least one of Sidgwick's criticisms of Kant's formalism, that "Kant never explains why the scoundrel does not express in a bad life his characteristic and freely chosen selfhood in the same way that a saint expresses his characteristic and freely chosen selfhood in a good one. Sidgwick's objection is decisive, I think ... This defect is made good, I believe, by the conception of the original position" (*TJ* 224).

This shows how, in spite of deep disagreements, Sidgwick remains an important and stimulating interlocutor for Rawls. In particular, the best way of understanding Rawls's complex notion of *constructivism* is probably to turn to the sharp opposition he draws, in an important section of *CP* (341–346, shortened in *PL* 90–92), between Sidgwick's rational intuitionism and his own Kantian constructivism. In contrast with Sidgwick's belief that there exist independent moral principles, Rawls's and "Kant's idea of autonomy requires that there exists no such order of given objects determining the first principles of right and justice among free and equal persons" (*CP* 345). The possibility of a constructivist doctrine was closed to Sidgwick (*CP* 342) because he did not recognize Kant's distinction between theoretical and practical reason: "practical reason is concerned with the *production* of objects according to a conception of those objects – for example, the conception of a just constitutional regime taken as the aim of political endeavor – while theoretical reason is concerned with the knowledge of given objects" (emphasis added, *PL* 93; Kant, *Critique of Practical Reason* Ak: V: 15). This is the reason why he was unable to conceive of the human person as no longer mainly a knower, but also as an autonomous "agent of construction" (*CP* 338 and *PL* 99). In that sense, rational intuitionism is as much a *heteronomous* doctrine as Hume's naturalism (*CP* 345 and *PL* 98). Constructivism, in contrast, insists on the agents' autonomy and the necessary doctrinal autonomy of the conception of justice that they should adopt as exemplified in the procedure of the original position.

Catherine Audard

SEE ALSO:

> *Conception of the good*
> *Constructivism: Kantian/political*
> *Deliberative rationality*
> *Dominant end theories*
> *Egoism*
> *Intuitionism*
> *Mill, John Stuart*
> *Plan of life*
> *Practical reason*
> *Utilitarianism*
> *Utility*

202.

SIN

R AWLS'S UNDERGRADUATE thesis at Princeton dealt primarily with the concepts of sin and faith. The former was defined as the repudiation and destruction of community, whereas the latter was defined as the affirmation and enhancing of community. The sort of relations that were *communal* were those between persons (including God as personal), relations that were *natural* were those between a person and an object, and relations that were *causal* were those between objects (*BIMSF* 113–114, 122, 193).

Egoism was seen as a type of sin wherein communal relations were turned into natural relations (e.g., when people were treated as objects). Egotism (with a "t") was a more basic type of sin that consisted in self-love. In fact, egoism was claimed to be an external manifestation of egotism such that the latter was really the master sin (*BIMSF* 122–123, 193, 203, 209, 211). Whereas egoism fails to embrace personal relations and settles for natural relations, egotism embraces personal relations only to destroy them from within.

At this early stage in his career Rawls anticipated a third sort of sin to appear in the future: despair. This was because the prime result of sin was aloneness, which was seen as the most terrible condition for a human being. Even Rawls's early view of sin was primarily social rather than metaphysical (*BIMSF* 206, 213). Despair is a type of hopelessness, suggesting that living without hope is a type of sin. One is reminded here of Rawls's later attempt to sustain reasonable hope for liberal democracies.

Although the root of sin was passion (specifically, in the passionate tendency toward self-love), and although the ancient Greeks gave a great deal of attention to passion, they did not arrive at an adequate conception of sin. The early Rawls's view of sin was heavily influenced by the Augustinianism of neo-orthodox theologians popular in the mid-decades of the twentieth century. This included the influence of original sin (*BIMSF* 145, 152, 171–173).

It is ironic, given his later stance, that the early Rawls saw the view of society as based on mutual advantage as sinful. At this point in his career he also saw both bad institutions and anxiety as signs of sinfulness. That is, he rejected the Manichean view that sin was due to a cause external to us. Rather, we deprave ourselves, which is the heart of the doctrine of original sin (*BIMSF* 189–192) when interpreted not literally as the inheritance of Adam's sin, but as a metaphor for humanity's tendency to foul its own nest, as it were.

Later in his career Rawls identified Kant's moral psychology as Augustinian in that our moral failures were seen by Kant as due to the exercise of our free power of choice (*LHMP* 294, 303). By contrast, Rousseau criticized the Augustinian doctrine of original sin in that he saw our moral failures as due to external causes (*LHPP* 205, 208–209).

In this regard the mature Rawls was more like Rousseau than Kant. He even came to see St. Augustine (along with Dostoyevsky) as one of the two "darkest minds" of Western thought (*LHPP* 302). Indeed, in his very late essay "On My Religion" he came to see the doctrine of original sin as "repugnant" (*BIMSF* 263). This strong language is surprising given that one of the reasons for deliberation behind a veil of ignorance is the pervasiveness of bias in theorizing about justice, a pervasiveness that makes sense on the Augustinian belief in original sin.

Rawls's repudiation of the doctrine of original sin is required to understand his view at the very end of *LP* to the effect that if a reasonably just society, or a global society of peoples, is not possible, then the explanation would probably be due to the inability of the members to subordinate their power to reasonable aims. If human beings are incurably self-centered (which Rawls denies), then Rawls wonders "whether it is worthwhile for human beings to live on the earth" (*LP* 128).

Daniel Dombrowski

SEE ALSO:

Faith
Moral psychology
Reasonable hope
Reconciliation
Religion
Rousseau, Jean-Jacques
Self-interest

203.

SOCIAL CHOICE THEORY

SOCIAL CHOICE THEORY is a formal analysis of collective decision-making rules, which construct a consistent social ranking of a set of alternatives on the basis of individual preferences over this set. Modern social choice theory begins with Kenneth J. Arrow's impossibility theorem. According to Arrow's theorem, there exists no collective decision-making rule that simultaneously satisfies four seemingly uncontroversial conditions; (1) unrestricted domain (a collective decision-making rule can take all logically possible orderings as its domain); (2) Pareto (if all individuals strictly prefer alternative x to y, then society would rank x above y); (3) independence of irrelevant alternatives (the social ranking of two alternatives depends only on individuals' preferences over these two alternatives); and (4) nondictatorship (the social ranking does not coincide with the ranking of an identified individual, whatever others may rank). This theorem is understood as a generalization of Condorcet's voting paradox (the majority rule may yield cyclical ranking of three alternatives). Arrow's theorem provoked the large body of work on axiomatic analysis of distributive principles, including Rawls's difference principle.

Within Arrow's analytical framework, the informational basis of social choice is restricted in several morally relevant respects. Two related types of informational restrictions are particularly important in order to understand the formal structure of Rawls's difference principle. First, it is assumed that individual preferences are ordinal and interpersonally incomparable. This is a standard assumption in modern welfare economics. Second, given the assumption that individual preferences are interpersonally incomparable, the information concerning interpersonal distribution is not taken into account. Arrow's framework is insensitive

779

to distributive justice. Arrow calls his own analytical framework "ordinal-utilitarian."

If collective decision-making rules should incorporate the concern for distributive justice, some sort of interpersonal comparison is required. The post-Arrow literature of social choice theory analyzes interpersonal comparisons in terms of utilities, and elucidates the formal structure of distributive principles and the meaning of different types of interpersonal comparisons. For example, if it is assumed that utility level is interpersonally comparable, then it is possible to identify the level of the worst-off individual, the second worst off, and so on. Thus, level comparability opens up a possibility for the maximin rule and its lexicographic extension, leximin. Rawls's difference principle can be seen as leximin if the notion of utility is taken to be primary goods. Rawls's difference principle is an egalitarian collective decision-making rule that avoids Arrow's impossibility result. Leximin only requires level comparability, not the comparability of the cardinal unit of utility (roughly speaking, the numeric value of the gains and losses for different individuals).

Iwao Hirose

SEE ALSO:

Arrow, Kenneth J.
Difference principle
Justice and interpersonal comparison
Maximin rule of choice
Sen, Amartya
Utility

204.

SOCIAL CONTRACT

F ROM EARLY IN his career, Rawls was attracted to the idea of the social contract as a way of developing a systematic alternative to utilitarianism – one that defended our intuitive conviction that there are limits to the aggregation of interests across persons, but that went beyond intuition by yielding a definite ranking of competing priorities. While the details of the argument from the original position have been much criticized, the general idea of an agreement about principles of institutional design reached under fair conditions can be seen as the key to Rawls's attempted reconciliation of liberty and equality. On the one hand, if the social order must be acceptable to everyone, it must be acceptable to minority religious and philosophical points of view, arguing for freedom of thought, conscience, and association. On the other hand, if the social order must be acceptable to everyone, it must be acceptable to the worse off, arguing that socioeconomic inequalities should benefit those with less. The social contract can thus be seen as the linchpin for Rawls's egalitarian liberalism.

Rawls's attempt to build on "the long tradition of contract doctrine" (*TJ* 14) has led to much confusion, however. For one thing, this tradition has two different strands. According to the first, Hobbesian view (sometimes referred to as "contractarian"), justice is the result of a prudential agreement between rational egoists roughly equal in power. According to the second ("contractualist") view, justice is a matter of respect for one's fellow citizens as free and equal moral persons, the requirements of which can be modeled as the result of a rational agreement between parties under fair conditions. Although it differs in fundamental ways from contractarianism, contractualism involves a thought experiment whose inhabitants bear some resemblance to the contractarian account of human nature, leading to criticisms of asocial individualism or "atomism." Because it aims to identify principles of justice via agreement of fairly situated parties, the original position cannot assume that the parties have notions of justice without begging the question. *We* care about justice, but the parties within what Rawls would eventually label his original position must have a more austere psychology, if they are to help us resolve our uncertainties and disagreements about what justice requires.

In 1958's "Justice as Fairness," Rawls presented early versions of his two principles of justice as the result of an agreement between self-interested but nonenvious parties similarly situated, and constrained to make a once and for all decision about the principles that would be used to assess all future complaints about their common institutions. Rawls acknowledged that his thought experiment was connected with the view we now label "contractarian," i.e. that justice represents a compromise between people who are unable securely to dominate one another, and therefore agree not to do wrong so as not to suffer it. As proponents of this position, Rawls cited Plato's Glaucon, Thucydides's Athenians from the Melian debate, Epicurus, Hobbes, and Hume. Rawls pointed out in response that he was not making any claims about typical human character, but simply describing the motivations of parties in the circumstances in which justice is a relevant virtue, which is when there are conflicting priorities for the design of social institutions, on the part of agents who take themselves to have legitimate claims (*CP* 56). It is important not to let the assumption of conflicting interests obscure the larger point of the contract device, however, which is to show that only where institutions satisfy principles that could be mutually acknowledged in fair conditions "can there be true community between persons" (*CP* 59). The problem with utilitarianism was that individuals are not conceived of as being related in any way, but as so many separate recipients of scarce resources. The satisfaction of their desires is taken to have value "irrespective of the moral relations between persons, say as members of a joint undertaking" (*CP* 65). This conception of justice as an efficient higher-order administrative decision brings out "the profound individualism" of classical utilitarianism, Rawls claimed. That this individualism is mistaken is evident from the fact that utilitarianism would permit one to argue that slavery is unjust because its advantages for the slaveholder do not outweigh its costs for slaves (*CP* 67). The advantages to the slaveholder shouldn't count in the first place, because this "office" or social position is not in accordance with principles that could be mutually acknowledged in a "general position" (*CP* 67). In contrast, when social practices satisfy principles that would be agreed to in a suitably general position, "persons...can face one another openly and support their respective positions by reference to principles which it is reasonable to expect each other to accept." When practices don't meet this standard, Rawls said "this will affect the quality of their social relations" (*CP* 58–59). Principles of justice establish a common point of view from which persons' conflicting claims may be adjudicated, Rawls would later say, establishing "the bonds of civic friendship" (*TJ* 5).

Rawls's use of the social contract is distinctive in a second respect. In so far as the contract tradition is understood in normative rather than strategic terms, the underlying principle is often taken to be "no authority without consent" (an idea common to Hobbes and Locke, despite their different accounts of the conditions necessary for genuine consent). However, Rawls was never much concerned with the social contract as an account of political obligation. Rawls was more indebted to Rousseau and Kant, in this respect. According to Rousseau, the fundamental problem that the social contract solved was that of finding a form of political association that protects each with the force of all while nonetheless leaving each as free as before, obeying himself alone (*Social Contract*, 2011 [1762], 164). The idea that whatever people freely agree to is legitimate does not solve that problem, because it says nothing about what form of society one should agree to. For Kant, the hypothetical nature of the contract is even clearer, since the contract is simply an "idea of reason" (1983 [1793], 77).

Already in "Justice as Fairness," Rawls insisted that the parties to his general position were not coming together for the first time to establish a particular society (*CP* 57–58). Rather, they were agreeing to principles for appraising social practices assumed to be already in existence. Rawls followed Hart in saying that the duty to follow the rules of social practices was a matter of fair play, for those having voluntarily accepted the benefits of a fair practice (*CP* 60–61). The main point of the contract device was to identify principles that would define fair practices, not to derive the obligation to obey institutional rules from (tacit) agreement. Even at this stage Rawls recognized that the social contract "overreached" as a theory of political obligation, while insisting that it expressed "an essential part of the concept of justice" (*CP* 71). In *TJ*, Rawls would further restrict the scope of political obligation. Acceptance of benefits had to be voluntary, but citizens are typically born and raised in a particular society and can only later leave with difficulty. Rawls therefore said that he accepted Hume's critique of Locke in "Of the Social Contract," at least as applied to citizens generally (*TJ* 296 n.2). Hume's first main argument against the idea of an original contract was that the poor peasant could not plausibly be said to have tacitly consented to obey the laws, simply by the fact of not having left upon reaching the age of majority, but that peasant surely did have a duty to obey, which therefore had to be based on something other than free agreement – utility. Rawls concluded that only political representatives and others holding higher office had a duty to obey the rules based on the principle of fair play; others were obligated to comply because of the natural duty of justice.

The idiosyncrasy of Rawls's understanding of the social contract tradition is illustrated by his account of the relationship between Locke and Hume in *Theory*. Hume's second main argument against an original contract was that the duty to keep agreements is itself grounded in utility, making it superfluous to ground political obligation in agreement as opposed to grounding it in utility directly. Rawls's response was to deny that Hume meant by utility what we take it to mean today, and to claim that Hume never really recognized Locke's "fundamental contention" (*TJ* 29), which was apparently not that voluntary agreement is the only legitimate source of obligation, but that universal benefit from a fair baseline is the master principle of justice. The role of equal rights in Locke's state of nature is to ensure that departures from this condition are permissible only if they benefit everyone (*TJ* 29). When Hume says that allegiance is grounded in utility, all he means is that "each man stands to gain" (*TJ* 29). There is therefore no conflict with Locke's contract doctrine, Rawls claims. In this discussion, and in his later *Lectures on the History of Political Philosophy*, Rawls treats Locke's basic claim as one about which institutional set-ups are just or legitimate, taking for granted that membership in a political society cannot generally be voluntary. At the same time, he claims that Hume's appeal to utility did not conflict with what Rawls took to be the central, anti-aggregative message of the contract doctrine, as applied to the problem of institutional design.

Andrew Lister

SEE ALSO:

Advantage, mutual vs. reciprocity
Constructivism: Kantian/political
Hart, H. L. A.
Hume, David
Kant, Immanuel
Liberal conception of justice
Locke, John
Reciprocity
Rousseau, Jean-Jacques

205.

SOCIAL MINIMUM

THE SOCIAL MINIMUM is designed to ensure that no one unwillingly falls below a minimum level of well-being. In *TJ* Rawls assigned to the transfer branch of government the responsibility for ensuring that "the claims of need" are satisfied (*TJ* 243–244). Rawls suggests that the social minimum could be fulfilled by, e.g., family allowances, unemployment insurance, or a graded income supplement. In *PL* he endorses Rodney Peffer's argument for a basic needs principle, lexically prior to the first principle, requiring that "citizens' basic needs be met, at least insofar as their being met is necessary for citizens to understand and to be able fruitfully to exercise those rights and liberties" (*PL* 7; *JF* 44; cf. Peffer 1990). But Rawls rejects Philippe van Parijs's argument that a social minimum should be guaranteed to everyone regardless of ability to work, arguing instead that "those who would surf off Malibu must find a way to support themselves and would not be entitled to public funds" (*PL* 181–182; cf. van Parijs 1991). The idea of basic needs appears also in *LP* where Rawls says that decent societies, which enjoy the right of noninterference, guarantee that basic needs are met. Failure to satisfy basic needs may give rise, on the part of other peoples, to the duty of assistance (*LP* 37–38).

The social minimum plays an important role in Rawls's rejection of utilitarianism. The principle of average utility fails as an alternative to the difference principle because it cannot ensure that everyone has a "reasonably satisfactory standard of living" (*TJ* 147). The principle of restricted utility, in contrast, does include a social minimum, but Rawls suspects that that principle, lacking an independent criterion for the minimum, would implicitly rely upon the difference principle (*TJ* 278). In *JF*, however, Rawls accepts Jeremy Waldron's argument that a proponent of the principle of restricted utility could set the social minimum at the lowest level required for "meeting the basic needs essential for a decent life" (*JF* 127–128) on the grounds that anything less would violate the strains of commitment (Waldron 1986).

In reply, Rawls argues that the social minimum must do more than satisfy basic needs. He admits that insofar as restricted utilitarianism requires only that citizens' essential needs be met, it can prevent one of the two ways in which the strains of commitment can be excessive. Because citizens are able to lead a "decent" life, they will not become "sullen and resentful... ready as the occasion arises to take violent action in protest against [their] condition" (*JF* 128). But, Rawls warns, this may not be sufficient to prevent the strains of commitment from being excessive in a second, milder way if citizens become "withdrawn and cynical" and "retreat into [their] social world" because the principles of justice "fail to engage [their] moral sensibility" (*JF* 128). It may therefore be necessary that the social minimum be higher than what is required to satisfy basic needs (*JF* 130). Rawls rejects welfare-state capitalism even though its "welfare provisions may be quite generous and guarantee a decent social minimum covering the basic needs" (*JF* 137–138). Instead, Rawls argues, the principles of justice can be satisfied only in a property-owning democracy (or under liberal socialism). To prevent inequalities that would threaten the fair value of the political liberties and fair equality of opportunity (*JF* 138), social institutions must "put in the hands of citizens generally... sufficient productive means for them to be fully cooperating members of society on a footing of equality" (*JF* 140). An adequate social minimum must ensure that the least advantaged are "in a position to manage their own affairs on a footing of a suitable degree of social and economic equality," not simply (as in welfare-state capitalism) "assist those who lose out through accident or misfortune" (*JF* 139).

Rawls often links the social minimum to the difference principle and says that the social minimum (i.e. the lifetime expectations of the least advantaged extending over future generations) should be maximized (*TJ* 252; *PL* 326; *JF* 129). But if the fair value of the political liberties (and fair equality of opportunity) permit less economic inequality than the difference principle alone would permit (*JF* 150), the social minimum might also have to be lower than it could otherwise be. This "guaranteeable level" would still have to be "quite satisfactory," such that the parties in the original position would care little about what could be gained above that level (*TJ* 134–135; *JF* 98–100). Although Rawls does not make this point, it would also seem that the principle of restricted utility, since it includes the fair value of the political liberties and fair equality of opportunity

Social minimum / 787

(*JF* 120), should, no less than justice as fairness, require a minimum sufficient to prevent the strains of commitment from being excessive in the second (milder) way. For both theories, the social minimum should be sufficient to block the development of "a discouraged and depressed underclass" which "feels left out and does not participate in the public political culture" (*JF* 140).

In *JF*, Rawls defends a more egalitarian conception of the social minimum than he started with in *TJ*. He recognizes the need not only for a social minimum guaranteeing the satisfaction of basic needs. This is a constitutional essential (*PL* 228–229, 166) and is included in any liberal political conception of justice (*PL* 157). But Rawls also (citing Rousseau) affirms the need for a social minimum, tied to the requirements of equal citizenship, requiring more than the satisfaction of basic biological (and psychological) needs (*JF* 132). This is the minimum required "when we take seriously the idea of society as a fair system of cooperation between citizens as free and equal" in which the least advantaged see themselves as "full members" (*JF* 129).

Walter E. Schaller

SEE ALSO:

Basic needs, principle of
Branches of government
Difference principle
Duty of assistance
Leisure
Strains of commitment
Two principles of justice (in justice as fairness)
Utilitarianism

206.

SOCIAL UNION

THE NOTION OF social union is central to *A Theory of Justice* in which the just society is described as a "social union of social unions" (*TJ* 462). In effect, the idea expresses Rawls's view of "human sociability" and is meant to deflect charges that his contract doctrine cannot account for the "value of community" (*TJ* 456).

According to Rawls, our social nature is all too often described in "a trivial" fashion (*TJ* 458). One repeatedly hears, for instance, that we are "social creatures" or that society is necessary for human life, for acquiring language and certain interests, even for our ability to think. These facts are not trivial but to claim that our social nature *consists* in them is inadequate, for all these facts are equally true of a group of egoists. Egoists too cannot learn to speak nor develop their selfish ways outside specific human communities. Genuine human sociability entails something more; it requires social union.

Rawls's idea of social union is drawn up in explicit contrast to that of "private society" or that form of social organization distinguished by two features: individuals comprising it have their own exclusive ends, either competing or independent, but in any case not complementary, and they view their social relations and institutions as means to these private ends (*TJ* 458). The "natural habitat" of this idea is the economic theory of competitive markets, and it can already be found in the thought of A. Smith and in Hegel's notion of civil society (*TJ* 459 n.4).

A social union, by contrast, is distinguished by the fact that members have shared final ends, they value their relations and common activities as ends in themselves, and there is an agreed-upon scheme of conduct leading to a complementary good for all. A social union is decidedly *not* a zero-sum game (one person's gain entailing another's loss) but exemplifies a win-win situation whereby "the successes and enjoyments of others are necessary and complementary to our own good" (*TJ* 458). This idea can be traced back to the writings of von Humboldt and Kant (*TJ* 459 n.4).

By way of illustration, Rawls relies on an example from the German Idealist tradition: that of a group of musicians playing in an orchestra. Here each has a different realized musical capacity and performs on a different instrument, but none could develop his individual skill, nor express his musical abilities, except by way of the collective achievement of all: in the actual play of the music. Humans enjoy and participate in each other's excellences for their own sake. "It is only in active cooperation with others that one's powers reach fruition. Only in a social union is the individual complete" (*TJ* 460 n.4). In his list of social unions Rawls includes the arts and science, religion, culture, sexual relationships, families, school, friendships, games, and the well-ordered society itself (*TJ* 460ff.). Significantly, the realm of work is absent.

What does Rawls mean by claiming that the just society is "a social union of social unions"? In a modern pluralist society citizens inevitably hold differing views of the good life and thus a modern political community cannot be a social union *simpliciter*; there is no one comprehensive good shared by all citizens. Still, a well-ordered society contains countless lesser unions of different types and sizes and may be conceived as "a social union of unions" (*TJ* 462). The only shared end in which all partake is that of realizing a conception of justice and prizing their democratic institutions as valuable in themselves. Ideally, there is also an agreed-upon score: the regulation of society's basic structure by Rawls's two principles of justice. Modern citizens express their common moral nature through their desire to act justly and by participating in the realization of just institutions.

In his later works, Rawls's thesis on social unity shifts slightly and becomes more "realistic" (*PL* xvi). The most reasonable basis for unity continues to be majority agreement on a conception of justice, but such agreement is now explicitly conceived as a "politically established social union" (*LHMP* 365) and not a moral one; it consists in a "reasonable overlapping consensus" on which citizens agree but often for very different reasons (*JF* 32). Justice as fairness remains suited for its unifying role, however, because its requirements are limited to the basic structure and it is now revealed as a "freestanding view": one that presupposes no comprehensive doctrine as its ground.

A few concerns may be raised with regard to the notion of social union. First, Rawls omits all mention of social union in *the realm of labor*. Although work should be "meaningful for all" and the worst aspects of the division of labor avoided

(*TJ* 464), he still accepts a major tenet of neo-economic economics whereby the market is the home of "private society" and there social relations remain instrumental. But should *we* accept this tenet? Not only have socialists long argued that cooperative work relations are possible and often superior, but more recently feminists have stressed that women's traditional labor of caring for others – whether in the private or public economic sphere (such as in health care) – hardly fits the old private competitive model.

So too, we might wonder whether Rawls's account of human sociability is *sufficient* for political unity. Again, socialists may be right that private ownership in the major means of production creates a rift between society's haves and its have-nots, which only grows larger (as in the US today). Perhaps we should revise our dominant conception of labor as aiming primarily at private gain.

Of course, Rawls's theory proffers various mechanisms to keep instrumental market relations in check, most importantly: (i) individual rights and liberties are fundamental and may never be traded for economic gain; (ii) his difference principle requires inequalities in the basic structure to work to the advantage of the "worst-off" group; and (iii) democratic elections should be publicly funded to keep the state from becoming a tool of the wealthy (*TJ* 198). Still, most of us spend *at least eight hours* a day at work. If this remains a realm of "private society" and the instrumental use of others, we may justifiably wonder how the average citizen will ever develop the strong *other-directedness required*, say, to vote for Rawls's difference principle, or to work for other political constraints on egoistic gain. Despite all its advances, a lacuna remains at the heart of Rawls's account of human sociability.

Sibyl A. Schwarzenbach

SEE ALSO:

Congruence
Culture, political vs. background
Egoism
Hegel, G. W. F.
Overlapping consensus
Reasonable pluralism
Well-ordered society

207.

SOCIALISM

S OME ON THE right wing of the political spectrum condemn Rawls and
Rawls's theory for being "socialist"; some others, on the left side of the
spectrum, claim that his theory is a species of "bourgeois ideology" and
is incompatible with socialism. Neither of these claims is true. At the theoretical level (before taking actual historical circumstances and realities into account),
Rawls's theory is compatible with certain kinds of socialism but does not require
any kind of socialism.

> Which of these systems [capitalist or socialist] and the many intermediate
> forms most fully answers to the requirements of justice ... depends in large
> part upon the traditions, institutions, and social forces of each country, and
> its particular historical circumstances. The political judgment in any given
> case will then turn on which variation is most likely to work out best in
> practice. (*TJ* 274/242)

Rawls takes private versus public "ownership of the means of production"
(*TJ* 266) to be the essential difference between capitalist ("private property") and
socialist economies (and societies): "the size of the public sector under socialism
(as measured by the fraction of total output produced by state-owned firms ...) is
much larger. In a private-property economy the number of publicly owned firms
is presumably small and in any event limited to special cases such as public utilities
and transportation" (*TJ* 235), while "under socialism the means of production
and natural resources are publicly owned" (*TJ* 242).

Public-sector firms in socialist economies can be managed either by "state
officials or workers' councils" (*TJ* 235) or "by agents appointed by [workers'

councils]" (*TJ* 248). Thus, the degree of workers' self-management does *not* come into the definition of "socialism." Perhaps inconsistently, in *PL* Rawls objects to Peffer's proposed social and economic (workplace) democracy principle because, Rawls writes, "it appears to require a socialist form of economic organization" (*PL* 7–8). But Rawls does not repeat this objection in *JF* 44.

Second, socialism is *not* defined by the extent to which public goods and welfare benefits are provided. "Since the proportion of social resources devoted to their production is distinct from the question of public ownership of the means of production, there is no necessary connection between the two. A private-property economy may allocate a large fraction of national income to these purposes, a socialist society a small one, and vice versa" (*TJ* 239). Therefore, social democratic societies – such as Scandinavian countries since World War II – are *not* socialist societies even though they devote a higher proportion of national income to public goods – at least assuming that the bulk of large-scale productive enterprises and investment capital is privately rather than publicly held in them.

Third, "there is no essential tie between the use of free markets and private ownership of the instruments of production" (*TJ* 239). "...this connection is a historical contingency in that, theoretically at least, a socialist regime can avail itself of the advantages of this system" (*TJ* 239). This means that "market socialism" is *not* a contradiction in terms, as some claim. In fact, "market institutions are common to both private-property [i.e. capitalist] and socialist regimes..." (*TJ* 241) since "All regimes will normally use the market to ration out the consumption goods actually produced." "But in a free market system [whether capitalist or socialist] the output of commodities is also guided as to kind and quantity by the preferences of households as shown by their purchases on the market." However, "In a socialist regime planners' preferences or collective decisions often have a larger part in determining the direction of production" (*TJ* 239) because the public sector owns and controls the bulk of investment capital. But "There is no necessity for comprehensive direct planning" in market socialist economies (*TJ* 239).

Moreover,

> It is perfectly consistent for a socialist regime to establish an interest rate to allocate resources among investment projects and to compute rental charges for the use of capital and scarce natural assets such as land and forests...It does not follow, however, that there need be private persons who as owners of these assets receive the monetary equivalents of these evaluations. Rather these accounting prices are indicators for drawing up

an efficient schedule of economic activities. Except in the case of work of all kinds, prices under socialism do not correspond to income paid over to private individuals. Instead, the income imputed to natural and collective assets accrues to the state, and therefore their prices have no distributive function. (*TJ* 241)

That is, in a socialist system no private individual receives an income from merely owning productive assets and allowing them to be used.

Market systems are more economically efficient than command economies because "any other procedure is administratively cumbersome" (*TJ* 239) and "The theory of general equilibrium" explains how, at least under ideal assumptions, markets lead to Pareto optimality (*TJ* 241). Thus, even though "market failures and imperfections are often serious...And the market fails altogether in the case of public goods" (*TJ* 241), government policy can compensate for these problems well enough to make real-world market economies more efficient than real-world command economies.

Moreover, "it is hard to see how, under ordinary circumstances anyway, certain aspects of a command society inconsistent with liberty can be avoided." A second major advantage of a market economy is that "a system of markets decentralizes the exercise of economic power." Moreover, "Both private-property and [liberal] socialist systems normally allow for the free choice of occupation and of one's place of work. It is only under command systems of either kind that this freedom is overtly interfered with" (*TJ* 239). These two facts provide a strong argument against command economies and, thus, in favor of market economies. But,

> a liberal socialist regime can also answer to the two principles of justice. We have only to suppose that the means of production are publicly owned and that firms are managed by workers' councils say, or by agents appointed by them. Collective decisions made democratically under the constitution determine the general features of the economy, such as the rate of saving and the proportion of society's production devoted to essential public goods. Given the resulting economic environment firms regulated by market forces conduct themselves much as before. (*TJ* 248; cf. *PL* 328; *JF* 138, 150, 178.)

"Some socialist have objected to all market institutions as inherently degrading, and they have hoped to set up an economy in which men are moved largely by social and altruistic concerns" (*TJ* 248). But "It seems improbable that the control of economic activity by the bureaucracy (whether centrally directed or guided by the agreements reached by industrial associations) would be more just on balance than control exercised by means of prices (assuming as always the necessary framework)" (*TJ* 248). "Moreover the theory of justice assumes a definite limit on the strength of social and altruistic motivation" (*TJ* 248). In fact, the type of society these critics of the market are proposing – e.g. Marx's vision of full-fledged communism or left anarchists' vision of a future society – "is a society in a certain sense beyond justice" (*TJ* 248) in that "It has eliminated the occasions when the appeal to the principles of right and justice is necessary" (*TJ* 248).

Rodney G. Peffer

SEE ALSO:

Basic structure of society
Branches of government
The economy
The market
Marx, Karl
Property-owning democracy

208.

SOCIETY OF PEOPLES

A SOCIETY OF PEOPLES refers to those peoples who follow the principles of external and internal justice that Rawls defends in *The Law of Peoples*. Theprinciples of external justice guarantee the freedom and independence of peoples, impose a duty of nonintervention, confer a right to wage war in self-defense, place limits on the conduct of war, grant the power to ratify (and the duty to observe) treaties, and require assisting economically burdened societies. The principles of internal justice guarantee basic human rights, which for Rawls consist in minimal rights to life (to personal security and means of subsistence), to liberty (to freedom from slavery, serfdom, forced labor), to personal property, to a measure of freedom of conscience and association, to formal equality (treating like cases alike), and to emigration. The principles of internal justice also require societies to contain some kind of consultative procedure through which their members' views are heard, either as individuals (as in liberal democracies, where individuals possess the right to vote) or as members of associations (for more communal societies, where associations, but not individuals, each have a say in decisions).

Absent from these internal requirements are more robust liberal rights and freedoms, such as democratic political rights, rights to nondiscrimination, and the generally broader scope that liberalism affords to freedom of religion, freedom of speech, freedom of association, and the like. Democratic political rights – understood according to the maxim, one-person, one-vote, where individuals are the bearers of the right to vote – are not required, as Rawls's internal principles allow for institutions in which individuals do not possess the right to vote (provided that they are consulted as members of associations). Rawls's principles do not require church–state separation either. Societies may be organized around religious comprehensive doctrines – essentially, a state religion – provided that they allow for the free exercise of other religions. The state religion may be liberal or nonliberal. Absent from the external requirements are liberal-egalitarian principles of economic distribution. For instance, there is no international equivalent of the difference principle. Instead, there is (merely) a duty to help burdened societies – those that are unable to satisfy the internal requirements due to unfavorable economic, social, or historical circumstances – realize their conceptions of domestic justice. Accordingly, Rawls claims that the principles that constitute his Law of Peoples are capacious enough to include both liberal and nonliberal – what Rawls calls *decent* – societies, and that this is a strength of his theory, insofar as it expresses liberalism's own principle of tolerance for other (legitimate) ways of ordering society.

The defense of these principles comes through a modified version of the original position. Whereas in the domestic version of Rawls's theory the parties in the original position are individuals, in the international version of his theory the parties are delegates that represent societies. In fact, Rawls runs two separate sessions of the international original position – one with delegates representing only liberal societies, another with delegates representing only decent societies – the first to demonstrate that the principles are an acceptable extension of liberal norms, the second to confirm their acceptability to nonliberal societies. In both cases, these delegates choose principles from behind a veil of ignorance that excludes knowledge of the size, population, military strength, natural resources, and economic development of their society. However, the delegates are permitted to know the conception of domestic justice of the society they represent. They are permitted to know, this means, that they do not represent what Rawls calls *outlaw* states, which he defines as states that are expansionist or violate basic human rights (or both). He maintains that delegates so situated would select principles of internal and external justice whose content is described above – principles that he refers to as the Law of Peoples. A society of peoples therefore consists of those peoples who follow, in their domestic and foreign relations, the internal and external requirements of the Law of Peoples. Standing in a relation of fair equality with one another, they now share a public political conception of justice.

Chris Naticchia

SEE ALSO:

Decent society
Human rights
Ideal and nonideal theory
Law of Peoples
Liberal people
Peoples

209.

SOPER, PHILIP

PHILIP SOPER (b. 1942) is an American legal and moral philosopher. In *A Theory of Law* (1984), Soper develops novel accounts of the law's normative force and of political obligation. Rawls draws on this work in his accounts of the common good idea of justice and legal systems in decent societies (*CP* 545, 546; *LP* 66, 67, 72; *PL* 109).

Soper argues that the law has normative force only when public officials sincerely believe the law serves justice or the common good. When officials sincerely believe the law does this for all, citizens have reason to respect it. This is so, even when any citizen might reasonably reject the official conception of justice or the common good as suboptimal or wrong-headed. This respect for the law amounts to a duty to defer when officials enforce the law.

Rawls does not define legal systems, but follows Soper as to when and how legal systems impose bona fide duties and obligations (*LP* 65–66). Like Soper, he holds that officials must be willing to defend, publicly and in good faith, laws requiring or forbidding conduct (*LP* 67). For Rawls, this means officials must reasonably see their law as consistent with their common good conception of justice.

Soper does not define justice or the common good since his account is generic and not specifically liberal. Further, he recognizes that there is reasonable disagreement over justice and the common good in all societies. However, Soper does argue that any account of justice or the common good must give some consideration to the interests of each member of society, though not necessarily equal consideration. Without this, some would have no reason to respect the law. Further, officials must connect the law to some conception of justice or the common good that is part of a discourse or tradition known to members. Otherwise, citizens will have reason to suspect that the law serves only the private interests of officials.

Since the law's normative force depends on official sincerity, members of a society may test official sincerity. Soper calls this the "right to discourse." Sincerity is difficult to judge, but members have reason to doubt officials who will not talk, who are careless with facts, or who cannot tie their political activity to some known understanding of justice or the common good. In such situations, citizens may doubt that officials sincerely see the law as promoting justice or the common good, and lose their reason for respecting the law. When law does not serve justice or the common good, it usually serves the interests of law-makers alone. The right to discourse is not a right to free speech, though, and is limited to this testing function.

Rawls draws on this right to discourse when he argues that decent peoples must respect dissent and allow different voices to be heard, and further that officials must address objections (*LP* 72). For Rawls, refusal to allow or to respond to dissent turns a cooperative scheme into a paternalistic one.

Walter J. Riker

SEE ALSO:

Common good idea of justice
Constitution and constitutional essentials
Decent societies
Law, system of
Political obligation

210.

SOVEREIGNTY

"Sovereignty" is not a topic or term that Rawls spends significant time on. (It barely appears in his extensive indexes.) But it, along with the closely related ideas of a sovereign and sovereign powers, are important for understanding several aspects of his work. Part of *The Law of Peoples*, the stability of justice as fairness, and Rawls's connection to others in the social contract tradition, are intimately related to his views on sovereignty and sovereign power. While these topics seem disparate, they have a close connection through the idea of sovereignty. Seeing this helps show the over-all unity of Rawls's thought.

The modern notion of sovereignty and of sovereign powers developed in the sixteenth and seventeenth centuries in the works of such thinkers as Jean Bodin in *Les six livres de la république* (the most relevant sections reprinted as *On Sovereignty* (1992 [1576])), Hugo Grotius in *The Rights of War and Peace* (2005 [1625]), and Thomas Hobbes in *Leviathan* (1994 [1651]) and other writings. These works were developed against the background of the wars of religion in Europe and the concurrent emergence of the modern state. The theories of sovereignty that developed provide answers to two problems that remain central to Rawls's works: how to secure the stability of a political order so that members of the society may flourish, and the proper relationship between distinct societies. The first of these questions has been central to Rawls since *TJ*, where Rawls provides an answer via the "congruence" argument. A new answer to this question is given in *PL*. Though rarely noted, Rawls's position is intimately tied to a theory of sovereignty, in that part of his goal is to show how the problem of stability may be solved without either a unified, unlimited sovereign or a slide into anarchist or minimal state views.

In the "traditional" views of sovereignty offered by Hobbes and Bodin, the purpose of the sovereign is to ensure the stability of the political order. Hobbes and Bodin both faced divided societies, torn apart by civil war, split loyalties, and religious persecution. Though Hobbes's view is better known to philosophers, Bodin's is perhaps the more influential statement of the "classic" or "traditional" view. On this account, a sovereign has the power of appointing magistrates, making and repealing laws, of making war, of hearing appeals, and the power of life and death. The sovereign is one whose power is not limited by any early laws as to its reach, function, or duration. Though the sovereign is bound by the power of God and ought to follow the laws of nature, he cannot be subject to anyone else, for if he were, he would not be sovereign, and therefore could not provide the needed stability. Even binding the sovereign by his own laws would make him unable to provide the needed stability. This view of sovereignty leads not only to a domestically unbounded sovereign, but also to the traditional approach to the sovereignty of states in international relations. On the traditional view, states reserved the right to fight wars to advance their interests, as they saw them. As Rawls notes, this idea is worked out most systematically by Clausewitz in his *On War* (1989 [1932]) (*LP* 25–26), but this follows from, and is explicit in, the traditional notion of sovereignty as formulated by Bodin and Hobbes. If a sovereign lacked the power to declare war, on the traditional account, this could only be because he (and so the state) was subject to some other power. But then, either this other power would be sovereign, or else sovereignty would be divided, and so unable to provide the requisite stability. The idea of a binding international law is therefore rejected by views such as Bodin's and Hobbes's, as incompatible with their solution to the pressing problem of stability.

Although the full importance of stability in Rawls's work only come to the fore in *PL*, it plays an important role throughout his work, and the answer he gives to the problem in *PL* has a close, if not always appreciated, connection to his rethinking of the idea of sovereignty in *LP*. Rawls recognizes that the problem of stability has an "uninteresting Hobbesian answer" (*PL* 391 n.27) but this answer is unacceptable for a society of free and equal democratic citizens. Whether such a society may be stable without an unlimited sovereign, and so "stable for the right reasons," is the burden of the last third of *TJ* and of much of *PL*. Here is not the place to review Rawls's account of stability. Rawls recognizes the role of a sovereign in enforcing laws, and so ensuring reciprocity among citizens – thereby solving one aspect of the "assurance problem" – but argues, in *TJ*, that the relationship of friendship and mutual trust based on a public sense of justice could form a partial alternative to the unlimited sovereign found in the traditional views of Bodin and Hobbes (*TJ* 497). This view is further modified in *PL* to take more explicit note of the problem posed by a plurality of comprehensive moral and political conceptions, with the idea of an "overlapping consensus" of reasonable views taking the place of a single (partially) comprehensive doctrine. Rawls therefore maintains the goal of providing a stable basis for society without depending on the unified, unlimited sovereign of the traditional view.

Rawls's most explicit treatment of sovereignty is in *LP*. Here Rawls is explicit that "peoples," the subject of the Law of Peoples, lack some of the traditional powers of sovereignty (*LP* 25). For reasons already given, peoples reject the "internal" aspects of traditional, unlimited sovereignty. A corollary of this is a rejection of the right to go to war to promote state interests. This right is part of the unlimited nature of the traditional view – no external power, and so no international law, could limit a sovereign if the supposed sovereign was to be sovereign in fact. But, once we reject the idea that unlimited sovereignty is required to solve the problem of stability, we must ask why traditional "external" sovereignty should be accepted. In *LHMP* Rawls considers Hegel's argument that states need traditional sovereignty, including the right to go to war to promote state interests, if they are to be recognized as equal individuals (*LHMP* 361). This claim is connected to the idea, accepted by Hegel, that the anarchic nature of international relations will, with great certainty, lead to war. Rawls, however, argues that both aspects of the argument are mistaken.

Rawls rejects states as the subjects of international relations and justice, replacing them with "peoples" – a population organized in a political way that gives them a moral character of their own. The nature of the sovereignty held by peoples arises from the Law of Peoples itself, and is limited to what peoples would agree to in the appropriate circumstance (*LP* 27). The interests of peoples are limited by considerations of reasonableness, and include only territorial integrity, security and safety of citizens, preservation of political institutions, and the liberty and culture of civil society (*LP* 29). (Rawls makes this point most explicitly in relation to liberal peoples, but it is clear that nonaggressiveness, accepting war only in the case of self-defense, and an ability to accept fair terms of cooperation are features of "decent societies" as well (*LP* 88).) Rawls follows Kant in holding that such peoples will not be warlike, thereby rejecting the other aspect of Hegel's argument for traditional sovereignty (*LP* 54; *LHMP* 361–362). The interests noted above, however, are significant and justify a large degree of independence for peoples. Intervention into the internal affairs of a society can only be justified in the case of grave human rights violations (*LP* 79–80). We see, then, how Rawls's revisionary answer to the stability problem leads him to greatly revise the traditional notion of sovereignty, while still maintaining certain aspects of it in a recognizable form.

Matt Lister

SEE ALSO:

Democratic peace
Hobbes, Thomas
Human rights
Just war theory
Law of Peoples
Peoples
Stability

211.

STABILITY

RAWLS CONSISTENTLY MAINTAINS that a theory of justice must be shown to be stable. Rawls famously declares that justice is "the first virtue of social institutions" (*TJ* 3). But after explaining that the goal of his work is to vindicate this conviction by showing that there can be a set of just principles that could regulate the actions and institutions of a well-ordered society, Rawls goes on to note that such a conception of justice is "not the only prerequisite for a viable human community. There are other fundamental social problems, in particular those of coordination, efficiency, and stability" (*TJ* 5). Of these three, stability poses the most challenging problem for Rawls's theory of justice.

"It is evident," continues Rawls, "that these three problems are connected with that of justice." But Rawls's two principles of justice address the first two problems directly, by explaining how the goals of coordination and efficiency are to be made consistent with the priority of justice. According to the first principle, individuals can justly coordinate their plans of action by recognizing a scheme of equal basic liberties which allow each person to pursue a conception of the good. According to the second principle, a society can justly pursue efficiency by permitting a scheme of competitive economic incentives, and their resulting inequalities, only to the extent that this scheme improves the situation of the worst off. But nothing in the two principles shows that Rawls's proposed scheme of social cooperation must be stable – which for Rawls means that the scheme "must be more or less regularly complied with and its basic rules willingly acted upon; and when infractions occur, stabilizing forces should exist that prevent further violations and tend to restore the arrangement" (*TJ* 6). The two principles of justice do not themselves imply that individuals will willingly follow them, even

Stability / 805

if their content is specified in a way that appropriately unifies the values of justice, coordination, and efficiency.

One way of getting individuals to comply with principles of justice, of course, is force. Thus Rawls notes that a classic statement of the problem of stability, and a classic solution to that problem, can be found in Hobbes (*TJ* 211). For Hobbes, the principles of justice are set out in his laws of nature, which direct all individuals, for the sake of self-preservation, to surrender their liberty to use violence against one another, insofar as all others are willing to do the same. Peace requires a mutual agreement, but nothing in the nature of an agreement guarantees that the parties will actually comply. My self-preservation is a reason for keeping my agreement only if others are complying with that agreement; if not, my willingness to cooperate becomes a weakness to be exploited, and thus a threat to the end of self-preservation. And so Hobbes famously argues that the laws of nature, on their own, are unstable. They require a sovereign power, authorized to make positive law, and thus not bound to any agreement, which in turn allows the sovereign to use force against anyone who violates the law. What we gain from the sovereign is the threat to others that assures their compliance with the laws of nature, and that assurance is what allows us to observe those laws for ourselves.

Now Rawls grants that a scheme of coercive sanctions for violations of justice is legitimate and even necessary; however, he makes clear that such a scheme belongs to what he calls nonideal as opposed to ideal theory (*TJ* 8–9; 211–212). By ideal theory, Rawls means a theory that assumes that individuals will comply with the principles that the theory has shown to be justified. A nonideal theory, by contrast, is a theory that tells us what we can and should do when particular individuals do not comply with the principles that have been shown (ideally) to be justified. For Rawls, penal sanctions are coercive measures designed to bring individuals into compliance with the principles of justice; they are not justified on their own, but can and should be used only to the extent that they are needed to ensure the continued compliance with the principles of justice.

There is a certain puzzle about why Rawls brings this distinction into play here. It is not as if anyone would have missed the fact that penal sanctions were external forces introduced to insure compliance with justice. Hobbes recognizes that subjection to the will of the sovereign can be "very miserable" (i.e. clearly not ideal), arguing only that it is better than the condition of civil war (in a nonideal world, it offers the better hope for self-preservation). If stability is about assuring compliance with justice, and penal sanctions are always necessary to assure that compliance, then it would seem obvious that the problem of stability is always to be addressed by nonideal theory. But Rawls is saying that the problem of stability also can, and should, be addressed by ideal theory. It is this idea that seems most puzzling. If ideal theory assumes that individuals will always comply with justified principles, then how can the problem of stability even arise for ideal theory?

The answer is that a space may remain between even our best theory of justice and what is justified to the individuals who need to comply with it. Such individuals still need to know: what reason do they have to act justly, given their other values and their relation to justice? Though one can nonideally comply with justice out of fear of legal sanctions, one should also be able to (ideally) comply with justice because acting justly makes rational sense (*TJ* 496–497; *JF* 185).

Despite his emphasis on the coercive power of the sovereign, Hobbes does have an answer to the problem of stability that belongs to ideal theory. One can obey the laws of nature out of fear of punishment, but one can also obey them because they provide security (provided that others are obeying, of course). Self-preservation is a good reason for acting justly, not just for obeying the sovereign. This is because Hobbes holds that our self-preservation is the best reason for doing anything, both in the state of nature and in civil society.

For Rawls, however, things are more complicated. Rawlsian citizens choose the principles of justice for themselves, but they do so behind the veil of ignorance, where they are unaware of their particular positions in society and their particular conceptions of the good. The constraints imposed by the veil ensure that the principles of justice are not simply self-interested, but they also divide our actual selves from the rational choices of the parties in the original position. As citizens of a Rawlsian society, we must be able to say why we have good reason to regard the choices of those parties as our own. Rawls's problem of stability thus takes on a very specific form: how can actual citizens, with particular identities and particular conceptions of the good, endorse complying with what they would have chosen in the original position, without reference to their identities and their conceptions of the good? The subtlety here is that any solution to this problem must directly address each citizen's conception of the good – exactly what was abstracted away in the argument for the principles of justice.

Rawls's argument for the stability of his justice as fairness shifted dramatically from *A Theory of Justice* to *Political Liberalism*. Indeed, he writes that the inadequacy of the earlier argument for stability was his main reason for writing the later book (*PL* xv–xvii). In the earlier book, Rawls argues for a kind of *congruence* between the two principles of justice and individual conceptions of the good. Since those individual conceptions will vary, Rawls develops what he calls a "thin theory of the good," assumed to be common to every fully developed (and hence thicker) conception. He calls this thin theory "goodness as rationality," with rationality understood in the merely instrumental sense used in the theory of rational choice, and also in the original position. The thin theory says that individuals will each have an interest in achieving the ends set out in their conceptions of the good, and of developing the means that will allow them to effectively pursue those ends. "The problem," writes Rawls, "is whether the regulative desire to adopt the standpoint of justice belongs to a person's own good when viewed in the light of the thin theory with no restrictions on information" (*TJ* 497).

Rawls's solution to this problem is a complex argument in moral psychology that sprawls across part III of *A Theory of Justice*. He argues first that individuals in a well-ordered society will normally be socialized to develop a sense of justice, and that this sense of justice will align with justice as fairness (*TJ* §§69–75, 76–77). To justify the first claim, Rawls appeals to a series of premises about developmental psychology. He argues that children with loving parents will come to identify with the moral demands imposed on them by their parents, and later come to understand those demands as rationally related to the rules required for any association that provides mutual support and advantage, and eventually as principles that hold even if they conflict with immediate self-interest. To justify the second claim, Rawls argues that the commitment to such principles is better supported by justice as fairness than with utilitarianism, since the principles that would be chosen in the original position have a better claim to be advancing the interests of each individual, taken as an individual. Well-socialized individuals will normally have an interest in developing and using the capacities that allow them to pursue their ends (the Aristotelian principle – *TJ* §65). These capacities can be better realized in what Humboldt called social unions (*TJ* §79), contexts that allow persons to develop and reinforce their powers interpersonally and institutionally. On the thin theory of the good, then, individuals have an interest in the flourishing of the social unions that would better allow them to realize their ends. And since a well-ordered society can be understood as a social union of social unions, there will be a kind of psychological congruence between the individual's sense of the good, now understood to include a commitment to social union, and that individual's sense of justice, understood as a commitment to the good of the well-ordered society. Individuals who cared only for their own goods against the good of justice would suffer a kind of psychological alienation, their individual goods cut off from both their sense of justice and the values of social union that could sustain their own individual goods (*TJ* §§85–86).

Rawls's later work questions not the psychological details of this argument for congruence but the fundamental premise on which any unified argument for congruence depends: that there is enough unity among the various conceptions of the good to formulate a thin theory of the good applicable to them all. Modern liberal societies are characterized by what Rawls calls the fact of pluralism: fundamental and ineradicable differences between conceptions of the good life. Further, this pluralism is reasonable pluralism: it is the result of different individuals reasoning to the best of their abilities about the nature of the good, and despite their most sincere and disciplined efforts to persuade one another, failing to reach agreement (*PL* xvi–xvii). Under conditions of reasonable pluralism, any Rawlsian argument for congruence is doubly inappropriate. It is unlikely to produce consensus, and it fails even to address the ways individuals reason diversely about their own goods. In his later work, Rawls speaks not simply of conceptions of the good but of the comprehensive doctrines that seek to justify them. A comprehensive doctrine is a historically established and ongoing exercise of practical reasoning about the nature of the good. In the language of the later work, it is as if Rawls's earlier argument for congruence had tried to show that justice as fairness was rational on the terms of every comprehensive doctrine. It is not simply that it is practically difficult to show that every comprehensive doctrine would affirm the congruence argument; it is also that it is the comprehensive doctrines themselves, as exercises of practical reasoning, and not Rawls's own theory, that must do the affirming. So instead of arguing that every comprehensive doctrine *will*, through a common line of reasoning, come to affirm the truth of political liberalism, the later Rawls argues instead that every reasonable comprehensive doctrine *can*, through its own favored lines of reasoning, come to affirm the rationality of political liberalism. Rawls thus hypothesizes the possibility of an overlapping consensus, through which different comprehensive doctrines justify political liberalism in their own ways (*PL* 133–172; *JF* 187).

As before, this new account of stability is the second half of a two-stage justification of the theory of justice. In the later work, Rawls argues first that the fact of reasonable pluralism demands that political arrangements, which rely on coercive laws, must be justified without reference to any particular comprehensive doctrine. Reasonableness, therefore, is a necessary condition of the rational justification of political arrangements under conditions of reasonable pluralism. Rawls then presents his theory of justice as a merely reasonable theory; i.e. he presents the constraints of the original position, which leads to the choice of the two principles of justice, as deriving solely from the requirement of reasonableness, from the need to abstract from the plurality of conceptions of the good life. Since the original position is intended as the sole framework for political justification, Rawls is thus arguing that reasonableness, itself only a necessary condition for political justification, is in political liberalism regarded as also a sufficient condition for political justification. The task of showing that merely reasonable political justification is also rationally sufficient is the later work's version of the original problem of the stability: why should citizens act on what would be chosen in the original position, in the light of their full conceptions of the good?

Since Rawls no longer presumes to speak for the various comprehensive doctrines, he can only hypothesize that they can come to an overlapping consensus around merely reasonable political justification. He does that by laying out what he calls a "model case" illustrating how different sorts of comprehensive doctrines might relate rational and reasonable justification (*PL* 145–149, 168–172). There are three options. First, a comprehensive doctrine might hold a conception of rationality that exactly matches the notion of the reasonable. This is comprehensive liberalism: political liberalism is justified because liberalism already holds the right account of practical justification. Second, a comprehensive doctrine might hold an account of practical justification thinner than that of the reasonable: this is a kind of pluralism, which might nonetheless regard liberal politics as one value worth having in a world of irreducibly plural goods. Finally, a comprehensive doctrine might defend a conception of practical justification thicker than that of the reasonable. This is illustrated by many traditional religious doctrines, which affirm deeper sources of rational authority, but might nonetheless view religious coercion in the political realm as inconsistent with the special relation individuals have to religious value. So whether a comprehensive doctrine is thicker, thinner, or tailored to the boundaries of the reasonable, there are familiar and recognizable routes for it to enter into an overlapping consensus around a merely political liberalism.

If overlapping consensus obtains, it is a rational consensus, justified by the deepest commitment of each reasonable comprehensive doctrine. In none of Rawls's work is stability simply a practical problem of compliance, to be solved through coercion or proper socialization. Rather it is a matter of showing that we have good reason to respect what would be chosen in the original position. In the early work, this is a matter of showing that our own goods cohere with a Rawlsian sense of justice. But that account unjustifiably assumes a Rawlsian account of our own goods (and perhaps also a comprehensive Rawlsian theory of justice). In the later work, these defects are made good by recasting the argument for stability as the claim that overlapping consensus of comprehensive doctrines can show the merely reasonable to be, for political purposes, fully rational.

Larry Krasnoff

SEE ALSO:

Congruence
Hobbes, Thomas
Ideal and nonideal theory
Moral person
Moral psychology
Reciprocity
Sense of justice
Social union
Thin and full theories of good

212.

STATESMAN AND DUTY OF STATESMANSHIP

JUSTICE AS FAIRNESS makes moral demands on all citizens. For example, Rawls holds that there are natural duties on all individuals that include, among others, duties "not to harm or injure another," "not to cause unnecessary suffering," and "to support and to comply with just institutions that exist and apply to us" (*TJ* 98, 99). But justice as fairness also holds that when individuals accept certain positions with special responsibility and authority, they put themselves under obligations that are more demanding than the moral requirements that apply to ordinary citizens (*TJ* 97). As an exercise in ideal theory, justice as fairness assumes that all individuals have a sense of justice (and are motivated to comply with it) at least above a certain minimal threshold. In this respect, they are all equal. However, even as part of ideal theory, Rawls notes that "individuals presumably have varying capacities for a sense of justice" above this threshold (*TJ* 443). And a higher-than-ordinary sensitivity to concerns of justice may be a qualification for certain social positions.

In *The Law of Peoples*, Rawls discusses moral demands in the highly nonideal condition of war. Among other requirements, he notes "so far as possible, the human rights of the members of the other side, both civilians and soldiers" must be respected (*LP* 96). One of the reasons for this is "to foreshadow during a war both the kind of peace they aim for and the kind of relations they seek" (*LP* 96). But this requires seeing beyond the immediate interests of a society to recognize their long-term goal of establishing a just peace and a society of peoples of mutual respect. While these duties apply to all individuals, they apply especially to soldiers and even more powerfully to their military commanders and political leaders.

Individuals in positions of great political and social power have special duties to identify paths toward achieving these longer-term ends and "to hold fast to the aim of gaining a just peace" (*LP* 98). These are the duties of statesmanship. A statesman is an honorific title attributed to those who fulfill these duties admirably. Rawls gives the examples of Washington and Lincoln. "Statesmen may have their own interests when they hold office, yet they must be selfless in their judgments and assessments of their society's fundamental interests and must not be swayed, especially in war, by passions of vindictiveness" (*LP* 97–98). Although Rawls does not mention it explicitly in this context, a statesman should also help steer his or her country toward fulfilling its duty of assistance. The duty of statesmen is to identify the path toward the creation of a peaceful and just society of peoples and then to keep his or her society on that path.

Jon Mandle

SEE ALSO:

> *Human rights*
> *Ideal and nonideal theory*
> *Just war theory*
> *Law of Peoples*

213.

STRAINS OF COMMITMENT

RAWLS WRITES THAT in selecting among alternate principles of justice we are to view the parties in the original position as permanently consigning those they represent to a particular scheme of cooperation; that is, to a basic structure for society that distributes rights and liberties, opportunities, and social and economic goods in specific ways. It is crucial, therefore, that the parties only select principles of justice that they believe actual people can fully endorse, or more precisely, principles to which agents who view society as a fair system of cooperation in which all are treated as free and equal can remain committed in thought and action over the course of an entire lifetime. Principles of justice that do not meet this criterion impose (excessive) strains of commitment on those who inhabit the society whose basic structure they specify, and therefore manifest two distinct, albeit related, defects in virtue of which they ought to be rejected. First, the selection of such principles in the original position exhibits bad faith. We ought not to endorse as standards regulating the basic structure of society principles of justice to which we are unlikely to remain true, since to do so is to display an inadequate (not to mention morally reprehensible) commitment to treating others justly. Rawls's use of contract terminology such as "commitment" and "bad faith" to make this argument reflects a conception of the principles of justice as the object of agreement between free and equal persons, and not (merely) as the object of rational choice by agents behind the veil of ignorance aiming to maximize the position of the worst off in society, as has sometimes been thought. Second, principles of justice that impose strains of commitment fail to generate stability for the right reasons. People who grow up in a society structured by such principles will not acquire a reasoned and informed allegiance to them; rather, whatever degree of stability that society enjoys will result largely from a combination of coercion, false consciousness, and alienation.

Rawls introduces the idea of the strains of commitment as part of an argument for why the parties in the original position will select the principles of justice he proposes over the principle of (maximal) average utility. Consider, first, the distribution of the basic liberties, such as freedom of thought and of conscience, the right to vote and participate in politics, and freedom of association. The parties in the original position know that the basic liberties protect the fundamental interests of citizens conceived of as free and equal. They also know that if they adopt Rawls's two principles of justice, then everyone will be guaranteed a highly satisfactory level of the basic liberties. Finally, they know that in certain circumstances, ones that plausibly might obtain, the principle of average utility will require that some members of society be deprived of one or more of their basic liberties. For example, the denial of freedom of conscience to a religious minority may well produce an increase in aggregate welfare. In light of this knowledge, the parties will recognize that the principle of average utility imposes excessive strains of commitment, and so ought to be rejected in favor of Rawls's two principles of justice. Given the realistic possibility of organizing society so that all could enjoy a fully adequate scheme of the basic liberties, what reason is there for a person who believes that all members of society should be treated as free and equal to accept a basic structure that might systematically deny her protection of one (or more) of her fundamental interests? None, Rawls answers, and so it exhibits bad faith to assert that in the original position the principle of average utility would be selected over the two principles of justice. Indeed, Rawls maintains that far from constituting a basic structure that all can affirm in thought and action, the principle of average utility will generate oppressive strains of commitment for those denied one or more of the basic liberties. They will view society's basic structure as imposed upon them, and bide their time in sullen resentment until the opportunity to overthrow it arises. Therefore a society in which all of the primary goods, including the basic liberties, are distributed according to the principle of average utility will fail to be stable for the right reasons; indeed, it may not be stable at all.

Suppose, however, that the parties in the original position select between Rawls's two principles of justice and a form of restricted utilitarianism in which the aim of maximizing average welfare only governs the distribution of income and wealth, but not the other primary goods. Furthermore, suppose that this goal may be pursued only once all members of society have had satisfied those needs essential for a decent human life. Here, too, Rawls appeals to the strains of commitment to argue that the parties will select the two principles; that is, that they will endorse the use of the difference principle rather than the principle of average utility to regulate the distribution of income and wealth in society. Though the less advantaged in a society organized along the lines of restricted utilitarianism will not view its basic structure as oppressive, neither will they view it as fully recognizing their status as free and equal citizens. Rather, when economic inequalities have no basis in a principle of reciprocity, the less advantaged will adopt a cynical attitude toward political society and feel estranged from it. They will experience what might be called alienating strains of commitment. The explanation for why this is so begins with Rawls's observation that contingencies such as native endowments that can give rise to economic inequality do so only because they are exercised within a basic social structure that depends on the cooperation of all. In a society in which economic inequalities are limited to those sanctioned by the difference principle (and consistent with the fair value of the political liberties and genuine equality of opportunity), the less advantaged will be able to view the greater life prospects enjoyed by the more advantaged as reciprocation for the latter's contribution to improving their own life prospects. Thus the less advantaged will still be able to conceive of political society as a fair system of cooperation in which all are regarded as free and equal, despite differences in income and wealth. The same is not true, however, for the less advantaged in a society organized according to restricted utilitarianism. Thus the selection of a utilitarian principle, even when restricted in the ways described above, will exhibit bad faith, since no one who is honest with herself will be able to view a society organized along such lines as a fair system of cooperation between free and equal citizens. Nor, for that very reason, will such a society be stable for the right reasons.

Two final points regarding the strains of commitment warrant a brief discussion. First, Rawls recognizes that any conception of justice has the potential to conflict with a person's legitimate interests, and in particular, those grounded in a person's permissible comprehensive doctrine. It follows that the use of the strains of commitment argument to defend the superiority of one conception of justice over another will likely involve a comparative claim; that is, an assertion that one conception of justice imposes fewer strains of commitment than does a rival conception. Second, Rawls employs the strains of commitment argument to defend the claim that a fully just and stable society will be one organized along the lines of his two proposed principles of justice as fairness rather than the principle of maximal average utility. That is, the argument figures in what Rawls calls ideal theory. Rawls does not intend his remarks on the strains of commitment to address the difficulties that those who benefit from past and present injustices might experience in transitioning to just institutional arrangements. This is a pressing question, to be sure, but it is a matter of nonideal, not ideal, theory.

David Lefkowitz

SEE ALSO:

> *Basic structure of society*
> *Facts, general (in OP argument and as part of justification)*
> *Lexical priority: liberty, opportunity, wealth*
> *Maximin rule of choice*
> *Mixed conceptions of justice*
> *Moral person*
> *Moral psychology*
> *The original position*
> *Two principles of justice (in justice as fairness)*
> *Utilitarianism*

214.

SUPREME COURT AND JUDICIAL REVIEW

JUDICIAL REVIEW AND constitutionalism play an important role in Rawls's thought on two large issues, namely, the institutionalization of the two principles of justice, and the Supreme Court as an "exemplar" of public reason.

Rawls thinks of his project as articulating a conception of justice specifically for a constitutional democracy. He seeks to show that the conception of justice originally outlined in part I of *A Theory of Justice* has institutional implications and can be extended into a "workable" political order that is "a reasonable approximation and extension of our considered judgments" (*TJ* 195). Hence, his theory requires some way of justifying an order of relations between majoritarian, legislative institutions, and adjudicative ones. Rawls does this through a procedure he calls "the four stage sequence of application." The first, best-known stage of this procedure involves parties in the original position selecting principles of justice for the basic structure of society, with "the veil of ignorance" fully drawn. The principles of justice must then be embodied in actual political institutions under conditions of "partial compliance," i.e., where political principles must be coercively enforced through law. As such, a set of political institutions can only be an "imperfect procedure" for implementing the principles of justice (*TJ* 201). However, its degree of imperfection is relative to its institutional design, and after selecting the two principles of justice, parties in the original position enter a "constitutional convention," where they become aware of general facts about their particular society and the types of political

817

institutions available to them. Rawls concludes that parties in the constitutional convention would opt to enumerate the basic liberties of the first principle in something like the American Bill of Rights and provide for a judicial mechanism of enforcing them. In other words, Rawls is inclined to treat basic liberties (along with questions of government structure) as "constitutional essentials," and social and economic inequality more as a matter of ordinary politics to be addressed in the third, legislative stage of application (*PL* 228–229).

Thus, Rawls believes that his theory of justice can accommodate, and in a way presupposes, the fundamental ideas of modern constitutionalism and the rule of law: distinctions between, on the one hand, "higher" law of constitutional principle and the constituent power of "We the People," and, on the other, "ordinary" law and political power. Ordinary law and politics is the "day-to-day" exercise of governmental power, rendered legitimate by a constitutional framework defined in its essentials "by the political ideal of a people to govern itself in a certain way" (*PL* 232), namely, through public reason informed by a conception of justice. Because this higher law represents the basic commitments a people undertakes in order to constitute itself as a democratic one, it must be regarded as more or less fixed and constant – although democratic ideals of justice embodied in a constitution may progressively evolve "to become broader and more inclusive" (as described by Bruce Ackerman's "dualist" conception of democracy) (*PL* 238), they cannot be legitimately renounced. This explains Rawls's contention (controversially, and contra Ackerman) that the Supreme Court would be right to refuse to acknowledge legislative attempts to amend the constitution in a way that repealed a basic commitment of democratic justice (e.g. revoking the First Amendment) (*PL* 239).

Rawls's reasons for institutionalizing the first principle of justice at the constitutional stage of application, while mostly leaving the second to the legislative stage, are complex. He takes it that the basic liberties are amenable to judicial enforcement through constitutional review: they are defined as bright lines of principle that ought, given the priority that they are accorded in the original position, to constrain political actors. Although of course new cases can raise difficult problems of application, and may be extremely controversial at the time of court decisions, the content of the basic liberties is supposed to be consistent over time, and constitutional courts staffed by legal professionals appear better equipped to provide for this than majoritarian, elected, representative institutions, in which actors have more immediate and parochial interests. Such an account of judicial review is provisional and instrumental: the object is to design a system of constitutional government that minimizes the likelihood of injustice; judicial review presents itself as a prudent mechanism for protecting constitutional essentials, but this may not be true under all historical circumstances (*PL* 240).

Rawls's concern with the consistency of the basic liberties goes beyond what has traditionally been seen as the rule of law's virtue of treating like cases alike. A crucial ingredient of Rawls's overlapping consensus is what he calls publicity conditions: "the principle of liberal legitimacy" requires that citizens of a constitutional democracy credibly believe that, at least on important issues pertaining to the basic structure, the laws that they are subject to are ones that they would be reasonably willing to impose on themselves (*PL* 137). This means that citizens should be aware that the conception of justice they are jointly committed to effectively shapes and constrains the lawmaking process (*PL* 66–67). Embedding the basic liberties in something like a Bill of Rights renders them public, along with guaranteeing that legislation is regularly subject to judicial review in order to ensure that it respects the basic liberties.

The question no doubt arises as to why Rawls embeds only the first principle of justice in the constitution, especially considering that, although the basic liberties are given priority in the original position, he acknowledges that their "fair value" depends on citizens' being practically and materially equipped to make use of them (*PL* 324–331; *JF* 176–179). And plainly, issues impacting the "fair value" of the basic liberties are frequently on the dockets of constitutional courts (e.g. nondiscrimination and equal protection issues). Some constitutional designers, notably in post-apartheid South Africa, have experimented with constitutional mandates of certain social and material conditions, and others have argued for constitutional welfare rights within a Rawlsian framework (Michelman 1972). While not ruling out such arrangements, Rawls holds that the material "adequacy" of the basic liberties cannot be effectively secured by the constitutional convention stage. The main reason is that he holds that violations of the basic liberties "are often plainly evident" in a way that violations of the difference principle are not (*TJ* 199): factors that affect patterns of inequality are a matter of complex social and economic policy requiring bureaucratic expertise, public feedback, and trial and error, among other tasks that legislatures are often better equipped to perform than courts (*TJ* 201).

This is not to say that Rawls thinks that the work of the Supreme Court is straightforward. For although the basic liberties as a whole have "priority," no one right or liberty within the "scheme" defined by the first principle (most generally, freedom of thought and conscience; of private and political association; of bodily integrity; and rights associated with the rule of law) should be thought of as an absolute rule that trumps other considerations, as, for example, property rights are often regarded in libertarian theories (*TJ* 203). Since Rawls's idea is to define a scheme of liberties equally adequate for the exercise of all citizens' moral powers, he endorses a "balancing" approach to constitutional jurisprudence, and while he does not hold that the constitution ought to (or can) mandate the fair value of the basic liberties, he is enthusiastic about legislative policies that aim to do so. From these considerations follow both Rawls's endorsement of the string of free speech decisions culminating in *Brandenburg* v. *Ohio* (1969), which expanded constitutionally protected speech to include "subversive" speech, and his dismay at *Buckley* v. *Valeo* (1976), in which the justices held the regulation of a certain form of political speech (campaign donations) aimed at making political liberties for all more equally adequate amounted to the restriction of what they regarded as an inviolable right of individuals to speak as they wish, using the means at their disposal (*PL* 340–363).

Finally, the constitution and the public interpretations of it offered by the Supreme Court can be a key node of public reason in a constitutional democracy, and provide a prominent "exemplar" for how it ought to be conducted. For in an overlapping consensus, citizens know one another to be commonly committed to a scheme of basic liberties, while not relying on a shared sectarian doctrine to undergird it. The Supreme Court manifests this understanding of the basic liberties by justifying itself to a diverse public, normally making arguments in favor of its decisions by appealing to established legal doctrine and "political values"; it seeks to articulate the basic principles of law that all are subject to in terms that all reasonable persons can accept (*PL* 232).

As such, Rawls holds that the Court provides an instructive example of how political justification in a well-ordered society ought to be conducted: reasonable citizens ought to concern themselves to publicly present their political views (at least those concerning fundamental matters) by employing the shared political values embodied in the political conception of justice, rather than

Supreme Court and judicial review / 821

"the whole truth" as they see it, by the lights of their comprehensive doctrine (*CP* 579).

Todd Hedrick

SEE ALSO:

Basic liberties
Constitution and constitutional essentials
Democracy
The four-stage sequence
Freedom of speech
Justification: freestanding/political
Legitimacy
Procedural justice
Public reason
Publicity
Rights, constitutional
Rule of law

T

215.

TAXATION

WHEN CONSIDERING THE institutions and policies of a society that would realize Rawls's principles of social justice, it is clear that the tax system would be an important part of a just basic structure (see e.g. *TJ* 234–235). However, despite the centrality of a system of taxation to the realization of justice in practice, Rawls does not give us a systematic account of the nature of taxation in a just society. Instead, his remarks on the subject are somewhat fragmentary, "illustrative and highly tentative" (*JF* 136), leaving us with a sketch that would need to have its details completed in practice through democratic deliberation at the legislative stage.

Rawls's clearest and least tentative remarks about taxation consist in his avowed aim of using the tax system to realize "the idea of regulating bequest and restricting inheritance" (*JF* 161), in connection with realizing fair equality of opportunity. Following the suggested forms of taxation described by James Meade in his description of a property-owning democracy (Meade 1964), Rawls endorses a highly progressive, recipient-oriented (rather than estate-oriented) form of taxation on bequests and capital transfers, "whereby the principle of progressive taxation is applied at the receiver's end," covering both cases of inheritance and gifts *inter vivos* (*TJ* 245; *JF* 161). Surprisingly, Rawls sees the aim of progressive taxation not as encompassing the goal of raising funds for the provision of public goods, "but solely to prevent concentrations of wealth that are considered inimical to background justice" (*JF* 161); in terms of the distinction made by Murphy and Nagel (2002, chapter 4), Rawls targets progressive taxation at the job of redistribution, and not as a way of funding public provision of services.

Rawls's thoughts on the use of the tax system to realize the difference principle, and to "raise the revenues that justice requires" (*TJ* 246), are in many ways more surprising than his views on taxation and fair equality of opportunity, and are indeed in some respects rather puzzling. Rawls rather tentatively endorses a proportional (NB *not* progressive) expenditure tax as a replacement for standard forms of income taxation, a substitution which he considers welcome on the grounds that an expenditure tax would tax people "according to how much they use of the goods and services produced and not according to how much they contribute" (*JF* 161), such that "it imposes a levy according to how much a person takes out of the common store of goods and not according to how much he contributes" (*TJ* 246). Rawls may be right that this thought is attractive "at the level of common sense precepts of justice" (*TJ* 246), but it is difficult to avoid the conclusion that its plausibility collapses under scrutiny. In a closed economy, one individual's expenditure just is another individual's income (given that, in Paul Krugman's phrase, "Your spending is my income, and my spending is your income" (Krugman 2012)), and so it seems muddled to talk of expenditure as extraction of goods from some common store. It may also seem problematic to endorse a tax system that would structurally disincentivize spending relative to saving as, given Keynes's "paradox of thrift," one should be aware of the depressive economic consequences it could produce (Keynes 1936, chapter 7).

Whatever the merits of expenditure vs. income taxation, it is particularly puzzling that Rawls here endorses a flat (i.e. proportionate) form of taxation rather than progressive taxation. His suggestion is that a flat tax may be more efficient, as it would do less to interfere with incentives, but no evidence is provided for this apparent supposition. Rawls suggests that policy-makers could aim at the rough satisfaction of the difference principle "by raising and lowering this [social] minimum and adjusting the constant marginal rate of taxation" (*JF* 161), but there seems no plausible reason to hamstring policy-makers to this restrictive set of options, rather than also allowing them to vary the number and particular thresholds of higher progressive marginal rates of taxation. It should, though, be emphasized here that Rawls is cautious and tentative on these questions, ceding technical questions of taxation policy to the province of "questions of political judgement" in a democratic society, suggesting that they are "not part of a theory of justice" (*TJ* 246). It should also be borne in mind that Rawls's discussion of income and expenditure taxation assume the background of a property-owning democracy with broadly dispersed holdings of capital (as guaranteed by the aggressive taxation, and subsequent redistribution, of transferred capital); he acknowledges that, under near-to-current conditions, "given the injustice of existing institutions, even steeply progressive income taxes" may be justified, all things considered (*TJ* 247).

The broadly Rawlsian approach to taxation perhaps finds its fullest expression to date in Liam Murphy and Thomas Nagel's *The Myth of Ownership: Taxes and Justice* (Murphy and Nagel 2002). In that book, Murphy and Nagel show that measures of tax equity in terms of horizontal and vertical equity, as deployed in the traditional public finance literature (e.g. Musgrave 1959), lose their salience when the tax system is treated as simply one aspect of the basic structure of society, and when property rights are understood as distributed through that basic structure. Once one rejects the "everyday libertarianism" that treats pretax income as a morally salient baseline for the assessment of tax systems, traditional measures of tax equity make no sense. It is notable that, although Murphy and Nagel's approach is fully Rawlsian in its structure and assumptions, they strongly dismiss a number of the particular views that Rawls is tempted to endorse: e.g. fairness-based arguments for favoring consumption as the tax base, and the preference for proportional rather than progressive taxes in funding public services. Much future work needs to be undertaken in thinking through the implications of a Rawlsian approach to taxation for the appropriate structure and justification of the taxation of environmental pollutants, land, capital, corporations, and financial transactions, as well as in addressing issues such as the proper balance between local, state, and even global, taxes.

Martin O'Neill and Thad Williamson

SEE ALSO:

Basic structure of society
Branches of government
Difference principle
Fair equality of opportunity
Four-stage sequence
Legitimate expectations
Nagel, Thomas
Property-owning democracy

216.

THIN AND FULL THEORIES OF GOOD

R AWLS FIRST DRAWS the distinction between the thin and the full theories of goodness in §60 of *A Theory of Justice*. The first and perhaps the most important thing to note about the distinction is that it is a distinction between two *theories* or *accounts* of goodness. It should not be conflated, as it sometimes is, with a very different distinction that is drawn by some of Rawls's critics. Communitarians sometimes oppose "thin" to "thick" and predicate these terms of *conceptions* of the good endorsed by members of Rawls's well-ordered society or by members of the actual societies with which we are familiar. But this is not the distinction Rawls is drawing. He opposes "thin," not to "thick," but to "full" and he applies both adjectives to accounts of what makes something good rather than to conceptions of the good.

The thin and full theories differ in two respects. First, they differ in the resources on which they draw. The full theory "takes the principles of justice as already secured" (*TJ* 349) and so draws on those principles to account for goodness, while the thin theory does not. This difference leads to the second difference, which is one of scope. The thin theory can account for the value of some goods, such as the primary goods. Indeed, Rawls says that he introduces the thin theory precisely to account for the value of those goods (*TJ* 347), though we shall see later that the thin theory can account for the value of other goods as well. Because the full theory draws on more philosophical resources than the thin theory does, it can account for values that the thin theory cannot. In particular, because the full theory draws on the principles of justice, it – unlike the thin theory (see *TJ* 381) – can account for various kinds of moral goodness. Among these is the goodness of the morally worthy person, who is good because she "has the moral sentiments that support adherence to" the principles of justice (*TJ* 384).

Though the thin and the full theories are different accounts of goodness, they are not unrelated. Rawls says that the full theory is a "develop[ment]" of the thin theory (*TJ* 382). Indeed, he might have gone further. Instead of saying in §60 that he was "distinguish[ing] between two theories of the good" (*TJ* 347), he might have said that he was drawing an important distinction within a single overarching account of goodness. To see why he might have said this, it will be useful to recall the main point of Rawls's overarching account of goodness in *TJ*, an account he calls "goodness as rationality."

Goodness as rationality is a "rational-desire" account of goodness. The central thesis of such accounts can be put, most crudely, as the claim that the good is the object of rational desire. Something is a good instance of its kind if it has the properties it is rational to want in things of that kind, given what things of that kind "are used for or expected to do" (*TJ* 351). To use one of Rawls's examples, a particular timepiece is a good watch if it has the properties it is rational to want in watches, given what watches are used for. But sometimes we speak of an object, not as a good example of the kind of thing it is, but as good *for* a person or as part of his good. Goodness as rationality can be used to explicate this kind of goodness as well. Something is good for a person if (i) it has the properties it is rational for him to want in things of that kind, given his aims and (ii) his aims are organized into a plan of life that is rational given his circumstances and abilities (*TJ* 350–351). Note that the way goodness as rationality accounts for a thing's goodness and for something's being good for a person are both "information-sensitive." What it is rational to want in things of a given kind can only be determined in light of information about what a known population normally uses things of that kind for. What it is rational for someone to want depends upon what he knows – or perhaps what he ought to know – about his own aims and how to achieve them.

Both the thin and the full theories of goodness use this rational-desire account of goodness, and so both give accounts of what makes something good and of what makes something good for a person that conform to its pattern. The differences between the thin and the full theories are differences between two accounts of goodness that apply the same template. The first of the differences mentioned above was that the full theory draws on greater philosophical resources than the thin theory. Since goodness as rationality is information-sensitive, that difference can now be redescribed this way. When the full theory accounts for the goodness of things and of persons, and for the goodness of things for persons, it uses Rawls's rational-desire account of goodness, but it uses a richer informational base than the thin theory does. The informational base of the full theory includes the principles of justice. The informational base of the thin theory does not. This difference between the informational bases of the two theories accounts for the second difference between them, the difference in scope. To see this, it will be useful to start by seeing how the thin theory accounts for the value of some of the goods that fall within its scope, the primary goods.

Rawls says that he introduces the thin theory of the good to secure "assumptions about the parties' motives in the original position" and, more specifically, about their motives to choose one principle or set of principles rather than another. In asserting the need for a theory of the good to secure these assumptions, Rawls may seem to be saying that if the parties are to have any motivation at all to choose, then there must be some things which appear good to them. But on rational-desire accounts of goodness, the goodness of something, or our perception of its goodness, does not explain the desire for it or account for the rationality of desiring it. Rather, to say that something is rationally desired by someone just is to say that it is good for him. So what Rawls means is that if parties in the original position are to be motivated to make a choice, there must be some things it is rational for them to want which they can get by adopting principles. Because of the veil of ignorance, they cannot want those things in light of their circumstances, abilities, aims or plans. If they are to make a choice, there must therefore be things it is rational for them to want regardless of their aims and plans or, as Rawls says, some things "it is rational to want...whatever else is wanted" (*TJ* 380). Those things are the primary goods. The rational desire to secure those goods motivates the parties' choice of principles of justice.

Thus the account of the value of the primary goods to parties in the original position follows the pattern of goodness as rationality. The primary goods are good for parties because it is rational for them to want them. Moreover, the account reflects the information-sensitivity of goodness as rationality, since the primary goods are good for the parties in the original position because they want them in light of what they know about their aims and plans. The original position is merely the limit case of this information-sensitivity, since the parties have no information about their own aims and plans at all. Finally, because the account of the value of the primary goods does not appeal to the content of Rawls's principles of justice – as it cannot if the primary goods provide the motivation for choosing among principles – that account is clearly provided by the thin theory of goodness.

In writings after *Theory of Justice*, Rawls gave increasing prominence to the claim that free and equal moral persons are thought of as having two moral powers: a capacity for a sense of justice and a capacity for a conception of the good. At the same time, he began to cite different reasons when explaining why parties in the original position want primary goods. Whereas in *Theory of Justice*, he said that primary goods are things "it is rational to want...whatever else is wanted" (*TJ* 380), in these later writings he described the primary goods as things which "are generally necessary as social conditions and all-purpose means to enable human beings to realize and exercise their moral powers and to pursue their final ends" (*CP* 314). Parties in the original position are then said to want the primary goods because of the interest they know they will have in developing and exercising their moral powers when they step out from behind the veil.

While this revision may constitute a significant change in what Rawls says about why the primary goods are wanted, it did not require a departure from his use of goodness as rationality to account for the value of primary goods for the parties in the original position. For in later writings as in *A Theory of Justice*, Rawls insisted that "the parties' preference for primary goods is rational" (*CP* 314). This insistence allowed him to maintain, as he had in *A Theory of Justice*, that the primary goods are good for the parties because it is rational for them to want them. Rawls's account of their goodness remained information-sensitive. In stressing the parties' interest in conditions and means needed to develop and exercise the moral powers, Rawls was merely adding to their information base by adding general information about their moral psychology. Because the information he added did not include or presuppose the principles of justice, Rawls enriched the parties' information base while staying within the thin theory.

Of course, primary goods are not good only for parties in the original position. They are good for members of the well-ordered society too. Their goodness for members of the well-ordered society can be accounted for in the same way as their goodness for parties in the original position. But many other things are thought to be good, and are good for members of the well-ordered society. An especially important case of goodness is the goodness of the morally worthy person. We will need to see how Rawls accounts for that.

We saw earlier that according to goodness as rationality, something is a good instance of its kind if it has the properties it is rational to want in things of that kind, given what things of that kind "are used for or expected to do" (*TJ* 351). If goodness as rationality is to account for the goodness of the morally worthy person, it must follow this template. We saw then that the account of a thing's goodness which is provided by goodness as rationality is information-sensitive because it depends upon the normal uses or expectations of a known population. The use of goodness as rationality to account for moral worth therefore depends upon the identification of the relevant population. The population Rawls chooses is, not surprisingly, the membership of a well-ordered society. And so he says that "a good person has the features of moral character that it is rational for members of a well-ordered society to want in their associates" (*TJ* 384). The goodness of the morally worthy person is accounted for by the rational desirability of those features.

Is this a plausible account of moral worth? In a well-ordered society, everyone knows she has a sense of justice and is inclined to abide by the constraints. It is therefore rational for each member of a well-ordered society to want others to abide by those constraints too rather than to take advantage of her (*TJ* 385). And so it is rational for each to want others to have a sense of justice and the other qualities of character that ease compliance with the demands of justice. That is, "the features of moral character that it is rational for members of the well-ordered society to want in their associates" are those qualities of character that we intuitively regard as the moral virtues. Of course, the contents of the principles of justice themselves must express what we regard as plausible demands, but Rawls thinks his do. Provided he is right about this, goodness as rationality can plausibly account for the goodness of the morally worthy person.

We have seen that Rawls also uses goodness as rationality to account for goodness *for persons*. If we think that it is good for members of the well-ordered society that their compatriots be just, then goodness as rationality must be able to account for that value as well. It should now be clear how it does so. It is rational for members of the well-ordered society to want their compatriots to be morally worthy because each knows that she has a sense of justice and, therefore, that her aims include the aim of being a just person herself. So the moral worth of others is something it is rational for each member of the well-ordered society to want in light of information about her aims and ends. It follows from goodness as rationality that having morally worthy compatriots is good for her.

Rawls's accounts of the goodness of the morally worthy person and of the value to members of the well-ordered society of having morally worthy compatriots – unlike his accounts of the goodness of the primary goods and of their value to the parties in the original position – appeal to the contents of the two principles of justice. They are therefore provided by the full rather than the thin account of goodness. But despite this difference in their informational bases, the

Thin and full theories of good / 833

former accounts – like the latter – follow the template of goodness of rationality and reflect its information-sensitivity. It seems that the full theory can therefore be described as one part of goodness as rationality. As if to confirm this, Rawls speaks at one point in *Theory of Justice* of "the full theory of goodness as rationality" (*TJ* 381).

Later, in *Political Liberalism*, Rawls equated goodness as rationality with the thin theory (*PL* 178). We might take this remark to express what Rawls thought all along and conclude that he never thought the full theory was part of goodness as rationality. But another possibility is that as Rawls's thought developed, he came to see that the distinction between the thin and the full theories was one he no longer needed, and that he dropped the full theory altogether while retaining goodness as rationality to account for the value of the primary goods. To see whether this is so, it will be helpful to ask why the full theory and the distinction between it and the thin theory were important to Rawls when he wrote *Theory of Justice*.

We have already seen that with an informational base that includes the principles of justice, Rawls thinks he can account for the goodness of the morally worthy person and the value to members of the well-ordered society of having morally worthy compatriots. He also thinks that with the principles of justice on hand, he can explicate other important ethical concepts such as "beneficence," "benevolence," and "supererogation" and show why persons and deeds that answer to them are good (*TJ* 381–385). Because Rawls's treatment of beneficence, benevolence, and supererogation appeals to the principles of justice, his account of their goodness – like his account of moral worth – is provided by the full theory.

As with moral worth, so with persons and deeds that are beneficent, benevolent, and supererogatory, Rawls needs the full theory to give a plausible account of their moral value. (See *TJ* 381.) If he did not appeal to principles of right and drew only on the thin theory, he would not be able to say what kinds of acts the benevolent or beneficent person actually performs or to claim plausibly that the actions classified as supererogatory are morally good ones. Thus "[d]eveloping the thin theory into the full theory via the original position is," Rawls says, "the essential step" in providing an account of moral goodness (*TJ* 382). Accounting for the moral value of beneficence, benevolence, supererogation and moral worth is something Rawls wants to do, since showing that the contract view can give an account of their moral goodness lends the contract view necessary credence (see *TJ* 349) and helps to make good on the promise that it can be extended beyond a theory of justice to "an entire ethical system" (*TJ* 15).

There is another task that the distinction between the thin and full theory is needed for, a task that is more central to the project of *A Theory of Justice*. Rawls says that the "central aim" of much of part III "is to prepare the way to settle the questions of stability and congruence" (*TJ* 347). Both the full and the thin theories of the good are used to help settle those questions.

Rawls gives a two-part answer to the question of whether justice as fairness would be stable (*TJ* 397). In the first part, laid out in *A Theory of Justice*, chapter 8, Rawls argues that members of the well-ordered society would acquire a sense of justice. Each would therefore have a strong desire to act from principles chosen in the original position. Those principles are, Rawls says, "collectively rational" (*TJ* 497). But what is collectively rational might not be individually rational. If it were rational for individual members of the well-ordered society to defect from the agreement reached in the original position or to uproot their sense of justice, then the well-ordered society would be undermined by well-known collective action problems. So in the second part of his treatment of stability, brought together in §86 of *A Theory of Justice*, Rawls argues that members of the well-ordered society would have and realize that they have strong rational desires to preserve their sense of justice. Preserving their sense of justice is, he argues, something that must be included in their rational plans. And since according to goodness as rationality, each person's good consists in the fulfillment of his rational plan, preserving the sense of justice would be – and would generally be known to be – good for each. Rawls concludes that "the right and the good are congruent" (*TJ* 450). Then "no reasonable and rational person in the well-ordered society is moved by rational considerations of the good not to honor what justice requires" (*CP* 487 n.30) and the well-ordered society would be stably just.

So described, Rawls's line of thought leaves open the question of what informational base members of the well-ordered society draw on when they judge that it is rational to preserve their sense of justice.

Suppose that that base includes their knowledge that they have a strong and rational desire to act from the principles that would be chosen in the original position. Then they would know that being just persons is something they strongly wish to do. Since that desire is strong and rational, it is a desire that should be included in their plans and its fulfillment would be good for them in the full sense "good." But in that case, the conclusions that they should plan to preserve their sense of justice and that doing so belongs to their good would be "obvious" and the argument for those conclusions would be "trivial" (*TJ* 498).

Thin and full theories of good / 835

If Rawls is to provide a nontrivial argument for those conclusions, the notion of goodness at work in the second part of the stability argument cannot be that accounted for by the full theory. That is why he says in *Theory of Justice*, §60:

> when we ask whether the sense of justice is a good, *the important question is clearly that defined by the thin theory*. We want to know whether having and maintaining a sense of justice is good (*in the thin sense*) for persons who are members of a well-ordered society. (*TJ* 350, emphases added)

To see how Rawls uses the thin theory for this purpose, note first that objects of desire are intentional objects, individuated by their descriptions. If, for example, the same referent is desired under three different descriptions, then there are three desires and three objects of desire. It may be that the description of one of those objects appeals to the content of the principles of justice, so that the rationality of desiring it depends upon the rationality of wanting to satisfy the principles. In that case, the value of that object is accounted for by the full theory. But if the other two objects are given by descriptions which do not appeal to the principles of justice, then their value – like the value of the primary goods – can be accounted for by the thin theory.

This is the case with a sense of justice. For according to Rawls's contract view, the phrase "a sense of justice" picks out a referent which can also be described as "a desire to act from mutually justifiable principles" and "a desire to act from principles that would be chosen in a contract the outcome of which is determined by our nature as free and equal rational beings." There are objects of desire answering to each of the three descriptions. The rationality of wanting the first, "a sense of justice," depends upon the rationality of wanting to honor Rawls's principles. Indeed, to desire a sense of justice just is to want to be the kind of person who wants to honor them. That is why the good of satisfying the desire is accounted for by the full theory. But the other two descriptions do not appeal to the content of the principles, and the rationality of wanting the objects they pick out does not depend on the rationality of honoring or of wanting to honor the principles of justice. Their value can therefore be accounted for by the thin theory and they fall within its scope.

Rawls argues that members of his well-ordered society would want to act from mutually justifiable principles and would want to act from principles which they would agree to as free and equal rational beings. The objects of those desires are given by descriptions which have the same referent as the phrase "sense of justice." What Rawls calls a "practical identity" therefore holds among the objects of all three desires (*TJ* 501). Members of the well-ordered society would therefore have what are, in effect, desires to maintain their sense of justice. Moreover, since members of the well-ordered society "have a lucid grasp of the public conception of justice" (*TJ* 501), they would be aware of the practical identity and aware that what they want – albeit under a different description – is to maintain their sense of justice. So even "when they assess their situation independently from the constraints of justice" (*TJ* 350), they would include the satisfaction of that desire in their rational plans. By the central claim of goodness as rationality, satisfying that desire therefore belongs to their good.

This argument – which greatly compresses Rawls's reasoning in *A Theory of Justice*, §86 – shows that the right and the good are congruent, and hence that the well-ordered society would be stably just. Yet the question of whether someone who wants to act from mutually justifiable principles and who wants to act from principles chosen in the right sort of social contract also wants to have and maintain a sense of justice is not a "trivial" question and it does not have "an obvious answer." Rather, it is a problem the solution to which depends upon the details of Rawls's theory. Clearly, his argument that a "practical identity" holds between the objects of the first two desires and the object of the third is crucial to the provision of an answer which is philosophically interesting. Because the value of those two objects is accounted for by the thin theory, the question of whether attaining them – and for that reason having and maintaining a sense of justice – is good for members of a well-ordered society is a question that uses "good" "in the thin sense." It is a question "defined by the thin theory."

Thus the distinction between the thin and the full theories is a distinction between two theories that follow the template of goodness as rationality, but that differ in their informational bases and scope. In *A Theory of Justice*, Rawls uses the full theory to explicate various kinds of moral goodness, showing how moral worthiness and other moral values fall within its scope. He used the distinction between thin and full, and the scope of the thin theory, to argue for congruence and stability. In the years following the publication of *A Theory of Justice*, his concern to present justice as fairness as a political conception of justice eclipsed his interest in showing how contract theory could be developed into "an entire ethical system" (*TJ* 15). The full theory went into eclipse along with this interest. Rawls also offered a different account of stability, one which did not rely upon the distinction between the thin and the full theories. Perhaps these changes explain why in later work, Rawls identified goodness as rationality with the thin

Thin and full theories of good / 837

theory and restricted its employment to just one of its uses in *A Theory of Justice*: that of accounting for the value of the primary goods to the parties in the original position.

Paul Weithman

SEE ALSO:

Conception of the good
Congruence
Goodness as rationality
Moral worth of persons
Plan of life
Primary goods, social
Sense of justice
Stability

217.

TOLERATION

TOLERATION IS a paradoxical political virtue. To tolerate the morally odious smacks of moral weakness. Yet to speak of toleration in the case of beliefs or practices that are morally acceptable also seems to speak poorly of the individual or group that practices toleration. To tolerate is to prescind from using the power one has to condemn or prohibit a practice of which one disapproves. But if the practice being tolerated is morally acceptable, then on the face of it there is no reason to disapprove of it in the first place. Thus the paradox: a political virtue that has been widely praised throughout history ends up being difficult to spell out without making the tolerators either morally spineless or overly censorious.

Rawls's forays into the discussion of toleration begin with the first of these two apparently unattractive postures. The question he asks, in an early essay on "Constitutional Liberty and the Concept of Justice," and then again in *A Theory of Justice*, is whether "tolerant sects" have the right to suppress "intolerant sects," where intolerance is defined as the rejection of the principle of equal liberty. Rawls argues that they do not. In his view, the widely held thought that the intolerant can be suppressed stems from a fallacious inference. Though it is true, Rawls claims, that the intolerant do not have a legitimate claim against those that would suppress them, it does not follow that the tolerant have the right to suppress them. Whether that right exists should be determined on the basis of principles of justice, rather than on the presence or absence of a legitimate claim on the part of the intolerant that they not be suppressed. The only conditions under which the tolerant can legitimately suppress the intolerant is if they have good grounds to believe that the latter pose a serious danger to security and to the stability of a system of equal liberty. In the absence of such a well-grounded fear, the goal of the tolerant sects should be to win the members over to the principles of a just system of laws. Suppression in the absence of a real threat expresses the view that members of intolerant sects are "incapable of a sense of justice" (*CP* 93). The goal should rather be to persuade those who hold intolerant beliefs to come to affirm just principles through the upholding of justice and equal liberty, on the assumption that "other things equal, those whose liberties are secured by a just system will acquire an allegiance to it" (*CP* 93).

Thus, in Rawls's view, religious freedom and freedom of conscience are only to be limited when threats to public order and liberty exist. Rawls's account provides us with a way of refuting the view according to which the toleration of some forms of immorality or injustice is itself a form of moral weakness. At least in some circumstances, toleration serves the cause of justice by better promoting the conditions under which those who labor under immoral or intolerant views, but who do not pose a threat to public order or to a system of liberty, might ultimately be won over to the cause of justice.

Rawls next addresses the question of toleration and of its legitimate scope in the context of his later work, which is premised on a deeper appreciation than his early work had manifested of the "fact of pluralism." The fact of pluralism denotes the existence within even a well-ordered society of a diversity of reasonable conceptions of the good, which may nonetheless be at odds with each other. (A conception is deemed "reasonable" when, contrary to the "intolerant sects" with which Rawls was concerned in his earlier writing on toleration, its adherents affirm a common political conception of justice despite their disagreements on larger philosophical or religious issues.)

The centrality of reasonable pluralism to Rawls's later work leads to a development of his views on toleration along two axes. First, such a pluralism convinces Rawls that the principle of toleration has to be applied to philosophy itself. That is, in the presence of substantial disagreement among reasonable persons, principles of justice must be thought of as grounded in purely political values, rather than in particular comprehensive conceptions of the good.

Second, Rawls is able to specify why toleration is required even among reasonable persons, that is, among persons who would have counted as "tolerant" in his earlier discussions of toleration. On Rawls's view, what makes it possible for reasonable persons to come to disagree with one another quite passionately about some of the most fundamental questions of life are what he refers to as the "burdens of judgment." Burdens of judgment are ineliminable aspects of the epistemic circumstances of human beings that make it the case that they will arrive at different conclusions about important philosophical questions, even when they are making as optimal a use of their cognitive capacities as can reasonably be expected. The circumstances have to do, for example, with the "vagueness" of concepts with which human judgment unavoidably operates, with the difficulties inherent in assessing evidence, and the like (*PL* 56–57).

When reasonable human agents make use of their cognitive capacities in the context of the burdens of judgment, they can nonetheless come to be quite bitterly divided on central questions of human existence. Being reasonable, they nonetheless tolerate one another, and prescind when they are in positions of political power from making use of that power to suppress those reasonable others with whom they disagree. This is because they recognize that it would be unreasonable to ground the justification of political coercion in a particular conception of the good while all the while acknowledging that reasonable others can come to hold different conceptions. "[R]easonable persons see that the burdens of judgment set limits on what can reasonably be justified to others, and so they endorse some form of liberty of conscience and freedom of thought" (*PL* 61). Rawls thus provides us with a way of understanding how toleration of morally acceptable views does not evince undue censoriousness.

Rawls returns to the theme of toleration in his final work, which deals with international justice. In *The Law of Peoples*, Rawls considers the question of the moral and political stance that liberal democracies ought to take up toward societies which, though they are illiberal, are nonetheless "decent," in that, though they might not be fully liberal, they nonetheless uphold basic human rights, engage in some form of political consultation, even though that consultation might not be *democratic* consultation, and permit some degree of political dissent (*LP* 61).

It has been argued by some that Rawls's argument merely applies to the international arena the views and arguments developed in his work in *Political Liberalism* and in the essays that were written around the same time. (See Tan 1998.) Aspects of Rawls's argument for the toleration of illiberal peoples certainly seem to borrow from the argument from the "fact of pluralism." Thus, for example, he writes that "[i]f all societies were required to be liberal, then the idea of political liberalism would fail to express due toleration for other acceptable ways (if such there are, as I assume) of ordering society" (*LP* 59). Thus, it would seem, Rawls is arguing that we ought to tolerate decent hierarchical societies for reasons analogous to those that require that we tolerate our reasonable fellow citizens who make use of their cognitive capacities within the context of the burdens of judgment and thus arrive at answers different from our own to life's most difficult and fundamental questions.

But Rawls's argument for the toleration of such societies also harks back to the kinds of arguments he made in his earliest work on toleration in the case of intolerant sects. There, to recall, he held that unless order and equal liberty are threatened by them, we ought to operate on the assumption that their members are capable of a "sense of justice," and to tolerate them while upholding just laws so as to set up conditions favorable to their ultimate "conversion."

Similarly, in *Law of Peoples*, Rawls argues, first, that we ought to make the charitable assumption when dealing with citizens of decent hierarchical societies that they possess the moral capacities that are required in order to change and evolve. In the case of "peoples," evidence of this moral nature is provided by the fact that their members possess "a certain proper pride and sense of honor; . . . a proper pride in their histories and achievements, as what I call a 'proper patriotism' allows" (*LP* 62). Second, he holds that, once it is ascertained that illiberal peoples are possessed of such a nature, and that they pose no threat to a liberal international order, then justice requires that they be tolerated because, as in the case of intolerant sects, toleration in the context of a just institutional order is likely to favor the gradual evolution of decent hierarchical societies toward liberalism. At the very least, it is likely to be more favorable to such an evolution than, say, political sanctions would be. Rawls writes: "The Law of Peoples considers this wider background basic structure and the merits of its political climate *in encouraging reforms in a liberal direction* as overriding the lack of liberal justice in decent societies" (*LP* 62, emphasis added).

Thus invocations of reasonable pluralism in *Law of Peoples* would seem to point toward a transfer of the argumentative strategy of *Political Liberalism* to the international sphere. Toleration aims not to lay the groundwork for the eventual convergence of all reasonable conceptions, but rather to ensure peace among such reasonable conceptions which, being reasonable, have no reason to change. But the justification of toleration as lying at the end of the day in the hope that decent hierarchical societies will ultimately change "in a liberal direction" indicates that Rawls is treating decent hierarchical societies much as he did intolerant sects. They are to be tolerated with a view to their ultimate convergence around liberal norms.

Daniel Weinstock

SEE ALSO:

Burdens of judgment
Decent societies
Law of Peoples
Liberty of conscience
The reasonable and the rational
Reasonable pluralism

218.

TRUTH

RUTH IS AN important topic here, not because Rawls developed a theory of truth as it applies to morality or political justice but because he studiously avoided doing so. From his earliest articles through the publication of *A Theory of Justice* in 1971, he developed a conception of moral and political justification that involved no starring role for the concept of truth. In his mature political liberalism, he took a step beyond that, and insisted that political liberalism should not avail itself of the concept of truth. Only in between, at the brief high-water mark of his Kantian constructivism (with the publication of "Kantian Constructivism in Moral Theory" in 1980) was Rawls tempted into offering the rudiments of an account of moral and political truth. With his turn to a "political, not metaphysical" approach less than a decade later, however, Rawls left off any development of these hints and instead took up the more self-denying stance just mentioned.

Rawls's principal motivation for avoiding any talk about truth in his later theory arose from his view that it is a deeply controversial matter what the nature of truth is, whether specifically in morality or more broadly. To understand his thinking on this topic, then, one needs to have some sense of what the controversies are.

Suppose I utter the following sentence in a conversational setting:

(W) "Outlawing freedom of religious worship is wrong."

In doing so, I seem to be making an assertion. It seems that, if I am mistaken and outlawing freedom of religious worship is not wrong, I have said something false. Some philosophers have suggested that anyone willing to "hold" or make moral assertions such as (W) is committed to "a 'minimal' kind of truth" in moral-ity (Estlund 2008, 28). Against this kind of move, John Mackie's "error theory" (1977) held that, although we are correct in taking ourselves to be asserting things when we utter statements like (W), all of our assertions about what is right or wrong are false. Mackie argues that although these moral assertions presume the existence of objective values, in fact there are none. If he is right, the kind of "commitment" to truth found in our language yields no substantial vindication of moral truth. Another traditional way to resist the appearance that there are moral truths is to suggest – as have a variety of ethical noncognitivists – that when we utter statements such as (W), we are not in fact asserting anything, but rather expressing one or another set of attitudes. It is deeply controversial whether or not expressivism (the currently favored version of noncognitivism) can adequately make sense of our practices of ethical argument and disagreement. When you reply with "No, it is not!" to my utterance of (W), you seem to be con-tradicting me – implying that what I said was false. Is this, too, an illusion? The nature of truth in general is of course also a deeply disputed philosophical topic.

For many philosophical projects, engaging in this controversy is unavoid-able. Starting with his earliest article, "Outline of a Decision Procedure for Ethics" (1951), however, Rawls set aside controversies about moral realism ver-sus noncognitivism in order to undertake a more practical task. His aim was to characterize a reasonable decision procedure for adjudicating conflicts among people. What interested him was whether any such procedure could yield justi-fied results, not whether these would be true. Although he narrowed and refined his question over time, it remained the same in kind. *TJ* prominently resisted a "Cartesian" conception of moral justification that assigns the concept of truth an essential role: "I do not claim for the principles of justice proposed that they are necessary truths or derivable from such truths. A conception of justice cannot be deduced from self-evident premises or conditions on principles; instead, its jus-tification is a matter of the mutual support of many considerations, of everything fitting together into one coherent view" (*TJ* 19).

In Rawls's later work on political liberalism, the Cartesian is replaced by the related character of the "rational intuitionist," who denies that the concepts of assertion and judgment suffice to carry the idea of (moral) truth because he also "views moral principles as being true or false of an independent order of values" (*PL* 114). Whether such a metaphysical add-on is needed in order to characterize truth in general remains one of the central philosophical controversies in the theory of truth.

On account of these perennial controversies, Rawls's mature writing avoids asserting that the principles he defends are "true." Instead, he applies "the principle of toleration to philosophy itself" (*CP* 435; *PL* 10, 154). To do so is to proceed in a way that tolerates as wide a range of philosophical views as possible, compatibly with developing political liberalism, while leaving room for the citizens themselves to discuss those views within the "background culture" (*PL*, 14) rather than in public reasoning about the constitutional essentials or other matters of basic justice. To be sure, Rawls engages in ethical arguments and purports to disagree with various philosophical opponents. Yet he is wary of invoking the idea of truth, suggesting alternatives such as reasonableness or correctness (*PL* 111).

Of course, he does not deny that the principles he defends are true, either. Rather, he avoids asserting or denying this, and instead defends them as reasonable, perhaps indeed the most reasonable principles of justice (e.g. *PL* 114). Some philosophers find this stance maddening. Replying to Jürgen Habermas, who insisted that Rawls could not avoid the question of the truth of his principles, Rawls blithely wrote, "I do not see why not" (*PL* 395). It would be a problem if Rawls's stance barred citizens from making explicit claims about truth in public reasoning. Cohen (2009b), who takes Rawls to hold this, argues that it is a mistake for Rawls to hold that the concept of truth is "unavailable" for this purpose. Yet Rawls never asserts that the concept of truth is unavailable, only that political liberalism will not avail itself of it. What he says is just that "political liberalism does not use the concept of truth applied to its own political (always moral) judgments" (*PL* 394; cf. xxii, 94, 114, 127). He does not bar citizens from deploying the concept in public reasoning, but only suggests, more mildly, that given the fact of reasonable pluralism, "the idea of the reasonable is more suitable" (*PL* 129).

Henry S. Richardson

SEE ALSO:

Avoidance, method of
Comprehensive doctrine
Constructivism: Kantian/political
Objectivity
Political liberalism, justice as fairness as
Rational intuitionism
The reasonable and the rational
Reasonable pluralism

219.

THE TWO PRINCIPLES OF JUSTICE (IN JUSTICE AS FAIRNESS)

R AWLS'S SUBSTANTIVE CONCEPTION of social justice, justice as fairness, includes two principles. They are an answer to this question: "viewing society as a fair system of cooperation between citizens regarded as free and equal, what principles of justice are most appropriate to specify basic rights and liberties, and to regulate social and economic inequalities in citizens' prospects over a complete life?" (*JF* 41). The following are three key formulations of the two principles:

FIRST PRINCIPLE

Each person is to have an equal right to the most extensive total system of equal basic liberties compatible with a similar system of liberty for all.

SECOND PRINCIPLE

Social and economic inequalities are to be arranged so that they are both: (a) to the greatest benefit of the least advantaged, consistent with the just savings principle, and (b) attached to offices and positions open to all under conditions of fair equality of opportunity. (*TJ* 266)

a. Each person has an equal claim to a fully adequate scheme of equal basic rights and liberties, which scheme is compatible with the same scheme for all; and in this scheme the equal political liberties, and only those liberties, are to be guaranteed their fair value.

b. Social and economic inequalities are to satisfy two conditions: first, they are to be attached to positions and offices open to all under conditions of fair equality of opportunity; and second, they are to be to

845

the greatest benefit of the least-advantaged members of society. (*PL* 5–6)

(a) Each person has the same indefeasible claim to a fully adequate scheme of equal basic liberties, which scheme is compatible with the same scheme of liberties for all; and

(b) Social and economic inequalities are to satisfy two conditions: first, they are to be attached to offices and positions open to all under conditions of fair equality of opportunity; and second, they are to be to the greatest benefit of the least-advantaged members of society (the difference principle). (*JF* 42–43)

All formulations require equal basic liberties (in the first principle), fair equality of opportunity and the difference principle (in the second principle). This entry does not focus on the corollary just savings principle discussed in *TJ*. When formulating the principles in *PL* and *JF* Rawls does not refer to just savings, but he assumes that it does apply.

To clarify the content of the principles we can consider five important points. First, the principles apply to the basic structure of society as a dynamic whole, and within that context the first principle applies primarily to the constitution and associated institutions (e.g. courts) while the second applies primarily to the economy and civil society and associated institutions (e.g. legislatures). Rawls claims that the two principles should guide the arrangement of two parts of the basic structure of society (*TJ* 53; *JF* 47–48). The first principle applies to those aspects of the social system that define the fundamental liberties of citizens. In justice as fairness, such basic liberties are given by a list that includes, for example,

> political liberty (the right to vote and hold public office) and freedom of speech and assembly; liberty of conscience and freedom of thought; freedom of the person, which includes freedom from psychological oppression and physical assault and dismemberment (integrity of the person); the right to hold personal property and freedom from arbitrary arrest and seizure as defined by the concept of the rule of law. (*TJ* 53)

The second principle concerns the apportionment of economic and social benefits. It guides the distribution of income and wealth and the mechanisms determining access to positions of authority and responsibility in the economic structure.

Two principles of justice (in justice as fairness) / 847

Second, the principles are arranged in a serial order. The first principle has priority over the second principle, and, in the second principle, fair equality of opportunity has priority over the difference principle. Thus, for example, a basic liberty can only be rendered less extensive if this would strengthen the total system of liberties shared by all, and it may be secured in a less than equal way only if this would be acceptable to those with the lesser liberty. It would not be just to limit basic liberties to increase the availability of economic benefits (*TJ* 266). This impermissibility of trade-offs between principles holds so long as we face "reasonably favorable conditions" (*JF* 47; *PL* 297; see also *TJ* 55, 132, 214–220).

Third, the two principles are a specification of a more general conception of justice according to which "All social values ... are to be distributed equally unless an unequal distribution of any, or all, of these values is to everyone's advantage" (*TJ* 54). Justice as fairness is an egalitarian conception of justice. It sees all persons as rational and reasonable cooperators, as having equal claims at the bar of justice. Equal distribution is always the appropriate default position in the division of social advantages, so that any departure requires a special justification that shows that everyone (and especially those who gain least) would be benefitted. (Sometimes such departures can indeed be justified for reasons of efficiency.)

Fourth, justice as fairness, like any other conception of justice, needs an objective metric to measure and compare persons' levels of advantage and to identify what goods justice aims to distribute. For this purpose, Rawls proposes a list of "social primary goods" that includes (i) basic rights and liberties; (ii) freedom of movement and free choice of occupation against a background of diverse opportunities; (iii) powers and prerogatives of offices and positions of authority and responsibility; (iv) income and wealth; and (v) the social bases of self-respect (*JF* 58–59). Thus, for example, the principle of equal liberty frames the distribution of (i) and (ii), the principle of fair equality of opportunity frames the distribution of (iii), and the difference principle frames the distribution of (iv). The social bases of self-respect are secured by the combined implementation of all the principles. Social primary goods are social because their distribution can be determined through the institutions of the basic structure, and they are primary because they are general means all rational persons are presumed to want for their pursuit of their ends (whatever these are) (*TJ* 54). The idea of primary goods is reformulated in Rawls's later work, to refer to the "various social conditions and all-purpose means that are generally necessary to enable citizens adequately to develop and fully exercise their two moral powers, and to pursue their determinate conceptions of the good" (*JF* 57).

Fifth, the principles are concerned with eliminating or mitigating morally arbitrary inequalities. Rawls mentions three kinds of contingencies that may lead to inequalities in people's life-prospects that are arbitrary from the moral point of view: family and social class of origin, native endowments, and good or bad fortune and luck (*TJ* 83; *JF* 55). Let us consider how the second principle accounts for this point. To do so, let us discuss, with Rawls, a series of progressively inclusive principles of economic equality: formal equality, liberal equality, and democratic equality (see *TJ* §§12–13). Formal equality demands nondiscrimination. For example, it disallows the arbitrary exclusion of applicants for jobs on the basis of their gender, ethnicity, or class of origin. This goes some way toward developing the idea of equality of opportunity. But Rawls's second principle goes further, including the idea of liberal equality. The principle of *fair* equality of opportunity requires that people have a fair chance to attain positions of advantage. It is not enough for careers to be "open to talents" (as in formal equality). People must also be given similar chances to develop whatever talents they are born with. "[S]upposing that there is a distribution of native endowments, those who have the same level of talent and ability, and the same willingness to use these gifts should have the same prospects of success regardless of their social class of origin, the class into which they are born and develop until the age of reason" (*JF* 44). Thus, for example, if Sarah and Maria have the same initial talents and motivation, it would be unjust if Sarah turns out to be more qualified for certain jobs simply because her parents could pay for excellent private education that was unavailable to Maria given her own parents' relative poverty. A just society would offer Maria affordable public education of the highest quality. However, liberal equality (and Rawls's principle of fair equality of opportunity) is still not enough. It does not fully address the impact of differing social circumstances (such as those resulting from features of the internal life of the family), and it is silent on inequalities due to differing natural endowments. The idea of democratic equality, which adds the difference principle to the principle of fair equality of opportunity, is more encompassing. The difference principle allows inequalities in income and wealth only when they work to the maximum benefit of the least advantaged. Thus, it might be acceptable that Maria earns more than Laura (who is less motivated or talented even if she comes from a similar social background). But a just society would include mechanisms ensuring that the privileged condition of people like Maria is coupled with benefits for people like Laura (through redistributive taxation, increased economic productivity, etc.). "We are led to the difference principle if we wish to set up a social system so that no one gains or loses from his arbitrary place in the distribution of

Two principles of justice (in justice as fairness) / 849

natural assets or his initial social position in society without giving or receiving compensating advantages in return" (*TJ* 87).

Some additional points regarding the principles are worth making. First, the first principle focuses on a set of liberties given by a list. It does not talk about liberty as such (*PL* 291–292; *JF* 44). Some conceivable liberties are not basic and have no priority. An example is private property in the means of production (as opposed to personal property, which is part of the list) (*TJ* 54). To determine which liberties are basic, in his later work Rawls suggests that "we consider what liberties provide the political and social conditions essential for the adequate development and full exercise of the two moral powers of free and equal persons" (*JF* 45; see *PL* 310–324). Thus liberty of conscience and freedom of association are supported by their relation to the capacity to formulate, revise, and pursue a conception of the good, and equal political liberties and freedom of thought are supported by their relation to the capacity for a sense of justice. Second, since liberties might clash with each other in practice, the first principle does not see any of them as absolute; instead, it calls for an adequate scheme in which the "central range" of each is protected (*TJ* 54; *PL* 295–298). To underscore these two points, and in response to powerful challenges by H. L. A. Hart, Rawls changed the formulation of the first principle in *PL* and *JF*, referring to an "adequate scheme" rather than to "the most extensive system" of basic liberties (see *PL* lecture VIII).

Third, Rawls acknowledges that the first principle may be preceded by a prior principle that requires that "citizens' basic needs be met, at least insofar as their being met is necessary for citizens to understand and to be able fruitfully to exercise [the first principle's] rights and liberties" (*PL* 7; *JF* 44). Fourth, the first principle includes the demand that the "fair value" of political liberties be secured. This means that we should ensure that "citizens similarly gifted and motivated have roughly an equal chance of influencing the government's policy and of attaining positions of authority irrespective of their economic and social class" (*JF* 46). This requirement has important distributive effects; for example, it disallows great economic inequalities because of their tendency to translate into political inequality (*TJ* 198–199).

Finally, the principles are selected and applied in a "four-stage sequence" that involves a progressive lifting of the veil of ignorance in the original position. The principles are first adopted behind a thick veil of ignorance that only allows general information about human psychology and social organization in the circumstances of justice. The first principle is then applied at the constitutional stage, the second principle at the legislative stage, and both are fully pursued at the final stage of day-to-day legal and political judgment (*JF* 48). A consequence of this sequence is that there may be different appropriate implementations of the principles for different social contexts. For example, Rawls considers five kinds of social systems in modern conditions: (a) laissez-faire capitalism, (b) welfare-state capitalism, (c) state socialism with a command economy, (d) property-owning democracy, and (e) liberal (democratic) socialism. Whereas Rawls thinks that (a), (b), and (c) involve violations of the two principles, he suggests that both (d) and (e) could provide full implementations, the choice among them depending on contextual considerations about the political culture and history of particular societies (*JF* §§41–42).

Pablo Gilabert

SEE ALSO:

Basic liberties
Basic structure of society
Difference principle
Equal opportunity, democratic interpretation
Lexical priority: liberty, opportunity, wealth
Liberal conception of justice
The original position
Primary goods, social
Reciprocity
Well-ordered society

U

220.

UNITY OF SELF

A PERSON IS a human being with the two moral powers – to form, revise and pursue a conception of the good and to propose and honor fair terms of social cooperation – with a determinate, if revisable, conception of her good. We may think of each person as a particular human life lived according to a rational and reasonable plan. She says who she is by stating her ends and purposes (*TJ* 358). Rawls argues that justice as fairness offers a distinctive conception of the unity of particular persons, or selves, so understood. He sets out this conception by way of contrast with the conception of the unity of particular persons, or selves, implicit in average utilitarianism, the most plausible teleological rival candidate conception of justice to justice as fairness. While this contrast is brought to its conclusion in §85 of *Theory*, Rawls begins to develop it in §§83 and 84. He aims to show, first, that average utilitarianism rests on a conception of the self (and so is likely, if institutionally embodied, to encourage in us a self-conception or self-understanding) that is neither descriptively accurate nor normatively attractive. He then argues, second, that justice as fairness rests on a distinct conception of the self (and so is likely, if institutionally embodied, to encourage in us a self-conception or self-understanding) that is both descriptively more plausible and normatively more attractive. This two-part comparative conclusion captures one of two general lines of objection Rawls presses specifically against average utilitarianism.

Suppose agents in the original position are asked to consider average utilitarianism as a candidate conception of justice. This option would appeal to them, Rawls argues, only if they conceive of the parties they represent as having no determinate character or will, no system of final ends, with which they identify and that they are fundamentally concerned to advance. Original position agents must conceive of the parties they represent not as *full* persons, with the two moral powers and a determinate conception of the good or system of final ends, but rather as *bare* persons, mere vessels for utility or sites of preference satisfaction, ready to take on any conception of the good or system of final ends (*TJ* 150–152).

The problem can be brought out as follows. Why might agents in the original position find average utilitarianism attractive? Because it purports to offer them a way to ensure for the parties they represent a basic social structure, with its various social positions, that maximizes average utility. But how are the parties they represent to understand this? Suppose the original position agent representing me comes to me and says: "Look, since I am behind the veil of ignorance and don't know the details of your conception of the good or system of final ends, and since I assume you have an equal probability of occupying any particular social position, I advanced your interests as best I could by committing you and your compatriots to a basic social structure that maximizes the average level of utility or preference satisfaction." It would be perfectly sensible for me to ask in reply: "Since you didn't and couldn't know the details of my or anyone else's conception of the good or system of final ends, how were you able to give any content at all to the idea of average utility or preference satisfaction?" Suppose the original position agent responds by saying: "I just supposed that what you really most cared about was to have as much utility or as high a level of preference satisfaction as possible." I should naturally respond by pointing out that while *I* do want as much utility or as high a level of preference satisfaction as possible, *I* want this relative to the particular conception of the good and system of final ends with which *I* identify. I wouldn't want to be someone else with their conception of the good and system of final ends just because they enjoyed a higher level of utility or preference satisfaction. But this seems to be what my imagined agent in the original position has committed me to. And I might properly complain that my agent has thereby misunderstood what I am as a particular person or self. To be sure, the point isn't that my agent should know and advance *my* determinate conception of the good or system of final ends. That would render the original position defective as a tool for representing my commitment to impartiality. But my agent should know that I have, and should advance my interests as a person with, *an identity given by a determinate conception of the good or system of final ends.* For that is what *I* am: a particular human life lived according to a rational and reasonable plan, not any old plan, but the plan with which I identify.

Now, the proponent of average utilitarianism might concede here that it would be a mistake for agents in the original position to understand and advance the interests of the parties they represent as if their identities were constituted merely by their aiming at preference satisfaction or utility maximization. A person does not say who she is by stating that she aims to satisfy her preferences or maximize her utility. And so, if the parties represented by agents in the original position are to be represented as full persons, then they must be represented as more than mere vessels for utility or sites of preference satisfaction. They must be represented as having a determinate system of final ends with which they identify. Of course, agents in the original position will not know the details, but they will know that they represent and are to advance the interests of parties with determinate systems of final ends.

These interests must have some structure or content if agents in the original position are to be able to reach any sort of conclusions regarding how best to serve the parties they represent. Rawls considers two possibilities. One is that notwithstanding the diversity of their systems of final ends, the parties are all committed to a particular final end as a dominant end and so share a rational basis for selecting and ordering all their final ends into particular systems. Agents in the original position might then advance the interests of the parties they represent by advancing their common interest in this dominant end. Of course, this dominant end would have to be identified and original position agents would have to be able to determine objectively whether they were advancing it for the parties they represent. Rawls doubts that this can be done (see, e.g., *TJ* §84). But more to the point here he argues that the positing of a dominant end by which persons select and order their final ends and so constitute their determinate identities or selves as full persons disfigures the self in the name of an overly narrow conception of system (*TJ* 486). The final ends to which persons are rationally drawn and in terms of which they constitute their determinate identities as full persons are many and heterogeneous, and while persons must rationally select from these ends and then order them in a consistent and coherent fashion in order to constitute their determinate identities as full persons, they need not do so by reference to any dominant end. Indeed, Rawls argues that the idea that we constitute ourselves as the particular persons we are by way of an algorithmic selection and ordering of final ends by reference to some dominant end is both descriptively inaccurate and normatively unattractive.

This fact is acknowledged by the second possibility Rawls considers and in the end endorses. On this view, two features of the parties' particular identities as full persons guide the reasoning of original position agents trying to advance their interests. The first is that the parties all share a fundamental interest in certain universal means, what Rawls calls primary goods, to their many and heterogeneous final ends. The second is that the parties all count two higher-order interests – in the development and exercise of each of their two moral powers – among their many and heterogeneous final ends constituting their determinate identities. In *Political Liberalism*, Rawls links primary goods and the two higher-order interests within the context of a political conception of the parties as full *citizens*, thereby providing agents in the original position with a single unified view of the interests they are to advance on behalf of the parties they represent. Knowing these two features of the parties' particular identities as full persons (or citizens), agents in the original position are able to advance their interests by securing for them the largest possible share of primary goods, taking special care to ensure a share adequate to the development and exercise of the two moral powers.

On this view, there are several things that constitute and explain the unity of parties represented as full persons or selves. (See *TJ* §85.) The first is that they deliberatively (though not algorithmically) rationally identify with their life plans, systems of final ends or conceptions of the good. A second is that they deliberate over only reasonable possibilities, ensuring that their life plans, systems of final ends or conceptions of the good express both their moral powers. A third is that they fully express their rational *individuality* through their life plans or systems of final ends since as between reasonable possibilities their deliberative rationality is given free play. A fourth is that because they count among their final ends a higher-order interest in reasonable relations, or political community, with their compatriots, they identify with the traditions and institutions of their society and so are reconciled without regret to deliberatively choosing between the realistic range of reasonable and rational life plans, systems of final ends or conceptions of the good they support. Finally, the parties may think of their individual life plans, systems of final ends or conceptions of the good as distinct subplans within a larger, more complex, comprehensive plan regulating the political community as a whole over time. Their unity as particular persons or selves is thereby bound up with the unity of both their political community and their compatriots as their own distinct particular persons or selves. Original position agents represent and advance the interests of parties who collectively and over time constitute

Unity of self / 857

themselves as the particular, full, unified persons – rational, reasonable, and with a determinate system of final ends – that they are.

David A. Reidy

SEE ALSO:

Communitarianism
Deliberative rationality
Dominant end theories
Moral person
Moral psychology
Plan of life
The reasonable and the rational

221.

UTILITARIANISM

UTILITARIANISM – IN PARTICULAR, *classical utilitarianism* – holds that a society is just when its major institutions are so arranged as to maximize the aggregate satisfaction of the rational desires of its members. Locating the good of society in the welfare of its individual members, utilitarianism has deep roots in the liberal philosophical tradition, being long associated with the defense of the importance of the liberty of the individual and of freedom of thought. It is a view whose initial plausibility and appeal is, Rawls suggests, undeniable (*TJ* 23).

Many will find this claim quite surprising. Utilitarian reasoning has, after all, a reputation for delivering conclusions about what justice requires that are often starkly at odds with our considered convictions. But the approach has certain virtues that make the idea that utilitarianism is the most rational way to assess the justice of a society's basic institutional arrangement structure surprisingly compelling.

Three are of particular importance. The first is that utilitarian theorizing about justice agrees with Rawls in taking the subject matter of concern to be how society's basic institutions – what Rawls calls the *basic structure* – ought to be organized so as to best serve the interests of its citizens.

Second, utilitarianism squarely faces what Rawls calls *the priority problem*. Any assessment of the justice of a society's basic structure will involve balancing various relevant considerations, such as equity, fairness, and efficiency. In many cases, these considerations will pull in different directions, so some decision will need to be made concerning how they ought to be weighted against one another as part of an all-things-considered assessment. The priority problem concerns what the criteria are that ought to guide this decision.

Intuitionism holds that there are no such criteria. How different considerations ought to be weighted against one another is just a matter of judgment, the basis of which cannot be rationally explicated. Rawls finds this position unsatisfactory, calling it "only half a conception of justice" (*TJ* 37). One of the roles of a public conception of justice in a well-regulated society is to provide a common point of view from which individual justice claims may be adjudicated. Constructing that point of view is only possible if individuals, who may disagree on the weighting of different considerations, have a shared basis for rationally examining and revising their views on this matter, as part of a process of reaching an agreement on those principles of justice, constitutive of the common point of view, that ought to regulate their society.

Utilitarians share both Rawls's dissatisfaction with intuitionism and his sense of the importance of a genuinely shared point of view from which justice claims can be adjudicated. They offer a constructive solution to the priority problem, proposing that how different considerations are to be weighted against one another ought to be settled by the utilitarian criterion of what is likely to maximize aggregate welfare. Unlike appeals to brute intuitions that may well in part be shaped by a background of unjust institutions, this is a clear, ethically appropriate, basis for rationally determining how different relevant considerations ought to be weighted.

Third, utilitarianism is a *teleological view*, defining what is right to do instrumentally, as that which, of the available alternatives, is most likely to maximize the good. The "good" in question can be filled in in different ways. What is essential to a view being teleological is that the good, whose production supplies the point of right action, be specified independently of considerations that, intuitively, have to do with doing what is morally right. A view that counted fairness as a good to be realized, for instance, would not count as teleological.

A teleological account is appealing in part because of its simplicity and clarity, factoring "our moral judgments into two classes, the one being characterized separately while the other is then connected with it by a maximizing principle" (*TJ* 22). But its appeal also draws heavily on a familiar and attractive general characterization of practical reasoning as being teleological in structure. On this picture, being practically prudentially rational is a matter of determining how best to achieve the fulfillment of the maximum number of one's goals or desires. Utilitarianism simply holds that, because morality is impartial, whose desires in particular end up being satisfied is irrelevant. The morally rational thing to do, therefore, is always that which is most likely to lead to the maximum number of rational desires being satisfied (the good here being the satisfaction of rational desire) (*TJ* 23–24).

The utilitarian picture of good moral reasoning is vividly depicted as the kind of reasoning appropriate to a rational, impartial, sympathetic spectator assessing the arrangement of society's basic institutions. Completely impartial, and with perfect knowledge of each person's desires, the spectator imaginatively identifies with each person in society, agglomerating the desires of each individual into a single system of desires that she alone is able to grasp, in effect fusing many persons into one (*TJ* 24). She determines what the basic structure ought to be rationally, using the same form of maximizing reasoning as "an entrepreneur deciding how to maximize his profit by producing this or that commodity, or that of a consumer deciding how to maximize his satisfaction by the purchase of this or that collection of goods" (*TJ* 24).

Though Rawls agrees that how the basic structure ought to be arranged is a matter for rational assessment, he argues that the utilitarian's extension of "the principle of rational prudence to the system of desires constructed by the impartial spectator" (*TJ* 26) is deeply mistaken. In treating the principle that ought to govern how benefits and burdens are distributed interpersonally, across lives, as identical to that which is appropriate to deciding how to distribute them intrapersonally, within a life, utilitarianism ends up ignoring the separateness of persons (*TJ* 24).

Rawls's thought is this: it is presumptively rational for a person to arrange her life so as to maximize the sum of the satisfaction of her rational desires. This will mean having to live, at some points in her life, with certain burdens (frustrated desires), but the compensation for doing so is greater benefits (more satisfied desires) at other points in her life. It is the person herself who is the beneficiary of a strategy of maximizing the sum of satisified rational desires. But in the interpersonal case, there is no single individual who enjoys this maximized sum. Rather, maximizing can result in a distribution of satisfaction with some having very few of their rational desires satisfied, seriously compromising their ability to lead a good life, while others have a great many of their desires satisfied.

This does not trouble the utilitarian because she takes the opportunity for each person being able to pursue a good life to be of derivative importance. What ultimately matters is that the sum of satisfied desires be maximized. Rawls's point is that, in detaching the desires to be satisfied from the individuals whose desires they are, the utilitarian loses sight of the fact that the system of desires constructed through the agglomeration of the desires of individuals is not any individual's system of desires. Once this is recognized, the idea that what one ought to do is to maximize the sum of rational desire satisfaction ceases to be compelling, in the way that it intuitively is in the individual case. If anything, the willingness of utilitarianism to sacrifice the interests of some individuals in order to achieve the maximal sum of desire satisfaction starts to make that goal look like a kind of fetish.

It is an essential feature of human societies that they are made up of a plurality of distinct persons with separate, often conflicting, systems of ends or goals around which their life plans are organized. Utilitarianism, in offering a way of reasoning about justice that suggests that the arrangement of society's basic institutions not offering a person an adequate opportunity to pursue his goals is somehow compensated for by this being necessary in order that the maximal aggregate good be realized, fails to take this fact sufficiently seriously. Rawls's own two principles of justice do a much better job of recognizing the importance to each individual of having an adequate opportunity to pursue his own rational plan of life, guaranteeing for each person the basic liberties and a satisfactory economic minimum.

At the heart of Rawls's critique of classical utilitarianism is the thought that it operates with a conception of society that fails to match the nature of our society as we know it. If, as Rawls suggests, "we assume that the correct regulative principle for anything depends on the nature of that thing" (*TJ* 25), we ought to think of principles of justice as for the regulation of society conceived of as not a single individual, but as a "scheme of cooperation for reciprocal advantage regulated by principles which persons would choose in an initial situation that is fair" (*TJ* 29).

Rawls models the constraints that constitute that fair initial situation with what he calls "the original position." Reasoning in the way the original position mandates does not, however, rule out the possibility that some form of normative utilitarian principle might be what is converged for the regulation of the basic structure.

The most likely candidate is the *principle of average utility*. It requires that the basic structure be arranged so as to maximize the average level of utility that a person in the society can be expected to enjoy. Intuitively, there is a reasonable case for thinking that this might be the principle chosen in the original position: if one assumes that one has an equal chance of occupying any of the social positions in society, and is concerned to maximize one's share of social resources, the average principle appears to ensure the best chance of a favorable outcome (*TJ* 147).

Rawls argues against the average view by envisioning the parties to the original position considering the choice between the principle of average utility and his two principles of justice, and offers several arguments in support of the conclusion that his two principles would be favored. The most widely discussed, and controversial, argument is one that appeals to the decision-theoretic maximin rule for choice under uncertainty.

Though the success of that formal argument is controversial, the intuitive version of it is reasonably clear and compelling. Echoing the argument against the classical view, what Rawls draws attention to is that a principle that directs that the average level be maximized is fully compatible with some having to bear living intolerable lives, marked by restricted civil liberties and little economic opportunity, in order that the others, who are already better off, can be better off still. Though utilitarians hold that, as an empirical matter, this is not what the average principle will mandate, nothing in the view in fact excludes such an outcome.

Rawls's two principles, on the other hand, guarantee each person an inviolable set of basic liberties and a satisfactory economic minimum. No individuals' interests are sacrificed for the sake of the others in the way the average utilitarianism permits. Choosing the two principles is arguably the best way for each behind the veil, concerned to advance her own individual interests and "having no basis for determining the probable nature of society, or [her] place in it" (*TJ* 134), to protect and advance her own interests.

Just as important as the arguments for the rationality of choosing his two principles, however, are the arguments he offers that appeal to plausible claims about the moral psychology of justice. They bring into relief serious weaknesses of the average principle that make it a poor candidate to serve the role of being a publicly affirmed principle of justice. Of particular relevance are the arguments appealing to the strains of commitment, the stability over time of a just social order regulated by the two principles, and the extent to which they support an ethos of both self-respect and interpersonal respect.

First, it is important to the parties to the original position that they identify principles for the regulation of the basic structure whose requirements it is psychologically realistic to expect all to comply with. The point of seeking principles of justice, after all, is not just to identify the principles, but to identify principles that it is reasonable to expect citizens to comply with as part of the realization of a just social order. Now, even if one thought that adopting the principle of average utility is the rational choice behind the veil of ignorance, it is still a risky choice. A person might well end up with both restricted liberties and substantially fewer resources with which to pursue her conception of the good than both what she had hoped for and what she would have had if the two principles of justice had been chosen.

It is this risk that creates the problem for the principle of average utility that Rawls calls "the strains of commitment." Parties to the original position are required to reach an agreement on principles in good faith. If there is a question as to whether each will be able to stick to the agreement to comply with a proposed principle, they must set it aside and choose from amongst the alternatives (*TJ* 153).

As a matter of general human psychology, it could be very difficult for an individual to comply with a principle of justice that requires her to accept the kinds of burdens the principle of average utility could impose on her when they are not necessarily mandated by the requirements of justice (*TJ* 153). If any plausible principle(s) of justice acceptable to all behind the veil of ignorance would result in her being seriously burdened in the way the principle of average utility permits, a person could, psychologically, accept being so burdened as simply what justice demands. But because Rawls's two principles do not even create a risk of anyone having to bear such a burden, it is clear that justice does not require that anyone have to make the kinds of sacrifices the average principle permits. Without this necessity, it is certainly psychologically understandable as to why even a just person would find it difficult to comply with the requirements of a principle that demanded such sacrifices of her.

Second, Rawls argues that a society regulated by the two principles is better able to maintain itself as a just society, or is more stable, over time than one regulated by the average principle. Stability, in the relevant sense, has to do with the fact that

> When the basic structure of a society is publicly known to satisfy its principles for an extended period of time, those subject to these arrangements tend to develop a desire to act in accordance with these principles and to do their part in institutions that exemplify them. A conception of justice is stable when the public recognition of its realization by the social system tends to bring about the corresponding sense of justice. (*TJ* 154)

A society regulated by the average principle is one that can demand that some individuals "accept the greater advantages of others as a sufficient reason for lower expectations over the whole course of our life" (*TJ* 175). This is a psychologically extreme demand if one accepts, as the average principle does, and in contrast to the classical utilitarian principle, a conception of society as a cooperative enterprise designed to advance the good of each of its members (something assumed when one asks what principles would be chosen in the original position). Securing compliance with such demands over time, and thus stability, requires inculcating in most citizens a psychological disposition to benevolence of a sufficiently high degree of intensity that they do not balk at such an extreme demand. This kind of disposition to so strongly identify with the interests of others is not easily achieved, and may just be psychologically unrealistic.

Rawls's first principle of justice, on the other hand, ensures that each person's liberty is secured, and in virtue of his second principle, there is a clear sense in which each benefits from social cooperation. The stability of a society governed by the two principles can then be explained without appealing to an inculcated disposition to benevolence, but by a plausible general "psychological law that persons tend to love, cherish, and support whatever affirms their own good. Since everyone's good is affirmed, all acquire inclinations to uphold the scheme" (*TJ* 155).

The final argument, concerning self-respect, draws attention to the importance that the principles of justice chosen in the original position will be publicly affirmed as such. Those principles have implications for a person's sense of self-respect, essential to a person's sense that his life plan is one worth carrying out (*TJ* 156). Self-respect, as Rawls notes, relies heavily on the respect of others. "Unless we feel that our endeavors are honored by them, it is difficult if not impossible for us to maintain the conviction that our ends are worth advancing" (*TJ* 156).

The average principle, by sanctioning an arrangement of basic institutions in a way that grants some lesser liberties and life prospects for the sake of others, allows individuals to regard one another "as a means to one another's welfare" (*TJ* 157), and lends itself to a psychological "weakening of our sense of the value of accomplishing our aims, when we must accept a lesser prospect of life for the sake of others" (*TJ* 57). A society regulated by the average principle, given human psychology, will be one in which, "men will find it more difficult to be confident of their own self-worth" (*TJ* 158).

The two principles of justice better express the respect of individuals for one another. First, they guarantee equal liberty for all. But more importantly, by "undertaking to regard the distribution of natural abilities as a collective asset so that the more fortunate are to benefit only in ways that help those who have lost out" (*TJ* 156), the importance of each person having the means and opportunity

Utilitarianism / 865

to carry out his rational life plan is clearly publicly recognized and affirmed. Rawls's two principles of justice, unlike the average principle, support, rather than erode, individual self-respect and the idea that each person has an inviolability founded on justice (*TJ* 3).

Rahul Kumar

SEE ALSO:

Intuitionism
Maximin rule of choice
Mill, John Stuart
Mixed conceptions of justice
Moral person
Moral psychology
The original position
Publicity
Sidgwick, Henry
Stability
Strains of commitment
Unity of self
Utility

222.

UTILITY

THE CONCEPT OF utility does not play a fundamental role in justice as fairness. Where other theories, most notably utilitarianism, rely on utility, justice as fairness relies on primary goods. It does so in two related places: the motivation of the parties in the original position and the content of the principles.

Rawls distinguishes "classic utilitarianism" from "average utilitarianism." The former is a teleological theory which requires the maximization of aggregate utility. Average utilitarianism, in contrast, "directs society to maximize not the total but the average utility (per capita)" (*TJ* 140). While Rawls associates classical utilitarianism with the idea of a "rational and impartial sympathetic spectator," he argues that average utilitarianism would be chosen by an individual in an initial choice situation similar but not identical to the original position. The justifications of these two forms of utilitarianism, he holds, are quite different: "while the average principle of utility is the ethic of a single rational individual (with no aversion to risk) who tries to maximize his own prospects, the classical doctrine is the ethic of perfect altruists" (*TJ* 164–165).

The two forms of utilitarianism are also distinguished by the understanding of utility on which they typically rely. As a teleological theory, classical utilitarianism must identify a good to be maximized, and do so without relying on any moral concepts or principles. There are many different teleological theories because there are many candidates for this good. But Rawls suggests, "Hedonism is, one might say, the symptomatic drift of teleological theories insofar as they try to formulate a clear and applicable method of moral reasoning" (*TJ* 490). Thus, one common interpretation of "utility," the one associated with classical utilitarianism and endorsed by Sidgwick (*TJ* 487), interprets utility as the experienced feeling of pleasure (or perhaps the balance of pleasure and pain, somehow combined). Rawls holds that taking pleasure to be a dominant end for purposes either of individual deliberation or the construction of a theory of justice is implausible. He objects: "Surely the preference for a certain attribute of feeling or sensation above all else is as unbalanced and inhuman as an overriding desire to maximize one's power over others or one's material wealth" (*TJ* 488). The parties in the original position certainly cannot assume that their only interest is in maximizing the feeling of pleasure. Likewise, they would not choose a hedonistic utilitarianism as the standard for evaluating the basic structure of their society.

Contemporary utilitarians typically take utility as an abstract measure of the degree to which a set of preferences is satisfied. On this interpretation, utility does not have any particular content because the preferences which it measures do not have any particular content. The preference set must, however, satisfy certain axioms in order for the utility function to be well defined. There are different ways of constructing this measure; perhaps the most common is due to John von Neumann and Oskar Morgenstern. Rawls discusses this construction in the context of comparing his two principles to a mixed conception that accepts his first principle and fair equality of opportunity, but substitutes for the difference principle "the principle of average utility constrained by a certain social minimum" (*TJ* 278). Even in this subordinate position, the utilitarian principle raises a number of problems associated with its reliance on utility rather than primary goods. For example: "It is necessary to arrive at some estimate of utility functions for different representative persons and to set up an interpersonal correspondence between them, and so on. The problems in doing this are so great and the approximations are so rough that deeply conflicting opinions may seem equally plausible to different persons" (*TJ* 282). Furthermore, any reliance on the actual preferences of real individuals will make justice dependent on "contingencies that are arbitrary from a moral point of view" (*TJ* 284). In a passage in the original edition of *TJ*, Rawls writes: "we want to go behind de facto preferences generated by given conditions" (*TJ*, original edition 155).

In the original position, the parties do not know their conception of the good. But they do know that they have "fundamental aims and interests" such as a "religious interest" and "the interest in the integrity of the person" as well as a "highest-order interest" in being able to "revise and alter their final ends" (*TJ* 131). In *Political Liberalism*, Rawls expands on these ideas, referring to "higher-order interests" in developing and maintaining the two moral powers (*PL* 18–19). The point is that Rawls assumes that the parties are not "barepersons" but are "determinate-persons: they have certain highest-order interests and fundamental ends...It is these interests and ends, whatever they are, which they must try to protect" (*TJ* 152). We could, if we wanted to, construct a kind of utility function for the parties based on these interests. Much of their utility functions would be unknown, of course, but the absolute priority given to maintaining the two moral powers over the satisfaction of other preferences would be assumed. Such a utility function would reflect not the empirical preferences of actual individuals but the normative model of the moral person (later: citizen) on which Rawls relies.

With respect to this utility function, the parties in the original position would maximize their expected utility by choosing the two principles. And indeed, the two principles would overlap with average utilitarianism defined with respect to this utility function. Rawls observes of this overlap that "we should be cheered if utilitarians can find, from within their own point of view, a way to endorse the ideas and principles of justice as fairness" (*JF* 107). However, Rawls distinguishes this approach from utilitarianism since "This constructed utility function is based on the needs and requirements of citizens – their fundamental interests – conceived as such persons; it is not based on people's actual preferences and interests" (*JF* 107). There is no assumption that the two principles will maximize average utility with respect to the actual preferences of individuals in a society. This is as it should be, Rawls holds, because the content of only certain interests and preferences – those associated with the normative model of the person – is relevant for the construction of the principles of justice.

Jon Mandle

SEE ALSO:

Altruism
Conception of the good
Hedonism
Justice and interpersonal comparison
Maximin rule of choice
Moral person
The original position
Primary goods, social
Rational choice theory
Strains of commitment
Utilitarianism

W

223.

WALZER, MICHAEL

AT SEVERAL POINTS in his writings Rawls indicates a debt to the political theorist Michael Walzer (b. 1935). Most noteworthy in this regard is the fact that Rawls's defense of just war theory in *LP* (95) does not depart in any significant respect from that of Walzer in his now classic work *Just and Unjust Wars* (2006). Rawls largely agrees with Walzer regarding issues in *jus ad bellum* (i.e. the justice *of* war), wherein a just cause to fight requires either that one be fighting in self-defense or in defense of the rights of aggrieved others, as well as issues in *jus in bello* (i.e. justice *in* war), wherein the rights of noncombatants should be respected.

Throughout his career, even when opposing the war in Vietnam, Rawls was like Walzer in seeing the refusal to participate in all war under all conditions as an "otherworldly" view that was integrally connected to sectarian doctrine. Such a view no more challenges the right to self-defense than a defense of celibacy challenges the right to get married (*TJ* 335).

Rawls also relies on Walzer in defense of the claim that a state has a right to defend its borders and to limit immigration (although the details of such limitation are not specified by Rawls) on the assumption that unless a definite agent is given responsibility of maintaining an asset, the asset tends to deteriorate (*LP* 39). Rawls even follows Walzer rather closely in the latter's controversial defense of a "supreme emergency exemption." Here Rawls claims (*LP* 98–99) that when civilization itself is threatened (as when the

Allies were on the verge of defeat early in World War II before the Battle of Stalingrad) then *jus in bello* constraints could be violated for the sake of justice.

Rawls relies on Walzer in another area of nonideal theory. He holds that there is more than one path that leads to toleration. In addition to the toleration of reasonable differences found in politically liberal states, there is something like this in consultation hierarchies as well, as evidenced historically in the Ottoman Empire and imaginatively in Kazanistan, the mythical consultation hierarchy discussed in *LP* (76).

In ideal theory Rawls also acknowledges a debt to Walzer in claiming that expertise in political philosophy does not entail a claim to rule or a claim to have authority, as would be suggested by philosopher-kings/queens. Nor is political philosophy required in the day-to-day activities of politicians, but this does not diminish the significance of questions in political philosophy. Rather, political philosophy finds its place in the education of citizens regarding the character of democratic thought and attitudes (*LHPP* 2, 7; *PL* lxi). Or again, we turn to political philosophy when our shared political understandings break down or when we are divided within ourselves on some political question. The deeper the conflict (as in the contemporary pervasiveness of pluralism), the higher the level of philosophical abstraction that is required in order to get an uncluttered view of its roots. That is, the Rawlsian work of abstraction is set in motion by deep political conflicts (*PL* 44, 46).

It should be noted that Rawls does not go as far as Walzer in seeing all political ties deriving from consensual acts, in that Rawls also acknowledges the force of natural duties (*TJ* 99). Even subjected minorities, for example, have a natural duty not to be cruel (*TJ* 330). It also seems fair to say that, despite Rawls's defense of associational freedoms, he is not as much of a "communitarian" as Walzer, whose view seems to require something like a shared (partially) comprehensive doctrine, in contrast to Rawls's stronger recognition of the fact of reasonable pluralism. That is, Walzer's view incorporates culture, and not only institutions, in a way that Rawls would resist.

Rawls makes it clear that justice could be reached either through a kind of liberal socialism or through a kind of liberal property-owning democracy, although it seems that he prefers the latter (e.g. *TJ* 239; *JF* 135–140). Walzer seems to lean in the direction of liberal socialism, yet both he and Rawls share many important critiques of contemporary society. One example is Walzer's emphasis on the unjust boundary crossing found in the abuse of money in politics and Rawls's emphasis on the "curse of money" in politics (*CP* 580).

Daniel Dombrowski

SEE ALSO:

Communitarianism
Culture: political vs. background
Decent societies
Democracy
Ideal and nonideal theory
Just war theory
Reasonable pluralism

224.

WELL-ORDERED SOCIETY

THE NOTION OF a well-ordered society has been a central idea in Rawls's thinking about justice at least since his great opus, *A Theory of Justice*, in which it plays a crucial role. The core idea of a well-ordered society is a society whose citizens all accept the same conception of justice, its institutions actually conform to that conception, and both of these facts are publicly known. By envisioning different societies, each organized by a particular conception of justice, and so each "well-ordered" in terms of that conception, we can get some traction on the question of which of the many conflicting conceptions of justice is the most reasonable, is the most worthy of adoption. Over time the idea of a well-ordered society has come to play an increasingly important role. In *Justice as Fairness: A Restatement*, Rawls presents the idea of a "well-ordered society" as one of two "companion fundamental ideas" to the "most fundamental idea in [his] conception of justice," which is the "idea of society as a fair system of social cooperation" (*JF* 5). (The second companion idea is the "idea of citizens...as free and equal persons.") Rawls offers a definition or explication of this term in each of his major writings, and in many papers as well. Though there are slight differences among these formulations, the core idea has remained fairly stable. A well-ordered society is "a society effectively regulated by a public conception of justice" (*JF* 8). What this means is glossed by three points:

> First, a well-ordered society is one "in which everyone accepts, and knows that everyone else accepts, the very same principles of justice" (*PL* 35) and that "knowledge is mutually recognized," as if the conception of justice "were a matter of public agreement" (*JF* 8).

Second, society's "basic structure...is publicly known, or with good reason believed, to satisfy these principles" (*PL* 35).

Third, its "citizens have a normally effective sense of justice...that enables them to understand and apply the publicly recognized principles of justice, and for the most part...act accordingly" (*JF* 9; cf. *PL* 35).

In *A Theory of Justice* Rawls adds that a well-ordered society is "designed to advance the good of its members" (4), and this idea is at least implicit in subsequent accounts. Of course, how that good is understood will differ among well-ordered societies.

The idea of a well-ordered society specifies the role a conception of justice must play in a society viewed as a system of social cooperation over time. Conceptions of justice that are incapable of effectively regulating a society are, he suggests, "seriously defective" (*JF* 9). The first and second conditions, for example, constitute a strong publicity condition (*PL* 66ff.), which rules out conceptions of justice that could not be publicly acknowledged, such as the account Plato offers in the *Republic* in which most of the members of society are deceived about the basis of their social order, or at most have access only to a metaphorical representation of its basis. Satisfying these conditions also requires a shared set of "beliefs relevant to political justice" that "can be supported...by publicly shared methods of inquiry and forms of reasoning" (*PL* 67). Without such shared beliefs and methods of inquiry they could hardly be said to know that the society's basic structure satisfies the principles of justice. Thus, a well-ordered society must include both a shared conception of justice and shared "guidelines of inquiry: principles of reasoning and the rules of evidence" (*PL* 224).

The third condition bears on the question of the stability of a conception of justice, that is, whether a society organized in accordance with a particular conception of justice functions in such a way that those who grow up and live in that society come to affirm its principles of justice, and to conform to them on appropriate occasions. One "conception of justice is more stable than another if the sense of justice that it tends to generate is stronger and more likely to override disruptive inclinations and if the institutions it allows foster weaker impulses and temptations to act unjustly" (*TJ* 398). Thus, the idea of a well-ordered society frames his discussion of the question of stability – explicitly in his earlier work (*TJ* §69) and implicitly in his later work.

Perhaps the most important implication of the idea of a well-ordered society is that no society can be well-ordered on the basis of principles of justice rooted in a single comprehensive doctrine if its members hold a plurality of comprehensive doctrines. In general, each doctrine will include an account of justice, one that reflects its various moral, philosophical, and theological commitments, and so pluralist societies are challenged to meet the first condition of a well-ordered society because its citizens will tend not to accept the same conception of justice. Even if one group had enough power to prevail over the others, and even if its doctrine were actually the correct or true doctrine, the society would not be well-ordered. This points to what is perhaps most distinctive to Rawls's thinking about social justice – that there could be a break between a society's being organized justly, that is, in accordance with the "correct" principles of justice (assuming there is such a set), and its being well-ordered. Others might argue that the proper concern of political philosophy is to understand what justice itself requires, even if practical constraints limit our ability to implement the correct principles of justice. By foregrounding the idea of a well-ordered society, one whose members all accept the same principles of justice, Rawls seems to suggest that no society can actually be just unless it is well-ordered.

The bulk of Rawls's later work was devoted to explaining how a society marked by what he called "reasonable" pluralism could develop a "political" conception of justice that would enable it to be well-ordered. The core idea is that the "political conception of justice" is not based on any particular comprehensive doctrine, and so if properly developed could be accepted by reasonable adherents of conflicting comprehensive doctrines. Thus, societies characterized by reasonable moral pluralism can only be well-ordered on the basis of a political conception of justice. In his last writings, notably "The Idea of Public Reason Revisited" (*CP* 573–615) and *Justice as Fairness*, Rawls came to see that citizens of a democratic and therefore morally pluralist society might not accept a single political conception of justice, but may accept any one of a family of political but liberal conceptions of justice, and still be well-ordered.

Societies organized according to a conception of justice rooted in a particular comprehensive doctrine – what he calls a common good conception of justice – can also be well-ordered, and so would be a system of social cooperation rather than one of mere social coordination, provided that there is widespread (though perhaps not completely universal) acceptance of the comprehensive doctrine that defines its "common good." One might think that a well-ordered society would require unanimous adherence to a particular conception of justice. Although that would be ideal, the demand for complete consensus may be too strong. As long as the human rights of minorities are respected and their numbers are small, Rawls seems to suggest that these dissenting groups could nonetheless endorse the society's being structured by the values of the overwhelming majority. They

Well-ordered society / 877

might think it would be unreasonable that they – whose numbers are so small – would block the overwhelming majority's realizing the way of life they cherish. For example, he imagines a decent Muslim society, and comments that "we may expect non-Muslim minorities to be less wedded to certain of the priorities than Muslim," but "that both Muslims and non-Muslims will understand and regard these priorities as significant" (*LP* 77). Rawls calls such societies "decent" societies to distinguish them from well-ordered liberal societies. Although societies that are well-ordered on the basis of a common good conception of justice are introduced in part to provide a contrast to societies ordered by a political conception of justice (*PL* 109–110), they figure mainly in his discussion of global justice.

J. Donald Moon

SEE ALSO:

Basic structure of society
Decent societies
Fundamental ideas (in justice as fairness)
Overlapping consensus
Public reason
Publicity
Reasonable pluralism
Stability

225.

WITTGENSTEIN, LUDWIG

RAWLS'S REFERENCES TO Wittgenstein in his published work are few and far apart. Nevertheless, Wittgenstein's influence on Rawls's thought, both directly and mediated through philosophers such as Norman Malcolm (one of Rawls's first teachers of philosophy at Princeton in the 1940s, and with whom he later worked at Cornell in the 1950s) and Burton Dreben (his colleague for many years at Harvard), may be considered more substantial than initial impressions would suggest.

A Theory of Justice contains just two references to Wittgenstein, both of which occur in part III of the book. In the discussion of the "Features of the Moral Sentiments" (*TJ* 420), Rawls characterizes his method of elucidating the main features of the moral sentiments "by considering the various questions that arise in trying to characterize them and the various feelings in which they are manifested" (*TJ* 420; see also *CP* 107) as being a Wittgensteinian method, "applying to the concept of the moral feelings the kind of inquiry carried out by Wittgenstein in the *Philosophical Investigations*" (*TJ* 420 n.17; Wittgenstein 1953).

Later in part III, in the discussion of "Hedonism as a Method of Choice" in §84, Rawls draws an analogy between, on the one hand, Wittgenstein's rejection of any reliable subjective criterion for distinguishing memories from imaginings, or beliefs from suppositions, and on the other hand, his own rejection of hedonism (and of any other monistic theory of the good), and his conclusion that "there is no dominant end the pursuit of which accords with our considered judgments of value" (*TJ* 489). Both Rawls and Wittgenstein understand themselves as resisting a certain kind of superficially attractive philosophical theorizing that would pay insufficient attention to the true complexity of the phenomena under investigation. Just as there is no feature that all instances of memory or imagination or belief have in common (as Rawls takes Wittgenstein to have shown), so too "it is antecedently unlikely that certain kinds of agreeable feelings can define a unit of account the use of which explains the possibility of rational deliberation. Neither pleasure nor any other determinate end can play the role that the hedonist would assign it" (*TJ* 489; see here also Rawls's reference to Anscombe 1957). Here, then, Wittgensteinian influence in terms of method has some role in explaining Rawls's rejection of any view of the good (such as hedonism) that pays insufficient attention to the plurality of values and value-judgments.

Hence, on both occasions where Wittgenstein is mentioned in *TJ*, Rawls is not relying on any particular substantive claims of Wittgenstein's, but is rather recording his debt to the kind of cautious and attentive philosophical methodology that Wittgenstein's work sought to embody. Wittgenstein's influence on Rawls here is to motivate mistrust of the pretensions of sweeping but uncareful theoretical claims, and instead to attend with care to the internal complexities of the questions they each address.

In the pre-*Theory* papers, the main use of Wittgenstein is one explicitly indebted to Norman Malcolm's elucidation of the Wittgensteinian idea of a criterion (see Malcolm 1954). In both "Justice as Fairness" and "Justice as Reciprocity," Rawls claims that acceptance of the duty of fair play is a basic criterion of participants in a common practice "recognizing one another as persons with similar interests and capacities"; in other words, accepting fair-play duties simply is part of mutual recognition between cooperators (*CP* 62, 212). His other short mention of Wittgenstein among the early papers is the admission, in "Two Concepts of Rules," that the idea of a "rule" may in fact be something akin to what Wittgenstein identified as a "family resemblance" concept (i.e. a concept without clear necessary and sufficient conditions for its application), rather than an idea falling under either of two neat conceptions. Notwithstanding this acknowledgment, Rawls suggests that this does not undermine his task of emphasizing and sharpening two particular conceptions of rules for the purposes of his argument.

When assessing the influence of Wittgenstein on the later stage of Rawls's thought, the figure of Burton Dreben looms large. Dreben, Rawls's longtime colleague and close friend, espoused a conception of philosophy that was deeply influenced by Wittgenstein's philosophical quietism, and his scepticism about the claims of philosophical theory. On Dreben's view, all philosophical claims involving an inflationary concept of truth are misguided, given that truth plays no substantive role in meaningful discourse. It is difficult to assess the degree to which

Dreben's (and Wittgenstein's) picture of philosophy might have played an important role in Rawls's move from comprehensive to political liberalism, and, as it were, from the true to the reasonable. Wittgenstein is not explicitly discussed in *Political Liberalism*, but in the Introduction to the book, Rawls describes his debt to Dreben as "beyond accounting" (*PL* xxxii). Later, in a reminiscence of Dreben published in 2001, Rawls described himself as "Burt's tutee" (Floyd and Shieh 2001, 423–426). Fascinating further evidence comes with Dreben's posthumously published essay "On Rawls and Political Liberalism," where he claims that there is "a very close connection" (Dreben 2003, 316) between Rawls and Wittgenstein (and Frege). When discussing Rawls's idea of public reason, Dreben says that, in public reason, "you try to keep highfalutin notions to a minimum. There is nothing that is so dangerous to gaining a proper conception of public reason as metaphysics, or Philosophy with a big 'P.' That is why I said, for me, there is a genuine connection between what I said here five years ago when talking about Frege and Wittgenstein, and now in talking about Rawls" (Dreben 2003, 345–346).

It is of course one thing to say that Rawls's move toward *political* liberalism would be welcomed by those, like Dreben, who endorse a Wittgensteinian conception of the status of philosophy, but it would be something much stronger to say that Rawls's shift to the political could have been in some ways motivated by Wittgensteinian considerations. One can suggest only that this is a fascinating issue, and one ripe for further investigation. Such an investigation might also interrogate the relationship between Rawls's views and Carnap's; Dreben wrote suggestively of "Rawls's claim that fruitful political philosophy need not (should not?) rest on any metaphysical or comprehensive philosophical position" as potentially one that would "add some weight to Carnap's fundamental attitude to the doing of philosophy" (Dreben 1995, 39). Rawls himself seemed to be intrigued and perplexed by the relationship between his own work in political philosophy and the broadly Wittgensteinian (or perhaps Carnapian?) conception of the discipline of philosophy endorsed by Dreben, as attested by Rawls's quizzical remarks made in his warm reminiscence of his colleague:

> The crucial questions in understanding Burt's view are: What is philosophical understanding? What is it the understanding of? How does understanding differ from having a theory? How do we know understanding when we have it? And why is it worth having? I wonder how I can give answers to these questions in my work in moral and political philosophy, whose aims Burt encourages and supports. Sometimes Burt indicates that

my normative moral and political inquiries do not belong to philosophy proper. Yet this raises the question, Why not? And what counts as philosophy? (Rawls in Floyd and Shieh 2001, 422)

Wittgenstein and Dreben both thought that philosophy should seek *understanding* rather than theoretical truths. Dreben seems to have believed that Rawls, in his later work, ascended to a form of political philosophy that made good on this ambition.

Martin O'Neill

SEE ALSO:

Happiness
Hedonism
Moral psychology
Moral sentiments
Moral theory
Political conception of justice
Rules (two concepts of)
Social cooperation
Truth

Bibliography

Anderson, Elizabeth. 1999. "What Is the Point of Equality?" *Ethics* 109: 287–337.

Anscombe, G. E. M. 1957. *Intention* (Blackwell).

Aquinas, Thomas. 2006 [1265–1274]. *Summa Theologiae: Questions on God*, ed. Brian Davies and Brian Leftow (Cambridge University Press).

Arneson, Richard. 1993. "Democratic Rights at National and Workplace Levels" in *The Idea of Democracy*, ed. David Copp, Jean Hampton, and John Roemer (Cambridge University Press).

   1999. "Against Rawlsian Equality of Opportunity," *Philosophical Studies* 93: 77–112.

   2000a. "Welfare Should Be the Currency of Justice," *Canadian Journal of Philosophy* 30: 497–524.

   2000b. "Luck Egalitarianism and Prioritarianism," *Ethics* 110: 339–349.

   2003. "Liberal Neutrality on the Good: An Autopsy" in *Perfectionism and Neutrality*, ed. Steven Wall and George Klosko (Rowman & Littlefield).

Arrow, Kenneth. 1973. "Some Ordinalist-Utilitarian Notes on Rawls's Theory of Justice," *The Journal of Philosophy* 70: 245–263.

   1977. "Extended Sympathy and the Possibility of Social Choice," *American Economic Review*, Supplementary issue of the Proceedings: 219–225.

Baehr, Amy, ed. 2004. *Varieties of Feminist Liberalism* (Rowman & Littlefield).

Baier, Kurt. 1989. "Justice and the Aims of Political Philosophy," *Ethics* 99: 771–790.

Barry, Brian. 1965. *Political Argument* (Routledge).

   1973. *The Liberal Theory of Justice* (Oxford University Press).

   1989. *Theories of Justice* (University of California Press).

   1995. "John Rawls and the Search for Stability," *Ethics* 105: 874–915.

Bedau, Hugo Adam, ed. 1969. *Civil Disobedience: Theory and Practice* (Pegasus).

Beitz, Charles. 1999. *Political Theory and International Relations*, revised edition (Princeton University Press).

   2009. *The Idea of Human Rights* (Oxford University Press).

Benhabib, Seyla. 1987. "The Generalized and the Concrete Other: The Kohlberg-Gilligan Controversy and Moral Theory" in *Women and Moral Theory*, ed. Eva Feder Kittay and Diana Meyers (Rowman & Littlefield).

   2004. "The Law of Peoples, Distributive Justice, and Migration," *Fordham Law Review* 72: 1761–1787.

Bentham, Jeremy. 2007 [1789]. *An Introduction to the Principles of Morals and Legislation* (Dover Publications).

Berlin, Isaiah. 1969. *Four Essays on Liberty* (Oxford University Press).

Bodin, Jean. 1992 [1576]. *On Sovereignty*, ed. Julian Franklin (Cambridge University Press).

Bojer, Hilde. 2003. *Distributional Justice: Theory and Measurement* (Routledge).

Bradley, F. H. 1927. *Ethical Studies* (Oxford University Press).

Brandt, Richard. 1964. "The Concepts of Obligation and Duty," *Mind* 73: 374–393.

1979. *A Theory of the Good and the Right* (Oxford University Press).

1990. "The Science of Man and Wide Reflective Equilibrium," *Ethics* 100: 259–278.

Buchanan, Allen. 2000. "Rawls's Law of Peoples: Rules for a Vanished Westphalian World," *Ethics* 110: 697–721.

2009. *Justice and Health Care* (Oxford University Press).

2010. *Human Rights, Legitimacy and the Use of Force* (Oxford University Press).

Buchanan, James and Gordon Tullock. 1962. *The Calculus of Consent: Logical Foundations of Constitutional Democracy* (University of Michigan Press).

Callan, Eamonn. 1997. *Creating Citizens* (Oxford University Press).

Carens, Joseph. 1987. "Aliens and Citizens: The Case for Open Borders," *Review of Politics* 49: 251–273.

1992. "Migration and Morality: A Liberal Egalitarian Perspective" in *Free Movement*, ed. Brian Barry (Penn State University Press).

Clausewitz, Carl von. 1989 [1832]. *On War*, ed. and trans. Michael Eliot Howard and Peter Paret (Princeton University Press).

Cohen, G. A. 1978. *Karl Marx's Theory of History: A Defense* (Oxford University Press).

1979. "The Labor Theory of Value and the Concept of Exploitation," *Philosophy and Public Affairs* 8: 338–360.

1989. "On the Currency of Egalitarian Justice," *Ethics* 99: 906–944.

1993. "Equality of What? On Welfare, Goods, and Capabilities" in *The Quality of Life*, ed. Martha Nussbaum and Amartya Sen (Oxford University Press).

1995. *Self-Ownership, Freedom, and Equality* (Cambridge University Press).

1997. "Where the Action is: On the Site of Distributive Justice," *Philosophy and Public Affairs* 26: 3–30.

2000. *If You're an Egalitarian, How Come You're So Rich?* (Harvard University Press).

2008. *Rescuing Justice and Equality* (Harvard University Press).

2009. *Why not Socialism?* (Princeton University Press).

2011. *On the Currency of Egalitarian Justice, and Other Essays in Political Philosophy*, ed. Michael Otsuka (Princeton University Press).

Cohen, Joshua. 2002. "For a Democratic Society" in *The Cambridge Companion to Rawls*, ed. Samuel Freeman (Cambridge University Press).

2009a. *Philosophy, Politics, Democracy: Selected Essays* (Harvard University Press).

2009b. "Truth and Public Reason," *Philosophy and Public Affairs* 37: 2–42.

2010. *The Arc of the Moral Universe and Other Essays* (Harvard University Press).

Costa, M. Victoria. 2011. *Rawls, Citizenship, and Education* (Routledge).

Daniels, Norman, ed. 1975. *Reading Rawls* (Basic Books).

1985. *Just Health Care* (Cambridge University Press).

1988. *Am I My Parents' Keeper?* (Oxford University Press).

1996. *Justice and Justification: Reflective Equilibrium in Theory and Practice* (Cambridge University Press).

2003. "Democratic Equality: Rawls's Complex Egalitarianism" in *The Cambridge Companion to Rawls*, ed. Samuel Freeman (Cambridge University Press).

884 / *Bibliography*

2008a. *Just Health: Meeting Health Needs Fairly* (Cambridge University Press).

2008b. "Justice between Adjacent Generations: Further Thoughts," *Journal of Political Philosophy* 16: 475–494.

2009. "Just Health: Replies and Further Thoughts," *Journal of Medical Ethics* 35: 36–41.

2011. "Reflective Equilibrium," in *The Stanford Encyclopedia of Philosophy*. http://plato.stanford.edu/entries/reflective-equilibrium/

Daniels, Norman, Bruce Kennedy, and Ichiro Kawachi. 2000. *Is Inequality Bad for Our Health?* (Beacon).

Daniels, Norman and James Sabin. 2008. *Setting Limits Fairly*, second edition (Oxford University Press).

Darwall, Stephen. 1976. "A Defense of the Kantian Interpretation," *Ethics* 86: 164–170.

Davion, Victoria and Clark Wolf, eds. 2000. *The Idea of a Political Liberalism* (Rowman & Littlefield).

Deigh, John. 1983. "Shame and Self-Esteem: A Critique," *Ethics* 93: 225–245.

Doppelt, Gerald. 1981. "Rawls' System of Justice: A Critique from the Left," *Nous* 15: 259–307.

2009. "The Place of Self-Respect in a Theory of Justice," *Inquiry* 52: 127–154.

Dowding, Keith, Robert Goodin, and Carole Pateman, eds. 2004. *Justice and Democracy: Essays for Brian Barry* (Cambridge University Press).

Doyle, Michael. 2006. "One World, Many Peoples: International Justice in John Rawls's *The Law of Peoples*," *Perspectives on Politics* 4: 109–120.

Dreben, Burton. 1995. "Cohen's Carnap, or Subjectivity Is in the Eye of the Beholder" in *Science, Politics and Social Practice*, ed. Kostas Gavroglu, John Stachel, and Marx Wartofsky (Kluwer).

2003. "On Rawls and Political Liberalism" in *The Cambridge Companion to Rawls*, ed. Samuel Freeman (Cambridge University Press).

Dworkin, Ronald. 1975. "The Original Position" in *Reading Rawls*, ed. Norman Daniels (Basic Books).

1981. "What Is Equality? Part 2: Equality of Resources," *Philosophy and Public Affairs* 10: 283–345.

1985. *A Matter of Principle* (Harvard University Press).

1986. *Law's Empire* (Harvard University Press).

2000. *Sovereign Virtue* (Harvard University Press).

2003. "Equality, Luck and Hierarchy," *Philosophy and Public Affairs* 31: 190–198.

Dyke, Charles. 1981. *Philosophy of Economics* (Prentice Hall).

Epstein, Richard. 1998. *Principles for a Free Society: Reconciling Individual Liberty with the Common Good* (Basic Books).

Estlund, David. 2008. *Democratic Authority: A Philosophical Framework* (Princeton University Press).

Farrelly, Colin. 2007. "Justice in Ideal Theory: A Refutation," *Political Studies* 55: 844–864.

Floyd, Juliet and Sanford Shieh, eds. 2001. *Future Pasts: The Analytic Tradition in Twentieth Century Philosophy* (Oxford University Press).

Freeman, Samuel. 2001. "Illiberal Libertarians: Why Libertarianism Is not a Liberal View," *Philosophy and Public Affairs* 29: 105–151.

ed. 2003a. *The Cambridge Companion to Rawls* (Cambridge University Press).

Bibliography / 885

2003b. "Congruence and the Good of Justice" in *The Cambridge Companion to Rawls*, ed. Samuel Freeman (Cambridge University Press).

2006a. "The Law of Peoples, Social Cooperation, Human Rights, and Distributive Justice," *Social Philosophy and Policy* 23: 29–63.

2006b. "Frontiers of Justice: The Capabilities Approach vs. Contractarianism – Book Review of *Frontiers of Justice*, Martha C. Nussbaum," *Texas Law Review* 85: 385–430.

2007a. *Justice and the Social Contract: Essays on Rawlsian Political Philosophy* (Oxford University Press).

2007b. *Rawls* (Routledge).

Friedman, Milton. 1962. *Capitalism and Freedom* (University of Chicago Press).

Galston, William. 1995. "Two Concepts of Liberalism," *Ethics* 105: 516–534.

Gilligan, Carol. 1982. *In a Different Voice: Psychological Theory and Women's Development* (Harvard University Press).

1987. "Moral Orientation and Moral Development" in *Women and Moral Theory*, ed. Eva Feder Kittay and Diana Meyers (Rowman & Littlefield).

2011. *Joining the Resistance* (Polity Press).

Goodman, Nelson. 1955. *Fact, Fiction, and Forecast* (Harvard University Press).

Gray, John. 1996. *Isaiah Berlin* (Princeton University Press).

Grotius, Hugo. 2005 [1625]. *The Rights of War and Peace*, ed. Richard Tuck (Liberty Fund).

Gutmann, Amy. 1980. *Liberal Equality* (Cambridge University Press).

1995. "Civic Education and Social Diversity," *Ethics* 105: 557–579.

2002. "Rawls on the Relationship between Liberalism and Democracy" in *The Cambridge Companion to Rawls*, ed. Samuel Freeman (Cambridge University Press).

Habermas, Jürgen. 1995. "Reconciliation through the Public Use of Reason: Remarks on John Rawls's Liberalism," *Journal of Philosophy* 92: 109–131.

1996. *Between Facts and Norms: Contributions to a Discourse Theory of Law and Democracy*, trans. William Rehg (MIT Press).

Hammond, Peter. 1991. "Interpersonal Comparisons of Utility: Why and How They Are and Should Be Made" in *Interpersonal Comparisons of Well-Being*, ed. Jon Elster and John Roemer (Cambridge University Press).

Harding, Walter. 1982. *The Days of Henry Thoreau: A Biography* (Dover).

Hare, R. M. 1973a. "Rawls' Theory of Justice – I," *Philosophical Quarterly* 23: 144–155.

1973b. "Rawls' Theory of Justice – II," *Philosophical Quarterly* 23: 241–252.

Harsanyi, John. 1953. "Cardinal Utility in Welfare Economics and in the Theory of Risk-Taking," *Journal of Political Economy* 61: 434–435.

1955. "Cardinal Welfare, Individualistic Ethics, and Interpersonal Comparisons of Utility," *Journal of Political Economy* 63: 309–321.

Hart, H. L. A. 1955. "Are There Any Natural Rights?" *Philosophical Review* 64: 175–191.

1958. "Legal and Moral Obligations" in *Essays in Moral Philosophy*, ed. A. I. Melden (University of Washington Press).

1968. "Prolegomenon to the Principles of Punishment" in *Punishment and Responsibility: Essays in the Philosophy of Law* (Oxford University Press).

1975. "Rawls on Liberty and Its Priority" in *Reading Rawls*, ed. Norman Daniels (Basic Books).

1994. *The Concept of Law*, second edition (Oxford University Press).

Hayek, Friedrich von. 1960. *The Constitution of Liberty* (Routledge and Kegan Paul).

Hayes, Jarrod. 2011. "Review Article: the Democratic Peace and the New Evolution of an Old Idea," *European Journal of International Relations*: 1–25.

Hegel, G. W. F. 1991 [1821]. *Elements of the Philosophy of Right*, ed. Allen W. Wood (Cambridge University Press).

Hill, Thomas E., Jr. 1994. "The Stability Problem in Political Liberalism," *Pacific Philosophical Quarterly* 75, 333–352.

Hobbes, Thomas. 1994 [1651]. *Leviathan*, ed. Edwin Curley (Hackett).

Holmes, Stephen and Cass Sunstein. 1999. *The Cost of Rights: Why Liberty Depends on Taxes* (Norton).

Hume, David. 1978 [1738]. *A Treatise of Human Nature*, second edition, ed. L. A. Selby-Bigge (Oxford University Press).

Johnson, Oliver. 1974. "The Kantian Interpretation," *Ethics* 85: 58–66.

Kamm, Frances. 1993. *Morality and Mortality*, volume I (Oxford University Press).

Kant, Immanuel. 1983. *Perpetual Peace and Other Essays*, trans. Ted Humphrey (Hackett). This volume includes "On the Proverb: That May Be True in Theory, but Is of No Practical Use" [1793] and "Perpetual Peace" [1795].

1996 [1797]. *The Metaphysics of Morals*, ed. Mary Gregor (Cambridge University Press).

1997a [1785]. *Groundwork of the Metaphysics of Morals*, ed. Mary Gregor (Cambridge University Press).

1997b [1788]. *Critique of Practical Reason*, ed. Mary Gregor (Cambridge University Press).

Keynes, J. M. 1936. *The General Theory of Employment, Interest and Money* (Macmillan).

Kelly, Paul. 2009. "Obituary: Brian Barry," *The Guardian* (30 March 2009): www.theguardian.com/books/2009/mar/31/brian-barry-philosophy

King, Martin Luther, Jr. 1987 [1958]. *Stride Toward Freedom: The Montgomery Story* (Harper & Brothers).

2000 [1964]. *Why We Can't Wait* (Signet Classics).

Kittay, Eva Feder. 1999. *Love's Labor: Essays on Women, Equality, and Dependency* (Routledge).

Klosko, George. 1987. "Presumptive Benefit, Fairness, and Political Obligation," *Philosophy and Public Affairs* 16: 241–259.

1994a. "Political Obligation and the Natural Duties of Justice," *Philosophy and Public Affairs* 23: 251–270.

1994b. "Rawls's Argument from Political Stability," *Columbia Law Review* 94: 1882–1897.

2000. *Democratic Procedures and Liberal Consensus* (Oxford University Press).

2004. *The Principle of Fairness and Political Obligation*, second edition (Rowman & Littlefield).

Knight, Frank. 1923. "The Ethics of Competition," *The Quarterly Journal of Economics* 37: 579–624.

Korsgaard, Christine. 1996. *The Sources of Normativity* (Cambridge University Press).

2009. *Self-Constitution: Agency, Identity, and Integrity* (Oxford University Press).

Krasnoff, Larry. 1998. "Consensus, Stability, and Normativity in Rawls's Political Liberalism," *Journal of Philosophy* 95: 269–292.

2014. "Kantian Constructivism" in *The Blackwell Companion to Rawls*, ed. Jon Mandle and David Reidy (Blackwell).

Bibliography / 887

Krouse, Richard and Michael McPherson. 1988. "Capitalism, 'Property-Owning Democracy,' and the Welfare State" in *Democracy and the Welfare State*, ed. Amy Gutmann (Princeton University Press).

Krugman, Paul. 2012. *End This Depression Now!* (W. W. Norton).

Kuper, Andrew. 2000. "Rawlsian Global Justice: Beyond the Law of Peoples to a Cosmopolitan Law of Persons," *Political Theory* 28: 640–674.

Kymlicka, Will. 1989. *Liberalism, Community and Culture* (Oxford University Press).

  1995. *Multicultural Citizenship: A Liberal Theory of Minority Rights* (Oxford University Press).

  2002. *Contemporary Political Philosophy: An Introduction*, second edition (Oxford University Press).

Larmore, Charles. 1996. *The Morals of Modernity* (Cambridge University Press).

  2003. "Public Reason" in *The Cambridge Companion to Rawls*, ed. Samuel Freeman (Cambridge University Press).

LeBar, Mark. 2008. "Aristotelian Constructivism," *Social Philosophy and Policy* 25: 182–213.

Leibniz, G. W. 1951 [1697]. "On the Ultimate Origin of Things" in *Leibniz*, ed. P. P. Weiner (Charles Scribner's Sons).

Lloyd, S. A. 1994. "Family Justice and Social Justice," *Pacific Philosophical Quarterly* 75: 353–371.

  1998. "Contemporary Uses of Hobbes's Political Philosophy" in *Rational Commitment and Social Justice*, ed. Jules Coleman and Christopher Morris (Cambridge University Press).

Locke, John. 1960 [1689]. *Two Treatises of Government*, ed. Peter Laslett (Cambridge University Press).

  1997 [1676]. *Essays on the Law of Nature* in *Political Essays*, ed. Mark Goldie (Cambridge University Press).

  2010 [1689]. *A Letter Concerning Toleration and Other Writings*, ed. Mark Goldie (Liberty Fund).

Lomasky, Loren. 1987. *Persons, Rights, and the Moral Community* (Oxford University Press).

MacCallum, Gerald. 1967. "Negative and Positive Freedom," *Philosophical Review* 76: 312–334.

Macedo, Stephen. 1995. "Liberal Civic Education and Religious Fundamentalism: The Case of God v. John Rawls?" *Ethics* 105: 468–496.

MacIntyre, Alasdair. 1984. *After Virtue*, second edition (Notre Dame University Press).

Mackie, John. 1977. *Ethics: Inventing Right and Wrong* (Penguin).

Malcolm, Norman. 1954. "Wittgenstein's *Philosophical Investigations*," *Philosophical Review* 63: 530–559.

Mandle, Jon. 2005. "Tolerating Injustice" in *The Political Philosophy of Cosmopolitanism*, ed. Gillian Brock and Harry Brighouse (Cambridge University Press).

  2006. *Global Justice* (Polity).

  2009. *Rawls's A Theory of Justice: An Introduction* (Cambridge University Press).

Martin, Rex. 1985. *Rawls and Rights* (Kansas University Press).

Martin, Rex and David Reidy, eds. 2006. *Rawls's Law of Peoples: A Realistic Utopia?* (Blackwell).

Marx, Karl. 1994 [1888]. "Theses on Feuerbach" in *Selected Writings*, ed. Lawrence H. Simon (Hackett).

McMahan, Jeff. 2000. "Moral Intuition" in *Blackwell Guide to Ethical Theory*, ed. Hugh LaFollette (Blackwell).

McMullin, Ernan. 1985. "Galilean Idealization," *Studies in the History and Philosophy of Science* 16: 247–273.

Meade, J. E. 1964. *Efficiency, Equality and the Ownership of Property* (George Allen & Unwin).

Michelman, Frank. 1972. "In Pursuit of Constitutional Welfare Rights: One View of Rawls' Theory of Justice," *University of Pennsylvania Law Review* 121: 962–1019.

Mill, John Stuart. 1991. *On Liberty and Other Essays*, ed. John Gray (Oxford University Press). This volume includes *On Liberty* [1859], *Utilitarianism* [1861] *Considerations on Representative Government* [1861], *The Subjection of Women* [1869].

2012 [1843]. *A System of Logic, Ratiocination and Inductive* (Cambridge University Press).

Moellendorf, Darrel. 2002. *Cosmopolitan Justice* (Westview Press).

2009. *Global Inequality Matters* (Palgrave Macmillan).

Mueller, Dennis. 2003. *Public Choice III* (Cambridge University Press).

Munoz-Dardé, Véronique. 1988. "John Rawls, Justice in and Justice of the Family," *The Philosophical Quarterly* 48: 335–352.

Murphy, Liam. 1998. "Institutions and the Demands of Justice," *Philosophy and Public Affairs* 27: 251–291.

Murphy, Liam and Thomas Nagel. 2002. *The Myth of Ownership: Taxes and Justice* (Oxford University Press).

Murray, John Courtney, S. J. 1965. *The Problem of Religious Freedom* (Newman Press).

Musgrave, R. A. 1959. *The Theory of Public Finance* (McGraw-Hill).

1974. "Maximin, Uncertainty, and the Leisure Trade-Off," *The Quarterly Journal of Economics* 88: 625–632.

Nagel, Thomas. 1975. "Rawls on Justice" in *Reading Rawls*, ed. Norman Daniels (Basic Books).

1991. *Equality and Partiality* (Oxford University Press).

1997. "Justice and Nature," *Oxford Journal of Legal Studies* 17: 303–321.

2003. "Rawls and Liberalism" in *The Cambridge Companion to Rawls*, ed. Samuel Freeman (Cambridge University Press).

2005. "The Problem of Global Justice," *Philosophy and Public Affairs* 33: 113–147.

Narveson, Jan. 1988. *The Libertarian Idea* (Temple University Press).

Nozick, Robert. 1974. *Anarchy, State, and Utopia* (Basic Books).

Nussbaum, Martha. 1993. "Non-Relative Virtues: An Aristotelian Approach" in *The Quality of Life*, ed. Martha Nussbaum and Amartya Sen (Oxford University Press).

1997. *Cultivating Humanity: A Classical Defense of Reform in Liberal Education* (Harvard University Press).

1999. *Sex and Social Justice* (Oxford University Press).

2000. *Women and Human Development: The Capabilities Approach* (Cambridge University Press).

2001. *Upheavals of Thought: The Intelligence of Emotions* (Cambridge University Press).

2003. "Rawls and Feminism" in *The Cambridge Companion to Rawls*, ed. Samuel Freeman (Cambridge University Press).

Bibliography / 889

2004. *Hiding from Humanity: Disgust, Shame, and the Law* (Princeton University Press).

2006. *Frontiers of Justice: Disability, Nationality, Species Membership* (Harvard University Press).

2010a. *From Disgust to Humanity: Sexual Orientation and Constitutional Law* (Oxford University Press).

2010b. *Not for Profit: Why Democracy Needs the Humanities* (Princeton University Press).

2011. *Creating Capabilities: The Human Development Approach* (Harvard University Press).

Nussbaum, Martha, and Amartya Sen, eds. 1993. *The Quality of Life* (Oxford University Press).

Okin, Susan Moller. 1989. *Justice, Gender and the Family* (Basic Books).

1999. *Is Multiculturalism Bad for Women?* (Princeton University Press).

2004. "Justice and Gender: An Unfinished Debate," *Fordham Law Review – Symposium: Rawls and the Law* 72: 1537–1567.

O'Neill, Martin and Thad Williamson, eds., 2012. *Property-Owning Democracy: Rawls and Beyond* (Wiley-Blackwell).

O'Neill, Onora. 1988. "Abstraction, Idealization, and Ideology in Ethics" in *Moral Philosophy and Contemporary Problems*, ed. J. D. G. Barnes (Cambridge University Press).

1989. *Constructions of Reason* (Cambridge University Press).

Parfit, Derek. 2002. "Equality or Priority" in *The Ideal of Equality*, ed. Matthew Clayton and Andrew Williams (Palgrave Macmillan).

Pateman, Carol. 1988. *The Sexual Contract* (Polity Press).

Patten, Alan. 2005. "Should We Stop Thinking about Poverty in Terms of Helping the Poor?" *Ethics & International Affairs* 19: 19–27.

Peart, Sandra and David Levy, eds. 2008. *The Street Porter and the Philosopher: Conversations on Analytical Egalitarianism* (University of Michigan Press).

Peffer, R. G. 1990. *Marxism, Morality, and Social Justice* (Princeton University Press).

Perelman, Chaïm. 1963. *The Idea of Justice and the Problem of Argument* (Routledge).

Pogge, Thomas. 1989. *Realizing Rawls* (Cornell University Press).

1992. "Cosmopolitanism and Sovereignty," *Ethics* 103: 48–75.

1994. "An Egalitarian Law of Peoples," *Philosophy and Public Affairs* 23: 195–224.

1995. "Three Problems with Contractarian-Consequentialist Ways of Assessing Social Institutions," *Social Philosophy and Policy* 12: 241–266.

1998a. "A Global Resources Dividend" in *Ethics of Consumption*, ed. David Crocker and Toby Linden (Rowman & Littlefield).

1998b. "The Categorical Imperative" in *Kant's Groundwork of the Metaphysics of Morals*, ed. Paul Guyer (Rowman & Littlefield).

2000. "On the Site of Distributive Justice: Reflections on Cohen and Murphy," *Philosophy and Public Affairs* 29: 137–169.

2002a. "Is Kant's *Rechtslehre* a 'Comprehensive Liberalism'?" in *Kant's* Metaphysics of Morals: *Interpretive Essays*, ed. Mark Timmons (Oxford University Press).

2002b. "Can the Capability Approach be Justified?" *Philosophical Topics* 30: 167–228.

2005. "Human Rights and Global Health: A Research Program," *Metaphilosophy* 36: 182–209.

2007 [1994]. *John Rawls: His Life and Theory of Justice*, trans. Michelle Kosch (Oxford University Press).

2008. *World Poverty and Human Rights*, second edition (Polity Press).

2012. "The Health Impact Fund: Enhancing Justice and Efficiency in Global Health," *Journal of Human Development and Capabilities* 13: 537–559.

Quong, Jonathan. 2005. "Disagreement, Asymmetry, and Liberal Legitimacy," *Politics, Philosophy, Economics* 4: 301–330.

2011. *Liberalism without Perfection* (Oxford University Press).

Ray, James. 1998. "Does Democracy Cause Peace?" *Annual Review of Political Science* 1: 27–46.

Raz, Joseph. 1998. "Disagreement in Politics," *American Journal of Jurisprudence* 43: 25–52.

Reidy, David. 1996. "Education for Citizenship in a Pluralist Liberal Democracy," *Journal of Value Inquiry* 30: 25–42.

2004. "Rawls on International Justice: A Defense," *Political Theory* 32: 291–319.

2006a. "Political Authority and Human Rights" in *Rawls's Law of Peoples: A Realistic Utopia?* ed. Rex Martin and David Reidy (Blackwell).

2006b. "Three Human Rights Agendas," *Canadian Journal of Law and Jurisprudence* 19: 237–254.

2007. "Reciprocity and Reasonable Disagreement: From Liberal to Democratic Legitimacy," *Philosophical Studies* 132: 243–291.

2010. "Human Rights and Liberal Toleration," *Canadian Journal of Law and Jurisprudence* 23: 287–317.

Riker, Walter. 2009. "The Democratic Peace is Not Democratic: On Behalf of Rawls's Decent Societies," *Political Studies* 57: 617–638.

Risse, Mathias. 2005. "Do We Owe the Global Poor Assistance or Rectification?" *Ethics & International Affairs* 19: 9–18.

Rorty, Richard. 1979. *Philosophy and the Mirror of Nature* (Princeton University Press).

1991. "The Priority of Democracy to Philosophy" in his *Objectivity, Relativism, and Truth: Philosophical Papers*, volume I (Cambridge University Press).

Ross, W. D. 1930. *The Right and the Good* (Oxford University Press).

Rousseau, Jean-Jacques. 2011 [1762]. *The Basic Political Writings*, ed. Donald A. Cress (Hackett).

Sandel, Michael. 1982. *Liberalism and the Limits of Justice* (revised edition 1998) (Cambridge University Press).

1998. *Democracy's Discontent* (Harvard University Press).

Sayre-McCord, Geoffrey. 1996. "Coherentist Epistemology and Moral Theory" in *Moral Knowledge?* ed. Walter Sinnot-Armstrong and Mark Timmons (Oxford University Press).

Scanlon, T. M. 1998. *What We Owe to Each Other* (Harvard University Press).

2003. *The Difficulty of Tolerance* (Cambridge University Press).

2006. "Justice, Responsibility, and the Demands of Equality" in *The Egalitarian Conscience: Essays in Honour of G. A. Cohen*, ed. Christine Sypnowich (Oxford University Press).

Scheffler, Samuel. 2001. "Justice and Desert in Liberal Theory" in *Boundaries and Allegiances* (Oxford University Press).

Bibliography / 891

2003a. "Rawls and Utilitarianism" in *The Cambridge Companion to Rawls*, ed. Samuel Freeman (Cambridge University Press).

2003b. "What Is Egalitarianism?" *Philosophy and Public Affairs* 31: 5–39.

Schmidtz, David. 2011. "Nonideal Theory: What It Is and What It Needs to Be," *Ethics* 121: 772–796.

Searle, John. 1969. *Speech Acts* (Cambridge University Press).

Sen, Amartya. 1980. "Equality of What?" in *The Tanner Lectures on Human Values*, vol. 1, ed. Sterling McMurrin (University of Utah Press).

1982. "Equality of What?" in his *Choice, Welfare, and Measurement* (Blackwell).

1985. "Well-being, Agency, and Freedom: The Dewey Lectures 1984," *Journal of Philosophy* 82: 169–221.

1987. *Commodities and Capabilities* (Oxford University Press).

1992. *Inequality Reexamined* (Harvard University Press).

1993. "Capability and Well-Being" in *The Quality of Life*, ed. Martha Nussbaum and Amartya Sen (Oxford University Press).

2009. *The Idea of Justice* (Harvard University Press).

Shapiro, Danny. 2007. *Is the Welfare State Justified?* (Cambridge University Press).

Shue, Henry. 1975. "Liberty and Self-Respect," *Ethics* 85: 195–203.

Sidgwick, Henry. 1888. "The Kantian Conception of Free Will," *Mind* 13: 405–412.

1981 [1874]. *The Methods of Ethics*, sixth edition (Hackett).

Simmons, A. John. 1979. *Moral Principles and Political Obligations* (Princeton University Press).

2001. *Justification and Legitimacy: Essays on Rights and Obligations* (Cambridge University Press).

2010. "Ideal and Nonideal Theory," *Philosophy and Public Affairs* 38: 5–36.

Simmons, A. John and Christopher Wellman. 2005. *Is There a Duty to Obey the Law?* (Cambridge University Press).

Soper, Philip. 1984. *A Theory of Law* (Harvard University Press).

Sreenivasan, Gopal. 2008. "Justice, Inequality and Health," in *The Stanford Encyclopedia of Philosophy*. http://plato.stanford.edu/entries/justice-inequality-health/

Sterba, James. 2008. "Completing the Kantian Project: From Rationality to Equality," *Proceedings and Addresses of the American Philosophical Association* 82: 47–83.

Tan, Kok-Chor. 1998. "Liberal Toleration in Rawls' Law of Peoples," *Ethics* 108: 276–295.

2000. *Toleration, Diversity, and Global Justice* (Pennsylvania State University Press).

Taylor, Charles. 1985. *Philosophical Papers*, volume II, *Philosophy and the Human Sciences* (Cambridge University Press).

1989. *Sources of the Self* (Harvard University Press)

1995. *Philosophical Arguments* (Harvard University Press).

Temkin, Larry. 2003. "Equality, Priority, or What?" *Economics and Philosophy* 19: 61–88.

Thoreau, Henry D. 1973 [1849]. "Thorea," in *Reform Papers: The Writings of Henry D. Thoreau*, ed. Wendell Glick (Princeton University Press).

Vallentyne, Peter. 2010. "Libertarianism" in *The Stanford Encyclopedia of Philosophy*, ed. Edward Zalta. http://plato.stansford.edu/archives

2011. "Nozick's Libertarian Theory of Justice" in *Anarchy, State, and Utopia – A Reappraisal*, ed. Ralf Bader and John Meadowcroft (Cambridge University Press).

van Parijs, Philippe. 1991. "Why Surfers Should Be Fed: The Liberal Case for an Unconditional Basic Income," *Philosophy and Public Affairs* 20: 101–131.

Waldron, Jeremy. 1986. "John Rawls and the Social Minimum," *Journal of Applied Philosophy* 3: 21–33.

1993. "Special Ties and Natural Duties," *Philosophy and Public Affairs* 22: 3–30.

Wall, Steven. 2002. "Is Public Justification Self-Defeating?" *American Philosophical Quarterly* 39: 385–394.

Walzer, Michael. 1983. *Spheres of Justice* (Basic Books).

2006. *Just and Unjust Wars*, fourth edition (Basic Books).

Weinstock, Daniel. 1994. "The Justification of Political Liberalism," *Pacific Philosophical Quarterly* 75: 165–185.

1997. "The Graying of Berlin," *Critical Review* 11: 481–501.

Weithman, Paul. 2000. "Citizenship and Public Reason" in *Natural Law and Public Reason*, ed. Robert George and Christopher Wolfe (Georgetown University Press).

2011. *Why Political Liberalism?* (Oxford University Press).

Wenar, Leif. 1995. "Political Liberalism: An Internal Critique," *Ethics* 106: 32–62.

Wenar, Leif and Branko Milanovic. 2009. "Are Liberal Peoples Peaceful?" *Journal of Political Philosophy* 17: 462–486.

Wicksell, Knut. 1958. "A New Principle of Just Taxation," in *Classics in the Theory of Public Finance*, ed. R. A. Musgrave and A. T. Peacock (Macmillan).

Williams, Andrew. 1995. "The Revisionist Difference Principle," *Canadian Journal of Philosophy* 25: 257–281.

Williams, Bernard. 1962. "The Idea of Equality" in *Philosophy, Politics, and Society*, ed. P. Laslett and W. G. Runciman (Blackwell).

1981. *Moral Luck* (Cambridge University Press).

Wittgenstein, Ludwig. 1953. *Philosophical Investigations*, ed. G. E. M. Anscombe and Rush Rhees (Oxford University Press).

Young, Iris. 1997. *Intersecting Voices: Dilemmas of Gender, Political Philosophy, and Policy* (Princeton University Press).

2006. "Taking the Basic Structure Seriously," *Perspectives on Politics* 4: 91–97.

Index

abortion, **3–4**, 88, 670–671, 720, 729
allocative justice, **7–8**, 57–58, 211, 217–219, 482, 652
altruism, 5, **9–10**, 94, 213, 363, 488, 566, 703, 794, 866
animals, **11–13**, 67, 252, 519, 566
Aquinas, Thomas, **14–16**, 20, 89, 719
Arendt, Hannah, 21, 100
Aristotelian principle, 13, **17–19**, 136–137, 170, 315, 501, 522, 604, 683, 762
Aristotle, 14, 15, 17, **20–22**, 81, 89, 100, 153, 344, 429, 566, 685, 719
Arneson, Richard, **23–24**, 271, 471
Arrow, Kenneth, **25–26**, 332, 383, 506, 779–780, 784
Augustine, 14, 15, 89, 719, 778
autonomy, **27–31**, **32–39**, 121, 156, 165, 296, 395–398, 399–402, 413, 445, 536, 600, 603, 727, 743
avoidance, method of, **40–41**, 101, 389, 624–625, 842–844

Barry, Brian, **45–46**, 59, 135
basic liberties, **47–49**, 102, 141–146, 295–296, 300–303, 330, 435–439, 440, 460–463, 494, 497, 504–506, 583, 643, 645, 728–730, 814, 817, 818, 845–850
basic needs, **50–54**, 82, 494, 785–787, 849
basic structure, **55–58**, 70, 113, 217–221, 279, 306, 417, 425, 499–500, 613, 732–734, 742, 846, 875
Beitz, Charles, **59–60**, 163, 413
benevolent absolutism, **61–62**, 378, 600
Bentham, Jeremy, 336, 356, 499, 500
Berlin, Isaiah, **63–64**, 457, 701
Bodin, Jean, 278, 718, 800–802
branches of government, 50, **65–68**, 481, 604, 785

Buchanan, Allen, **69–70**, 601
Buchanan, James, 662–663
burdened societies, **71–73**, 226–228, 600
burdens of judgment, **74–77**, 98, 127, 267, 461, 626, 700–702, 839–840

capabilities, 23, **81–83**, 180, 263, 332, 383, 565–567, 610, 676, 766
care, **84–86**, 283, 285–286, 332–335, 517, 525, 660, 769, 790
Catholicism, 4, 76, **87–89**, 278, 463, 619, 721
chain-connection, **90–91**
circumstances of justice, 10, **92–96**, 267, 330, 355, 488–489, 581, 700
citizen, 52, 83, **97–99**, 131, 179, 296–297, 344, 418, 423, 508, 512–519, 527, 613, 631, 723
civic humanism, 21, **100–101**, 102, 123
civic republicanism, 21, 32, **102–103**, 756
civil disobedience, **104–107**, 139–140, 403–404, 461, 552
close-knitness, 90–91, **108–110**
Cohen, G. A., 56, 109, **111–114**, 180, 220, 268, 270, 471–473, 475, 489, 543, 645, 646, 714–715, 733–734, 844
Cohen, Joshua, **115–116**, 190
common good idea of justice, 15, 20, 89, **117–118**, 159, 183–184, 742, 756, 798, 876
communitarianism, 95, **119–125**, 339, 755–756, 871–873
comprehensive doctrine, 76, 77, **126–129**, 130, 173, 253, 445–446, 447–451, 588–593, 612–613, 616–617, 621–622, 666–672, 695, 700–702, 842–844
conception of the good, 126, **130–132**, 297, 314–317, 342–345, 501, 514, 606–607
congruence, xix, **133–138**, 529, 770, 807, 834–836

894 / *Index*

conscientious refusal, 104, **139–140**, 380, 461, 721

constitution and constitutional essentials, 51, 57, **141–146**, 229, 291, 419, 424–425, 666–668, 728–730, 787, 817–821

constitutional consensus, 51, **147–148**, 591, 592, 621

constructivism, 113, **149–156**, 397–398, 432, 533–538, 579, 632, 635–639, 685–687, 775–776

cooperation and coordination, 5–6, 61, 93, **157–161**, 273–276, 296, 306, 352, 385, 703–706, 768

cosmopolitanism, 46, 59, **162–168**, 341, 413, 496–498

counting principles, **169–170**, 186–187

culture, **171–175**, 407–408, 599, 664–665, 668, 844

Daniels, Norman, **179–181**, 271, 332–335

decent societies, 117–118, 166, **182–185**, 196–197, 350, 599–601, 840, 877

deliberative rationality, 169, **186–189**, 224, 315, 606, 775

democracy, 115, **190–194**, 195–196, 210, 334–335, 352, 458, 483, 653, 670

democratic peace, **195–197**, 380, 690, 802

deontological vs. teleological theories, 20, **198–201**, 602, 607, 650, 725, 859–860

desert, **202–205**, 213, 218, 428–430, 453–454, 483–484, 709–710

desires, 8, 170, 187, **206–208**, 356, 527, 636

Dewey, John, **209–210**

difference principle, 23, 51, 90, 108–110, 113, 180, **211–216**, 245, 261, 421, 453, 474, 494, 563, 584, 704–705, 709–710, 785–787, 826, 845–850

distributive justice, xvii, 7–8, 57–58, 92, 163, 202–205, **217–221**, 239–247, 651–653

dominant end theories, 16, 188, **222–225**, 337, 855, 878

Dreben, Burton, xix, 304, 878, 879–881

duty of assistance, 38, 164–166, **226–228**, 412, 796, 812

duty of civility, 194, **229–233**, 351, 559, 666–672

Dworkin, Ronald, 112, **234–235**, 386–387, 471–473, 558

economy, 65–66, **239–247**, 481–485, 486–492, 656–661, 791–794

egoism, 9, 14, 22, 93, 134, **248–251**, 659, 726, 760, 773, 777

environment, 11–13, **252–255**

envy, 22, **256–258**, 363, 523–524, 580, 741, 763

equal opportunity, 45, 66, 180, 212, **259–263**, 269–272, 280, 332–333, 583, 657, 731, 825, 845–850

facts, **267–268**, 688, 714

fair value of political liberties, 66, 106, 190–193, 294, 303, 458, 657, 660, 819–820, 845, 849

fairness, principle of, 57, **273–276**, 548, 575, 628–630, 655, 783

faith, **277–278**, 431

family, 56, 270, **279–283**, 285–287, 320, 470, 507, 577

feminism, 85, 270, **284–287**, 470, 566, 577–578, 790

formal justice, 20, **288–289**, 350, 369, 386, 745

four-stage sequence, **290–292**, 333, 361, 662, 817, 849

freedom, 47–49, **293–299**, 457–459, 517, 666

freedom of speech, 192, **300–303**, 438, 458, 820

Freeman, Samuel, 185, **304–305**, 352, 415, 489, 650

friendship, 135, 136, 194, 508, 515, 526, 670, 704, 760, 770, 789

Fuller, Lon, 289, 747

fundamental ideas, 55–58, 157–161, 171, **306–307**, 388–389, 512–519, 579–585, 589–590, 614, 664–665, 874–877

games, 17, **311–313**, 327, 368, 508, 546–547, 692, 788, 789

goodness as rationality, 186–189, **314–317**, 539, 606, 828–837

guilt, 136, **318–321**, 469, 514, 520–521, 525, 530–531, 760, 769–770

Habermas, Jürgen, 36, 174, 619, 701, 844

happiness, 21, **325–326**, 342, 606

Harsanyi, John, 25, **327–328**, 506, 684

Hart, H. L. A., 48, 295, **329–331**, 368, 385, 418, 574, 628, 747, 849

health and healthcare, 25, 82, 179–180, 271, **332–335**, 660

hedonism, 188, 224, **336–338**, 866, 878

Hegel, G. W. F., **339–341**, 488, 688, 707, 723, 788, 802

Index / 895

higher-order interests, 28, 48, 296, **342–345**, 438, 494, 644–645, 867

Hobbes, Thomas, **346–348**, 544, 685, 757, 782, 800–802, \({805}, 805, 806

human rights, 51, 60, 61, 69, 183, **349–353**, 377–381, 586, 610, 735–736

Hume, David, 30, 93–94, 207, **354–357**, 481, 685, 782, 783

ideal and nonideal theory, 226, 274–275, **361–364**, 377, 437, 586, 766, 805–806

individualism, 119, 163, 234, 339, **365–367**, 445, 487, 757

institutions, 55–58, 354, **368–370**, 386, 499, 575, 643, 766

interpersonal comparisons, 25, **382–384**, 643–647, 779, 847, 867

intuitionism, **371–373**, 431, 435, 640, 739, 773

just war theory, 139, 350, **377–381**, 586, 811–812, 871

justice between generations, 180, 211, 240, 254, 452, 660–661, 845

justice, concept of, 217–221, 311, **385–387**, 580

justification, 171–175, 229–233, 307, 311, **388–389**, **390–391**, 692–697, 711–716

Kant, Immanuel, 27–30, 154, 199, 298, 338–341, **395–398**, 399–402, 445, 635–636, 685, 775, 778

Kantian interpretation, 30, 396, **399–402**

King, Martin Luther, Jr., 16, 140, **403–404**

Kohlberg, Lawrence, 84, **405–406**, 507, 675

Kymlicka, Will, **407–408**

Law of Peoples, 52–54, 61–62, 69–70, 162–168, 226–228, 349–353, 377–381, **411–416**, 671–672, 698–699, 795–797, 840–841

law, system of, 57, 288, 330, **417–419**, 745–749

least-advantaged position, 211–216, 294, **420–421**, 433, 786

legitimacy, 115, 185, 349, 415, **422–427**, 449, 464–467, 666–667, 704, 728, 819

legitimate expectations, 57, 202–203, **428–432**, 454, 540

Leibniz, G. W., 14, 298, 428, 432, 685

leisure, **431–432**, 644

lexical priority, 23, 47, 51, 271, 372, **435–439**, 440, 608, 626, 763, 766, 847

liberalism, 234, 284, **440–441**, **442–444**, **445–446**, **447–451**, 488, 543, 557–560, 597–598, 616–622, 627

libertarianism, **452–456**, 481, 561–564, 626, 653, 827

liberty of conscience, 88, 294, 350, 437, 458, **460–463**, 839, 849

Locke, John, 278, 293, 355–356, **464–467**, 476, 562, 717, 783–784

love, 135, 193, 281, 320, **468–470**, 507, 525, 530, 721, 769

luck egalitarianism, 8, 24, 112, 180, 271, **471–477**, 610, 709–710

Malcolm, Norman, xvi, xvii, 878, 879

market, 239, 244–245, 260, **481–485**, 543, 641–642, 652, 792–793

Marx, Karl, xviii, 95, 111, 246, 294, 485, **486–492**, 656, 659–660

maximin, 23, 45, 211, 256, 328, 421, **493–495**, 684, 780, 862

migration, 423, **496–498**, 871

Mill, John Stuart, xvii, 18, 279, 284, 298–299, 300, 366, 445, **499–503**, 535, 660, 750

mixed conceptions of justice, **504–506**, 584–585, 603, 675–676, 785, 814–815, 867

moral education, 30, 207, 286, **507–511**, 632–633

moral person, 4, 11, 98, 112, 149, 153, 296–297, 307, 342–345, **512–519**, 572, 681, 853

moral psychology, xix, 17, 206–208, 279–283, 318–321, 405–406, 468–470, 501, 507–511, **520–527**, 528–532, 705–706, 741–744, 768–772, 807–808

moral sentiments, 318, 521, **528–532**, 632

moral theory, **533–538**, 539, 588, 771, 773

moral worth, 202–205, 484, 517, 533, **539–540**, 725, 831–832

Nagel, Thomas, 363, 364, 366, **543–545**, 718, 827

Nash point, **546–547**

natural duties, 16, 275, **548–550**, **551–552**, 574, 811

natural duty of justice, 274, 275, 548, 551–552, 575, 628–630

natural talents, 203–204, 212, 261, 267, 270, 453, 455–456, 475, 489, **553–556**

neutrality, 24, 64, 121, 122, 235, 343–345, 509, **557–560**, 755

896 / *Index*

Nozick, Robert, 111–112, 337, 429, 452–456, 473, 483, **561–564**, 663
Nussbaum, Martha, 81, **565–567**, 646, 676

objectivity, 536, 543, **571–573**, 687
obligations, 273–276, 548, **574–576**, 811
Okin, Susan Moller, 86, **577–578**, 646
original position, 28, 122, 151, 267, 290, 307, 312, 327, 399–400, 411–412, 493, 548, 571–573, **579–585**, 637, 725–727, 758, 813–816, 861–865
outlaw states, 350, 377, 415, **586–587**, 600
overlapping consensus, 46, 137, 147–148, **588–593**, 614, 638–639, 664, 689, 707, 808–810

paternalism, **597–598**, 799
peoples, 341, 414, 442–444, 502, 519, **599–601**, 795–797, 802–803
perfectionism, 18, 20, 199, 253, 432, 440, 499, **602–605**
plan of life, 18, 130, 169, 315, 325–326, **606–607**, 775, 853
Plato, 14, 15, 30, 89, 157, 270, 432, 685, 719, 782, 875
Pogge, Thomas, 163, 165, 185, 414, 438, **608–611**
political liberalism, 40–41, 88, 97, 126–129, 171–175, 229–233, 347, 388–389, 422–427, 446, 447–451, 588–593, **612–615, 616–622, 623–627**, 631–634, 666–672, 692–697, 700–702, 876
political obligation, 105, 139–140, 273–276, 465, 551, 575, **628–630**, 783, 798
political virtues, 102, 509, 626, **631–634**, 649
practical reason, 114, 153, 170, 188, 222–225, 356, **635–639**, 692
precepts of justice, 435, **640–642**, 747
primary goods, 20, 23, 25, 81–83, 112, 215, 241–243, 342–345, 366, 382–384, 433–434, 441, 474, 581, **643–647**, 762, 765, 828–831, 847
priority of right over good, 198–201, 607, **648–650**, 725–727, 755
procedural justice, 57, 142, 215, 221, 334–335, 386, 429, 482, **651–653**
promising, 276, 576, **654–655**, 751, 759
property-owning democracy, 103, 245, 482, **656–661**, 786, 825
public choice theory, **662–663**

public political culture, 171–175, 192, 207, 227, 412–413, 512, 589, 614, **664–665**
public reason, 74, 171–172, 193–194, 229–233, 403–404, 424–425, 559–560, **666–672**, 676–677, 820–821
publicity, 114, 158, 288, 368, 592, **673–677**, 726, 875

race, 16, 107, 214, 267, 276, 334, 403–404, **681–682**
rational choice theory, 312, 327–328, 547, **683–684**
rational intuitionism, 21, 356, 371, 432, 572, 635, **685–687**, 714, 740, 843
realistic utopia, 362, 414, **688–691**, 698, 708
reasonable and rational, 127, 512–519, 633–634, 636–637, **692–697**, 700–702, 768
reasonable hope, **698–699**, 708, 718, 777
reasonable pluralism, 74, 95–96, 123, 131, 267, 522, 588, 612, 689, **700–702**
reciprocity, 5–6, 9, 61, 134, 158, 213–214, 354, 423, 514, 626, 666, **703–706**, 769, 770, 815
reconciliation, 391, 688, 700, **707–708**
redress, 202–205, **709–710**
reflective equilibrium, 20, 179, 210, 340, 536, 573, 582, **711–716**, 771
religion, 12–13, 14–16, 87–89, 232, 277–278, 460–463, 465, **717–722**, 777–778
respect for persons, 30, 38, 77, 233, 517, 549, 647, **723–724**, 746, 864–865
right, 120, 198–201, 248, 533, 648–650, 673, **725–727**, 758
rights, 47–49, 349–353, **728–730, 731–736**
Rorty, Richard, **737–738**
Ross, W. D., 21, 371, 428, 685, **739–740**
Rousseau, Jean-Jacques, xviii, 100, 293, 297, 688, **741–744**, 778, 783
rule of law, 288, 330, **745–749**
rules, two concepts of, 311, 329, 501, 655, 748, **750–752**, 879

Sandel, Michael, 119, 122, 339, 483, **755–756**
Scanlon, T. M., 59, 304, **757–759**
self-interest, 248–251, 285, 405, 662, 743, **760–761**, 782
self-respect, 18, 193, 243, 257, 604, 646–647, 723, 741, **762–764**, 864–865
Sen, Amartya, 81, 332, 364, 383–384, 547, 646, 676, **765–767**

Index / 897

sense of justice, 20, 105, 133–138, 342–345, 468–470, 520–527, 528–532, **768–772**, 807, 834–836, 875

shame, **318–321**, 514, 525, 530–531, 566, 741

Sidgwick, Henry, 288, 356, 400, 499, 534, 685, **773–776**, 866

sin, xxi, 277, 717, 718, **777–778**

Smith, Adam, 157, 259, 788

social choice theory, 25, 765, **779–780**

social contract, 355, 464–467, 580, **781–784**

social minimum, 50–54, 66, 481, 505, 626, 657, **785–787**, 862

social union, 19, 312, 502, 503, **788–790**, 807

socialism, 482, 484, 486–487, 502, 658, 790, **791–794**

Society of Peoples, 182–185, 195–197, 255, 412, 497, 690–691, **795–797**

Soper, Philip, 747, **798–799**

sovereignty, **800–803**

stability, 30, 104–105, 133–138, 249, 346, 520–527, 551, 588–593, 673–675, 800–803, **804–810**, 863–864

Stace, Walter, xvi

statesman and duty of statesmanship, 587, **811–812**

strains of commitment, 280, 438, 494, 524, 583, 786, **813–816**, 862–863

supreme court and judicial review, 145, 231, 291, 419, 748–749, **817–821**

taxation, 65–67, 244, 270, 424, 429, 433, 482, 489, 544, 609, 652, 660, **825–827**

thin and full theories of good, 82, 133–134, 198–199, 249, 315–316, 522, 539, 644, 649, 807, **828–837**

toleration, 15, 88, 166–168, 182–185, 278, 415, 461, 627, 717–722, **838–841**

trust, 136, 319–321, 469, 507–508, 525, 530, 576, 654, 670, 760, 770

truth, 40–41, 534, 536, 572, 617, **842–844**

two principles of justice, 211–216, 220–221, 259, 299, 656–661, **845–850**

unity of self, 119, 188, 224, 535, 607, 755, **853–857**

utilitarianism, xvii, 9, 25, 48, 199, 327–328, 355, 365, 435, 494, 499–503, 504–506, 583–585, 640, 734, 750–752, 782, 814, 853–855, **858–865**, 866, 868

utility, 25, 327, 382–384, 500–501, 775, **866–868**

Walzer, Michael, 120, 272, 755, **871–873**

well-ordered society, 306, 361, 540, 617, 649, 703, 728, 763, **874–877**

Wittgenstein, Ludwig, xvi, xvii, 224, **878–881**

For EU product safety concerns, contact us at Calle de José Abascal, 56–1º,
28003 Madrid, Spain or eugpsr@cambridge.org.

www.ingramcontent.com/pod-product-compliance
Ingram Content Group UK Ltd.
Pitfield, Milton Keynes, MK11 3LW, UK
UKHW030654060825
461487UK00011B/963